THE PAPERS OF

WOODROW WILSON

VOLUME 16
1905-1907

SPONSORED BY THE WOODROW WILSON
FOUNDATION
AND PRINCETON UNIVERSITY

THE PAPERS OF

WOODROW
WILSON

ARTHUR S. LINK, *EDITOR*

DAVID W. HIRST AND JOHN E. LITTLE

ASSOCIATE EDITORS

JEAN MACLACHLAN AND SYLVIA E. FONTIJN

CONTRIBUTING EDITORS

M. HALSEY THOMAS, *CONSULTING EDITOR*

JOHN M. MULDER, *EDITORIAL ASSISTANT*

Volume 16 · 1905-1907

PRINCETON, NEW JERSEY

PRINCETON UNIVERSITY PRESS

1973

Printed in the United States of America
by Princeton University Press
Princeton, New Jersey

INTRODUCTION

THIS volume, covering the period from mid-February 1905 to mid-January 1907, documents notable events and developments in Wilson's life and the history of Princeton University.

In the opening pages, we find Wilson organizing the Princeton alumni in the first systematic campaign among them to raise money for what would be called, for want of a better term, as Wilson said, the preceptorial system. Its aim was to bring students and teachers into close contact and make students "reading men" who mastered subjects instead of pupils who merely listened to lectures and memorized textbooks. The necessary funds assured, Wilson sets out after frequent consultation with departmental heads to recruit some fifty of the most promising young teacher-scholars in the country. Almost overnight, the preceptorial system revolutionizes the intellectual life of Princeton.

Years of excessive work take their toll in late May 1906, when Wilson suffers a major stroke that seems for a moment to threaten his life and leaves him partially blind in the left eye and temporarily disabled in the right arm. He goes for the summer and early autumn to his beloved Lake District of England, for rest and restoration.

Returning in apparent good health to Princeton in early October 1906, Wilson plunges at once into the life of the University. Then, in a report to the Board of Trustees in December, he proposes his quadrangle plan for the abolition of the upper-class eating clubs and the grouping of all undergraduates in a number of quadrangles, or colleges, where they would live and eat. After presenting his plan and appointing a committee of trustees to consider it, Wilson leaves for a vacation in Bermuda.

Meanwhile, as the documents also reveal, Wilson gains some national political attention when George Harvey, editor of *Harper's Weekly*, suggests him for the Democratic presidential nomination in a speech in 1906 to the Lotos Club in New York. This "nomination" sets off widespread discussion among newspaper editors and conservative Democrats who are pleased by Wilson's forceful denunciations of the Democracy of William Jennings Bryan and the nationalistic progressivism of Theodore Roosevelt. Moreover, as this volume ends, Wilson is thrust into the political arena once again when Harvey and James Smith, Jr., leader of conservative Democrats in New Jersey, organize a movement, in opposition to progressives, to make Wilson the New Jersey Democratic senatorial nominee in 1907.

Other documents generously illustrate the history of Princeton University during this period 1905-1907, when Wilson was at the peak of his leadership—undergraduate life, curricular matters, the continuing development of the campus and its buildings, alumni affairs, and numerous other topics.

Readers are again reminded that *The Papers of Woodrow Wilson* is a continuing series; that persons, institutions, and events that figure prominently in earlier volumes are not re-identified in subsequent ones; and that the Index to each volume gives cross references to fullest earlier identifications. We reiterate that it is our practice to print texts *verbatim et literatim*, repairing words and phrases only where necessary for clarity and ease of reading, and that we make silent corrections only of obvious errors in typed copies.

We are grateful to Mrs. Bryant Putney of Princeton University Press for help in copyediting, and to Miss Marjorie Sirlouis for deciphering Wilson's shorthand. We welcome Sylvia E. Fontijn and John M. Mulder to our staff and also Lewis Bateman to the editorial staff of Princeton University Press.

THE EDITORS

Princeton, New Jersey
February 14, 1973

CONTENTS

CONTENTS xvii

ILLUSTRATIONS

Following page 330

TEXT ILLUSTRATIONS

ABBREVIATIONS

ALI	autograph letter initialed
ALS	autograph letter(s) signed
APS	autograph postcard signed
CCL	carbon copy of letter
CCLI	carbon copy of letter initialed
EAW	Ellen Axson Wilson
hw	handwritten, handwriting
HwCL	handwritten copy of letter
HwL	handwritten letter
Hw MS	handwritten manuscript
MS	manuscript
PCL	printed copy of letter
sh	shorthand
TC	typed copy
TCL	typed copy of letter
TL	typed letter
TLS	typed letter(s) signed
T MS	typed manuscript
T MS S	typed manuscript signed
TR	typed report
TRS	typed report signed
WW	Woodrow Wilson
WWhw	Woodrow Wilson handwriting, handwritten
WWhw MS	Woodrow Wilson handwritten manuscript
WWsh	Woodrow Wilson shorthand
WWsh MS	Woodrow Wilson shorthand manuscript
WWT	Woodrow Wilson typed
WWT MS	Woodrow Wilson typed manuscript
WWTCL	Woodrow Wilson typed copy of letter
WWTLS	Woodrow Wilson typed letter(s) signed
WWTRS	Woodrow Wilson typed report signed

ABBREVIATIONS FOR COLLECTIONS AND LIBRARIES

Following the National Union Catalog
of the Library of Congress

CtY	Yale University
DLC	Library of Congress
DNA	U.S. National Archives
ICU	University of Chicago
MH	Harvard University
MH-Ar	Harvard University Archives
MiU-C	University of Michigan, William L. Clements Library
MoSHi	Missouri Historical Society
Nc-Ar	North Carolina State Department of Archives and History
NcD	Duke University
NjP	Princeton University

xxii ABBREVIATIONS AND SYMBOLS

NjR	Rutgers University
NN	New York Public Library
NNC	Columbia University
NRU	University of Rochester
OClWHi	Western Reserve Historical Society
PBL	Lehigh University
PPAmP	American Philosophical Society
PSt	Pennsylvania State University
RSB Coll., DLC	Ray Stannard Baker Collection of Wilsoniana, Library of Congress
TNJ	Joint University Libraries
TSewU	University of the South
TxHR	Rice University
TxU	University of Texas
UA, NjP	University Archives, Princeton University
ViU	University of Virginia
WC, NjP	Woodrow Wilson Collection, Princeton University
WP, DLC	Woodrow Wilson Papers, Library of Congress
WU	University of Wisconsin
WWP, UA, NjP	Woodrow Wilson Papers, University Archives, Princeton University

SYMBOLS

[Feb. 18, 1905]	publication date of a published writing; also date of document when date is not part of text
[c. June 1, 1905]	latest composition date of a published writing
[[Oct. 31, 1905]]	delivery date of a speech if publication date differs
*	denotes first mention of each of the original preceptors appointed in 1905. Extensive biographical information about all appointees is printed at Dec. 14, 1905.

THE PAPERS OF

WOODROW WILSON

VOLUME 16

1905-1907

THE PAPERS OF

WOODROW WILSON

A News Item

[Feb. 18, 1905]

President Wilson returned to Princeton on Wednesday the 15th, looking and feeling very well after his three weeks' rest at Palm Beach, Florida. He had been absent from Princeton just eight weeks,—two weeks longer than was anticipated, an unexpected complication having followed the operation at the Presbyterian Hospital in New York.[1] During the President's absence his Annual Report to the Trustees[2] has gone through the press, and an edition of 8,000 is now being distributed from the University Secretary's office, to our graduates, other colleges and leading preparatory schools.

Printed in the *Princeton Alumni Weekly*, v (Feb. 18, 1905), 317.
[1] See WW to R. Bridges, Dec. 9, 1904, n. 1; the two news items printed at Jan. 7, 1905; and the news item printed at Jan. 21, 1905, all in Vol. 15.
[2] It is printed at Dec. 8, 1904, Vol. 15.

An Announcement by Robert Bridges and a Statement by Wilson

[c. Feb. 18, 1905]

THE COMMITTEE OF FIFTY
OF PRINCETON UNIVERSITY

The recent publication of the report of the Treasurer of Princeton University[1] has revealed for the first time to the Alumni that the imposing work of the whole University is conducted on the income of $2,700,000 of invested funds. For the instruction of 1500 students by a faculty of more than one hundred picked men, leaders in their various lines of work, and for the maintenance of the great material plant of the University itself there is an endowment which is hardly the equivalent of many moderate private fortunes. The work has been made possible only through intelligent management and the personal generosity of a few individuals, and the self-denying and persistent efforts of

[1] The report of Henry Green Duffield, Treasurer of Princeton University, was printed as part of the Annual Report of the President for 1904. A summary of Duffield's report appeared in "The First Public Statement of the Finances of Princeton University," *Princeton Alumni Weekly*, v (Jan. 28, 1905), 271-73.

a faculty devoted to the best interests of the University. The time has now come when the Alumni must take part in this work with great vigor and unanimity if the University is not to retrograde.

The Board of Trustees, at its meeting in December, authorized the President to appoint a Committee of Fifty "to provide for the immediate necessities and future development of the University." Mr. Cleveland H. Dodge, '79, was appointed Chairman of this Committee made up of picked men from the Alumni, a full list of which is appended.

Princeton University is in competition with the largest and oldest Universities in the East, and it is also in direct and keen competition with the remarkable group of small colleges, toward which many of the best informed educators have of recent years been directing their students. Princeton must meet the competition of the former with an endowment of one-half or one-third of the older institutions; it must meet the competition of the latter with a teaching force entirely inadequate to give the student that personal attention which is the great merit of the small college. Soon after his inauguration President Wilson propounded his scheme for the introduction of the Tutorial system at Princeton,[2] which he believes will immensely add to the efficiency of Princeton in this competition, and efficiency above all things is what Princeton needs. A brief statement of this system by President Wilson is enclosed herewith. To put it in operation would require the income of $2,500,000; and this is only one of the large plans, formulated after earnest investigation, which the University must carry out if it is to keep its place among the foremost institutions of learning.

The Committee of Fifty have therefore undertaken a vigorous campaign to provide the immediate funds for carrying on these projects. We cannot wait for the millions that are necessary as a permanent endowment; we must have at least $150,000.00 annually to enable the President to begin now some of these necessary projects. This sum of money the Alumni can and will give. The Committee propose to canvass the whole body of Alumni for this purpose. Several ways in which they may give to the

[2] Wilson had first suggested adoption of a "modified form . . . of the English tutorial system" in his Annual Report in 1902 (printed at Oct. 21, 1902, Vol. 14). He also mentioned the idea in speeches to the Chicago and New York alumni in the autumn of 1902 (see the news report printed at Nov. 29, 1902, and the speech text printed at Dec. 9, 1902, both in Vol. 14). Wilson referred to the concept again in his letter to Andrew Carnegie of April 17, 1903 (also in Vol. 14). Finally, he spoke approvingly of the Oxford tutorial system, though without specific reference to Princeton, in his address, "The College Course and Methods of Instruction," printed at Dec. 12, 1903, in Vol. 15.

University will be put before them. First of all, large sums for the permanent endowment are most desired; but if any donor prefers, the Committee will be glad to have him agree to give annually the interest on the capital sum which he can at some future time pay over as a whole. Others will perhaps agree to give annual amounts for a limited term of years. All of the money so raised is to be devoted to the present needs of the University.

Mr. George W. Burleigh, '92, of 52 Wall Street, New York City,[3] has been elected permanent secretary of the Committee of Fifty and will visit the various cities and explain to them in detail the needs of the University and the plans of this Committee to meet them. He will be glad to furnish further information to anyone desiring it.[4]

The Committee.

NEW YORK CITY.
Cleveland H. Dodge, '79
Chairman
John L. Cadwalader, '56
James W. Alexander, '60
John W. Aitken, '69
Adrian H. Joline, '70
Charles Scribner, '75
Percy R. Pyne, '78
Cornelius C. Cuyler, '79
Edward W. Sheldon, '79
Pliny Fisk, '81
William C. Osborn, '83
Matthew C. Fleming, '86
Charles W. McAlpin, '88
C. Ledyard Blair, '90
George W. Burleigh, '92
Secretary
Andrew C. Imbrie, '95
Albert G. Milbank, '96

NEW JERSEY.
Archibald D. Russell,
Hugh H. Hamill, '71
Adrian Riker, '79
Philip N. Jackson, '81
Uzal H. McCarter, '82

PHILADELPHIA AND VICINITY.
J. Dundas Lippincott, '61
Alexander Van Rensselaer, '71
Thomas H. Atherton, '74
Bayard Henry, '76

Henry B. Thompson, '77
Frank C. Roberts, '83
John Y. Boyd, '84
Algernon B. Roberts, '96

BALTIMORE AND WASHINGTON.
Frederick D. McKenney, '84
John F. Wilkins, '94
Walter B. Brooks, Jr., '79
Lawrason Riggs, '83
Robert Garrett, '97

PITTSBURG AND VICINITY.
Nathaniel Ewing, Jr., '69
William Scott, '68
James R. MacFarlane, '78
John I. Shaw, '81
Joseph B. Shea, '85
James H. Lockhart, '87
Benjamin F. Jones, Jr., '91

CHICAGO.
Samuel Baker, '65
David B. Jones, '76
Cyrus H. McCormick, '79
James B. Walter [Waller], Jr., '79
James S. Harlan, '83
William B. McIlvaine, '85
William H. Forsyth, '88

ST. LOUIS.
John D. Davis, '72
Rolla Wells, '76
P. Taylor Bryan, '82
Edward F. Goltra, '87

[3] George William Burleigh, Princeton 1892, New York lawyer and businessman.
[4] This seems to have been the first organized effort by an American college or university to mobilize its alumni in a systematic campaign for regular financial contributions. As future documents will reveal, the idea of "capitalizing the good will of the alumni" originated with Wilson.

STATEMENT OF THE TUTORIAL SYSTEM[5]

By President Wilson

The object of the tutorial system is to give the undergraduate in a great university the advantage of the same sort of close and intimate contact and council with his instructors that the undergraduate of the small college enjoys. The advantage of the small college is that the student comes into immediate contact with the best minds of the teaching body and has their individual attention; its disadvantage is that the small college lacks the broad community life and the quickening rivalries of the great university. The advantage of the great university lies in its stimulating life. It is a sort of little world in itself. It is more apt than the small college, moreover, to have in its faculty some of the most original and inspiring men of science and of letters that the country affords; but its disadvantage is that the student cannot get at these men; meets them only as a member of a large class to which they lecture; gets their influence diluted by the general mass of men in whose company he hears them; seldom feels any trace of their personal influence on him or has a chance to take their counsel direct from their own lips.

The tutorial system is meant to import into the great university the methods and personal contact between teacher and pupil which are characteristic of the small college, and so gain the advantages of both. This can be done only by multiplying teachers, by multiplying the number of well-paid teachers, and using them for the instruction, not of large classes, but of small groups of students, whose guides, counsellors, and friends they will be in their work.

It is meant also to change the method of the student's own work, to make a reading man of him instead of a mere pupil receiving instruction. The method of the tutorial system is to give a man subjects to read up, and to supply him with advice and assistance in his reading,—advisors who will be practically accessible at all times, and who will be guides to the best reading and to the best method of reading. This is the only manly, stimulating way to prepare for an examination, to prepare to be examined on great subjects, not simply upon a particular text book, or the lectures of a particular lecturer. Lectures and classroom work should supplement independent reading only for the sake of stimulation and systematic drill. Under such a system the most interesting men in the teaching body would have an opportunity to gain personal access to the student, and the greater lecturers

[5] There is a WWsh draft of this statement in WP, DLC.

would be constantly supplemented and interpreted by tutors who would guide the men's reading.

The only drawback to the system is its expense; the expense of getting a great many more teachers and paying enough to get good ones. It would require at Princeton two and a half millions to set the system up upon anything like a systematic basis. But no more distinguished gift could be made to American education; no gift more adapted to revivify and strengthen university training; no gift more certain to bring fame to the giver.[6]

Printed documents (WP, DLC).

[6] This announcement and statement were printed in the *Princeton Alumni Weekly*, v (Feb. 25, 1905), 333-35, and given wide publicity by the newspapers. Wilson later described what would soon be called the preceptorial system in much greater detail. See, e.g., his articles printed at April 28 and June 24, 1905; the news reports printed at April 17 and June 14, 1905; and his Annual Report to the Board of Trustees, printed at Dec. 14, 1905.

A News Item

[Feb. 20, 1905]

CHRISTIAN CONFERENCE.

Closing Sessions Held in Murray-Dodge Hall
Saturday and Sunday.

The second annual conference of the leaders of Christian work in the East[1] held its closing session yesterday afternoon in Murray-Dodge Hall.

The three sessions held on Saturday were devoted largely to a consideration of methods of work. Saturday's meetings began with a devotional exercise of fifteen minutes, at 9.30 a.m. President Wilson then addressed the conference, welcoming the delegates to Princeton.

Printed in the *Daily Princetonian*, Feb. 20, 1905.

[1] This was a conference of leaders of Christian work among students, held from February 17 through February 19, 1905, which dealt especially with problems of religious work in professional schools on the eastern seaboard.

From Winthrop More Daniels, with Enclosure

My dear Wilson: Princeton, N. J.   Feb. 21, 1905.

The Department of History and Politics authorized me to inform you that with the assistance of six "Preceptors,"[1] the Department thinks it will be able to inaugurate the tutorial system.[2] This estimate of six Preceptors is based on the assumptions: 1st., that the tutorial system will not apply to Sophomore year.[3] (There are 240 in the Soph. History) 2nd., that the number enrolled next year in the Department does not exceed the number enrolled this year.

The Department also desired to express to you its preference for assigning each "Preceptor" exclusively to one of the three sections of the Dept. (History, Politics, or Economics). This undivided control by any section, such as History, over its "Preceptors" will simplify the problem of administering the tutorial system. If the "Preceptor" owed a divided allegiance, it is apprehended that difficulties might result. It was suggested that a "Preceptor," after giving one term's work exclusively to a given subject—let us say, History—might be transferred the next term with advantage to a cognate field—for example, Politics. He will thus secure some variety of work and broadening of interests without endangering the system of centralized control.

The Department also requested me to call your attention to the fact, that the amount of collateral reading required by this tutorial system may occasion difficulty on the score of furnishing an adequate supply of books. Many students, it is feared, will not feel able to purchase the number of books that will be required each term: and the Library will be unable to provide a sufficiency of duplicate copies. I append a table, the virtual counterpart of the one employed to compute the amount of tutorial service required in our meeting this afternoon.

Very sincerely yours,   W. M. Daniels

ALS (WP, DLC).

[1] This is the first use of this term in documents known to the Editors.

[2] This statement would seem to indicate that Wilson had already decided to launch the tutorial, or preceptorial, system. One can only assume that he was not merely anticipating the success of the Committee of Fifty's campaign but had received pledges of sufficient support from trustees and other friends of the university to guarantee the operation of the preceptorial system during its first years.

[3] The preceptorial system was intended to apply to all Princeton undergraduates in the humanities and social sciences and, wherever practicable, in the scientific departments. In practice, the new system seems to have been confined largely to upperclassmen in its first year, and its later extension to underclassmen was left to the discretion of the individual departments. For example, the sophomore course in general history was not conducted under the preceptorial system in 1905-1906, but in 1906-1907 a new sophomore course in medieval history, prerequisite to much of the upperclass work of the Department of History, Politics, and Economics, was given with a combination of lectures and precepts.

E N C L O S U R E

Table

For computing amount of tutorial service that *each week* will be required in the Dept. of History and Politics.

N.B. This Table proceeds on the assumption that each Preceptor will take at each conference period of one hour not more than 12 men. The Table assumes that of the 3 hours devoted weekly to each course only one will be occupied by the tutorial conference, except in Jr. Economics where 2 of the 3 hours will be so occupied.

Junior Year

Course.	No. of Electors (this year)	Hours of tutoring required weekly	Hours of tutoring given by professors weekly	
Politics	125	10	0	(The President is not expected to tutor)
History	120	10	2	(Because of the demands of Soph. History)
Economics	120	20	4	

Senior Year

Course.	No. of Electors	Hours of tutoring required	Hours given
Politics	{ 110	10	2
	{ 40	3	2
History	{ 120	10	2
	{ 170	15	2
Economics	60 (45 in 2d term)	5 (4 in 2d term)	2
		83 (82 in 2d term)	16

Total number of hours of tutorial service
   required per week   83 (82)
Number thereof contributed by the
   present staff per week   16 (16)

Net number required of Preceptors in the Dept.
   per week   67 (66.)

Should the Preceptor take not more than 10 men at a given conference, the number of hours would be increased to about 80 hours per week.

On the basis of 66 hours per week each Preceptor must give 11 or 12 hours' instruction weekly besides correcting written recitation papers

On the basis of 80 hours per week each Preceptor must give 13 or 14 hours' instruction weekly, besides correcting written recitation papers.

Hw MS (WP, DLC).

From Fred Neher

My dear Dr. Wilson: Princeton, 22 Feb. 1905.

In accordance with your request I send you in the following a memorandum of the matters concerning the Department of Chemistry which I brought to your consideration in our interview of 20 Feb.:

REDUCTION OF EXTRA TUITION FEE FOR ACADEMIC STUDENTS TAKING PRACTICAL WORK IN CHEMISTRY. For many years but one chemical course involving laboratory work was open to Academic students and, by way of compensation to the School of Science for the extra expense of laboratory maintenance entailed by this course and in view of the disparity between the tuition charges in the two undergraduate departments, a special so-called "tuition" fee of $10.00 was reported against all men electing the course. Six years ago when, in connection with the establishment of the Department of "Organic" Chemistry, other courses involving laboratory work were opened to Academic students, I was directed to report a similar charge *each term* for each Academic student working in my laboratory. At the time of the reorganization of the chemical courses last year, as a result of which Academic and School of Science students are now admitted on an equal footing to the courses offered by the consolidated department, the matter of the proper extra fees for Academic students escaped attention, so that during the present year we have had no choice but to follow the established custom and charge each Academic student $10.00 each term. In view of the fact that the difference in tuition for the two classes of students is but $10.00 a year at present it would be fairer to all concerned to make this fee hereafter but $5.00 per term. The number of men involved averages *at present* about twenty per term,—a difference in revenue of c. $700.00 each year. For the past five years there have been about twenty such men each term.

WITHDRAWAL OF MR. VAN NEST. I had also to notify you of the intention of Mr. J. S. Van Nest of resigning his position as an instructor on our staff in order to study abroad. In this connection I suggested the advisability of waiting a year before seeking another man to assist in the work of the department in place of Mr. Van Nest. While having no direct right to speak with reference to the manning of the courses in mineralogy, I also ventured the opinion that this work also could be carried out without the help of a man in Mr. Van Nest's place.

SALARIES   I also felt it at once a duty and a pleasure to request that steps be taken to secure an in-crease of Dr. Foster's salary to $1,300[1] and that Mr. Woodward be made an instructor and given an instructor's salary ($800.00?)[2] Both requests were based upon the proved merit of the men together with the facts that they carry heavy schedules and are taking increasingly important shares in the work of the department.

I further asked you to try to arrange for an increase in my own salary,[3] partly on the grounds already taken in the letter containing a similar request which I wrote you toward the close of the last academic year,[4] partly because my father's prolonged illness, necessitating his withdrawal from business affairs, makes the amount of my salary a matter of far more pressing moment to me than it has ever been hitherto.[5]

Regretting the necessity for again burdening you with this latter request at this time, I am,

Very sincerely yours,   Fred Neher.

TLS (WP, DLC) with WWhw marginal comments not printed.
[1] William Foster, Jr., Instructor in Chemistry. Foster was promoted to Assistant Professor for the academic year 1905-1906, and his salary was increased to $1,800 per annum.
[2] Truman Stephen Woodward, Assistant in General Chemistry. Woodward was not made an Instructor until 1906, but his salary for 1905-1906 was $800.
[3] Neher's salary at this time was $2,000 per annum.
[4] This letter is missing.
[5] His salary for 1905-1906 was increased to $2,500.

A News Report of an After-Dinner Talk in New York

[Feb. 23, 1905]

DIFFICULT TO BE A REAL STATESMAN

Dr. Woodrow Wilson Tells Descendants of Revolutionary Warriors of the Great Problems.

At the annual banquet of the Sons of the Revolution last night at Delmonico's there was a notable list of speakers. Edward Wetmore,[1] the president, presided. The speakers were Woodrow Wilson, president of Princeton University, who spoke to the toast, "George Washington"; James M. Beck,[2] "The Principles Established by the Revolution"; William D. Murphy,[3] "Our Flag—Yesterday, To-day and To-morrow," and "The Army," Brigadied [Brigadier] General Frederick Dent Grant.[4]

Dr. Wilson said there were those whose courage he admired more than their principles, particularly as to their position in regard to our possessions. The persons referred to, he said, had recently shifted their ground. Washington would have been the last man to say his advice applied to one generation would be pertinent to another and later generation. Washington had cautioned us as to what alliances we formed. The keynote of what Washington left was not imperative standards of policy but precepts of character. His idea was that each generation could decide its own standards.

"Did it ever occur to you," continued Dr. Wilson, "that we are really a leaderless people? No one man has the right to declare the whole policy of the nation. Each portion of the government has its own peculiar functions, each fitting into the other forming a perfect whole."

"There is no country in the world where public statesmanship is so difficult as in this our own country. Statesmanship consists in developing thoughtful citizens.

"If our statesmen are true and honest their efforts as private statesmen will lift this country to the highest possible pinnacle. The best citizens and statesmen are those who ascertain and speak the truth and have no private axe to grind."

Dr. Wilson declared that it requires no backbone to be with the majority, and he did not consider it [un-]American to dispute with the majority. The American flag, said he, stood for the greatest "kick" in history. It stood for the minority. He declared he did not say that because he is a democrat. That is, he said, he was a democrat until certain things happened in 1896. Since then he had been trying to find a party fitted to his conscience.[5]

Printed in the *New York Herald*, Feb. 23, 1905; some editorial headings omitted.
[1] Edmund Wetmore, New York lawyer.
[2] James Montgomery Beck, corporation lawyer of New York.
[3] Real estate broker of New York.
[4] A son of Ulysses S. Grant, at this time commander of the Department of the East.
[5] There is a brief WWhw outline of these remarks, dated Feb. 22, 1905, in WP, DLC.

To Walter Hines Page

My dear Mr. Page: Princeton, N. J.   24 Feby, 1905.

Thank you most sincerely for your kind note of Jany 23d.[1] After my five weeks in the hospital I went to Palm Beach, and I have just now returned from my rest there feeling completely well again. I very much appreciate your kind thoughtfulness in the matter.

Always,   Cordially yours,   Woodrow Wilson

TLS (W. H. Page Papers, MH).
  [1] It is missing.

To Azel Washburn Hazen

My dear Dr. Hazen: Princeton, N. J.   24 Feby, 1905.

I greatly appreciate your kind note of Jany 24th.[1] I have only just returned from Palm Beach whither the doctor sent me after my five weeks in the hospital. The operation went perfectly well and I have recovered my strength completely, returning to my work with real zest.

Every evidence of your affection gives me the keenest pleasure and Mrs. Wilson joins me in affectionate regard both to Mrs. Hazen and yourself.

Always,
          Cordially and faithfully yours,   Woodrow Wilson

TLS (in possession of Frances Hazen Bulkeley).
  [1] It is missing.

Notes for an Address

Address: "The People's Forum," New Rochelle.[1]   26 Feb. 1905
          The Individual and the Organization.
Question lies beneath all Society.
  1) Qu. of Politics,—not our present theme.
  2) "   " *private statesmanship.*
      Individual responsibility under a free polity.
      Patriotism,—what?
  3) Qu. of individual advantage and development.
      Liberty, what?
      Equality: 1) a free field and
                2) no favour
      In order to realize 2) we have imperiled 1).
      E. g. Labour union restrictions
                Tariff
      Competition, to bring out capacity and develop natural
          inequality.

Natural Inequality
Enrichment of Society
Heartening of Individual
Penalizing of inefficiency.

WWhw MS (WP, DLC).
1 For earlier correspondence concerning this address, see M. J. Keogh to
WW, June 21 and July 16, 1904, both in Vol. 15.

A News Report of an Address on Trusts and Labor Unions at New Rochelle, New York

[Feb. 27, 1905]

WILSON FOR PUBLICITY.

President Wilson, of Princeton University, delivered an address yesterday before the New-Rochelle People's Forum on the subject, "The Individual and the Organization." He discussed principally the labor unions and the trusts. He said he favored the plan to compel more publicity regarding trusts and corporations.[1] He said:

If we are to give them our money, they must at least let us trouble them to see their consciences. If we could only see the souls of the boards of directors and know how much they weighed, then we would know whether it would be safe to invest our money in them or not. A good soul, I should imagine, would tip the scales upward and a bad soul tip them in the other direction.

We can't abolish the trusts. We must moralize them. . . .

Dr. Wilson . . . said the trust question was one regarding which the people should not make too much haste, but they should see that men who were trusted were trustworthy. The thing that kept water in stocks, he said, was secrecy.

Dr. Wilson advised the audience to beware of books relating to political theories, as they were dangerous. He went on:

The peril in this world is the number of good people who are radically wrong. We say too often of a political leader, "He is a good man," and then rush helter skelter after him.

There is no objection to an organization which does not crush individuals, but there is every objection to an organization which does crush them. Undoubtedly, the success of a democratic government rests upon equality. The kind of equality we want is the kind maintained on athletic fields, where they see that the course is kept clear, that there is no fouling and that every one gets an equal start.

The objection I have to labor unions is that they drag the highest man to the level of the lowest. I must demur with the labor unions when they say that you must award the dull the same as you award those with special gifts. I was an enthusiastic labor advocate, and I am yet a supporter of all unions that are conducted in a proper manner, but some of the rules which are promulgated at present are unfair and irrational.

A man in the back of the hall said he would take issue with Dr. Wilson's statement that employers were compelled to pay a maximum rate of wages to dull men. He said that in his union wages were not set for either the superior or the inferior man, but for the medium man, and were only about what were necessary for the support of himself and family.

Dr. Wilson replied that no doubt these conditions were found to [in] his particular union, but he told of a union which limited the number of bricks to be laid each day to 300 a man, when a good man could easily lay 1,000 a day.

Printed in the *New York Tribune*, Feb. 27, 1905; two editorial headings omitted.
1 This was probably a reference to the work of the Bureau of Corporations of the United States Department of Commerce and Labor. The Bureau was established in February 1903 for the purpose of gathering information to enable the President to make recommendations to Congress for legislation, and the Commissioner of Corporations was empowered to compel testimony and the production of documents. The Bureau, soon organized under the capable leadership of Commissioner James Rudolph Garfield, set to work investigating various corporate enterprises, most notably the beef-packing industry. However, apparently for political reasons, President Theodore Roosevelt chose not to make public any of the reports of the Bureau until after his election to the presidency in his own right in 1904. In his Annual Message to Congress of December 6, 1904, Roosevelt announced that the Bureau would "make a special report on the beef industry." There was considerable public interest in the anticipated release of this report, aroused especially by sensational journalistic exposés of the "Beef Trust" being published at this very time. See Arthur M. Johnson, "Theodore Roosevelt and the Bureau of Corporations," *Mississippi Valley Historical Review*, XLV (March 1959), 571-90.

From Melancthon Williams Jacobus

[Hartford, Conn.]
My dear President Wilson: February 28th, 1905.

I have just received from Mr. McAlpin the information for which I was about to inquire in a letter to you this morning, regarding the time and place for the meeting of the Curriculum Committee next week. I have sent out in this mail the necessary notice to each member of the Committee, omitting the name of Dr. [Simon John] McPherson whose resignation from the Committee I believe was accepted by the Board at the last meeting, and in whose place I do not recall any one as having been placed by the Board. If I am in error on this last point, kindly give me the name of the member added to the Committee so that I may give him immediate notice of the meeting.[1]

What I was more anxious to ask you about, however, in my letter of inquiry was what your idea is regarding the character of the report from our Committee to be presented to the Board at this meeting. On the schedule adopted by the Board for meetings and reports of committees, the Curriculum Committee is to give a preliminary report at the March meeting of the Board, and its second and final report at the June meeting. I should be very glad indeed to have your ideas as to what our report for this meeting should contain, and shall be only too glad to follow out such suggestions as you have to make.

I have been holding for some time, until you could get back to Princeton and be in some sort of strength for such things, the enclosures[2] which I herewith forward to you. They have to do, as you see, with the educational problems which are being worked out in the West, especially at the point as to whether education shall be commercial in so adjusting the curriculum as to allow men to get through their professional education by short cuts, or whether it shall be thoroughly cultural, having for its one aim an out-rounded preparation of a man for life. I think you will be interested in what Dean Main[3] has to say, and also in the action taken by the Faculty of Grinnell College, in the adjustment

Purpose and point of view everything.[5] of their curriculum for meeting professional school needs.[4] In face of such adjustment, it seems to me all protestations as to a cultural purpose lose very considerably their worth and value.

Hoping that you have been greatly benefited by your rest, and that you will be able to finish the academic year without taxing very much your vitality, so that you can be fresh and strong for next year's work, I am

Most cordially yours, M W Jacobus

TLS (WP, DLC).

[1] McPherson resigned at the meeting of the Board of Trustees on December 8, 1904. The board elected John De Witt to succeed him on March 9, 1905.

[2] J. H. T. Main to M. Jacobus, Dec. 20, 1904, TCL (WP, DLC); policy statement concerning cooperation between Iowa College (later Grinnell College) and certain professional schools, TC (WP, DLC).

[3] John Hanson Thomas Main, at this time Dean of the Faculty of Iowa College. He became president of the college in 1906 and served in that capacity for twenty-five years.

[4] Main's letter and the accompanying statement described the efforts of Iowa College to coordinate its program of studies with the requirements of professional schools of medicine, technology, theology, and law in order that its students might receive credit from the professional schools for a portion of their undergraduate work. Main insisted, however, that the courses offered in fields related to professional work had not been introduced as pre-professional courses but had been established in the curriculum for some time and were perfectly acceptable as subjects in the liberal arts. "We have not," he wrote, "departed in any

respect from our cultural ideals. We are simply making an adjustment with these institutions on the basis of work already offered,—work that has its place independently of any ulterior consideration in the college curriculum."

5 WWhw.

From Charles Greene Rockwood, Jr., to the President and Board of Trustees of Princeton University

Dear Sirs   Princeton, N. J.   March 1 1905

As it seems desirable for various reasons, partly in view of my wifes health, that I should spend the next winter in Europe with my family, and as such an interruption in my work might not well agree with the new methods of instruction which I understand are expected to go into effect during the next college year, I have thought it best that I should retire at this time from the active service of the University, and I beg therefore to offer to your honorable body my resignation of the office of Professor of Mathematics, the same to take effect at the close of the present college year, on July 1, 1905.

In thus proposing to lay aside the duties of the position to which I have given, in unbroken series, twenty eight of the best years of my life, I wish to say that my regard for the institution which I have served so long is not in any wise diminished, and I shall always be ready in the future, as in the past, to advance the interests of the University in any way that may be open to me.

With thanks for the consideration that has been accorded me since I came to Princeton in 1877, I beg to remain

very respectfully   C. G. Rockwood Jr.
Professor of Mathematics.

ALS (Trustees' Papers, UA, NjP).

Allan Marquand to the Board of Trustees of Princeton University

Dear Sirs: Princeton.   March 2, 1905.

The time has come when the enlargement of the Art Museum may be called an urgent necessity.

The basement is now filled with casts of sculpture and there is no available space to house the casts which represent the Princeton expeditions to Syria.[1] It is moreover being used for classes in architecture. This is not only a makeshift for the classes in architecture, but an injury to the collection of casts.

The main floor is crowded with the collection of pottery presented by Mr W. C. Prime[2] and several barrels full of pottery and porcelain of the Livingston Collection[3] have remained in the Museum for several years unopened for lack of room.

The upper story is not large enough to house the books and photographs which are ready to be presented and at the same time provide for the exhibition of the paintings and other objects already in possession.

A lecture hall in conjunction with the Museum is also most desirable.

In order to stimulate the completion of the building I hereby offer to the University my collection of art books, photographs and slides, roughly estimated as consisting of 5000 books, 5000 slides and 30,000 photographs and valued at $40 000, on condition that the building be enlarged to provide a suitable working library, a lecture hall and a room for architectural draughting.[4]

Yours very truly   Allan Marquand

ALS (WP, DLC).

[1] About these expeditions, see the Committee on the Curriculum to the Board of Trustees, June 13, 1904, n. 1, Vol. 15.

[2] William Cowper Prime, Princeton 1843, who died at his home in New York on February 13, 1905, had been Professor of the History of Art at Princeton since 1883, although he had not been active for some years. His valuable collection of ceramics, presented to Princeton in 1882, was the nucleus of the university's Museum of Historic Art.

[3] A collection of early American pottery presented by Mrs. William Smith Livingston.

[4] No permanent addition was made to the Museum of Historic Art until 1922, when McCormick Hall (a gift of the McCormick family) was completed on a site adjacent to the old building. Actually, Marquand presented his collection to the university on October 14, 1907, at which time he stipulated only that a "suitable" librarian be provided to care for it.

To Robert Garrett

My dear Mr. Garrett: Princeton, N. J.   March 3, 1905.

I inclose the letter which I promised to write to your brother.[1] I hope I have written it in a way that will seem to you best, and I shall regard it as a great favor of [if] you will kindly forward it to him.

I had the pleasure of a few words with Mrs. Garrett[2] on the street yesterday and she delighted me by telling me that you had decided not to become a Trustee of Johns Hopkins. I appreciate this decision all the more because I know the kind of sacrifice it involves, and yet I hope that my pleasure in it is not altogether selfish.

With warm regard,

Faithfully yours,   Woodrow Wilson

¹ That is, John Work Garrett, Princeton 1895. Both Robert and John W. Garrett had subscribed to the Emergency Fund established in the winter of 1904 (see WW to J. W. Garrett, Feb. 5, 1904; WW to R. Garrett, June 29, 1904; and R. Garrett to WW, July 4, 1904, all in Vol. 15). Wilson's letter to John W. Garrett concerned a subscription to the new funds being raised by the Committee of Fifty. See R. Garrett to WW, March 4, 1905, and WW to C. H. Dodge, Oct. 24, 1905.
² Robert Garrett and his mother, Alice Dickinson Whitridge (Mrs. Thomas Harrison) Garrett, maintained a residence at 50 Library Place, Wilson's former home.

To Winthrop More Daniels

My dear Daniels,   Princeton, N. J.   3 March, 1905

The enclosed papers contain all the "leads" I have as yet in the matter of preceptors. The Smith is the very pale boy, of fine stuff, whose brother (Schuyler)¹ (they were both of '01) was the handsomest, most distinguished looking man of his class²

Faithfully Yrs.,   Woodrow Wilson

¹ Howard Alexander Smith, New York lawyer, and Wilson Schuyler Smith, banker of New York. They were twins.
² See H. A. Smith to WW, May 1, 1905, n. 1.

To Ralph Barton Perry¹

My dear Mr. Perry: Princeton, N. J.   March 4, 1905

You may have heard, either through the newspapers or our own publications, that we are about to set up here a system of instruction by tutors, not unlike that which has so long been in successful operation at Oxford. Of course it is not our purpose to imitate Oxford and upset all the accepted methods among ourselves, but merely to graft well established principles upon our present way of teaching.

We want to make reading men of the undergraduates and wish to give them the best teachers we can possibly find to be their guides, philosophers, and friends in the process.

I am taking the liberty of writing you this letter to ask if you are sufficiently interested in the plan to be willing to consider the question whether you would yourself care to accept an appointment as tutor (or preceptor, as we shall probably choose to call the new officer) under the new system. We mean to give these new appointments dignity by raising them to a rank equivalent to that of Asst-professor and by paying as much as $1800 by way of salary. I know that you will tell me very frankly how you feel about the whole thing and about coming back to Princeton.

If you would like to go into the matter at all, I will be more than happy to take it up with you, either by letter or in a personal interview.

    With much regard,

               Sincerely yours,   Woodrow Wilson

TCL (in possession of Henry W. Bragdon).
   [1] Princeton 1896; Ph.D., Harvard, 1899; at this time Instructor in Philosophy at Harvard.

From Robert Garrett

My dear Mr. Wilson: [Princeton, N. J.]   March 4, 1905.

    Thank you very much for your letter with which you enclosed the one to my brother. I shall send this on to him within a few days, as soon as I can get a chance to jot down my views, such as they are, upon the subject of the change in the endowment plans. I thank you also for what you say concerning the Hopkins trusteeship. I decided that it would probably in the end prove fairer to decline the invitation to join the board in view of the fact that I should probably find it difficult to give my whole heart to the work at all times.

               Yours very sincerely,   [Robert Garrett]

CCL (Selected Corr. of R. Garrett, NjP).

A News Report of an Announcement
About McCosh Hall

                                 [March 4, 1905]

    The welcome announcement was made by President Wilson this week that Princeton is to have the new recitation hall so long needed. It is to be given by several benefactors of Princeton, who desire that their names shall not be announced at present.[1] But we understand that the money required for a handsome building, to cost perhaps as much as $300,000, is assured, and that it will be started next summer and completed in time for the academic year 1906-7.

    The site chosen for the new recitation hall is that portion of the old academy lot running along the north side of McCosh Walk. And it is to be called, very appropriately, McCosh Hall. While the plans for the building have not yet been drawn, competing architects must adhere to the collegiate Gothic style of the buildings erected in recent years on the campus. The recitation hall will extend from the rear of Marquand Chapel to Washington Road, and, possibly, it may turn the corner and run northward a short distance toward the School of Science. It is planned as the first of a projected group to form a new quadrangle of buildings surrounding the academy lot. There will be the much needed lecture halls for the use of both the Academic Department and the School of Science, and a considerable number of conference rooms somewhat similar to the seminar rooms of the University Library, for use in carrying out the preceptorial system described by President Wilson in the last number of The Weekly. This generous gift, by the way, is not a part of the $2,500,000 endowment fund to be raised by the Committee of Fifty, the main object of that fund being to put into effect the preceptorial system.

Printed in the *Princeton Alumni Weekly*, v (March 4, 1905), 349.

[1] The Minutes of the Board of Trustees of Princeton University for the period 1905 to 1908 reveal that the principal contributors to the McCosh Hall building fund were Cleveland Hoadley Dodge, Sarah Hoadley (Mrs. William Earl) Dodge (mother of C. H. Dodge), Moses Taylor Pyne, Percy Rivington Pyne, Archibald Douglas Russell, and Albertina Pyne (Mrs. Archibald D.) Russell.

To Ralph Barton Perry

My dear Dr. Perry: Princeton, N. J.   March 6, 1905

Thank you for your prompt answer to my letter.[1] I take pleasure in replying to the questions you put as particularly as I can in the circumstances. Of course it will take a number of years to adjust the new system to our own precedents, and I daresay that the tutorial function will differ in different departments, but I can give you a somewhat definite answer to each of your questions.

The tutorial function is not to be entirely specialized and isolated. The tutor will probably do some class work as well, though his tutorial work would be much the most important.

The amount of time the tutor is to devote to tutorial work will necessarily be somewhat indefinite, depending upon the size of the classes and the possibility of combining the men for instruction in small groups, but I should expect that it would require some four or five hours a day to do the tutorial work as it should be done. It would be our expectation and hope that we could mass these hours each day, so that a considerable portion of the day would be free for the tutor's own private use.

The tutors who showed unusual qualities would certainly be in line for promotion to a professorship. I do not think that it would be wise to make the tutors an isolated and exceptional group, notwithstanding they must exercise a very distinct and special function.

I hope that these are satisfactory answers to your questions, and that I shall hear from you again very frankly.[2]

Always,

Cordially yours,   Woodrow Wilson

TCL (H. W. Bragdon Coll., NjP).
[1] It is missing.
[2] Further correspondence concerning this matter is missing, but Perry did not accept the appointment at Princeton. He was promoted to Assistant Professor of Philosophy at Harvard in 1905.

To the Board of Trustees of Princeton University

Princeton, New Jersey, March 8, 1905.

The Committee on Honorary Degrees at a meeting held this day after consideration voted to recommend to the Board of Trustees for adoption and for incorporation in the By-Laws of the Trustees the following

Standards to be observed in conferring Honorary degrees:

LL.D.

1: Distinguished services to the state, to learning, or to mankind, coupled with—
2: Intellectual gifts and moral qualities which entitle him to rank with men of culture and high principle.

D.D.

1: Distinguished services to Christianity or to Christian philanthropy beyond the limits of a single locality, coupled with—
2: Intellectual gifts, displayed either by writing or otherwise, which give him rank with scholars and naturally suggest his recognition by a great University.

L.H.D.

1: Distinguished services to letters, art, music, or education, coupled with—
2: Intellectual and moral qualities which give him place among cultivated gentlemen.

D.Sc.

1: Distinguished service to science—coupled with—
2: Personal qualities and a kind of learning which entitles him to recognition by a learned educational body of high standing.

◇

The Committee recommend for the degree of
LL.D.
The Hon. George Brinton McClellan, Class of 1886, Mayor of the City of New York.

Andrew James McCosh, M.D., Class of 1877.

It is hoped that Sir William Mather[1] and James Curtis Hepburn, M.D.,[2] on whom it was voted to confer the degrees of LL.D. last year, may be present to receive the degrees at the coming Commencement.[3]

The Committee recommend for the degree of
D.D.
The Rev. Professor James Denney, of Glasgow, Scotland.[4]

It is hoped that the Rev. Allen Henry Brown[5] and the Rev. James Walter Lowrie,[6] on whom it was voted to confer the degree of D.D. last year, may be present to receive the degrees at the coming Commencement.[7]

The Committee recommend for the degree of
D.Sc.
Arthur Everett Shipley, of Christ's College, Cambridge, England.[8]

Woodrow Wilson   Chairman.

TRS (Trustees' Papers, UA, NjP).

[1] British industrialist and former Member of Parliament.

[2] Hepburn, Princeton 1832, had served as a medical missionary in Singapore and Amoy, China, from 1840 to 1845. In 1859, he became one of the earliest American missionaries to Japan, where he remained until 1892. In 1867, he published a Japanese-English dictionary, a pioneering work, and was also primarily responsible for one of the earliest translations of the Bible from English into Japanese. In 1905 he was living in retirement in East Orange, New Jersey, and, at the age of ninety, was the oldest living graduate of Princeton University.

[3] Both men received their honorary degrees at Commencement on June 14, 1905.

[4] Scottish theologian, Professor of New Testament Language, Literature, and Theology at the United Free Church College in Glasgow.

[5] Active for many years in Presbyterian mission work in various communities on the New Jersey shore. At this time he was living in Atlantic City.

[6] Princeton 1876; Presbyterian missionary in China since 1883.

[7] Brown and Lowrie also received their degrees on June 14, 1905.

[8] Zoologist, Fellow and Tutor in Natural Science at Christ's College and University Lecturer on Invertebrate Zoology. He did not receive his honorary degree from Princeton until 1906.

To Henry Oothout Milliken[1]

My dear Mr. Milliken: Princeton, N. J.   March 9, 1905.

Allow me to thank you most sincerely for your kindness in sending Mrs. Wilson and me tickets to the Dress Rehearsal of the Triangle Club on March 15th.[2] We shall look forward with great pleasure to being present.

Sincerely yours,   Woodrow Wilson

TLS (WC, NjP).

  [1] Princeton 1905, president of the Triangle Club, 1904-1905.

  [2] *The Pretenders*, book by John Matter '05 and James Dayton Voorhees '05, and lyrics and music by Kenneth Sherman Clark '05.

Henry Burchard Fine to the Board of Trustees' Committee on Morals and Discipline

Gentlemen: Princeton University, March 9, 1905.

Within the period covered by this report the Faculty has been asked to suspend one student for intoxication and another for disorderly conduct. There have been no other cases requiring serious discipline.

Under our rules of examination and standing 71 students were dropped at the end of the first term as against 75 last year. They were distributed among the several classes and departments as follows:

	Ac.	B.S.	C.E.
Seniors	2	1	0
Juniors	4	3	3
Sophomores	2	8	3
Freshmen	6	23	6
	—	—	—
	14	35	12

S.S. [School of Science] Specials—First year, 5—Upper Class, 5—Total, 10.

It will be observed that of the 71 men dropped, 40, or more than half, were either Freshmen or first year Specials. The remaining 31 constitute little more than 3% of the total enrolment in the three upper classes—surely not a large percentage of failures when account is taken of the fact that it includes every student who came under our rules.

The large mortality among the first year men is due in part to inadequate preparation and in part to excessive idleness. It may be said of nearly all the dropped Freshmen that while they had received preparatory instruction which enabled them to pass enough of the entrance examinations to gain admission to college, they had not been really trained with any degree of thoroughness in the subjects on which the work of Freshman year depends.

But it should also be said that despite their inadequate preparation a large number of these men might have survived the mid-year examinations had they shown reasonable diligence during the term. Twice in the course of the term the roll of the class was carefully reviewed and on both occasions all students who were found to be below the passing mark in any considerable portion of their work were turned over to me for a personal warning and a letter home. Almost every one of the Freshmen now dropped received one or both of these warnings. In these personal interviews with the men I soon discovered that they had come to college with a notion that an hour or two of study a day was quite enough for a "university man" to do, and that the rest of the day was meant for idle pleasure. I did what I could to disabuse their minds of this folly, but as the event has proved, with only small success. At first they would not take seriously what I had to say regarding the fate in store for them if they persisted in their foolish ways, and then quite suddenly, some three or four weeks before the end of the term, they became frightened and began cramming at a rate they could not stand and so disqualified themselves nervously to a degree for meeting the examinations.

I have taken pains to describe this situation at some length since I fear that it may repeat itself. We shall not be able to deal satisfactorily with our Freshmen until the time comes when they can be accommodated in college dormitories. The idleness of which I have just spoken manifests itself in its extreme form in the lodging houses of the town where large numbers of the Freshmen are collected.

I may add that about the middle of the term I warned all upperclassmen who were reported to me as being below the passing mark in half of their work. These warnings seem to have had a salutory effect, the students having taken them seriously.

Returning to the table, it will be noticed that this year, as last, the number of dropped B.S. men exceeds that of the A.B. and C.E. men combined. But this is mainly due to the weakness of the B.S. Freshmen. It is to be expected that the Freshman loss will be greatest in the B.S. course until it is realized that at Princeton this course is as serious as either the A.B. or the C.E. course.

I wish to call particular attention to the improved showing made by the C.E. Department, from which but 12 men were dropped—a loss of only 7% as against 10% last year. The fact that but 6 Freshmen were dropped is an evidence that the notion which is somewhat prevalent that because the entrance requirements of the C.E. Department are lower than those of the A.B. and B.S. Departments, the poorest class of students congregate there is not well founded. I am inclined to think that most of the students now in our C.E. Department are there with the serious purpose of fitting themselves for the engineering profession, and not because, wishing to reside in Princeton for a time, they found it easier to gain enrolment in that Department than in either of the others.

The number dropped from the A.B. Department is one less this year than last and is in fact so small that I am inclined to think it has reached its minimum. The number dropped, 14, is but 2% of the number enrolled, 659, in this Department.

The number dropped from the B.S. Department is also slightly less than last year. It is, however, 10% of the total enrolment in the Department. But this large percentage of the whole is due to the heavy loss among the Freshmen. The three upper classes have suffered a loss of only a little over 3%.

Taken as a whole, the statistics which I have given show that a strict enforcement of our rules of examinations and standing results in a very moderate loss of students except in the Freshman class. The reason is obvious. Our standards are not excessively high. Any student who possesses ordinary ability and who will consent to be reasonably diligent can easily reach them. Since we began to enforce the rules with strictness the students have taken them into serious account and their diligence has been greatly increased. It is because the Freshmen cannot be made at the start to realize what the strict enforcement of a rule means that they suffer in their first examinations so much more heavily than the three upper classes.

In this connection it may be of interest to remark that of the students dropped at this time last year and who returned last Fall, as they were allowed to do under our rules, only 3 have failed again. Previous to the adoption of our present rules the majority of such men failed. To judge from our recent experience, a majority of the dropped students return to college, when they are allowed to do so, and, as just illustrated, are successful in their subsequent work.

Finally I wish to call attention to the fact that while the new course of study is much more exacting than the old, especailly [especially] in the upper years, it has not caused an increase in the number of failures.

Respectfully submitted,

H.B. Fine   Dean of the Faculty.

TRS (Trustees' Papers, UA, NjP).

From the Minutes of the Board of Trustees of Princeton University

[March 9, 1905]

The Trustees of Princeton University met in stated session in the Trustees' Room in the Chancellor Green Library at Princeton, New Jersey, at eleven o'clock on Thursday morning, March 9, 1905.

The President of the University in the chair.

The meeting was opened with prayer by Dr. [George Black] Stewart. . . .

The report of the Committee on Honorary Degrees was accepted and the recommendations of the Committee adopted except the one to incorporate in the By-Laws the standards to be observed in conferring Honorary Degrees.

"Minutes of the Trustees of Princeton University, June 1901-Jan. 1908," bound minute book (UA, NjP).

To Williamson Updike Vreeland

My dear Prof. Vreeland: Princeton, N. J.   March 10, 1905.

The inclosed letter from Philip Churchman[1] explains itself. I think I already know your judgment about him, but perhaps I ought to ask for it again with regard to the new openings.[2] Will you not let me hear from you or see you soon about it?[3]

Always,
            Cordially and faithfully yours,   Woodrow Wilson

TLS (WC, NjP).
[1] Princeton 1896; Instructor in French, 1900-1904; at this time Instructor in French at the United States Naval Academy.
[2] That is, whether he should be considered for a preceptorship.
[3] He was not appointed.

From Charles Williston McAlpin

My dear Dr. Wilson: [Princeton, N. J.]   March 9, [10], 1905.

At the meeting of the Trustees held yesterday the resignation of Professor Rockwood was accepted and you were directed to convey to Professor Rockwood the appreciation by the Trustees of his long and faithful services to the College and the University.

            Sincerely yours,   [C. W. McAlpin] Secretary.

CCL (McAlpin File, UA, NjP).

From Samuel Henry Butcher

Dear President Wilson,   [London]   March 10, 1905
Your kind letter has given me genuine pleasure.[1] It is so delightful to think that you retain so friendly a remembrance of your passing guest (one of so many) at Princeton.[2] For myself I shall always recall those days with a sense of warm gratitude, & cherish what I believe the lawyers call 'animus revertendi.'
                    Yours Sincerely   S. H. Butcher

ALS (WP, DLC).
 [1] Wilson had probably written to thank Butcher for a copy of his *Harvard Lectures on Greek Subjects* (London and New York, 1904). The book, inscribed "With the Author's Compliments," is in the Wilson Library, DLC.
 [2] About his visit to Princeton, see WW to EAW, April 26, 1904, Vol. 15.

Ellen Axson Wilson to Anna Harris[1]

My dear Friend,   Princeton, March 11, 1905.
I have been wishing and meaning to write you for many months, but it has been such a troubled year with me, and my own immediate family has been so scattered and so ravenous for home letters, that I have sadly neglected all other friends[.] Two of my girls are at college now,[2] and Madge is in Italy for the winter; and having a *rapturous* time. She went in Oct. to stay a year,—travelling of course next summer in the more northern countries. And poor Stockton is also away on a very different errand. He has been for three months in *bed* in Phila. with complete nervous exhaustion, and melancholia. It is the second collapse in two years; he was in the same condition for six months year before last. All the fall he was struggling desperately to keep out of that pit, yet slipping steadily down inch by inch. It was *terrible*. I hardly know how either of us lived through it, for he depends altogether on me for help when he is in such case. At last it was arranged for him to go to this Phila. specialist, just two days before Woodrow and I were to go to the New York hospital where he was to be operated upon. (That too had been hanging over us for six months.) But Stockton is much better now and very cheerful and hopeful; and the doctor,—who really seems to know what he is about more than any of the others he has been to,—assures us that by next fall he will be better than he has been for many years. So the poor fellow has another chance. It is *wonderful* that he should have made such a brilliant record for himself with such dreadful health as he has had for years. The boys are wild over him, both as a man and a lecturer,

voting him formally "the most popular professor"; and the trustees show the most extraordinary regard and appreciation of him. They are always telling Woodrow that "they cannot allow him to be 'hard' on so valuable and remarkable a man just because he is a relative." So while Woodrow was at the hospital it was settled without consulting him that Stockton should have another year off on full salary, the second since he has been here.[3]

Woodrow, I am glad to say, has come through his troubles finely and is going to be stronger,—able to take more exercise,—than for several years past. We were away nine weeks, five at the hospital and four in Fla. We had a delightful holiday at Palm Beach and it did us both worlds of good. The climate there is almost too good to be true. Indeed now that we are back again amid[4]

ALS (WC, NjP).

[1] Mrs. Wilson's girlhood friend of Rome, Ga.

[2] Margaret and Jessie, both at the Woman's College of Baltimore (now Goucher College).

[3] Axson had also been promoted to Professor of English by the Board of Trustees on December 8, 1904.

[4] The balance of this letter is missing.

A News Item

[March 11, 1905]

President Wilson '79, Dr. J. C. Hepburn '32, Rev. Dr. Wilton Merle Smith '77, and Cleveland H. Dodge '79 are members of the General Committee for the Japanese Relief Fund, to provide "aid for the sick and wounded in both armies and the destitute widows and children of the soldiers killed in the Russo-Japanese War."

Printed in the *Princeton Alumni Weekly*, v (March 11, 1905), 369.

Two Letters to Winthrop More Daniels

My dear Daniels: Princeton, N. J.   March 13, 1905.

This letter about Mr. [Hiram] Bingham* makes the case look very promising indeed. Had we not better have him down and have a look at him?

Faithfully yours,   Woodrow Wilson

* One of the original preceptors appointed in 1905. In his Annual Report to the Board of Trustees, printed at December 14, 1905, Wilson provides extensive biographical information about all new appointees in 1905. Such persons are denoted by a large asterisk where they are first mentioned in this volume.

My dear Daniels: Princeton, N. J.   March 14, 1905.

Thank you for letting me see Andrew's letter,[1] which seems to me quite helpful. Evidently, we must strike for Hiram Bingham. I like your suggestion about Keener[2] very much indeed and will seek an early conversation with you about it.

I inclose two letters sent me this morning by [William Milligan] Sloane.

Cordially yours,   Woodrow Wilson

TLS (Wilson-Daniels Corr., CtY).

[1] Abram Piatt Andrew, Princeton 1893, at this time Assistant Professor of Economics at Harvard.

[2] Perhaps John Henry Keener, Princeton 1897, A.M., 1898, who was teaching at the Lawrenceville School. Keener had entered college at the age of thirty-three and by graduation had won a notable reputation as a tutor of his fellow-students. However, if he or any other Keener was being considered for an appointment at Princeton, he did not receive it. John Henry Keener remained at the Lawrenceville School until his death in 1911.

From Edward Nelson Teall[1]

Dear Sir: New York, Mar. 15, '05

Probably you will have noticed already the enclosed article.[2] Whether it may prove pleasing or otherwise to you, I think I am doing right in sending it to you.

The article is based upon your public report—and I hope that has been properly interpreted, and nothing said that could possibly be injurious to you or to the University.

Very sincerely,   Edward N. Teall. ('02)

ALS (WP, DLC).

[1] Princeton 1902, on the editorial staff of the New York *Sun*.

[2] The enclosure was a clipping of an editorial in the New York *Sun*, March 15, 1905, which discussed with favorable comment Wilson's plan for the tutorial, or preceptorial, system.

From Robert Shoemaker Dana[1]

Dear Doctor,   Morrisville, Pa., March 15th, 1905.

I have just seen a statement made in the public paper that you have expressed yourself as "doubting the utility of the worship of the flag as now taught in the public schools."[2] Will you please be kind enough to state if this report is correct. If not, please state what you did say that has led to this report, and the reasons for the making of the above, or any similar remarks if such have been made. As Special Aide of the Grand Army of the Republic, I have now, with others, been engaged for several years in endeavoring to instill into the minds of the children as high a spirit of patriotism and love for their country as possible, thereby fitting them the better for their duties as citizens. The Grand Army of the Republic would not be too hasty in its conclusions, and as Special Aide for the Department of New Jersey, I would ask an early reply to the above. You will thereby greatly oblige,

Most respectfully yours,   Robert S. Dana, M.D.,
Special Aide of G. A. R. for Dep't of N. J.
Post Office Address, Morrisville, Pa.

PCL (WP, DLC).
[1] A retired physician of Morrisville, Pa., who identifies himself more fully in his letter.
[2] In Wilson's address to the New Rochelle, N. Y., People's Forum on February 26, 1905.

Notes for an Address

18 March, 1905
Pittsburgh Alumni

No amount of money or strength of plan could of themselves "do as much for the cause of higher learning in ten years as Johns Hopkins does in one term, and not as much for the promotion of manhood and citizenship in a year as Princeton does in a week."[1]

Princeton's scholarship stands for sound thinking and an all-round release of the faculties as *vs.* narrow, particularistic, technical training, *holding that the end of knowledge is life.*

Object *now* to establish intimate connection bet. her scholarship and her life. The means?

1) Preceptorial system
2) Graduate College
   Upon wh. will follow self-expression in larger fields of action, thought, and literature.

Thus we shall get conspicuous leadership and, by consequence, a very sobering sense of responsibility

But a pleasurable sense of responsibility, after all,—because a responsibility for maintaining high ideals.

WWhw MS (WP, DLC).
[1] About the authorship of this quotation, see n. 1 to the news report printed at April 15, 1903, Vol. 14.

A News Report of an Alumni Meeting in Pittsburgh

[March 19, 1905]

PRINCETON MEN PAY TRIBUTE TO ALMA MATER

Four Hundred Tigers Make Banquet Hall of Schenley Ring.

PRESIDENT'S WORDS

Woodrow Wilson Tells of the Present
and Plans for the Future.

If Princeton University does not attain the pre-eminent standing for which President Wilson and his faculty are striving it will not be the fault of the Princeton Club of Western Pennsylvania. Because the Triangle Club of Old Nassau was here on a conquest Princeton men from the entire western portion of the State arranged a complimentary dinner to the visitors last evening at the Hotel Schenley, and included as guests President Wilson, Dean West and others.

The real feature of the evening, excepting the address of the head of the university, was the singing of the graduates and students. From "Old Nassau," sung by the multitude afoot, to the singing of favorite selections from "The Pretenders," the Tigers proved themselves masters of melody and princes of good-fellowship. There were over 400 of them to help along the merriment, and the smallest undergraduate was of as much importance as the most-talked-of alumnus.

There was a brief reception which began at 6:30 o'clock, and soon afterward the assemblage, headed by President Wilson and J. B. Shea,[1] President of Princeton Club of Western Pennsylvania, marched into the banquet hall. Decorations of orange and black were in evidence in all parts of the hall, from Princeton markers on the tables to streamers about the walls. The members and guests took their places according to the year of their graduation as designated by figures on the tables, the first beginning with 1854. The menus were engraved in the Princeton colors, with the Tiger's head on the cover and each inside page. . . .

Woodrow Wilson, President of "Greater Princeton," was introduced by President Shea as "The Ruler of the Tiger." There was continued applause. As a speaker he has the admirable art of terseness, humor and intermittent solidity of thought. He amused one minute and convinced the next. President Wilson devoted most of his time to the Graduate College and incidentally registered a sound remonstrance against the "money colleges."

---

[1] Joseph Bernard Shea, Princeton 1885, department store executive in Pittsburgh.

When this was done there were whispers of "Stanford" and "Chicago," although President Wilson, oblivious to all about him, continued his notable address for the preservation of the "great principle of Princeton." He said in part:

"Such a full-throated welcome is enough to hearten anyone. Here in Pittsburg the Princeton pulse beats stronger than any place I know, and it is gratifying to be among you. I admire the ease with which you get your presidents."

This was interrupted with good-natured laughter, which was quickly quelled by the speaker adding:

"I refer to Dr. Shaw[2] and Mr. Shea. But it is a serious matter, this thing of being a President and posing as such before an assemblage of this kind. When I was last here[3] Dr. White[4] had much fun at my expense while dealing in reminiscences in which he referred to my family, which used to live in these parts.[5] This reminded me of the old adage of 'Tell the truth and shame the family.'[6]

"Posing before you as President of Princeton reminds me of the woman who visited a circus where she saw a man reading through a two-inch board, a newspaper. After watching him for a brief period she remarked: 'Let me out. This is no place for me with such thin things on.'"

President Wilson, after a few insinuations regarding himself and his office, spoke of the gratification and satisfaction he derived from reading certain newspaper items, and as an illustration he read this: "No amount of money or strength of plan could of themselves do as much for the cause of higher learning in 10 years as Johns Hopkins does in one term, and not so much for the promotion of manhood and citizenship in a year as Princeton does in a week."

Continuing, he said: "The mere expenditure of money out of hand does not make a great university, but it is by genius and genius alone. During the 150 years that Princeton has been established we have not succeeded owing to one set of men or money.

[2] James Prestley Shaw, M.D., Princeton 1886. Until recently, Shaw had been President of the Princeton Club of Western Pennsylvania.
[3] Wilson had addressed the Pittsburgh alumni on March 7, 1903. See the news report printed at March 8, 1903, Vol. 14.
[4] Thomas Henry White, M.D., Princeton 1867, Vice President of the Princeton Club of Western Pennsylvania.
[5] Wilson's memory was faulty at this point. It was John Adams Wilson '73, Woodrow Wilson's first cousin, who spoke in 1903 of the Wilson family in the Pittsburgh area.
[6] This quotation appeared as the entry for the week beginning January 1, 1905, in Ethel Watts Mumford, Oliver Herford, and Addison Mizner, *The Entirely New Cynic's Calendar of Revised Wisdom* 1905 (San Francisco, 1904).

"Manhood and citizenship are much involved in Princeton's scholarship—manhood and citizenship backed not by good intentions, but by knowledge and common sense. Yet, I believe Princeton's scholarship stands for sound thinking—an all-round release of the faculties as versus narrowness, particularities, technical training—holding that the end of knowledge is life. A scholarship not as a means of livelihood, but a method of life.

"At the university there is created a quick power of mind where one is lifted to see beyond a horizon of commonplace things. The university is a great community where there is developed the best fellowship and manhood and citizenship. I pray that pedantic learning—as commonly accepted—may never creep into Princeton. It is necessary for technical learning, as more men require it than can ever enter Princeton, but I hope that our university will soar above this."

Here President Wilson spoke for the faculty, saying that each member was "as good a fellow as the collegian." This created a merry "ha ha." The point he aimed to make was the contemplated establishment of a connection of good-fellowship between the faculty and undergraduates.

He said that he had heard rumors of "revolution" which called him "leader," but as to the usages and customs of Princeton he declared none would be destroyed except the bringing closer together of the students and faculty.

This will be accomplished, he explained, by appointing about 50 professors, who, for the want of a better term at present, will be known as preceptors. This list will be augmented by the faculty, who will also act as preceptors in order to become better acquainted with the undergraduates.

Speaking of college education or learning in general the speaker said he does not understand how a man without learning can carry his head over the crowd—how he can possibly hope to see the proper arrangement of life. In this respect he spoke of the character of man, what lies within, as against the physical make-up.

"A wonderful thing about Princeton," he said, "is how it has got along on such slender capital. When I look at the annual budget my thoughts turn to the remark of an Irish friend who, during a game of cards, lost $5,000. He explained, however, that he had lost only $5. I hope that the good will of the alumni will be capitalized at a good sum."

The remainder of his address was devoted to the Graduate College or the Residential College, which is to be composed of the cream of the graduates. He said that achievement counts; that the man who lives in memory is dead, and that Princetonians' accomplishments will be founded on memory, plus achievement, plus confident hope.

Dean West of the Graduate School spoke of the Residential College and paid a glowing tribute to President Wilson. . . .

Printed in the *Pittsburg Dispatch*, March 19, 1905; some editorial headings omitted.

To Robert Shoemaker Dana

My Dear Sir: Princeton, N. J., March 21st, 1905.

An absence for some days from home has prevented my replying sooner to your letter of March 15th.

I would say in reply that the quotation you saw in the newspaper from an address which I recently delivered in New Rochelle, N. Y., was, as usual, given only in part. I, of course, have no criticism to make of the respect and veneration taught our school children for the flag of the United States. The passage from which the quotation was taken was merely devoted to the plea that the children, instead of being taught a mere blind reverence, should be more discriminatingly instructed as to what the flag stood for. I am sorry that the address was extemporaneous and that I cannot send you the passage as I uttered it. Allow me to add that while I am perfectly willing to tell any citizen of the United States what I have said and what I think on a subject of this kind, the intimation which your letter seems to contain, that the Grand Army of the Republic is at liberty to call their fellow-citizens to account for public utterances, *seems to me both offensive and ridiculous.*

Very truly yours,   Woodrow Wilson

PCL (WP, DLC).

To Edgar Odell Lovett

My dear Prof. Lovett: Princeton, N. J.   March 21, 1905.

Would it be possible and convenient for you to attend the Installation of President Alderman at the University of Virginia as Princeton's representative? I know that they are anxious to have a Princeton delegate, and I also know that a strong preference is that you should be that delegate.

I know also that you will not need urging to go if it is possible for you to do so, and I can assure you that it would give me personal gratification if you found it possible to go.[1]

Cordially and sincerely yours,   Woodrow Wilson

TLS (E. O. Lovett Papers, TxHR).
[1] Lovett represented Princeton at the inauguration of Edwin Anderson Alderman as first President of the University of Virginia on April 13, 1905.

To the Secretary of the American Philosophical Society

Princeton, N. J.   March 21, 1905.

Mr. Woodrow Wilson desires to thank the American Philosophical Society for the kind invitation to be present at the annual dinner of the Society on Friday evening, April 14th at 7:30, and accepts the invitation with pleasure.

TL (Archives, PPAmP).

A News Report

[March 23, 1905]

ANNUAL BANQUET

Of The Daily Princetonian, Held at the Inn Last Evening.

The seventh annual banquet of The Daily Princetonian was held last evening at the Princeton Inn. The dinner was the largest ever given by the Princetonian, one hundred covers being laid. The banquet began at half-past eight and concluded with the toast by President Wilson. . . .

President Woodrow Wilson responded to the toast, "Princeton University." We must not look ahead only a few years if we are to be true Princeton men, but we must look into the future and prepare ourselves for it, as Princeton looks to us to uphold her name. Living in histories and the stories of men who are gone will not assist us, but by profiting by their experience, we are better enabled to face the world. The great objection to a technical course of education is that it has the tendency to train a man's mind in certain channels while a liberal course of education gives a man an all-around training and better fits him for a broad career. The real Princeton spirit is that which binds us together by agreement on the great principles to which our lives are devoted. The bond of union is that community of thought which comes from sharing a purpose in the things that are worth while, from concerted action in the things we believe in. There must be some universities where men can think the general things of the world. Princeton's strength is not material but spiritual.[1]

Printed in the *Daily Princetonian*, March 23, 1905.
   [1] There is a WWhw outline of these remarks, dated March 22, 1905, in WP, DLC.

To Robert Kilburn Root*

My dear Sir: Princeton, N. J.   March 23, 1905

We are just about instituting in Princeton a Tutorial system based upon that at Oxford, for the purpose of bringing the undergraduates and the faculty into closer and more efficient relations. In order to give the appointments made under the new system the dignity which ought to attach to them, we have determined to give the preceptors appointed (for that is the name by which they will be called) the rank and privileges of Assistant-Professors, so that they will be in line for promotion to Professorships if an opportunity should offer, and the salary paid the preceptors will range from $1500 to $2000. The appointments will at first be for a term of years, but with the same prospect of permanency that all such appointments should have when the work done is perfectly satisfactory.

Of course it is impossible in a letter to describe as I should wish them described, our plans for the operation of this system, and I am therefore taking the liberty of writing you to ask if you would be willing to have your name considered for one of the appointments, and whether, in case you should be willing, you could make it convenient, at some early date, to come to Princeton or arrange for an interview with me in New York City.

I know that your friend Professor Hibben would wish to be very cordially remembered to you if he knew I were writing.
                    Very sincerely yours,   Woodrow Wilson

Printed in William Starr Myers (ed.), *Woodrow Wilson: Some Princeton Memories* (Princeton, N. J., 1946), pp. 13-14.

From Charles Scribner

Dear Mr. Wilson: New-York   March 24, 1905.

Your letter[1] arrives as I was about to write you regarding the fellowship. I am glad you approve it but I must write a word or two of explanation.

Not very long ago Professor Hunt and Professor Parrott expressed a wish that there could be an additional University fellowship for next year in order that they might keep at Princeton one of the men whom they valued very highly—Mr. [William Harry] Clemons I think. I was willing to provide the additional fellowship for the year but a week ago I received a letter from Professor Parrott stating that Mr. Clemons would be retained as an instructor, owing to the installation of the tutorial system, and suggesting that the extra fellowship be thrown open to seniors and graduates. In response to this I proposed that it be made a competitive fellowship for seniors only on the same basis as the other college fellowships and that I would provide the money for three years. It is rather late to manage it for this year but the professors in the English Department think it can be done satisfactorily. At the end of the three years I hope some way will be found for continuing the fellowship. I think Dr. van Dyke has some plan for that—possibly in connection with a reunion of his own class. I know he is greatly interested in having this fellowship as he thinks it will stimulate the undergraduates. I hope it will be of service in connection with the University fellowship in turning out good men for tutors. I write all this because I wish you to understand how the proposal came about, though perhaps Professor Hunt has already told you most of it.

In any public announcement of this fellowship I prefer that my name should not be mentioned. I do not wish to make any mystery of [it]; it is only for three years and no name is necessary.[2]   Yours sincerely,   Charles Scribner

TLS (WP, DLC).
    [1] It is missing.
    [2] The fellowship was described in the Princeton catalogue for 1905-1906 as follows: "Special Fellowship in English—This fellowship, yielding $500 to the holder, is awarded for the year 1905-1906 through the liberality of Mr. Charles Scribner, of the Class of 1875."
    As Scribner indicated, the fellowship was offered for three years, that is, through the academic year 1907-1908. In 1908, Henry van Dyke's Class of 1873 established a very generous fellowship in English literature.

A News Report of a Talk in Philadelphia

[March 25, 1905]

COLLEGE MEN GREET HEAD OF PRINCETON

University Club Entertains
Woodrow Wilson at Reception and Dinner.

A reception to President Woodrow Wilson, of Princeton, was given last night at the University Club. Several hundred members of the club attended.

Preceding the reception, Dr. Wilson was entertained at dinner by the Board of Governors of the club. All the decorations of table and dining hall were suggestive of Princeton. Orange and Black bunting was draped on the walls, there were yellow flowers in black receptacles, and the candle shades were of the same colors. Within the inclosure, surrounded by the circular table, was the famed Princeton Tiger, lithe and fierce-looking, and partly hidden in a miniature jungle.

Two speeches were made at the dinner. John Cadwalader, president of the Board of Governors, welcomed the guest of honor and testified to the appreciation in which President Wilson is held by university men everywhere.

To this Dr. Wilson replied that he was glad to meet men of university training and education who have a community of interest in the promotion of higher ideals.

"It is important that university men should take the place in public life for which they are fitted," said Dr. Wilson.

"There should be a community of interest among university men in seeking to advance the welfare of their fellows. Their relation to each other is more important in some respects than their relation to public life. Yet, every man who is educated and trained in college has a duty to his country by reason of the privileges he has enjoyed.

"In certain university men there lingers a trace of the college provincialism. This should be forgotten, and, while college loyalty is not without its value, the general term 'university man' should supersede that of Princeton man or Pennsylvania man or Yale man to a great extent. That is why I value greatly such an occasion as this, when we meet on the common interest of being university men."

Printed in the Philadelphia *North American*, March 25, 1905; one editorial heading omitted.

From Marion Phar Hilliard[1]

Dear Dr. Wilson:　　　East Orange, New Jersey, March 25, 1905.

A year ago I was one of many who gathered in a lecture room of the University of New York to hear what you had to say to us about the teaching of history in the grammar grades.[2]

As I listened to you I experienced the exquisite delight born of the realization that a truth long groped for in the dark is suddenly and clearly revealed. Ever since I have been trying to teach history, a sense of its profound value as a means of spiritual development has been deepening in my mind; but how to perform I saw not until "that happy day.["] It was as if you had said to me, "I will show you clearly the truths of which you have been vaguely conscious." Your clear-cut phrases were so sharply engraved upon my memory that they have become my professional creed.

Since then I have been trying with all my might to give my pupils "a conceiving imagination" of the periods of history we have studied. Tho' I am much hampered by text books and examinations, the work has been a delight to me.

I send you by this mail some specimens of what my pupils have done. If you feel that I have done anything at all toward helping them to "live our history in their imagination," will you tell me so? You will make me very happy by so doing at a time when I feel the need of encouragement. And it will help me just as much if you will point out the defects. These are representative papers; I have many others that are quite as well written. But I have a special fondness for these papers; so perhaps you will be so kind as to return them. I hope you will not feel I have taken too great a liberty in sending them. I feel a special need of help and criticism just now.

Sincerely yours,   (Miss) Marion Phar Hilliard

ALS (WP, DLC).
₁ Teacher of history and English in the grammar schools of East Orange, N. J.
₂ See WW to EAW, March 21, 1904, n. 2, Vol. 15.

To Winthrop More Daniels

My dear Daniels: Princeton, N. J.   March 27, 1905.

Here is another candidate into whose claims we may find it worth while to look.

I assumed on Saturday that you were as much pleased with Bingham as I was and I definitely offered him an appointment. He will certainly accept if certain family arrangements do not prevent.

Always,
Cordially and faithfully yours,   Woodrow Wilson

TLS (Wilson-Daniels Corr., CtY).

From Winthrop More Daniels, with Enclosure

My dear Wilson: Princeton, N. J.   Mch. 27, 1905.

I enclose a large batch of replies with their accompanying testimonials.[1] Of the four men who are concerned it is clear that

W. Roy Smith of Bryn Mawr[2] cannot be longer considered at present, as he admits that he is in honor bound to stay in his present place for one more year.

I should say that Trenholme of the Univ. of Missouri[3] ought not to be encouraged, purely on financial grounds. He now receives $1850, and is on the way to receive more in the near future; is married and has two children. He has sent me a copy of his study of "The Right of Sanctuary in England"[4] and his testimonials are strong. If we were looking for a professor of History, his claims would be fairly strong, *prima facie.*

Mr. A. B. Wolfe[5] who writes from St. Louis was named by Prof. Carver of Harvard,[6] and seconded by Andrew, tho' not very enthusiastically. A close examination of his letter does not predispose me much in his favor.

The last of the four is one of our own graduates, McIlwain,* now at Miami University, Oxford, Ohio. He took his graduate course in history at Harvard, and sends me a MS. thesis on "The Development of the Jury in England[.]" You will note that he is ready to be in Princeton for an interview bet. Mch 24 and April 4th. Will you advise me whether to name a date when he could see you here, or will you write him directly? Have you written to Viles?[7]   Yours very Sincerely,   W. M. Daniels

[1] The enclosures were W. R. Smith to W. M. Daniels, March 24, 1905, ALS (WP, DLC); N. M. Trenholme to W. M. Daniels, March 23, 1905, TLS (WP, DLC); A. B. Wolfe to W. M. Daniels, March 23, 1905, TLS (WP, DLC); Charles W. Colby, testimonial in behalf of N. M. Trenholme, TC (WP, DLC); Charles Gross, testimonial in behalf of N. M. Trenholme, TC (WP, DLC); Albert B. Hart, testimonial in behalf of N. M. Trenholme, TC (WP, DLC); and Benjamin Watkins, testimonial in behalf of N. M. Trenholme, TC (WP, DLC).

[2] William Roy Smith, Associate in History at Bryn Mawr College.

[3] Norman Maclaren Trenholme, Assistant Professor of History at the University of Missouri. He was promoted to Professor of History later in the year.

[4] Norman Maclaren Trenholme, *The Right of Sanctuary in England: A Study in Institutional History* (Columbia, Mo., 1903).

[5] Albert Benedict Wolfe, Instructor in History at McKinley High School in St. Louis. He received the Ph.D. in economics from Harvard in 1905.

[6] Thomas Nixon Carver, David A. Wells Professor of Political Economy at Harvard.

[7] Jonas Viles, Instructor in History at the University of Missouri.

ENCLOSURE

Charles Howard McIlwain to Winthrop More Daniels

Dear Sir: Oxford, Ohio   March 22, 1905.

Your letter of March 20 has been received, and I have noted your description of the qualifications and duties of the tutors under the new system to be adopted at Princeton.

I am willing to consider a definite offer of one of these positions.

The spring vacation here begins on Friday, March 24, and ends on Tuesday, April 4. At any time within those dates I could come to Princeton.

For two or three years I have been busy at some work which will, I hope, come out eventually as one of the Harvard Historical Studies,[1] but as yet I have published nothing. I will send under separate cover one or two things I wrote some time ago, though not for publication.

Very truly yours,   C. H. McIlwain.

I could be in Princeton by Thursday next, or by Wednesday if I could hear in time that this date was satisfactory to you.

ALS (WP, DLC).

[1] He was probably referring to the work which ultimately appeared as Peter Wraxall, *An Abridgment of the Indian Affairs . . . Transacted in the Colony of New York, From the Year 1678 to the Year 1751*, ed. with an introduction by Charles Howard McIlwain, "Harvard Historical Studies," Vol. xxi (Cambridge, Mass., 1915). By this date, however, McIlwain had also published *The High Court of Parliament and its Supremacy* . . . (New Haven, Conn., 1910).

Notes for an Address to Detroit Alumni

30 March, 1905

To the Princeton Men at Dinner

Present tasks:

Reorganization of undergraduate training

1) *The new course of study*
2) *The preceptorial system*: to make reading men and promote independent and discriminating thoughtfulness.

Hopes: The sort of stimulation we want can come only thr. the spirit and ideals of scholarship.

1) *Pure Science* as a liberal, rather than professional, study.
2) *A Graduate College* of residence.

WWhw MS (WP, DLC).

A News Report of Two Addresses in Detroit

[March 31, 1905]

HAILED WITH COLLEGE YELL

Principal Wilson, of Princeton, Heartily Received.

When Rev. Dr. A. H. Barr,[1] of the Jefferson Avenue Presbyterian church, ended his introduction of President Woodrow Wilson, of Princeton university, last night, the 200 members of the University club, assembled in their hall, arose and, with one accord, greeted their guest with the time-honored Princeton yell.

In his subsequent address President Wilson proved himself worthy of the enthusiastic welcome accorded him.

"We constantly hear that education ought to be modern and of the day in which we live," he said. "I cannot help suspecting that the man who takes this position must have voted for Bryan. Why? Because Bryan believes that this country can maintain its monetary standard without reference to the remainder of the world, and these other people seem to think they can maintain a standard of education without reference to other generations. A generation that cuts itself off from preceding generations cannot tell whence it came or whither it is going."

President Wilson spoke of the value of acquiring the power of analyzing that which is not seeable, because then it will be easy to dissect that which may be cut to pieces with a knife. By way of illustration of a point, the speaker referred to Tammany.

"The strength of Tammany lies in her union. Privately, her passions are good. She stands by those affiliated with her. Publicly, she stands for the art of getting at the resources of New York City, so that she may make her benevolences possible. Until the reformers can organize as Tammany has organized, they can never successfully keep the field against her. You can understand Tammany by reading your Bible, because in that book you find human nature in all its phases."[2]

As a climax to an argument for an educated and "traveled" mind, President Wilson stated that he believes in individual and social ethics. The individual in things that concern him alone must never swerve from the path that duty and conscience point out. In social ethics, persons must "get together" and find a common ground upon which to work.

Preceding the lecture, about twenty-five Princeton alumni tendered a dinner to President Wilson at the Detroit club. Rev. J. M. Barkley[3] was toastmaster and other universities were represented, as follows: Yale, Truman H. Newberry; Harvard, Fred M. Alger; University of Michigan, Henry M. Campbell.[4] Dr. Wilson made a fine address after the dinner, detailing the latest changes in the courses of study at Princeton.

Printed in the *Detroit Free Press*, March 31, 1905; two editorial headings omitted.
[1] Alfred Hamilton Barr, Princeton 1889.
[2] Here Wilson was probably in part reflecting the observations of Henry Jones Ford in "Municipal Corruption," *Political Science Quarterly*, XIX (Dec. 1904), 673-86, which was a review essay of Lincoln Steffens, *The Shame of the Cities* (New York, 1904). Ford said that Steffens' descriptions of boss rule and munici-

pal corruption, although unquestionably accurate, did not go to the heart of the matter. Responsibility in city government had been so diffused by the proliferation and division of power that effective government was impossible through prevailing constitutional forms. The boss and the machine were in fact the one unifying force in municipal politics and the one agency capable of governing. "It is better," Ford wrote, "that government and social activity should go on in any way than that they should not go on at all." Moreover, he continued, the machine had served a significant social service by assimilating diverse immigrant groups into the mainstream of American political life.

[3] James Morrison Barkley, Princeton 1876, pastor of the Third Presbyterian Church in Detroit.

[4] Truman Handy Newberry, Yale 1885, Detroit businessman and capitalist, soon to be appointed Assistant Secretary of the Navy; Frederick Moulton Alger, Harvard 1899, businessman of Detroit; and Henry Monroe Campbell, Michigan 1876, lawyer of Detroit.

A News Report of an Address in Ann Arbor, Michigan

[April 1, 1905]

THE SCHOOLMASTERS HAVE LEFT CITY

President Wilson, of Princeton, Gave Address Last Night

The 40th annual meeting of the Michigan Schoolmasters' club and the meeting of the Michigan Academy of Science were brought to a conclusion today, and the big delegation of school teachers have returned to their homes. The attendance was a record-breaker and the session was voted by all who attended to be especially interesting.

One of the most brilliant addresses on the S. L. A. Course or of the Michigan Schoolmasters' club, was given last evening[1] by President Woodrow Wilson of Princeton University, on "The University and the Nation."

"One thing I like about living at a university["], said this president of one of the greatest institutions, "is that a man may take time in a university to think a little—if he has anything to think with.

"Your universities are not to make money; they are not on the same footing as any other enterprise you have built up["]; but just what their relation is to the nation, was the burden of Prof. Wilson's discourse, presented as they live it at Princeton.

"Individual achievements have back of them the force of a common motive—public spirit—to which every man is summoned to contribute, and in every one of us dwells this force that gives strength in the making of a nation. Herein lies the key to the greatness of America.

"Your universities," continued Prof. Wilson, "are intended to be your vehicles of spirit. They are intended to provide a little quiet space, where a man may cloister himself and draw apart from the confused field of business and pore upon the map of life.

"And what are you going to study? If your interest is bent upon your profession alone, you are not in the university at all. You cannot study by rule of thumb, but you must see your work in its relation to the community.

"If you can get a fellow to liberate himself and release his mind from its thralldom, so that there comes into his consciousness something more than a particular interest, then you have educated him and made him a university man.

"The university ought to communicate the 'travel[ed] mind,' the 'liberal mind,' and the 'political mind,' meaning by the latter, the temper of affairs.

"The function of our universities is in essence, a vehicle of spirit to enable you to discover your souls and use them in the service of your fellowmen, to see your opportunities, and to know how wide they are in the pursuit of the truth, which is the daily task, and is to be extracted from the daily task.

"When we have gained this conception, then we have become university men.

"What we want is places of learning where the youth may stretch and emancipate his mind; finding through this freedom those ideals in which the hope of humanity dwells."[2]

Printed in the *Ann Arbor*, Mich., *Daily Argus*, April 1, 1905; some editorial headings omitted.

[1] Wilson spoke under the auspices both of the Michigan Student Lecture Association and of the Michigan Schoolmasters' Club.

[2] There is a WWhw outline of this address, dated March 31, 1905, in WP, DLC.

From Oren Root[1]

Dear Sir: Clinton, N. Y., April 3 1905

I crave pardon for intrusion. I have no claim whatever upon your attention and no excuse to urge save that I am getting to be a veteran teacher. I began in 1856—the year of my graduation and—save for three years during which while nominally a lawyer, I continued my reading of mathematics and actively interested myself in schools—I have taught since then. I have had a somewhat varied experience: college tutor, academy principal, western university professor, city school superintendent, president of a small college. For sixteen years, I taught literature, history, and oratory. In 1880, I reverted to mathematics as my father's successor here.

You do not need light or strength in the matters you have undertaken at Princeton. I write thinking merely that it may please you a little to have hearty indorsement even from an old chap up on the Oneida hills.

Your plan for what you call a "tutorial university" has been a pet notion of mine since I came to this college as tutor in 1860. I have talked it in conventions of High School teachers, in State Association at our New York Regents Convocation, in the National Association. In my work and in my administration, I have always since 1860, sectionized my classes. When I returned here in 1880, I at once asked the faculty to arrange for a division of my classes into sections not larger than 15. I call every man for recitation at every exercise. I study the boys and there is no monotony in teaching the same subjects year after year. The boy problems are new every year. Since 1880, my colleagues in our faculty have followed my example and save in a few upperclass subjects, we have few exercises with numbers exceeding twenty. This to my mind has been the proper work of the small college; to reach every man so constantly that he can get away from your influence only by positive struggle: to arouse the sluggish, to steady the brilliant careless fellow, to touch a key somewhere which answers with personal interest in mathematics[,] to ascertain what each particular boy needs and make direct effort to supply that need. I have failed perhaps too often but I have sometimes succeeded.

Your plan will place this advantage of the small college, in connection with the abundant facilities and the ample, vigorous inspiration of a great university[.] Your plan—as I understand it, differs from the long usage of Yale, Harvard, Williams & others, in that it is your purpose to place your "twenties" under able and experienced teachers. At other large aggregations, young men are appointed on small salaries, to stay a year or two while they prepare for other things. Incidental teaching is good only by accident.

No educational proposition, my dear Sir, has so carried me away as this plan of yours. If successful and if adopted by other great universities as it must be ultimately in some form, it will settle the question as to the supremacy of the university in our system of so called "higher education[.]" It is vastly better for the great mass of young men than the methods at Oxford and Cambridge or at Berlin.

My only adverse thought is as to the size of your groups. When my sections exceed fifteen I find myself often discontented with my results.

The Annapolis groups of ten are best: I consider fifteen the limit in most subjects for really satisfactory work.

Your plan will cost money: all good things do. You can get it. People will see that it is folly to have cheap machinery to do university work[.]

Our mills do not use poor machines to spin cotton! Why do it to spin character.

You can get the men as well as the money. Were I thirty years younger, I should rejoice to have such opportunity to do great work in making men and to grow while doing it. There are lonely men, scholarly, broad, manly men, working practically unsupported who will delight to put time & brain & heart into the tutorial work at Princeton[.]

Again I crave pardon. But as I turn your proposition over in my mind it so pleases me, that the boy in me would shout.

With assurance of great respect

Very truly yours   Oren Root

ALS (WP, DLC).
[1] Professor of Mathematics at Hamilton College and brother of Elihu Root. Professor Root and his father, also named Oren Root, between them taught mathematics at Hamilton for over half a century.

To Charles Grosvenor Osgood, Jr.*

My dear Dr. Osgood: Princeton, N. J.   8 April, 1905.

It gives me great pleasure to ask if you would be willing to accept an appointment in Princeton as Preceptor in English under our new arrangement at a salary of $2000.

I have no legal right to make you this as an offer outright, because all appointments rest with the Board of Trustees, but you will understand of course that it is only a legal limitation, and I am asking for your authority to present your name to the proper Committee of the Board.

Hoping most sincerely that you will feel inclined to accept, and that you will find work in Princeton most pleasant and profitable,

Cordially and sincerely yours,   Woodrow Wilson

TLS (WC, NjP).

To Cyrus Hall McCormick

My dear Cyrus: Princeton, N. J.   8 April, 1905.

I confidently expect to attend the meeting in Kansas City[1] and don't quite understand Mr. Thacher's[2] excitement. I wrote him that I would certainly be there unless prevented by ill health, and I am glad to say that I see no prospects of being prevented

by that cause. I quite agree with you that it is very desirable indeed that the Faculty should be represented.

Hoping that you are all very well,

Faithfully yours,   Woodrow Wilson

TLS (WP, DLC).
    [1] The sixth annual meeting of the Western Association of Princeton Clubs
on May 13, 1905. See the news report printed at May 14, 1905.
    [2] John Hamilton Thacher, Princeton 1895, lawyer and Assistant City Coun-
sellor of Kansas City, secretary and treasurer of the Western Association of
Princeton Clubs. He was elected president at the meeting on May 13, 1905.

To Charles Howard McIlwain

My dear Mr. McIlwain: Princeton, N. J.   10 April, 1905.

It was a pleasure to see you in Princeton the other day and
to know that you were willing to consider an appointment here
as Preceptor under our new arrangements.

Inasmuch as the Preceptors are to have the rank of Assistant-
professors, they must of course be elected by the Board and I
have not the right of appointment, but I write to ask if I may
have your consent to nominate you for the position for a term
of five years at the salary of $2000 a year.

Cordially and sincerely yours,   Woodrow Wilson

TLS (WC, NjP).

A News Report of an Address in Newark, New Jersey

[April 11, 1905]

THE UNIVERSITY AND THE NATION

President Wilson Addresses Members of
Presbyterian Union[1] on that Topic.

Addressing an audience which taxed the capacity of the Rose-
ville Presbyterian Church, Dr. Woodrow Wilson, president of
Princeton University, spoke for three-quarters of an hour last
night on the effect institutions of learning have on the affairs of
the country. It was the sixty-ninth reception of the Presbyterian
Union. In addition to Dr. Wilson's address there was a musical
program.

Charles G. Titsworth[2] was chairman of the meeting and introduced Dr. Wilson, who had for his subject "The University and
the Nation." The speaker began by saying that the thought upper-
most in the minds of all parents who send their sons to college
is what are the sons fitted for and what will the college make

of them. There are no institutions, he said, but what are related
in some way to the life of a nation. It would be a rash undertaking to try and analyze, to try and find any single thread to the
labyrinth of thought between the university and the nation, and
yet the two have some things in common. Every one is proud
of the achievement of the nation, he said, but no one is proud
of individual achievement.

"Public service is our word, public welfare our ideal," said the
speaker. "There is one word, 'noble,' which we use recklessly.
This word 'noble' must not be applied to men who have not been
big hearted enough to serve the nation while serving themselves.
Our[s] is a task acquired only by united effort. All government
springs up as a sort of voluntary effort, voluntary association let
us say, and every sort of power we have had has been a voluntary
power. We boast that we do not have to wait; what we do springs
out of our own purposes. It is astonishing how the affairs of the
country have prospered, because we boast of liberty. We cannot
boast that we are the monopolists of purity. We were the first to
give a home to liberty and to recognize her as deserving of a
comfortable shelter. And yet it is a singular circumstance that
we who live among a public-spirited community, we who like
to talk of liberty and what we have done for her, should allow
this community to be so ill-governed. What puzzles foreigners
the most is that in the midst of corruption we devote so much
time to praising the purity of the nation. If we have energy
sufficient, and use it aright, we can lift the nation along upon
the path of progress. We are close upon the time when we cannot afford to neglect the power of government much longer; we
must begin to pay more attention to house cleaning."

Dr. Wilson went on to say that the country had grown materially during the past decade and that we no longer are concerned alone in national affairs, but in international affairs also.

"The time has come to ask yourselves questions. Do you want
aggrandizement? Do you want to be the arbiter of nations?[3] You
have found you cannot be provincials longer. There are some
who advise us not to bother with the future. 'Let us be modern,
they say, and take care of the present.' Establish a standard of
educational value of our own, irrespective of all other governments. I take it that these advisers voted for Bryan. We must
establish a coin of educational value. The nations who strike
principles universally are the nations which are universally successful.

"And now we come to where the modern university takes its
part. It must not be bewildered. It must know what to do. Some

say its sole duty should be to inform. Inform the modern youngster about the modern world in four years? Such a task is as
ridiculous as it sounds. Others say make a scholar of this modern
youngster. This cannot be done in four years either. Judging
from myself, it has not been done in forty-eight years. But we
can teach a spirit of scholarship, and this is what the modern
university is striving to do."

The speaker alluded to book learning, declaring it was the
natural impulse of a healthy man to reject books, that a healthy
man would much prefer to be out doors using his muscles than
to be cooped up with a bit of literature in front of him. The
only reason books are read, he said, was because the reader
could not know all men. If all authors were living, he said, and
the reader had the time to meet and talk with them, their books
would not be read. It is delving into affairs that have been, however, that makes the desire to read.

"We cannot steer by the future; we must steer by the past. The
past is all our capital to trade on. The past is only found on the
printed page. We read of the past: otherwise we would not know
who we were."

Printed in the *Newark Evening News*, April 11, 1905; some editorial headings
omitted.

[1] An association of Presbyterian laymen who usually met monthly for discussion of literary, contemporary, and religious subjects.

[2] Charles Grant Titsworth, Princeton 1881, lawyer of Newark.

[3] He referred to President Theodore Roosevelt's negotiations with Russia and
Japan for an end to the Russo-Japanese War. Rumors of these negotiations were
common at this time. For example, the *New York Times*, March 31, 1905,
printed a report from St. Petersburg stating that Roosevelt had been formally
selected as mediator by both countries.

From William Jennings Bryan

My Dear Sir: Lincoln, Nebraska, April 11, 1905

According to a provision in the will of the late Philo Sherman
Bennett, of New Haven, Connecticut,—a copy of which provision
will be found at the end of this letter—I am authorized to select
twenty-five colleges or universities and turn over to them Four
Hundred Dollars ($400) each, the money to be invested by the
college and the annual proceeds used for a prize for the best
essay discussing the principles of free government.

As the bulk of Mr. Bennett's property was in New York, an
inheritance tax was collected in that state and also in Connecticut, the state of his residence. The tax in the state of New York
was 5% and the tax in the state of Connecticut will be 3%, and
as these taxes come out of the beneficiary, they will reduce each

Four Hundred Dollars to the extent of thirty-two dollars, but as there will probably be a little interest, the reduction may not be quite that much.

If the trustees of your university are willing to accept this money and invest it, and arrange for the giving of this annual prize from the proceeds of the investment, please let me know, and I shall send you a check for the amount, together with a receipt to be signed, as soon as I can determine the exact amount to be given to each college. I have personally established a similar prize in nineteen of the state universities, and have been gratified to find that the prize has had the desired effect in stimulating the students to a study of the science of goverment.

Yours truly,   W. J. Bryan

ARTICLE 17 OF BENNETT WILL.

I give and bequeath to William J. Bryan, of Lincoln, Nebraska, the sum of Ten Thousand Dollars ($10,000) in trust, however, to pay to twenty-five colleges or universities, to be selected by him, the sum of Four Hundred Dollars ($400) each. Said sum of Four Hundred Dollars to be invested by each college receiving the same and the annual proceeds used for a prize for the best essay discussing the principles of free goverment.

P.S. As your University has a more commanding influence than the state university, of your state, I have decided to give you preference over the state university if the trustees of your university are willing to establish the prize.[1]

TLS (WP, DLC).

[1] The Princeton trustees accepted the bequest and established the Philo Sherman Bennett Prize in Political Science, to be awarded to that member of the Junior or Senior Class who wrote the best essay on the principles of free government. The subject of the essay was set by the Professor of Politics.

To Duane Reed Stuart*

My dear Sir: Princeton, N. J.   12 April, 1905.

It gives me real pleasure to ask you if you will permit me to nominate you to our Board of Trustees for appointment as Preceptor in Classics at Princeton for a term of five years at the salary of $2000 a year.

As the Preceptors under the new system will have the rank of Assistant-professors, they must of course be elected by the Board of Trustees and I therefore have not the power of appointment, only of nomination to the Board. However, I think you

need have no apprehension of miscarriage as between nomination and election.

Permit me to add that in offering you this nomination for a
fixed term, I do not wish to be understood as meaning that promotion will be precluded for that term.[1] It gives me pleasure to
say that we are particularly anxious to associate you with ourselves in the interesting and important work we are entering upon and that I shall hope to do everything possible to make your
connection with Princeton comfortable, satisfactory and even
delightful. It is not possible, at the outset, for us to offer a salary
of more than $2000 in connection with these new appointments,
but I shall hope that it will not be necessary to maintain that
minimum in the case of those who render exceptionally valuable
and distinguished services to the University.

With much regard,

Cordially yours,   Woodrow Wilson

TLS (in possession of Duane Reed Stuart, Jr.).
[1] Stuart was promoted to professor in 1907.

To Gordon Hall Gerould*

My dear Mr. Gerould: Princeton, N. J.   12 April, 1905.

It gives me great pleasure to ask, on the recommendation of
the English Department of the University, if you will permit me
to nominate you to our Board of Trustees as Preceptor in English.

I have not the power of appointment, inasmuch as the preceptors under our new system will have the rank of Assistant-professors and must therefore be elected by the Board, but I hope that
you will allow me to nominate you for a term of three years at
the salary of $2000. a year.

It was a great pleasure to meet you the other day and I shall
look forward to our association here with the greatest interest
and satisfaction.

Let me add that the limitation of the appointment to a term of
years carries with it no sort of implication that the appointment
is temporary.

Very cordially yours,   Woodrow Wilson

TLS (WC, NjP).

To Charles Grosvenor Osgood, Jr.

My dear Mr. Osgood: Princeton, N. J. 13 April, 1905.

I very cheerfully consent to your having longer time to consider our wish to have you here as a Preceptor, and I sincerely hope that the consideration will lead to a decision favorable to your coming. We are sincerely anxious to have you.

The last paragraph of your letter[1] leads me to fear that perhaps you may think that our methods will be chiefly serviceable for the poorer sort of students. The part that interests us most is that the best students ought to be greatly stimulated by such instruction and that the delight of teaching will be decidedly increased. Sincerely yours, Woodrow Wilson

TLS (Selected Papers of C. G. Osgood, NjP).
[1] It is missing.

Notes for an After-Dinner Speech[1]

13 April, 1905 9:45 P.M.[2]

Banquet, *Am. Philosophical Society* Philadelphia, 14 Apr. '05
Toast: *Benjamin Franklin*

Centuries the dramatic units of our history:
A century of colonization.
A century of war, to clear the stage.
A century of nation-making.
A century of ——— ?

Samples: Englishmen: Hamilton, Madison
Americans: Marshall, Webster.
Provincials: Jno. Adams, Calhoun
Mixed: Jefferson, Benton.

Americanism progressive, optimistic, unpedantic, unprovincial, unspeculative, unfastidious; "in a sense unrefined, because full of rude force; but prompted by large and generous motives, and often as tolerant as it is resolute."

Franklin: self-made, serviceable, of the people;
One region his birthplace, another his home;
His philosophy homely, practical, witty.
Favoured independence, organization, union.
Stood for the democratic law of self-selection
Fitted for the frontier.

Others—Washington, Clay, Jackson, Lincoln

WWhw MS (WP, DLC).
[1] A news report of Wilson's speech is printed at April 15, 1905.
[2] Wilson's composition date.

From Charles Howard McIlwain

Dear Sir: Oxford, Ohio, April 13, 1905.

Your very kind letter of April 10 was received.

I appreciate the honor you have done me, and desire that you would consider me a candidate for an appointment as Preceptor on the terms mentioned in your letter.

I request that you will present my name if you see fit to do so.

Very sincerely,   C. H. McIlwain

ALS (WP, DLC).

From David Magie, Jr.*

My dear Dr. Wilson,   Princeton.   April 13, 1905.

It gives me great pleasure to accept your kind offer to nominate me to the Board of Trustees for the position of Preceptor in Classics, and I appreciate very highly the honor that you have conferred upon me in making me this offer. I feel very grateful too for the cordiality of your invitation to participate in this new system which must arouse the enthusiasm of every lover of Princeton, and by means of which our University must inevitably rise to a pitch of excellence in the educational world, to which not even she has ever attained before.

Very sincerely yours,   David Magie, Jr.

ALS (WP, DLC).

From Andrew Carnegie

Confidential

Dear Sir,   New York: April 14th, 1905

I propose handing over $10,000,000 in 5% Bonds to a commission, as I did to the Research Commission in Washington,[1] and to the Commission for Scotch Universities,[2] the revenue to provide retiring pensions for the teaching staff of universities, colleges, and technical schools under such conditions as the Trustees may from time to time adopt. I am able now to say expert calculation proves that the revenue will be sufficient for the purpose.[3]

I hope you will do me the favor to act as one of the first trustees, who will be (with few exceptions) like yourself, the Presidents of educational institutions. A prompt reply by wire will greatly oblige.   Very truly yours,   Andrew Carnegie

TLS (WP, DLC).
[1] That is, the Carnegie Institution of Washington, established in 1901.

² The Carnegie Trust for the Universities of Scotland, established in 1901 for the support of the universities of St. Andrews, Aberdeen, Edinburgh, and Glasgow, and for scholarships for students of Scottish birth or extraction in these universities.

³ Carnegie was about to establish the Carnegie Teachers Pension Fund, with an endowment of $10,000,000 in bonds of the United States Steel Corp. The original Board of Trustees included twenty-two college and university presidents and three non-academicians, under the chairmanship of Henry Smith Pritchett, President of the Massachusetts Institute of Technology. Teachers in universities, colleges, and technical schools in the United States and Canada were to be eligible to apply for pensions without regard to race, sex, or creed. However, teachers in sectarian and state-supported institutions were not eligible. At first incorporated in New York State in 1905, the Carnegie Teachers Pension Fund received a charter from Congress in 1906 and became the Carnegie Foundation for the Advancement of Teaching. In practice, the trustees of the foundation set the standards under which institutions were admitted to participation in the program, and thus in time the foundation gained much power as an informal accrediting agency and did much to raise academic standards in the United States and Canada. In 1908, Carnegie gave an additional $5,000,000 to provide for pensions for teachers in state-supported institutions. By 1915, however, the number of pensioners had become so large that it was obvious that the system of free pensions could not continue indefinitely. A detailed study of the problem by the foundation led to the creation in 1917 of an independent legal reserve life insurance company called the Teachers Insurance and Annuity Association of America, the initial funding for which was provided by the Carnegie Corporation of New York. From 1918 onward, the TIAA entered into contractual relationships with individual educational institutions under which it established life insurance and annuity programs for faculty and administrators on a contributory basis, the institution paying part of the premiums and the individual the balance. This system continues to the present day. See Joseph F. Wall, *Andrew Carnegie* (New York, 1970), pp. 870-79.

From Andrew Runni Anderson*

My dear Sir,   Madison, Wisconsin, April 14, 1905.

I have the honor to acknowledge your letter of the 12th inst., and to state in answer thereto that I shall be most happy to have you nominate me to your Board of Trustees for appointment as Preceptor in the Classics for a term of three years at the salary of $1800. per year.

Let me say that I am in the fullest accord with the system which you are about to inaugurate, and that, if elected, I shall contribute everything in my power toward its success, and that I shall devote myself unremittingly to the responsibilities of the position.

Very sincerely yours,   Andrew R. Anderson.

ALS (WP, DLC).

From Ernest Ludlow Bogart*

My dear President Wilson: Oberlin, Ohio, April 14, 1905.

In reply to your letter of April 10, offering me a position for five years at a salary of $2000 a year under the new preceptorship arrangement, I may say that I accept gladly this opportunity to enroll myself again at Princeton. As Professor Daniels has explained the situation, I understand that such an appointment carries with it in general the opportunities now enjoyed by Assistant-professors, for a man to win his spurs and ultimate promotion. Believing, as I sincerely do, in Princeton and her development—particularly along these new lines—I am glad to invest myself in my *Alma Mater*. President King[1] has signified his willingness to accept my resignation from my position here. I should be glad at your convenience to learn further of my duties at Princeton, and especially to what extent it is planned to give the new men an opportunity to lecture.

With many thanks for your cordial letter, I am

Very sincerely yours,   Ernest L. Bogart

TLS (WP, DLC).
[1] Henry Churchill King, President of Oberlin College.

From Fred Le Roy Hutson*

My dear Dr. Wilson: [Princeton, N. J.]   Apr. 14, 1905.

Your kind letter of Apr. 12 in which you ask to nominate me for appointment as Preceptor in the University was received.

In reply, I wish to thank you for honoring me in this way and to express my willingness that you should nominate me.

I wish also to express my deep appreciation of the cordiality of your letter and to assure you that, should the Trustees act favorably upon my nomination, I shall devote to the new position the best effort of which I am capable.

Very sincerely yours,   F. L. Hutson.

ALS (WP, DLC).

A News Report of an After-Dinner Talk to the American Philosophical Society

[April 15, 1905]

Dr. Woodrow Wilson, President of Princeton,
Extols Benjamin Franklin as the
Typical American

An elaborate banquet at the Bellevue-Stratford ended what was unanimously proclaimed the most successful session ever held by the society. In the red room the philosophers and their guests partook of the good cheer and listened to able addresses made by several of their number. President Edgar F. Smith[1] was toastmaster.

Dr. Woodrow Wilson, president of Princeton University, in responding to the toast "The Memory of Franklin," said:

"It remains for me to review Franklin in his relation to the history of the country and as a typical American. Many features of his character and mind seem to me to place him in the character of a typical American. But to place him as such we would have to make him a canon.

"Franklin's life stands near the last of the second act and at the beginning of the third act of making our nation.

After giving a sketch of the growth of the country in bygone centuries, Doctor Wilson said:

"America has developed in a spreading wedge into the West. You cannot imagine a man more fitted for the frontier than Benjamin Franklin. He could invent a pump and organize a philosophical society. He was a man adaptable to the conditions of the case, whatever they might be. He could see when the lightning was ready to be drawn down and when the streets were ready to be swept.

"Your American, whether you take the type of Benjamin Franklin or George Washington, is the man of adaptabilities, ever ready to seize the phases that come to his notice. Until 1890 the census takers were enabled to draw a frontier on our maps. It was not an accident that we annexed the Philippines. We had to have a frontier; we got into the habit, and needed one. The characteristic American is an exploiter.

"There was no more admirable exploiter than Benjamin Franklin. He illustrated what is the real process of democracy. The real process is self-selection. The power of America is that she is willing to give to any man who is willing to select himself for the gift.

"All these things entitle Franklin to be called perhaps the par excellent American. He deserves to be remembered as an example of what we can do.

"Bred by himself, educated by no one in particular, he brought himself to be among the front rank. It would be amiss to praise Franklin because we are all Americans, and we would be praising ourselves. But we can say this is the kind of man we can produce, and this is the kind of man we hope we shall produce."

Printed in the Philadelphia *Public Ledger*, April 15, 1905; two editorial headings omitted.

[1] Edgar Fahs Smith, President of the American Philosophical Society and Vice-Provost of the University of Pennsylvania.

To Frederick Jackson Turner

My dear Turner: Princeton, N. J.   15 April, 1905.

Will you be good enough to tell me what you know of the personality and accomplishments of M. N. Beddall[1] who is now teaching at the High School at Boone, Iowa?

As you probably know, we are selecting a large number of men to put into operation here next year, in modified and Americanized form, the Oxford Tutorial system. Inasmuch as the men we choose will have to come into intimate association with the undergraduates, meeting them individually or in small groups, in an informal fashion, and acting as their guides, philosophers and friends in their reading, their personality is even more important than their scholarship, but their scholarship should be of a very humane sort which would give them quick sympathy for tyros.

I would like some particular information, therefore, with regard to Mr. Beddall's scholarship in History and Economics (for he would be called upon to teach both) and even more particularly about his personality and antecedents. I hope I am not asking too much in asking you for this information or to be put in the way of obtaining it.

It is a pleasure to have any occasion to write to you and hear from you again. I sincerely hope that Mrs. Turner and you are both very well.

Cordially and sincerely yours,   Woodrow Wilson

TLS (Archives, WU).
[1] Marcus Melvin Beddall, Wisconsin 1897.

From Gordon Hall Gerould

My dear President Wilson: Bryn Mawr, Pa., April 15, 1905

I was unable to see President Thomas[1] until this afternoon, and so to reply to your very kind letter of Thursday. After some conversation, Miss Thomas promised to ask the Trustees to release me from my engagement with the College for next year. They are to meet, she tells me, on Friday next. I think that it is now safe, accordingly, for me to say that I shall be very glad to have you nominate me to the Trustees of Princeton on the terms which you suggest. Though I shall not be legally free to accept the appointment till after the meeting of our Board, no impediment is now likely to be placed in my way here.

It gives me the liveliest pleasure to be able to look forward to working under your direction on the details of an educational scheme which promises so much. I feel sure that I shall find my work in the University exceedingly interesting; and I hope to be useful.   Faithfully yours,   G. H. Gerould

TLS (WP, DLC).
[1] Martha Carey Thomas, President of Bryn Mawr College.

From Roger Bruce Cash Johnson*

My dear President Wilson,   Oxford: Ohio   April 15/1905.

I wish to thank you for your very kind letter. It is, I assure you, an honor for me to be invited to come to Princeton to engage in the new work you have planned. I need hardly say, however, that I do not regard lightly the responsibility involved. I shall come to you (if the Board so elect) uncertain of my fitness for the important work but desirous of doing everything in my power to make myself worthy of the confidence you seem to place in me.

What it has cost me to make this decision, I think Professor Ormond may have told you. I am coming at a financial sacrifice, which, of course, means much to one whose salary has been as small as mine. Immediate creature comfort would have bidden me to remain here.

But having decided to come, I shall come heart and soul, leaving the future on 'the laps of the Gods,' but in the meantime doing what my hands find to do, in fulfilling the new duties to which I have committed myself.

I wish to thank you again for your faith and confidence in me and to assure you that I shall do everything in my power to contribute in the department of Philosophy, at least, something towards the success of your policy.

                    Very sincerely   Roger B. C. Johnson

ALS (WP, DLC).

From Haven Darling Brackett[1]

Dear Sir,   Worcester, Mass.   Apr 15, 1905.

Your letter of April 12th reached me duly. After weighing the matter carefully I have decided that I am unwilling to leave my present position to accept the position at Princeton at the salary which you mentioned[.] Thanking you and the classical teachers at Princeton for the honor conveyed by the proposition which you have made to me, I beg to remain

                    Yours very sincerely   Haven D. Brackett

ALS (WP, DLC).
[1] Instructor in Greek at Clark University.

From Duane Reed Stuart

My dear Sir: Detroit, April 15, 1905.

Your letter reached me yesterday just as I was leaving Ann Arbor. I was not hoping that my conversation with Professor West would materialize before my visit to Princeton and I am gratified that you have seen fit to take my name into consideration for nomination to the Board of Trustees.

I have followed with the greatest interest and sympathy the progress of your changes in the system at Princeton and I wish to confess frankly that I find the outlook very attractive. I am not, however, ready to pledge myself until I have looked over the ground at Princeton and have bored Professor West with a few more questions. I am under contract with the University of Michigan for two more years and, although release is a mere matter of form with us, I hesitate to bind myself to come to Princeton just at present. I shall certainly be able to give you a definite answer—if you care to wait for one—soon after my return to Ann Arbor. With many thanks for your courtesy and for the kindly interest you were good enough to express, I am

Very respectfully yours Duane Reed Stuart.

ALS (WP, DLC).

From Douglas Labaree Buffum*

My dear Sir: New Haven, Conn., April 15th, 1905

I have just received your letter of the 14th inst. asking if I would accept nomination to the position of Preceptor in Modern Languages for a term of two years at $2000 a year.

It gives me great pleasure to inform you that I shall be very glad to accept this offer.

Very truly yours, Douglas Labaree Buffum

ALS (WP, DLC).

From Harold Ripley Hastings*

My dear Sir, Madison, Wis. April 15, 1905.

Your letter of the 12th inst., offering to nominate me for appointment as preceptor in the Classical Department of Princeton came today. I thank you heartily for the honor, and if the Trustees endorse the nomination, I shall be very glad of the opportunity to become identified with the new system and to contribute something, if possible, to its success.

Yours very sincerely Harold R. Hastings.

ALS (WP, DLC).

From Christian Frederick Gauss*

My dear President Wilson: South Bethlehem, Pa., April 15 1905

I wish gratefully to acknowledge the honor which you have done me in offering to nominate me to your Board of Trustees for a Preceptorship in Modern Languages at Princeton. During my pleasant visit at the university I discussed fully with Professor Vreeland any points which might have inclined me to hesitate and he was able to reassure me upon all of them. It is with much pleasure, therefore, that I now put my name and case into your hands with best hopes for its successful issue, and thank you sincerely for your courtesy and interest in me. With all regard,   Yours, very truly,   Christian Gauss

ALS (WP, DLC).

From Charles Brewster Randolph[1]

My dear Sir: Worcester, Mass.   April 15, 1905

Permit me to thank you for your letter of April 12th, and for the honor which you show me in proposing to present my name for this office to your Board of Trustees.

Princeton attracts me strongly; I have given this matter very earnest thought, and if circumstances were somewhat different I should accept your kind offer. But as affairs have shaped themselves here it seems to my advantage to remain in my present position.

Again thanking you, I am
                Very sincerely yours   Charles B. Randolph

TLS (WP, DLC).
[1] Instructor in Greek and Latin at Clark University.

A News Report

[April 17, 1905]

PRESS CLUB BANQUET.

President Wilson Describes the New Tutorial System.

The Press Club banquet held at the Inn on Saturday evening [April 15] was one of the most interesting and successful ever given. . . .

President Wilson, the last speaker, gave a complete description of the preceptorial system in replying to the toast "Practical Journalism in University Life." He first complimented the Press Club on the efficiency its members have shown in observing the best interests of the University through the newspapers. He continued in substance as follows:

The new preceptorial system is not to be merely an extension of the system of class room work by enlarging the Faculty and making the classes smaller. No matter how small a class may be, bright men who won't work and dull men who can't work, are invariably ranked together, and treated with the same hard and fast methods with little resulting benefit. Class room work is never calculated to deeply interest a man in study. The tutorial system is a plan to get hold of the personal equation of each man, giving him freedom with some guidance, in the things toward which his taste runs, and showing him his weak points and training him to see the value in the things which he does not naturally like. Under this plan each man will be treated individually, with the purpose of putting zest into his work. The tutor will bring out and strengthen the individual characteristics of each man.

The importance of the whole system lies in the character of the men who are being obtained. In the first place they are being selected along very careful lines, and only those will be taken who feel a certain love for the place, and who are in entire sympathy with its spirit, and understand the scope of the plan which is being developed. They are to be selected primarily upon their stand-[ing] as gentlemen, as men who are companionable, clubable, whose personal qualities of association give them influence over the minds of younger men. If their qualities as gentlemen and as scholars conflict, the former will win them the place. It has been found that when a man at another institution has been invited here, he is immediately offered inducements to stay where he is. These are the kind of men wanted.

The new system is not done for advertisement but in order that the best men of the country shall be attracted here, and that Princeton shall turn out a body of men, possessing such sound learning, such high development in all the essential characteristics of manliness, that whenever there is anything really difficult to be done in the nation, Princeton and Princeton men will have to be consulted for advice and counsel.

Printed in the *Daily Princetonian*, April 17, 1905.

A News Report of a Religious Address in Trenton

[April 17, 1905]

PRINCETON PRESIDENT ADDRESSED Y.M.C.A.

President Woodrow Wilson of Princeton university was the speaker at the mens' meeting held in Association hall yesterday afternoon under the auspices of the Y.M.C.A. He talked on "The profit of Belief," and addressed one of the largest audiences of the season at this service.

The theme was taken from Job 28:28, "The fear of the Lord that is wisdom, and to depart from evil is understanding." President Wilson in his introduction said the fear of the Lord referred to was not the fear of dread, but that which takes heed and is afraid to disobey. The true fear of the Lord, he said, was adjustment to the Lord, which leads one to act with the Lord.

The speaker said no scientific proof of the existence of God could be given, and the question is often raised in this intensely practical age, "Why should I fear what I do not know?" True wisdom, it was explained, is not the knowledge of things merely, but the perception of the value of things. It does not necessarily require much brains to have this wisdom.

Mr. Wilson showed that happiness is not physical, but a condition of the mind, and a man would soon find that "to depart from evil" is an adjustment that would bring real happiness and show the way to God.

The speaker pleaded for less doctrine and more simplicity in the approach to Christ. Christ's life, he said, if brought into the life of a man would make that man ashamed of evil things. Referring again to those who refuse to believe what they cannot prove, Mr. Wilson claimed that it was not so much a case of cannot believe, as won't believe. Many men, he said, refuse to believe in God because it makes them uncomfortable. Their lives are not right and the approach to God emphasizes the fact. It was stated that the will must act first in believing and a man can believe what he wills to believe.

Continuing, Dr. Wilson said: "Life is seeking adjustment to the forces of the world. The true fear of God is connecting life with His transcendent powers, then the adjustment that brings true happiness becomes an easy matter. This is an age of temptation, and nine men out of ten will go as far into evil as they can without being caught, and yet expect success, but the text gives the true way of finding success.

"No man in this audience, if he stops to think, will deny that the spirit lives after death. Don't stake everything on physical success. After you are dead your spirit will swing on in the same line it swung in this life. There can be no change then."[1]

John A. Campbell,[2] president of the association and a graduate of Princeton, introduced President Wilson.

Printed in the Trenton *True American*, April 17, 1905; two editorial headings omitted.
[1] For this address, Wilson used the notes printed at Jan. 13, 1895, Vol. 9.
[2] John Alexander Campbell, Princeton 1877, businessman and civic leader of Trenton.

From the Minutes of the Princeton University Faculty

5 p.m.   April 17, 1905

. . . The Committee on the Course of Study reported a course of study for the Department of Engineering;[1] the Entrance Requirements, as reported, were adopted as follows:

In 1907 there will be added, to the present requirements,
> *History*; one and one only of
>> 1. American History and Civil Government
>> 2. English History
>> 3. Ancient History.

Beginning in 1907 no student will be admitted to the C.E. Freshman Year until he has passed in all the mathematical subjects required for entrance.

In 1908 and thereafter two of the three languages, Latin (1, 2, 3, 4), French A, German A, will be required.

In 1909, and thereafter the Latin requirement will be increased by the addition of Virgil A (six books) and Sallust (Catiline).

The Undergraduate Course of Study as reported was adopted as follows:

Freshman Year.

First Term		Second Term	
Courses	Hours a week	Courses	Hours a week
English	2	English	2
Lab. Phys., French, Germ.	6	Lab. Phys., French, Germ.	6
Math	4	Math	4
Chem.	3	Chem	3
Graphics	2	Geodesy	2
	17		17

Sophomore Year

Gen. Physics	3	Gen Physics	3
Math 21	3	Math 22	3
Math	2	Math.	2
Mineral.	3	Geology	3
Graphics	3	Graphics	3
Geod.	3	Geodesy	3
	17		17

Junior Year.

Anal. Mech. 33	3	Anal. Mech. 34	3
Gen. Astron.	3	Pract. Astron.	2
Graph. Statics	3	Mech. Materials	4
Mater. Construction	2	Geodesy	5
Geodesy	4	Graphics	3
Graphics	2		17
	17		

Senior Year.

Framed Structures	5	Framed Structures	3
Motors	3	Motors	3
Hydraulics	2	Water Works	2
Graphics	2	Sewerage	2
Geodesy	3	Roads	2
Laboratory	2	Mason. Structures	2
	17	Methods of Construction	2
		Laboratory	1
			17

"Minutes of the University Faculty of Princeton University Beginning in September, 1902 Ending June 1914," bound minute book (UA, NjP).

1 Actually, the department had been, and continued to be, known as the "Department of Civil Engineering," since this was still the only type of work in engineering available to Princeton undergraduates. The only other engineering program at Princeton at this time was a two-year graduate course in electrical engineering offered by Professor Cyrus F. Brackett and Assistant Professor Howard McClenahan of the Department of Physics.

The undergraduate program in civil engineering had always been a completely prescribed one with no elective subjects whatever, and it continued so under the revised program described above. The new program represented an upgrading of the former course of study and hence a rounding out of the general reform of the Princeton curriculum described in the Editorial Note, "The New Princeton Course of Study," printed in Volume 15 of this series.

The revision of the entrance requirements was intended to bring the civil engineering program substantially into line with the requirements for candidates for other undergraduate degrees, especially the B.S. and Litt.B. degrees. The requirements in English literature were already the same for all candidates. The new requirement in history was the one already required of all other candidates. The requirements in mathematics for civil engineering candidates were the same as those for B.S. and Litt.B. students. However, the statement that from 1907 onward no student was to be admitted to the freshman year until he had passed all of the mathematics requirements for entrance indicates clearly that heretofore the administration of the requirements had been lax. The language requirements for 1908 and afterward were still somewhat more lenient than those for Litt.B. and B.S. candidates, who had no option but to present Latin, including the Virgil and Sallust requirements, together with either French and German or some combination of advanced work in French or German and either elementary physics or chemistry. On the other hand, civil engineering candidates, unlike Litt.B. and B.S. candidates, had an absolute requirement to present either physics or chemistry upon entrance.

The civil engineering program was under intensive re-examination during the academic year 1904-1905. Indicative of this was the fact that the Princeton catalogue for 1904-1905, unlike those which preceded and followed it, contained no general statement of the methods and objectives of the Department of Civil Engineering and no schematic outline of its program of study. A comparison of the outlines and descriptions of the courses in the catalogue for 1903-1904 and in the one for 1905-1906 reveals a considerable amount of shifting of courses from one year to another and a great deal of revision of the content of specific courses. The greatly revised statement of the methods and objectives of the program included in the catalogue for 1905-1906 indicates clearly what the faculty was attempting to accomplish. The additions to the old statement are especially significant: "In arranging the course in civil engineering care has been taken to give the student the benefit of as much general training in the earlier years as the claims upon his time made by his later technical studies will permit." In line with this objective, all courses taken in the freshman year were to be the same as those taken by other undergraduates except for those in chemistry, graphics, and geodesy. While the work of the sophomore year was more specialized, the courses in general physics and mathematics were taken in common with students in other departments. Moreover, the course in general physics had been shifted from the junior to the sophomore year, thus enhancing the preparatory nature of the first two years of the program.

The revised general statement continued: "A very large proportion of the strictly technical studies of the course cannot be profitably pursued without a thorough previous preparation in mathematics; especial attention is therefore given in the earlier part of the course to imparting to the students in civil engineering a sound working knowledge of the ordinary divisions of that science, inclusive of analytical mechanics, and a high degree of proficiency therein is exacted from all candidates for the degree of C.E." The new course program included more class hours devoted to courses in mathematics, but, much more significant, the scope and content of the individual courses had been greatly revised and enriched, and all were given by the staff of the Department of Mathematics. The course in analytical mechanics, for example, was to be given either by James Hopwood Jeans, the brilliant English mathematician just added to the Princeton faculty in 1905, or by the promising young preceptor, Luther P. Eisenhart.

On paper at least, the technical courses of the junior and senior years seemed to be changed very little, though there were to be more class exercises in some courses, and there was a specific allocation of time in the senior year for "Laboratory Work in Civil Engineering." However, the description of the engineering facilities in the university catalogue for 1905-1906 reveals that significant changes had taken place in this area also: "During the past year the facilities for instructing students in laboratory work in civil engineering have been greatly enlarged by the provision and equipment, through the generosity of the trustees of the John C. Green estate, of a separate building to be devoted entirely to the laboratory work of the Department of Civil Engineering." The building was located on Washington Road between Nassau and William Streets, on the site of the present Green Hall. The catalogue, after describing the building and its equipment in some detail, went on to state: "The additional apparatus has been carefully chosen with a view to its value as a means of cultivating the perceptive faculties of the student, of stimulating originality of thought, and of making clear many points in the later studies of the course which otherwise might remain ill-defined because imperfectly conceived." Thus, at least to some degree, even the more purely technical portions of the program in civil engineering were being revised as much as possible to produce thinking men rather than mere technicians.

The reader who wishes to make a more thorough comparative study of the old program and the new one should examine the statements of intent of the

Department of Civil Engineering, the schematic outlines of the course of study, and the descriptions of the courses in the Princeton catalogues for 1903-1904 and 1905-1906.

From Edwin Moore Rankin*

My dear President Wilson: Princeton, N. J., April 17, 1905.

Permit me to express my cordial appreciation of the honor you do me in offering me the position of a Preceptor in the Department of Classics in Princeton University. It will give me pleasure to have my name presented to the Board of Trustees for this position.

The system to be inaugurated next year enlists my hearty approval and sympathetic interest. It would afford me genuine satisfaction to contribute my full share towards its success.

Very sincerely yours,   Edwin M. Rankin.

ALS (WP, DLC).

To Andrew Carnegie

Confidential.

My dear Mr. Carnegie: Princeton, N. J.   18 April, 1905.

It will give me great pleasure to serve as you desire, as one of the first Trustees of the fund which you are establishing to provide a retiring pension for the teaching staff of Universities, Colleges and Technical Schools, and I very much appreciate the compliment you have paid me in asking me to serve in such a capacity. I should expect this fund to be most beneficent in many ways.

With much regard,

Sincerely yours,   Woodrow Wilson

TLS (A. Carnegie Papers, DLC).

From Donald Cameron*

Dear Sir: Waco, Texas.   Apr. 18, 1905.

I will be glad to have you nominate me to the Board of Trustees for appointment as Preceptor in the Department of Classics on the terms you mention.

Thanking you for your invitation, which I very much appreciate, I am   Very sincerely yours,   Donald Cameron.

ALS (WP, DLC).

From Robert Herndon Fife, Jr.[1]

My dear President Wilson,   Middletown, Conn., April 18, 1905.

Although I cannot as yet answer definitely regarding the matter in question, I hasten to thank you for the very kind and cordial letter which you have written me regarding the position at Princeton. I appreciate fully what you say regarding the outlook there and the inspiring character of the work. The prospect is a most alluring one to me; indeed, I may as well confess that a chair at Princeton has been to some extent the goal of my ambition ever since I decided to give my life to teaching.

Much to my disappointment, I was unable to confer with our President[2] regarding the question until this morning; and at his urgent request, I have written Professor Vreedland [Vreeland], asking him, if possible and convenient, to allow me to postpone final action until next Monday, in order to give President Raymond time to consider the question in all of its bearings, and, if necessary, to confer with a committee of Trustees regarding it. This is as unexpected as it was unsolicited on my part. The Wesleyan authorities have, however, always accorded me such fair and courteous treatment, that I feel it would be highly unjust for me to act without hearing their side of the case.

My visit to Princeton was full of enlightenment to me in many ways. I am deeply interested both pedagogically and personally in the success of the plan which you are inaugurating there; and if in the course of human events, I should become an active function in carrying it out, I should expect to give zll [all] of my energy toward its success.[3]

With cordial greetings, I am
                    Very respectfully yours,   Robert H. Fife

TLS (WP, DLC).
  [1] Associate Professor of German at Wesleyan University.
  [2] Bradford Paul Raymond, President of Wesleyan since 1889.
  [3] See R. H. Fife, Jr. to WW, April 26, 1905.

From Jonas Viles

Dear Sir;   Columbia [Mo.], April 18, 1905.

Your letter of April 12 was all that I expected it to be; it removed all doubt as to the character and future of the Preceptorship. It was my expectation and hope that I could write you a definite answer to-day, but when I submitted your letter, as I had promised to do, to the chairman of the Executive Board here, he earnestly requested me to defer a formal answer until the Board,

which meets next week, could submit a formal proposition to me.
The chairman has been very kind to me and, reluctantly, I consented, without pledging myself in any way. I hope that my desire to be courteous to Mr Williams[1] has not led me into even an
apparent discourtesy to you.

If this delay is to inconvenience you, either because of a meeting of the Princeton Board, the possibility of securing another
man, or for any other reason, please telegraph me at my expense
and I will decide at once.[2] With all apologies for this delay, I am
Very sincerely yours,   Jonas Viles.

ALS (WP, DLC).
[1] Walter Williams, Chairman of the Board of Curators of the University of
Missouri.
[2] See WW to W. M. Daniels, May 1, 1905, n. 2.

From Moses Taylor Pyne

My dear Woodrow: New York   April 18, 1905.

I return Mr. Bryan's letter regarding the bequest of the late
Philo S. Bennett of New Haven. I have consulted Mr. Cuyler, Mr.
Dodge and others, and the universal opinion seems to be that although it is very small in amount nevertheless it would be un-
gracious to refuse, especially as the refusal might be used to our
disadvantage, and in this I agree.
Very sincerely yours,   M Taylor Pyne

TLS (WP, DLC).

From James Henry Lockhart

My Dear Dr. Wilson: Pittsburgh, April 19, 1905.

Your letter of the 13th instant has been received and carefully
noted.

I expect to be married next Tuesday evening,[1] and am very
busy at present, but will just take a few moments to write and
tell you that in order to help out the Committee of Fifty, I will
subscribe $10,000.00 toward the $150,000.00 fund they are endeavoring to raise, and I prefer to make this a single donation.
Later on I may be in the position and feel like making an Annual
Subscription for a definite number of years, but cannot tell at
present.

Will you please give me an idea at your earliest convenience
as to when they would expect this subscription paid, and I will
try to arrange matters in some way, before I leave home.

I was delighted to see you and Dr. West when you were in Pittsburgh,[2] and regretted that I could not see you both at the dinner.

With kindest regards and best wishes not only for yourself, but also for our beloved "Old Nassau," I am,

Yours very truly,   James H. Lockhart.

P.S. As with former subscriptions, please enter this as from "An Alumnus," as I do not wish to have my name appear.

J.H.L.

TLS (WP, DLC).
    [1] He married Florence Dilworth on April 25, 1905.
    [2] That is, when they spoke at the dinner of the Princeton Club of Western Pennsylvania on March 18, 1905. See the news report printed at March 19, 1905.

From Charles Grosvenor Osgood, Jr.

My dear President Wilson: New Haven, Conn.   April 19, 1905.

It gives me pleasure to say that I have decided to accept your informal offer of a preceptorship in English in Princeton. As you mentioned no term of years in your first letter, may I ask whether the term implied was five years or not?

In my last letter I think I said that the new arrangement at Princeton encourages one to think that by its help much may be accomplished with students which has hitherto been impracticable. It was not students of lesser abilities that I had in mind, but rather the better class of man, who, under the present arrangement of herding forty to fifty men in a classroom, are far too much neglected.

My address for the next week will be Wellsboro, Penna.

I wish to thank you heartily for your kindness in allowing me so much time for consideration of your offer. I hope my delay has not inconvenienced you.

Sincerely yours,   Charles G. Osgood, Jr.

ALS (WP, DLC).

From Robert Kilburn Root

My dear Dr. Wilson,   Atlantic City.   April 19, 1905.

It is with very great pleasure and with deep appreciation of the honor you have done me that I accept the position as preceptor at Princeton offered me in Professor Hunt's letter of April 18. As nothing is said about the length of the appointment, am I right in understanding that it is for five years? You will remember that you thought that such an arrangement could be made in my case.

Among the attractions which draw me to Princeton, not the least is the thought that I shall be working under your personal guidance.[1]

Very sincerely yours, Robert K. Root.

ALS (WP, DLC).

[1] About his interview with Wilson and its impact upon him, Root later wrote: "To such an invitation, so graciously expressed, a young instructor, though reasonably contented where he is, does not say 'no.' And a salary of $2,000 was, according to the standards of 1905, a very handsome stipend. But as I journeyed to Princeton on a bright day in early April, I had misgivings as to this new-fangled method of teaching and more personally as to whether a Yale man could be happy in Princeton.

"My interview lasted some forty minutes. Mr. Wilson asked me no questions about myself, but spoke with winning eloquence about his plans for Princeton. Before five minutes had passed I knew that I was in the presence of a very great man. Of course I was not sufficiently a prophet to foresee the scope of his subsequent achievement, that his great qualities of mind and spirit were to make themselves felt not only in academe but throughout the country and the whole circuit of the world. But I did recognize that I had never before talked face to face with so compelling a person. Before the talk was over my loyalties were entirely committed to him. Had Woodrow Wilson asked me to go with him and work under him while he inaugurated a new university in Kamchatka or Senegambia I would have said 'yes' without further question." Robert K. Root, "Wilson and the Preceptors," in William Starr Myers (ed.), *Woodrow Wilson: Some Princeton Memories* (Princeton, N. J., 1946), pp. 14-15.

From John Duncan Spaeth*

My dear Dr. Wilson   Philadelphia   [c. April 19, 1905]

I have told Professor Thompson[1] that I have decided to accept the position of Preceptor in the English Department at Princeton.

Although you were kind enough to allow me until next Monday to consider, I feel that further delay would only make it more difficult for me to adhere to a decision which, all things considered, I am convinced is right and best.

Yours very respectfully   J Duncan Spaeth.

ALS (WP, DLC).

[1] Robert Ellis Thompson, President of Central High School in Philadelphia, where Spaeth was Professor of English Language.

News Reports of Two Addresses in Alabama

[April 21, 1905]

MR. WILSON AT MARION.

Large and Representative Audience Heard
Distinguished Speaker.

Marion, April 21.—(Special.)—The most noteworthy event in the sixty years of Marion academic history was the coming of

President Woodrow Wilson of Princeton University to deliver the annual Government Day address before the students of the Marion Military Institute last evening.

The chapel of the Institute was filled to overflowing with the largest and most representative audience ever assembled in Marion. Distinguished visitors from every section of Alabama and from other States bore fitting tribute by their presence to the appreciation of the honor of President Wilson's coming. A delightful reception was given President Wilson by the faculty and ladies of the Institute after the address.

The address itself well repaid those who came from the farthest distance. Replete with wisdom, it was charming in its simplicity of style and felicitous appropriateness. President Wilson paid high tribute to the endeavor in self-government so successfully undertaken by the students of the institute and showed in a masterful manner that education was above all a training to the temper of affairs through a community of life and effort. Education is not merely acquiring information, but a process of life. This process of life can come only through four years of community life in college. Its fruit is not knowledge, but action, and such action must be a community of effort to effect any enduring good. This community of effort comes of training to the temper of affairs and this temper of affairs is the object of democratic education and a necessity of democratic government—education in the halls of debate and under an honor system of self-government; education as a process of life in a community of human fellowship.

The students of the institute accorded President Wilson an ovartion [ovation] after the address and the large audience were enthusiastic in its appreciation. Never in the long history of Marion has a man so won the hearts of its people as did President Wilson by his charming personality and his inspiring message to the students of the institute. Princeton renders the people of Alabama and the South the highest service by such counsel from its distinguished chief executive to the youth of our land.[1]

[1] For other accounts of Wilson's visit to and address at the Marion Military Institute, see the *Marion*, Ala., *Institute Bulletin*, III (July 1905), 14-16, and *ibid.*, IX (July 1914), 28-29.

SPOKE TO STUDENTS.

Princeton President at Dallas Academy, Selma.

Selma, April 21.—(Special.)—Dr. Woodrow Wilson, president of Princeton University, was for four hours to-day the guest of Selma.

Arriving in this city from Marion, where he spoke last night to the Judson College and Marion Military Institute students, the eminent educator addressed the student body of Dallas Academy, one of the principal institutions of learning in Dallas County. This afternoon at 4 o'clock Dr. Wilson left for Montgomery.

Dr. Wilson arrived in Selma at noon today from Marion. He was met by a delegation composed of Mayor V. B. Atkins, Professor Hardaway, Hon. L. G. Jeffries and Colonel W. R. Nelson, representing Dallas Academy and J. F. Hooper, president of the Commercial and Industrial Association.

After the greeting at the Union passenger station Dr. Wilson was driven to the home of Dr. and Mrs. F. G. DuBose, whose guest he was at luncheon from 12:30 o'clock until 1:30 o'clock. From the home of Dr. DuBose Dr. Wilson was driven to Dallas Academy High School and before a large audience of students and spectators he made a short address which he delivered especially to the student body of the institution.

From 2:30 o'clock until train time Dr. Wilson was at the home of Dr. DuBose where he was visited by prominent citizens of this city including members of the alumni of Princeton.

Dr. Wilson was invited to come to Selma by telegram yesterday by Professor Hardaway, principal of Dallas Academy, Colonel W. R. Nelson and Hon. H. S. D. Mallory, of the Board of Trustees.

Printed in the *Montgomery*, Ala., *Advertiser*, April 22, 1905.

From Hopson Owen Murfee

Dear Doctor Wilson: [Marion, Ala.] 21 April 1905

The boys have had so much to say of your words to them last night, that I must express again my grateful appreciation of your kindness in coming to give them counsel and courage in their life and work. Their enthusiasm and appreciation is fine to see.

My heart goes up in gratitude to God for your coming into my life, now into the life of our little home, and into the lives of our boys—those who heard your living words last night and those who shall read them, I trust, in after years on [in] the Journal of the Council and Commons.[1]

Queenie (that is Mrs. Murfee) joins me in grateful remembrance. Faithfully yours H. O. Murfee

ALS (WP, DLC).
[1] That is, the *Marion Institute Bulletin*. The Council and Commons were the organs of student self-government and the honor system at the Marion Military Institute.

A News Report of an Address in Montgomery, Alabama

[April 22, 1905]

FINE ADDRESS BY DR. WILSON

President of Princeton in Montgomery.

A masterful defense of the American university as a factor in the national and the international life was made last night by Dr. Woodrow Wilson, President of Princeton University, who spoke on "The University and the Nation" at the Girls' High School, corner of Lawrence and High Streets, before a large and appreciative audience.

Flashing arguments were used by Dr. Wilson in answer to the materialism of today. Men plodding on in the swirl of commercial life, he said, have either affected contempt for the cloistered intellect or felt it. With the brilliant historian who is head of one of the leading universities in the republic there is a different idea of the student. He expressed his firm belief that it is well to cloister the mind in the right pauses of life and view quietly the horizon of activity.

Dr. Wilson carried to the hearts of his hearers that the freedom of America is not alone for the accumulation of fortunes, but, what is more sublime, the elevation of our motives.

"Great fortunes are piled up in this free nation," said the distinguished speaker, "but fortunes can be piled up as well in worlds that are not free. It is in the elevation of our motives that we can and must take advantage of this freedom."

The historian almost spoke epigrams in his remarkable exaltation of the college and its life. The historian on the platform is none other than the historian in volume. That was the opinion of those members of the audience who heard him.

The audience in a way was an ideal one. It comprised some of the most cultured men and women of Montgomery. The feature was that not all were old men and women, but a great many young ladies and young men were there to hear and to be charmed by the choice diction and forceful utterances of the distinguished teacher and writer.

The speaker presented his message to the people of Montgomery in that incisive and hew-to-the-line style that marks his books. He impressed his audience that, being a philosopher and a historian in one, he amply realizes that "history is philosophy teaching by example." It was a message, however, not to Montgomerians, but to the world. Defended by Dr. Wilson, it was the opinion of the audience last evening that the university is the citadel of the world-at-large. In another figure of speech he himself called it "the vehicle of spirits."

The audience began gathering as soon as a fire across the street, which consumed a residence, began to smoulder. Frank P. Glass of Montgomery introduced the speaker.

Prominent alumni of Princeton sat in a semi-circle to the right and the left of the visitor. In the number on the rostrum also sat well-known citizens of Montgomery who are not alumni of that institution, but admirers of the great educator.

In his introduction, Mr. Glass, of a class of the seventies, lauded Princeton in all its long history. He told of the beginning of the University 160 years ago. He related how its progress was interrupted by the War of the Revolution, but arose in its vigor and advanced in the eyes of the nation ever afterwards. The great percentage of Southern students in Princeton both before and after the War between the States was referred to by Mr. Glass. The wonderful ability of Dr. Wilson as the head of the University now is being demonstrated by his successful performance of the giant task of raising two and a half millions of dollars for the further upbuilding of the institution. This was the amount he said he would raise when he was inducted into the presidency[1] and he is on a road to apparently sure success.

In beginning his address, Dr. Wilson expressed his appreciation of the opportunity to stand before the audience that faced him. He said his hearers, were strangers to him in form until he saw the orange and black festoons about him on the stage. These colors brought him home, being the adopted colors of Princeton. He said there is no use in this land of ours in being strangers anywhere. We think substantially the same thoughts and are a part of the same Republic.

A comparison was made by the speaker of strictly technical colleges and real universities. It was charged that technical colleges are often misnomers for universities. He would not try for one moment to disparage the technical institutions for they certainly have an important place in this world, but he viewed with some concern the money applied to these schools from year to year which could be more equitably diverted to the university proper.

The trend of all technical schools today, as noted by the speaker, is to teaching true science and less and less of the applied detail. Benefactors are gradually realizing that even in colleges

[1] Glass was mistaken. Wilson, in 1902, had announced a total fund-raising goal for Princeton of $12,500,000.

of applied science the fact must ever hold that we cannot learn everything.

Dr. Wilson said that the nation is only one grand dramatic unit. We have passed through one century in starting the republic, a second in "getting rid of that complication, the French," and a third in clearing the stage for the real drama that is to come, and in the fourth the first act is really to begin.

The question was asked, "What is to be the culmination of this drama?" It was asked what we are going to do with the first act. He said in boasting of where America stands today, we have no right to look to her achievements except to regard the motives which were behind them. We must know what to do for our country in character and not in meaningless detail if he [we] would work out the right culmination of the great drama.

The speaker then turned into the philosophy of broader life than domestic life. The people of this age must look beyond the hills that shut us in our homes. The world that lies about us should be known and known for what it is. The Babel that split the tongue of nations split not only the tongue, but scattered temperaments as well. Some humorous passages were indulged here by Dr. Wilson who ridiculed the domestic fiend to whom the Cynic's almanac recently said, "Tell the truth and shame your family."[2]

Dr. Wilson said the coming citizens of manhood and philanthropy are to have international minds. Our cousins abroad must be searched and it should be known what they are doing and what they are thinking. If we confine ourselves to the homes where we live and live and move only in their environment we do not know where we are, according to Dr. Wilson. We do not know where we are and we cannot tell where we are "until we know what and where the rest of the world is."

Another phase of university life is the indispensable regard for what those who have been before us have done. It is a fallacy, said Mr. Wilson, to say that we disconnect from what has gone before us. In the walls of the universities, in quietude and separation, there are the opportunities to see the great map of things done by the fathers of long ago. In the same atmosphere the young man is surcharged with that sentiment that follows him all through the life of this commercial age. The horizon of untrained motives are seen from the high mount and indelibly impressed on his mind so that when he dips down into the vortex of industrial frenzy he can look back and nurse the sentiment

[2] See n. 6 to the news report printed at March 19, 1905.

that he once caught sight of a life not so tainted. At the college there is to be found the "vehicle of spirits" and it is to be found nowhere else.

The historian has no particular delight in reading books. In fact, he says, he takes it that a degree of resolution is necessary for him to read a book. He does not delight in "distressing his young men with constant tasks." Notwithstanding this, there is an essence in communing with those who have gone before and it is not policy to "wait until we can get with them to talk with them." With all his early theological training, the speaker said he is not sure anyway that he is going just where these ancients are and he preferred reading them now.

Dr. Wilson emphasized two qualities of mind that the university guarantees to the student who seeks it aright. One of these is a travelled mind and the other is discriminating. He humorously remarked that many people we see have travelled bodies, but not so often are to be experienced the travelled minds. For benefit to oneself it is the mind that travels and not the body. This probably accounts for the queer characters we meet within our travels, according to the speaker. They have only their bodies with them or if their minds "they are concealed somewhere about their persons."

These men reminded the speaker of a recent characterization of a certain head. One friend asked another what sort of head it was that had come into sight.

"Head? That's no head," said the other, "that's only a knot God Almighty has put on him to keep his body from ravelling out."

The discriminating mind is taught by the university life because there is the chance there of cultivating it which is impossible in the commercial realm. The man who has not a discriminating mind was almost defined by Dr. Wilson as a man who enjoye [enjoys] holding an opinion today with "the expectation of giving it up tomorrow." He revels in the delight that he has held an opinion and it was all right for the time although it had to fall down. More respect for the man who clings to his opinion with sincerity Dr. Wilson says he has than for the man without discrimination.

One of the charming illustrations of the catholicity of mind and the infection of ideals to be found in universities was given by Dr. Wilson who traced the freshmen through their four years. They go in with different minds apparently and do not know one another. Yet when they go out into the world they are one homogeneous mass, reeking with the ideals that were distributed among them by the dispensations of the university.

Dr. Wilson who reached here at 6 o'clock yesterday evening from Marion is the guest of F. P. Glass while he is in the city. He will leave early this morning for Princeton University accompanied by Mr. Glass.

Printed in the *Montgomery*, Ala., *Advertiser*, April 22, 1905; some editorial headings omitted.

From Andrew Carnegie

Dear Sir,   New York: April 24th, 1905

Thanks for your kind acceptance of the Trusteeship.

I have instructed my Financial Secretary, Mr. R. A. Franks, President of the Home Trust Company, Hoboken, N. J., to transfer Ten Millions of Dollars of Bonds to the Trustees when organized.

Messrs. Vanderlip[1] and Pritchett will proceed to obtain data from all the institutions concerned for use at the meeting of the Trustees when it is convened early in November next (at my house, Wednesday, November 15th—two o'clock). The gift will be announced after I sail for Europe next Wednesday and the whole subject will be before the faculties of the various institutions and will no doubt be fully discussed during the coming summer months, especially by the Trustees as they may happen to meet each other or others interested. In the meantime a corporation will be organized.

It is thought that these few months will be profitably spent in this manner, so that when the Trustees meet in November they will have much valuable information to build upon.

Much will depend upon finding the right man for permanent Secretary to organize the office and working plans for disbursing the funds. It is hoped the Trustees will be on the lookout for the indispensable man.[2]

Very truly yours,   Andrew Carnegie

TLS (WP, DLC).

[1] Frank Arthur Vanderlip, Vice President of the National City Bank of New York.

[2] The trustees in 1906 elected Henry Smith Pritchett as the first President of the Carnegie Foundation for the Advancement of Teaching.

From Morris William Croll*

Dear Doctor Wilson,   Philada. April 24, 1905.
I am very glad to learn that I have been appointed to an instructorship in Princeton for the year 1905-6. I accept the position, and will give my best efforts to the work.
         Yours Respectfully,   Morris W. Croll

ALS (WP, DLC).

From George Tyler Northup*

My dear Dr. Wilson: Williamstown [Mass.]   April 24 [1905].
I shall be very glad to accept your appointment as Preceptor of modern languages. Kindly excuse my delay in acknowledging your letter. I have only just received it having returned to town after an absence of several days.
         Very sincerely yours   George T. Northup.

ALS (WP, DLC).

From Gordon Hall Gerould

My dear President Wilson: Bryn Mawr, Pa., April 24, 1905
The Trustees of Bryn Mawr have released me from my engagement here, so Miss Thomas informs me. Thus I can now formally accept the invitation of Princeton, which I do with the happiest anticipations of the work and the life in the University.
With many thanks for your personal kindness,
         Faithfully yours,   G. H. Gerould

ALS (WP, DLC).

To Gordon Hall Gerould

My dear Mr. Gerould: Princeton, N. J.   25 April, 1905.
It is with real gratification that I read your letter received this morning and I will take pleasure in presenting your name to the proper committee of the Board at a very early date. It gives me the greatest pleasure to look forward to being associated with you in our work here.
         Cordially and sincerely yours,   Woodrow Wilson

TLS (WC, NjP).

From Robert Herndon Fife, Jr.

My dear President Wilson,   Middletown, Conn.   April 26, 1905.

Somewhat later than I had hoped, our President returned to-day from a conference with a committee of Trustees. He tells me that the college authorities have promoted me to a full professorship here, with a corresponding increase of salary. This action was altogether unsought on my part, and altogether unlooked-for when I laid the matter before him; but it creates a situation which prompts me, although very reluctantly, to give way to the pressure here and decide to remain. I am keenly alive to the prospects at Princeton, and the prestige and opportunities for usefulness which it offers in ever-increasing ratio; but the independence of the position here, as the permanent head of the German department, is irresistibly attractive. It is with keen regret that I turn aside from what may be the only opportunity to enroll myself with a university toward which I feel so strong an attraction. I shall, however, watch the developement of your plan of instruction with great interest.

I have written Professor Vreedland, and hope the delay in the matter has not caused him trouble. In conclusion, please let me thank you again for your cordial letter. The most pleasant part of the affair has been the opportunity of making the pdrsonal [personal] acquaintance of yourself and others who are building at Princeton.

With renewed regrets, I am,
                        Very respectfully yours,   Robert H. Fife.

TLS (WP, DLC).

To Edgar Odell Lovett, with Enclosure

My dear Dr. Lovett: Princeton, N. J.   27 April, 1905.

The inclosed letter from Russell explains itself. I am entirely in sympathy with all of it except his suggestion that he should be immediately be made Assistant-professor at a salary of $1500. I think this is decidedly presumptuous, but of course I understand the character of the man and do not attach any great importance to such a suggestion. I should be very glad, as you know, to assure Russell of an appointment as Instructor when he is ready to take it, and if you think it best to promise him so far ahead I would be very much obliged if you would write to him. I think you know, after our conversations, how I feel about the matter in all respects.[1]   Faithfully yours,   Woodrow Wilson

TLS (E. O. Lovett Papers, TxHR).
¹ Henry Norris Russell, Princeton 1897, was appointed Instructor in Astronomy beginning 1905-1906 at a salary of $1,000.

E N C L O S U R E

From Henry Norris Russell

My dear Dr. Wilson,   Capri, April, 6, 1905

I am very glad to hear that you have recovered from your recent illness, and are able once more for University work. So I would like to ask your consideration of certain things which Professor Young and Professor Lovett advised me to write to you about, but with which I did not wish to occupy you while you were ill.

When I was in Princeton last January, I had conversations with them, which led me to hope that I might be connected with the Astronomical Department at Princeton in the near future. I told them of some of the ways in which I thought I could do useful work at Princeton, and they approved of my ideas, and recommended me to tell you something about them.

The field in which I think an additional member of our staff, —I speak as a Princeton man,—could do most good is that of Physical Astronomy,—or, as it is usually called now-a-days, Astrophysics. It is in this branch of Astronomy that the greatest advances of recent years have been made,—thanks chiefly to modern spectroscopic and photographic methods—and the most important unsolved problems of the science are at present astrophysical;—for example, the constitution of the Sun, the explanation of the different types of stellar spectra, of the phenomena of variable and new stars, and of the nebulae. All these problems lead up to the greater one of stellar evolution—the answer, as far as may be, to this question. How did our universe reach its present form, and what will become of it?

There is undoubtedly room for a professor of Astrophysics in Princeton, without danger of duplication of any one else's work. Of the present members of the astronomical staff, Professor Lovett's interests lie in the region of theoretical and mathematical astronomy, while Professor Reed¹ is an observer. There is a large field lying between the regions in which they are at work, and it is in this field that I believe I could work to advantage. I have always been particularly interested in Astrophysics, and have had unusually good opportunities to study it—at first under Professor Young, and recently at Cambridge, which I have found an excellent place to learn the modern methods of research.

I refer especially to astronomical photography. The work which I have been doing for the Carnegie Institution[2] is of this character, and in the course of it I have seen very clearly how much room there is for similar work in America. Thousands of photographs of the stars are being taken in America every year. A large number of these are suitable for measurement,—that is, measures of the images of stars on the plates will give the relative positions of these stars in the sky with a higher degree of accuracy than direct observations with ordinary telescopes can afford.

But only a very few of the plates are being measured. In this respect European astronomers are far ahead of us. As an example of the value of the new methods which they have developed, I may mention some recent work of Professor Kapteyn,[3] who finds that, for determining the proper motions of the stars, two photographs taken ten years apart are as good as a pair of ordinary meridian observations of the old sort at an interval of a century.

How important this saving of time is, appears when it is considered that the study of these small proper motions gives us the only way we have of determining the distance and size of the Milky Way, and the structure of the stellar universe.

There are many other problems in which photography is equally valuable, such as the measurement of the distances of the nearer stars, (on which I am now at work), the discovery and observation of minor planets and satellites, and so on.

Plenty of people in America can take good photographs, but there are not more than half-a-dozen men in the country who are familiar with the modern ways of measuring them, and of reducing the result to a useful form. Yet such work requires no expensive equipment. All the apparatus necessary for the very best work can be bought for a thousand dollars.

I have gone into these details because I think that this is a sort of research that could be peculiarly well carried on at Princeton. If we obtained an adequate endowment, we could set up a photographic telescope of our own; but, even without this, we could get plates from other observatories, and work at them. This is being done all the time in Europe. In fact, Professor Kapteyn of Groningen has made a distinguished reputation for himself and his University in the astronomical world by such work, although he has no observatory, and not even a small telescope.

I may add that such work is of great educational value, and one of the best things for graduate students that I have ever come across. I should be very glad to do such research work at Princeton; but at the same time I would like to do my share of the lecturing and teaching work of the Astronomical Department. What I have seen of the tutorial system at Cambridge has put me in very hearty sympathy with what I read of the proposed preceptorial system at Princeton, and I should feel it a privilege to assist in its establishment, and to do what I could to make "reading men" of those whom I taught.

Owing to the long rest necessitated by my late attack of typhoid, my work as Research Assistant to the Carnegie Institution has been delayed, and will keep me busy for a year to come, but I will be free in the summer of 1906, before the beginning of the academic year.

I would hope that any position which I might have in Princeton would lead ultimately to a Professorship of Astrophysics and a permanent connection with the University.

As I shall have been for three years a member of the staff of a scientific institution, I think that the title of Assistant Professor, and a salary of $1500 a year, would not be unreasonable to suggest at the start.

If these considerations should commend themselves to the Trustees, there would be advantages in early action upon them. If I could be appointed to a place in Princeton—the appointment to take effect in 1906—I would be free to devote my spare time to some of the admirable opportunities which Cambridge offers for the study of mathematical and spectroscopic Astronomy.

In any case, I should be very greatly obliged to you for any advice that you cared to give me upon this matter. My permanent address is The Observatory, Cambridge, England.

Pardon my troubling you with such a long letter. It is due to the natural enthusiasm of a Princeton man at the hope of a return to his Alma Mater.

I cannot close without thanking you once more for the recommendation to the authorities of Cambridge University which you so kindly gave me two years ago, which helped me greatly in starting my work there.[4]

With sincere good wishes, I am

Yours very truly   Henry Norris Russell

ALS (E. O. Lovett Papers, TxHR).

[1] William Maxwell Reed, Assistant Professor of Practical Astronomy at Princeton, 1901-1905.

[2] Russell had been a research student at King's College, Cambridge, in 1902-1903. From 1903 to 1905, he served as research assistant for the Carnegie Institution of Washington, stationed at the Cambridge Observatory.

[3] Jacobus Cornelis Kapteyn, noted Dutch astronomer, Professor of Astronomy and Theoretical Mechanics at the University of Groningen.

[4] See WW to the Registrar of Cambridge University, Aug. 27, 1902, Vol. 14.

To Winthrop More Daniels

My dear Daniels: Princeton, N. J.   27 April, 1905.

I saw [Henry Robinson] Shipman* and [Charles Worthen] Spencer*; was very much pleased with the latter, but very little with the former, who seemed to me decidedly stiff and unadaptible. Perhaps you had a closer interview with him and formed a different opinion. I will have a talk with you soon about them.

Cordially and sincerely yours,   Woodrow Wilson

TLS (Wilson-Daniels Corr., CtY).

An Article on the Preceptorial System

[April 28, 1905]

THE PRECEPTORS.

President Wilson Describes the New
System to be Introduced.

President Wilson has written the following article on the tutorial system at the request of The Daily Princetonian:

The new methods of instruction which are to be introduced next year will not be at all revolutionary in character, but they will involve a great many interesting changes. There will be fewer lectures and fewer class room exercises in the various courses, in order to make way for personal conference between the student and the instructor. The present staff of the University will take an active part in this conference work, and it will be the chief business of the gentlemen who are to be added to the Faculty; so that the whole aspect of instruction will be materially altered. The students will be met by their instructors, either singly or in groups. When groups are formed they will be made up of men who are found to have substantially the same preliminary training, the same capacity for work, and the same tastes and aptitudes in what they undertake. Those who cannot thus be classified, or who stand in any special need of individual assistance, will be met singly and assisted in the way best suited to them.

It is expected that each undergraduate will be assigned, for the work of the department which he chooses, to some one Preceptor who will be his guide in all the reading and work of the department, so that the course may be drawn together, so far as he is concerned, into a single body and studied as a related group, rather than singly and separately under different masters. It is hoped that in this way the student may be relieved from constant drill in those subjects which he carries most easily and in which he needs little assistance, and will be supplied with the best possible aids in those parts of his studies which come harder to him and in which the stimulation of direct contact with trained scholars is of vital consequence to him. The Preceptors will not set the examinations and will therefore be more free to cover the subjects broadly in their dealings with their pupils.

There will naturally be a good deal of written work connected with this sort of instruction. The students will be frequently called on to submit brief reports of one kind or another, to their Preceptors, very much as they do now in the various thesis courses, though more informally; and it is expected that all of this written work will be judged of with regard to the English in which it is written, as well as in respect of its subject matter, so that the men will be given constant drill in the correct use of the English language and in the development of their power to express ideas.

The general theory of the system is that college work ought to be radically different in method from school work; that the men ought not be given the impression that they are merely getting up tasks, learning the lectures and ideas of particular instructors, or mastering text books, but should feel that they are reading up great subjects for their own sake. In order to enable them to do this reading intelligently they will be directed by their Preceptors to the books which will best acquaint them with the chief matters involved in their several studies. The lectures will be not so much the subject matter of their study as incidental aids to the studying they are doing. The object of the lecturer will naturally be to give the greatest possible amount of stimulation and to expound the more difficult or the more interesting portions of the subject in hand.

Such a system ought certainly to give the student a greater feeling of independence and the distinct impression that he is handling himself not as a pupil merely, but of his own initiative, though under competent guides and in intimate association with scholarly teachers, who serve him not only for guidance, but for stimulation of the best kind.

This, in outline, is the plan to which we are looking forward with the greatest interest and in the confident hope that it may make the studies of the University both vital and delightful.

WOODROW WILSON.

Printed in the *Daily Princetonian*, April 28, 1905.

To Robert Bridges

My dear Bob: Princeton, N. J.   28 April, 1905.

I am just dropping you a hasty note to tell you of a terrible sorrow that has fallen on Mrs. Wilson and me. Edward Axson, her younger brother, his wife and child were drowned on Wednesday at Creighton, Georgia.[1] Their bodies are being brought North and we are expecting to bury them in a plot of our own at 2 o'clock to-morrow Saturday the 29th.

Always—   Affectionately yours,   Woodrow Wilson

TLS (WC, NjP).
    [1] Edward William Axson, his wife, Florence Choate Leach Axson, and their son, Edward Stockton Axson (born June 2, 1903) were drowned on April 26, 1905, in the swift waters of the Etowah River near Creighton, Georgia, where Axson was employed as Superintendent and General Manager of the Franklin Gold Mining Company.
    "They were driving in a two-seated carriage attached to a team not thoroughly accustomed to travelling together, but apparently steady and manageable. It was necessary to cross the river by means of a flat ferry-boat, which was moored to the bank at the foot of a winding road leading down from the hill above. This they had almost gained, when, without warning, the horses swerved, took fright, and dashed out upon the flat and off at the farther end, the carriage almost reversing itself in the fall, so that they sank, entangled, right where the horses plunged. With his wife on one arm and his child on the other, Eddie made the bravest possible fight for life—for their lives. . . .
    "The three of them lie in one grave in the Wilson plot in Princeton Cemetery. The marker bears this inscription:
    " 'They were pleasant in their lives, and in their deaths they were not divided.' "
Arthur M. Kennedy, compiler and ed., *Princeton University 1897: Fiftieth Anniversary Book* (Princeton, N. J., 1947), p. 13.

From George Howe III

                                        Chapel Hill, N. C.
Dear Uncle Woodrow & Aunt Ellie,   April 29, 1905

The shock has stunned me completely. I cannot think about it, and I am totally unable to give any expression to my grief. You will most probably laugh at me, but I think I loved him as dearly as either one of you did. I wish I could write some words of comfort, but I need comfort myself. I try to get some out of the thought that no one is left to mourn the others. I never knew Florence and had so long looked forward to having her with us. But Ed I did know.

I wish I could get some particulars of the accident. Sometime as soon as possible write me what you have learned. And if there is anything I can do that will be of even the slightest service to you, please do not hesitate to tell me of it. You know how gladly I would do [it]. I thought, when I read your telegram, that there was perhaps a need of my presence conveyed in the last sentence. But I did not want to act foolishly, and therefore telegraphed back to find out. If I could help in no way then, maybe I can now in straightening out matters which you have no time for. If so please call on me.

Maisie[1] is not with me. I felt the shock all the more for that reason. You have heard, I suppose, that they have forced Dr. Flinn to resign his position after sixteen years of service.[2] He is soon to be adrift with nothing to do,[3] and now they are beginning to break up the old home. The loss of home & all the anxieties concerning the future movements of the family have made the past winter rather a hard one for them all. I have sent Maisie home early that she might be in the old place a little while before it is upset. Then she will be needed in the packing & sorting of her things. So I suppose I shall not have her back again for about three months.

Our house is coming on very slowly. We are both well & news from Mother & Annie is good.

Dear people, you know that all our sympathy is yours. May God comfort you.

With unbounded love & sympathy　George Howe.

ALS (WP, DLC).
[1] His wife, Margaret Smyth Flinn, whom he had married on October 27, 1903, in Columbia, S. C.
[2] The Rev. Dr. John William Flinn, Chaplain and Professor of Philosophy at South Carolina College since 1888. The trustees requested Flinn's resignation because "he was generally regarded as an ineffective teacher." Daniel W. Hollis, *University of South Carolina* (2 vols., Columbia, S. C., 1951-56), II, 215.
[3] Actually, Dr. Flinn became a professor at South Carolina College for Women in Columbia, S. C., where he served until his death in 1907.

Duane Reed Stuart to Andrew Fleming West

My dear Mr. West:　　　　[Ann Arbor, Mich.]　April 29, 1905.

Your note and the cheque were duly received and would have been acknowledged some days ago, had I not waited in the hope that I might have something definite to write to you.

Mrs. Stuart and I have been sore troubled in mind since our return from the East, and have spent much time in trying to transform what are undeniably our wishes into horses. The eternal question of ways and means has thrust itself in continually. I wish sincerely that we were in a position to accept your offer without giving a thought to other considerations. Then nothing they could offer here could keep me. Unfortunately we are not free lances financially. They have promised to recommend me for a Junior Professorship at $2000 in case I promise in advance to accept it and I must give them a definite answer by the eighth or the ninth of May. Of course there may be a miscarriage when the matter comes before the Regents but the Assistant Professorship is a certainty and, to tell the truth, I know we can live comfortably on $1600 here. I hesitate to try it on $2000 at Princeton. Then the promotion here must come more rapidly than you would have any reason for giving it to me at Princeton. To put it differently, I doubt if I could be as much service to you as they seem to think I can here.

I have written to you thus frankly because I promised to inform you before I rejected your offer. I feel sure that I shall have much to regret if I do not come but, as conditions are at present, I hesitate to say "Yes."

Mrs. Stuart joins me in kindness remembrances.

                    Faithfully yours   Duane Reed Stuart

ALS (WP, DLC).

To Winthrop More Daniels

My dear Daniels: Princeton, N. J.   May 1, 1905.

I shall, I feel confident, be at home next Saturday, the 6th of May, and I am just writing Mr. Scott of Toronto,[1] asking him to come on to see us on that day.

I am very much interested in what you say about Shipman and shall, of course, feel very much inclined to follow your judgment in the matter. Do you happen to know what Spencer's present situation and salary are?

I am sorry to say that a telegram received on Saturday informs me that Viles cannot accept,[2] so that one of our birds has escaped.

        Always—   Faithfully yours,   Woodrow Wilson

TLS (Wilson-Daniels Corr., CtY).
  [1] T. Fraser Scott, M.A. (Edin.), Lecturer in Political Science and Economics at the University of Toronto.
  [2] It is missing. Viles was promoted to Assistant Professor of History by the University of Missouri.

From John Howell Westcott

Dear Woodrow,   Saranac Lake, N.Y.   May 1, 1905

We have read today the sorrowful news of your loss of Ed Axson & his wife and child. How can we express our sympathy for you and Mrs. Wilson in this sudden and mysterious trial. In your own words "God disposes," and that is our sure ground of comfort and confidence.

They all went together to the better life. In my moments of discouragement[1] I can find it in my heart to envy them but I remember it is our duty not to be discouraged.

Yours always   J. H. Westcott

ALS (WP, DLC).
[1] Over the illness of his wife, Edith Sampson Westcott, who died on September 6, 1905.

From Howard Alexander Smith

My dear Dr. Wilson,   [New York]   May the first [1905].

I have talked the proposition over with Mrs. Smith and my father and have decided to accept the position of instructor in your courses next year. I hope if things go alright that I may be fitted for a preceptorship the following year, if I find that it agrees with me well enough to stay. My plan now is to go down to Princeton the end of this week or early next week, and want to call on you again to find out about my duties more specifically and also to find out the books you expect to require next year, so that I can read up this summer. Now that the matter is decided I am more than happy at the prospect, and particularly as I hope to have the benefit of your guidance and help in my work.[1]

Always sincerely yours   H. Alexander Smith

ALS (WP, DLC).
[1] As it turned out, Smith was unable to serve. At this time, he was already suffering from tuberculosis, and his health deteriorated so rapidly during the next few months that he was forced to spend the summer of 1905 in a sanitarium in the Adirondacks. In the autumn of 1905, he moved with his family to Colorado Springs. See William M. Leary, Jr., "Smith of New Jersey: A Biography of H. Alexander Smith, United States Senator from New Jersey, 1944-1959" (Ph.D. dissertation, Princeton University, 1966), pp. 7-8.

From Blanche Wilder Bellamy[1]

My dear Dr. Wilson,   [Brooklyn, N.Y.]   May first, 1905.

You will not, I am sure, remember Mrs. Bellamy who had the pleasure of dining with you at Miss Cutting's last winter.[2] I am she, however, & I write a word of thanks to you & congratulations to Princeton on the new plan of instruction to be inaugurated there.

We have just sent a young nephew,[3] the son of Mr. Edward Bellamy,[4] through Harvard. He has taken the four years' work in three years & gained the "magna cum laude." He is but twenty, & has had no fault found with him at any point or for any cause.

He tells me that there is *not one* Professor, instructor or tutor at Harvard to whom he can go for a letter of recommendation as a teacher; not one who would recognize him, except as a name on a list. If from education the *man* is to be withdrawn, & only the extract of information remains, how long will it be worth while to struggle to send our boys to college? "I sing arms *and the man*," my Virgil reads, & so does my Educational Creed. For your stride in the right direction all the Colleges are your debtors!

Most Appreciatively Yours,   Blanche Wilder Bellamy.

ALS (WP, DLC).
₁ Mrs. Frederick Putnam Bellamy, author and editor.
₂ See Wilson's diary entry printed at Feb. 11, 1904, Vol. 15. "Miss Cutting" was Elizabeth Brown Cutting.
₃ Paul Bellamy, Harvard 1905, who went on to a notable career as reporter, managing editor, and editor of the Cleveland *Plain Dealer*, 1907-53.
₄ Edward Bellamy, the utopian novelist, who had died on May 22, 1898.

To Benjamin Lawton Wiggins[1]

Princeton, N. J.

My dear Vice-Chancellor Wiggins: 4 May, 1905.

I do not know any place I would rather go to than Sewaunee, but unhappily I find it impossible to accept any Commencement invitations. My duties here for several weeks before and several weeks after our own Commencement are of such an engrossing character that I feel it would be unconscientious for me to absent myself from Princeton.

Allow me to thank you most cordially for your invitation and to assure you that I regard it as a great compliment, and also to express my unaffected regret that I cannot accept.

Very sincerely yours,   [Woodrow Wilson]

TL (TSewU).
₁ Professor of Greek and Vice-Chancellor of the University of the South.

From Donald Alexander Mac Rae*

Dear Sir: Ithaca, N. Y.   May 4, 1905.

In reply to your letter of yesterday, I beg to state that I willingly accept your kind offer to nominate me as a Preceptor in Classics at Princeton for a term of three years at a salary of two thousand dollars.

Permit me to say that I shall do all in my power to merit the kind confidence which you and your colleagues of the Classical Department of Princeton have shown in me.

Yours very sincerely,   Donald A. Mac Rae.

ALS (WP, DLC).

A News Report of a Religious Talk

[May 5, 1905]
PHILADELPHIAN SOCIETY.[1]

Regular Weekly Meeting Addressed
by President Wilson Last Evening.

President Wilson addressed the regular weekly meeting of the Philadelphian Society last evening in Murray Hall. The theme of the address was the deliberate government of the thoughts, and by way of introduction the speaker read the passage from the fourth chapter of Philippians, beginning with the eighth verse: "Finally brethren, whatsoever things are true," and ending with the exhortation, "think on these things." This familiar passage, said the speaker, establishes the principle that a man may be the final arbiter of his mental environment. He may choose his thoughts, he may use those selective faculties with which he is endowed and make his intellectual surroundings wholesome and pure, as he may by the same process choose his company and make his social circle just what he wishes, illiterate and coarse or cultured and refined. And by this very choice of companions our thoughts themselves are chosen, for they are in a large measure suggested and prompted by the people with whom we come in daily contact. The potency of these voluntary thoughts, by which we may change our whole mental scene is vast, when properly directed. By them, we may, in the midst of labors rest ourselves, in the midst of excitement calm ourselves, and in the midst of sorrow be soothed. High company and its train of higher thoughts may be cultivated in many ways: by books, rich legacies of noble men, by the observations of nature and communion with her, and finally by choosing the company of true christian men.[2]

Printed in the *Daily Princetonian*, May 5, 1905.
  [1] About this organization, see n. 1 to the news item printed at Nov. 1, 1890, Vol. 7.
  [2] For this address, Wilson used the notes printed at Sept. 21, 1902, Vol. 14.

From Walter Taylor Marvin*

My Dear Sir: Cleveland, Ohio. May 8th, 1905.
    I received your letter of May second last Thursday, and have delayed sending my answer to you until today, at the request of President Thwing.[1] I hope that this delay has caused you no inconvenience.

I shall be most happy to have you nominate me as a Preceptor in Philosophy, and I deeply appreciate the honor Princeton confers upon me.

Very sincerely yours,   Walter T. Marvin

ALS (WP, DLC).
  [1] Charles Franklin Thwing, President of Western Reserve University and Adelbert College since 1890.

To Winthrop More Daniels

My dear Daniels: Princeton, N. J.   9 May, 1905.

I have written [Royal] Meeker,* Shipman and Spencer, offering them appointments, but I have thought it on the whole best not to offer an appointment to Van Tyne.[1] I am, as you know, about to start for Kansas City and I will not write to Scott until I get back. If, in the meantime, you think it best that we should see Archer,[2] about whom [Robert McNutt] McElroy spoke to me yesterday afternoon, will you not be kind enough to make arrangements to have him down here next week?

Always—

Cordially and sincerely yours,   Woodrow Wilson

TLS (Wilson-Daniels Corr., CtY).
  [1] Claude Halsted Van Tyne, Assistant Professor of History at the University of Michigan.
  [2] He is unknown to the Editors.

A News Item

[May 10, 1905]

CAMPUS IMPROVEMENTS.

During the coming summer the lecture room of the First Presbyterian Church[1] is to be torn down, and the house on the lot immediately to the west will be taken away, adding about eighty feet to the open frontage of the campus on Nassau Street. By an arrangement with the church authorities, the University is to build an addition to the church at its southern end, to take the place of the lecture room.[2] The matter is now in the hands of the architect. The residence of Professor Cornwall on the adjoining lot is to be moved to Morven Street, on the Stockton property. The eighty odd feet thus to be added to the front campus, together with the lot where the residence of the late Treasurer Osborn formerly stood, will give an open space of about 125 feet in front of Alexander Hall, and will permit the widening of the present narrow driveway, thus obtaining a suitable entrance to Alexander Hall.

Printed in the *Daily Princetonian*, May 10, 1905.
¹ That is, the assembly room used as the facilities of the Sunday School by the First Church.
² It consisted of a chapel with a seating capacity of 300 and other rooms for Sunday School purposes and was completed in early 1907. Actually, the university contributed $7,750 toward the cost of the new structure, with the congregation paying the balance of about $10,750.

From Arthur Lincoln Frothingham, Jr., with Enclosure

Dear Sir   Rome¹   May 10/05

I beg to enclose a letter of resignation which I would ask you to kindly present to the board of Trustees, to take effect at the end of the present term.

I have seen many archaeologists during the last eight months, especially during the Archaeological Congress at Athens, and I can see that those who have accomplished something worth while are those attached to institutions that leave them free to give no lectures at all or to lecture on what they happen at the time to be busy with for their own research work. And after all, as Prof. Sayce² said to me: "There are hundreds of good teachers & administrators, but the born archaeologist is very rare."

So I feel that the present course is under the circumstances the very best for me, & I shall try to make up for lost time. Still, I do feel that the years of teaching have given me an experience that will help me to understand & address the public.

I hope to be back again in Princeton in the autumn, feeling as much at home as ever in the old atmosphere of friends, and as much as ever a Princeton man.

Yours very sincerely,   A. L. Frothingham, jr.

ALS (WP, DLC).
¹ Frothingham was on leave in Rome during the academic year 1904-1905.
² Archibald Henry Sayce, Professor of Assyriology at Oxford University since 1891.

ENCLOSURE

Arthur Lincoln Frothingham, Jr., to the Board of Trustees of Princeton University

Gentlemen   Rome, Italy   May 10, 1905

I feel obliged, after seventeen years of service as full professor, to offer my resignation to the Board.

It is with regret that I sever a connection that has been so pleasant and honorable, but I feel as if the original work which is my special province, & which I have been obliged for a number of years to abandon almost entirely on account of the increased requirements of teaching, can with difficulty be carried on in connection with this University.

I would ask as a favor that the material at present in my Seminar Room, purchased out of a fund raised by myself, should be added to the general collection in the Library, instead of to any special Collection, so that its use may be unrestricted.

Very respectfully A. L. Frothingham, jr.

ALS (Trustees' Papers, UA, NjP).

From Royal Meeker

Dear Sir: Collegeville, Pa., May 10, 1905

Your communication of the 9th inst. is at hand. I shall be very much pleased if you will present my name to the Board of Trustees of Princeton University as a preceptor in History and Politics. I anticipate a most pleasant and profitable year at Princeton under your administration. I trust that I may fit into your most excellent plan, and prove myself worthy of the responsibility attaching to the position of preceptor in Princeton University.

Thanking you for your kindness, I am

Yours sincerely, Royal Meeker

ALS (WP, DLC).

From Harper and Brothers

Dear Mr. Wilson,   New York May 11th, 1905.

The unbound sheets of your History have gone forward to you as requested in your letter of May 8th. As to the inquiry you make touching the sales of the History, we appreciate the cordial courtesy of its presentation. It seems only fair in replying to call your attention to what we believe to be a fact,—that no history and no literary work of any kind (excluding fiction) of a similar number of words, has brought to the author as great a revenue as your American Nation[1] has, in the same time. When the fact is recalled that the History was really projected as a one volume (or at most a two volume) work, that it could with decent fairness have been so produced, that it was expanded into five volumes largely because of the initiative of the publisher, and in that shape made such a magnificent showing:—when these things are considered, we believe you will recognize with us that the publisher has been of service. We confidently believe that no history in America has had as much spent on it in advertising and circularization, and we believe that no other house in the world could have sold more.

It is a fixed rule with us not to dispose of any plates or publications in which we are interested. We do not believe there is any firm which can sell or would sell as many volumes as we can sell and do sell. No mere money consideration would induce us to part with any important book which has once borne our imprint.

Please do not read into this letter anything save the most earnest desire to be of service to you and to meet your wishes. We do not believe, we *know* that no other House can sell more by reputable methods than we can, and we had fondly looked forward with hope to other volumes from your pen.

Yours very truly,   Harper & Brothers.

TLS (WP, DLC).
¹ That is, Wilson's *A History of the American People.*

From Charles Hodge Jones*

Dear Sir: Port Deposit, Md.   May 11, 1905.

At the request of Dean West, I write to accept the offer of an Instructorship for next year at a salary of twelve hundred dollars. This offer was made to me on Wednesday, May tenth, by Dean West at a conference to which he had summoned me.

Yours very truly,   Charles H. Jones.

ALS (WP, DLC).

A News Report about Wilson's Arrival in Kansas City

[May 12, 1905]

DR. WOODROW WILSON HERE

President of Princeton Talks of University Education.

Dr. Woodrow Wilson, president of Princeton university, arrived in Kansas City last night. He came all the way from the New Jersey home of the school to attend a convention of the Western Princeton Alumni clubs and will return Saturday night to the East. His chief address while here will be to the convention delegates at the University club Saturday night. The future of Princeton will be his theme.

John H. Thacher, E. D. Ellison and W. G. Mellier met Dr. Wilson at the depot and escorted him to the Hotel Baltimore.

Dr. Wilson was a member of the class of 1879, Mr. Mellier of the class of 1880. In response to an inquiry Dr. Wilson declared it was his belief that the tendency of young Americans toward securing a college education was growing, not falling off.

"Business men tell me this," he said. "They say, too, that they want college men. The operation of modern business requires men who can see things as systems, just as a general operates his armies without seeing the battlefield, just as men play chess without seeing the board. They keep it before their minds. One cannot do that without mental training. The college career supplies this.

["]This applies not only to the sciences but to the classical studies. A president of the Illinois Central Railroad company[1] told me he preferred men who had received a classical education in the administrative department. He declared they went farther, though they did not start as rapidly as those without it.

"Princeton is growing just like a tree, it seems impossible to stop the growth. We have more students now than we can comfortably care for. A new and much needed dormitory is to be started as soon as the contract can be let. There is to be a new recitation hall built in the autumn. We get our students from all over the country. It is a good thing to have the young men from different parts of the country mix. A South Carolinian, of a philosophical turn of mind, once told a Princeton representative: "I reckon there's a good many things down here we'uns don't know about and there's a good many things up there you'uns don't know about. Mixin' larns both of us." There is sound philosophy in that remark.

"The East, I think, is beginning to understand the West better. There are some parts of the East, though, that will never understand the West. I have learned many things about the West in my visits to it which I should never have known otherwise."

Dr. Wilson believes that strong class organization is an important feature of college life.

"The seniors rule the college," he said. "It is noticeable what an effect it has on the rest of the college if the seniors are weak. If the class has no natural leaders, the whole college feels it. If there are strong men in the senior class their rule is as supreme as that of kings. There are two members of the Princeton faculty who were seniors when I was a freshman.[2] I still have that feeling of reverence for them when I meet them now as I had when in school.

"There are a good many rich persons coming to Princeton to live just now. I regret it, because it destroys the simplicity of the place. Fortunately, those who have come so far are not ostentatious."

Dr. Wilson will be kept busy during his stay in Kansas City. This morning he will speak at the Central and Manual Training high schools and this afternoon at the Phroso academy.³ There will follow a dinner at the Country club this afternoon and a reception at the University club to-night. Dr. Wilson was asked what he would speak about at the high schools.

"I really do not know," he replied. "I wish I did. I am hoping that I shall wake up with some ideas in the morning. I haven't any to-night."

Printed in the *Kansas City Times*, May 12, 1906; some editorial headings omitted.
¹ Stuyvesant Fish, President of the Illinois Central Railroad from 1887 to 1906.
² Either Wilson's memory betrayed him or he was misquoted. There was no member of the Class of 1876 on the faculty at this time. Wilson was probably thinking of the Class of 1877, whose membership in the Princeton faculty included William Libbey, Alexander Thomas Ormond, William Berryman Scott, and John Howell Westcott.
³ The Prosso Preparatory School, a private, nonsectarian day and boarding school for boys, offering college preparatory courses.

An Editorial About Wilson

[May 12, 1905]

PRESIDENT WOODROW WILSON.

President Woodrow Wilson of Princeton university remarked to a Kansas City newspaper man yesterday that he had learned many things on his visits to the West. In return it may be said that the West has learned several things from President Wilson. Such of its sons as have attended Princeton university within the last fifteen years have felt the influence of that stimulating personality. To many more American history has been raised from the dead by the genial yet penetrating interpretation of this representative of the new school of historians.

There are plenty of men scattered over the country who recall the delight with which they read a little volume of Johns Hopkins university studies on "Congressional Government" published a score of years ago. That was before the days of such elaborate studies of American administration as have been embodied in the works of Bryce and [Henry Jones] Ford and Ostrogorski, and its method of going behind the theory of government to a study of its practical workings, while familiar in England, was novel enough in America. Readers of the book discovered that its author was a Johns Hopkins graduate who after a brief experience in the practice of law had gone into college work and they looked with anticipation for other writings.

Since that time Woodrow Wilson has had an audience for everything that he has cared to write. A Virginian with a Northern training, he has been particularly fortunate in his exposition of the Southern point of view of the issues leading to the Civil war, while his human interest and his gift for expression have vivified the record which he has transcribed. Indeed, there are people who have a quarrel with Princeton university for conferring upon him an office which they have feared might overwhelm him with administrative details and so prevent him from continuing his historical work.

It may not, perhaps, be amiss to express the hope that President Wilson finds his visits to the West as delightful as the West finds President Wilson.

Printed in the *Kansas City Star*, May 12, 1905.

A News Report of Speeches in Kansas City

[May 12, 1905]
THREE TALKS BY DR. WILSON

HIGH SCHOOLS VISITED BY THE PRESIDENT OF PRINCETON.

The Necessity for Reading Books and Studying "Dead" Languages Explained to the Pupils— The Advantages of Education Described.

Dr. Woodrow Wilson, president of Princeton university, visited the three Kansas City High schools this forenoon and at each school made a brief talk to the students. He went first to Central High school, then to the Manual Training High school and finally to the Westport High school.

At the Central High school President Wilson was introduced by Prof. Cammack, who told of the many educators of renown who have spoken at the school and said President Wilson stood second to none of the great men the school had heard.

President Wilson introduced his speech with a little explanation that would make a Missourian wonder if he had not at some time listened to some of the state's political orators. "It was very good of these gentlemen who brought me here," he said, "to leave me free to talk on any subject. The easiest subject to talk on is the one you know least about. There is such a freedom in speaking on subjects that one does not understand. There is no restraint because of facts if one does not know the facts. We are convinced of a good many things that are not so and we like to talk about them."

Laughter and applause greeted this odd introduction. Then the speaker talked seriously. "One thing we are justly convinced of," he said, "and that is the advantage of education. People ask: What is the particular use of this or that study? This is a work-a-day world, where we are all busy providing the essential physical things for ourselves and families. I have heard the usefulness of studies questioned, but I never heard a man object to gymnasium exercise because he did not expect to earn his living by doing a double trapeze act with a partner. We go into the gymnasium to get the body in good physical condition, to strengthen the muscles and build up the system. So you go into college to get your mental faculties in such state that you can take care of yourself anywhere. You build up the mind in college as you build up the body in the gymnasium.

"Why defend the study of classics? You won't conduct your business correspondence in Latin. You don't study Greek so you can go to Greece and talk with the modern Greeks in their own language. But these languages, though you call them dead languages, are alive with literature that is of great value to the student. It is a part of the life and literature of our own age. It fertilizes the mind and puts you in the current of the best there is in our modern civilization. It helps to equip you for modern citizenship. Be more than a mere citizen of your craft, be a citizen of your city and state in the broadest possible sense.

"I am disinclined to sit down and read a book. In reading your position is not the healthy, natural position. It is not easy for the lungs. You sit indoors. It is more pleasant to be outside where the air is fresher. The only reason I read a book is because I cannot see and converse with the man who wrote it. It is the only way I can find out his ideas and learn what he knows. It would be much better if I could talk with the writer, but very often he is dead or too far away.

"A book only partly expresses what the author means. I have written books myself. You are expected to make a book symmetrical. Sometimes in doing it you deal with things you do not fully understand. Then you write things you don't know and pray that nobody will stand on the weak parts until they break through. You read because you want to get at the mind and soul of the writer and the things he knew. That broadens the mind and makes its grasp of things stronger. Did you ever think that the reason man controlled the animal kingdom is because of his mind. You are not as strong as the lion. You are not as beautiful as some animals or as cunning as others, but you have the one great power of mind and the power to draw from the reservoir of the minds of all the men and women in the world. The cultivation of the mind is the best and most profitable thing you can do."

Printed in the *Kansas City Star*, May 12, 1905; two editorial headings omitted.

A News Item About McCosh Hall

[May 13, 1905]

Seven architects have entered the competition and submitted plans for McCosh Hall, the new recitation building projected for the Academy lot back of Marquand Chapel, the money for which, President Wilson announced some time ago, is already provided by benefactors of the University whose names have not been made public. On the basis of the several sets of plans submitted, the successful architect is to be chosen in the near future,[1] though additional drawings will no doubt be required before the final designs are accepted. It is announced, however, that McCosh Hall will probably be built of stone, and that in style it will be similar to the imposing buildings erected on the campus in the last few years. In addition to numerous lecture and recitation rooms of the size required for ordinary classes, there are to be two large halls, one to seat four hundred, the other big enough for six hundred. Also there are to be about twenty rooms for preceptors. It is hoped that work may be started on the hall during the summer.

Printed in the *Princeton Alumni Weekly*, v (May 13, 1905), 519.
[1] See the news item printed at May 20, 1905.

A News Report

[May 14, 1905]

HE SPOKE FOR PRINCETON.

Dr. Woodrow Wilson at the Western
Association's Dinner.

Woodrow Wilson, president of Princeton university, was the guest of honor at the annual meeting and banquet of the Western Association of Princeton Clubs held yesterday in the city. At 1 o'clock yesterday the delegates to the meeting took a special car at Twelfth street and Broadway and rode to Westport. There they were met by tallyhos and were driven to the Country club, where luncheon was served from 2 to 4 o'clock. The election of officers was held after the luncheon. . . .

The annual dinner of the association was held last night in the University club. The invocation was by the Rev. Paul B. Jenkins. . . .

Dr. Wilson's address was loudly applauded. It reviewed the achievements of Princeton university and made some predictions as to its future.

Printed in the *Kansas City Star*, May 14, 1905.

From Duane Reed Stuart

My dear Sir: Ann Arbor, Michigan.   May 15, 1905.

I have written to Professor West signifying my willingness to come to Princeton on the terms proposed in his last letter. May I, therefore, authorize you to present my name to the Board of Trustees for appointment as Preceptor in Classics? Trusting that I may be of service in the work at Princeton if the Board act favorably on the nomination, and assuring you of my high regard I am

Yours sincerely   Duane Reed Stuart

ALS (WP, DLC).

From La Rue Van Hook*

My dear Sir: Saint Louis, Missouri. May 15th, 1905.

Dean West writes me that the Classical Dept. has recommended me to you for a position as preceptor in Classics.

I write therefore, accepting the position and desire that my name be presented to the Trustees.

I look forward with pleasure to my work at Princeton.

Very sincerely yours,   La Rue Van Hook.

ALS (WP, DLC).

From Charles Worthen Spencer

My dear Sir: Hamilton, New York.   16 May 1905

In reply to your favor of the 9th instant, proposing to nominate me to the Trustees of Princeton University for a Preceptorship in History and Politics, I have the honor to accept your proposal with great heartiness. I find the attractions at Princeton very strong, among the chief of which is the prospect of working under your direction.

I presume that a nomination is equivalent to an election and that I may safely mention the matter and present my resignation to the Trustees of Colgate University?

        Very sincerely yours,   Charles Worthen Spencer

TLS (WP, DLC).

To Palmer Chamberlaine Ricketts, Jr.

My dear Mr. Ricketts: Princeton, N. J.   17 May, 1905.

Thank you most sincerely for your kind letter of May 11th. I have just returned from a trip to the West and Mrs. Wilson has also been absent from Princeton for the past week.

I know that she will be as grateful to you as I am for your kind words of sympathy. The blow was indeed overwhelming. Although Mrs. Wilson has been singularly brave and steady under it, I do not yet feel entirely reassured as to the consequences. Fortunately, she is made of wonderful stuff.

    With warm regards,

        Cordially and sincerely yours,   Woodrow Wilson

TLS (in possession of Bruce Gimelson).

A News Item

[May 18, 1905]

DINNER TO PROFESSOR YOUNG.

Unusual Mark of Esteem Conferred Upon Him by Members of the Faculty.

A dinner was given last evening by the University Faculty in honor of Professor Charles Augustus Young at the Princeton Inn. The parlor in which the dinner was held was brilliantly lighted and the tables were handsomely decorated with flowers.

After-dinner speeches were made by the following gentlemen: President Woodrow Wilson, Ex-President Francis L. Patton, M. Taylor Pyne '77, Professor Magie, Dr. Henry van Dyke, and Professor Brackett.

Dr. Henry van Dyke read a poem written in honor of the occasion, and a letter was also read from the Hon. Grover Cleveland who was unable to be present.

After Professor Brackett, the last speaker, had finished, the following toast was proposed, to which Professor Young responded most fittingly:

"He through heaven,
That opened wide its blazing portals, led
To God's eternal house direct the way,
A broad and ample road, whose dust is gold,
And pavement stars."[1]

Professor Young was made the recipient of a handsome silver loving cup, Professor Brackett making the presentation with a few words appreciative of Professor Young's services.

Printed in the *Daily Princetonian*, May 18, 1905.
  [1] John Milton, *Paradise Lost*, Book VII, lines 574-78.

From Charles Augustus Young

Dear Dr. Wilson: [Princeton, N. J.]   May 18 1905

I want to thank you most heartily for your part in the planning and arrangement of the dinner last evening as well as for your speech. The occasion was one I shall never forget, and I shall hand its memory down to my children and their children after them. It was the highest, most appreciated, honor that ever came to me.

Cordially & gratefully yours   C. A. Young

ALS (WP, DLC).

To Arthur Lincoln Frothingham, Jr.

Princeton, N. J.
My dear Professor Frothingham: May 20, 1905.

Allow me to acknowledge the receipt of your favor of May 10th, inclosing your letter of resignation to the Board of Trustees, and to thank you most sincerely for the cordial way in which you express your future intentions with regard to living in Princeton. I am sure that I speak for everyone concerned when I say that you will be most welcome and that the old relations will be most cordially maintained.

I know that there will be universal regret that it is necessary for you to break your long standing connection with the University and that everyone will hope that it will redound greatly to the benefit of your own studies.

Always—

Sincerely yours,   Woodrow Wilson

TLS (WC, NjP).

From Donald Cameron

Dear Sir: Waco, Texas. May 20, 1905.

Some two weeks after I had written you that I would accept the appointment of Preceptor in Classics Prof. West wrote me that the department had not heard from me. I wrote Prof. West at once saying again that I would accept the appointment, but I did not write a second time to you as I should have done.

I write you this thinking that even at this late day it might chance to be useful in preventing a misunderstanding.

Very sincerely yours,   Donald Cameron.

ALS (WP, DLC).

A News Item

[May 20, 1905]

The committee in charge of McCosh Hall, the new recitation building projected for the Academy lot back of Marquand Chapel, have selected as its architect Mr. R. C. Gildersleeve of New York,[1] the son of Prof. B. L. Gildersleeve '49 of Johns Hopkins University, and the architect of Upper and Lower Pyne, the Nassau street dormitories opposite the front campus.

Printed in the *Princeton Alumni Weekly*, v (May 20, 1905), 538.
[1] Raleigh Colston Gildersleeve, Johns Hopkins 1888.

From Henry Robinson Shipman

My dear President Wilson,   Hanover, N. H.   May 21, 1905.

It would give me a great deal of pleasure to go to you as Preceptor in History and Politics for a term of three years at a salary of $1500.   Yours very sincerely   Henry R. Shipman.

ALS (WP, DLC).

From the Minutes of the Session of the Second Presbyterian Church of Princeton, New Jersey

May 24 1905

The Session met in the lecture room at 8 P.M. and was opened with prayer. Present as Moderator Rev. F. W. Loetscher, Elders Fisher, Freund, Wilson, Van Dyke.[1] . . .

After an expression of opinion from each one present concerning the services of Dr. de Vries as pastor of the Church,[2] Elder

Wilson was appointed a committee to prepare a resolution to be put in the minutes of the Session and to be presented to Presbytery.

After prayer, adjourned.

H. N. Van Dyke, Clerk.

"Minutes of the Session 1898-1914, Second Presbyterian Church, Princeton, N.J.," bound minute book (St. Andrew's Presbyterian Church, Princeton, N. J.), p. 53.

[1] Frederick William Loetscher, Frederick Fisher, Louis W. Freund, and Henry Nevius Van Dyke.

[2] The Rev. Dr. John Hendrik de Vries, who had announced his resignation as pastor of the Second Presbyterian Church.

A Tribute

[c. May 24, 1905]

RESOLVED: That the Session express to the Presbytery, in presenting the resolution of the congregation, their very warm admiration of the character, the gifts and the attainments of Dr. deVries, his unusual power and expository insight as a preacher, his energy and diligence as a pastor, his unremitting devotion to every part of his duty, and recognize in the most cordial manner the very substantial services he has rendered the Church. They feel that in losing him they are losing a most faithful and devoted friend and fellow laborer; that his influence has always been in the direction of the things that are purest and highest, his doctrine always true to the word of divine Scripture, his counsel helpful and right; that the removal of the heavy debt which rested upon the church at the beginning of his pastorate and the material improvement of the church property have been in no small measure due to his work and zeal; and that his labours have been crowned with benefits to the church which make it his permanent and grateful debtor.[1]

> Woodrow Wilson
> Louis W. Freund.
> Frederick Fisher
> Matthew Bergen
> H. N. Van Dyke, Clerk[2]

T MS S (in possession of Henry Batholomew Cox).

[1] There is a WWhw draft of this resolution in WP, DLC.

[2] This resolution was presented to a special meeting of New Brunswick Presbytery in the First Presbyterian Church of Trenton on May 29, 1905. It was printed in the *Princeton Press*, June 3, 1905.

From Oliver Samuel Tonks*

My dear President Wilson: New York, May 25, 1905.

I shall be happy to have you nominate me to your Board of Trustees on the terms you mentioned. I thank you for the offer
                              Yours sincerely   Oliver S. Tonks.

ALS (WP, DLC).

To Andrew Cunningham McLaughlin[1]

                                        Princeton, N. J.
My dear Professor McLaughlin: May 30, 1905.

Your letter,[2] sent by special delivery, makes me fear that we may have done Mr. Van Tyne some disservice in not writing to him since his visit here. We were extremely pleased with the man himself, and of course knew before we saw him how enviable a place he already occupies as a student of American history. But my talk with Dr. Van Tyne convinced me that he would really take very little interest in our new Preceptorial system as such and that he would himself be happiest and freest where he could have a University appointment of the usual kind with an opportunity to confine himself to one subject of study and to writing. For these reasons we had ceased to consider [h]is name, though we felt that we were thereby turning away a very unusual and brilliant man.

I would esteem it a courtesy if you would lay these reasons before Dr. Van Tyne himself, with the expression of our warm regard.   Very sincerely yours,   Woodrow Wilson

TLS (C. H. Van Tyne Papers, MiU-C).
   [1] Professor of American History at the University of Michigan. However, he was on leave during the academic years 1903-1905 to serve as Director of the Bureau of Historical Research of the Carnegie Institution of Washington.
   [2] It is missing.

From Hamilton Ford Allen*

My dear Mr. Wilson: Washington, Pa. May 31, 1905.

I am sorry to have delayed so long to give you a definite answer in regard to the offer for next year. Dr. Moffat[1] did not return until yesterday, and did not give me a definite answer until this morning. He said that the college could not afford to give me a year's leave of absence, but I have no hesitation in accepting your offer for next year, as I think that the prestige of having taught a year at Princeton will be well worth the sacrifice. I am sure that the fact that I have taught a year at Princeton, together with the good-will of the faculty, which I shall strive earnestly to gain, will enable me to get a good position for the following year.

Therefore, as I said in my telegram, I accept with thanks the offer made in your kind letter of the twenty-fourth.

Yours very respectfully,   Hamilton Ford Allen.

TLS (WP, DLC).
1 The Rev. Dr. James David Moffat, President of Washington and Jefferson College.

An Article

[c. June 1, 1905]

THE PRINCETON PRECEPTORIAL SYSTEM

The system of preceptorial instruction which we are about to elaborate at Princeton is no new or novel notion of our own, but based upon almost universal experience, upon what every teacher must have found out for himself, whether by way of interpreting his failures or of interpreting his successes; he always gets his best results by direct, personal, intimate intercourse with his pupils, not as a class but as individuals.

College instructors have long observed that their teaching is rendered more effective by dividing large classes into small sections and making each section small enough to enable them to get frequently at each member of the class in the process of test and drill. But even this division of large classes into small sections has not been satisfactory. The sections were usually made up either alphabetically or according to marks or grades received by members of the class in written tests or examinations on the subjects they were studying, the best students being put in one section, the next best in the next, and so on to the dullest in the lowest section. Now, it so happens that God has not classified men's abilities either alphabetically or according to their performances in examinations. I need not urge that he has not used the alphabet; neither will it require much argument to prove to experienced teachers that he has not adjusted gifts to the processes of examination. It by no means always turns out that the men who have got themselves by examination into the first section of the class are the brightest men in the class, or that those who allow themselves to fall into the lowest section are the dullest. The lowest division, in fact, often contains the greatest variety: very bright men, who will not use their gifts in their studies; very dull men, who have no gifts to use, and mediocre men, who are lazy. Separating the class into sections in either of the two ways most commonly employed is certainly a way of dividing it, but it is not an intelligent way of classifying the individuals who compose it. The intention of the preceptorial system is to enable the instructors to handle the men assigned them either singly or in classified groups, in which men of like training, aptitudes and needs are united.

But the system involves much more than a change of method. It is meant not only, in time, to supersede entirely the old-fashioned "recitation," but also to affect very materially the subject matter of study, to give the undergraduates their proper release from being school boys, to introduce them to the privileges of maturity and independence by putting them in the way of doing their own reading instead of "getting up" lectures or "lessons." The subject matter of their studies is not to be the lectures of their professors or the handful of text-books, the narrow round of technical exercises set for them under the ordinary methods, but the reading which they should do for themselves in order to get a real first-hand command of the leading ideas, principles and processes of the subjects which they are studying. Their exercises with their preceptors are not to be recitations, but conferences, in which, by means of any method of report or discussion that may prove serviceable and satisfactory, the preceptors may test, guide and stimulate their reading. The governing idea is to be that they are getting up *subjects*—getting them up with the assistance of lecturers, libraries and a body of preceptors who are their guides, philosophers and friends. The process is intended to be one of reading, comparing, reflecting; not cramming, but daily methodical study.

One great incidental advantage is expected to accrue to the study of English. The reports of the undergraduates to the preceptors on the reading they are doing will naturally very often be written reports, and it is to be expected that all such reports will be judged of as English as well as with regard to the accuracy or inaccuracy of their subject matter. If not written in good English, they will have to be written over again, and if it turns out that any man cannot use his mother tongue correctly and with some degree of elegance, upon being so corrected and held to a standard of expression, he is to be handed over to the English department for fundamental training. The constant daily necessity to know his own language and to use it properly upon all sorts of subjects will certainly be the most vital system of "theme writing" yet devised, and may be expected to have a quality of reality

about it which the formal written exercises of English departments have generally lacked. The men will be using their mother
tongue in careful writing, not for the sake of the language itself,
but for the sake of releasing ideas and stating facts. Style will
be a means and not an end; and it should never in any kind of
writing be anything else.

In brief, the system will be a method of study, a means of
familiarizing the undergraduate with the chief authorities, conceptions and orders of work in his fields of study. The preceptors
will not set the examinations. That would turn them into mere
coaches, coaching for final tests which they themselves were to
set. They are, rather, to be fellow students, expositors, advisors,
to see that the right work is done by themselves taking part in it.

They will not, however, be a body of men segregated and set
apart from the general body of the faculty. The present staff of
the university will also do preceptorial work; the new preceptors
will take some part in the lecture and regular class work, which
will still go forward; they will be members of the faculty, indis-
tinguishable in privilege and rank from their colleagues. The fundamental object of the system would be defeated if any sharp
line of division were drawn in the faculty between the several
kinds of teachers, for the fundamental object is to draw faculty
and undergraduates together into a common body of students,
old and young, among whom a real community of interest, pursuit and feeling will prevail. The preceptors will only have more
conference work to do than their colleagues. It will be their chief,
if not their distinctive, function to devote their energies to the
intimate work of counsel and guidance I have tried to character-
ize and describe.

It is our confident hope that such changes will bring about very
gratifying results: that the undergraduate will take more pleasure in his studies, derive more profit and stimulation from them,
and that the instructor will find vital intercourse with his pupils
give place to dull routine. There will be more work done, but it
will be less burdensome both to teacher and pupil, more normal,
less like a body of tasks and more like a natural enjoyment of
science and letters.[1]

Printed in the *Independent*, LIX (Aug. 3, 1905), 239-40.
[1] There is a WWsh draft of this article in WP, DLC.

From Edward Samuel Corwin*

Dear Sir: Philadelphia—June 3 [1905].

I wish to thank you for your offer to nominate me for the position mentioned in your communication of this date. I shall accept the position with the greatest pleasure.

Yours sincerely   Edward S. Corwin

ALS (WP, DLC).

To James Julius Chambers[1]

My dear Mr. Chambers: Princeton, N. J.   June 3, 1905.

I am very much mortified that you should have come to Princeton only to find me away on the day I had appointed for an interview. I telegraphed the day before, sending the telegram to your house address as given in the New York directory, and in as much as you had said in your letter that you would not come to Princeton until the morning of the day you were to see me, I took it for granted that the telegram would reach you.

Allow me to express my very deep regret at having put you to this inconvenience and to apologize for my apparent remissness.[2]

Cordially and sincerely yours,   Woodrow Wilson

TLS (de Coppet Coll., NjP).
    [1] Free-lance journalist and author of New York; former managing editor of the *New York Herald* and the New York *World*.
    [2] Further correspondence between Wilson and Chambers is missing. However, it seems probable that Chambers made arrangements by telephone for an early meeting, and that he was the author of the interview with Wilson printed at June 11, 1905.

From John William Basore*

My dear President Wilson: Baltimore, Md., June 5, 1905.

In acknowledgment of your favor of June third, I beg to say that I have wired my resignation to the University of California and hope to be able to signify promptly an unconditional acceptance of your offer.

Most Sincerely yours,   John W. Basore.

ALS (WP, DLC).

To Hamilton Holt

My dear Mr. Holt: Princeton, N. J.   June 7, 1905.

Thank you very much for your letter of June 6th.[1] It would give me pleasure to make such an addition to my article on the Preceptorial system as you suggest, were I not fearful lest it should involve me in some embarrassments. I might seem to be drawing some comparisons between the character of the men heretofore chosen for the Faculty and the character of the men chosen to be Preceptors, for I should have to dwell upon the fact that we have been chosing them with the principal view to their character, the disposition being whenever necessary to prefer a gentleman of somewhat inferior attainments in scholarship to a fully equipped scholar who was not a gentleman. I think you would see how delicate a matter this would be to handle.

I thank you very much for your letter and am particularly pleased that you think the changes we are about to make serviceable and sensible.

Cordially and sincerely yours,   Woodrow Wilson

TLS (PBL).
[1] It is missing.

To Winthrop More Daniels

My dear Daniels: Princeton, N. J.   June 7, 1905.

This is certainly an extraordinary letter from Van Tyne[1] and, in conjunction with other things that have come to my notice, it makes me rather glad that we did not ask him here. I think your letter to him excellent and I am myself writing him a brief note.

Cordially and sincerely yours,   Woodrow Wilson

TLS (Wilson-Daniels Corr., CtY).
[1] The Van Tyne letter is missing from the papers of Winthrop More Daniels, now in the possession of R. Balfour Daniels.

To Claude Halstead Van Tyne

My dear Mr. Van Tyne: Princeton, N. J.   June 7, 1905.

I learn with real distress from Professor Daniels that you, and perhaps Prof. McLaughlin also, think that my letter to Prof. Mc-Laughlin contained between the lines an intimation that you had shown some kind of bad faith in your dealings with us. No such notion ever entered my head for a moment. I knew that you came on in perfect good faith and all that I meant to say was that, after my conversation with you, I felt convinced that you would not be happy in doing the miscellaneous teaching over the wide field which we shall be obliged to exact of our Preceptors. I am very much mortified that I should have expressed myself so clumsily as to have conveyed so erroneous an impression.

Cordially and sincerely yours,   Woodrow Wilson

TLS (C. H. Van Tyne Papers, MiU-C).

From John William Basore

My dear Dr. Wilson: Baltimore Md., June 8, 1905.

I have been surprised by the possibility of having a personal interview with President Wheeler[1] here, and write to express my readiness to accept the position of Preceptor in Classics upon the terms indicated in your recent letter.

I shall come with genuine interest in the distinctive features of the new work and hope that by zeal I may contribute to its success.   Very sincerely yours,   John W. Basore.

ALS (WP, DLC).
[1] Benjamin Ide Wheeler, President of the University of California.

From Charles Henry Smyth, Jr.*

My dear Sir: Clinton, N. Y., June 8, 1905.

It gives me great pleasure to reply in the affirmative to your very kind letter of the 7th. inst., asking if you may present my name to your Board of Trustees for election as Professor of Geology.

The position is, in every way, attractive to me, and the cordiality of your invitation adds much to my pleasure in accepting it.

Let me assure you that it will be my most earnest endeavor to prove worthy of your confidence.

Very truly yours,   C H Smyth Jr.

TLS (WP, DLC).

From Harvey Waterman Thayer*

My dear Sir,   Brooklyn, New York   June 8. 1905.

Your letter is just received. In reply to your question I desire to say that I shall be happy to accept the nomination to the position of Preceptor for the coming year under the conditions which you indicate. I shall look forward with pleasure to the new work at Princeton, and trust that I may be able to make my services useful to the University.

Yours sincerely,   Harvey W. Thayer

ALS (WP, DLC).

From Hopson Owen Murfee

My dear Dr. Wilson: Marion, Alabama.   10 June 1905

We appreciate your kindness in offering to write something for the Journal of the Council after Commencement.[1] You have already rendered us inestimable service by your coming into the school and by your message to our boys. I wish that you might know how appreciative they are, and what great good you have done. Four of our finest boys have decided to go to Princeton, three next year and one the following year. They are:

H. H. Tippin, Gulfport, Mississippi
W. H. Tippin,   "   "
W. F. Pratt,   "   "
F. S. Fountain, Burnt Corn, Alabama[2]

Three of these have attained the highest rank in their studies, and the fourth is a boy of unusual ability. They would appreciate copies of the Princeton catalogue; and I should like to have a copy of the current catalogue with information of conditions of admission.

I have just returned from the session of the Alabama Educational Association where I heard many gratifying expressions of appreciation of your visit to Alabama.

Mrs. Murfee, and all the members of our household, join me in grateful remembrance.

Very sincerely yours   H. O. Murfee

TLS (WP, DLC).
[1] Wilson was unable to contribute to the *Marion Institute Bulletin*.
[2] None of the four boys mentioned entered Princeton.

An Interview

[June 11, 1905]

COLLEGE ENGLISH IS BAD, SAYS PRINCETON'S HEAD

President Woodrow Wilson Deplores the Modern Neglect of
the Study of our Own Language in Higher Education.
Newspaper English Remarkably Good

Are college graduates lacking in ability to handle the English language well?

President Woodrow Wilson, of Princeton University, says that they are, and that not enough attention is given in college curriculums to instruction in English composition.

When asked what he considered the most conspicuous shortcoming in the present scheme of college instruction he unhesitatingly answered:

"The lack of study of our own language. To my way of thinking the knowledge of English has been most wofully neglected. Very few students, and very few others, for that matter, can write English and express their exact thoughts in a clear, simple and comprehensible manner. They devote their minds to thinking of the style to be followed, and to worrying whether or not a sentence is correct rather than to a direct expression of the meaning. People are inclined to write simply words without any substance or body to them, or any clear meaning. They are handicapped in their expressions by trying to follow a certain routine of style and keep in a correct rut of language.

"It is having a very bad effect on our literature, and vigorous methods should be taken at once to correct the evil. The average American when he sits down to write anything will display a prodigal waste of words and a miserly array of thought.

"Next year we shall begin to take steps here to correct it by making each student write daily reports upon his work. The attempts in the past to correct the evil by having students write theses on various subjects seem to have had no effect. The trouble is just as great as ever, or greater. The reports will be criticised without regard to the correctness of the statements made, but as to the way the statements are expressed. Those who do not pass muster will be returned to be done over again, and when we come across any 'howlers' the writer will be exiled to a class in preliminary instruction. By this method we hope to get the students into the way of writing just what they would say without being hampered by any style or conventionality of expression. We want to encourage their imagination in the use of words and lead them out of the beaten and worn paths of the language.

"Style in writing is something I do not believe in. It sets a limit to expression and is a wet blanket on thought. The possibilities of the English language are very great, and have yet to be fully developed."

"Do you object to what is known as fine writing and flowers of speech?"

"Oh, not entirely. Flowery writing should be indulged in with great discretion, however. The same principle applies to it as does to architecture. You can build a structure and ornament it to its improvement, but you cannot build ornamentation and have a structure that will stand."

"Do you expect this coaching in clear writing will also work inversely and teach the students to speak better?"

"It should, certainly."

"In which do you find the average student most deficient—writing or speaking English?"

"In speaking, I should say, for in talking he is apt to thoughtlessly take short cuts in the language and indulge in slang."

"Do you resent the incorporation of slang words in the acceptedly correct language?"

"It requires the drawing of a very fine line between the slang that is a new, forceful and expressive word and the slang that is simply vulgar. Only usage and time can tell exactly which is which. Correct language is absorbing slang words all the time and I suppose always has. I presume the expression in the Bible, 'by the skin of his teeth' was once slang. It is a very sure thing, though, that we are using fewer French words than formerly, and Latin expressions have almost entirely been dropped.

"It is the fashion among a certain class to rather sneer at what they are pleased to call 'newspaper English.' These gentlemen should look at home before committing themselves, and remedy their own shortcomings and their laboriously correct style of writing. I think the English used in newspaper articles is remarkably good. It is generally terse and clear and right to the point, and tells in a simple way exactly what the writer wants to say. It is most surprising to me to understand how the reporters, writing as they do so hurriedly and under such a great pressure, are able to write so well. I can hardly comprehend it.

"None need be afraid of spoiling their taste for good English by reading newspapers. The articles are almost always delightfully free from stiltedness and trite conventionality, which is more than can be said of the average collegian's effusions."

President Wilson is a man who always means what he says, and says it directly and clearly. In appearance he bears a striking resemblance to Mr. George Ade, a dramatist, except that he is not quite as tall as the funny man from Indiana.

Mr. Wilson has a habit when speaking of pointing his finger at you to emphasize a statement. In fact, he uses his hands a great deal when talking and makes gestures with the ease and facility of an actor. He neither looks nor acts in accordance with the old popular conception of the head of a great university. Thick dark hair, dark brown eyes, a straight nose and a long, smooth shaven sun-burned face give him the appearance of a typical young American business man rather than the dignified head of a college faculty. In manner he is jovial and whole souled, and his laugh comes easily and noisily.

Just now, at commencement time, it is interesting to learn what the college commencements of 1905 show.

Toward what general class of occupation is the tendency of the army of young men now graduating from college?

Are the professions still overcrowded and is the modern rush into scientific and business pursuits still at its height?

Does commercialism offer more opportunities of preferment than professionalism?

These are the questions that thousands of young men and their parents and thinking people generally are asking themselves just now. That classical education was on the decline has been apparent to every one with an eye half opened to the signs of the times for ten years past. The colleges had flooded the country with ministers, lawyers and doctors. There was an enormous surplus of them, and in consequence a large percentage were forced to be idle or take up some other occupation.

Then came a reaction with the great industrial development. Young men sniffed at Latin and Greek and literature generally and went pell mell up to their necks into mathematics, chemistry and the exact sciences. It seemed as though every active young man with college aspirations was ambitious to be an engineer of some kind or an architect until now the scientific pursuits are quite as crowded as were the professional.

"The question of whether science or business, or the professions offer the best inducements to college graduates is one that is very hard to answer," said President Wilson. "At present I think my ideas on the subject are in only a half baked condition. I have not actually come to a conclusion on the matter, although I have given it a great deal of thought and study and intend to give it a great deal more in the near future.

"There is no doubt that it is a subject of very great importance, not only to the young men who are graduating, but to the future welfare of the country. I am, you know, a writer rather than a talker, and like all writers, I dislike to commit myself until I am absolutely sure of the ground I stand on. Then, too, you must remember that I am new on this job. I am not one of the veteran college presidents, but only a junior, and perhaps my opportunities for observation have not yet been sufficient to entitle me to talk with conviction.

"I do not think, however, that classical education is done for by any means and that the time has come to lay it on the shelf."

"You do not think then that the time devoted to the study of the classics is time wasted?"

"Certainly not. I have no patience with the cry for 'practical education,' as it is called, although that is not an intelligent way to put it. What I mean is the near-sighted demand that youngsters should not study or be taught anything in college that they will not have a direct use for in after life. Everything of that nature is termed impractical. How absurd that is when you come to look at it carefully! For instance, there is nothing done in the gymnasium that a man is ever likely to do afterward in his study or his office. None ever make use of the horizontal bar or the trapeze to further their business interests, to promote scientific investigations or to help in literary research, and yet nobody disputes the fact that exercise in the gymnasium is thoroughly practical. It strengthens the muscles and gives the man a clearer brain to carry on his real work, whatever it is. Study of any kind disciplines the mental faculties and makes them supple and better fitted to tackle problems."

"You believe then in a comprehensive course of education, embracing both scientific as well as classical elements?"

"Most assuredly I do, if the student can possibly find the time to take them up. A minister is better off for having studied calculus and an engineer for having read the Latin authors. The study of any subject always makes for improvement and is a benefit whether the student ever had occasion to use the knowledge gained or not.["]

"You do not think a special line of education is advisable?"

"Not if a comprehensive one can be had."

"Is not there at present an inclination to run to specialties in education?"

"I am afraid there is and it is to be deplored, as it only develops a part of the brain. The other parts of the brain are left to wither up and become dwarfed."

"Which leads in the number of college students throughout the country at present, the scientific or classical courses?"

"Including the technical schools, I should think that the scientific courses had considerably the best of it just now. In the State universities the scientific students far outnumber the others."

"But you think this condition is likely to be changed?"

"I would not be surprised if there was soon a revival in classical study. We are making plans here to test the question of the advisability of the two kinds. It will, I think, when we get it under way, be a practical test that will give us much valuable data to work upon."

"What occupation predominates in those selected by the members of the present graduating class here at Princeton?"

"It is somewhat remarkable that there is very little variance here from year to year in what the boys select to become. A great many naturally go into business, the majority without any question. In the professions the law has the first place, although a great many elect to become physicians. That seems to be a profession that is growing in popularity among college men."

"How about the ministry?"

"The number of candidates is perceptibly decreasing. I am not armed with any exact information on the subject and only know what my theological friends have told me, but they all unite in saying that there is a great scarcity of candidates for the ministry just now. Of course, this should not be so, but it is easy to understand why it is so. The material benefits offered by other professions are much greater than those to be had in preaching the gospel, and it is not to be wondered at that young men select a career where the chances of worldly prosperity seem to be the brightest. That ministers get smaller pay than other professional men is a well known fact, and much to be regretted. It is also a question in political economy that I cannot undertake to explain or offer a remedy for."

"All young men leave college nowadays with a determination to do something, do they not?"

"Ah, yes, we no longer graduate a 'gentleman of leisure' class. They all have ambitions and aims. They all want to do something and they take pride in announcing what line of work they have picked out. It is the fashion for every American to have some occupation, you know. There is not one of the boys but that would be ashamed to admit he intended to lead a life of idleness. Human drones are out of date. They are not a little bit popular in this age of enterprise and progress."

"Is the enthusiasm for knowledge of Latin and Greek on the wane or not?"

"Well, I don't think there is much enthusiasm for it and I doubt if there ever was. The study of Latin, however, is steadily increasing. It is being taught more than it ever was. And in the preparatory schools and academies all over the country the study of Latin has become very general. On the other hand, the time and attention given to Greek is just as steadily and rapidly decreasing. Within the last few years Greek has dropped to a very minor and unimportant place in the curriculums.

"Neither of the languages has ever been genuinely popular with the majority of students, largely due to the fact, I think, that they have been regarded solely as the study of syntax and etamology [etymology]. That, of course, was mainly due to the methods of instruction. The boys were wont to regard the study of Latin as the dry and stupid analysis of a language; a grind that had to be endured but could not be interesting. I know I thought of it that way when I was a student.

"How many young men do you suppose ever read Caesar's commentaries with any pleasure? They only looked upon it as so many sentences to be translated and parsed. Few ever realized that it is an absorbing work full of vitality and human interest. It was written by one of the world's greatest generals and is a record of his own battles and achievements. The subject alone would prevent its being dull. The only other book at all like it is Grant's memoirs, and nobody ever thought that dull. College students would read Grant's memoirs with great enjoyment, but would shy at Caesar's commentaries, and heartily dread to read them.["]

Printed in the *New York Herald*, June 11, 1905; editorial sub-headings omitted.

A Sermon

BACCALAUREATE ADDRESS, 11 June, 1905.

I suppose that in a sense it is true, as satirical critics of university training like to suppose,—and have supposed generation after generation without troubling themselves to re-examine the facts, —that men just graduating from college are unsophisticated, as the world judges sophistication, and that they go out, at some risk of ridiculous mistake, into a world which will certainly chill and sober them with many painful but instructive surprises. I am inclined to believe, however, that their simplicity is exaggerated, their ignorance misconstrued. At any rate in places like Princeton, where they have been members of a self-governing community, fundamentally democratic in its constitution, and have not been kept in leading strings in matters of conduct, they are not now the innocent youngsters and easily gulled tyros they may formerly have been. They often step out into the world of affairs with not a little self-possession, not a little power to comprehend. The slowness and awkwardness with which they adjust themselves arise as much from the singular and oftentimes irrational disorder of the new relations into which they are thrust as from their own inaptness to perceive and act in the midst of practical business; and the disorder of those relationships was never greater than it is to-day.

The modern world confuses very practiced thinkers, throws very experienced guides out of their way. Not because it is so big, or even because it is so multiform and various. Bigness is not confusing if its proportions display upon examination a symmetry of fixed relations. Variety is not confusing, multiformity does not distract the careful and observant eye, if unity be anywhere discoverable, if the crowding elements be anywhere drawn into ranks and orders. The college bred man, if he be indeed bred and not simply cast and stamped like a senseless coin, would look with a comprehending eye on system, whatever the variety of detail. He naturally seeks a series, a governing arrangement and principle, and can hardly be wondered at if he cannot understand what the understanding has never forged together. Things new and old jostle one another in our day and live in no peace or concord, arrange no *modus vivendi* among them. The new do not seem to have sprung from the old. Their lineage and connection seem undetermined and accidental. The tendencies which sway them are gathered nowhere into any one great drift or current, but swirl hither and thither in confused and lawless eddies, in giddy mazes which the eye despairs of following. The age desires law but cannot find it, seeks order but does not discover it, would be led but knows not whom to follow. Who does walk through it with complete sophistication and self-mastery; who does thread its labyrinth confident of his clue, sure of coming upon the thing he seeks? The blundering of the lad is only a little more evident, a little less artfully concealed, than the blundering of the experienced man of the world. There are many high and earnest strivings, there is much patient, much exalted hope, much noble purpose, much steadfast belief in the divine rectitude of fortune and event; but there is more, much more, distraction and blind trust in chance, mad running after what rash adventure may bring of gain and pleasure.

We seek to regulate our life and are baffled. Law will not come at our bidding or merely because of our need. No sufficient rule of guidance seems to be anywhere discoverable. Thoughtful men turn themselves about in every direction crying "Is there nothing that can quiet us, give us confidence, assurance, peace?" There are even those amongst us who turn to the ancient, tranquil, patient East for quietness of spirit, and envy the Orient its calm

of deadened energy. A recent writer,[1] with satirical intent, no
doubt, and a purpose he has no wish to conceal to cast ridicule
upon the frantic energy of modern communities, that pile up
power and know not how to use it, and yet, it may be, with half
serious admiration of the placid East, has avowed his disgust with
the turmoil of aimless industry which fills the life of Europe and
America with cheerless abundance, and has calmly proclaimed
his preference for the monotonous levels of existence to be found
in China's secluded kingdom, teeming with its close-packed
millions, where each may hope to find little more than his daily
dole of food and the common comfort of shelter, but where there
is peace without plenty, and the satisfactions of an undisturbed
mind, not doubting dull duty or slighting the daily task, content
with its present, undismayed by fear of its future, neither restless
nor in haste.

No doubt the days of the oriental show singularly serene upon
the surface, and are a happy thing for the jaded minds of our own
men and women to look upon. They hide within them, it may be,
for those who live them thoughtfully and hold their spirits true
to the calm counsels of their ancient creeds, conceptions of life
and duty which satisfy if they do not save. Why should they not
take solace and content from a belief which seems without date
or beginning and has held within its formulas the ages through
an immemorial civilization which no process of mere time seems
able to impair? If quietness of spirit were all, if that life were life
enough in which fear and doubt were set at rest and the blood
bidden go its slow pace of dull content as if very sluggishness
were a law of health, one might easily persuade himself that it
were enviable to be as the patient, unchanging peoples of the
East are, with whom life slips by like a watch in the night. But we
are of another creed and impulse. We cannot believe that there
is health where there is no growth, where old wrongs go always
unrighted and new wrongs do not spring up simply because nothing changes; where men do not desire and therefore do not
struggle; where habit and long endurance are the pillars of the
temple of peace. For us, alike by nature and by faith, such ways

[1] Wilson was almost certainly referring to the anonymous author of *Letters
from a Chinese Official: Being an Eastern View of Western Civilization* (New
York, 1903). This brief book, originally published in London in 1901 under the
title *Letters from John Chinaman*, had stirred considerable controversy over its
highly critical view of western civilization as contrasted with a very favorable
view of Chinese culture and society. The author was later revealed to be the
English historian, political philosopher, and man of letters, Goldsworthy Lowes
Dickinson. Wilson's attention was probably drawn to the work by John Huston
Finley, who included a brief review of the American edition in his regular
column, "Letters and Life," in *The Lamp*, xxviii (April 1904), 229-30.

of life, such quiescences of thought are impossible. Our powers stir too imperiously within us, and our consciences tell us that we should use them: the quietude of inaction is not peace but imprisonment. Our ideal is never here: it is yonder. We pursue it upon a rising path, upon which it costs many a struggle to maintain our footing, along which it costs many an eager effort to breast our way. Peace we can have only with the confidence that we are right, only with the hope that we shall attain; and it is not peace that we seek, but victory.

But victory in what,—victory *over* what? As we pour [pore] upon our chart of life to-day where do the main routes of happiness and achievement seem to us to run? To the mines, to the marts of trade, to the stock exchanges, to places of political power, to places of adventure and daring? Do you not see that it is a matter of indifference whither you go: that all the difference to you will lie in the cargo you carry,—not the cargo of capital, of credits, of merchandise, of knowledge, of expertness, of aptitude or energy, —but in your purpose? What sort of happiness are you in quest of? You are preparing to enjoy the world, but are you preparing to enjoy yourself? You know that if you be ill nothing will go well with you: good fortune will sit as uncomfortably upon you as bad; and, if bodily health be thus indispensable to you, is there no such thing as spiritual health? Will not distempers of the mind and spirit as easily mar your fortunes? If success in material undertakings were the sure way to happiness, how many more amongst us would be happy! Happiness is not for the purchaser. The sweet influences of contentment are not outside of you, but within you. Your mind and your heart are your only real kingdom. Rule and purify them and all your life answers to their governance.

It is so that I read the opening words of the sixty-seventh Psalm: "God be merciful unto us, and bless us; and cause His face to shine upon us; that thy way may be known upon earth, thy saving health among all nations." "Thy saving health"! How the beautiful phrase sinks into our hearts! It is like rain upon dry ground!

What is a University but a place wherein to establish the health and natural vigor of our minds? And that is not done by knowledge. Knowledge is the mere food and tonic of the mind, learning merely its exercise. Its health is established, its strength increased, by right action upon these things. They minister to its health, but they do not constitute it. Moreover, though the psychologists dissect and anatomize the mind for our instruction, they do not and cannot in fact take it apart. It is immersed in matter, but it is itself spirit. Our hearts and our intellects are not in fact distinct. Our emotions sweeten our thinking, our hearts give character to our minds. As the spirit is turned so will the mind direct. Our spiritual health, our very rectitude of thinking, is determined by purity of motive, elevation of ideal, the visions of hope and the plannings of purpose. If God should be merciful unto us and bless us, and should cause his face to shine upon us, how should that make known his way upon earth, his saving health among all nations? No doubt because we should see in his face, as his merciful presence enabled us to look upon it, such counsels of confidence and of peace as would enter into our own spirits to rule them, release their powers by means of a perfect revelation of what is the true and acceptable and rewarding way of life, convince them once for all of their own nature and destiny.

In looking upon you to-day, as in writing the words I am reading, I have wondered if your four years in this place which we love have brought you saving health. It is a question which touches the life of the university in every part, in every vital process, both within and without the class-room; it is also a question concerning the use you have yourselves made of the things that might have rendered you strong in every function of your natures. Has the life you have lived here, have the things you have pondered and held your thoughts to served to clarify your purposes, rectify your judgments, and set you free from perplexing conjectures? The ideal object of education is at once to develope and to simplify the mind,—simplify it by a perfect adjustment to its uses and to its environment; and such is health. In "saving" health there is not only this ease and adaptation but also a full pulse of ardent vigor, which fills action with zest, existence itself with grateful ardours of satisfaction. There is no such saving health in the sad, submissive peace of a Chinese country-side. There is no such saving health in mere industry, in mere striving after achievement. The modern struggle for wealth is more like a consuming fever than like a right function of health. There is in many of our material achievements a touch of frenzy and distemper. Our energy is stimulated to the pitch of intoxication, lacks poise, overleaps the bounds alike of prudence and of pleasure, hurries us panting to beds of exhaustion and of sickness, where the physician's task is to get the heat and turmoil out of our blood.

No doubt our spirits were given us for quieter uses, for contemplation as well as for the breathless efforts of a too eager race; and our education has been singularly barren and aside from the mark if it has not shown us the springs of contemplation which lie in our natures, the sweet counsels of reassurance and of guidance which fill our days with light when we harken to the Father of our Spirits and are still in his presence. The influences have been very strong amongst us which ought to make these things evident to all who give any heed or regard to them. Some of the most manly and attractive of your comrades have illustrated among you every day how thoughts of God and of our long destiny lift the thought and temper the judgment. If you have not realized that this was an essential part of education, the true refining process of the mind, it has been because you gave it no heed; if you have not been consciously touched by this, I venture to hope that you have been unconsciously, and that in unfolding it to you now I am speaking of things in fact familiar.

The mind of the oriental is quieted by his religion, his undoubting belief in the fixed, unchangeable order of the life he lives. He is the servant of Fate, and were a fool to kick against the pricks. It is after a very different way that you think of your life. You are of the same spirit with your maker, not his slave, but, if you will, his partner. It is the object of his saving grace to make his thoughts your thoughts, his purposes your purposes; and your spirit is never so free as when that gracious wonder has been wrought. This is the peace that falls upon you when his face shines upon you. This is that saving health which clarifies and ractifies [rectifies] the processes of your nature.

The metaphor, if metaphor it be, is the more perfect because it has so exact a correspondence with our own observation and experience. We know how easy hope and quietness are to the man who is well, physically well, whose vital forces are in everything free of clog and impediment. Fear seems to be cast out by the mere confident flow of the blood; doubt seems to creep in only where there is functional disorder; and the physician seems oftentimes to stand nearer the sources of our happiness than the minister. Your pessimist is seldom a well man. If you cannot mend his digestion you may not change his philosophy. And so I say, if it be a metaphor, this metaphor of health gives us the right criteria of happiness. We know that, the ordinary signs notwithstanding, spiritual health may come, does come, without bodily health, by the grace and revelation of God even to the weak and suffering. It has laws and sources of its own. Physical disorder may impede it but cannot destroy or preclude it. Many a noble invalid has illustrated its reality and beauty, many a militant dyspeptic has overcome himself and all adversaries of God by means of it.

This saving health of the spirit, like the saving physical health that purges the body of all distemper, has very positive laws, very unmistakable conditions. Its marks and elements we know. Where it is present it is plain that spiritual nutrition comes from a true perception of moral values. The doubts and disorders of our age, whether they touch us as individuals or only as communities, arise, I think you will agree with me in saying, out of our temporary confusion as to moral values in the new circumstances of enterprise, the new methods and difficulties of industry, we find our lives in contact with. Reform would be easy, could we but perceive them. Even rectitude of intention waits on enlightenment, purpose on knowledge. The light of creeds and codes is slow to penetrate the nebulous mass of our present social structure, which is changing but is not yet formed. The saving health of moral sanity among the nations of the earth waits, as usual, upon the thought and purpose of the individuals who compose them. You will see, therefore, how our responsibility is increased as men who are called upon to perceive, to assess, to estimate, to value, to make choice. In the choice of our callings, in the application of our energies, in the mastery we seek and the service we offer, we are looked to to exercise conscious, deliberate moral preferences.

It is odd, as it is impressive, how everything that a man touches takes tone and character from himself, no matter how trivial it may be, how like mere routine, how little like a great transaction. You are never a mere automaton. If you were, the things you produced would give evidence, by their very uniformity and lack of distinction, of the unthinking machinery which gave them form. You are spirit, whether you will or no; you are character, whether your will be right or wrong, and the thing which you touch is distinguishable. Educated men, whether their education be of the school or of affairs, are in a very real sense trustees of the moral assets of the world. Their doctrine of life holds at its heart the world's weal or ruin. That is the reason why I said that when you spread your chart of life before you and plan your journey, it is not the direction you take that is of first and most vital consequence, but the object with which you trade at this port or that. The most trivial occupation may be dignified by the spirit in which it is undertaken and the manner in which it is pursued. Nothing is ignoble to which a noble man may in good conscience devote his energies.

But it is not enough to be void of offence. You would not yourself be satisfied with that. There is a positive obligation resting upon us as well as a negative, a duty to create good as well as to avoid evil. Our function in life is not that of critics merely, to perceive that this is good and that evil, prefer the one and reject the other, as a critic of art might buy the objects of his admiration and leave the ugly to the vulgar. We must trade with our trust estate and increase it. We must be active lovers of the good, propagandists of the excellent.

But the standard? It is easy enough to talk of assessing moral values and of increasing the stock of good in the world, but what is good and what is evil, for us individually and for the world in which we live? May we not determine that deep question by our experience, candidly interrogated and interpreted,—by the peace, the ardour, the satisfaction our spirits get from our own days and their tasks,—by the tonic health we get from one course of action, the restlessness, the bitterness, the disappointment and weariness we get from another? You do not have to go to a doctor to ascertain that you feel well; you do not have to go to a casuist or to a minister to find whether your conscience is at ease, your heart at peace with itself. Your studies here have widened the field of your thought; they must have widened also the field of your moral perception and given you fuller intimations than you ever had before of the true satisfactions of action and endeavor. Here lies the world before you. You go out into it an enlightened spirit. What do you mean to seek; what do you expect to find? You may count success to be of this kind or of that, but one thing I can predict with the utmost confidence: you shall not find happiness without health, and health lies in the constant rectification of the spirit, its love of the truth, its instinctive sincerity, its action without fear and without corruption of motive, its self-sufficing energy and independence. It is God's power in the heart. It is the spirit's consciousness of its immediate connection with his will and purpose. It is his saving health, which must be known among all nations before peace will come and life be widened in all its outlooks.

I do not see how the spirit of learning can be separated or divorced from the spirit of religion. At its heart lies that which is ideal, which elevates and enobles, while it quickens the pulse and fills the lungs with a new and vivifying breath,—the love of truth, the desire to see with the eyes of the mind, to see the things which are invisible and which stand fast through all generations. Once let this ardour get into your veins and you cannot afterwards sit content with the material evidences of your success. They cannot express you: they cannot mean to the world at large what you mean to yourself. More than that, they cannot live after you in any close enough association with your name to satisfy your hope and your vision of what is to be, unless you have so handled and disposed them as to fill them with a spirit, an uplifted, foreseeing spirit, which shall make them forever your own, a monument and sign of the heart that beat in all that you did. Your only fame in this world is the permanent record here of the spirit you have carried into the next world: there can be no severance of the one immortality from the other.

And I take the saving health of our spirits to be nothing less than obedience to the law of their immortality. This is a law of existence, not only, but also of growth or decadence. The soul that lives and has its powers quickened for a full age of health and wholesome zest will show always clear and constant progress in its vital processes. Its strength will increase, and with its strength its aptitude for happiness as well as for achievement. In life there can be no stagnation; so long as its processes persist there will be progression, advance, development.

It is worth your while to observe that the power of a man's life increases in direct proportion to the simplification of his motive. It is that which brings concentration, confidence, and definiteness of action, precision of aim, exact adaptation of means; and the tendency of our lives is more and more to concentrate as we advance in years upon some one favourite object and ambition. As the process unfolds itself our true characters are revealed to the world: it is known for certain, whatever our attempted concealments, whether we are noble or ignoble, small or great, of fine stuff or base. There is in some men a terrible simplification, an intense concentration upon evil objects, upon low and selfish aims, which seems to sweep the very moral law itself away with their success, until the thing which they seek is accomplished and at an end, and we see it laid alongside the standard measurements of time and circumstance. Then its futility is disclosed, its ugliness, its evident symptoms as if of disease and distemper. We see it to have been wrought under the heat of a destroying fever. There is another simplification which is the simplification of saving health, of a self-forgetting love which clears all the courses of life of whatever impedes the beneficent and the right, a love of God and of our fellow men, the happiness that comes of service and of a life that moves to the grave, not as towards death, but as towards a sweet fruition of every hope. This is your clue to the labyrinth: not to search for yourself, but for a way of service which will make you greater than yourself.

GENTLEMEN OF THE GRADUATING CLASS: I hope, I believe, that you have found this moral for yourselves in this place. The object of our teaching, however imperfectly realized, has been to enable you to see life whole,—not as a thing of parts and patches, but as a thing entire, undivided, woven of spirit and of matter, governed by laws of thought as well as of material force, a thing to use for happiness and greatness as well as for gain and aggrandizement. We love Princeton as a place of companionships, of comradeships, of close and delightful commerce with friends; and I would remind you that your love for your friend is a more intimate element of your health and your happiness than your love for yourself. Let it stand as an image and standard of what it is you go forth into the larger fields of the world to seek. You have here had friendship, satisfying friendship, in the midst of daily tasks. It has sweetened every hour of study and of recreation. So will it be in the new occupations of the world of business and of professional life. See that you widen your friendship to the men about you in your new places of labour until life seem to you like a series of friendly purposes that include the community and the nation itself. Serve all good things with all your might, and peace and health and happiness will come to you with every breath you draw. This is the regulation of which our disordered age stands in need!

This is always a solemn day, this day of our last service together, this last conference concerning our duty and our destiny; but there is confidence in this parting as well as sorrow and foreboding: for we know the spirit of this place, deepened and sanctified by generations of good men and faithful gone before us. We cannot but take a deep draught of this tonic air of duty and of self-forgetting love with us as we go, as we turn to the effort of our permanent work. God grant that you may be blessed and favoured and enlightened and vouchsafed all saving health![2]

T MS (WP, DLC).
[2] There is a WWhw outline and a WWsh draft of this address in WP, DLC.

The Curriculum Committee to the Board of Trustees
of Princeton University, with Enclosure

[Princeton, N. J.,

GENTLEMEN OF THE BOARD: c. June 12, 1905]

The Committee on the Curriculum in presenting their report for the year desire to remind the Board that the year just closing has witnessed two innovations in the administration of the courses of study which together are likely to prove a reformation to University education in this country little less than revolution:

(1) the adoption of the so called departmental system of study;
(2) the adoption of the preceptorial method of instruction.

The former of these has been in working practically through
the year—the present Senior class not being open to its privileges.
The only comment to be made upon the working is that it has
been so smooth as to call for no comment. One of the provisions
of the system is that members of the Junior and Senior classes
shall have the privilege of changing the departments in which
they have chosen their studies, if there is dissatisfaction with
their choice. It is significant that less than twelve of the Juniors
called for any change, practically the entire University body, both
students and professors, are more than satisfied with the system
in their experience of its results.

The latter of these innovations is in condition now to be formally recommended to the Board for establishment and to be put
into practical operation with the opening of this next academic
year.

In connection with the general rearrangement of studies under
the new system the committee desire to report to the Board that
such changes have been made in the C.E. Course as:

(1) To bring the C.E. Entrance Requirements up to those now
obtaining in the B.S. and Litt.B. courses.

(2) To incorporate all those portions of the C.E. curriculum
concerned with General Science into the new system, while the
purely technical portions of the curriculum are left unchanged.

The details of these changes are herewith submitted in a copy
of the report presented to the University Faculty April 17, 1905,
by the Committee on the Course of Study.[1] (File A)[2]

Further the committee desire to report the following changes
in courses of study as reported to the University Faculty June 5,
1905, by the Committee on the Course of Study. (File B)[3]

RECOMMENDATIONS

(I) The committee recommend the approval of the above
mentioned changes of course as reported to the University
Faculty April 12 [17] and June 5, by the Committee on the
Course of Study.

II. In connection with the preceptorial method of instruction
the committee at a special meeting in the City of New York received from the President certain recommendations which they
voted to lay before the Board with their approval. These recommendations are now presented to the Board as follows:

1. That there be established in connection with the instruction of the University the position of preceptor, the

occupant of which position shall have the full rank and privileges of assistant professor.

2. That appointment to this position shall be for a term of years and not permanently.

3. That the following named persons be appointed to said positions for the terms and at the salaries connected with their respective names, the salaries having been approved by the Finance Committee. (File C)

III. The committee recommend the following changes in the Faculty:

1. That William K. Prentice be advanced from Assistant Professor of Greek to Professor of Greek.

2. That John H. Coney be advanced from Assistant Professor of History to Professor of History.

3. That Hamilton Ford Allen of Washington and Jefferson College, be appointed Professor of Latin for one year to fill out the second year of Professor Carter's leave of absence. This appointment is to take the place of that of Professor Grant Showerman, whose service was eminently acceptable, but whose leave of absence from his own University terminates with this year.

4. That Charles Henry Smyth Jr., of Hamilton College, be appointed Professor of Geology at a salary of $3,000, said salary having been approved by the Finance Committee.

5. That George A. Hulett* of the University of Michigan, be appointed Assistant Professor of Chemistry at a salary of $2,000, said salary having been approved by the Finance Committee.

6. That Lucius Hopkins Miller* of the Class of 1897 be appointed Assistant Professor of Biblical Instruction at a salary of $2,500 said salary having been approved by the Finance Committee.

IV. The committee recommend that the President be authorized, in consultation with his colleagues on the Faculty, to simplify the titles of the various chairs, except in cases where the titles are already determined by Deeds of Gifts.

V. That the resignation of A. L. Frothingham, Jr. as Professor of Ancient History and Archaeology be accepted in accordance with his communication to the Board herewith submitted. (File D)[4]

VI. The Committee recommend that the name of Professor Charles G. Rockwood be retained upon the roll of the Faculty with the title of Professor of Mathematics, Emeritus.

VII. In the matter of an informal meeting of the Board with the Faculty of the University, referred to the committee for consideration and report, the recommendation of the committee is

"That the President be requested, if convenient to himself and Mrs. Wilson, to arrange for a Social Reception of the Board of Trustees and the Faculty of the University at Prospect on the evening immediately preceding this next October meeting of the Board."

Respectfully submitted, Melancthon W. Jacobus
John J. McCook
John DeWitt
David B. Jones.
D. R. Frazer.
Geo B. Stewart[5]

TRS (Trustees' Papers, UA, NjP).
[1] It is printed at April 17, 1905.
[2] Not printed.
[3] Not printed.
[4] A. L. Frothingham, Jr., to the Board of Trustees of Princeton University, May 10, enclosed in A. L. Frothingham, Jr., to WW, May 10, 1905.
[5] This report was approved by the Board of Trustees at its meeting on June 12, 1905.

ENCLOSURE

[C]

Preceptors:

Philosophy:	Roger B. C. Johnson, (Miami)	5 yrs.	$2000
	Wilmon Henry Sheldon* (Columbia)	5 yrs.	$2000
	Adam-Leroy Jones,* (Columbia)	5 yrs.	$2000
	Walter T. Marvin (Adelbert)	5 yrs.	$2000
	Edward G. Spaulding,*	5 yrs.	$2000
History and	Edward G. Elliott,* (Princeton)	5 yrs.	$2000
Politics	Hiram Bingham (Harvard),	3 yrs.	$2000
	Ernest L. Bogart (Oberlin),	5 yrs.	$2000
	C. H. McIlwain (Miami),	5 yrs.	$2000
	Royal Meeker, (Ursinus),	1 yr.	$1500
	H. R. Shipman (Dartmouth)	3 yrs.	$1500
	Charles W. Spencer (Colgate)	3 yrs.	$2000
	Edward S. Corwin (Mich.),	1 yr.	$1600
Art and Archaeology:	Oliver S. Tonks (Columbia),	3 yrs.	$1500
Classics:	David Magie, jr., (Princeton),	5 yrs.	$2000
	E. M. Rankin, (Princeton),	3 yrs.	$1500

	F. L. Hutson, (Princeton),	3 yrs.	$1500
	Andrew A [R]. Anderson (Wisconsin),	3 yrs.	$1800
	Donald Cameron (Texas),	3 yrs.	$1500
	Harold R. Hastings (Wisconsin),	3 yrs.	$1500
	George D. Kellogg* (Williams),	5 yrs.	$2000
	Duane Reed Stuart (Michigan),	5 yrs.	$2000
	Donald A. MacRae (Cornell),	3 yrs.	$2000
	LaRue VanHook (Washington, St. Louis),	3 yrs.	$1500
	John W. Basore (Hampden-Sydney),	3 yrs.	$1600
English:	Charles G. Osgood (Yale),	5 yrs.	$2000
	Nathaniel E. Griffin* (Johns Hopkins),	1 yr.	$1400
	G. H. Gerould (Bryn Mawr),	5 yrs.	$2000
	Hardin Craig* (Princeton),	5 yrs.	$2000
	A. W. Long* (Princeton),	5 yrs.	$1800
	F. C. M[a]cDonald* (Lake Forest),	5 yrs.	$1600
	R. K. Root (Yale),	5 yrs.	$2000
	John Duncan Spaeth (Central High School, Philadelphia),	5 yrs.	$2000
Modern Languages:	George M. Priest* (Princeton),	5 yrs.	$2000
	William Koren* (Princeton),	5 yrs.	$1800
	Frank L. Critchlow* (Princeton),	5 yrs.	$1500
	A. A. Moore* (Cornell),	3 yrs.	$1500
	Christian Gauss (Lehigh),	3 yrs.	$2000
	D. L. Buffum (Yale),	2 yrs.	$2000
	George T. Northup (Williams),	1 yr.	$1400
	Harvey W. Thayer (N. Y. City College),	1 yr.	$1500
Mathematics:	L. P. Eisenhart* (Princeton),	5 yrs.	$2000
	William Gillespie* (Princeton),	5 yrs.	$1800
	G. A. Bliss* (Missouri),	5 yrs.	$2000
Geology:	Marcus S. Farr* (Princeton),	5 yrs.	$500[1]

WWhw and WWT MS (Trustees' Papers, UA, NjP).
[1] Farr had been Curator of Vertebrate Paleontology since 1900 at a salary of $1,500. This salary was continued, and he received an additional $500.

From the Minutes of the Board of Trustees of Princeton University

[June 12, 1905]

  The Trustees of Princeton University met in stated session in the Trustees' Room in the Chancellor Green Library, Princeton, New Jersey, at eleven o'clock on Monday morning, June 12, 1905. . . .

REPORT OF COMMITTEE ON PROCURING FUNDS

Mr. Dodge, Chairman of the Committee on Procuring Funds for the University reported. The report was accepted and is as follows:

A year ago, the most pressing need of the University was for a Lecture and Recitation Hall to re-enforce the existing unsanitary and inadequate building,[1] and the Trustees passed a Resolution in June 1904,[2] authorizing the President to appoint a large Committee to canvas for funds for this purpose.

At that time, the annual deficit of the University was about $20,000. and an emergency fund has been created to secure annual pledges for three years of $100,000 to meet the deficit, and eventually provide an endowment to cover it.

Maenwhile [Meanwhile], the larger plans for the development of the University were in abeyance, and there seemed no likelihood of their being carried out at an early date.

When the President asked the writer of this report, to accept the Chairmanship of the Committee to raise funds for the new Lecture Hall, and others were called into consultation, all felt that in view of the recent canvas for the gymnasium and emergency fund, a new canvas for the large sum needed to erect the new hall, would be difficult, and would fatally defer the President's plans for the teaching force.

The whole matter was laid before a few friends of the University, through whose prompt generosity funds were pledged sufficient to erect the new hall, and at the October meeting of the Trustees the action of the June meeting was amended authorizing the President to appoint a Committee of Fifty to secure funds for the internal development of the University.[3]

A committee of Alumni, representing different sections of the country was appointed, and met promptly to organize.

When it was realized that in order to meet the annual deficit, to adequately increase the salaries of the existing teaching force, and to supply the fifty new men needed for President Wilson's preceptorial scheme, an additional income representing the interest at 4% on three-and-a-quarter million dollars, the Committee was staggered, and felt that the securing of such a large endowment was impossible.

It did not seem feasible to secure any very large gifts, especially in view of the fact that some of the most generous friends of the University were already pledged to large cash gifts for the new

[1] That is, Dickinson Hall.
[2] The trustees adopted this resolution, in fact, on October 21, 1904.
[3] The trustees took this action, actually, on December 8, 1904.

hall. The situation seemed hopeless, when it was suggested that the goodwill of the Alumni be capitalized; that as many gifts as possible for permanent endowment be secured, and that the balance of the necessary income be raised by annual gifts from the Alumni and other friends.

It was realized that many of the wealthy alumni could not immediately pay a large sum for endowment, but might be willing to promise such a sum and pay annual interest thereon until such time as they could pay the principal; that others would pledge an annual sum for a term of years, and that there were others who would only give from year to year, but whose permanent interest and annual support could be depended upon.

To meet these three different forms of gift, contract pledges were drawn up by a Trust lawyer, and printed.

With the co-operation of the President and Finance Committee, it was arranged that the Emergency Fund should be merged into the new fund and the managers of the Alumni Fund agreed to assist the Committee of Fifty in its work.

Mr. George W. Burleigh was elected Secretary of the Committee, and it was arranged that he should give most of his time to the management of the canvas, assisting the various members of the Committee in different localities in soliciting funds.

All the expenses of the Committee were underwritten by a few of its members.

A presentation of the whole matter, written by Mr. Robert Bridges, was sent with the President's report and Financial Statement to every alumnus, which elicited great interest.

With the aid of the President and other Trustees, a large number of friends of the University were at once appealed to, with results fully justifying our faith in Princeton's loyal alumni.

About this time, we were encouraged by the turning over to the University of Mrs. Brown's legacy,[4] which will augment its income by an amount equal to about $10,000. per year; by the maturing of the plans for the Alumni dormitory,[5] which within a year will add $3,000. more per annum, and further, by the increase of the Jesup Fund[6] to $60,000., the income of which,

4 About this bequest, see WW to L. H. Miller, March 18, 1903, n. 2, Vol. 14.
5 The dormitory under construction and soon to be named Patton Hall, about which there is much correspondence in Vol. 15.
6 Morris Ketchum Jesup had just given an additional $10,000 in bonds to augment the endowment of the Morris K. Jesup Fund. His original gift of $25,000 had been made in June 1900 "to be kept as a fund, the income from same to be applied to the uses of the University, as the Trustees might deem best." (Entry of June 11, 1900, in "Minutes of the Trustees of Princeton University, 1898-1901," bound minute book, UA, NjP). Jesup subsequently added $10,000 to the fund in December 1902 and $15,000 in March 1904.

namely—$3000. has been assigned by the donor for the purposes of the Committee of Fifty.

On the three forms of pledges already named, the Committee has secured—

per annum

1st. Promises for permanent endowment of $420,000. bearing interest at 5%, or .... $21,000.

2nd. Promises for annual gifts pledged for five years, or until further notice .... 51,610.

3rd. Gifts for one year, most of which we feel confident will be renewed .... 21,950.

Including therefore, the Brown legacy, the Jesup Fund, and the Alumni dormitory, the permanent funds of the University have been increased since a year ago, about $800,000 or

	$37,000 per annum
Special Gifts for this year	21,950 " "
In annual pledges, ...	52,610 " "
Total	$111,560

Enough will be paid before the close of this fiscal year, July 31st, to cover the deficiency of the year; to pay off the floating indebtedness of about $18,000. and leave a surplus for next year.

GIFT OF $10,000 FROM A MEMBER OF THE CORPORATION OF HARVARD UNIVERSITY. In addition to these amounts, the Chairman of the Committee has received a most touching and graceful gift of $10,000 from a member of the corporation of Harvard University, and one of Harvard's leading alumni, who is the leader of the effort to secure additional funds for Harvard.[7] This was given without any solicitation, a token of his kindly feeling and goodwill for Princeton, as indicated by the following extract from his letter accompanying the gift: "If you like to create a fellowship from Harvard University, pray do so, leaving away any personal allusion. The names of our great universities have great value and will last forever, mine has none, nor should it last. This is a gift kindly meant to mark the respect and esteem from one university to another, which feeling will be mutual when received by Princeton. You and I receive strength and value, if any, from our respective universities."

The Committee hopes that some action may be taken by the Board of Trustees, which will show its appreciation of this generous and graceful act.

---

[7] He was Henry Lee Higginson, prominent investment banker of Boston.

The Committee is greatly chagrined that the wider and more general canvas of all the Alumni which it purposed to undertake during the past four months, has been checked by the prolonged illness of its Secretary. We feel, however, that we have made a fair start, and have warrant for confident hope that before another year has elapsed our more matured efforts will result in securing a regular income for the University, sufficient for all its immediate needs.

We have made no effort to raise funds for the graduate school, feeling that the other needs named are more pressing, and that when the preceptorial scheme has been inaugurated, the absolute necessity of the graduate school would become so apparent, that the needed funds would speedily be forthcoming.

In conclusion, we wish to emphasize our appreciation of the assistance continually and unsparingly rendered by the President of the University, and tha [the] Chairman of the Finance Committee, without which it would have been difficult for us to have accomplished anything.

THANKS TO DONOR OF $10,000 AND DISPOSITION OF GIFT

On motion of Mr. Dodge, seconded by Mr. Cleveland, the following resolution was adopted:

RESOLVED that the cordial thanks of the Board of Trustees be tendered to the generous donor of the sum of $10,000 given by him an alumnus of Harvard University as a token of his kindly feeling and goodwill for Princeton.

That the Finance Committee be instructed to invest this sum as a special endowment of a Fellowship, the name and purpose of which shall be determined by the President of the University.[8]

[8] See C. W. McAlpin to WW, Oct. 11, 1905, n. 1.

From Gilbert Ames Bliss

Dear Sir: Chicago, June 12, 1905.

Your letter concerning the Preceptorship in Mathematics at Princeton, was forwarded to me here. I shall be glad to have you present my name to the Board of Trustees for the appointment as Preceptor, for a term of five years, at the salary of $2000 per year, as you suggest. I am anticipating the work with much pleasure.

My address until the end of August is the University of Chicago.   Respectfully yours   G. A. Bliss.

ALS (WP, DLC).

From Charles Williston McAlpin

My dear Dr. Wilson: [Princeton, N. J.]   June 13, 1905.

The following quotation from the Report of the Committee of Fifty was referred to you in order that you might prepare a suitable acknowledgment:

"In addition to these amounts, the Chairman of the Committee has received a most touching and graceful gift of $10,000 from a member of the corporation of Harvard University, and one of Harvard's leading alumni, who is the leader of the effort to secure additional funds for Harvard. This was given without any solicitation, a token of his kindly feeling and goodwill for Princeton, as indicated by the following extract from his letter accompanying the gift: 'If you like to create a fellowship from Harvard University, pray do so, leaving away any personal allusion. The names of our great universities have great value and will last forever, mine has none, nor should it last. This is a gift kindly meant to mark the respect and esteem from one university to another, which feeling will be mutual when received by Princeton. You and I receive strength and value, if any, from our respective universities.' "

The Committee hopes that some action may be taken by the Board of Trustees, which will show its appreciation of this generous and graceful act.[1]

                    Sincerely yours,   [C. W. McAlpin] Secretary.

CCL (McAlpin File, UA, NjP).
[1] See WW to C. H. Dodge, June 15, 1905.

A News Report

[June 14, 1905]

PRESIDENT WILSON'S ADDRESS.

158th Commencement Marked by Announcement of Notable Gifts.

The 158th annual commencement was held in Alexander Hall this morning at 10.30. The procession of Trustees, members of the Faculty and alumni, followed by the class of 1905, formed in front of Nassau Hall at 10.15, and marched to Alexander Hall. The exercises were opened with music followed by prayer.

Charles Christopher Mierow of New Jersey delivered the Latin Salutatory. Morton [Merton] S. Fales of New York, then delivered an oration on "Education, a Public Benefit." After a musical selection, Raymond Blaine Fosdick[1] of New York delivered an oration on the subject, "The Other Half." Samuel Harries Daddow of Pennsylvania and Willard Voorhees VanDoren of New York were excused from delivering their orations.

After an intermission of ten minutes the awards of prizes and fellowships were announced. The conferring of degrees on the members of the graduating class and the conferring of honorary degrees then took place.

Norman Mattoon Thomas[2] of Pennsylvania, delivered the Valedictory, and the exercises closed with prayer and benediction.

The following is a summary of President Wilson's address at the Commencement exercises in Alexander Hall this morning:

President Wilson in his address to-day made announcements which mark an extraordinary degree of progress and prosperity on the part of the University. In the first place, he announced the gift to the University by the generosity of a number of Alumni, of 336 acres of land, the beautiful tract known as the Olden farm of 96 acres, which lies beyond Washington Road immediately

[1] Born in Buffalo, N. Y., June 9, 1883. A.B., Princeton, 1905; A.M., 1906. LL.B., New York Law School, 1908. Assistant Corporation Counsel, New York City, 1908-10; Commissioner of Accounts, 1910-1913. Studied European and American police systems for the Rockefeller Bureau of Social Hygiene, 1914-16. Special representative of the Secretary of War on the Mexican border, 1916. Chairman, Commission on Training Camp Activities of the War and Navy Departments, 1917-18. Special Representative of the War Department in France, 1918-19; civilian aide to General John J. Pershing, 1919. Under-Secretary-General of the League of Nations, 1919-20. Practiced law as member of the New York firm of Curtis, Fosdick and Belknap, 1920-1936. President of the Rockefeller Foundation and of the General Education Board, 1936-48. Member at various times of the Board of Directors of the Woodrow Wilson Foundation. Author of numerous books. Died July 18, 1972.

[2] Born in Marion, Ohio, Nov. 20, 1884. A.B., Princeton, 1905. B.D., Union Theological Seminary, 1911. Social worker in New York, 1905-10. Associate pastor, Brick Presbyterian Church of New York, 1910-1911. Ordained to the Presbyterian ministry in 1911. Pastor of the East Harlem Presbyterian Church and chairman of the American Parish, a federation of churches and social agencies in the immigrant neighborhoods of New York, 1911-18. The outbreak of the First World War led Thomas toward socialism and Christian pacifism. In 1917 he joined the Fellowship of Reconciliation and the American Union Against Militarism and was a co-founder of the latter organization's Civil Liberties Bureau (later the American Civil Liberties Union). Founder and editor of *The World Tomorrow*, 1918-21. He resigned his church positions in 1918 and demitted the ministry in 1931. Joined the Socialist Party in 1918. Associate editor of the New York *Nation*, 1921-22. Director of the League for Industrial Democracy, 1922-37. In 1924 he ran for Governor of New York on the Socialist ticket; in later years he ran for governor, Mayor of New York City, and other local and state offices. Socialist candidate for President in 1928, 1932, 1936, 1940, 1944, and 1948. Author of many books, pamphlets, and articles. Died Dec. 19, 1968.

contiguous to the grounds of the University, and the almost equally beautiful tract of 240 acres known as the Springdale property, which is in close proximity to the property of the University and which is now used as the playing course of the Princeton Golf Club. These splendid additions to the extensive grounds already in the hands of the University more than double the amount of land available for building and other uses. The Olden farm in its lower portion lies along the course of the lake now being constructed through the generosity of Mr. Carnegie.

In addition to these gifts of land, Dr. Wilson announced much more important gifts of revenue. The Alumni Committee of Fifty, recently appointed by the authority of the Board of Trustees, has already succeeded, after only two or three months' work, in assuring the University of an additional income of more than $100,000 per annum. Much of this is supported by promised gifts of permanent endowment; the rest is secured by promises which render the University secure in assuming that it will have continuous command of the revenue represented by the subscriptions.

In view of these gifts, the University is about, Dr. Wilson said, to enter upon a notable development by the inception of the new Preceptorial system. Fifty new men are next year to be added to the Faculty, under the title of Preceptors, whose chief function will be to keep in constant touch with the undergraduates as guides, advisers, and testers of their reading. Lectures are to be much less relied on. The old-fashioned quizzes, recitations and tests are in large part to give way to conferences of individuals and small groups of men with their instructors. The men are to "get up" not the lectures of a particular man or the dicta of a particular text writer, but the leading authorities on the subjects they are studying, and are to have frequent conferences with their Preceptors about their reading, in order that it may be properly directed and tested. The present members of the Faculty, as well as the new Preceptors, are to take part in this conference work. The old time separation of Professor and student is to be broken down and the students are once more to come into personal touch with their instructors as in the small colleges. But there is to be this essential difference from the old methods of the small colleges, that this personal touch is to be informal: its purpose, not recitation, but the direct conference of reading men, reading as if they were grown up, not as if they were still school boys.

It will be seen at once that this method of teaching is first of all chiefly intended for the reading departments. The laboratory departments of the University sadly need more laboratory room;

they also need more assistants in the laboratories, but their method is already that of personal contact between teacher and pupil. It is in effect their laboratory method which is now being extended to the reading courses. The laboratory courses also need Preceptors to drill men in the general conceptions of science by reading and conference, but their need in this respect is less pressing than that of the other departments: their methods of teaching are already more efficient than those of the other departments of the University. Dr. Wilson none the less emphasized the need of the University for more laboratory facilities and for more teachers in the laboratory sciences, and expressed the earnest hope that they may be the next beneficiaries of the generous friends of the University. Pure science is now, in the scheme of the University, one of the chief factors of culture and intellectual training, and every effort is being made to give science its deserved prominence in the course of study.

President Wilson was also able to announce that a very gratifying beginning had been made in realizing the cherished hopes of the University for a Graduate College. The necessity for such an institution—not the mere multiplication of courses of study, but the establishment of a comfortable residential college as a distinct unit of the University—has now become more than ever evident and pressing, because of the institution of the Preceptorial system, which makes it necessary that the University should supply itself in some systematic way with teachers trained in her own methods and accustomed to her own traditions and points of view. A beautiful private estate on Bayard Lane, one of the most beautiful in Princeton, has just been bought by friends of the University, and its excellent residence and park-like grounds will at once be put at the service of the Graduate School as a place of residence for the Fellows and the most promising advanced students of the University.[3] This at last gives the Graduate School the prospect of early realization. Under the influence of Dean West this development ought now to take shape very rapidly. Its growth and endowment, the object which the University author-

[3] Actually, the estate, Merwick, had been purchased by Moses Taylor Pyne, who continued to hold title to it during the years when it was used by the university as a residence for graduate students. It had most recently been the residence of George Lansing Raymond, who gave up his Professorship of Aesthetics at Princeton in 1905 to reside in Washington and teach at the George Washington University. Merwick, located at 83 Bayard Lane, was bounded by the residences of Henry van Dyke and William Milligan Sloane. The house was spacious and, by October 1905, twelve graduate students were in residence, and five others took their meals there. Howard Crosby Butler was the first master in residence. Merwick continued to be used as a residence for graduate students until the completion of the Graduate College in 1913.

ities have now most at heart, will give Princeton an Institution of unique character and importance.

President Wilson also announced the gift of McCosh Hall by several generous graduates.[4]

Printed in the *Daily Princetonian*, June 14, 1905.
[4] There is a WWsh draft of this statement in WP, DLC.

A News Report of a Speech at the Alumni Luncheon

[June 14, 1905]

The annual Alumni Luncheon was held yesterday afternoon at 1 o'clock, in the Gymnasium. About seven hundred graduates were present. Mr. Adrian H. Joline '70, who acted as toastmaster, welcomed those present and then introduced President Wilson as the first speaker.

President Wilson in the greater part of his speech discussed the fundamental advantages of the Preceptorial System. He said in part that the proposed plan was no experiment and was bound to succeed. The essential purpose of the scheme is to group men not by alphabetical order, but by their aptitudes, training, tastes, and acquirements. The men who have no characteristics in common with any of their classmates will be treated individually. The purpose of every student is to combine ideas and ideals, and the Preceptorial System is designed to accomplish this. The plan is essentially a scheme of partnership between the preceptors and the undergraduates, by means of which every man may be guided into the paths for which he is best suited and thus fully develop his talents.

In addition he said that education in the University is a branch of statesmanship. Princeton must supply this country with thoughtful men, who will stand behind the statesmen, for the life of a nation depends upon the thought and principle of its people. No man in these troublesome times can distinguish the right course of action unless he has a broad and intellectual mind.

In closing, President Wilson exhorted the graduates to enter the rush and turmoil of public life with their course of action clearly mapped out in advance and thus have a definite goal to aim for.

Printed in the *Daily Princetonian*, June 14, 1905; editorial headings omitted.

To Cleveland Hoadley Dodge

My dear Mr. Dodge: Princeton, N. J.   June 15, 1905.

Since we are not to know who the very generous donor was, who presented to the University $10,000 as a token of friendship from Harvard, I take the liberty of expressing to him through you what are, I am sure, the feelings of all concerned.

It seems to me a gift of really touching significance. I am sure that the feeling between Harvard and Princeton as centers of learning has always been of the most cordial character, but gifts of this kind are so exceptional and the purpose of this gift is so beautiful, that I feel that it will undoubtedly produce between the two Universities a more intimate feeling of friendship. I hope that you will express to the donor our profound appreciation and genuine admiration of his public spirited generosity.

Cordially and sincerely yours,   Woodrow Wilson

TLS (H. L. Higginson Coll., MH-BA).

To Winthrop More Daniels

My dear Daniels,   Princeton, N. J.   17 June, 1905.

In view of the new methods of instruction to be employed next year, I write to request that, with the aid of your colleagues in your Department, you will be kind enough to prepare a list of the books which we mean to require all the men in the courses of our Department to use during the year, in order that the list may be laid before the Library Committee of the Faculty before the term opens.

The Committee will meet on the Monday preceding the opening of the University in September, and it will probably be necessary for it to authorize the purchase of a large number of duplicates of all the books on such lists, in order to avoid putting on the undergraduates the whole burden of buying the copies that will be needed.

With much regard,

Sincerely Yours,   Woodrow Wilson

WWTLS (Wilson-Daniels Corr., CtY).

From Hiram Bingham

My dear President Wilson,   Cambridge [Mass.] June 17, 1905.

Considerably to my surprise and delight I have received the announcement of my election as preceptor for *three* years. I supposed from your conversation with me at the University Club that my appointment was to be for one year only, so this news is very pleasant. I am looking forward with keen anticipation to the work at Princeton.

Wishing you a very pleasant summer, and again thanking you for the honor of this appointment, I remain, my dear President Wilson,   Faithfully yours,   Hiram Bingham

TLS (WP, DLC).

A News Item

[June 18, 1905]

SONS OF REVOLUTION ON PRINCETON CAMPUS

Celebrate Evacuation of
Philadelphia by Visit to Battlefield.

WELCOMED BY WILSON

Three hundred strong, the Pennsylvania Society of Sons of the Revolution yesterday observed their annual custom of celebrating the anniversary of the evacuation of Philadelphia and the simultaneous retirement of the American army from its winter quarters at Valley Forge by making a pilgrimage to the battlefield of Princeton.

The exercises were opened by an invocation by the Rev. Dr. G. Woolsey Hodge, rector of the Church of the Ascension, Broad and South streets. Woodrow Wilson, president of Princeton University, made the address of welcome. "I do not feel that Princeton University can properly boast of this historic spot, for it has not made it so," said Mr. Wilson. "That Princeton is the site of a decisive battle is not by virtue of the university, but I am proud of the fact that many of the thoughtful and able men of the Revolution were bred here."

Printed in the Philadelphia *North American*, June 18, 1905.

From Eleanor Glasgow Voorhis[1]

My dear Professor Wilson,   New York.   June 19th, 1905.

We are very anxious to consult with you in regard to some historic literary material which we have. Mr. Wells,[2] of Harper Brothers, suggested our writing to you on this subject, some time ago.

Our manuscript collection of papers, letters, &c. pertains to my Great Grandfather, General William Clark of the Lewis &

Clark Expedition.[3] The journey across the continent has been so fully published, we do not wish to repeat that. My mother's idea is to have [published] the "Life & Letters of William Clark," which have never been given to the public, & to have for our Editor the very best and highest historic & literary authority. Hence, our earnest wish to consult with you. Our collection has been pronounced of rare and unique interest, by men who understand. There are manuscript documents & letters of Madison, Thomas Jefferson, Monroe, John Quincy Adams, & many other distinguished men, including Lafayette & Prince Paul of Würtemburg.

If you are to be in New York during this week or next, we should be glad to show you this material in our home. Can you appoint a time to come with convenience to yourself? If this be impossible & you could arrange to see us in Princeton, my mother & I would try to go there for an afternoon, as we are eager to have your opinion, & hope you would feel that you could be the Editor of this work.[4] In any case, please be so kind as to let us consult with you. Your splendid "History of the American people" makes us doubly desire your advice. Please be so kind as to let me have a word of reply, as to whether we may hope to see you & when.   Yours very truly,   Eleanor Glasgow Voorhis

ALS (WP, DLC).
    [1] Unmarried great-granddaughter of General William Clark. She lived with her mother, Julia Clark Voorhis, at 73 East 92nd St., New York.
    [2] Thomas Bucklin Wells, Associate Editor of *Harper's Magazine* since 1902.
    [3] The Voorhis collection was quite extensive. In addition to the documents specifically mentioned in this letter, it included journals of William Clark for 1805 and 1806, as well as manuscripts and memorabilia of George Rogers Clark. There is a description of the William Clark materials in the Voorhis collection in Reuben Gold Thwaites (ed.), *Original Journals of the Lewis and Clark Expedition, 1804-1806* . . . (8 vols., New York, 1904-1905), I, l-li. The collection was ultimately given to the Missouri Historical Society in St. Louis.
    [4] As Eleanor G. Voorhis to WW, June 25, 1905, indicates, Wilson had to decline the task of editing the Clark manuscripts. However, Reuben Gold Thwaites had long since been in contact with the Voorhis ladies and had printed numerous documents from their collection in the work already cited. No separate biography of William Clark has ever been published.

Raleigh Colston Gildersleeve to Moses Taylor Pyne

My dear Mr. Pyne: N. Y.   June 20th, 1905.

In answer to your letter, would say that I am glad my designs for the alteration of Nassau Hall[1] met with the approval in general of the Committee.

The throne can be very easily suppressed. As to the extent of the oak wainscot, after seeing your hall I do not think that anyone can feel that the oak wainscot does not have its effect even though it is to a large extent covered with portraits. Your hall has some very large pictures in it, and yet the feeling that the wainscot is really behind the pictures gives it richness.

There is a substitute for wainscot which is very ingenious, that is, a sort of paper or cloth on which is applied a veneer of oak. This can be pasted on the walls and simple trim and mouldings can be put around it and can be finished so that it would take a shrewd observer to know that the wainscot was not entirely of solid wood. In doing this it would be desirable to have the panels quite large, and by this means we could reduce the cost considerably.

In regard to your query as to what progress has been made with McCosh Hall, I have been waiting to hear from Prof. [Henry Dallas] Thompson and from the Committee which is to take charge of the building. I have not yet received my drawings nor have I heard anything about the project since I turned over the last perspective to you on June 8th.

Faithfully yours,   Raleigh C Gildersleeve

TLS (WP, DLC).
1 That is, the construction of a Faculty Room in Nassau Hall, the details of which will unfold in subsequent documents.

From Charles Williston McAlpin

My dear Dr. Wilson: [Princeton, N. J.]   June 21, 1905.

Mr. Dodge writes me that he handed his resolution about the gift of $10,000 from a member of the Harvard Corporation to you; can you give me a copy of it for the Minutes?

The chairmen of all but two of the Standing Committees of the Board have been chosen and if you can give me your vote on these two I can proceed with the printing of the lists.

The vote for a chairman of the Committee on Faculty Minutes stands, Dr. Stewart 2, Mr. Davis 1.

The vote for chairman of the Committee on Morals and Discipline stands, Dr. Dixon 3, Mr. Dod 1.

For secretary of the latter committee the vote stands, Mr. Dod 2, Mr. Davis 2. Dr. Henry, Dean Fine, and yourself have not voted.

I am sorry that I missed you this afternoon, but I hope to have the pleasure of seeing you next Wednesday. If, however, you do not expect to be in Princeton on the 28th will you let me know at Morristown what day I can see you before your departure. I know of no matter of importance to bring to your attention, but I would like to see you before you leave.

Very sincerely yours,   [C. W. McAlpin] Secretary.

CCL (McAlpin File, UA, NjP).

To Charles Williston McAlpin

My dear Mr. McAlpin: Princeton, N. J.   23 June, 1905.

My votes in regard to the chairmenships which are still unfilled would be for Dr. Stewart as Chairman of the Committee on Faculty Minutes; Dr. Dixon as Chairman of the Committee on Morals and Discipline, and for the Secretary of the Committee on Morals and Discipline I should vote for Mr. Davis.

I take pleasure in enclosing the resolution which Mr. Dodge handed me in regard to the gift of $10,000 from a member of the Harvard Corporation.[1] Mr. Dodge handed it to me with a notion that I might alter it, but it seems to me excellent as it stands.

Always

Cordially and faithfully yours,   Woodrow Wilson

TLS (McAlpin File, UA, NjP).

[1] Missing in the McAlpin File, this resolution is reproduced in the Minutes of the Board of Trustees printed at June 12, 1905.

An Article About the Preceptorial System

[June 24, 1905]

NEW PLANS FOR PRINCETON

By Woodrow Wilson

The object of the preceptorial system is to prevent the disintegration of the university, its disintegration in that essential feature of all vital teaching, the intimate acquaintance and contact of pupils and teacher. Mere increase of numbers separates them. As a university grows in numbers professors and students draw apart, have hardly a speaking acquaintance with one another. Lectures bring them into the same room, but not into vital touch. No matter how strong and interesting a lecturer may be, his contact with his hearers is not personal: they are only an audience, and get only such flavor of his personality as may inevitably get into the sentences he utters, into the tone and manner in which he utters them. Even when he meets his classes in small sections for quizzes, recitations, oral tests, the contact is hardly more intimate. There is a stiffness about the intercourse, a formality, a restraint: he sits behind a desk upon a dais; they sit in rows in front of him, and are prodded to expose their ignorance.

The small college escapes this difficulty, in large part by very reason of its smallness. The total number of its students is small; the instructors generally meet their pupils in many different classes; teachers and pupils become personally known to each other by constant contact and daily meetings in many places. The vitality and fruitfulness of their contact arise out of their acquaintance with one another, the impression the personality of the teacher makes upon the pupil, and the direct appeal the pupil's needs makes to the teacher's interest and sympathy: the profit is not derived from the formal intercourse of the class-room so much as from the personal touch and the mutual understanding which exist because of their knowledge of each other outside of the class-room.

The large university, teeming with hundreds of growing youngsters, ought not to forego this fruitful process of comradeship if it can possibly get the advantage of it by any feasible arrangement. The other advantages of the large university are so great, its larger library, its greater variety of gifted men, its quickening life amidst the hosts of its graduates and undergraduates, its ampler resources, and completer equipment; it should find a way by which its students may be given an intimate use of these things instead of being held off at arm's length, as if their very multitude made the full use of the university by them impossible. Intimate access to their teachers is the first and chief step by which to bring this about. Graduate students have it already; undergraduates should have it too.

It is Princeton's plan, with this object in view, to add at once to her teaching force, to add fifty "preceptors,"—as she will call them, for want of a better name,—whose special duty it shall be to deal with their pupils outside of the class-room. The preceptors are to be members of the faculty, not distinguishable from the rest in rank and privilege, and the present members of the faculty are to undertake preceptorial work in order that the new and closer contact may be brought about all along the line; but for the new men the preceptorial work will be the chief function. It will be their duty to take the students in the several departments, either singly or in groups, and by every serviceable method give them counsel, guidance, and stimulation in their work. Dull men and very bright and ambitious men they will probably have to take singly. Groups will have to be made up by careful classification, combining men of like training, acquirements, and aptitudes. But the object will be always the same,—not to hear "recitations" on fixed text-books, but to discuss, to sift, to test the reading done by the men in their several courses, so that the men may feel that the preceptors are in some sense their fellow students and friendly guides in their outside reading, the reading by which lectures are to be supplemented and the more formal discussion of the class-room broadened and made part of an independent scheme of study. By such means college work may be made to seem something more than a sublimated kind of school work, and may be made to rest not upon the dictum of the teacher in the class-room or of the author of a particular textbook, but upon something like first-hand acquaintance with the chief authorities on the several subjects studied.

It is the tutorial system of Oxford adapted to American conditions and to the traditions of American colleges. The lecture and the formal class exercise are not to be abandoned, but they are to be very much less relied on, are to be considered only a part, and that not the chief part, of the process of college instruction. The chief part is to be the reading done with the preceptors.

There will naturally be a great deal of written work connected with it. The preceptors will certainly find that the most serviceable way of ascertaining what reading the men are doing, and with how much thoroughness and intelligence they are doing it, is to require written reports of them, brief, it may be, but definite, critical, at once a collation of what they have been reading and a commentary upon it. These reports will incidentally be judged as pieces of English, as well as with reference to their adequacy and accuracy. If they are incorrectly or inelegantly written, they will be given back to be rewritten; and if any man cannot express himself accurately and with some degree of propriety and elegance, he will be handed over to the English department for fundamental drill. It is one of the reproaches of our American colleges and universities that their graduates are not trained in the correct use of their mother tongue. "Theme writing"—that is, constant, deliberate exercise in English composition,—does not seem to supply the training that is necessary. Its most radical defect is that it is a means for making men write for the sake of writing, for the sake of the language and the style. The object of the use of language, the only legitimate object of the development of style, is the release of ideas, the clear statement of fact, the adequate embodiment in words of some image or conception of the mind. The reports of the students to their preceptors will furnish at least a natural motive for expression, and will furnish, besides, a great variety of themes which must be taken seriously. When every piece of written work done in the university, examination papers included, is required to be in correct English, the English department of the university can afford to give over its laborious addiction to "themes."

Another thing which is expected to give naturalness to the preceptorial system is that the preceptors are not to set the examinations, but are to read with their men in subjects upon which their colleagues set the tests; and the examinations are to be upon subjects, not upon a particular course of lectures merely, delivered by the examiner. The lectures are to be only one means of setting forth the subjects, one means of stimulating interest in great fields of study: the chief means is to be conferences with the preceptors, following no cut-and-dried routine, limited to no single text-book or view, but intended to give the men at least an introduction to the literature of the subjects considered.

The rule, moreover, is not to be that for each subject a man will have a particular preceptor. At Princeton the students select "departments" of study, and the "departments" are as inclusive as "philosophy," "history and politics," "classics," and "modern languages." Each undergraduate is to be assigned to one preceptor for all the courses or studies of his department, in order that he may have at least an adequate conception of their co-ordination, their connection, their vital union as a *body* of studies.

Such reading, so free from artificial trammels and done in constant conference with helpful scholars, ought to impart to study a new reality, ought to give college men a sense of having been emancipated from school and mere tutelage, and given the responsibilities as well as the opportunities of maturity. They are challenged to read, to look about them in great subjects, and discover the world of thought. No doubt more work will be done under the new stimulus than is done now, but it will not, if properly directed, be burdensome, dull, a task, a matter of reluctance, as too much college work is now. It is really a pleasure to use your mind, if you have one, and many a man who now never dreams what fun it is to have ideas and to explore the world of thought, may be expected, in his intercourse with his preceptors, to find learning a rare form of enjoyment, the use of his faculties a new indulgence. He may even discover his soul, and find its spiritual relations to the world of men and affairs.[1]

Printed in *Harper's Weekly*, XLIX (June 24, 1905), 904.
[1] There is a WWsh draft of this article in WP, DLC.

From Eleanor Glasgow Voorhis

My dear President Wilson,   [New York] June 25th, 1905.

My Mother & I thank you heartily for your kind letter. We shall count it a very great pleasure & privilege to see you in our own home, as you so kindly say you will call, after July eighth. We cannot easily relinquish our strong wish to have you edit the book which we are considering, but if that be impossible, we shall greatly value your opinion & advice.

We shall be glad to show you our historic collection of old manuscripts, letters, &c when you come, & hope you can arrange to dine with us at seven o'clock. Would Tuesday, the eleventh of July be convenient for you? If not, will you kindly name a time that suits you during that week? Later in the summer we hope to visit the Lewis & Clark Exposition,[1] but shall be in the city for several weeks to come.

Again with our earnest thanks for your kindness, I am
          Very sincerely yours,   Eleanor Glasgow Voorhis.

ALS (WP, DLC).
  [1] The Lewis and Clark Centennial Exposition, held at Portland, Ore., from June 1 to October 15, 1905.

From Raleigh Colston Gildersleeve

Dear Sir: N. Y.   June 29th, 1905.

I am sending you under separate cover revised plans of the 1st and 2nd floors of McCosh Hall, and I would beg to draw your attention to certain changes which have been made in the plans which seem to meet with the wishes that have been expressed by the different authorities with whom I have conferred in regard to the needs of the building. First,—In regard to the shape of the class rooms,—These rooms have been made longer and narrower than in the original plan. This affords the Professor greater ease in supervising the class, although it, of course, entails using a louder tone of voice than if the room were approximately square as was shown on the first plan. This arrangement also results in enabling me to narrow up the building nine feet and it lengthens the entire building. It also makes the rooms lighter and the construction more economical. One entry and one staircase have been added so that no entry serves more than three hundred and fifty students. The class rooms have been arranged so that there are now but three class rooms in the entire building lighted only from the south. I have rearranged the staircase, so as to effect economy of space and have no recesses whatever in the halls.

The toilet rooms in each unit for the use of the Professor are indicated, as there seemed to be some difference of opinion as to the
omission of them. The plan provides for five preceptorial rooms
in addition to the twenty called for in the original programme.
In the case of the two which can be entered only from the rooms
with a capacity for 13 students, it would seem wise to combine
each of these with one of the adjoining preceptorial rooms, which
would give two class rooms of a size between that of the preceptorial room and the rooms with a capacity of 50 students. This is
merely a suggestion, however.

A rough calculation of the number of square feet called for
in the revised plans shows the slight increase of 500 Sq. ft., but
the cubical contents will be decreased slightly below the original
plan and the construction will be more economical.

Another change in the plans to which your attention is invited
is at the recess on the quad's side of the passage to McCosh Walk.
This recess has been widened and shortened so that the room for
the 65 students facing on the quad. will be better lighted and
quieter than in the original plan.

These revised plans contemplate a building as long as that
shown in the scheme submitted for the general arrangement of
the completed quad., but the building itself will be narrower than
there shown. The number of main class rooms is not affected nor
their seating capacity.

I would request that you take these plans under consideration
and let me hear from you at your convenience in regard to any
further changes that you would like to have made.

Faithfully yours,   Raleigh C Gildersleeve

TLS (WP, DLC).

To R. D. Compton[1]

My dear Sir: Princeton, N. J.   June 30, 1905.

I am writing to ask if you will not send me some circulars and
let me know your terms for boarders by the week. My party would
consist of myself and my wife and two duaghters [daughters] and
we should wish two double rooms, each with two single beds in
them. Inasmuch as we should expect to make a considerable stay
we should, of course, wish rooms with a pleasant outlook and as
airy as possible, but I am obliged to look for rooms at moderate
prices and therefore beg that you will quote me the best terms
possible within the limits of comfort.

I should hope that the circulars you send will contain some account of the surrounding country and the sports available.

Sincerely yours,   Woodrow Wilson

TLS (NNC).
[1] Proprietor of the Cragsmoor Inn, Cragsmoor, Catskill, N. Y.

From John Wesley Young,* with Enclosure

Dear Sir,   Columbus, Ohio, July 6, 1905.

Enclosed you will please find my formal application for the preceptorship which was under discussion between Professor Thompson and myself a few days ago, when I had the pleasure of visiting Princeton and calling upon you. I am acting on the advice of Professor Thompson in sending the application in duplicate, one copy to you and one to him.

Hoping to hear of favorable action by the committee soon, and in such an event anticipating a most pleasant and profitable year at Princeton, I beg to remain.

Yours very respectfully,   J. W. Young

E N C L O S U R E

John Wesley Young to the Board of Trustees of Princeton University

Gentlemen: Columbus, Ohio, July 6, 1905.

I hereby apply for a Preceptorship in Mathematics in Princeton University at a salary of $1500 a year, the duties of the position to begin with the opening of the college year 1905-1906.

Very respectfully yours,   John W. Young

TLS (WP, DLC).

From Raleigh Colston Gildersleeve

Dear Sir: N. Y.   July 8, 1905.

I have yours of June 30th in regard to the Council Chamber in North College.[1] I finished up the revised drawings and specifications for the work in the Council Chamber and sent them to the different contractors immediately after our interview of Tuesday, June 27th, and have just received the estimate on the cost and have written Mr. Pyne concerning them. The estimate on the cost of the preliminary work, that is, removing the cases[2] and setting them up in the unused portion of the Library, taking out the galleries, removing the skylight and putting on new roof and the plain plastering is the sum of $2995. The estimates on the cost of the interior work are Matthews $12600., The Hiss Co. $14765. and The Hayden Co. about $18000. These estimates do not include heating or electric lighting or electric fixtures. These items, however, will be comparatively small. In order to lose no time my working details are being pushed through and will be ready to be turned over to the cabinet maker by the time he is ready to take his measurements.

I sent you on Saturday revised plans for McCosh Hall which seem to meet all the conditions which were imposed.

Should it finally be decided to make an enclosed quad., as you suggested, this could be placed the distance back from Marquand Chapel which you desire and would come between the two entrances east of the rear of the Chapel so that would only darken two 50 student rooms and two preceptorial rooms.

Mr. Pyne has written me requesting me to hurry the work on McCosh Hall as much as possible, and I am now only waiting for the criticisms on the plans which were sent you, Mr. Pyne and Professor Thompson on Saturday, before starting my working drawings.

Faithfully yours,   Raleigh C Gildersleeve

P.S. Since writing the above I have received your letter for which I thank you. Mr. Pyne has also informed me that the plans seemed quite satisfactory. I shall therefore begin the working drawings forthwith.

Faithfully yours,   Raleigh C Gildersleeve

TLS (WP, DLC).

[1] That is, the Faculty Room in Nassau Hall.

[2] The Museum of Geology and Archaeology occupied the southern and eastern wings of Nassau Hall. The collections of the Archaeological Department were moved to the University Library to make way for the new Faculty Room.

To R. D. Compton

My dear Sir,   Princeton, N. J.   10 July, 1905.

It was a real dissapointment to us not to be able to take advantage of your kind offer of special terms and accommodations, made in your letter of the second of July. A later consideration of our summer plans determined us to join the colony of artists at Lyme, Connecticut, where Mrs. Wilson will have a much coveted opportunity to return to her old artistic pursuits.[1]

We shall hope at some other time to avail ourselves of the hospitality of Cragsmoor Inn.

Very sincerely Yours,   Woodrow Wilson

WWTLS (NNC).
[1] According to Stockton Axson, Wilson insisted that his wife renew her painting as a means of therapy for her grief over the death of her brother, Edward William Axson. R. S. Baker, interviews with Stockton Axson, Feb. 8, 10 and 11, 1925 (RSB Coll. DLC).

To Williamson Updike Vreeland

My dear Professor Vreeland: Princeton, N. J.   July 10, 1905.

I am sincerely obliged to you for your kind letter of July 5th. On the strength of it I ran down to Lyme on Saturday and came back early yesterday morning. I have engaged two rooms with Miss Thibets[1] and am very much attracted by the place indeed; so that you may expect us by the end of this week to have established ourselves with her.

I am sincerely obliged to you for the trouble you have taken for us and shall look forward with real pleasure to seeing you frequently during the summer.

In haste,

Cordially and sincerely yours,   Woodrow Wilson

TLS (WC, NjP).
[1] Whose first name is unknown and who ran a girls' boarding school during the academic year and a boardinghouse during the summer in a large frame structure, Boxwood, in Lyme, Conn.

From Raleigh Colston Gildersleeve

Dear President Wilson: N. Y.   July 11th, 1905.

I was very sorry not to have been able to meet you on Friday last, but I had an important engagement with the Building Committee to visit the School at Tarrytown.

My partner, Mr. [Harry Warren] Tuttle, tells me that you were pleased with the arrangement and design of the table at the end of Nassau Hall. I shall note what you have to say in regard to fencing off McCosh Walk and handling the building materials from the north side of the site.

I shall be very glad to see Mr. Sutton[1] on Friday morning between 10 and 12 if this suit[s] his convenience.

Faithfully yours,   Raleigh C Gildersleeve

TLS (WP, DLC).
[1] Possibly Carr Kemper Sutton, Princeton 1905, who might have been interested in work in the field of architecture.

From John Grier Hibben

My dear Woodrow,   Redfield [N.Y.], July 14/05

We have just received your letter & are greatly distressed that you & Mrs. Wilson should be undergoing such a strain of anxiety about Stockton Axson.[1] I feel that he put too great a burden upon Mrs. Wilson in his unexpected appearance in Princeton. If the plan for him can be carried out, it will I think straighten matters out wonderfully. As soon as his mind is eased about the past, he will find courage to face the present. Your report about Lyme sounds most fascinating and in that atmosphere Mrs. Wilson cannot fail to get out of herself and become absorbed in her art. She has been so brave in the midst of all her troubles, & we hail with joy anything which will bring her relief of mind & the possibility of new & diverting occupation. We are having a very delightful visit, with the family all together, & the many attractions on the stream & in the forest. There is however again & again a tug towards Princeton, & our dear friends there. It does seem a long time to be away, but we will return to the old scenes with renewed zest. We will be eager to hear from you when you are settled at Lyme. I hope that you too will find some real recreation & be able to lose yourself awhile in some absorbing pursuit.

We send a great deal of love to you & Mrs. Wilson. Jenny will write in a day or two

Yours affectionately   Jack.

ALS (WP, DLC).
[1] Stockton Axson had been suffering from nervous prostration and acute melancholia and was apparently still in a Philadelphia hospital. See EAW to Anna Harris, March 11, 1905.

To Charles Freeman Williams McClure

"Boxwood["], Lyme, Connecticut,
My dear McClure,   17 July, 1905.

I am afraid that you think me rather cavalier and not a little negligent to have overlooked your kind invitation to visit the biological laboratory. The fact of the matter is, that I did not overlook it. I simply found myself tied up every day in some round of business from which it was impossible to escape. Pray forgive me, and pray do not give up expecting me to visit your domain with the deepest interest and the most sincere desire to learn its needs and opportunities.

I hope that you will have a refreshing summer and will feel fit for anything in the autumn.

With warm regard,

Cordially and faithfully Yours,   Woodrow Wilson

WWTLS (McClure Zoological Autograph Coll., NjP).

To Benjamin Wistar Morris III

My dear Mr. Morris,   Lyme, Connecticut, 18 July 1905.

We are established here at the above type-written address, and I am ready to add my signature to the contracts with Bishop and Prior[1] whenewer [whenever] you may find it convenient to send them to me.

I hope that you are weathering this heat successfully and that I may soon see you running over here from Fenwick Point.

With much regard,

Sincerely Yours,   Woodrow Wilson

WWTLS (WC, NjP).

[1] The general contract for the construction of the ten-class dormitory, later named Patton Hall, awarded to the John Wilson Bishop Co. of Worcester, Mass., and the contract for the limestone work, awarded to Thomas H. Prior and Sons of Trenton, N. J.

From Henry Burchard Fine

My dear Tommy,   Amsterdam, July 18th 1905

Today or at least before the week ends I mean to send you a cablegram: "Strongly advise immediately making Jeans[1] the offer explained in my letter of the fifteenth."[2] For I have come to the conclusion that we have an opportunity which we can not afford to lose. I saw a great deal of Jeans before I left Cambridge and I made very careful inquiries of those who know most about him and the result of it all was the conviction that he would prove a brilliant teacher—the only point about which I was not perfectly assured when I wrote my letter of the fifteenth. He is most attractive personally and in conversation shows greater quickness and keenness of mind than almost any Englishman I have met, as well as much humor. I have talked with him very closely about his notions of teaching applied to mathematics (Mechanics and Mathematical Physics) and they seem to me admirable and likely to interest our students exceedingly. Furthermore those who know about J.'s teaching speak most highly of it.

Of course the great reason for calling him is his extraordinary scientific ability. Thomson (J. J.) and Forsyth (head of the Math. Dept. at Cambridge)[3] agree in pronouncing him already the foremost math. physicist in Great Britain (of course counting out Lord Kelvin[4] and J. J. Thomson himself, if you choose to rate him among the *math.* physicists.) If we get him we shall secure for Princeton the *leading* place among the American universities in mathematical science. He will come if he receives the call described in my letter of the fifteenth—a call to teach applied math. at a salary of $3500, the number of hours to be given to classroom & preceptorial work to be same as in case of other men in the Department.

The reason for urgency is this. He has been asked, as Brown[5] & Wick Scott[6] were, to be a member of the official party going to South Africa,[7] and this matter should be settled one way or the other before the day set for his sailing, namely July 30. If he receives the call to Princeton and I urge him to give up the trip to S. Africa he will do so. If he is not to receive the call to Princeton at once, he will of course go to S. Africa and will then not be back again in Cambridge until Oct. 7th.

Thomson (J. J.) is tremendously interested in our getting Jeans—for he has a great affection for Princeton[8] and he sees in this appointment the most important step that can be taken in giving Princeton the leading place in Math & *Phys.* science in America. He thinks that Jeans would at once attract all students of Math. Phys. to Princeton. He says too that this is probably our *one chance* to get him, there being a likelihood of his being called to Liverpool before another year begins. Then too other American universities, Columbia among them, are on the lookout for a man of Jeans make-up. And according to T. there is no other man of anything like J.'s quality in Gt. Britain. I think that the appointment of Jeans would be a far better & more distinguished one than that of Brown of Haverford; and I am sure that he will make a better teacher than Brown.

Affectionately yours,   H. B. Fine

ALS (WP, DLC).
1 James Hopwood Jeans (1877-1946), Fellow of Trinity College, Cambridge, since 1901; University Lecturer, 1904-1905. Professor of Applied Mathematics, Princeton, 1905-1909. Stokes Lecturer at Cambridge, 1910-1912. Jeans had already published an important work, *Dynamical Theory of Gases*, in 1904. He was elected Fellow of the Royal Society in 1906. After resigning the Stokes Lecturership in 1912, he held no regular position, living first in London and, after 1918, at his estate, Cleveland Lodge, in Dorking, England. In addition to important contributions to the fields of mathematics, theoretical physics, and astronomy, he was later to become important as a popularizer of science, writing several well-known books in the field. Knighted in 1928.
2 This letter is missing.
3 Joseph John Thomson, Cavendish Professor of Experimental Physics at

Cambridge University, and Andrew Russell Forsyth, Sadlerian Professor of Pure Mathematics.

[4] William Thomson, 1st Baron Kelvin, at this time Chancellor of the University of Glasgow.

[5] Ernest William Brown, born in England and educated at Cambridge, at this time Professor of Mathematics at Haverford College.

[6] William Berryman Scott.

[7] The British Association for the Advancement of Science met in various cities and toured other areas of the several British colonies of South Africa from August 15 to September 17, 1905. See *Report of the Seventy-Fifth Meeting of the British Association for the Advancement of Science; South Africa, August and September 1905* (London, 1906), and William Berryman Scott, *Some Memories of a Palaeontologist* (Princeton, N. J., 1939), pp. 262-75.

[8] Thomson had been awarded an honorary LL.D. at Princeton's Sesquicentennial in 1896.

From Henry Burchard Fine

Amsterdam, July 19 1905

Strongly advise immediately making Jeans offer outlined in letter mailed on fourteenth   Fine

Hw telegram (WP, DLC).

From Jenny Davidson Hibben

Redfield, N. Y.

My dear Mr. Wilson,   Wednesday [July 19, 1905]

Jack & I were rewarded last night, when we drove to the village for the mail, to find your letters, & to our delight postmarked *Lyme*. I am so glad that you are away from Princeton, & what really dreadful times you and Mrs. Wilson have had since we left you! I do hope that you both have a few weeks of rest & peace before you, for you can not endure much more. If Mr. Axson could come to some definite decision I suppose you would feel the most intense relief. I think uncertainty is so hard to bear—& with you & Mrs. Wilson to have all his future undecided will mean, I am afraid, a summer filled with anxious thought. I know full well how *good* you both are, & how conscientiously you will try to fill your minds with other things—but I am afraid it will not be easy to do it. . . .

We leave on Monday, & plan to go to Greensboro [Vt.] by Lake George & Ticonderoga stopping one night at Lake George & the next at Bennington Vt.

The name "Boxwood" at the top of your letter makes me think your boarding place may possibly be "Boxwood Hall" where one of Jack's cousins went to school a few years ago. She thought it & Lyme such a fascinating place.

Be sure and tell me about Margaret & Miss Axson when you write.

I feel already as if we had been away from Princeton & our old, sweet, life there many weeks, & yet I realize how good it is for all of us to have this change. You must gather health & strength, if you can in the weeks to come. I wrote dear Mrs. Wilson last Sunday, but had to send the letter to Princeton—it will be forwarded to her, doubtless. Mrs. Harper writes me from *Princeton*, that Mrs. Westcott[1] shows a slight improvement.

Dear love to you & Mrs. Wilson. We miss you very, very much & our talks can not be made up by letters.

Ever yours   Jenny D. Hibben

ALS (WP, DLC); P.S. omitted
[1] Edith Sampson (Mrs. John Howell) Westcott, who died on September 6, 1905.

Two Letters from Henry Dallas Thompson

Dear Wilson: Princeton, N. J.   July 21, 1905

I have received word from *N. R. Wilson*[1] that he will arrive from Chicago on next Monday morning, July 24—as a candidate for a "$1500 preceptorship in Mathematics, with the rank of Asst. Profr., the appointment to be for 3 yrs." I had previously written Mr. Wilson that the University would pay one-half the R.R. fare, if the position was *not* offered to him. "He is BA (double first class) and M.A. from the University of Toronto; he has studied at Cornell (one summer) and Chicago (6½ quarters). He has had one years experience in teaching . . . in the Royal Military College (the Canadian West Point) & four years' in University work as lecturer in Wesley College, University of Manitoba. During the past year he has been fellow in the Univ. of Chicago, teaching the first quarter." Profr. Moore of Chicago,[2] who[se] judgement in these matters is rather good writes of him —"He is taking his doctorate this August. . . . Personally & as a teacher, and in mathematical scholarship & research purpose and ability he is just the type of man you seek. . . . He is personally like Gillespie, only dark instead of fair (sic!) and his antecedents at Toronto & Chicago are similar." "He has a $1600 post in one of the constituent colleges of the Univ. of Manitoba." This last all from Profr. Moore.

This is all the information I hear about him. I will try to get Magie to look at him also while he is here—and send him on to see you. I will try to let you know by wire before he reaches you what we think of him.

I will send him on to see you on Monday, if he gets here on time. Will you therefore *at once* telegraph me if he can*not* see you Monday and Tuesday. If I do not hear from you I will understand that you will be ready to have him call upon you.

I recapitulate:

Preceptors fixed		Instructors fixed		Besides these Fine gets	
Eisenhart	2000	Hun	1000	Englishman	200
Gillespie	2000	Stromquist (stays)[3]	1000	Veblen*	150
Bliss	2000	Underhill	1000	& possibly we can get	
J. W. Young	1500	MacInnes[4]	1000	(?) N.R. Wilson	150
		Morrow[5]		keeping, for increase,	
		(In Kellogg's place)[6]	750	this year or next	$ 65

Very truly yours   H. D. Thompson

[1] Norman Richard Wilson.
[2] Eliakim Hastings Moore, Professor and Head of the Department of Mathematics, University of Chicago.
[3] John Gale Hun and Carl Eben Stromquist, already Instructors in Mathematics.
[4] Anthony Lispenard Underhill and Charles Ranald MacInnes were appointed Instructors in Mathematics for the academic year 1905-1906.
[5] Emerson Boyd Morrow, Princeton 1904, at this time a graduate student at Princeton. He was appointed Instructor in Mathematics as of the academic year 1905-1906.
[6] Oliver Dimon Kellogg, Instructor in Mathematics, who had accepted an assistant professorship at the University of Missouri.

My dear Wilson: Princeton, N. J.   July 24, 1905

Mr. N. R. Wilson has been here this morning, and he has gone on to New York and may come on to see you. I *think* that he would be successful but I am not all together *sure* that he knows enough of the American boy to get along with our students. I have frankly told him that this is my opinion—that I was in favor of advising you to offer him the $1500 preceptorship, but I was not sure that it would be the wisest thing for him to accept it, as he has a perfectly sure position in Manitoba at more than $1500, while here he would have no chance to advance and might not get along. I think that you will have to take the responsibility of deciding what to do about him if he comes on to you at Lyme.[1]

I am

Very faithfully yours,   H. D. Thompson

ALS (WP, DLC).
[1] It is not known whether N. R. Wilson went to Lyme. However, H. D. Thompson to WW, July 26, 1905, indicates that he decided to withdraw his candidacy for the preceptorship.

To Charles William Kent

My dear Kent,   Lyme, Connecticut, 25 July, 1905.

With many misgivings, for the autumn is to be full, for me, with undertakings of the first consequence to Princeton, I accept your kind invitation to deliver the chief morning address at the coming dedication of Madison Hall on the morning of October twentieth next.[1] Will you not be kind enough to send me particulars of the projected programme at your earliest convenience?

Excuse the haste with which this is written, and accept my warmest assurances that it is a genuine pleasure to be able to do something you want me to do. I am glad that you are so much enjoying yourself at Madison.[2]

Always,

Cordially Yours,   Woodrow Wilson

WWTLS (Tucker-Harrison-Smith Coll., ViU).
[1] A news report of Wilson's address is printed at Oct. 21, 1905.
[2] Kent was teaching in the summer school of the University of Wisconsin.

From Raleigh Colston Gildersleeve

My dear President Wilson: N. Y.   July 25th, 1905.

I had a talk with Mr. Pyne in regard to the alteration of Nassau Hall and McCosh Hall, the tenor of which, I think, should be reported to you. Mr. Pyne expressed himself as being very desirous of obtaining exact estimates on the cost of these pieces of work at the earliest moment possible, although he does not wish to delay the work unduly. Inasmuch as several changes have been recently made in the alterations at Nassau Hall and a certain amount of time must elapse before the estimates can be put into complete shape, he instructed me to accept Matthews' preliminary estimate on the cost of the work on the Hall, and instructed me to obtain exact estimates on the total cost as soon as possible.

In regard to McCosh Hall, he thought it would be well to make a contract for the foundation work and while the excavation and foundation are being done, to proceed to obtain estimates on the cost of all the work necessary to complete the building, but not to do anything further until the total cost can be ascertained.

The only practical question about which I am now in doubt, is in regard to the large rooms in McCosh Hall accommodating 400 to 600; these are the rooms in which the floors will be sloped. In order to obtain the amount of slope I should like to know whether or not the the lecturer should be on a platform or on the floor, and whether or not it it desirable for the top of his desk to be visible from the different seats. I have asked Mr. Pyne about this who refers me to Prof. Thompson, to whom I have written. I should appreciate very much an expression of your views in regard to this matter, as we are engaged in redesigning the elevations and the matter is of much importance in determining the heights and locations of the windows.

Faithfully yours,   Raleigh C. Gildersleeve.

TLS (WP, DLC).

From Henry Dallas Thompson

Dear Wilson: Princeton, N. J.   July 26, 1905

As I promised Mr. N. R. Wilson one half of his railroad fare, will you please have the Treasurer send a check for $24.08 to Mr. Norman R. Wilson, Box 206, Cobourg, Ont., Canada. Could you do this very soon as Mr. Duffield tells me that he leaves Princeton the first part of next week. I have Mr. Wilson's itemized statement regarding the amount, which is doubtless correct, and which I can send to you if you so wish. I have a letter from Mr. Wilson which closes all our negotiations with him.

I, also, have received a letter from Fine regarding Jeans; and I am delighted that you have decided to call him. If he comes, it will give us a start in just the line we want.

The offering of $3500 to Jeans will leave us but $650 of the amount which we have been counting on for next year, and we are still one man short. While it is possible that we might find some very young man for that amount, it is not a sure thing that we shall be able to do so. Can we go up to $1,000 (i.e. $350 extra) for this last Instructor? I will of course do nothing in this matter until I hear from you.

The arrangement of the $17,900 is now as follows

Prof. J. H. Jeans	$3500
Prec. Eisenhart	2000
Prec. Gillespie	2000
Prec. Bliss	2000
Prec. J. W. Young	1500
Prec. (Veblen)	1500
Inst. Hun	1000
" Stromquist	1000
" Underhill	1000

"	MacInnes	1000
"	Morrow	750
"	(Instructor?)	650

$17,900

With the hope that you are having as much of a rest as you can hope with these things coming up all the time, I am

Very faithfully yours,   H. D. Thompson

ALS (WP, DLC).

To Benjamin Wistar Morris III

My dear Mr. Morris,   Lyme, Connecticut, 28 July, 1905.

Excuse my delay in returning the contracts. A hundred things, small and great, have delayed me. I hope you have not been inconvenienced.

With warmest regard,

Cordially Yours,   Woodrow Wilson

WWTLS (WC, NjP).

From Henry Burchard Fine

My dear Tommy,   Grindelwald, July 29, 1905.

Your cablegram reached Professor Forsythe in good time and I am delighted to say that Jeans has accepted. This puts us in possession of the man who is regarded in England as possessing higher genius for applied mathematics than any other young man in Great Britain and from whom work is already anticipated comparable in quality with that of Lord Kelvin and J. J. Thomson. And as I have already written you, he is highly cultivated, attractive in appearance, and not only is a gentleman but is quite willing to look like one (which I find is not true of all Englishmen even in academic circles.)

Finally I heard in Cambridge nothing but praise of the teaching he has done. As I think I wrote you, Miss Meyer,[1] the Professor of Mathematics at Girton, told me that Mr. Jeans had taught a number of the Girton girls and that his work with them was such that she had come to regard him as the one young mathematician of brilliant talents who could be counted on to adapt his teaching to his pupil—who could arouse enthusiasm in an able pupil and yet be willing to take great pains to clear away the difficulties of a dull one. Indeed Miss Meyer's very frank concern lest I should succeed in persuading Jeans to leave Cambridge was as satisfying testimony as I could have wished on the only point about which I felt the need of additional assurance after my first interview with him. After my second talk with him, I may add, I was so fully convinced that he possessed in a very high degree the abilities of the teacher and that if he came to Princeton he would throw himself into the work of instruction with real heartiness, that I was almost ready to recommend him for our chair of applied mathematics without further investigation.

Jeans would have given up the trip to South Africa altogether could he have known a little earlier that he was to have the Princeton call. But after my letter to you was written he found that as Secretary of his section of the British Association it was his duty to decide either for or against going early in the present week. He therefore decided to go but has made arrangements whereby he is to remain in S. Africa only for the meeting of the Association at Cape Town. He then returns to Cambridge, attends to a few necessary matters of business there, and then sails for America in time to reach Princeton by Saturday, Sept. 23rd.

You would have been delighted at Thomson's enthusiastic interest in our getting Jeans. "Now," said he, "get sufficient laboratory equipment and another experimental physicist who is full of ideas and you will have at Princeton the greatest school of applied mathematics & physical science in America and one of the greatest in the world." For Thomson insists that Jeans' equal is not to be found anywhere else, and he has a very warm place in his heart for Princeton and regards it as possessing the ideal environment for the great school of applied mathematics and purely physical science which he evidently longs to see established in America.

Of course the situation created by Jeans coming to Princeton makes a strong appeal to my imagination. I have felt for some years that the great need of mathematical science in America was the presence among us of a first rate applied mathematician such as are produced nowadays in Cambridge only. And now I see a man of that sort coming to Princeton—and not a man of great promise merely, but one who, though young, has already won for himself rank among the leaders in the science. Surely I may be excused in these circumstances if I indulge myself in enthusiastic anticipation. I cannot tell you, Tommy, how much I appreciate your willingness to give me a free hand in this matter. It was a case where promptness was necessary. It was plainly Thomson's opinion that if we waited a year we were likely to miss getting Jeans altogether. He had not until our call received the academic recognition he desired, but Thomson has been receiving inquiries about him from the University of Liverpool and from another British university the name of which I forget, which made it seem likely that before the year closed he would accept a post in Great Britain from which it would be far more difficult to dislodge him than from a Cambridge lectureship.

Last evening I received a letter from O. D. Kellogg telling me that he had accepted the Assistant Professorship in Mathematics at the University of Missouri from which we have just called Bliss. It was my first intimation of the fact, for Thompson has not deigned to send me so much as a line regarding his doings for the Math. Dept. For personal reasons I am sorry to have Kellogg go. He is also a fine mathematician. But he was not really succeeding in his class room work and had gotten the unfortunate reputation with the Freshmen of being unintelligible, for all practical purposes, to a dull student. He might have overcome all this (though I am by no means sure that he would), but to have promoted him now in order to keep him would in my opinion, as in yours & Thompson's, not have been warranted. But I wish that Thompson would write me and put at rest my misgivings that through the loss of Kellogg (and perhaps that of Stromquist[2] also) we stand in danger of starting the year short handed in mathematics. I shall write Thompson again and *demand* information.

We have had a delightful journey thus far. After a few days in London we visited Gerrans[3] at Oxford, who entertained us charmingly, and then J. J. Thomson & his wife in Cambridge, where of course we enjoyed ourselves greatly. We then crossed to Holland and travelled somewhat leisurely to Switzerland, arriving last Monday in Grindelwald, where we shall probably remain for the next two weeks. Our movements after that are not yet fully decided upon except that we are to remain in Switzerland until the last week in August, when we go to Tours. I sail from Cherbourg Sept. 7th & am due in Princeton Sept. 16th.

I hope that you and yours are having a delightful summer and that you are getting thoroughly rested. With kindest regards to Mrs. Wilson & yourself, in which Mrs. Fine joins me, I am as ever

Affectionately yours,   H. B. Fine

(My address is Care British Linen Co. Bank, Threadneedle St. London)

ALS (WP, DLC).
¹ Margaret Theodora Meyer, Lecturer and Director of Studies in Mathematics, Girton College.
² Stromquist remained at Princeton until 1909, serving as Preceptor in Mathematics in 1908-1909.
³ Henry Tresawna Gerrans, Tutor and Mathematical Lecturer at Worcester College, Oxford. See A. F. West to WW, Oct. 4, 1902, Vol. 14.

From Jesse Benedict Carter

My dear Mr. Wilson,   London, England, July 31, 1905.

For the last few months the conviction has been growing in me that it would not be possible for Mrs. Carter to live in Princeton for a number of years to come, and I have been struggling with the question of what my *own* duty was in the matter. If it had been possible I would have come to you and talked the matter over, but that was not possible, and letters are well enough to give results but of very little use to indicate the preliminary processes of decision, and so I have had to work the thing out for myself and to give you the bald result with all its blunt angles of decision. And I am afraid that even now at this distance, it will not be possible for me to do what I would like to do—let you know the whole story of the struggle—and I must therefore ask the supreme boon of friendship—the building of the bridges of trust across the gaps of my narrative. When it became clear that my wife could not go back to Princeton for a long time I tried hard to persuade myself that I could go back without her, but I have decided that that would not be right. But that once established—and I succeeded in doing so only last week—then of course I ought to tell you about it and set your hands free as soon as I could—hence this resignation.

As for date on which it takes effect, I would leave that entirely to your pleasure. I have suggested the end of the *coming* academic year because it would give you a year in which to fill the actual blank before it became a theoretical one as well, and also because it would enable me to work a *second* year in the Roman School as Princeton's representative, since my appointment was for two years. As for the salary ($500) which would normally accrue to me in this coming year I hope that you will allow me to consider it merely as a loan to be repaid as soon as I can sell my house in Princeton.[1]

As for the future I have, to be sure, nothing but *possibilities*, but I have a work to do, and *fortunately* my longing for work does not end in sentiment, as I have a living to earn. I suppose we shall live in Rome which in spite of its apparent drawbacks agrees with Mrs. Carter better than almost any other place in the world, and where I have personally a better chance of being useful with my present equipment of knowledge and experience. In case the Roman school should find some use for me, I would gladly work with them. Naturally I have thought of this possibility in these weeks of debate, but the possibility is at best merely remote. However I shall find something to do.[2]

My *head* has been speaking in this letter, giving the ultimate message of my heart. I did not dare to let my heart speak—that would only confuse the situation because it would speak on both sides at once. But my heart is with you and your work just as truly as when I wrote you the day before I sailed from America,[3] and the thing that would make me happiest in the world would be in some way to prove my *devotion* in spite of my separation— Who knows but what that may be possible?

Faithfully yours   Jesse Benedict Carter

ALS (WP, DLC).
  [1] See J. B. Carter to WW, June 29, 1904, Vol. 15, in which he thanked Wilson very warmly.
  [2] In fact, he became Director of the American School of Classical Studies in Rome in 1907.
  [3] J. B. Carter to WW, June 29, 1904, Vol. 15.

From Charles Williston McAlpin

Dear Sir: [Princeton, N. J.]   July 31, 1905.

The vote for Chairman and Secretary of the Committee on Morals and Discipline has resulted as follows:

Chairman, Rev. John Dixon, D.D.

Secretary, Mr. John D. Davis.

Sincerely yours,   [C. W. McAlpin] Secretary

CCL (McAlpin File, UA, NjP).

To Williamson Updike Vreeland

My dear Mr. Vreeland,   Lyme, Connecticut, 2 August, 1905.

I take the liberty of sending you a letter from Laurason Riggs,[1] of Baltimore, which explains itself, and which belongs, of course, to your Committee.[2] It needs no further reply at present than I have already made. I have written to Mr. Riggs to say that, while I could not bind the Faculty in such a matter, I would myself be entirely in favour of granting Mr. McSherry the credits he asks for.[3]

I have a long letter from Frank Glass, '77, of Montgomery, Ala.,[4] about his boy, Frank, junior, who was, you remember, dropped on account of deficiencies resulting from illness. The boy, it seems, understood that "if he dropped back a year he was to be relieved of all existing conditions, that he was to start with a clean page." He had, his father tells me, "a lot of extra work put on him, on account of the changed curriculum, that did not come in his own Soph. year. He says he had about six (6) hours of extra work, and he understood it was to cover all old conditions."

The father is a sensible man and writes to me for advice as to whether he should keep the boy in college or take him out. I have got a pleasant impression of the son; know how genuine his embarrassments were in connection with his long and serious illness; and would personally like to see him stay, if that is possible under the rules without a burden such as an indifferent student is unlikely to be able to carry successfully. Will you not tell me what you think I ought to say to the father. The boy represents that he is being harshly dealt with,—which of course is not so by intention, and probably not so in any sense.[5]

With warmest regard,

Always,

Faithfully and cordially Yours,   Woodrow Wilson

WWTLS (WC, NjP).

[1] Lawrason Riggs, Princeton 1883, lawyer of Baltimore.

[2] The Faculty Committee on Examinations and Standing, of which Vreeland was secretary.

[3] Solomon Hillen MacSherry of Roland Park, Md. He entered Princeton as a freshman in 1905 and remained only through his sophomore year.

[4] It is missing.

[5] Franklin Purnell Glass, who had entered Princeton in 1902, was graduated in 1907. For an earlier discussion of his academic difficulties, see F. P. Glass to WW, Oct. 2, 1903, Vol. 15.

To Charles William Kent

My dear Kent,   Lyme, Connecticut, 2 August, 1905.

Thank you for your cordial letter of the thirtieth of July,[1] and pardon my slip: I meant to accept for the nineteenth, not for the twentieth. The latter date would be impossible for me, indeed.

I am afraid that Mrs. Wilson will not be able to accompany me; but you may be sure she will if she can, and she greatly appreciates the invitation which you so kindly urge.

With warmest regard,

Cordially and sincerely Yours,   Woodrow Wilson

WWTLS (Tucker-Harrison-Smith Coll., ViU).
1 It is missing.

To Benjamin Wistar Morris III

My dear Mr. Morris,   Lyme, Connecticut, 2 August, 1905.

I send you, enclosed, the receipts you ask for, or, rather, the acceptances.

With cordial regard,

Faithfully Yours,   Woodrow Wilson

WWTLS (WC, NjP).

From Charles Williston McAlpin

My dear Dr. Wilson: [Princeton, N. J.]   August 2, 1905.

I had intended not to bother you with any University problems this summer, but a question has arisen in connection with the University Scholarships that I would like your advice on.

The rule states that the ten Class "A" Scholarships shall be assigned to first group men in the order of seniority of class and that the thirty Class "B" Scholarships shall be assigned to second group men in the order of seniority of class. This year there are four 1906 men and nine 1907 men in the first general group (this refers only to men who have received remission of tuition). There are sixteen 1906 men in the second group and eighteen 1907 men in the second group. The question in my mind is should the three surplus first group men in 1907, who cannot be given Class "A" scholarships, be given Class "B" scholarships to the exclusion of the three men standing lowest in the second group.

As there are thirty-four in the second group in 1906 and 1907 the four lowest men in 1907 will be debarred in any case. The point is, should the three lowest men in the first group of 1907 lose the University Scholarship or should they receive a Class "B" scholarship and the next three lowest men in the second group be debarred?

According to the strict letter of the law I suppose the three men in the first group of 1907 should be the ones to suffer, but in view of the fact that these scholarships were created to encourage high standing it seems a pity that a man who has stood in the first group should receive less in the way of remission of tuition than a man who has stood in the second group.

I expect to leave for the West on Saturday to be gone until September 9th. If you wish to postpone your decision until my return I think there will be nothing lost by the delay, but if you decide now and will advise Mr. [John Rogers] Williams I will leave directions with him how to proceed in the matter.

Everything is quiet in town and the machinery of the University seems to be running smoothly. During the recent hot spell I was overcome by the heat, but fortunately the attack was not severe and at present I feel as well as ever. With kind regards to Mrs. Wilson, believe me,

        Very sincerely yours,   [C. W. McAlpin] Secretary.

CCL (McAlpin File, UA, NjP).

From John Grier Hibben

My dear Woodrow   Greensboro [Vt.]   Aug 3/1905.

I have recently heard from [Bliss] Perry an item of news which will interest you I know, and which moreover I think you ought to know. It seems that President Eliot has for some time been sounding Perry as to the possibility of his accepting a permanent position at Harvard. Last winter Perry lectured there in the place of Barret Wendell. This summer Mr. Eliot has made an offer to Perry in definite form,—either a position as full professor of English giving his whole time to the work, or a position in which he is to deliver two courses each year & at the same time carry on his editorial work. In the latter case Mr. Eliot states that whenever the editorial work may be given up, a full permanent position awaits him. Knowing your desire often expressed to have Perry some day in Princeton again, I felt that you ought to know of this critical juncture of affairs, for if anything is to be done to induce Perry to return to Princeton, some indication should be given to him of Princeton's attitude in respect to the present situation. Perry has told me that he does not think that he will stay with the Atlantic more than two years & then he wishes to take a year abroad. This gives three years before he wishes to settle again to academic work unless President Eliot should compel him by his importunity to commit himself to Harvard at once.

I mention this because any offer you should feel inclined to make Perry would not have to be made good until three years from now. That would give ample time to raise money sufficient to endow his chair. I feel that you could secure the money from the Alumni if you have Perry's name as the bait, for he was always so popular with his students, & they would be generous in a response made on his behalf. I imagine that Eliot has offered him $5000—the salary of the full professor at Harvard. I think that possibly you might secure that amount for Perry in the form of a graduate school professorship. It would start the beginnings of a graduate group of professors, & I believe that the idea has always been to make the salary of such chairs the sum of $5000. Such a position of course would not preclude the undergraduate teaching. I feel that if Princeton wishes Perry, then Harvard's offer must be met by as high an amount of salary.

I have thrown out these suggestions as they have come to mind & that you may know fully how the matter appears to me. Perry is now in Boston & does not know of my writing to you. The whole subject of the Harvard offer he wishes to be kept secret, & yet I felt that it was but fair to you that you should be advised of the situation.

We are enjoying your letters, & the good news which comes from you of Mrs. Wilson's delight in her new pursuit. We are having a most restful & charming summer. We think & speak of you often. Jenny joins in love to you all

Your affectionate friend   John Grier Hibben

We have just heard that Mrs. Westcott is sinking rapidly

ALS (WP, DLC).

To John Rogers Williams

My dear Mr. Williams,   Lyme, Connecticut, 5 August, 1905.

In reply to Mr. McAlpin's question about the "A" and "B" scholarships, I would say that it seems to me that it would be best to give Class "B" scholarships to the three surplus first group men in 1907, to the exclusion of the three men standing lowest in the second group who would otherwise to [be] eligible. It would be wholly inequitable to deprive the first group men in question of the benefit of their standing in such a way.

Hoping that you are well,

Sincerely Yours,   Woodrow Wilson

WWTLS (McAlpin File, UA, NjP).

To Benjamin Wistar Morris III

My dear Mr. Morris,   Lyme, Connecticut, 5 August, 1905.

After Mr. Cuyler's return nothing but formal contracts need be sent to me for my signature: everything done under a general contract already signed may be regarded as authorized by the principal contract which bears my signature. But, in his and Mr.

Pyne's absence, I will be glad to give the necessary authorizations. I am sending Prior's bill to the Treasurer of the University to-day. He is out of town, but will return before long.

With warmest regard,

Cordially Yours,   Woodrow Wilson

WWTLS (WC, NjP).

From John Grier Hibben

My dear Woodrow   Greensboro [Vt.]   Aug 7/05

I have just received your letter in reference to Perry. Since writing you last week, Perry has heard again from Mr Eliot, and in a letter which Perry showed me, Mr. Eliot offers him the Smith Chair of Belles Lettres[1][,] a chair which has been vacant since Lowell's death, & with it a full salary & privilege of continuing his editorial work indefinitely. Mr Eliot states that he has not before regarded any one as a sufficiently worthy successor of Lowell. I feel that if you decide to do anything in Perry's case you will have to act immediately, as Perry is being pressed for an answer to the Harvard offer. Perry told me that after his conversation with you a year or so ago he did not wish to decide this matter without your being advised of it. Whatever your decision I think he would appreciate a letter from you on the subject. There is of course a distinction which naturally attaches to such a chair as the one now offered to Perry, & it appeals to him very strongly I can see. However the old ties binding him to Princeton are very strong & an offer of an equal salary to that of Harvard might have some influence upon him. I think he expects to make his decision & reply to Harvard in a few days.

We have heard nothing further from the Westcotts. It would be a relief to learn that the strain is over.

With much love to you all

Your affectionate friend   John Grier Hibben

ALS (WP, DLC).
[1] As it turned out, the duties of the Smith Professor of the French and Spanish Languages and Literature and Professor of Belles Lettres were divided, with Perry becoming Professor of English Literature in 1906 and Jeremiah Denis Matthias Ford becoming Smith Professor of the French and Spanish Languages in 1907.

To Theodore Roosevelt

My dear Mr. President,   Lyme, Connecticut, 8 August, 1905.

I hear with the greatest pleasure that you are expecting to attend the foot ball game to be played between West Point and

Annapolis next November at Princeton, and I write to ask if you will not give Mrs. Wilson and me the honour and pleasure of lunching with us, with your party, on that day. We would not make it a tedious or elaborate "function"; our only object would be to give you a pleasant and comfortable meal and to put "Prospect," our home, at your service.

Mr. Munn, of the Scientific American,[1] wrote me, before I knew of the possibility of your attending the game, that he had invited you to lunch as his guest at the Ivy Club; but he has, with the greatest courtesy and generosity, yielded to my very earnest desire to have you and your party at "Prospect."

With warmest regard,

Sincerely Yours,   Woodrow Wilson

WWTLS (T. Roosevelt Papers, DLC).
[1] Charles Allen Munn, Princeton 1881, son of Orson Desaix Munn, who was for many years co-editor and publisher of *Scientific American*. Charles Allen Munn succeeded his father as co-editor and publisher on the latter's death in 1907.

Gutzon Borglum to Benjamin Wistar Morris III, with Enclosure

My dear Mr. Morris   [New York, c. Aug. 8, 1905]

I have sent the above to Pres. Wilson because I do not think they have shown me the consideration, the work I did for them deserves.

There is little use, I think, in not being honestly frank about these things—and I do feel they should not have again expected me to do a mass of work for them at prices impossible to produce the work, as their provision indicated.

Sincerely Yours   Gutzon Borglum

ALS (WC, NjP).

From Gutzon Borglum

My dear sir—   New York, Aug. 8th, 1905.

About two months ago I was asked by Mr. Morris to give estimates upon the sculpture work for the new Dormitories.[1] Mr. Morris also stated that there was a very small money provision considering the character of the work and the amount to be done, and for that reason, apologized for asking me to do it—but explained it was your wish, or the committee's, that I do thw [the] work. This was natural and consistant as the work upon the 79 Dormitory had been executed at a very considerable loss to me. Of course, the amount of work done then (some sixty different models) was in excess of contract and at my own volition entirely and the five hundred dollars paid barely covered the disbursements I made for the work. This, I say, was at my own volition and was due to friendships and a desire on my part to give to the sculpture of the building—if I had anything to do with it—a real character. What seems to have happened is that those circumstances have been entirely forgotten and the cost to the class of '79 used as a basis for the estimates upon this work. The figures I give for the work as planned by the architect are not really sculptor's prices and do not admit of much more than ordinary modeler's profits.

Yours very truly,   [Gutzon Borglum]

TCL (WC, NjP).
¹ That is, the dormitory later named Patton Hall.

To Bliss Perry

My dear Perry,   Lyme, Conn.   9 August, 1905.

Thank you most sincerely for giving Hibben leave to tell me of Pres. Eliot's proposals to you. I need not tell you that they deeply disturb me. We have nothing so distinguished to offer you as the successorship to Lowell—nothing but a welcome back to a great group of friends who love you and a part in what we all believe to be the assured coming greatness of Princeton; but, as you know, I have fondly counted on having you back with us when you had had enough of editorship and wish an academic berth again, and it will be one of the memorable disappointments of my administration if we do not get you.

This letter is only preliminary. It will be several days yet before I can hear from the chairman of the Finance com. whom I feel bound to consult, if possible, before laying a definite proposition before you. If you feel that you must reply to Mr. Eliot at once, pray let me know and I will act on my own responsibility: but if you can spare me a day or two more, do so, and I shall very much appreciate it.

Meanwhile, think kindly on Princeton and on the ties that naturally bind you to it. If there is no chair there that Lowell has occupied may there not be a chair which you have yourself made and made worthy of ambition in another generation? We are going to do notable things at Princeton, God helping us, and I

should rejoice to have you our close partner in our great undertakings.

Mrs. Wilson joins me in all cordial messages, and hopes more
than she can say to have a chance to claim Mrs. Perry again,
and I am,

As always,

Faithfully & cordially Yours,   Woodrow Wilson

HwCL (B. Perry Papers, MH).

From Theodore Roosevelt

My dear President Wilson: Oyster Bay, N. Y., August 9, 1905.

Indeed I accept with the greatest pleasure your kind invitation
for lunch on the day of the West Point-Annapolis game. Pray
thank Mrs. Wilson. I shall look forward to seeing you.[1]

Sincerely yours,   Theodore Roosevelt

TLS (Letterpress Books, T. Roosevelt Papers, DLC).
[1] A news report of Roosevelt's visit to Princeton is printed at Dec. 4, 1905.

To Benjamin Wistar Morris III

My dear Mr. Morris,   Lyme, Connecticut, 10 August, 1905.

Will you not interpret this letter for me. I do not know the
figures,—either those of Mr. Borglum's estimate or of the Committee's appropriation; so that I feel unable to form an opinion
or to reply to Mr. Borglum's letter.

Would it not be well to call Mr. Pyne's attention to the matter.
The carvings cannot wisely be neglected or skimped.

With much regard,

Sincerely Yours,   Woodrow Wilson

WWTLS (WC, NjP).

From Moses Taylor Pyne

My dear Woodrow   N E Harbor [Me.] Aug 11/05

I have submitted your letter to Messrs [Archibald Douglas]
Russell & [Bayard] Henry (in confidence) who are staying here.

We all three feel that we cannot afford to lose Perry & that we
must have faith in the future.

You had better write to him or better yet see him & close with
him on the terms you mentioned if you are satisfied we cannot

do better. $5000 is rather higher than our norm, & perhaps the Lowell endowment is less. Cannot you find out from Eliot's report wh. contains the Treasurer's statement.

I suppose you have recd Jesse Carter's letter & resignation. Had we not better continue him as a member of the Faculty on nominal pay until his wife's health improves. . . .[1]

Sincerely yrs   M Taylor Pyne

ALS (WP, DLC).

[1] He was in fact kept on the roster of the Princeton faculty until 1907, but the trustees' records do not reveal whether he continued to receive a nominal salary.

From Raleigh Colston Gildersleeve

Dear President Wilson: N. Y.   August 11th, 1905.

McCosh Hall has been entirely restudied now and I am sending you prints of our studies of the new elevations, and also the seating plans for the two large rooms and their galleries. These seating plans I am also sending to Mr. [Henry Conrad] Bunn, Prof. Thompson and Mr. Pyne, as I wish to be sure that they are satisfactory before finishing up the working drawings. In addition to the studies at small scale, I have well under way the large scale details of the exterior. When these details are completed we can reduce them to the small scale without any difficulty and then everything will agree.

I wish to say a word about the method which I propose to use in lighting the Council Chamber so as to see if it meets with your approbation. This was to be effected as follows,—By two large chandeliers dropping from the ceiling, by two standards on the President's desk and around the walls of the room by means of tall standard lights set between the windows and at the ends of the room. The position of these will be shown on the plan by the little receptacle indication, which is like this ⌦.

I am expecting to have an estimate in the course of a few days on the cost of the cut stone work for McCosh Hall in accordance with the design shown on the prints sent you to-day. When I have received it I shall be able to tell very closely how much the building will cost complete, and then whatever modifications to meet the situation, can be effected.

I trust you will let me know when there is any chance of your coming to New York, as I should like very much of being certain of seeing you.

Yours faithfully,   Raleigh C Gildersleeve

TLS (WP, DLC).

From Benjamin Wistar Morris III

My dear Dr. Wilson: New York   Aug. 11, 1905
    Replying to your letter of the 10th. enclosing letter from Mr.
Borglum of the 8th., I would say in explanation that the allowance I had made for the models on the Ten Class Building, and
which was reported to the Building Committee at the Meeting of
June 8th., was $1000.00[,] being twice the amount awarded to
Mr. Borglum for his work on the '79 Dormitory. During the last
month I have taken figures for the modelling work from Mr.
Borglum, [Leon J.] Neumann & [Louis M.] Even and Paul
Wiehle,[1] whose figures are respectively:
$2,110.00
1,500.00
1,400.00
on the same number of models. The price that I had allowed for
this work was evidently not sufficient but was made up as I said
before on Mr. Borglum's former price, allowing twice that
amount, knowing that there would be more and larger models
on this new Building. As Mr. Borglum was unwilling to reduce
his price, I awarded the work to Mr. Wiehle, who is a Sculptor,
not a mere "modeller," who has had excellent training and experience in work in Paris; and, since he has come to America
has done considerable modelling for me and for other well-known
Architects. I believe that Mr. Wiehle's work will be entirely satisfactory and I did not feel justified in accepting the higher bid
of Mr. Borglum.
    It may be that Mr. Borglum would produce some of the models,
which would be better than Mr. Wihele's [Wiehle's]. On the other
hand, Mr. Borglum is not an architectural sculptor and most of
the models that we shall need are distinctly architectural models.
I have given Mr. Wiehle verbal acceptance of his work and he
is now engaged in making the studies. Mr. Borglum has been
unsuccessful in fair competition, but if you wish further consideration given to him in this matter will you kindly let me know
immediately. Mr. Pyne I learn will not be home before Sept.
10th. and we shall need the models before that time.
                    Yours very truly,   B. W. Morris Jr.
                                [per] W. A. Payne[2]

TLS (WP, DLC).
    [1] All sculptors of New York.
    [2] William Arthur Payne, who had recently become an architectural assistant
to Morris.

To Benjamin Wistar Morris III

My dear Mr. Morris,   Lyme, Connecticut, 12 August, 1905.

I entirely approve your assignment of the carving designs to Wiehle. I sent Mr. Borglum's letter to you only because I had heard nothing of the matter and did not understand what he wrote. His letter read as if he were doing, or going to do, the work and felt that we were wronging him in the matter of pay. What you have done is perfectly right, and I can answer Mr. B's letter intelligently. Thank you for the explanation.

With warm regard,

Sincerely Yours,   Woodrow Wilson

WWTLS (WC, NjP).

To Gutzon Borglum

My dear Mr. Borglum,   Lyme, Connecticut, 12 August, 1905.

Your letter of the eighth of August has been forwarded to me here.

I am very sorry that Mr. Morris was unable to assign the designing work for the new dormitory to you. He of course had to be guided by economic considerations and was obliged to give the work to the lowest bidder. But I am sure that he appreciates as much as I do the work you did for us in connection with Seventy-Nine Hall. We shall always regard it as one of the most interesting things on the campus.

With much regard and sincere regret,

Very truly Yours,   Woodrow Wilson

WWTLS (photostat in the G. Borglum Papers, DLC).

From Henry Burchard Fine

My dear Tommy,   Grindelwald, Aug 12, 1905

On Aug 10th I met Veblen. He impressed me as being a man of unusual ability and good sense and as likely to be eminently successful as an instructor both in class room and in preceptorial conferences. On the surface he is somewhat lacking in polish & while never showing embarassment in the use of his mental faculties—indeed both Mrs. Fine and I found him very bright and interesting in conversation—he doesn't always know how to dispose of his hands & feet to the best advantage. But I am very confident that at Princeton he would soon make good his defi-

ciencies on that side—especially since, as he very ingenuously
told me, he is conscious of his deficiencies & desirous of remedy-
ing them. He seemed to be wholly free from freshness and self
conceit, and, best of all, to be a hearty, sincere, and high minded
young fellow. I confess that I took a strong liking to him personally, and when I considered his ability and attainments as a
mathematician, his success as a teacher in the University of Chicago, and his evident interest in teaching as well as in scientific
work, together with the fine personal qualities which he clearly
possesses, I felt no hesitancy about making him the offer which
it was agreed between you and me I was to make him in case I
thought well of him when I had met him—namely the offer of a
preceptorship at $1500. He at once accepted this offer and has
already written to Chicago resigning his post there. It may interest you to know that I have just learned through Thompson
that had Dickson of Chicago[1] been called to Northwestern, Veblen
was to have been promoted to Dickson's post—an assistant professorship—which is evidence enough of the high esteem in
which he is held at Chicago. He expects to arrive in Princeton,
ready to begin work there, by Sept. 16. When you come to make
the formal recommendation of his appointment—I mean the
recommendation to the Trustees—it had better be, I think, in
the same terms as that of J. W. Young, who, Thompson writes
me, has already received an appointment to a $1500 preceptor-
ship. As Veblen will be travelling almost continually from now
on until college opens, I told him that he was not to expect a
formal notice from you as to his appointment until after his
arrival in Princeton.

We are still in Grindelwald, all of us well and enjoying the
life of the Swiss Alps to the utmost. Someday next week we shall
migrate to Geneva and after a short stay there go on to Paris.
By the end of the third week in August we expect to arrive in
Tours where, as you recall, it is our plan that Mrs Fine and the
children shall settle for this winter. I shall say good by to them
just in time to catch the *Philadelphia* of the American Line sailing from Cherbourg Sept 9th & back in New York Sept 16th.

With kindest regards to Mrs. Wilson,

Sincerely Yours, as ever,   H. B. Fine

ALS (WP, DLC).
[1] Leonard Eugene Dickson, Assistant Professor of Mathematics at the University of Chicago.

From Jenny Davidson Hibben

My dear Mr. Wilson   Greensboro, Vt.   Aug. 15, 1905.

Your two letters were so welcome this morning that I hasten to answer mine immediately. All of your news was of the greatest interest to Jack & to me. Mr. Fine's delightful letter, I return in this one. Mr. *Jeans* sounds as if he were all any college could wish for. Jesse Carter's resignation was sure to come sooner or later, & while I grant you his brilliancy, I should think you would be glad to know what he means to do—his restless spirit never would have been satisfied with his position, even in Princeton— he always has seemed to me the very living embodiment of selfish ambition[,] an ambition so different from *some* other men in Princeton!

As for poor Mr. Axson, I don't know whether to be glad or sorry that he is not to marry. Your letter before the last one in which you quoted so largely from his was so peaceful—& almost happy in tone.

Mr. Perry has shown us your two letters,[1] they were lovely & all that he could ask. He & Mrs. Perry are off to-day for a trip to Quebec—for a week—& very happy to be going away from all care & responsibility. Their present plan is, I mean, for the future, to go to Europe as a family next July, Mr. Perry to stay with them until February, studying in Italy most of the time. Mr. Eliot wants him to teach Comparative Literature & Mr. Perry must familiarize himself with Italian writers. In Feb. he would leave Mrs. Perry & the children & come back to Cambridge & join them again the following summer.[2] We have no further news from dear Mrs. Westcott. . . .

Every here & there, a branch of a tree has turned red, & I know my beloved Autumn is coming—the golden rod & asters are here too!

Jack joins me in dear love to you & Mrs. Wilson, & we hope all these anxieties have not been too much for you this summer. Another year you & Mrs. Ellen must go to Europe & see Kipling's lovely country.   Ever yours—Jenny D. Hibben

ALS (WP, DLC).

[1] Wilson's second letter, in which he offered the professorship to Perry, is missing.

[2] Perry had obviously already decided to accept the Harvard professorship. His appointment as Professor of English Literature was announced in March 1906. He taught half time until his final resignation as editor of the *Atlantic Monthly*, effective August 1, 1909. Perry did go to Europe in the summer of 1906, returning in January 1907 to continue his editing of the *Atlantic Monthly* and begin his teaching at Harvard. For further details, see Bliss Perry, *And Gladly Teach: Reminiscences* (Boston and New York, 1935), pp. 190-98.

To Benjamin Wistar Morris III

My dear Mr. Morris,   Lyme, Connecticut, 22 August, 1905.

I have received your letter of the eighteenth of August,[1] and will give it as early consideration as possible. The matter of the heating of the new dormitory and the installation of pumps is evidently of the first consequence, and I should wish the members of the proper committees of the Board of Trustees to be consulted. I will consult them as fast as I can get at them.

With much regard,

Sincerely Yours,   Woodrow Wilson

WWTLS (WC, NjP).
[1] It is missing.

From Jesse Benedict Carter

My dear Mr. Wilson,   London, England.   August 24, 1905.

If ever a letter was an *answer*—a *response*—to another—your letter which I received yesterday was to mine, and I thank you for it with all my heart. Hard as it was to make up my mind to leave Princeton, it was almost harder to feel that perhaps somehow you would not understand, and I was willing to be misunderstood if necessary—but *not* by *you*.

Instead you have read *not* what I wrote but what I *thought* when I wrote what I did write—and you have taken me so *fully* at my word, that it seems as though we had talked it all over. That is all I can say now. As for your words of appreciation of me and my work, I hope I may grow to be far more worthy of them than I am now, but that makes them only the more of an inspiration to carry me forward into the new life whatever it is to be.

Mrs. Carter joins me in warmest regards to Mrs. Wilson and yourself   Faithfully yours   Jesse Benedict Carter.

ALS (WP, DLC).

From Raleigh Colston Gildersleeve, with Enclosure

Dear President Wilson: N. Y.   Aug. 24th, 1905.

Enclosed you will please find copy of a letter in regard to the Council Chamber which I am sending to Mr. Pyne, and which I think explains itself.

I am sending you under separate cover the plans for McCosh Hall and the Council Chamber which you left with me, and in addition prints of the revised elevations of the turrets which show the changes you wished to see. I trust they express your wishes.

I have looked into the question of seats used in Columbia University, and find they give very good satisfaction and they are much less bulky than those in use in Princeton. I have also taken up the question of the arrangement of the seats and see no possible way of arranging them with the aisles between them in the large rooms with raised floors where the seats are arranged in curved lines. The number of seatings would be also very much reduced. The representative of the Furniture Co. which manufactures these chairs tells me that they are never arranged with individual aisles in the large rooms or in rooms with raised floors where the seats are arranged in curves, and the reason why this is so is very apparent when the seats are indicated on the plans.

Very sincerely yours,   Raleigh C Gildersleeve

TLS (WP, DLC).

From Raleigh Colston Gildersleeve

Dear President Wilson: N. Y.   August 23rd, 1905.

I am sorry to say that I have struck a snag in connection with the Council Chamber at Princeton. You may remember that Mr. Matthews gave me the estimate which I submitted to you for the preliminary work, including a new roof over the building, carrying out cases, etc., and doing the entire wood work for $15,595. There were certain changes made after this estimate was received, notably taking out the canopy at the back of the room and putting in a raised dais with a long desk. These increased Matthews' estimate $635. which will bring the total up to $16,230. Thinking that this was settled I sent him on Aug. 10th all the working drawings for the job. After waiting a week he writes me that the cabinet maker has backed out of the figure that he gave him and is unwilling to do the work for the amount of his first estimate. Matthews therefore asked for $4,500. more for the work. I have obtained from the Hiss Company, who are excellent cabinet makers and are doing the work on the Cottage Club for McKim, Mead & White, an estimate of $14,600 as against Matthews' estimate for the same work of $17,100. I have obtained figures on the rest of the work for finishing the room and the complete amounts are as follows,—

The Hiss Co., Interior Work	14600.	
Rough work	2995.	
Heating	1775.	
Cutting	110.	Total $22,904.
Electric wiring	510.	
Electric fan for ventilating	249.	
Strengthening roof trusses	380.	
Gas piping	48.	
Floor repaired	110.	
Architect	2127.	

The difference between Matthews' estimate on the interior wood work and the ornamental plaster work, etc., including the dais, and the estimate of the Hiss Co. of $14,600. will be, I think, money well spent; because I am convinced that cabinet makers of the standing of the Hiss Co. will undoubtedly give the university far better value than Matthews could, especially if he has to shop around to get the work done cheaper, and we also save a profit of about $1500. which Matthews has added for his services.

The item "Strengthening roof trusses" I took upon myself the responsibility of adding, as, when the roof was removed and I could make a thorough examination of them, I was not at all satisfied that they should be left without being reinforced. They are of a very old type, and while I do not anticipate there being any serious difficulty with them now I should not have been willing to incur the responsibility of putting the weight of the chandeliers on them without taking this precaution.

The item of heating includes a very complete system of heating and ventilation of the room, and changing the air in the room every 15 minutes if the fan is put in, and every 30 minutes if the fan is not put in.

The figures herewith submitted include all the finish of the room with the exception of the chandeliers and standards, designs for which are being prepared.

I beg to inquire whether I shall accept these figures on behalf of the University and order the work.

Regretting very much the delay for which I cannot feel myself responsible, believe me,

Sincerely yours,   Raleigh C Gildersleeve

TLS (WP, DLC).

From Moses Taylor Pyne

My dear Woodrow   North East Harbor [Me.] Aug 25/05

Please read enclosed.[1] I suppose we had better follow the advice in the letter as we save a good deal over Matthew's bid. I am sorry his man went back on his estimate.

To save time, if you agree, will you kindly communicate directly with Gildersleeve & oblg

Yours very truly   M Taylor Pyne

ALS (WP, DLC).

[1] R. C. Gildersleeve to M. T. Pyne, Aug. 23, 1905, TLS (WP, DLC), the text of which is identical with that of R. C. Gildersleeve to WW, Aug. 23, 1905.

From Melancthon Williams Jacobus

My dear President Wilson: London.   29 August 1905

It has occurred to me that it would be well for you to have in your possession before the opening of the Seminary year a copy of the terms and conditions which Mrs. Jacobus[1] and I suggest as those which shall govern the Fellowship she has given to the University

These conditions are copied from those presented to and accepted by the Seminary Board of Trustees at Hartford in connection with a similar Fellowship established there by Mrs. Jacobus this last Spring.

They indicate her general desire as to the establishment and maintaining of the Fellowship and she would be glad if they could be carried out. At the same time she recognizes that the two situations are somewhat different and her request is that her suggestions be gone over by yourself and Dean West for such betterment as you might think advisable in the case.

She feels that it will be quite possible to meet all the requirements of the different situations and still preserve the general principles she has laid down—viz: (1) a separate fund (2) a general excellence of scholarship rather than a definite competitive examination, as the basis of award (3) an appropriation of unused income in the direction of further Fellowships.[2]

We sail for home on the 12 Sept so that you may address me in reply at Hartford

Hoping that the summer has been most beneficial to you in a real rest and recuperation

I am   Yours faithfully   M. W. Jacobus

ALS (WP, DLC).

¹ Clara Cooley Jacobus.
² For a description of this fellowship, see C. W. McAlpin to WW, Nov. 8, 1905, n. 2.

To Benjamin Wistar Morris III

My dear Mr. Morris,   Lyme, Connecticut, 30 August, 1905.
I return herewith two copies of the agreement with Mr. Wiehle concerning the models, with my signature.
I am expecting to return to Princeton next week, and will then take up the matter of the pumps for final settlement.
With much regard,
Faithfully Yours,   Woodrow Wilson

WWTLS (WC, NjP).

From Raleigh Colston Gildersleeve

Dear President Wilson: N. Y.   September 1st, 1905.
Enclosed you will please find two copies of the contract with The Hiss Company for the Interior Finish of the Council Chamber, Nassau Hall, which I beg that you will sign and retain one copy, returning me the other. I also enclose notice of contract awarded to Worrell, Shinn & Co. for Heating, Ventilating and Gas piping.   Faithfully yours,   Raleigh C Gildersleeve

TLS (WP, DLC).

To Charles Howard McIlwain

Princeton, N. J.
My dear Professor McIlwain: 15 September, 1905.
I write to ask that you will be kind enough to come to "Prospect" on Monday evening next, the 18th of September, to attend an informal conference which I wish to hold on that evening.¹
Sincerely yours,   Woodrow Wilson

TLS (WC, NjP).
¹ For a discussion of the preceptorial system.

Notes for a Talk to the Preceptors

[c. Sept. 18, 1905]
Preceptors
1. *Make-up of examination*
An examination on a *Subject*—or (a) in the lectures (b) in the reading?

2. Choice, methods, and object of reading. Definition of the field. Preceptors *not* assistants to professors.

    "   " coaches.

The preceptors *have charge* of their men. Independence in reading.

WWhw MS (WWP, UA, NjP).

From Richard Ludwig Enno Littmann

Dear Mr. President: Rome   Sept. 19, 1905.

At the beginning of the new College year, the second year of my absence from Princeton, I wish to tell you about my whereabouts and my plans for the coming winter.

My friends [Howard Crosby] Butler and [William Kelly] Prentice will undoubtedly have reported to you personally what our work has been in Syria, and soon you will have a printed preliminary report about our expedition.[1] The epigraphical results have gone far beyond any expectation. The most important fact is that from the new Safaïtic (more than 1000) and Nabataean (more than 100) inscriptions a great deal of the language, the history, the religion and civilization of the ancient Northern Arabs in the time from Christ to Mohammed can be reconstrued.

When I came home from Syria, I spent about two months with my family, quite busy, among other things working up a short history of Ethiopic literature. From the 10th to the 15th of August I had the great pleasure to be with Dean Fine's family at Grindelwald. From that time I have been in Italy preparing for Abyssinia. I shall leave Naples about the 10th of October and arrive in Massaua about the 20th. My main object is to gather philological material concerning the two main languages of Abyssinia, viz. the Tigray and the Tigré. I should like to write grammar and dictionary of both. The "Tigré language," which is of great importance for Comparative Semitic Philology, has no grammar or dictionary so far, and it is very appropriate that Princeton should help to explore it. But besides this I hope to be able to make some excavations at two or three ruins of ancient Abyssinia and to find some inscriptions contributing to the knowledge of its history and civilization. My address from October until the beginning of May will be Asmara, Colonia Eritrea (Italian East-Africa). If I am not there the post office will forward my mail.

I was very glad to hear that the reorganization of our University has made such splendid progress under your auspices.

Asking to be kindly remembered to Mrs. Wilson, Miss Axson and Stockton Axson, I remain

very faithfully yours   Enno Littmann.

ALS (WP, DLC).

[1] H. C. Butler and E. Littmann, "Preliminary Report of the Princeton University Expedition to Syria," *American Journal of Archaeology*, 2nd Series, IX (1905), 389-410. There is a pamphlet reprint of this article in the Princeton University Library.

Two Letters to Daniel Moreau Barringer

My dear Moreau: Princeton, N. J.   Sept 20, 1905.

I will be very glad indeed to look over the sketch[1] as you request, and if you will send it to me, I will do what I can with it and forward it at once to Mr. Van Noppen.[2] I need not tell you that I am delighted to do anything I can for you.

In greatest haste,

Affectionately yours,   Woodrow Wilson

[1] It was a biographical sketch of Barringer, undoubtedly written by himself.
[2] Charles Leonard Van Noppen, publisher of Greensboro, N. C.

My dear Moreau: Princeton, N. J.   21 Sept, 1905.

The sketch reached me yesterday and I have taken real pleasure in signing it. It goes forward to Mr. Van Noppen to-day. Unhappily, I have not had time to do more than touch its sentences here and there, but you may be sure that it has given me real gratification to do you even this slight service.[1]

Affectionately yours,   Woodrow Wilson

TLS (D. M. Barringer Papers, NjP).

[1] It appeared in Samuel A'Court Ashe (ed.), *Biographical History of North Carolina from Colonial Times to the Present* (8 vols., Greensboro, N. C., 1905-17), I, 145-47.

A News Item

[Sept. 22, 1905]

FORMAL EXERCISES

In Connection with the Opening of the University,
Held Yesterday Afternoon.

The exercises in connection with the formal opening of the University were held in Marquand Chapel at three o'clock yesterday afternoon. The Trustees and members of the Faculty, in academic costume, formed at the Library and entered the Chapel in a procession. President Wilson presided and after the opening prayer and the reading of a passage from the nineteenth Psalm, addressed the faculty and students on the occasion of the beginning of the one hundred and fifty-ninth college year. He said that one of the features of the opening of the college is the hope and enthusiasm which is instilled into the hearts of both the faculty and students. A special feature of the opening this year, he said, is the large number of men who are members of the faculty for the first time. The President extended a most cordial welcome to these men and said that they would find that the spirit of comradeship is just as firm in the faculty as in the undergraduate body. They could therefore well look forward to a pleasant year's work.

In welcoming the Freshman Class, he said that Princeton enjoyed a distinct spirit of her own to which every entering man should devote himself. The influences of life at Princeton should make the members of the University broadminded men, both mentally and spiritually.[1]

The exercises were concluded with a benediction by the Reverend Dr. Henry.[2]

Printed in the *Daily Princetonian*, Sept. 22, 1905.
[1] There is a brief WWhw outline of this talk dated Sept. 21, 1905, in WP, DLC.
[2] Rev. Dr. Alexander Henry, Jr., of Philadelphia, Princeton 1870, Secretary of the Presbyterian Board of Publication and Sabbath School Work.

A News Report

[Sept. 25, 1905]

FRESHMAN RECEPTION.

Class of 1909 Entertained by Philadelphian
Society Saturday Evening.

The annual reception to the Freshman Class was held in Murray-Dodge Hall on Saturday evening. . . .

President Wilson was the last speaker of the evening. He said that the teaching body of the University had the greatest interest in the men, for it prepared them for the long struggle to come. The last twenty-five years have brought such a change to our country, as it has spread and broadened, that each man has a greater responsibility placed upon him as a citizen. The men must prepare to uphold this responsibility here in college. They must learn not for the sake of learning but to be able to think afterwards. Every one should work to the utmost to go out into life as fit as possible for the struggle and prepared to uphold the honor of Princeton before the world.

Printed in the *Daily Princetonian*, Sept. 25, 1905.

A News Report of a Religious Talk

[Sept. 29, 1905]

PHILADELPHIAN SOCIETY.

First Weekly Meeting, Addressed by President Wilson.
Subject, "University Spirit."

The first mid-week meeting of the Philadelphian Society was held in Murray Hall last evening. President Wilson was the speaker, and took as his subject "University Spirit." He said in part that many wrongly think there is a difference between the spirit of intellect and that of knowledge. This view is very narrow; the spirit is not really divided; the soul is an undivided thing. A perfect university spirit untouched by religion, cannot be conceived.

Fortunately, he said, the cloistered idea of religion is no more. Religion is not only for the sound, but also for the sinful—we must not be selfish in our religion. The real university spirit is freedom of mind and of spirit. The more one sees of life, the more perfect and stimulating does he conceive Christianity to be. Christianity breeds wisdom, which is acquired not by being born with a good brain, but by exposing the brain to the influence of the world. Books can be successfully approached only by their friends, otherwise they are dry or uninteresting.

The old saying, "A gentleman and a scholar," is a very good one. A real gentleman is a thoroughly cultivated citizen of the world. Some men look distastefully on knowledge. No man is intellectual who does not at some time of the day talk of some substantial intellectual subject. A real university man should be at ease in every class of society, both the highest and the lowest. In conclusion the speaker made an appeal for an added touch of intellectuality, which he believed would make the union of Princeton men the greatest and most lasting in the country, both in the minds of men and in that of our Creator.[1]

Printed in the *Daily Princetonian*, Sept. 29, 1905.
[1] For this address, Wilson used a brief WWT outline, dated Nov. 6, 1902, in WP, DLC.

From Anson Phelps Stokes, Jr.[1]

[New Haven, Conn.]

My dear President Wilson,   October 2, 1905.

I should be very glad if you could give me confidentially your judgment with reference to Rev. Mr. Vernam,[2] pastor of the College Church at Dartmouth. I am told that he has preached acceptably at Princeton, and if you have a high opinion of his usefulness as a college preacher, I should be very glad to extend him an invitation to come to Yale.

I remember how you told me once of the difficulties that you had in getting the right kind of preachers to interest the Princeton students. Possibly the list which I enclose herewith, taken from the Bulletin of last Saturday, will be of interest to you. All of the preachers given who are coming for two Sundays have been at Yale several times before and are most successful, while only a few of the others represent new names.

With kindest regards, I am

Faithfully yours,   Anson Phelps Stokes, Jr.

TLS (Stokes Letter Books, Archives, CtY).
    ¹ Secretary of Yale University.
    ² Ambrose White Vernon, Princeton 1891, pastor of the Church of Christ and Professor of Biblical Literature at Dartmouth College.

To Anson Phelps Stokes, Jr.

My dear Mr. Stokes: Princeton, N. J.   3 October, 1905.

I am very glad to reply to your letter of October 2nd. Mr. Vernon is, we think, one of the most interesting of the younger preachers who come to us. He is thoughtful without being radical and his sermons have a delightful mixture of excellence of form and freshness of matter. I think it would be thoroughly worth your while to hear him.

Allow me to thank you for your kindness in sending me the list of your preachers for the year. It will be a very useful sort of suggestion.

Cordially and sincerely yours,   Woodrow Wilson

TLS (A. P. Stokes, Jr., Papers, Archives, CtY).

A News Report

[Oct. 7, 1905]

THE NEW FACULTY ROOM.

Work in This Department Well Started.
To be Called the "Council Chamber."

The remodeling of the south wing of Old North to form a new Faculty room called the "Council Chamber," is well advanced. The small room in the University Offices building¹ that has been used for the Faculty meetings has been entirely outgrown and for a long time the need has been felt for a larger and more convenient place of meeting. Raleigh C. Gildersleeve of New York City, is the architect for the new room. The builder's contract requires that it be finished before December 1. The designers expect it to be the finest Council Chamber in the country. The room is to be 76 feet long, 36 feet wide and 30 feet high.

The entrance, through the hallway in Old North, is to be remodeled to make it more imposing. Immediately inside the door are to be two columns supporting the pediment ornamented with the Princeton seal. The floor is to be of stone and at the south end of the room opposite the entrance is to be a raised dais for the President and the Secretaries.

The large windows on the sides are to be divided by columns into a large window and two narrow ones. A high wainscot will serve as a base for the columns and pilasters at the window groups.

The wood work throughout will be of English oak, so treated as to bring out the natural peculiarity and beauty of the wood. The color will be a soft, rich brown. This wood forms an excellent background for portraits, with which the walls are to be covered.

The plan is ultimately to make Old North an administration building by transferring all the University Offices to new quarters in it.

Printed in the *Daily Princetonian*, Oct. 7, 1905.
   [1] The building then known as the "University Offices" is situated west of Nassau Hall. Built in 1803, it is the third oldest building on the Princeton campus and is now called Stanhope Hall in honor of Samuel Stanhope Smith, seventh President of the College of New Jersey. In 1905, it contained, in addition to the old faculty room, the offices of the Treasurer, Registrar, and Curator of Grounds and Buildings.

To Cyrus Hall McCormick

My dear Cyrus: Princeton, N. J.   11 October, 1905.

If I have not written sooner to thank you for your very delightful letter from Paris,[1] you may be sure that it was not because I did not appreciate it. It brought me more cheer and gratification that [than] I could easily make you believe, and I certainly hope that you are coming on to the Trustee meeting next week and that we may then have an opportunity for a good talk.

Mrs. Wilson joins me in most cordial messages to you, and I am, as always—

          Affectionately yours,   Woodrow Wilson

TLS (WP, DLC).
   [1] It is missing.

From Charles Williston McAlpin

My dear Dr. Wilson: [Princeton, N. J.]   October 11, 1905.

In Mr. Dodge's resolution about the Ten Thousand Dollars given by an alumnus of Harvard, which was adopted by the Board at the June meeting, it was voted

> "That the Finance Committee be instructed to invest this sum as a special endowment of a Fellowship, the name and purpose of which shall be determined by the President of the University."

Will you be good enough to advise me at your earliest convenience of your decision in this matter in order that I may have the material for insertion in the catalogue?[1]

Very sincerely yours,   [C. W. McAlpin] Secretary.

CCL (McAlpin File, UA. NjP).
[1] The money was used to establish a University Fellowship in Chemistry. The Princeton catalogue for 1905-1906 said that it was "founded in 1905 by the generosity of one of the Fellows of Harvard University," and that its holder would receive the income on the investment of $10,000.

To Endicott Peabody[1]

My dear Dr. Peabody: Princeton, N. J.   13 October, 1905.

I am wondering if you will be generous enough to preach for us in our University Chapel on the morning of November 5th. It would give us the greatest gratification to have you here and to hear you and I sincerely hope that it will be possible for you to accept.

The honorarium—$50—suffices at any rate for travelling expenses and Mrs. Wilson and I hope, if you can come, you will be our guest while here.[2]

Cordially and sincerely yours,   Woodrow Wilson

TLS (E. Peabody Papers, MH).
[1] Headmaster of the Groton School, Groton, Mass.
[2] He preached in Marquand Chapel on Nov. 5, 1905.

To Charles William Kent

My dear Kent: Princeton, N. J.   14 October, 1905.

Mr. [Cleveland H.] Dodge and I are coming down together. We shall start on Wednesday[1] by the train which leaves New York at one oclock and shall reach Charlott[e]sville at 10:30 that night.

I am afraid that we shall both be obliged to leave at seven oclock on the evening of the 19th, in order to get back for imperative engagements the next day.

Thank you very much indeed for your letter about the programme. It seems to me very admirably conceived. Mr. Dodge and I are both looking forward to the visit with the keenest interest and pleasure.

> Cordially and sincerely yours,   Woodrow Wilson

TLS (Tucker-Harrison-Smith Coll., ViU).
  [1] Oct. 18, 1905.

Notes for an Address of Dedication[1]

10/14/95 [05][2]

Madison Hall, University of Va., 19 Oct., 1905.

Reasons for being present:
  1. Affection for the U. of Va.
  2. Life-long friendship with Dodge[.] (His work in such kind)
  3. Madison and Princeton
  4. Deep interest in what the building stands for.

The Religious and the Intellectual Life.
  An Association[3] like this stands at the springs of life.
    The field of "Life,"—its time? Its content?
  Whatever a man *does* constitutes his life,—*whenever he does it.*
    He does not live only during the hours when he has put work by.
    Study is life
    Writing is life,—*some* writing, notably poetry.
    Exploration is life, and all invention
    Industry, of whatever kind, is life.
    Business is life.
  The *field* of life
  The *motive* of life
    The object of Education
      Orientation
      Stimulation
  The law of life
  A university without religion.
  Religion, the *atmosphere*, the *motive* of life.
    Love of country? ⎫
    Love of fame?   ⎬ The *standard*? The *criterion*?
    Love of truth?   ⎭

The Object of Education, not (specific knowledge, not skill, but
   A. *Orientation*, with regard to
     (1) Knowledge
     (2) Life.
   B. *Stimulation*, the supplying of the moral and intellectual
     motives of action,—giving sight, and chart, of the goals
     of life.

Love, the law of life
Self-forgetting love the law of immortality and of noble fame.

A university without quick religious life a furnace without fire,—a pursuit without goal,—a measurement without standard.

WWhw MS (WP, DLC).
  [1] A news report of this affair is printed at Oct. 21, 1905.
  [2] Wilson's composition date.
  [3] The Y.M.C.A.

From Charles Augustus Young

Hanover N. H.
My dear President Wilson,   October, 19th '05

When I received my notice of a University Faculty Meeting for the 14th, and your invitation for tomorrow evening, I was puzzled at first; but on noticing that they were both addressed to me here, (not to Princeton, & then *forwarded*) I was greatly pleased, for I saw in them a token of remembrance and a recognition of me as still a member of your Faculty although emeritus. And I am glad to be so remembered and recognized.

We are having a delightful autumn here, and are very comfortably settled in our new old home. But I still look back to Princeton with regrets, and the wish that I could look in on you for a day or two.

Professor Lovett and the Alumni Weekly keep me pretty fairly well informed of the Princeton news, & I have heard now and then from others. I have been especially glad to hear how well Mrs. Wilson and you are looking, & how finely the preceptorship plan seems to be working out.

My daughter[1] joins me in sending kindest regards to you both.

With all best wishes for your health and success, and regrets that I cannot meet the "members of the Board of Trustees" at your house tomorrow evening, I remain
        Yours sincerely   C. A. Young

ALS (WP, DLC).
  [1] Clara Adelaide Young Hitchcock, widow of Hiram Augustus Hitchcock, a former Associate Professor of Civil Engineering at Dartmouth College.

A News Report of a Dedication Ceremony
at the University of Virginia

[Oct. 21, 1905]

MADISON HALL DEDICATED.

Speeches by Dr. Alderman, Dr. Woodrow Wilson
of Princeton, Mr. Dodge and others.
A large and enthusiastic attendence.

Perhaps no greater feast could come to the young men of the
University of Virginia than that offered last Thursday at the dedication exerciees [exercises] of Madison Hall. Probably five hundred students were present to do honor to the givers of the splendid new home of the Young Men's Christian Association, and
indeed the home, if they choose to use it, of every man in the
University.

The exercises were opened by prayer by Dr. Hume[1] of the
University of North Carolina.

Following this Mr. Cleveland H. Dodge, in the name of his
mother,[2] presented the building to the University. . . .

In accepting the gift in the name of the various factors in
University life Dr. Alderman said:

"I have the honor to accept with gratitude and pride, Mr.
Dodge, the gift of Madison Hall, which you have tendered so
heartily and graciously and which shall bear testimony always
to the generous wisdom of Mrs. William Earl Dodge and Miss
Grace Dodge,[3] and yourself."

He then went on in a way peculiarly his own, to voice the
thanks of the men to Mr. Dodge, and through him to the other
doners [donors] of the Hall.

Dr. Woodrow Wilson, President of Princeton University, was
next introduced, and his speech brought forth the greatest enthusiasm from the student body.

Dr. Wilson speaks with fluency and much force and magnetism. He is a graduate of the University and one of whom
we are proud. The appreciation of the men was well expressed
in the long continued applause which his speech elicited.

We cannot publish Dr. Wilson's speech for lack of space but
in his opening words Dr. Wilson struck a note of friendship that
it is well and fit to include in this article. He said:

Mr. McIlhany,[4] Mr. President and Gentlemen:
It is with very many emotions that I find myself in this place.
As I dwell with a very great affection upon the familiar features
of this old place, I realize by the movement in my spirit that I

am also a son of the University of Virginia, and I rejoice to believe that as Mr. Dodge has said, there are many connections, not merely of inter-collegiate courtesy, but of personal affection, between Princeton and the University.

I was struck before leaving home at the number of personal messages with which I was charged to bear to individuals in this place, both connected with the University and surrounding the University, as if there were a number of persons at Princeton who looked at this as the site of many of their friendships. Certainly my own feeling, as I come back, is stirred in many directions.

I remember friendships, still I am happy to say, persisting, which began in this place, which have been among the most cheering and heartening influences of my life. I remember ambitions which took definite shape here, which I have tried to work out in the years intervening. There is a certain geographical peculiarity about this place and its environments. It is less obvious now than when I was here as a student. In those days there were fewer roads and fewer paths. We almost always went from one point to another along the invariable route of travel, and the consequence is that these paths now seem thronged with ghosts; images of things that happened long ago, the echoes of conversations held long ago and forgotten until the imagery of the eye brought them back by the association of places, and it is difficult for a man to travel those old lines that were so familiar to our feet without being taken back to a very happy period of youth, and beginnings where often lie the springs of life

Then, there was another sort of affection which led me to come on this occasion. Mr. Dodge and I have been almost life-long friends. We have been friends ever since boys together in college, and I need not tell you that the men who know him intimately love him very much. You know a man when you see him! (Loud applause) And I want to say to you that what he could not in his modesty have said; that this gift is not single and unique for the Dodge family, though they have long thought of it and long cherished the hope to make it. They have made similar gifts to Mr. Dodge's Alma Mater, Princeton, and to Columbia. Buildings of this kind in which they have put into enduring shape their interest in the service of God among the men who are getting intellectual preparation for life.

Mr. Dodge belongs to that small and choice group of men who know what the real privileges of wealth are, and who exemplify to the country the uses which men should make of their principal in the use of their property.

Then, there is that direct tie between this place and Princeton which is represented in the character and person of James Madison for whom this building is named. But it were the work of supererogation to say anything of Madison in Virginia.

The benediction was pronounced by Dr. John Wm. Jones of Richmond,[5] formerly a chaplain of the University.

Printed in the University of Virginia *College Topics*, xvii (Oct. 21, 1905), 1, 4.
   [1] Thomas Hume, Professor of English Literature at the University of North Carolina.
   [2] Sarah Hoadley (Mrs. William Earl) Dodge.
   [3] Cleveland Dodge's sister.
   [4] The Rev. Hugh Milton McIlhany, Jr., Ph.D., General Secretary of the Y.M.C.A. at the University of Virginia.
   [5] The Rev. Dr. John William Jones, retired Baptist minister, historian of the South, and biographer of Robert E. Lee.

An Appeal

[Oct. 21, 1905]

One of the useful purposes served by the John Miller House,[1] 16 Witherspoon street, is the opportunity that it affords for maintaining a free reading room for men. Two of its large rooms are set aside for this purpose. They are furnished and heated and lighted and provided with a considerable range of periodical literature. Under the personal supervision of Mr. Samuel Smith[2] they are open every evening throughout the winter and spring from 6.30 until 9.30. The need for such provision in Princeton is very great this year, and it is highly desirable that the rooms be opened not later than the first of November. Thus far they have been maintained by comparatively few residents whose annual subscriptions have ranged from twenty-five cents to twenty-five dollars. This year it is hoped that by making a general appeal to all of the residents of Princeton a sum will be raised large enough not merely to maintain the work but greatly to increase its usefulness. Subscriptions in any amount may be sent to Mrs. E. F. Perrine,[3] care of the Hon. Grover Cleveland, Bayard Lane, or to Mr. O. H. Hubbard,[4] or left in passing at Mr. Hubbard's office, 38 Nassau street.

Signed,   Bayard Stockton,
Margaret Miller,
O. H. Hubbard,
Woodrow Wilson,
Walter A. Wyckoff,
Trustees.

Printed in the *Princeton Press*, Oct. 21, 1905.

¹ Named in memory of the Rev. John Miller, long-time minister in Princeton. Margaret Miller, mentioned below, was his daughter. The Editors have been unable to find any information about the founding of the John Miller House.
² Probably Samuel Smith, blacksmith, of 219 Nassau St.
³ Emma Harmon Folsom Perrine, mother-in-law of Grover Cleveland, who lived with the Clevelands in Princeton.
⁴ Oliver H. Hubbard, in the real estate business in Princeton.

The Curriculum Committee to the Board of Trustees of Princeton University

[Princeton, N. J., c. Oct. 21, 1905]

Although this is not a meeting of the Board when the Committee on Curriculum is expected to present one of its principal reports, there are certain recommendations which we feel should be laid before you for action.

1. Foremost among these is the recommendation that the following two persons be appointed as Preceptors in Mathematics with the rank of Assistant Professors.

> JOHN W. YOUNG—of the North Western University—for 3 years at salary of $1500—the salary already having been approved by the Finance Committee.
>
> OSWALD VEBLEN—of Chicago University—for three years at a salary of $1500—the salary having already been approved by the Finance Committee.

This recommendation is made with all the more heartiness because of the evidence which is already forthcoming of the admirable working of the system—evidence which we have doubtless fully expected, but which will be none the less welcome. . . .

2. The Committee further recommend the appointment of

> 1. JAMES HOPWOOD JEANS, A.M. Lecturer at the University of Cambridge, as Professor of Applied Mathematics.
> 2. HOWARD CROSBY BUTLER, Instructor in Art and Archaeology as Professor of Art and Archaeology.
> 3. WILLIAM FOSTER, JR. Instructor in Chemistry, as Assistant Professor of Chemistry.

3. The Committee recommend the Board's approval of the appointment of the following Instructors:

> 1. ALFRED E. RICHARDS of Lehigh University. ⎫
> 2. CHARLES R[E]. MATHEWS   ⎬ In Modern
>   of Johns Hopkins University.   ⎪ Languages
> 3. CHARLES E. LYON of Williams College.   ⎭
>
> 4. C. R. MACINNES   ⎫
> 5. A. L. UNDERHILL ⎬ In Mathematics
> 6. E. B. MORROW   ⎭

7. R. S. DUGAN In Astronomy
8. WILLIAM J. SINCLAIR in Geology
9. R. E. TRONE ⎱
10. C. J. DAVISSON ⎰ In Physics
11. H. W. MARCH ⎰
12. JOSEPH RUDD GREENWOOD Instructor in Civil
    Engineering. . . .

5. The following communication from Professor William Alfred Packard was laid before the Committee through the President:

PRINCETON UNIVERSITY New Jersey

"My dear President Wilson: Oct. 11, 1905.

I hereby present, through you, to the Board of Trustees of the University, my request that I be retired at their next meeting, Oct. 21st. from further service in my Professorship.

I make this request in view of the long term of my service (since 1870), of my age, and of some conditions of health, all which considerations make me feel such retirement to be due to the just claims of the University and needful to myself.

I beg to add the assurance of my most grateful appreciation of the privilege I have had of so long and happy service in association with the Trustees and with the Faculty of the College and University, and also that of witnessing the steady expansion of the Institution in all its interests during successive administrations never more full of life and promise than now. I am, ever, for the Board of Trustees, and for yourself,

Most respectfully and faithfully,

(Signed) WILLIAM A. PACKARD."

The Committee, with a deep sense of regret at the necessity compelling the resignation, recommend that it be accepted, and that Professor Packard be retained on the Faculty as *Professor Emeritus of Latin* at a salary of $1500—and that he be allowed the free occupancy of his house,[1] so long as it be not needed by the University.

6. The Committee recommend approval of the President's action in accepting from the Estate of the late Philo Sherman Bennett of New Haven, the sum of $400 for the founding of the PHILO SHERMAN BENNETT PRIZE IN POLITICAL SCIENCE.

Melancthon W. Jacobus, Chair'm
D. R. Frazer.
Geo B Stewart
John J McCook
John De Witt[2]

TRS (Trustees' Papers, UA, NjP).
1 On College Place.
2 This report was approved by the trustees on Oct. 21, 1905.

Henry Burchard Fine to the Board of Trustees' Committee on Morals and Discipline

Gentlemen: PRINCETON UNIVERSITY, OCTOBER 21, 1905.

I beg to submit the following report:

The number of students dropped last June for deficiencies in scholarship was 57, namely, 6 Juniors, 16 Sophomores, 22 Freshmen and 13 Special Students. Of the regular students in this list only 7 were candidates for the A.B. degree.

Of the 75 men dropped last February, 41 have re-entered college this Fall, or about two-thirds of those who were at liberty to return.

It is already evident that the newly instituted preceptorial system is greatly increasing the industry of our undergraduates and their interest in their work. It is to be expected therefore that hereafter a much smaller number of students will be dropped because of failure in their studies.

The total number of new students enrolled this year and now present in Princeton is 427 as against 443 last year. They are distributed among the classes as in the following table in which I have given the corresponding figures of last year:

	1905	1904
Freshman A.B.	188	148
B.S. & Litt.B.	109	136
C.E.	92	75
Total	389	359
Special students	19	61
Seniors Acad.	3	6
" S.S.	1	4
Juniors Acad.	1	1
" S.S.	4	2
Sophomores Acad.	6	9
" S.S.	4	1
Grand total	427	443

It will be observed that the number of new Freshmen is 30 greater than last year, but that there has been a slight falling off in the number of students added to the upper classes, and a marked decrease in the number of new special students. The reason that the enrolment of new specials is so small is that this year, for the first time, we have refused to admit to special courses candidates whose sole reason for wishing such a course was that they had not sufficient preparation to secure admission as regular students. That the quality of the preparation of the Freshmen is unusually good is indicated by the fact that 29% of the members of the class were admitted without conditions and 30% with but one condition each.

About 40% of the Freshmen are Presbyterians and nearly 30% Episcopalians. There are 25 Methodists, 21 Congregationalists, 16 Roman Catholics, 12 Lutherans, 9 Baptists, 8 Unitarians, 5 Dutch Reformed, 5 German Reformed, 3 Jews, 1 Universalist, 1 Christian Scientist, 1 Schwenckfelder, and 17 seem to have no church affiliations. Approximately one-half of the Freshmen are communicants of the churches with which they are connected.

The average age of the Freshmen class at entrance is eighteen years and ten months.

At a special meeting of the Faculty on October 15th. the following resolutions as to chapel attendance were adopted on the recommendation of the Dean and the Committee on Attendance:

1 That hereafter on weekdays a single chapel service be held from 8:55 to 9:05 A.M.
That the first class-room exercise begin at 8 A.M. instead of 8:05 and end at 8:50.
That the second class-room exercise begin at 9:10.
This reduces each of the first two class-room periods to fifty minutes but leaves them free from conflict with the chapel service.

2 That the system of marking chapel attendance be changed— That the students be not assigned seats as heretofore, but that they write their names on cards provided for the purpose and on leaving the chapel hand these cards to persons designated to receive them.

3 That every undergraduate student be required to be present twice each week at morning prayers in the chapel unless excused by the President or the Committee on Attendance. If a student at any time falls short of this requirement by four absences, he must during the next two weeks attend four times in addition to the four times provided for. Failure to comply with this rule will render him liable to suspension.

4 That every undergraduate student be required to attend the stated services in the chapel on Sunday unless excused

by the President or the Committee on Attendance. If a
student not thus excused shall in any quarter absent himself more than three times he will become liable to discipline.

It should be said first of all that these resolutions, coupled with
the provision agreed to by the Faculty that hereafter the Committee on Attendance is to accept no excuses for absence from
morning chapel, will secure a much better attendance at the
chapel services than we were able to obtain last year and a more
general and regular attendance than for many years past.

For under the regulations until now in force a student has
been free to absent himself as often as twice a week without
penalty and to distribute his absences at will through the quarter
or half-term. And since this allowance of absences has not been
large enough to warrant the Committee on Attendance in refus-
ing to accept any excuse, and it is not possible to distinguish between excuses which are really genuine and those which are only
apparently so, many absences have been incurred, with and without good reason, in excess of the gratuity.

What made the situation last year so particularly bad was that
it did not prove possible, as was expected when the new schedule
of hours was adopted, so to arrange the schedule of every student
that he was free to attend one or other of the chapel services
every week day. As a matter of fact, great numbers of the students were thus free but three days a week and others but two
days. The new plan meets this difficulty by providing an interval
for the chapel service between the first and second class-room
periods.

It is possible by the penalty of suspension to enforce a more
frequent attendance at morning chapel than our students have
grown accustomed to and than will be secured by the proposed
plan, but under existing conditions such a course seems to the
Faculty unreasonable, and, therefore, unwise. Experience has
taught us that no requirement will operate fairly if excuses for
absence are to be accepted. And if account be taken of the accidental causes which may prevent attendance, of the constantly
increasing demands made on a student's time by his studies,
laboratory or field work, of preceptorial appointments which on
certain days may find him at a distance from the chapel near the
time of service, it will be realized that for a majority of the students at least, a requirement of attendance regularly twice a
week can be no more easily met nowadays than the requirement
of attendance four times a week used to be when nearly every

student had a class-room exercise immediately after the chapel service.   Respectfully submitted,   H. B. Fine

TRS (Trustees' Papers, UA, NjP).

Alexander Thomas Ormond *et al.* to the Board of Trustees of Princeton University

PRINCETON, N. J. [c. Oct. 21, 1905]

TO THE HONOURABLE THE BOARD OF TRUSTEES OF PRINCETON UNIVERSITY

We, the undersigned, members of a joint committee of The American Whig and Cliosophic Societies respectfully present for your consideration the following:

It is well known that the membership of the two societies has declined to such a point that it is impossible for the members of the Societies to meet the ordinary running expenses, when economically administered.

Furthermore, the formation of the Freshman Union,[1] though it may ultimately lead to greater interest in hall work, will for the present still further diminish the membership and decrease the income.

We recall the important function which the Literary Societies perform in furnishing instruction and practice in practical literary work, and the fact that no extended opportunities are given for similar work in the University curriculum. We consider the Literary Societies an important part of the educational apparatus of the University and believe that their loss from the university life would be disastrous.

We, therefore, respectfully petition your honourable body to recognize the position of the Literary Societies in our scheme of education by assisting them in their financial difficulties. The most effective way in which this can be done is for the university to assume the cost of heating and lighting the halls. If you do this there is every prospect that the Literary Societies will be able to retain the place which is theirs by long tradition in our intellectual life.

We remain,

Yours very respectfully,   A. T. Ormond
Clayton W. Greene[2]
W. F. Magie
Geo. B. Stewart jr.[3]

TLS (Trustees' Papers, UA, NjP).

[1] The plan for a Freshman Debating Union was described by the *Daily Princetonian*, March 30, 1905. Any freshman might join the proposed organization, and work in the Union was to be the basis for election to Whig and Clio for the upperclass years. A news report in *Daily Princetonian*, Sept. 25, 1904, indicated that the Union was to begin operations in the very near future. However, an editorial in the issue of October 26, 1905, revealed that the plan had been dropped: "After considerable discussion the plan for a Freshman debate union has been rejected by the Halls as impracticable under present circumstances. The two literary Societies will therefore elect members in the usual way."

[2] Clayton Wellington Greene '06.

[3] George Black Stewart, Jr. '06.

From the Minutes of the Board of Trustees of Princeton University

[Oct. 21, 1905]

The Trustees of Princeton University met in stated session in the Trustees' Room in the Chancellor Green Library, Princeton, New Jersey, at eleven o'clock on Saturday morning October 21, 1905. . . .

COMMITTEE TO CONSIDER AND REPORT ON COMMUNICATION FROM HALLS

On motion duly seconded it was

RESOLVED that a committee of three be appointed by the chair to consider and report on the matter of the financial condition of Whig and Clio Halls.

In accordance with this resolution the President of the University appointed a committee consisting of Trustees Pyne, Dodge, and Garrett.[1]

[1] This committee was enlarged in December 1905. Its final report is printed at March 7, 1906.

To Cleveland Hoadley Dodge

My dear Cleve: Princeton, N. J.   24 October, 1905.

I am sorry to say that Robert Garrett told me after the Luncheon last Saturday that his brother did not care to bind himself to make an annual payment to the fund of the Committee of Fifty. He will, however, complete the payments he promised under the old emergency fund.

On the other hand, Mr. John Garrett offers to subscribe $100,000 to the endowment side of the Committee's fund, contingent upon the completion of the endowment of the Preceptorial system. In other words, he will subscribe $100,000 provided the two and a half millions necessary to endow that system, is raised entire[,] his subscription being included.

Robert Garrett seemed deeply disappointed that his brother had taken this position, but of course it is in a way very liberal and may assist us in the big task of getting the complete endowment.

Always,

Cordially and faithfully yours,   Woodrow Wilson

TLS (WC, NjP).

From William Alfred Packard

My dear President Wilson: [Princeton, N. J.]   Oct. 25, 1905.

Your note, informing me of the action of the Trustees last Saturday in response to my request for retirement, is just received.

I hasten to acknowledge most gratefully their very kind and generous provisions made for my title, and pension, and continued residence in my house here. I cannot duly express how much I value the added assurances, from them and you, of personal esteem and of appreciation of my services in the University, so far beyond my conscious deserving. I am most deeply touched by it all, and by the cordial and gracious expression of it from your hand.

Believe me, ever,

Very faithfully yours,   Wm. A. Packard.

ALS (WP, DLC).

A News Item

[Oct. 27, 1905]

HALL MASS MEETING.

Large Meeting of Freshmen Addressed
by Representatives of Two Halls.[1]

A mass meeting of the interests of the Halls was held last evening in Murray Hall. President Wilson presided, and in his opening remarks said:

"Inspiration received in Halls has had a great deal to do with the past history of the College. The records show that the Halls have trained men for speaking and have been a medium for men going into public life."

Dean West in behalf of Clio Hall then spoke. . . .

President Wilson closed the meeting with a few forcible remarks upon what had already been said.

Printed in the *Daily Princetonian*, Oct. 27, 1905.
¹ The American Whig and Cliosophic Societies.

Notes for a Speech to an Undergraduate Club

27 Oct., '05¹

*Princeton Municipal Club.*²   27 October, 1905.

The College Man in Municipal Politics.
Need of university men *as affairs thicken.*
The men of the Revolution (Hamilton, Madison, Washington) Mr. Roosevelt as Englishmen regard him.
Study of Politics in the universities now different from the former abstract discussions. *Mr. Jerome's* erroneous assumption.³
Go in as things are.
(1) for the sake of knowing,
(2) of helping in the detailed processes,
(3) of keeping the public informed.
As things ought to be?
Why bosses?
Because politics is now a business.
Politics is a business only because of the multiplicity of elective offices.
REFORM=*Publicity*
Simplification, the exposition of which and the agitation for which would form an inestimable service, and just the service for which university men are fitted.

WWT MS (WP, DLC).
¹ Wilson's composition date.
² The meeting of this newly organized undergraduate club scheduled for October 27, 1905, was postponed for unknown reasons to November 3, 1905, when Professor Harry A. Garfield spoke. Wilson did not address the club during the academic year 1905-1906.
³ "Mr. Jerome" was undoubtedly William Travers Jerome, the colorful District Attorney for New York County from 1901 to 1909. The Editors have been unable to find any specific statement among his frequent speeches and statements to the press that fits the context of Wilson's remark.

From the Minutes of the Session of the Second Presbyterian Church of Princeton, New Jersey

Oct. 27 [1905]

The Session met at noon in Dr. DeWitt's study¹ and was constituted with prayer. Present, the Moderator, Rev. Dr. DeWitt, Elders Fisher, Freund, Wilson, Van Dyke.

The minutes of Oct. 9 were read and approved. It was resolved that a meeting of the congregation be held in the lecture room of the Church on Monday, Nov. 6, at 7.30 P.M., for the consideration of a communication from the First Church with reference to a union of the two churches,[2] and for any other business that may arise.

Also, that Rev. McLanahan of Lawrenceville[3] be asked to moderate the Congregational meeting.

The Moderator pronounced the Benediction, and the Session adjourned.   H. N. Van Dyke, Clerk

[Dr. DeWitt thought that he himself ought not to be moderator of the Cong. meeting, as he was a resident of Princeton and a member of the First Church.

As Mr. McLanahan was ill, Dr. Studdiford[4] acted as Moderator][5]

[1] The Rev. Dr. John De Witt, Princeton 1861, Archibald Alexander Professor of Church History at Princeton Theological Seminary, who was serving as the Stated Supply of the Second Presbyterian Church.

[2] Both the First and the Second Presbyterian Church were without regular pastors at this time, and the congregation of the former, at a meeting on October 24, 1905, had voted that "this congregation considers union with the Second Church desirable." A special committee headed by John Grier Hibben was named to communicate the resolution to the Second Presbyterian Church. See Arthur S. Link (ed.), *The First Presbyterian Church of Princeton: Two Centuries of History* (Princeton, N. J., 1967), p. 85.

[3] The Rev. Samuel McLanahan, Princeton 1873, pastor of the Lawrenceville Presbyterian Church.

[4] The Rev. Dr. Samuel Miller Studdiford, pastor emeritus of the Third Presbyterian Church of Trenton.

[5] This entry, including the brackets, was written in the margin some time later by Van Dyke.

Notes for an Address[1]

SCHOOLMASTERS OF QUEENS.   28 October, 1905.

THE UNIVERSITY AND THE SCHOOLS.

The University for only *some* of the pupils of the schools.

The old school vs. the new

The ideal vs. the useful.

The University to teach a broader, more deliberate *utility*.

WE MUST DISCRIMINATE

Technical vs. *university* training.

Relation of the University to the technical school.

The modern industrial and commercial world.

The engineer also by necessity a statesman.

To the University belongs the deeper training of

The point of view.

The temper of mind
Aptitude for affairs
Citizenship of the world.
University studies:

Pure science ⎱
Philosophy ⎰ The human spirit and its relations
Literature ⎰ to the world in which it lives.

The University an assessor for the schools, an assessor *of values,* and of *intellectual processes.*

WWT MS (WP, DLC).
[1] No report of this address appeared in any New York newspaper.

An Appeal

[Oct. 28, 1905]

THE JOHN MILLER HOUSE.

In preparing the Free Reading Rooms in the John Miller House, 16 Witherspoon Street, for an early opening, those in charge will be glad to receive donations of equipment as well as of money. Among the articles which can be turned there to ready uses are framed pictures, comfortable chairs, rugs, bound volumes of illustrated periodicals and the like. The House is open every Friday afternoon from three o'clock until five, and gifts for the Reading Rooms will be gratefully received.

Mrs. E. F. Perrine, Sec'y.

Bayard Stockton,
Margaret Miller,
O. H. Hubbard,
Woodrow Wilson,
Walter A. Wyckoff,
        Trustees.

Printed in the *Princeton Press,* Oct. 28, 1905.

Remarks in New York at the Opening Exercises of the Institute of Musical Art[1]

[[Oct. 31, 1905]]

Mr. President,[2] and Ladies and Gentlemen:

When I first received the invitation to appear on the same platform with a distinguished musician,[3] I hesitated, but the purposes of this Institution seemed to me so noble and inspiring that I could not resist the temptation.

I have long been a lover of music, but I must admit that to some extent I feel like Boswell. Boswell, you know, told Doctor Johnson that music had so powerful an effect upon him that when he heard it, it either greatly depressed him or wrought him up mentally to a great degree. "Then why do you listen to it?" replied Doctor Johnson. "If it made such a fool of me, I should not hear it."

And yet there is a certain fine self-indulgence in appreciating to the full what is best in music. It is truly a fine nature indeed to which all that there is in good music is completely intelligible.

As I understand Mr. Damrosch, he wants not so much to teach a man expression as to give him something to express. I never heard sounder views on education. I have often thought that the difficulty with the American people is that they are too little touched by the nice art of what we call expression. We are not patient enough. We are not severe enough in our taste. We are in so great a hurry to do something that we leave all the nice detail uncompleted. We do not even commence the last finishing touches. We are not even solicitous enough toward having our fine instruments in absolutely perfect condition and tone.

Still, the need to have a first-rank composition to play is just as important as the temper of your instrument. If we are devoting a great deal of time to the power of expression, what are we devoting time to express? What have we to express as a nation?

I have often thought that the difficulty with the everyday talk of the present period, the conversation of the great numbers of people, and the talk of the press, is that they are able to say anything but have nothing to say. I sometimes believe that the trouble is not with the man's equipment but with the man himself, when he says nothing worth while. The American people have perhaps so far nothing to express except taste and appreciation. If we are to judge by our history so far, we have not yet any national word to say in the form of music. For America is not yet ready to express itself. It is not sure of itself. It lacks centralization. But we are learning. Not only are we learning music, but also the form of expression. And some day, when the spirit is perfected within us, we will accomplish great things.

Just as a lad in college is sometimes brought under the supervision of rhetoric teachers before he has anything to say, so this nation ought to be taught expression before it has anything to say. And then when the national impulse comes, it will not lack expression.

Composite America is being merged together. She is as yet only in a process of formulation.

It is not from my blood—the Scotch-Irish—that American music is now springing. That blood is good to fight with but not to play the violin with. It is not from her own blood that America is getting her musicians, but from the German blood, from the Scandinavian blood, from the Polish blood, from the Hungarian blood. From those nationalities which are being combined in this country, she is now separately getting her musical inspirations, and when these are once merged into the single impulse, then there will be American musicians and American music.

Our present music writes memories. It does not direct events; it does not show aspirations and purposes. It calls out of the past. Those phrases of music that are in our ears are the result of old impulses. We shall exchange single impulses for national ones when our composite stage is past. Some day will come an outlet for the true American spirit, after it has, as a result of fusion, really arrived.

America is now speechless with the things she intends to do. In New York City and elsewhere in the United States the springs of sentiment are covered up—covered up by concrete. If you will but unseal these springs, you will see the real sentiment beneath. Unseal them![4]

Printed in Frank Damrosch, *Institute of Musical Art, 1905-1926* (New York, 1936), pp. 59-62.

[1] The Institute of Musical Art was founded by Frank Heino Damrosch by means of a gift of $500,000 by James Loeb, a retired New York banker and philanthropist. Rudolph Edward Schirmer, Princeton 1880, was closely associated with Damrosch in the founding of the school and was a member of the original board of trustees. Cornelius C. Cuyler was president of the board until his death in 1909. The Institute merged with the Juilliard Graduate School in 1926, becoming the undergraduate division of the combined Juilliard School of Music. For further details on the early years of the Institute and a complete record of the opening exercises, see Frank Damrosch, *Institute of Musical Art, 1905-1926* (New York, 1936).

[2] Cornelius C. Cuyler.

[3] Frank H. Damrosch, Director of the Institute of Musical Art.

[4] There is a brief WWhw outline of these remarks dated Oct. 31, 1905, in WP, DLC.

A News Report

[Nov. 1, 1905]

OPEN INSTITUTE OF MUSICAL ART

Mr. C. C. Cuyler, the President, Assisted by
Dr. Damrosch and Other Prominent Men.

Before a large and fashionable audience the formal opening exercises of the Institute of Musical Art were held yesterday afternoon in the gothic hall of the old Lenox mansion, at Twelfth street and Fifth avenue, where this institution, founded by the late James Loeb,[1] has been comfortably housed.

The Institute's president, Mr. C. C. Cuyler, presided at the exercises, which included addresses by Dr. Frank Damrosch, director of the school, Dr. Woodrow Wilson, president of Princeton University, and Professor Felix Adler.[2]. . .

Dr. Wilson, referring to Mr. Damrosch's explanation of the school and its objects, said, in part: "I never heard sounder views of education. We Americans are not yet sure of ourselves.

"We have not yet a national word to say in music or anything else. In the meantime by such means as this school which Mr. Damrosch is inaugurating we are to be taught one mean of expression. When our national impulse comes, then will come the expression. The present America is speechless with the mighty things it means to do."

Professor Adler spoke along the same lines, although he took issue with Dr. Wilson's point that America had not yet anything national to say. He believed that this institute's highest service to American art was to be in its keeping in this country young men and women at their most receptive and creative time of life.

He also anticipated the time when the institute should become a centre for the spreading of general culture, not merely musical education.

Printed in the *New York Herald*, Nov. 1, 1905; one editorial heading omitted.
    [1] Actually, he did not die until 1933.
    [2] Founder of the Society for Ethical Culture and Professor of Political and Social Ethics at Columbia University.

A News Report About the Plans for McCosh Hall

[Nov. 4, 1905]

The picture of McCosh Hall on the opposite page shows the view of Princeton's new recitation building from the corner of Washington Road and McCosh Walk, and gives a good idea of the architecture of this handsome addition to the University's material equipment. . . .

The interior arrangement of McCosh Hall provides for a large lecture room to accommodate six hundred, another one seating four hundred, and two smaller lecture rooms with seating capacity for two hundred and fifty and one hundred and fifty; there will be fourteen recitation rooms, four to seat seventy-five each, four to seat sixty-five each, and six to seat fifty each; and twenty-six rooms for preceptorial conferences, making forty-four rooms all told. There are to be nine separate entrances, in six of which stairs will lead to the second floor, an arrangement specially designed to allow the maximum ease of ingress and egress and the minimum of confusion and noise. The total length of the building will be about four hundred feet on McCosh Walk, with an L on Washington Road of one hundred feet, the L to contain the large lecture room, on the second floor. The walls are to be of gray Indiana limestone, and the building is designed to be thoroughly fireproof. The excavating for McCosh Hall, which was started recently by the contractor, Mr. William R. Matthews of Princeton, is now well under way, and it is expected that contracts for work on the rest of the building will be awarded soon, so that the material may be prepared in time for the opening of the building season in the spring, and the work effectively pushed during the summer.

Printed in the *Princeton Alumni Weekly*, vi (Nov. 4, 1905), 83-84.

A News Report About Plans for a Faculty Room in Nassau Hall

[Nov. 4, 1905]

In the south wing of Old North, where the ancient mastodon has held sway over the ossified birds and beasts of the secondary, tertiary, quarternary, etc., ages, and the gigantic reptiles have frightened juvenile visitors time out of mind, a "Senate Chamber" is under construction, the collections of the Museum of Geology and Archaeology having been moved to the south stack of the University Library, to make room for a larger hall for the meetings of the university faculty. This improvement has also been designed by Mr. Raleigh C. Gildersleeve. The plans provide for an imposing assembly room seventy-six feet in length, thirty-six feet wide, and thirty feet high. The large windows on the east and west sides of the wing are to be divided by free standing columns, and a rich cornice will be carried around the room, at a height of about twenty feet from the floor, the intervening walls to be panelled in English oak. A vaulted ceiling will be pierced by lunettes over each window. At the south end of the room there will be a raised dais for the President and other officers, and the entrance, through the hallway of Old North, is to be remodelled to make it more in harmony with the imposing faculty chamber. The money for these improvements comes from the Van Wickle fund,[1] which was left for the double purpose of building the Fitz-Randolph Gateway and providing the more adequate university offices which Princeton's growth demands. Ultimately, it is expected that Nassau Hall will become the central administration building of the University.

Printed in the *Princeton Alumni Weekly*, vi (Nov. 4, 1905), 84.
    [1] This was a bequest, received by the university in 1900, from Augustus Stout Van Wickle (1856-98), A.B., Brown University, 1876, coal operator and banker of Hazleton, Pa. In his will, Van Wickle left $25,000 to Princeton "for memorial entrance gates . . . in memory of his ancestor Nathaniel Fitz Randolph." In a codicil to his will, he gave an additional $20,000 "to be used for the same purpose, my idea being to combine an administration or registrar's building with the entrance gates." (See the entry for the meeting of March 8, 1900, in "Minutes of the Trustees of Princeton University, Dec. 1898-Mar. 1901," bound minute book, UA, NjP.) Van Wickle also left $45,000 to his alma mater, Brown University, which resulted in the construction of an administration building and a set of "Van Wickle Gates."

To John Grier Hibben

Dearest Jack,   Princeton, Monday evening 6 Nov [1905]
    I beg that you and Mrs. Hibben will forgive me for my boorish behaviour. When the black mood gets on me I seem to forget that I was bred a gentleman. I hope that you will both believe that I am one in *some* essential way. I cannot ask you to love me if I cannot give you reason to respect me.
    In great shame,
                    Your devoted friend,   Woodrow Wilson

ALS (photostat in WC, NjP).

From Theodore Roosevelt

My dear Mr. Wilson: [Washington]   November 6, 1905.
    Many thanks for your note of the 4th instant.[1] About how many people would you be willing to entertain? You see, I shall have several members of my own family, and also, I hope, the Secretaries of War and the Navy,[2] and perhaps a couple of Assistant Secretaries and their wives. Now Mrs. Wilson and you must not crowd your house. Mrs. Roosevelt and I will come, of course, and if you will tell us how many people you can accommodate we will bring them with us and any extra people can take lunch on the car. Would it not perhaps be more convenient for you if we all took lunch on the car and simply came up to visit you just before the game?[3] How far are the grounds from the train and from your house, and what time is the game called?
                    Sincerely yours,   Theodore Roosevelt

TLS (Letterpress Books, T. Roosevelt Papers, DLC).
    [1] It is missing.

2 William Howard Taft and Charles Joseph Bonaparte.
3 See T. Roosevelt to WW, Nov. 24, 1905, and the news report printed at Dec. 4, 1905.

Notes for a Speech to the Princeton Alumni Association of the Oranges[1]

8 Nov., 1905[2]

Princeton's Future.   Orange Alumni, 9 Nov., 1905.

Present methods implanting *the spirit of study,*—from which will be bred a combination of hard-headedness and intellectual definiteness with a spirit of idealism.

We are dealing with the spirits rather than with the fortunes of men, and yet inevitably with their fortunes, too,—for what they *are* that they will *do.*

We shall do everything possible by way of stimulation,—E.g. perfecting of the preceptorial method and the creation of the Graduate School. *But* stimulation wd. be of comparatively small service were disintegration to follow it. In order to enthusiasm there must be the community of constant, general, intimate contact. *Therefore*—

No more students than dormitory room.

The drawing together of numbers, as they come, into geographical units.[3]

The surrounding of the central core of undergraduates, thus taught and thus united, with as various an apparatus of experiment and original study as possible,—the obvious connections of the University with the world of progress

For the undergraduates themselves definite, determinate bodies of knowledge; around them the curious and attractive tracts of exploration and discovery.

WWhw MS (WP, DLC).
1 A news report of this affair is printed at Nov. 10, 1905.
2 Wilson's composition date.
3 As the news report of this address also reveals, this is the first intimation in the documentary record that Wilson was beginning to conceive of what would later be called the quadrangle plan—the grouping of undergraduates into residential colleges based in part upon the undergraduate eating clubs. Wilson first formally proposed the quadrangle plan in the Supplementary Report to the Board of Trustees printed at Dec. 13, 1906.

From Charles Williston McAlpin

[Princeton, N. J.]

My dear President Wilson: November 8, 1905.

I beg to acknowledge receipt of your letter of the 7th inst.[1] enclosing the statement of "THE PORTER OGDEN JACOBUS FEL-

LOWSHIP," which I am inserting with the other University Fellowships in the new catalogue.[2]

I am,   Sincerely yours,   [C. W. McAlpin]

CCL (McAlpin File, UA, NjP).
  [1] It is missing.
  [2] The statement read as follows: "THE PORTER OGDEN JACOBUS FELLOWSHIP
Established in 1905 by the generosity of Mrs. Clara Cooley Jacobus. This Fellowship will be conferred upon that regularly enrolled student of the graduate school
who, in the judgment of the University Faculty, shall have evinced the highest
scholarly excellence in his graduate work during the year. The appointee to this
fellowship receives the income from an endowment of $25,000 and is expected
to devote himself exclusively to study under the direction of the Faculty." *Catalogue of Princeton University . . . 1905-1906* (Princeton, N. J., 1905), pp. 227-28.

A News Report of an Alumni Dinner in
East Orange, New Jersey

[Nov. 10, 1905]

Princeton's sons, to the number of ninety-nine, with a liberal
sprinkling of Yale, Harvard, Brown and Amherst grads and some
unattached people, sat down in Berkeley Hall, East Orange, last
night at the second annual dinner of the Princeton Alumni
Association of the Oranges. It was a typical Princeton gathering,
with plenty of orange colored flags, banners of orange and black,
chrysanthemums of the yellow hue and an immense tiger, which
proudly marched around the room, and then executed a two-step.

President Woodrow Wilson, Dean Andrew F. West, Senator-
elect Everett Colby[1] and Albert C. Wall[2] were the speakers of
the occasion, following Robert E. Annin, president of the association, who, as usual, had introductory remarks which teemed
with satire. His introduction of Dean West was particularly
felicitous, embracing a poem in which some of the dean's characteristics were shown up. Then there was a letter from Grover
Cleveland, which was received with much enthusiasm. Altogether
the dinner was one of the most successful college affairs ever
given in the Oranges. . . .

A cordial greeting was given Mr. Colby when he rose to speak
to the toast, "The Duty of To-day." He said:

"We need in public life to-day more reformers who know their
business. We have a number of amateurs who, with the very best
intentions in the world, fail to make good and accomplish results simply because they don't understand the game. The re-

  [1] Wealthy Newark lawyer and Republican member of the House of Assembly,
who had just been elected to the New Jersey Senate. During his three years in
the lower house, Colby had gradually assumed leadership of the reform element
in his party, soon to be called the "New Idea" group.
  [2] Albert Chandler Wall, Princeton 1886, lawyer of Jersey City.

former, as a rule, fails to appreciate that in politics, as in any other walk of life, the man who wants to do good work must know all about the materials which he handles. And he works with men. The banker knows the value of securities, the artist the composition of his colors, the sculptor the character and substance of his marble; so the political reformer must have accurate knowledge of men, and the conditions that go to make up political life.

"A good illustration of the ignorance that prevails on the part of a great many intelligent voters and reformers is found in the fight which is now being conducted in so many States against what is known as the 'boss.' Why has this great fight come upon us so suddenly? Why has it not been done before? Why have we allowed ourselves to be imposed upon for years, sitting quietly by while the bosses, through their alliance with the corporations, sold us out and capitalized our inertia? The answer is this: The reformers who captained our side in previous fights didn't know the rules of the game, and we were disqualified in the first round. For instance, take the impression that prevailed about a 'machine' or a 'boss' before Folk, of Missouri, cleared up the mystery.[3] We imagined the headquarters of a 'boss' to look something like the office of the criminal Moriatti[4] in 'Sherlock Holmes.' We pictured a wonderful human mechanism, the ramifying parts of which reached out into every ward and district of a great city, and were controlled and governed in some mysterious way by the giant intellect of the 'boss.' We saw in our imaginations shadowy figures enter by secret doors, in a back alley, hold a whispered conversation with the great man, and then disappear to start in motion as though by magic every wheel of the wonderful machine.

"That was our impression of a 'boss,' all powerful, invulnerable, impregnable, phantom qualities, all[,] but qualities, nevertheless, that the reformers failed to analyze and understand. Then Folk came along and pricked the bubble, and it was discovered that the all-powerful 'boss' was but a creature of our imaginations,

[3] Joseph Wingate Folk as a circuit attorney in St. Louis had rebelled against the political machine which had made possible his appointment and had gone on to make a national reputation as a battler against graft, bribery, and misgovernment in the city. One of Folk's targets was the local Democratic boss, Ed Butler, whom Folk had had arrested and convicted for bribery. Folk's election to the governorship of Missouri in November 1904 and his continuing success in exposing corruption seemed to prove, in illustration of Colby's remark, that an aroused electorate could reduce the most entrenched political machine and its leaders to impotence.

[4] He was of course referring to Sherlock Holmes's great antagonist, Professor James Moriarty.

and, like the Lybian giant Antaeus, lifted from the dough bag and the ballot-box, his power oozes away, his mysterious machine topples like a house built of cards, and he stands before us revealed as he is—nothing but a man, but a real man for all that, whatever his political morals and convictions may be.

"Now the boss and all his breed must go, but if he is to go the reformers who put him out have got to give the people something better. It won't do in politics any more than in religion to tear down without giving something better in its place, and the boss system met in no small measure a real and legitimate demand for a human element to stand between the law-makers and the people. The boss was the man originally whom the people looked [to] for help; he understood the needs of the poor and the conditions under which they lived; they could see him, they could touch him, they could go to him and they knew he would do for them. It was nothing more or less than human sympathy that formerly gave the boss his hold, and when he let go of that and cashed it in for power or influence, he fell. It is this sympathy and confidence that the reformer must give to the people if he hopes to be of any service. Now they are mistrusted, because the people at large see a little mean streak in some reformers and a lack of true sympathy.

"The people now feel as if reformers were trying to reform them just for the sake of reforming them, and not because it's going to make their lives brighter and happier. They look upon a reformer as a man who is more pleased to get a man in jail than to do a kind act; and I know such men myself, and they say that if reformers among themselves can't show a better sporting spirit than they do they don't want to be reformed, and I don't blame them. In other words, we need a deeper knowledge of humanity and less self-satisfaction with our own righteousness. We need more reformers; but by reformers I mean men who understand, who feel, who see, who know; broad men, generous men, open-minded and open-hearted men and men with a will to do. That is the great need, and it is 'the duty of today' to prepare ourselves for the future work of giving a lift and a helping hand to those less fortunate than ourselves."

President Wilson spoke on the future needs and aims of the institution of which he is the head and devoted considerable time to a narration of what should be done for the undergraduates. Speaking of them, he said:

"We are trying to stimulate these youngsters to the willing daily use of their faculties. The continual use of them makes them serviceable for use. They will in time get what constitutes intellectual power, that hardheadedness, definiteness, precision and easy co-ordination in the things they are doing.

"Education simply means that a man makes simple and easy use of the faculties about him. The great trouble with colleges is that the undergraduates have not been taught to work. They did not learn the daily pressure and compulsion of duty that is imperative in the shop, office or laboratory. The undergraduate must learn to use himself. One of the things we have tried to do, but which has been futile so far, is the attempt to teach men how to govern their fortunes. A man cannot do that until he learns to command himself."

Dr. Wilson referred to the recent victory of Everett Colby and the point it emphasized and, continuing, said:

"Mr. Colby will not be more useful to his individual constituents than many a Tammany politician is to his individual constituent for whom he does favors. There is a wide gulf of difference between the two, though, and the latter wins the true love of his constituency and illustrates that private welfare is somewhat involved in public welfare."

Dr. Wilson declared that the problem Princeton had to face now was the mere increase in numbers. He said that with the new methods of instruction there was certain to be an increase in the college roll, and the only way it could be regulated was to be more punctillious in the entrance examinations. The real difficulty at Princeton, as at other places that have grown too fast, he declared, was to keep the solidarity and retain the whole as an individual community. He said a big dormitory should be provided where all the undergraduates might be housed and when the limit of accommodation was reached to check the influx.

The speaker suggested a plan whereby the existing class clubs might be made the nuclei of small educational communities which could be allowed to gradually grow until in the course of time they might become institutions of learning known the world over. This, he said, he believed was worth thinking over.

Printed in the *Newark Evening News*, Nov. 10, 1905; editorial headings omitted.

A News Item

[Nov. 11, 1905]

The congregation of the Second Presbyterian Church at a meeting on Monday evening,[1] discussed the advisability of merg-

ing the two Presbyterian Churches of Princeton.² The majority
of those present considered organic union of the churches undesirable at present.³

Printed in the *Princeton Press*, Nov. 11, 1905.
¹ November 6, 1905.
² According to a very strong Princeton oral tradition, Wilson was the leader
of the group in the Second Presbyterian Church supporting union with the First
Church.
³ The vote was forty-six to fifty-nine.

A News Report of an Address on Education in Providence

[Nov. 12, 1905]

PRESIDENT WILSON AT BARNARD CLUB.¹

At the fall meeting of the Barnard Club, held yesterday afternoon at the Trocadero, about 150 members and guests enjoyed
the good dinner served and listened to a most interesting address
delivered by President Woodrow Wilson, Ph.D., LL.D., of Princeton University, the guest of honor of the club.

President Wilson discussed the topic, "The University and the
School," the subject of liberal education being brought before the
meeting in a sense that made it particularly interesting to those
assembled. He brought out many points that have been under
discussion by leading educators, compared old standards with
the new and went into some detail regarding the immense material tasks and undertakings of the modern world. The mechanic
was compared with the intellectual capitalist and the relation
was considered in an original manner.

At 12:30 o'clock a reception was held in the Trocadero parlors,
President Charles S. Chapin² of the Barnard Club presenting the
club members to President Wilson. Dinner was served at 1 o'clock
and at 2:30 p.m. the formal meeting of the club was held.

President Chapin presided at the meeting and introduced President Wilson, who was received with applause. In part the speaker
said there is a very slight connection between the university and

¹ The Barnard Club of Providence was a group of educators and citizens interested in educational improvement. One of its activities was the establishment
and support of the Barnard Club Library, a section of the Providence Public
Library designed to serve the needs of Rhode Island teachers and school administrators. The club was named after the nineteenth century educational reformer, Henry Barnard, who served as the first United States Commissioner of
Education from 1867 to 1870. Although Barnard was most active in Connecticut,
he did serve as the Rhode Island Governor's "agent" for school reform from
1843 to 1849. In this capacity, he was one of the founders of the Rhode Island
Institute of Instruction in 1845.
² Charles Sumner Chapin, Principal of the Rhode Island State Normal School.

the school for the reason that it is the minority of school graduates who turn their faces toward the university or college. To
solve the university and school question the basis of their utilities
must be considered. Education is training the mind to enable it
to grasp any topic. In the case of the technical schools some years
ago the process of mining, mechanical engineering, etc., could
be taught, he said, because the number of processes was limited
then, "but now you would restrict the student in all his after life
by so confining him to the practical. It is the principle that must
be taught, and no teacher is needed at his elbow to familiarize
the student with the processes.

"I don't find that mathematics come into very great practical
use in my line, although it is called a practical science," he continued. "The modern world is a complex world. Some of its
complexity can be seen in some of the things recently uncovered,
notably the insurance investigation.[3] We are witnessing all
around us the divorcement of the private life and the business
life of the citizen.

"Years ago these men may have invested their own money in
undertakings, believing them to be sound, and after finding that
the risk was passed they felt they could vote to invest the company funds in the same investment. But such action makes the
property increase in value and the directors can then sell out.
They will have used the funds of the society to enhance the value
of the property. They then could use the funds of the society
to start a company, and after such a company is successful they
can sell out and receive profits which belong to the company.
As directors of a big corporation they are investing trust funds
in something which they have for sale.

"They are in the midst of transactions in which the world has
had no experience except in the present generation. They have
not translated their old moral principles into the new practices.
The world must translate its old moral principles into new practices in order to meet new conditions. We must find our relations
with the rest of the world and the process of education is the
training of the mind to find itself in such relation. We need
the power of perception of values. You teachers must deal with the
spirits of men in order that they may adjust those spirits to
the part of the world in which they live.

"It's perfectly possible to make the intellectual mechanic a
mechanical working mind. I contrast the mechanic with the in-

[3] Wilson referred to the investigation of seventeen insurance companies then
under way by a committee of the New York legislature, whose chief counsel was
Charles Evans Hughes. For a fuller discussion of this matter, see WW et al. to
J. J. McCook and C. B. Alexander, Dec. 29, 1905, n. 1.

tellectual capitalist, who is the person whose mind is adjustable to the present circumstance. Do you realize there is one adjective never applied to mankind for success alone? I mean the word 'Noble.' Unless his character is beyond selfishness and reproach he is not given that title.

"What are you to teach? I have a duty to teach the classics. The suitable subject matter of education is made up of those subjects which are completed and certain. You will find the classics definitative, containing the complete record of the world to their time. Why do you put the concrete of language training over these most interesting historical reviews? What boy knows that Caesar's Commentaries should be placed alongside Grant's Memoirs? But you can't get the boy or world interested in anything that has no juice. As for mathematics, we do not teach the youngsters that for the pleasure it gives. As for the modern languages, they are an insufficient substitute for the classics because they contain just what our own speech contains, while the classics are entirely different. I think you ought to teach boys the Roman history which is not true as well as that which is true. It is impossible to teach the contents of modern literatures without including the erroneous history of the ancients.[4]

"You msut [must] get rid of the idea that education consists of information. Education is the process of limbering up the mental powers. No amount of information alone makes an educated man. Libraries are places where our information can be laid up where we can get at it easily, so we do not have to carry around a derrick to lift ourselves up every time we wish to impart information. The educated man knows where and how to get his information; the ignorant man does not.

"The men who have fertilized the world of knowledge are those who have leaped into the world of hypothesis, deserting the world of facts. Are we after the teaching of processes which are simply information? Did you ever realize the immorality of teaching a child psychology? It's absolutely immoral to try experiments on a child. Have we any right before we know what we are about to try experiments on children?

"The schools and universities have the task to debate and determine their utilities. We must determine intellectual, spiritual, utilities. Shall we brag of the educational system of the United States unless we are forming the stuff that shall rule with widest, broadest education? If the world is misled and misgoverned by the United States it is to us that the blame will be

[4] For a fuller exposition of this point of view, see Wilson's essay on the teaching of ancient history printed at Oct. 15, 1889, Vol. 6.

traceable. Shall we go along always near-sighted, seeing nothing but our hands? Shall we continue to make students who see in education only the means to a living? Shall we not rather see the spirit of the man and work for its development?"[5] . . .

President Wilson was a guest at the University Club last evening and after the party of about 125 members and guests had enjoyed a dinner he delivered an interesting address.

Printed in the *Providence Journal*, Nov. 12, 1905; some editorial headings omitted.
    [5] There is a brief WWhw outline of this address, dated Nov. 11, 1905, in WP, DLC.

Notes for a Talk[1]

Monday Night Club[2]   13 Nov., 1905
Princeton Ideals

The country now looks to Princeton.

This Club one of the mediating instrumentalities of our university life.

True and false standards of utility.
    The technical studies ⎫
    With foundations   ⎬ "Business" now in
    Without foundations ⎭ every sense *life*.

What Princeton stands for:
    Literature   ⎫
    History   ⎪
    Philosophy ⎬ as *Utilities*
    Science   ⎭

Practical Idealists.

WWhw MS (WP, DLC).
    [1] No Princeton newspaper or periodical reported this address.
    [2] Established by the Class of 1894, this organization, whose members consisted entirely of seniors, met weekly for discussion of philosophical, scientific, and literary subjects.

From Cornelius Cuyler Cuyler

My Dear Woodrow,   New York.   Nov 14/05
    Many thanks for your very charming letter of the 13th.[1] There are no congratulations I esteem more highly, or *as* highly I may say, as those from so dear and sincere a friend as yourself. I trust

you may have the pleasure of seeing Mrs Lord before long at my home. I know you are already acquainted with her.

I am prepared to deliver to the Trustees $5000. U. S. Steel Sinking Fund 5% Bonds the income of which can be used to aid some needy but good student each year. I want this little fund to bear the name of a warm friend of mine, and who was also a good one of yours, who died suddenly in August—Andrew White Green.[2] I await your suggestions but hope it may meet your views to have the fund bear his name.[3] As I told you when here he left no near relatives at all. With kindest regards

Sincerely Yours   C C Cuyler

ALS (WP, DLC).

[1] Wilson had just written to congratulate Cuyler upon his engagement to the widow, May, or Mary, Townsend Nicoll (Mrs. James Brown) Lord. They were married on March 3, 1906.

[2] A member of the Union Club and man about town, he had been employed in the naval office of the New York Custom House for the past forty years. He died suddenly in New York Hospital on August 2, 1905.

[3] The trustees accepted the gift, which was actually a legacy from Green to Cuyler, on December 14, 1905, and established the Andrew White Green Scholarship.

To Charles Freeman Williams McClure

Princeton, N. J.

My dear Professor McClure: 16 November, 1905.

I find myself somewhat at a loss to answer the inclosed letter.[1] Will you not be kind enough to do so, or if you prefer, to indicate to me the way in which it should be answered?

There is another matter about which I wish to speak to you, but have found it impossible to get to your laboratory at the proper time. Some of the men have found it impossible to get to Chapel because of some of their classes being held continuously from eight to ten during the first days of the week. I daresay that it was through inadvertence that this arrangement was made, because it was the distinct rule of the Faculty that there should be no classes between 8:50 and 9:12. Pardon me for calling your attention to this matter, but these little questions of detail are constantly coming to me.

Very sincerely,   Woodrow Wilson

TLS (McClure Zoological Autograph Coll., NjP).

[1] It is missing.

A News Report

[Nov. 17, 1905]

MEETING OF TRUSTEES OF CARNEGIE FOUNDATION.

The first meeting of the board of trustees of the Carnegie foundation was held on Tuesday at Mr. Carnegie's residence, 1093 Fifth Avenue, New York City. This fund of $10,000,000 was given by Mr. Carnegie last May for the pensioning of college professors who have become incapacitated. It produces a yearly income of $500,000 and is designed to relieve not only professors incapacitated by age, illness or accident, but also the families of deceased professors, in case of need.

The presidents of twenty-four universities, colleges and preparatory schools were present, all of the trustees named in the deed of gift being on hand, with the exception of President Harper, of the University of Chicago. Sessions were held both in the morning and in the afternoon, and the trustees were entertained at luncheon by Mr. Carnegie.

Henry S. Pritchett, president of the Massachusetts Institute of Technology, was elected chairman of the executive committee which is composed of the following men: President Woodrow Wilson '79, President [Nicholas Murray] Butler of Columbia, Provost [Charles Custis] Harrison of the University of Pennsylvania, President [Alexander Crombie] Humphreys of Stevens Institute, Mr. F. A. Vanderlip, vice-president of the National City Bank, and Robert A. Franks, Mr. Carnegie's financial secretary.

Numerous applications for pensions have already been received, but no action will be taken on them until the executive committee has completed its plans.

Printed in the *Daily Princetonian*, Nov. 17, 1905.

From Cornelius Cuyler Cuyler

My Dear Woodrow: New York. Nov 17/05

Many thanks for your kind favor of the 16th. You will know that I think of little else but Princeton outside of my family and business and some day I hope if my health is spared to be able to do something handsome for the University. It is a continual pleasure to me to meet you and to feel that a classmate of whom I think so highly is at the head of the Institution. I do not think you can understand how the alumni are rallying around you and this year I think should be a very fruitful one for the University.

Cleve [Dodge] is back and in fine shape. I expect to have a talk with him soon about finances. I am today writing Pyne as Chairman of the Finance Committee formally offering the $5000. to the University, of the A. W. Green fund.

Yours sincerely   C C Cuyler

ALS (WP, DLC).

A News Report of a Dedicatory Address
in Philadelphia

[Nov. 18, 1905]

N. E. MANUAL TRAINING SCHOOL IS DEDICATED

Woodrow Wilson's Address

The Northeast Manual Training School at Eighth street and Lehigh avenue, built at the cost of more than a quarter of a million dollars by the city, was dedicated yesterday. A number of prominent educators, including Dr. Woodrow Wilson, president of Princeton University, participated in the exercises.

Doctor Wilson pronounced the school one of the most useful in this country, and said that the type to which it belongs has a most important bearing on the nation's future. Mayor Weaver[1] was also one of the dedicating party and eulogized the school and its work.

Several hundred students, headed by a band and carrying the school colors—red and black—paraded from the new school building to Broad and Dauphin streets where, at 2:30 o'clock, they met Mayor Weaver and Doctor Wilson and many guests. These latter were in automobiles. Cheering vociferously, the schoolboys surrounded the autos and escorted them to the Training School. The main lecture room was decorated with class banners. Into this 800 relatives and friends of the schoolboys had filed p[r]eviously to the arrival of the students and the guests of honor. The school orchestra, under the leadership of Prof. A. Oswald Michner, struck up "Blaze Away," as Dr. Andrew J. Morrison, principal of the school, entered, followed by the dedicating party. These, with the alumni association, were accorded seats of honor on the stage, and the ceremonies began.

The Rev. Dr. Charles Wood[2] made the invocation. Dr. Walter Stewart Cornell,[3] president of the alumni association, introduced Thomas Shallcross,[4] who presided. In introducing Doctor Wilson as the first speaker Mr. Shallcross referred to him as the ablest educator in America, with one exception—Dr. Andrew J. Morrison, the principal.

"The object of a school of this sort is not to overemphasize any one feature of education," said Dr. Wilson. "America cannot attain supremacy without skilled hands as well as skilled minds. I rejoice to see manual training made part of the high school training and to see it recognized as a part of a liberal education. We depend upon liberal education. We do not want the narrowness of being able to do only one thing. That capability to do many things is the test of Americanism. Until 1890 the real test of Americanism was the fitness to live on the frontier. Benjamin Franklin was a glowing example of such a man.

"The distinctive note of Americanism is fitness for anything and also the most complex thing. The man who can play the boss of the gang in any work to be done is the man the country needs— the man who can take off his coat and do things himself.

"We must have an intellectual frontier. The real education is the education which apprises a man where he stands in the knowledge of his generation. A man in the desert says, 'I have lost myself.' He is mistaken. He has lost everything else but himself. Man is never lost. The object of knowledge is to know how you stand in the world, or, as the German says, to orient yourself.

"We must make for a student a sort of circle of knowledge, and when he goes around that circle he has boxed the compass. There is no reason for reading books except to discover the experience of another man. We wish to be made free of the world of men. The complete circle is being made in modern school methods. Educators are seeing that things material and immaterial are being treated. I like to see gymnasiums in schools. The gymnastics of the mind fit it for all that the world needs done. Beware of the man who has his mind in athletic shape.

"If you want your son educated well look for the school which has a complete circle of education, so that no part of his mind may become atrophied from disuse. I think with Doctor Holmes that many self-made men are 'remarkable considering who made them.'[5] As parents and voters I appeal to you not to allow yourselves to be deceived as to the word practical."

Printed in the Philadelphia *Public Ledger*, Nov. 18, 1905; some editorial headings omitted.

[1] John Weaver, Mayor of Philadelphia since 1903. An independent Republican, he was active in the reform of municipal franchises and other abuses.

[2] Pastor of the Second Presbyterian Church of Philadelphia.

[3] A physician, he was sometime Director of Medical Inspection of Public Schools in Philadelphia and lecturer in the college and medical school of the University of Pennsylvania.

4 A Philadelphia businessman.
5 See Oliver Wendell Holmes, *The Autocrat of the Breakfast Table*, Chapter 1.

Notes for an Address[1]

Inter-Church Conference on Federation[2]

Carnegie Hall, 19 Nov., '05

Mediation of Youth in Christian Progress.

Progress not a thing of *radical* change, but of progressive modification under the pressure of circumstance, purpose, and desire.

Youth conservative: does not originate its own convictions.

Youth progressive: does not measure or discriminate its convictions, but pushes them in the *mass*.

Its conviction not so apt to be of dogma as of motive and object.
Informed by doctrine, but not making doctrine its end.

Like the action of volunteer troops
Ignorant of danger
Impatient and negligent of discipline when in action
Sweeping over obstacles or ignoring them

Function of youth in Christian progress:
To push ideals rather than ideas.

Why Y.M.C.A. succeeds where missions fail,—
Because its desire, not to teach with definite dogmatic intent, but to lead, to help.

The key to all youthful effort,
Ardour, devotion, self-slaying love.
Devotion to what?
To Christ: *What would Christ have done in our day, in our place, with our opportunities?*
We can know only by the study of Christ at first hand,—"the Church's one foundation," the foundation of *all* the churches!

WWhw MS (WP, DLC).
1 News reports of this address follow.
2 The Inter-Church Conference on Federation met in Carnegie Hall in New York, November 15-21, 1905. The conference, sponsored by the National Federation of Churches, drafted the constitution of the Federal Council of the Churches of Christ in America, which was established in 1908 after ratification of the constitution by a number of major Protestant denominations. Among the speakers at the Inter-Church Conference on Federation were Jacob A. Riis, John Wanamaker, the Rev. Dr. Washington Gladden, and Associate Justice David J. Brewer. Wilson's address was part of a special program designed to encourage support for church youth programs.

Two News Reports of an Address in New York
on Youth and Christian Progress

[Nov. 20, 1905]

YOUNG MEN THE SAFEST,
SAYS WOODROW WILSON

President Woodrow Wilson of Princeton University spoke at a meeting in the interest of young people's religious organizations, held in connection with the Inter-Church Conference on Federation, in Carnegie Hall yesterday afternoon. The big auditorium was filled, and there was an overflow meeting in the Broadway Tabernacle, near by.

John R. Mott, Secretary of the International Committee, presided. Among those on the platform with him were Bishop Greer,[1] the Rev. Dr. William H. Roberts,[2] Robert E. Speer, Secretary of the Presbyterian Board of Foreign Missions, and Silas McBee, Editor of The Churchman.

In introducing President Wilson Mr. Mott told of progress in various bodies in young people's effort. The Young Men's Christian Association, he said, is a noticeable example of this cooperation.

"There is a mighty task before us," he [Wilson] said, "and it welds us together. It is to make the United States a mighty Christian Nation, and to christianize the world."

One statement that President Wilson made was taken by his hearers as an expression of opinion on the matter of the exclusion of the Unitarian delegates from the conference.[3]

"I know I speak on controversial ground here," he said, "but before I got to this platform I spoke for a few moments with several gentlemen of those faiths which teach salvation by character. I regard such an enterprise as one of despair. Just how you may feel about your character I do not know, but I know how I feel about my own. I would not care to offer it as a certificate of my salvation. If I started out to make character I would be a prig. I may say I do not care to make an odious creature of myself."

President Wilson's subject was "The Mediation of Youth in Christian Progress." "It is well to ask," he said, "if it is possible to intrust progress to young men. Generally young men are regarded as radicals. This is a popular misconception. The most conservative persons I ever met are college undergraduates.

"The radicals," he continued, "are the men past middle life. They have come to taste bitterly, and their ambitions are checked or cooled. These are the desperate radicals—the men who would clear the stage that they might begin anew. It is not the youngster of hope, but the man near the darkness of despair who is your man of destruction.

"It is your youngster who catches his conviction in a lump. We older fellows split hairs, and discriminate closely, and wear out our progressive vitality in doing so. Your youngster moves forward with a rash confidence that seems blind to us older men. He forges ahead and overcomes obstacles that seasoned men, knowing their bigness, would falter at.

"The pushing things in this world are ideals, not ideas. One ideal is worth twenty ideas in propulsive force. No naked idea is fit to become an ideal until we illuminate it, dress it up, and give it a halo that properly does not belong to it. We live by poetry, not by prose, and we live only as we see visions, and not as we have discriminating minds."

As a concrete example of illustration of his theories on dogma the speaker cited the work of the Young Men's Christian Association in Japan.

"There," he said, "success has been achieved not because a maximum of dogma has been taught, but because a minimum is taught. If, as some hold, greater success has been achieved there by this organization than by some of the missionary bodies, I think it is perhaps because of this.

"Here at home a minimum of faith can be made the faith of all the churches. It might seem a duty of the united Church to lead men in general rather than to communicate an individual dogma."

Printed in the *New York Times*, Nov. 20, 1905; some editorial headings omitted.

1 The Rt. Rev. David Hummell Greer, Bishop Coadjutor of the Diocese of New York, Protestant Episcopal Church. Upon the death of Bishop Henry Codman Potter in 1908, Greer became Bishop of the Diocese of New York.

2 Stated Clerk of the General Assembly of the Presbyterian Church in the U.S.A. He was one of the principal organizers of the Inter-Church Conference on Federation and served as its permanent chairman.

3 The exclusion of Unitarian delegates was a source of considerable debate prior to and during the conference. The executive committee decided to extend invitations to local church federations, as well as to the national headquarters of some denominations. No invitation was sent to the Unitarians, and when some arrived with church federation groups from New England, they were not admitted as delegates by the credentials committee. On November 20, the conference formally voted to admit into the proposed Federal Council of the Churches of Christ in America only evangelical denominations and those which affirmed the divinity of Jesus Christ. See the New York *Evening Post*, Nov. 20, 1905, and the *New York Tribune*, Nov. 21, 1905.

DR. WILSON HITS AT EXCLUDED FAITHS

Dr. Woodrow Wilson, president of Princeton University, was one of the speakers at a meeting in the interest of young men's and women's religious organizations, held in connection with the Inter-church Conference on Federation in Carnegie Hall yesterday afternoon. Long before the organ prelude began the big auditorium was filled. There was an overflow meeting in the Broadway Tabernacle near by.

John R. Mott, secretary of the International Committee, presided. Bishop Greer pronounced the benediction.

"There is a mighty task before us," Dr. Wilson said, "and it welds us together. It is to make the United States a mighty Christian nation, and to Christianize the world."

One statement he made was taken by his hearers to show a clear alignment of opinion on the matter of the exclusion of the Unitarian delegates from the Conference.

"I know I touch controversial ground here," he said, "but before I came to this platform I spoke for a few moments with several men of those faiths which teach salvation by character. I regard such an enterprise as one of despair. Just how you may feel about your character I do not know, but I would not care to offer my character as a certificate of my salvation. If I started out to make character I would be a prig. I may say I do not care to make an odious creature of myself.

"Character is a by product. If one sets out to make a by product by itself for itself he spoils the main product. If a man centres his powers in himself one of two things happens, he racks himself to pieces or else he stands still.

"A church that pads itself with doctrine and thus betakes itself out of direct contact with the Son of God is far less effective than a church that is in direct contact with Christ. Some men pad themselves about so well with doctrine that virtually they are in padded cells."

Printed in the *New York Herald*, Nov. 20, 1905; some editorial headings omitted.

To Minot Judson Savage[1]

My dear Sir: Princeton, N. J.   22 November, 1905.

In reply to your letter of November 21st I would say that the paragraph you have marked in the inclosed clipping[2] is quoted with substantial correctness, but, as usual, it is torn from its connections and therefore I fear bears a false intimation.

My point was that to devote one's self to the formation of one's own character is to fail of the very object; that the object of life is service, self-sacrificing, self-forgetting service, and that in this enterprise character is a by-product; that the main product would be injured if the by-product were too consciously regarded.

I need hardly say that those papers are utterly mistaken which have represented me as intending, even in the most indirect manner, to cast any slur upon the Unitarian faith. If I understand that faith correctly, its contention is substantially that which I have just now stated. I have never understood that it made character an object in itself.

Very sincerely yours,   Woodrow Wilson

TLS (WC, NjP).
1 Pastor of the Church of the Messiah (Unitarian) in New York. A Congregationalist during his early ministry, he became a Unitarian in 1873 and thereafter served churches in Chicago, Boston, and New York.
2 Both Dr. Savage's letter and the clipping are missing.

From Ernest Dressel North[1]

My dear President Wilson: New York   November 22: 1905

I want to tell you how much Mrs. North and I enjoyed your address on Sunday afternoon at Carnegie Hall

It was timely, original, and most suggestive, in fact it was as near model as such a speech could possibly be.

We particularly enjoyed your analysis of ideas & ideals and all you said about conservatism

I never heard you make a speech before and was highly delighted with your voice and manner[.] I hope the meeting will result in lasting good, and that all the men who participated in its deliberations will some day be as famous as the Signers. This note is meant to let you know that you had some keen listeners

With kind regards, I am

Yours very truly   Ernest Dressel North

ALS (WP, DLC).
1 A rare book and manuscript dealer in New York, who resided in Summit, N. J.

To Louis Wiley[1]

Princeton, N. J.

My dear Mr. Wiley: 23 November, 1905.

I very warmly appreciate your kind invitation to be your guest at the annual dinner of the Society of the Genesee, but I am sorry to say that I am already promised for the evening of January 27th.[2] Please accept my warm thanks and the expressions of my sincere regret.   Very truly yours,   Woodrow Wilson

TLS (L. Wiley Papers, NRU).
1 At this time working in the business management department of the *New*

York Times, he was promoted to business manager of that newspaper in 1906. He had earlier lived for nine years in Rochester, N. Y., hence his association with the Society of the Genesee.

2 He was to speak to the University Club of Brooklyn. See the news item printed at Jan. 28, 1906.

A News Report of a Religious Talk

[Nov. 23, 1905]

SEMINARY Y.M.C.A. ADDRESSED BY
PRESIDENT WILSON LAST EVENING.

President Woodrow Wilson '79, addressed the regular Wednesday evening prayer meeting of the [Princeton Theological] Seminary Y.M.C.A. in Stuart Hall last night. He took his text from 2 Timothy II, 3-4: "Thou therefore endure hardship, as a good soldier of Jesus Christ. No man that warreth entangleth himself with the affairs of this life." He spoke in general of the virtue of simplicity, in part as follows:

This is a passage in which good advice is given to those entering the ministry, but I am going to speak of a far simpler subject, that of simplicity itself. I see no virtue in simplicity for its own sake, but only as it is co-ordinate with things of greater complexity. There is a fine simplicity in the complex picture of a great artist. It is this simplicity of combination that I have come to commend to you this evening.

The ideal simplicity is that of the human frame, which comes from complete co-ordination. I have classified the clergymen whom I have met into two classes: those who wish to seem men of the world, and those who wish to hold aloof from the world. The ideal minister is that happy medium who concentrates his thoughts on what his profession is for, and who is in the ministry not for his own sake, but for the sake of others. A man may inveigh against a thing one day and the next day enter into it with zest, but it is he who stands up and speaks from the heart, who is the real factor in the progress of society. He who strips himself of every purpose save that of serving his Lord and Master is the true soldier of the Cross.

Printed in the *Daily Princetonian*, Nov. 23, 1905.

To Minot Judson Savage

My dear Sir:　　　　　　　　Princeton, N. J.　24 November 1905.

Allow me to thank you for your note of November 23rd and to say that you have my most hearty permission to quote my recent letter to you from your pulpit. The misconstruction of what I said at Carnegie Hall has distressed me very much and I could wish that every possible means were taken to correct it.

Sincerely yours,   Woodrow Wilson

TLS (WC, NjP).

From Theodore Roosevelt

[Washington]

My dear President Wilson: November 24, 1905.

I thank you for your very great courtesy. I now find that Miss Carow[1] will not be with us. The Secretary of War and Mrs. Taft have with them the wife of the Assistant Secretary of War[2] and Mrs. Oliver,[3] and three Ambassadors and their wives,[4] so that they will all lunch together on their car. This means that there will be three places less at your lunch. Do let me thank you again for your kindness. I am looking forward to seeing you.

Faithfully yours,   Theodore Roosevelt

TLS (Letterpress Books, T. Roosevelt Papers, DLC).
[1] Emily Carow, President Roosevelt's sister-in-law.
[2] Marion Rathbone (Mrs. Robert Shaw) Oliver.
[3] An unidentified member of the Oliver family.
[4] The three ambassadors and their wives were the British Ambassador, Sir Henry Mortimer Durand and Lady (Ella Sandys) Durand; the French Ambassador, Jean Jules Jusserand and Elise Richards Jusserand; and the German Ambassador, Hermann Speck von Sternburg and Lillian Langham Speck von Sternburg.

From Richard Ludwig Enno Littmann

Gheleb, Colonia Eritrea,
Dear Mr. President: Nov. 24th, 1905.

While quietly at work on the Tigre language in this little place far away from civilization I received suddenly a telegram through a messenger who had been running for nine hours. The telegram was from Berlin asking me to lead a German expedition to Axum in Abyssinia.

I had no time to loose. I cabled at once to Mr. Robert Garrett who sent me here to Abyssinia. He answered that he would certainly permit me to accept the offer if I thought it wise. Now I do not only think it wise, but consider it my scientific duty to go. Alone I could have done very little work at Axum, but with an expedition and with architects I believe that very important work can be done. I apologize sincerely that I had to accept without asking your consent. For the time from January until May 1906

I am to serve the German expedition but without salary. I hope this does not interfere with my position in America, since you were kind enough to give me leave of absence for two years. However, I know I am running a risk but I had to do it.

My work here is exceedingly interesting. I am studying the only Semitic language that is left to be studied, the only one of which no grammar exists. I am collecting fables, tales, legends and songs, studying the customs and beliefs of the people. All that will fill several volumes of Princeton University Publications.[1]

Asking to be kindly remembered to your family and wishing you and all Princeton a very happy Christmas and New Year I remain   Very faithfully yours   Enno Littmann

ALS (WP, DLC).
[1] On the basis of this work, Littmann produced *The Princeton University Expedition to Abyssinia, 1905-1906* (4 vols., Leiden, 1910-15).

From the Minutes of the Session of the Second
Presbyterian Church of Princeton, New Jersey

Nov. 25 [1905]

The Session met at noon in Dr. DeWitt's study: Present, the Moderator, Dr. DeWitt, Elders Fisher, Freund, Van Dyke. The meeting was opened with prayer by the Moderator. The minutes for Nov. 13 were read and approved.

Letters of dismission, to the First Presbyterian Church of Princeton, were granted to the following:

Henry Green Duffield	Woodrow Wilson
Florence M. Duffield	Ellen A. Wilson
Samuel Ross Winans	Margaret Wilson
Sarah M. Winans	Jessie W. Wilson
Louis W. Freund	Sarah E. Duffield
Wilhelmina Freund	Helen K. Duffield
Katie Freund	Sarah Green Duffield
Annie R. Burke	Margaret C. Duffield
Helen Bardwell Briner	George Barry Duffield
Kate Laura Davis	Edith L. Flanagan
Bevie Naughton	Sarah M. Latourette
Margaret Sutherland	Marion Spence
Florence Sutherland	C. L. Spence
John G. Durner	Anna E. Anderson
Henry B. Fine	Carrie Anderson
Mary B. Fine	Ida A. McKaig

The resignations of Woodrow Wilson[1] and Louis W. Freund from active service as Elders in the Second Church were presented and accepted.

After the benediction, adjourned

H. N. Van Dyke, Clerk

[1] The Wilsons were received into the membership of the First Presbyterian Church by its Session on November 29, 1905.

A News Announcement of Wilson's Visit to Nashville

[Nov. 27, 1905]

PRES. WILSON OF PRINCETON
TO ATTEND ALUMNI BANQUET

Prominent Educator and Writer Visiting at Home
of Nashville Relative—Address to Nashville Teachers.

Dr. Woodrow Wilson, President of Princeton University, reached the city Saturday night[1] and is a guest at the home of Mr. and Mrs. J. R. Wilson at 1012 Fifteenth Avenue, South.[2] Dr. Wilson went to Bell Buckle this morning, where he will deliver an address before Prof. Webb's school[3] to-day, returning to Nashville this evening. To-morrow from 4 to 6 p.m. he will be given a reception at the home of Judge and Mrs. Robert Ewing[4] at 421 Seventh Avenue, North; to-morrow night he will be the guest of honor and principal speaker at the Princeton alumni banquet, which will be given at the Maxwell House, and Wednesday night he will address the Nashville Teachers' Association at Watkins Hall. Dr. Wilson will leave for Princeton Thursday morning so as to reach home in time to receive President Theodore Roosevelt and other distinguished guests who will go to Princeton to attend the army and navy football game, which will be played there next Saturday. . . .

Printed in the *Nashville Banner*, Nov. 27, 1905.
[1] November 25, 1905.
[2] Joseph R. Wilson, Jr., had moved to Nashville in 1904 to join the editorial staff of the *Nashville Banner*.
[3] The Webb School, headed by the distinguished educator, William Robert Webb. No newspaper or school publication reported this address.
[4] Robert Ewing and Harriet Hoyt Ewing, Mrs. Wilson's first cousin.

A News Report of an Alumni Meeting in Nashville

[Nov. 29, 1905]

PRINCETON MEN OF TENNESSEE

Honor President Woodrow Wilson with Banquet.

The banquet and first reunion of the Princeton Alumni Association of Tennessee was one of the most enjoyable occasions of the kind ever held in this city. An elegant feast was served to guests from all over the South at the Maxwell House, with President Woodrow Wilson of the Princeton University as the especial guest of honor. The table was decorated with La France roses and the columns in the big dining-hall were entwined with the old gold and black of Princeton. Around the banquet board the true Princeton spirit prevailed, and the singing of the old songs such as "Old Nassau," and the triangle song, the cheering of the speakers in the familiar Princeton slogan, "The Locomotive," brought joy to the hearts of young and old alumni alike.

Just after coffee and cigars had been served, and before the toasts, a short business session was held, at which W. L. Granbery[1] was made President of the Tennessee Alumni Association, which was formed. . . .

Mr. Granbery, when he was through with the business, came down, as he said, to what was the pleasant part of the occasion. He said that it was the first time a Princeton University Alumni Association in Tennessee had had the President of their alma mater to pay them a visit.

He introduced Dr. Wilson, who was given a "locomotive" yell in the most approved manner.

Dr. Wilson said it was hard for a man to do the handsome pose when there were men in the assemblage who had seen him in a thousand and one poses not so handsome. Continuing, he said in part:

"A man who is President of Princeton has something to stand for which he did not himself make and which he could not destroy. It is not within his power to alter the character of the office. It is his duty to enhance the beauty of the traditions attached thereto. A Princeton man is born into the spirit of Princeton.

"If Princeton stands for anything, it stands for the tradition of liberal culture. I am afraid that not all of our universities know what liberal culture is. Their views have become greatly narrowed in many cases. Americans are narrowed in one way by the German university training. Americans trained in American universities moulded on German ideals are more narrowed than ever. Much learning makes a person mad, we are told. Many specialists are mad about some one line. They know only one thing. One point I expect to urge upon the public school teachers is that we devote ourselves to the practical side of education. I believe a man is dangerous to the country in proportion as he is provincial instead of national in his sympathies. Princeton stands for a broader view of life in all its phases.

"In educating a man you are dealing with his spirit, and nothing but his spirit. I do not decry technical education for the majority of the people, but we are speaking now of the university's sphere. Any number of technical schools in any locality could not constitute a university.

"University-bred men, if they live true to their inheritance, will be the leaders of the world. When you deal with a man's spirit you are dealing with his career. Is it not true that your lives are great in proportion as you know the goal toward which you are bound and keep towards it? There is one erroneous expression which we use. We speak of a man losing himself in a desert. As a matter of fact, he has lost everything but himself.

"This business of education is locating ourselves in relation to the thoughts and deeds of the world.

"The great thing of undergraduate education is teaching the lads the same thing. Even if they are fallacies, make them the same fallacies. I believe we should determine what bodies of knowledge we are going to teach, and then teach those bodies of knowledge as if we didn't doubt they were true. In taking the undergraduate through college we are taking him to the frontier of the world; the graduate student goes beyond the frontier into the field of adventure and romance. I believe that is the way to get the true aims of study. Anybody, though, can build an ideal, but the constant discouragement is how to bring it to consummation. You can't make a scholar in a year, but there is not even hope of ultimate success unless we can in some way teach him the pleasures of education.

"One thing of which I was glad to be informed a short time ago is that boys have to work now because it is interesting. A man said to me the other day that college life was being ruined and that men actually talked of their studies at the students' clubs. The great desiring that most minds have to make is what is really interesting.

"I don't know that many American professors realize the reproach that has attached to them in England and Germany. The reproach has been ignorance and they have been regarded as a lot of specialists, but that is another story. I have known chemists, for instance, who could not speak their mother tongue.

"What is needed in society is that structural iron in the law.

"The perfect acquaintance with a single member of the family of knowledge, however desirable, is not the only thing we should seek—we should labor to instill culture in its broadest sense.

"One of the objects we are seeking at Princeton is to get men classified in little groups of four or five of like men—men of like tastes—and not according to the alphabet or their class standing. Don't distress boys by training them in things in which they will naturally train themselves, but devote your attention to instruction in things wherein their progress is slow. Our new system at Princeton is not that a man choose from a lot of electives, but he selects a department. We are trying to get rid of the elective habit. It is not teaching a man a subject to examine him in regard to your own views on that subject. I don't see how it can be done, but if we could get rid of examinations altogether it would be a blessing. It is not a part of life for a man to know what my views are on jurisprudence, but every man should know the jurists' views of the structure of society.

"The only salvation for commercial mankind is for him to find out that business is life. We hope to make the student understand that study is life. Nothing is more demoralizing than the purpose that a boy is 'preparing for life' when he is in college. When you realize that men on their graduating day have lived more than half of life you see the fallacy of this. The man who really takes the four years of undergraduate's life seriously is living the quickest time of his life.["]

Printed in the *Nashville Banner*, Nov. 29, 1905; some editorial headings omitted.
  1 William Langley Granbery, a lawyer of Nashville. A member of the Class of 1885, he had left Princeton in 1883.

From Henry Mitchell MacCracken,[1] with Enclosure

Dear President: New York, Nov. 29, 1905.

I enclose a copy of an action adopted by the corporation of New York University, Wednesday, November 29th. We have fixed the meeting for Friday, December 8th, at 10:30 A.M., in a parlor of the Murray Hill Hotel, Fourth Avenue, near 42nd Street, New York City.[2]

We shall be happy to have your delegates as our guests at lunch in the Hotel at one o'clock.

We heartily desire that your university may be able to send an acceptance.[3]   Very truly yours,   Henry M. MacCracken

TLS (WP, DLC).

¹ Chancellor of New York University.
² As the enclosure indicates, the conference was being called to determine whether intercollegiate football should be abolished or reformed—issues being very hotly discussed throughout the nation at this time.
³ Wilson's reply is missing. However, the *New York Times*, Dec. 7, 1905, quoted him as saying, "We do not as yet feel prepared to take part in such a conference." "This declaration," the *New York Times* commented, "is in line with Princeton's known sympathy with the game and her disposition to do everything in a sane and reasonable way to remedy faults in the game, but to frown upon any hasty action during this time of undue excitement antagonistic to the sport."

E N C L O S U R E

[Nov. 29, 1905]

The Faculty of the College and the Faculty of the School of Applied Science of New York University, respectfully request the Council of the University to call a conference of twenty colleges and universities under the following invitation:

Upon the unanimous recommendation of the Faculty of the College of Arts and the Faculty of the School of Applied Science, New York University invites each of the nineteen colleges and universities whose football team has played with the team of this University in any year since its organization in 1895, to a conference to consider such questions as the following:

First. Ought the present game of football to be abolished?

Second. If not, what steps should be taken to secure its thorough reform?

Third. If abolished, what game or games may be possible in its place in the opinion of the athletic representatives in attendance.

Each college or university is invited to send a representative of its faculties and a representative of its athletic organization, making a possible membership of forty.

It is deemed proper to add that the delegates from New York University, on the unanimous recommendation of the Committee on Student Organizations, are instructed to support the first resolution that the present game of football ought to be abolished. It is understood that the decision of the conference will not bind any college participating.

NOTE.

The following are the nineteen universities and colleges described above:

Union, Syracuse, Hamilton, Wesleyan, Lehigh, Rutgers, Trinity, Haverford, Rensellaer [Rensselaer], Stevens, West Point

Princeton, Columbia, Fordham, Ursinus, Lafayette, Rochester, Amherst, and Swarthmore.

The teams of the eight last named have each played only a single game with the team of New York University.

The Council of New York University unanimously adopted the above action as requested, November 29, 1905.[1]

T MS (WP, DLC).
[1] Thirteen institutions sent representatives to the New York University conference on December 8. After five hours of strenuous debate, they decided by a two-thirds vote to retain football as a major sport, but only after making such reforms as to render the game less dangerous and devising rules to make detection of brutal and foul play more certain. The delegates also voted to invite all leading colleges and universities to a second meeting on December 28, 1905, for the purpose of establishing an association that would include colleges and universities across the country.

From John Huston Finley

Dear Woodrow Wilson: [New York]   Nov. 29, 1905.

In reviewing my reasons for thanksgiving, I find very near the top of the list something that has given me a very great happiness and pride, opposite your name. This is a belated and very small partial payment, but you will let it tell you, what I often try to tell Him, how grateful I am and increasingly, for the friendship which through years you gave to my brother Rob[1] and for that other friendship which you have given me out of such a store as few men have ever had. I am prouder of the friendship than of the honor which came to me through you last June,[2] and when you know that I prize the honor above that which could come to me from any other institution in all this country, you will be told something you must already know about my valuation of that which I have held and do hold above it.

Ever yours   John H. Finley

ALS (WP, DLC).
[1] Robert Johnston Finley, who had died on June 8, 1897. See WW to A. Shaw, June 21, 1897, n. 3, Vol. 10.
[2] When he received the LL.D. degree from Princeton University.

A News Report

[Nov. 30, 1905]

ABLE LECTURE ON EDUCATION

President Wilson of Princeton Addresses
Nashville Teachers' Association.

President Woodrow Wilson of Princeton University delivered an able lecture at Watkins Hall last night under the auspices of

Nashville Teachers' Association, his subject being "Liberal Education." The lecture was one of the most original ever heard in Nashville. There was a large and cultured audience present who gave the speaker the closest attention throughout. The lecture made a deep impression, emphasizing, as it did, certain phases of the question of education which had not before been presented in such an interesting form from a Nashville platform. . . .

Dr. Wilson said in part:

"I feel perhaps that we are at a critical stage in the educational development of our country for we have tried many new schemes and have become tired of them. We want to make our methods modern. We say to ourselves that we have kept many things that are old-fashioned and we desire a change. People have been contending that education should be modern and adapted to the times.

"For example, we say this is a material age, but we cannot say whether we are to be material or not. We do not have to prove our national supremacy, we admit it. The greatness of the United States in the material world is its capacity for power. Our supremacy depends on the guiding mind.

"The thing I would have you discriminate is that technical training which all must have and the liberal education which some may have.

"We speak of the greatness of the United States, and it is great, but the question now is what we are to do with our greatness? Our education must be a matter of statesmanship. Everything we have been proud of in America has found its residence in fair thinking. The ability to conceive what must be done with the races as races is the essential difference between America and other countries. Ideal thinking has produced the things worthy of the pride of American people. They have promulgated the doctrine of individual liberty.

"Differences of opinion are said to be un-American. Why, the American flag stands for the biggest kick on record. It stands for the greatest resistance. The American revolution was opposed by a majority of the colonists. The flag stands for individual opinions. The white stripes on the flag represent the parchment upon which was inscribed the doctrine of American liberty, and the red stripes the blood with which that liberty was bought.

"We have accumulated wealth and power, but have we been studying the problem of swinging this great mass to some good purpose? We are in danger of making provincials of ourselves. If we are going to give the United States nothing but a technical training, the great mass of the people will be among those who have only heard of those things that are known to be true."

Dr. Wilson here enlarged upon and illustrated in a striking manner the necessity for a liberal education. He emphasized the necessity for having a knowledge of things outside of one's special individual sphere of endeavor. He declared that education is not modern unless we make of ourselves citizens of the modern world. Liberal education must precede technical education. We must know more than the things we are doing. "What is a liberal education as distinguished from an illiberal education?" asked the speaker. "It consists," continued Dr. Wilson, "of the study with some particular end in view and not for some particular profession."

The speaker approved the study of the ancient languages and literature, as well as of higher mathematics, as a training for the mind. The means of a liberal education is to be found in the literature of the world. The masters of the race are those whose minds have been schooled for a mastery. Education is a part of the process of popular leadership. America is the first country to undertake a systematic education. Education is not information, but consists of the ability to use information as a stimulus to the mind.

Dr. Wilson left this morning for his home in New Jersey. He expressed great pleasure at the opportunity of visiting Nashville and meeting so many of her cultured people, expressing the hope that he may be able to return at no distant date.

Printed in the *Nashville Banner*, Nov. 30, 1905; some editorial headings omitted.

A News Report

[Dec. 4. 1905]

ARMY AND NAVY CROWD

Fills Princeton. President Roosevelt
at Prospect. Poor Train Facilities.

The eleventh annual football game between the Army and Navy played on University Field on Saturday, resulted in a tie game,[1] the first of the series. The Army scored first and held this lead until the last few minutes of the game, when the Navy by a magnificent show of strength, seized an opportunity and scored an equal number of points. . . .

The most important event of the day outside of the game was the appearance of President Roosevelt and party. The Presidential party arrived in Princeton shortly after twelve o'clock and was met at the station by President Wilson. The party was driven in carriages up University Place to Nassau Street–under guard of a cordon of police–thence down Nassau Street to the Chapel Road and so to Prospect. At the station and along the short line of march the President was greeted with cheers and the waving of flags and handkerchiefs. Those entertained by President and Mrs. Wilson at luncheon were: President and Mrs. Theodore Roosevelt, Mr. and Mrs. Douglas Robinson, and Miss Corinne Robinson,[2] Hon. Elihu Root, Secretary of State; Mr. Newbery, Assistant Secretary of the Navy, and Mrs. Newbery;[3] Brigadier General [Albert Leopold] Mills, Superiniendent [Superintendent] of the Military Academy, and Mrs. Mills;[4] Admiral [James Hoban] Sands, Superintendent of the Naval Academy; Mr. W[illiam]. Loeb, Jr., Secretary to the President; Mr. Charles A. Munn,[5] and Captain and Mrs. Cowles.[6]

Printed in the *Daily Princetonian*, Dec. 4, 1905.
[1] The score was 6 to 6.
[2] Douglas Robinson, a New York real estate magnate; Corinne Roosevelt Robinson, President Roosevelt's sister; and their daughter.
[3] Truman Handy Newberry and Harriet Josephine Barnes Newberry.
[4] Alada Thurston Paddock Mills.
[5] Identified in WW to T. Roosevelt, Aug. 8, 1905, n. 1
[6] Captain William Sheffield Cowles, U.S.N., commander of *U.S.S. Missouri*, and Anna Roosevelt Cowles, the President's sister.

A News Report of a Wesleyan Alumni Banquet in New York

[Dec. 9, 1905]

AMERICA'S MORALS A COLLEGE TRUST

"What Has the General Public to Do with Learning?" Asks Princeton's Head.

At the Hotel Savoy the Wesleyan University Club of New York held its thirty-seventh annual meeting and dinner last night, with a large attendance. D. L. Robertson, '78, president of the club, was toastmaster, and the speakers were the Rev. Dr. Bradford Raymond, LL.D., president of Wesleyan University; Woodrow Wilson, president of Princeton University; H. I. Harriman, '95, delegate from Boston Alumni Club; William D. Leonard, '78, representing the alumni, and Guy W. Rogers, '06, representative of the undergraduates. . . .

President Wilson, of Princeton, said in part:

"In later days educators have fallen into the knack of following instead of leading. I have been astonished at the cowardice of educated men. The self-made man is a remarkable product considering who made him. We need expert assistance to aid our fellow men. It is necessary for the educated man to be a bread winner, but they are not any more successful as bread winners than the self-made man although they work in different channels.

"The object of education is to discover the realities of life, not to make a living. Realities are only discovered on the broad field of observation. They say business is business, which I understand to mean business is not moral.

"If business be corrupt then life must be corrupt. We are making life and the universities must distinguish themselves from factories. We are making men for the nation and not for any particular occupation.

"What has the general public got to do with learning? I am not saying this cynically. The educated man—the university man—must always be in the minority. He is a singular but a necessary person. If we only had more memory we would not have to settle the silver question every generation.

"I believe we should regard ourselves as the trustees of America's morals.

"I don't belong to the republican party though the rest of the country does. I'm waiting for a party of my own. As the republican party is the whole of the country, I am its guest."

Printed in the *New York Herald*, Dec. 9, 1905; some editorial headings omitted.

A News Item About a Talk in Hartford

[Dec. 12, 1905]

PRESIDENT WILSON TO 20TH CENTURY CLUB.

Tells About Preceptorial System at Princeton University.

The Twentieth Century Club held a most successful meeting at the Hartford Club last evening with President Woodrow Wilson of Princeton as the speaker. Professor M. W. Jacobus, president of the Twentieth Century, himself one of the corporation of Princeton, introduced its president in a graceful speech and then Dr. Wilson spoke on "University Ideals," being in effect an elucidation of the preceptorial system, which he has recently inaugurated at the university.[1] The speaker has a charming way of putting things and a delicious humor, so that a serious and, as the watches proved afterwards, a rather long talk seemed all too short and was of continuing and lively interest. At the close a rising vote of thanks was given to President Wilson.

Printed in the *Hartford Courant*, Dec. 12, 1905.
[1] There is a brief WWhw outline of this talk, dated Dec. 11, 1905, in WP, DLC.

To the Board of Trustees of Princeton University

[Princeton, N. J.] DECEMBER 14, 1905
GENTLEMEN OF THE BOARD OF TRUSTEES:

I take pleasure in submitting to you my annual report upon the affairs of the University.

The most noticeable and noteworthy changes in the University since my last report are to be found in the personnel of the Faculty. Four members of the Faculty who had become our familiar friends have retired from it, and fifty-three new members have been added to it.

Professor William Alfred Packard, Professor Charles Augustus Young, Professor Charles Greene Rockwood and Professor Arthur Lincoln Frothingham have retired from active work as teachers.

Dr. Packard was appointed Professor of the Latin Language and Literature and of the Science of Language in 1870, at the age of forty, and now, at the age of seventy-five, unimpaired in faculty, lays down his work after thirty-five years association with the University, not because his health is broken, but because it has become necessary carefully to conserve it. I had the pleasure of being one of Dr. Packard's pupils and feel that I can speak with personal knowledge of the deep and abiding impression he made as a teacher, the impression of exquisite refinement, of precise scholarship, united with discriminating taste and a quick literary feeling. His influence as a scholar and a gentleman has touched generation after generation of undergraduates in subtle ways of which he has probably himself been unaware, and he has a right to look back with pride upon a life in which he has, with a distinction all his own, maintained the scholarly traditions of a singularly accomplished family.

Professor Packard continues to live with us; Professor Young has, to our great loss, removed to his old family home at Hanover, N. H. His contributions to scientific knowledge all the world is cognizant of, but only those who were privileged to be his associates can know the loss of stimulation that came with his departure from among us. Professor Young was appointed to the chair of Astronomy in 1877, when in his forty-third year, and had given to the University, when he retired last June, twenty-eight of the best years of his life. And certainly no years of service as a teacher have ever yielded a finer fruitage. It was hard to determine which most to admire in Professor Young, his achievements or his modesty. He has ever been a true man of science, approaching the great secrets of Nature with the simplicity, the eagerness, and the piety of a child, and using great powers without thought of self. Both his achievement as an investigator and his nobility as a man will long serve us as an inspiration and an example.

Professor Rockwood was appointed Associate Professor of Pure and Applied Mathematics in 1877, and Professor of Mathematics the following year, so that his term of service has been exactly coincident with that of Professor Young. Professor Rockwood is, however, nine years Professor Young's junior and leaves us, to enjoy a well-earned leisure and opportunity of travel, while still in the midst of years of full vigor. The University owes him a debt of grateful appreciation for services rendered, not only through many years of uninterrupted labor, but also with singular unselfishness and devotion.

Professor Frothingham leaves us, after nineteen years' service in the Faculty, to devote himself, at the maturity of his powers, to free investigation in the field of Archæology in connection with which his name has become so widely and so favorably known. His equipment for the work to which he has devoted himself is most unusual and complete, being quickened by both learning and enthusiasm; and we sincerely felicitate him upon his opportunity to push his inquiries forward with the entire freedom afforded him by a release from exacting academic engagements.

On the 13th of February, 1905, our true friend and one-time colleague, William Cowper Prime, was taken away by death. The influence of his enlightened life, enriched by the interests of the versatile scholar and the liberal man of letters, was at one time very directly felt here in Princeton in the development of our instruction in Art and Archæology, and we had for some time the privilege of retaining his name upon our Faculty list as Professor of the History of Art. His death removes a notable figure and leaves us to mourn an influential friend.

The new appointments of the year have been very numerous and have introduced into our Faculty an infusion of fresh strength which must permanently distinguish the present academic year as a notable turning point in the development of the University.

Mr. James Hopwood Jeans, Master of Arts of Trinity College, Cambridge (1902), comes to us this year as Professor of Applied Mathematics, fresh from the associations and the unusual training of that distinguished school of mathematicians and physicists which has persisted for so many generations at Cambridge and which has maintained with such handsome usury the spiritual inheritance directly transmitted to it from Sir

Isaac Newton. Mr. Jeans was elected Fellow of Trinity College in 1901, and in 1904 was appointed University Lecturer.

Dr. Charles Henry Smyth, a member of the Faculty of Hamilton College since 1891, comes to us as Professor of Geology. His academic training he received from the School of Mines of Columbia University, from which University he received the degree of Bachelor of Philosophy in 1888 and the degree of Doctor of Philosophy in 1890. During the year 1900-01 he studied at the University of Heidelberg. He has been connected with the geological survey work both of the Federal Government and of the government of the State of New York and has won an enviable reputation as an authority upon physical and petrographical Geology.

Mr. Howard Crosby Butler, since 1895 lecturer on Architecture, is this year advanced to the rank of Professor of Art and Archæology, an advance which he has earned not only by unusual success as a teacher and by very solid attainments as a scholar, but also by the remarkable success of the archæological explorations in Syria, of 1899-1900 and 1904-05, which he directed with such distinguished ability. Mr. Butler, after graduating from Princeton in 1892, was twice Fellow in Archæology here and pursued advanced studies in the school of Archæology in Columbia University, the American School of Classical Studies at Rome, and the American School of Classical Studies at Athens.

Dr. George Augustus Hulett, whom we welcome back to Princeton as Assistant Professor of Physical Chemistry, was graduated Bachelor of Arts here in 1892 in the same class with Mr. Butler and served the University as Assistant in Chemistry during the four years which followed his graduation. Since leaving Princeton in 1896 he has taken the degree of Doctor of Philosophy, after two years of study, at the University of Leipzig (1898) and has served the University of Michigan for five years most acceptably, first as Instructor in Chemistry and then as Assistant Professor of Physical Chemistry. By his researches he has established a reputation, which bids fair to grow with the facilities afforded him for investigation, as an investigator and elucidator of those chemico-physical problems which are now drawing physicists and chemists together into the same laboratories.

Dr. William Foster, promoted from the rank of Assistant in Chemistry to that of Assistant Professor, was graduated Bachelor of Arts from Hartford College, Kentucky, in 1892; was a special student in science at Vanderbilt University during the year 1892-93; and from 1893 to 1895 was Instructor in Science and Mathematics at his Alma Mater. He became a graduate student at Princeton in 1895 and received the degree of Doctor of Philosophy from the University in 1899; having meanwhile, from 1896 to 1898, been Assistant in Chemistry. During the year 1899-1900 he served as Professor of Chemistry at the Central University of Kentucky. In 1900 he returned to Princeton as Instructor, and has served in that capacity, with constant and increasing efficiency, for five years.

Mr. Lucius Hopkins Miller, who becomes Assistant Professor of Biblical Instruction, was graduated Bachelor of Arts from Princeton in 1897, Master of Arts in 1899. He was for the two years following his graduation General Secretary of the Philadelphian Society, serving with singular efficiency and helpfulness. From 1899 to 1902 he taught in the Syrian Protestant College, at Beyrout, Syria, first as Instructor in English and the Bible, and afterwards as Instructor in Bible and Assistant Principal of the Preparatory Department. In 1902 he returned to this country and entered Union Theological Seminary, where he remained until called to Princeton. From 1903 to 1905, in connection with his studies in New York, he acted as Instructor in Biblical History and Director of Religious Work at the Hill School at Pottstown, Pennsylvania.

Dr. Hamilton Ford Allen, who takes Professor Jesse Benedict Carter's place for the year, was graduated Bachelor of Arts from Williams College in 1888; taught Latin and Greek in Allen Academy, Chicago, from 1888 to 1892; and pursued advanced studies in Classics at the University of Berlin from 1892 to 1894. In 1897 he was graduated from the McCormick Theological Seminary, and during the two following years studied at the University of Chicago, during the first year as Orme Smith Fellow from McCormick Seminary and during the second as Fellow in Biblical and Patristic Greek by appointment from the University of Chicago itself. He spent the summer of 1899 as a student at the University of Leipzig and the winter of 1899-1900 in the American School of Classical Studies at Athens, paying particular attention to modern Greek. Two years, 1900-02, he again spent as Fellow at the University of Chicago. Since 1902 he has been Professor of Latin at Washington and Jefferson College.

We found it necessary last year, in view of the contemplated changes in our methods of instruction, to create a new title, that of *Preceptor*, carrying with it the rank of Assistant Professor; and forty-seven Preceptors have been appointed,—gentlemen who constitute in every way a most notable addition to our Faculty and who have entered into their work here with an intelligence and enthusiasm wholly delightful. I give their names, for convenience, in the order of the Departments as classified under our course of study.

Dr. Roger Bruce Cash Johnson, Preceptor in Philosophy, was graduated Bachelor of Arts from Princeton with the Class of 1887; was Fellow in Philosophy here from 1887 to 1888; and from 1888 to 1905 Professor of Philosophy at Miami University. In 1900 he received from Princeton the degree of Doctor of Philosophy.

Dr. Adam Leroy Jones, Preceptor in Philosophy, was graduated Bachelor of Arts from Williams College in 1895, earned his degree as Doctor of Philosophy at Columbia University in 1898, and has since 1898 been connected with the teaching staff of Columbia University, from 1898 to 1901 as Assistant in Philosophy, from 1901 to 1902 as Lecturer, and from 1902 to 1905 as Tutor.

Dr. Walter Taylor Marvin, Preceptor in Philosophy, was graduated Bachelor of Arts from Columbia University in 1893; pursued advanced studies in Philosophy at the University of Jena, 1893-94, at Columbia, 1894-97, and at the Universities of Halle and Bonn, 1897-98, receiving the degree of Doctor of Philosophy from Bonn in 1898; was Assistant in Philosophy at Columbia from 1898 to 1899, Instructor in Philosophy at Western Reserve University from 1899 to 1903, and Assistant Professor from 1903 to 1905, when called here.

Dr. Wilmon Henry Sheldon, Preceptor in Philosophy, was graduated Bachelor of Arts from Harvard University in 1895, Master of Arts in 1896, and Doctor of Philosophy in 1899; was Assistant in Philosophy at Harvard from 1898 to 1899, and Assistant in Philosophy at the University of Wisconsin from 1899 to 1900; was Austin Teaching Fellow at Harvard from 1900 to 1901, and in 1901 joined the teaching staff of Columbia University, where from 1901 to 1903 he was Assistant in Philosophy, and from 1903 to 1905 Tutor in Philosophy.

Dr. Edward Gleason Spaulding, Preceptor in Philosophy, was graduated Bachelor of Arts from the University of Vermont in 1894, specializing in Chemistry, and Master of Arts at Columbia University in 1896, specializing in Physics. Transferring his interest to philosophy, he pursued advanced studies in that field at the University of Bonn, from which he received the degree of Doctor of Philosophy in 1900. Since 1900 he has been Instructor in Philosophy and Psychology at the College of the City of New York, and since 1904 has been on the physiological staff of the Marine Biological Laboratory at Woods Holl [Hole], Mass.

Dr. Hiram Bingham, Preceptor in History, Politics, and Economics, was graduated Bachelor of Arts from Yale University in 1898, and subsequently pursued advanced studies at the University of California, 1899-1900, and at Harvard University, 1900-05, receiving the degree of Master of Arts both from the University of California and from Harvard, and from Harvard the degree of Doctor of Philosophy. At the University of California he served during the year 1900 as University Extension Lecturer, and during his residence at Harvard he served one year as Assistant in History, two years as Austin Teaching Fellow in History, and two years as Curator of South American History and Literature in the library of the University.

Dr. Ernest Ludlow Bogart, Preceptor in History, Politics, and Economics, was graduated Bachelor of Arts from Princeton in 1890, and after graduation pursued advanced studies at the University of Halle, the University of Berlin, Columbia University, and Princeton, being the Southeast Club University Fellow in Social Science during the year 1895-96. He received the degree of Master of Arts from Princeton in 1896, and the degree of Doctor of Philosophy from Halle in 1897. From 1898 to 1900 he was Assistant Professor of Economics and Social Science at Indiana University, and from 1900 to 1905 Professor of Economics and Sociology at Oberlin College.

Dr. Edward Samuel Corwin, Preceptor in History, Politics, and Economics, was graduated Bachelor of Philosophy from the University of Michigan in 1900, taught history in the High School of Ishpeming, Michigan, during the academic year 1900-01. From 1902 to 1904 he was Assistant in American History at the University of Michigan, at the same time studying for his doctorate. In 1904 he went to the University of Pennsylvania as Harrison Fellow in American History, and from that University he received the degree of Doctor of Philosophy in 1905, just before coming to Princeton.

Dr. Edward Graham Elliott, Preceptor in History, Politics, and Economics, was graduated Bachelor of Arts from Princeton in 1897, and taught school at Bolton, Tenn., during the year following his graduation. From 1898 to 1900 he was Instructor in Latin in the John C. Green School of Science, and in 1900 received the degree of Master of Arts from the University. The same year he turned from classical studies to studies in jurisprudence and politics and pursued work in those fields during the years 1900-02 in German universities, chiefly the University of Heidelberg, from which in 1902 he received the degree of Doctor of Philosophy. Since 1902 he has been Instructor in Jurisprudence at Princeton.

Mr. Charles Howard McIlwain, Preceptor in History, Politics, and Economics, was graduated Bachelor of Arts from Princeton in 1894. From 1894 to 1897 he studied Law with a view to its practice, and in 1897 was admitted to the bar of Allegheny County, Pa. In 1898 he received the degree of Master of Arts from Princeton and turned from law to teaching. From 1898 to 1901 he taught Latin and History in the Kiskiminetas Springs School at Saltsburg, Pa., the school in which he had been prepared for the University. From 1901 to 1903 he pursued advanced studies at Harvard University and received from that University in 1903 the degree of Master of Arts. Since 1903 he has been Professor of History at Miami University.

Mr. Royal Meeker, Preceptor in History, Politics, and Economics, was graduated Bachelor of Science from Iowa State College in 1898. From 1899 to 1902 he was a graduate student at Columbia University, being Fellow in Finance during the year 1901-02. From 1903 to 1904 he pursued advanced studies at the University of Leipzig, and in 1904 was appointed to the chair of History and Political Science at Ursinus College, whence he came to Princeton.

Dr. Henry Robinson Shipman, Preceptor in History, Politics, and Economics, was graduated Bachelor of Arts from Yale University in 1899, and, after pursuing advanced studies at Harvard, received from that University in 1901 the degree of Master of Arts, and in 1904 the degree of Doctor of Philosophy. From 1902 to 1904 he was Assistant in History at Harvard University, and during the year which preceded his coming to Princeton he was Instructor in History at Dartmouth College.

Dr. Charles Worthen Spencer, Preceptor in History, Politics, and Economics, was graduated Bachelor of Arts from Colby College in 1890. From 1890 to 1892 he was Instructor in Science and Ancient History at Hebron Academy, Hebron, Maine. From 1892 to 1895 he pursued advanced studies in history, politics, economics, and sociology at the University of Chicago and at Columbia University. In 1895 he was appointed Townshend Scholar at Harvard University, and in 1896 was appointed Professor of History at Colgate University, where he remained until he received an appointment here. During the year 1900-1901 he held the position of University Fellow in Columbia University, from which University he received, in 1905, the degree of Doctor of Philosophy.

Dr. Oliver Samuel Tonks, Preceptor in Art and Archæology, was graduated Bachelor of Arts from Harvard University in 1898, Master of Arts in 1899, and Doctor of Philosophy in 1903; was Instructor in Greek in the University of Vermont during the academic year 1903-1904, and Lecturer in Greek at Columbia University during the year 1904-1905. During the year 1902-1903 he was Assistant Curator of the Department of Classical Art in the Museum of Fine Arts at Boston.

Dr. Andrew Runni Anderson, Preceptor in Classics, was graduated Bachelor of Arts from the University of Wisconsin in 1900; pursued advanced studies in classics at the University of Wisconsin, 1900-1901, and at Harvard, 1901-1903, receiving from Harvard in 1903 the degree of Doctor of Philosophy; was travelling Fellow from Harvard, 1903-1904; and from 1904 to 1905 was Instructor in Greek at the University of Wisconsin.

Dr. John William Basore, Preceptor in Classics, was graduated Bachelor of Arts from Hampden-Sidney [Sydney] College in 1893. From 1893 to 1895 he taught Latin, Greek, and English, first in the Lewisburg (West Virginia) University School, and then in the Locust Dale Academy, Virginia. From 1895 to 1899 he pursued advanced studies at Johns Hopkins University, holding during one of his year's residence there a Fellowship in Latin; and in 1899 received from that University the degree of Doctor of Philosophy. During the year 1899-1900 he was Professor of Latin at Hampden-Sidney [Sydney] College. During the winter of 1900-1901 he studied at the University of Leipzig and in the Libraries of Milan and Paris. Since 1901 he has been an Instructor in Latin at the University of California.

Dr. Donald Cameron, Preceptor in Classics, was graduated Bachelor of Arts from the University of Texas in 1895, and received the degree of Master of Arts from that University in 1896. From 1895 to 1897 he pursued advanced studies at the University of Texas, first as teaching Fellow and then as Tutor. From 1897 to 1899 he taught Latin and Greek in the High School of San Antonio. From 1899 to 1902 he was a graduate student at Harvard University, and during the year 1902-1903 was Travelling Fellow from Harvard, studying in Italy, Germany, and Greece. From 1903 to 1904 he was Instructor in Greek at the University of Texas and from 1904 to 1905 acted as Professor of Greek at Baylor University.

Mr. Harold Ripley Hastings, Preceptor in Classics, was graduated Bachelor of Arts from Dartmouth College in 1900; gave instruction in classics at St. Paul's School, Concord, New Hampshire, during the year following his graduation; received the degree of Master of Arts from Harvard University in 1902; was Charles Elliott [Eliot] Norton Fellow in Greek Studies at the American School of Classical Studies at Athens, 1902-1903 and Fellow of the Archæological Institute of America at the same school during the year following; and during the year 1904-1905 was a Fellow in Greek at the University of Wisconsin.

Mr. Fred Leroy Hutson, Preceptor in Classics, was graduated Bachelor of Arts from Denison University in 1896; during the year which followed his graduation was Principal and Instructor in Latin and Greek in the Granville High School; and from 1897 to 1899 was Instructor in Greek at Denison, where he was again Instructor from 1900 to 1902, after having taken a year of advanced study at Chicago University. During the year 1902-1903 he was Fellow in Greek in Chicago University; and in 1903 he became Instructor in Greek at Princeton. He had served the University two years when promoted to a preceptorship.

Dr. George Dwight Kellogg, Preceptor in Classics, was graduated Bachelor of Arts from Yale University in 1895, and pursued advanced studies at that University until 1898, when he received the degree of Doctor of Philosophy. During the year 1896-1897 he served as Assistant in Latin at Yale, and during the year 1898-1899 as Instructor. From 1899 to 1900 he was a Fellow at the American School of Classical Studies at Rome, and from 1900 to 1903 again Tutor in Latin at Yale. For the two years preceding his appointment to a preceptorship here he was Assistant Professor of Latin and Greek at Williams College. Since 1901 he has been in charge of the Latin studies at the summer school at Chautauqua.

Dr. Donald Alexander MacRae, Preceptor in Classics, was graduated Bachelor of Arts from Dalhousie College, Halifax, Nova Scotia, in 1898, and after his graduation pursued advanced studies in classics at Cornell University from 1898 to 1900, receiving the degree of Master of Arts in 1899. From 1900 to 1905 he was Instructor in Greek at Cornell; and in 1905 he received from that University the degree of Doctor of Philosophy.

Dr. David Magie, Preceptor in Classics, was graduated Bachelor of Arts from Princeton in 1897; was Master at Lawrenceville School during the year 1897-1898; returned to Princeton for graduate study in 1898; and in 1899 received the degree of Master of Arts. From 1899 to 1901 he was Instructor in Latin here. From 1901 to 1904 he studied in Germany and Italy and in 1904 received from the University of Halle the degree of Doctor of Philosophy. In 1904 he resumed his duties as Instructor in Latin in Princeton.

Dr. Edwin Moore Rankin, Preceptor in Classics, was graduated Bachelor of Arts from Vanderbilt University in 1896. In 1897 he received from the same University the degree of Master of Arts, after a year of graduate study, and in 1898 the same degree from Harvard University. During the year 1899-1900 he served in the Faculty of Weatherford College, Weatherford, Texas, first as Professor of Latin and Modern Languages and then as Professor of Latin and Greek. Returning to Harvard in 1901, he devoted two more years to advanced study in classics, and in 1903 received from that University the degree of Doctor of Philosophy. Since 1903 he has been Instructor in Latin at Princeton.

Dr. Duane Reed Stuart, Preceptor in Classics, was graduated Bachelor of Arts from the University of Michigan in 1896, and was graduate Fellow at that University from 1896-1898. During the year 1898-1899 he studied at the American School of Classical Studies at Athens and at the University of Munich. In 1901 he received the degree of Doctor of Philosophy from the University of Michigan. From 1901 to 1904 he was Instructor in Greek and Latin, and from 1904 to 1905 Assistant Professor of Latin and Greek at the University of Michigan.

Dr. LaRue Van Hook, Preceptor in Classics, graduated Bachelor of Arts from the University of Michigan in 1899. In 1899 he took up graduate study in classics at the University of Chicago, and from 1900 to 1902 and again from 1903 to 1904 was Fellow in Greek at that University. During the year 1901-1902 he was a student in Germany and at the American School of Classical Studies at Athens. During the academic year 1902-1903 he acted as Professor of Greek at the University of Colorado. In 1904 he received the degree of Doctor of Philosophy from the University of Chicago, while serving as Instructor in Greek and Latin in Bradley Polytechnic Institute at Peoria, Illinois. The following year he became Instructor in Greek and Latin at Washington University, St. Louis, whence he came to Princeton.

Dr. Hardin Craig, Preceptor in English, was graduated Bachelor of Arts from Center [Centre] College, Kentucky, in 1897. During the year following his graduation he taught Latin and Greek at Stanford Academy, Kentucky. From 1898 to 1901 he was a graduate student in English at Princeton, studying also during the summers of 1899, 1900, and 1901 in the Graduate School of English in the University of Chicago, and receiving from Princeton in 1899 the degree of Master of Arts, and in 1901 the degree of Doctor of Philosophy. During the years 1899-

1901 he held the Charles Scribner Fellowship in English. From 1901 to 1902 he served as Instructor in English here. From 1902 to 1903 he pursued advanced studies abroad, first, during the summer semester, at Jena, and then at Oxford. In 1903 he resumed his duties as Instructor in English at Princeton.

Mr. Gordon Hall Gerould, Preceptor in English, was graduated Bachelor of Arts from Dartmouth College in 1899. From 1899 to 1900 he was Parker Travelling Fellow of Dartmouth, studying at Paris and Oxford, and receiving the degree of Bachelor of Letters from Oxford in 1901. From 1901 to 1905 he has been connected with the teaching staff of Bryn Mawr College, having been Reader in English there from 1901 to 1902 and Associate in English from 1902 to 1905.

Dr. Nathaniel Edward Griffin, Preceptor in English, was graduated Bachelor of Arts from the Johns Hopkins University in 1894, and earned his degree of Doctor of Philosophy from the same University in 1899. During the year 1899-1900 he taught at the University of Iowa, during the years 1900-1903 at Wells College, during the year 1903-1904 at the University of Vermont, and during last year at Johns Hopkins University.

Mr. Augustus White Long, Preceptor in English, was graduated Bachelor of Arts from the University of North Carolina in 1885; was Professor of English in Trinity College, North Carolina, from 1885 to 1887, graduate student in English at the Johns Hopkins University during 1887-1888, Professor of English in Wofford College, South Carolina, from 1888 to 1890, and graduate student at Harvard University from 1890 to 1893, receiving from Harvard in 1891 the degree of Master of Arts. He was English Master at Lawrenceville School from 1893 to 1902, and in 1902 became Instructor in English at Princeton.

Mr. Francis Charles MacDonald, Preceptor in English, was graduated Bachelor of Arts from Princeton in 1896; taught in schools and as private tutor, 1896-1899; was assistant in the Princeton University Library, 1899-1901, and in the Princeton Theological Seminary Library, 1901-1902; and was Instructor in English in Lake Forest College, 1902-1905.

Dr. Charles Grosvenor Osgood, Preceptor in English, was graduated Bachelor of Arts from Yale University in 1894, and after graduation for two years taught Latin and Greek at the Susquehanna Institute, Towanda, Pennsylvania. He then turned his attention to English and after three years graduate study at Yale received from that University in 1899 the degree of Doctor of Philosophy. After a brief service as Assistant Professor in the

University of Colorado, he became, in June, 1900, Instructor in English at Yale University, a position which he retained until called to Princeton.

Dr. Robert Killburn Root, Preceptor in English, was graduated Bachelor of Arts from Yale University in 1898, and from 1899 to 1905 was Instructor in English in that University, receiving in 1902 the degree of Doctor of Philosophy.

Dr. John Duncan Spaeth, Preceptor in English, was graduated Bachelor of Arts from the University of Pennsylvania in 1888, and Doctor of Philosophy from the University of Leipzig in 1892. In 1893 he became Assistant Professor of English in Gustavus Adolphus College, St. Peter, Minnesota, and in 1894 Instructor in English, Latin, and History in the Central High School of Philadelphia. The following year he was made Professor of English in that school, and continued in that chair until called to Princeton. In connection with his regular teaching duties he has been lecturer for the Philadelphia Free Library, the New York Board of Education, and the University Extension Society.

Dr. Douglas Labaree Buffum, Preceptor in Modern Languages, was graduated Bachelor of Arts and Master of Arts from the University of Virginia in 1898. From 1898 to 1900 he was Instructor in Latin and French in the Marion Military Institute, Marion, Alabama, being during the second of the two years Assistant Superintendent of the School. During the year 1900-1901 he was again at the University of Virginia following the courses in Latin and the Romance languages; and during the summer of 1901 he followed the courses in French linguistics and literature at the University of Grenoble. From 1901 to 1904 he was a student in the Romance languages at the Johns Hopkins University; held during the last of those three years the fellowship of the department; and received in 1904 the degree of Doctor of Philosophy. During the academic year 1904-1905 he was Instructor in French in Yale University.

Dr. Frank Linley Critchlow, Preceptor in Modern Languages, was graduated Bachelor of Arts from Princeton in 1896, Master of Arts in 1897. During the years 1898 and 1899 he served as Instructor in French and German in the Pingry School at Elizabeth, New Jersey. From 1899 to 1902 he was a graduate student at the Johns Hopkins University, from which, in 1893 [1903], he received the degree of Doctor of Philosophy. Since 1902 he has been an Instructor in French at Princeton.

Mr. Christian Gauss, Preceptor in Modern Languages, was graduated Bachelor of Arts from the University of Michigan; and

Master of Arts in 1899 after study in Paris. In 1899 he became Instructor in French at the University of Michigan; in 1901 Instructor in Modern Languages at Lehigh University; and in 1903 Assistant Professor of Modern Languages at Lehigh. He was called from that institution to Princeton.

Mr. William Koren, Preceptor in Modern Languages, was graduated Bachelor of Arts from Luther College, Decorah, Iowa, from which institution he also received the degree of Master of Arts. Subsequently he was graduated from Concordia Theological Seminary at St. Louis. From 1889 to 1902 he taught German and Greek at Luther College. From 1892 to 1894 he studied German philology and literature at the Universities of Graustock and Leipzig, and during the year following pursued additional advanced courses at the University of Chicago. From 1895 to 1900 he taught French and English literature at Iowa Wesleyan University, Mt. Pleasant, Iowa. The year 1900-1901 he spent in the study of the French language and literature at the University of Geneva. In 1901 he was appointed Instructor in Princeton.

Mr. Alfred Austin Moore, Preceptor in Modern Languages, was graduated Bachelor of Arts from Hamilton College in 1890; studied in the Universities of Freiburg, i B. and Heidelberg from 1893 to 1895; and was Instructor in Romance languages at Cornell University from 1896 until called to Princeton.

Mr. George Tyler Northup, Preceptor in Modern Languages, was graduated Bachelor of Arts from Williams College in 1897; from 1900 to 1903 he was a graduate student at Chicago University, during the last of those three years holding a fellowship; and from 1903 to 1905 he occupied the position of Instructor in Romance Languages at Williams College.

Mr. George Madison Priest, Preceptor in Modern Languages, was graduated Bachelor of Arts from Princeton in 1894, studied at the University of Berlin during the winter of 1894-1895, and became Instructor in German in the John C. Green School of Science in 1895. In 1896 he received from Princeton the degree of Master of Arts. The winter of 1901-1902 he spent at the Universities of Marburg and Jena. In 1902 he resumed his work as Instructor in German at Princeton.

Dr. Harvey Waterman Thayer, Preceptor in Modern Languages, was graduated Bachelor of Arts from Bowdoin College in 1895, and was graduated with the same degree from Harvard University the following year. The two ensuing years he taught modern languages in the University of Maine. The year 1898-1899 he spent at the University of Leipzig. During the academic years 1899-1901 he was Instructor in German in the St. Louis Normal High School. The year 1901-1902 he spent at Columbia University as Fellow in the Germanic Languages and Literatures. He received from that University in 1904 the degree of Doctor of Philosophy. From 1902 to 1905 he taught in the Pratt Institute of Brooklyn, and had been acting for only a few months of 1905 as Tutor in German at the College of the City of New York when called to Princeton.

Dr. Gilbert Ames Bliss, Preceptor in Mathematics, was graduated Bachelor of Science from the University of Chicago in 1897, Master of Science in 1898, Doctor of Philosophy in 1900, holding during his last year of residence there a Fellowship in Mathematics. During the years 1900-1902 he was Instructor in Mathematics at the University of Minnesota; during the year 1902-1903 he studied at the University of Göttingen. He spent the academic year 1903-1904 as Associate in Mathematics at the University of Chicago. In 1904 he became Assistant Professor of Mathematics at the University of Missouri, which position he resigned to come to Princeton.

Dr. Luther Pfahler Eisenhart, Preceptor in Mathematics, was graduated Bachelor of Arts from Pennsylvania College at Gettysburg in 1896, and during the year which followed his graduation taught mathematics and physics in the preparatory department of that college. During the three years 1897-1900 he was a graduate student in mathematics, physics, and astronomy at the Johns Hopkins University, during the last of those three years holding a fellowship, and receiving the degree of Doctor of Philosophy in June, 1900. In the autumn of that year he became Instructor in Mathematics at Princeton, a position which he held until his present promotion.

Dr. William Gillespie, Preceptor in Mathematics, was graduated Bachelor of Arts from Toronto University in 1893, spent the years from 1893 to 1897 in advanced study at the University of Chicago, and since 1897 has been connected with the teaching staff of Princeton. He received in 1899 from the University of Chicago the degree of Doctor of Philosophy.

Dr. Oswald Veblen, Preceptor in Mathematics, was graduated Bachelor of Arts from the University of Iowa in 1898 and with the same degree from Harvard in 1900. From 1900 to 1903 he pursued graduate studies in Chicago University, holding a fellowship there throughout that period and receiving the degree of Doctor of Philosophy at the close of it. From 1903 until called to Princeton he was Associate in Mathematics at Chicago.

Dr. John Wesley Young, Preceptor in Mathematics, was graduated Bachelor of Philosophy from Ohio State University in 1899, Master of Arts from Cornell University in 1901, and Doctor of Philosophy from Cornell in 1904. From 1899 to 1900 he was Fellow and Assistant in Mathematics at the Ohio State University; from 1900 to 1901 Oliver Graduate Scholar, and from 1901 to 1902 Erastus Brooks Fellow in Mathematics at Cornell. In 1902 he was appointed Assistant in Mathematics at Cornell, and in 1903 Instructor in Mathematics at Northwestern University, whence he came to join our own staff of instruction.

Dr. Marcus Stults Farr, Preceptor in Geology, was graduated Bachelor of Arts from Princeton in 1892; from 1892 to 1893 was Fellow in Biology at Princeton, taking the degree of Master of Science in 1893; was Fellow in Zoölogy at the University of Chicago 1893-1894, and received from that University in 1894 the degree of Master of Arts; was graduate student at Princeton 1894-1896 and received from Princeton in 1896 the degree of Doctor of Science; was Assistant in the Paleontological Laboratory in Princeton from 1896 to 1898, Assistant Zoölogist at the New York State Museum at Albany from 1898 to 1900, and from 1900 to 1905 Assistant in Geology at Princeton.

These appointments followed very fortunately upon our recent thorough reconstitution of the course of study.[1] In that reconsideration of the subject matter of our teaching we gave a new co-ordination to the studies of the University and effected an arrangement which has given to the undergraduate's choice of studies a new touch of system and consistency. These changes have afforded us a definite and satisfactory basis for reconsidering also and improving our methods of instruction. A year ago, when I submitted my last report to you, I did not venture even to hope that I was so soon to be able to set about reforms which for more than twelve years past have seemed to me the only effectual means of making university instruction the helpful and efficient thing it should be. I have now the great happiness of realizing that these reforms have already been effected with ease and enthusiasm, that Princeton is likely to be privileged to show how, even in a great University, the close and intimate contact of pupil and teacher may even in the midst of the modern variety of studies, be restored and maintained. Our object in so largely recruiting our Faculty has been to take our instruction as much as possible out of the formal class-rooms and get it into the lives of the undergraduates, depending less on lectures and written

[1] See the Editorial Note, "The New Princeton Course of Study," Vol. 15.

tests and more on personal conference and intimate counsel. Our preceptors, with a very few exceptions, devote themselves exclusively to private conference with the men under their charge upon the reading they are expected to do in their several courses. The new appointments have not been made in the laboratory departments, where direct personal contact between teacher and pupil has long been a matter-of-course method of instruction, but in what may be called the "reading" departments. We are trying to get away from the idea, born of the old system of lectures and quizzes, that a course in any subject consists of a particular teacher's lectures or the conning of a particular text-book, and to act upon the very different idea that a course is a subject of study to be got up by as thorough and extensive reading as possible outside the class-room; that the class-room is merely a place of test and review, and that lectures, no matter how authoritative the lecturer, are no more than a means of directing, broadening, illuminating, or supplementing the student's reading.

Accordingly, the function of the preceptor is that of guide, philosopher, and friend. In each department of study each undergraduate who choses the department, or who is pursuing all the courses offered in it in his year, is assigned to a Preceptor, to whom he reports and with whom he confers upon all of his reading in those courses. We try to limit the number of men assigned to one Preceptor so that they may not be too numerous to receive individual attention. He meets them at frequent intervals, singly or in small groups, usually in his own private study or in some one of the smaller and quieter rooms of the University, and uses any method that seems to him most suitable to the individuals he is dealing with in endeavoring to give their work thoroughness and breadth; and the work they do with him is not of the character of mere preparation for examinations or mere drill in the rudiments of the subject, but is based upon books chosen as carefully as possible for the purpose of enabling them to cover their subjects intelligently.

And the gentlemen I have named are not the only preceptors. We are all preceptors. Under the new course of study the undergraduates choose not only a department with all of its courses, but also a few other electives which they follow without attempting all the courses of the departments to which those electives belong. The lecturers who conduct the courses thus singly or separately chosen themselves act as preceptors for these students, members of their classes but not of their departments, in respect of the reading that must be done in those subjects; and our new method is making its hold good upon all of us.

One way of stating the nature of the change is to say that now the reading of subjects is the real work of the University and not intermittent study for examinations: that the term work, as we have been accustomed to call it, stands out as the whole duty of the student; and the amount of work done by the undergraduates has increased amazingly. But this is a much too formal way of stating the change. It looks at its surface and not within it. It is not the amount of work done that pleases us so much as its character and the willingness and zest with which it is undertaken. The greater subjects of study pursued at a University, those which constitute the elements of a well-considered course of undergraduate training, are of course intrinsically interesting; but the trouble has been that the undergraduates did not find it out. They did tasks, they did not pursue interests. Our pleasure in observing the change that has come about by reason of our new methods of instruction comes from seeing the manifest increase of willingness and interest with which the undergraduates now pursue their studies. The new system has been in operation but a little more than two months and yet it has affected the habits of the University almost as much as if it were an ancient institution. The undergraduates have welcomed it most cordially and have fallen in with it with singular ease and comprehension, and we feel that both authority and opinion are working together towards a common end,—the rejuvenation of study.

At the close of the last Academic year a "Senior Society" was formed upon the initiative and by the action of leading undergraduates, which has already proved an invaluable aid in the development of the unwritten constitution of the excellent system of self-government under which we live with regard to all that concerns our university life.[2] The Society is made up by the election of fifteen members of the Senior class, chosen as representatives of all the undergraduate activities: from the honor lists, the undergraduate publications, the dramatic and musical societies, the athletic teams and managers, and men of

2 The Senior Society was organized in June 1905 by the Class of 1906. According to its constitution, it consisted of twenty-one members, not fifteen as Wilson stated, who were leaders of various social, literary, and sports organizations. They were chosen by the society's members of the graduating class. The purpose of the organization, according to its constitution, was to reward those students who had achieved positions of leadership and to represent a cross section of undergraduates in discussions with the Board of Trustees and the faculty "for the purpose of connected effort along any line where such effort seems necessary and advisable." See the *Daily Princetonian*, June 14, 1905.

recognized social influence. Certainly this year we recognize in its members men who are really leaders of undergraduate opinion, and it has been with both pleasure and profit that the Dean of the University and I have called them into consultation upon matters of moment in which it was not only proper but desirable that authority should wait upon opinion.

The reconstitution of the general courses of undergraduate study in the Academic department and in Science effected during the year 1903-1904 was followed last year by a corresponding revision of the courses of study and of the entrance requirements in the department of Civil Engineering.[3] The entrance requirements were so amended that they will, after 1909, be substantially the same as those for the courses leading to the degrees of Bachelor of Science and Bachelor of Letters. In one particular, however, they will be singular. In 1907, and thereafter, no student will be admitted as a Freshman in the Civil Engineering course until he has passed all the mathematical subjects required for entrance. In other words, no one will be admitted with a condition in any part of his mathematics. Mathematics constitutes so essential a part of almost every study of the Engineering course that experience has taught us the futility of admitting to that course anyone insufficiently prepared in the mathematical studies.

In reconstituting the course of study we have sought to make the first two years, years not of technical study, but of drill in the fundamental scientific subjects like mathematics, physics, chemistry, mineralogy, and geology and of training in English and the modern languages. All the technical and strictly professional studies except geodesy and graphics, in which drill must begin early and be long continued, are placed upon the schedules of Junior and Senior years. We think that as it now stands the Engineering course is at once as thorough and as liberal as we can make it within the strait limits of four years. It ought, if we had the means and a free hand in the matter, to be made a graduate course, to be pursued after thorough training in general science and as liberal a programme of undergraduate study as possible.

A change has been brought about this year in connection with the administration of our Graduate School, which is likely, we believe, to be the beginning of a notable development. By the great generosity of a faithful friend of the University,[4] "Merwick,"

[3] See n. 1 to the Minutes of the Princeton University Faculty printed at April 17, 1905.
[4] Moses Taylor Pyne.

the delightful residence on Bayard Lane lately occupied by Professor George Lansing Raymond, has been purchased and fitted up as a house of residence for as many of the graduate students of the University as it can accommodate. The house is comfortable and spacious, stands in beautiful grounds ornamented with delightful shade trees, and, under the care of Professor Howard Crosby Butler, has at once become an institution among us. We believe that in this graduate house we have a sure prophecy of the Graduate College for which we so eagerly hope as the crowning distinction of Princeton's later development as a University.

The number of graduate students, which was last year ninety-four, is this year one hundred and six. Of this number thirty-three are devoting themselves exclusively to graduate study and seventy-three are combining graduate study with work in the Princeton Theological Seminary. Of the thirty-three regular graduate students, twelve have rooms at "Merwick" and twenty take their meals there. Professor Butler is also of course in residence at "Merwick" and presides over the little academic household.

The following table shows the number admitted to the University as undergraduates this year as compared with last:

	1904.			1905.		
	Acad.	S. S.	Total.	Acad.	S. S.	Total.
Freshmen without conditions	54	34	88	75	59	134
Freshmen with conditions	100	188	288	121	156	277
Specials	24	41	65	....	....	48
Seniors	7	4	11	4	1	5
Juniors	2	2	4	1	2	3
Sophomores	10	1	11	4	4	8
	197	270	467	205	222	475

Of the Freshmen admitted upon examination in 1904, nineteen, for one reason or another, did not come. Of those admitted this year, twenty did not come. So that the corrected figures for the two years are: 1904, 448; 1905, 455. The actual number of Freshmen who entered the University in 1904, exclusive of first year special students, was 357; in 1905, 391; a gain of 34 in the entrance figures of this year as compared with those of last year. To these statistics the following, for the full information of the Board, should be added:

	1904.			1905.		
	Acad.	S. S.	Total.	Acad.	S. S.	Total.
Examined but not admitted	24	41	65	19	50	69
Preliminary and partial examination	225	260	485	185	252	437

In the number of preliminary and partial examinations there is a falling off of forty-eight as compared with last year, a decrease which we believe to be accounted for by the fact that last year no fee was charged for entrance examinations and large numbers of boys at preparatory schools tried the examinations for the sake of getting our certificates without any intention of coming to Princeton. This year we adopted the practice of other universities in charging a fee. It may be presumed, therefore, that those who took our examinations were bona fide candidates for entrance.

The total undergraduate enrollment in the University is 1,280, and was last year 1,283. The gain of 34 in the number of Freshmen is more than offset by the loss of 72 from the last entering class during their first year at the University. The present Sophomore class, which numbered 357 at entrance, has an enrollment of only 285. We have reason to believe that the very much more careful application of our entrance tests this year resulted in the admission of fewer men who are likely to fail during their first year, the year of severe trying-out processes.

Two new buildings are now being erected, one the dormitory given by the ten classes, 1892-1901, a portion of which is already partially roofed and which gives promise of being entirely completed and ready for occupation by the opening of the next academic year, and McCosh Hall, the gift of a small group of loyal friends of the University who are also devoted to the memory of Dr. James McCosh. The foundations of McCosh Hall have been completed and will be allowed to settle during the winter. It is hoped that the work on the building can be very rapidly pushed forward in the spring and that it may be ready for occupation by the first of January, 1907. When it is finished we shall have in beautiful form what we have for so many years so much needed, —a commodious and convenient building for all sorts of class exercises and for the smaller sort of occasional public gatherings.

The Fitz-Randolph gateway and fence are completed, and now frame the front of Nassau Hall and the original plot of ground upon which the college was built in a manner at once beautiful and appropriate.

The Treasurer's statement, appended to this Report, is this year cast in a new form, which distinguishes in separate items the sums spent for administration and for the several departments of instruction in the University, and which will, it is hoped, display the finances of the University in a more intelligible and significant way than before.

In that statement will be found a record of the first year's result of the work of the Committee of Fifty, through whose efforts the money has been provided for our new work of instruction and for most of the improvements which we are carrying into effect. That Committee has become a vital instrument of our life. Respectfully submitted, WOODROW WILSON.[5]

Printed document (WP, DLC).
[5] There is a WWsh draft of this report in WP, DLC.

Henry Burchard Fine to the Board of Trustees' Committee on Morals and Discipline

Gentlemen: PRINCETON UNIVERSITY, DECEMBER 14, 1905.

I beg to submit the following report:

The regulations for morning chapel which were approved by the Board of Trustees at its last meeting have thus far worked very satisfactorily. The daily attendance has been excellent. It has averaged more than 400 and has never fallen below 300. Inasmuch as the students consider the new requirement fair and reasonable they attend willingly and take part in the service with good spirit. Enough members of the choir are present each morning really to lead the singing, which, as a consequence, has been very good. The card system of recording attendance has caused no confusion and has given rise to no abuses. Of course it was to be expected that among over 1200 undergraduates there would be some who could learn by experience only that the new requirement was not to be evaded by excuse. I have had to suspend 12 students thus far for chapel absences.

I have not been called upon to administer any discipline more serious than this since the term began. This Fall the undergraduates are far more interested in their studies than heretofore. There is certainly less idleness among them, and it may therefore be reasonably inferred less dissipation.

Respectfully submitted, H. B. Fine

TRS (Trustees' Papers, UA, NjP).

From the Minutes of the Board of Trustees of Princeton University

[Dec. 14, 1905]

The Trustees of Princeton University met in stated session in the Trustee's Room in the Chancellor Green Library, Princeton,

New Jersey, at eleven o'clock on Thursday morning December 14, 1905. . . .

NO REPORT FROM COMMITTEE ON FINANCIAL
CONDITIONS OF THE HALLS

The President of the University stated that one member of the Committee appointed to consider and report on the financial condition of the Halls had asked to be excused from service on the committee and that in consequence the Committee was not prepared to make a report.

COMMITTEE ON FINANCIAL CONDITION OF THE
HALLS INCREASED

On motion of Mr. Henry, seconded by Mr. Cuyler, it was
RESOLVED that the Committee on the subject of the financial condition of Whig and Clio Halls be increased to six and that the duties of the committee be enlarged to take in the general condition and welfare of these societies.

In accordance with this resolution the President of the University appointed the following committee:

Cleveland H. Dodge
Robert Garrett
John D. Davis
Bayard Henry
Henry W. Green
John L. Cadwalader[1]

[1] This committee's report is printed at March 7, 1906.

From Charles Williston McAlpin

[Princeton, N. J.]
Dear President Wilson: December 14, 1905.

In reply to your letter of the 13th inst. I have sent Mr. [Arthur Hugh Urquhart] Colquhoun, the Secretary of Toronto University,[1] the only article dealing with the Preceptorial System which we have, namely the brief statement prepared by yourself for the Committee of Fifty circular. I have called his attention to your article in "THE INDEPENDENT" of August 3rd last and which he will doubtless find in the Library of Toronto University. When this article came out I tried to secure a number of copies of THE INDEPENDENT but they informed me that the issue had been exhausted.

As we have many inquiries concerning the system and as this article is the only official statement of any length that has yet

appeared I think I will ask the permission of THE INDEPENDENT
to reprint it in pamphlet form if you approve the idea.

I remain,   Very sincerely yours,   [C. W. McAlpin]

CCL (McAlpin File, UA, NjP).
1 In fact, Colquhoun was at this time secretary of a special Royal Commission
of the Province of Ontario to inquire into the affairs of the University of Toronto.

An Address at Swarthmore College

[[Dec. 15, 1905]]

THE UNIVERSITY AND THE NATION.*

It is a great pleasure to find myself in this well known college
town, which I have never had the opportunity to visit before, and
which I esteem myself poor in not having known sooner. I feel
that I have undertaken to discuss before you a very great theme,
but you know there is a certain nautical advantage in giving
yourself plenty of sea room. I am sure that I can find room to
turn in in the great topic I have set myself to speak about. The
"university" would alone be a sufficient theme. The "university
and the nation" adds to the theme of education that of national
life and national affairs.

It would be very difficult for any one to know America well
enough to assess it, and I suppose that we are all keenly aware
that in our day America is coming to mean something new, that
the America described to us by the historian is not the America
in which we live, and that the era in which we live is producing
an America which will be new to the history of the world. I suppose that there is no country anywhere looked to with more
expectation of new things,—with apprehension by the European,
with hope by those who sympathize with the things which she
has professed in the past. Our own attitude has always been an
attitude of admiration, that easy admiration which is self-admira-
tion. We are very much in the attitude towards ourselves of a
lawyer friend of mine, who meeting two other members of the
bar, asked what they were discussing. They said they were discussing the question as to who was the leading practitioner at
the bar. "I am," he said. "How do you prove it?" "I don't have to
prove it; I admit it." Our own attitude toward our greatness is
very much the same. We don't have to prove it, we admit it. We
have always admitted it, and have even boasted of the size of the
continent as if we [were responsible for] of its size, because we
took possession of it, and we may say one is as large as the things

* An address in Parrish Hall, Swarthmore College, December 15, 1905. From
a stenographic report.

he takes possession of. . . .[1] I suppose that even yet we are not proud simply because of the material accumulations made by Americans, or the material power gathered together by the American nation. There have been other nations as fully equipped for mastery or dominion as we are or are likely to be, and they have not had histories which would encourage us to repeat the annals that characterized them in the days succeeding their supremacy. America is not the first to feel herself called to ruling the world, but if she rules the world well she will be the first to do that. And I suppose that in our hearts we know that we shall rule the world and rule it well or ill, as we do or do not maintain our characters as idealists. America is not great because of the things she holds in her hand, but because of the things she holds in her heart, because of the visions she has seen; and she will lose her greatness if in her too sophisticated majority she forgets the visions of her youth. It is not because we will have and hold the fleetest ships and most irresistible armies that we shall deserve the annals we started out to write, but as we use these armies and navies to do the just thing and to serve mankind.

We used to boast of our success as makers of government, but we do not boast any longer. There is hardly a great city in Europe which is not better governed than any American city. There is hardly a national government in Europe which is not more efficient and economically organized than the government of the United States. We waste our time electing a multitude of persons who are inexperienced in the functions for which we choose them, and their inexperience makes our government difficult and costly. We have not invented the best government. Mr. Bagehot used to say that because we had succeeded in running the Constitution of the United States it was not to be concluded that the Constitution of the United States was an excellent constitution, "because," he said, "Americans can run any constitution. They are ingenious enough, they are mature enough, they are steadfast enough to manage any system of constitutions, and because persons who know how to conduct themselves are conducting themselves well, it does not prove that the system under which they live is the best system."

We cannot any longer be proud of having the best institutions in the world. Of what should we be proud then? Of meaning to use our institutions for something grander than anything that has ever before been held as a national ideal.

The beauty of free institutions is that every man is put upon his honor to deserve to belong to the free community. We have

[1] This and following elisions in the original text.

very whimsical conceptions of what liberty is. It is difficult to say what it is, but easy to say what it is not. Liberty is not freedom from restraint. Take the phrase with reference to a boat. We say that she sails free. Do we mean that she is defying the forces of nature? No, we mean that she is adjusted to the forces of nature; she is going their way and therefore free. I am free in a false sense to climb to the roof of this building and to jump off, but when I jump off I am no longer free. Nature says to me, "Thou fool, I gave thee an understanding of the laws of nature, and thou hast defied them. Henceforth thou art my prisoner and hast no freedom at all." Just so surely as you defy the fixed laws of moral and of physical life you have forfeited your freedom. The man who thinks he is free to follow vice is simply a fool that allows himself to load his wrists with chains. Any man is free to load himself with chains, but if he is wise he will remain free and adjust himself to the profoundest laws of life. And we remain free if we adjust ourselves to the necessities of social relationships, and if we remain true to them. . . .

If there is any nation in the world which should be served by the school and the university it is the nation whose freedom depends on knowledge. De Tocqueville used to say of our institutions that they required a variety of information and a nicety of discrimination on the part of the citizen unparalleled anywhere else. How, therefore, are we to enable this nation to maintain her freedom? By clarifying her knowledge. Only as we know shall we live. The beauty of study, the beauty of all academic exercise, is that men profess at an[y] rate to have devoted themselves to the service of truth, find it where they may, find it as they may; and the man who throttles inquiry, who embarrasses the freedom of any portion of the mind, is an enemy not only of learning, but also of freedom and of the very social structure itself. It is for this high destiny, this destiny political as well as intellectual that the university is set up in a free country. We talk about universities being designed to produce citizens. Yes; but by a particular process of enlightenment; the flooding in of light on all that the human mind seeks to know, so that man shall no longer stumble because of ignorance in paths which are crossed by deep shadows, but that light shall blaze everywhere and man walk as seeing his way and able to guide his footsteps. So the university is intended for a particular function. A nation like ours is nothing single, it is plural, it is multiform, it is multifarious, complex, and what we have never understood is that the university is not for everybody. The university is for a minority and for a small minority, small not absolutely but relatively to the whole number. There is nothing restrictive, nothing exclusive in the small minority chosen for university training, because it is self-chosen. The vital[i]ty of democracy lies in this one thing[:] that every individual is free to choose for himself any career or achievement that he cares to aspire to, unlimited by class, by social condition, by social prejudice, but free to rise to anything that is not above his strength. . . . So that the minority that frequents the halls of the university is a self-chosen minority, chosen by reason of ambition, theoretically at any rate. I cannot pass that sentence without qualification, because I know many are not chosen by themselves but by their parents, and parents are apt to be mistaken. There is a proverb, "You can lead an ass to knowledge, but you cannot make him think." There are individuals, individual undergraduates, who are certainly in the wrong place. I have been reminded once and again of the remark of a friend of mine who after twenty years as a teacher declared that the human mind had infinite resources for resisting the introduction of knowledge; and I must admit that some of the men sent to the university illustrate these infinite resources. Nevertheless it is true that a considerable percentage are there because bidden by their own spirits to be there. So long, however, as the lad whose spirit bids him be a university man is free to be a university man, the principle that I am insisting on is a valid principle. A great many persons answer me when I broach the subject of liberal education that we must have technical education, and so we should. Who said we shouldn't? We must have manual training and technical education and the limited training which is needed for the practical uses of business for the vast majority of youngsters who are trained in this country. But it doesn't follow that we must not have the other kind also. And I for one maintain that unless a minority desires and gets a liberal education the ship of State will be without its pilots. For what is a liberal education? An education which gives a man something besides skill. I have sometimes thought of the man who has nothing but skill as a sort of intellectual mechanic. There are certain things he can do with his faculties admirably well, but he cannot do anything else with them. Yet for the affairs of the nation to be properly conducted somebody must have enlightened visions about things and pursuits out of which he is not making his own bread and butter. . . .

We have an erroneous way of speaking of a man having lost his way in the desert as having lost himself. That is the only thing he has not lost. *He* is there. The trouble with him is he has lost everything else in the world. If he knew where any

fixed thing in the world was he could steer by it and get somewhere. As it is he walks hopelessly in a circle towards the left.
If we walk vaguely in an open space we tend to walk to the left
and to complete a circle and to go on walking in the same circle.
But just as soon as you orient yourself (to use a fine German
phrase) and know where the east is, then you know where the
north is, and the south and the west, and you can steer and get
somewhere. Translated into terms of the intellectual life, you
have the liberal education, that which relates yourself with something like a sweep of horizon to the rest of the world. Somebody,
if the world is to be guided, must pore upon the whole matter of
life; somebody must seek a coign of vantage from which to see
the plan [plain] of human life, to see the broad highways of industry and commerce and the by-paths and frontiers beyond
which human life has not gone, and where the region of discovery lies.

Printed in the Swarthmore, Pa., *Swarthmorean*, I (Jan. 25, 1906), 2-3; *ibid.*,
Feb. 1, 1906, pp. 2-3.

From the Minutes of the Princeton University Faculty

5 p.m.   December 18, 1905.

The Faculty met, the President presiding. . . .

A communication from the national Football Conference[1] was
referred with power to the Committee on Out-Door Sports, acting
with the President.

[1] That is, the group formed at the meeting in New York on December 8, 1905.
The communication, which is missing, was an invitation to send a representative
to the general meeting planned for December 28, 1905.

An Announcement

[Dec. 18, 1905]

President Wilson and the faculty Committee on Out-Door
Sports of Princeton University announced today, as the principal
changes in the methods of playing and conducting football which
Princeton believes to be essential for the proper reformation of
the game, and will urge very earnestly on all suitable occasions,
the following:

1. That in the playing of the game all interference be abolished;

2. That all coaching by men who are paid in any way, directly
or indirectly, or who receive their expenses, or any part of them,
be done away with; and

3. That the number of intercollegiate contests be very much decreased and the length of the season for such contest correspondingly shortened.

The first suggestion is for the purpose of abolishing all mass plays and of restoring the original open game.

The second suggestion is designed to place the game upon a purely amateur footing, and to restore to the players themselves the initiative of which, in recent years, they have been deprived.

The object of the third suggestion is to decrease the amount of time and energy which the players are now obliged to devote to the game.

The committee has instructed Princeton's representative upon the Rules Committee,[1] Mr. J. B. Fine, to urge upon that committee the acceptance of the first suggestion.

WWT MS with WWhw emendations (WWP, UA, NjP).
[1] The Intercollegiate Rules Committee, formed on March 13, 1896, by representatives from Cornell, Harvard, the Naval Academy, Pennsylvania, Princeton, and Yale. The University of Chicago was admitted to membership in 1904.

To Henry Mitchell MacCracken

My dear Sir: Princeton, N. J.   19 December, 1905.

Not until yesterday afternoon was I able to present to the University Faculty the invitation you were kind enough to convey to Princeton in behalf of the National Foot Ball Conference of Universities and Colleges.

I need not assure you of our very deep interest in the whole question of the reform of the game of foot ball. We have of course been giving it very careful and very extended consideration. We have, indeed, come to conclusions so definite and comprehensive that we could go into such a conference as that proposed for the 28th of December only to urge our own conclusions.

In view of these facts it is our feeling that we should not seek to be represented in the approaching conference, though we sincerely wish for it the most useful results. We should not wish to appear to attend it only to insist upon a particular view of the case.[1]

I take the liberty of sending you a brief statement of our conclusions.

Very sincerely yours,   Woodrow Wilson

TLS (draft) (WWP, UA, NjP).
[1] The conference met in New York on the scheduled date. The *New York Times*, Dec. 29, 1905, reported that representatives from sixty-two institutions, after a long and stormy session, voted to establish a continuing association, the National Intercollegiate Football Conference, and to appoint a Conference Rules

Committee to seek joint meetings and possible amalgamation with the Intercollegiate Rules Committee. The new association changed its name within a
year to the Intercollegiate Athletic Association and in 1910 assumed its present
title, the National Collegiate Athletic Association.

To William Rainey Harper

My dear Dr. Harper: Princeton, N. J.   20 December, 1905.

We yesterday afternoon held our last University Faculty meeting before the Christmas vacation and I gathered from the members present so strong an impression of their feeling of sympathy
and admiration for you that I am giving myself the pleasure of
sending you this Christmas greeting.

You may be sure that the qualities you have shown in so simple
and so beautiful a way during your illness have won an admiration from us all which is nothing short of affection and personal
loyalty and I know that I am only expressing the views of every
man here when I send you a greeting from our very hearts.[1]

Faithfully and sincerely yours,   Woodrow Wilson

TLS (W. R. Harper Papers, ICU).
[1] President Harper was suffering from a terminal case of cancer. He died on
January 10, 1906.

From Melancthon Williams Jacobus

[Hartford, Conn.]
My dear President Wilson: December 20th, 1905.

I thank you for your kind inquiry of the 18th inst., and I am
glad to say that it was no illness of a serious nature that prevented my being present at the Board. I had really been in no
condition for some days preceding your visit, and matters grew
worse until Wednesday when the doctor sent me to bed where I
remained until the latter part of the week. But I am up and at
my work again, though not exactly in good shape.

I was greatly disappointed to miss the meeting, for I wished
especially to hear your annual report, and I am wondering
whether Mr. McAlpin could, without much inconvenience, send
me a rescript of it, together with a statement of such matters of
importance as were discussed and transacted at the meeting of
the Board. My interest in Princeton will not allow me to remain
out of touch with what is being done, for any length of time.

I am going to take this opportunity of telling you that Hartford has been talking about your address ever since you left
here, and bids fair to continue to do so for some time to come.
I can say it to you, for I think we know each other well enough

for you to understand the genuineness of the statement, that it was far and away the finest thing that has ever been given to the Twentieth Century Club,[1] and we have had some notable men from the East and the West and the South.

Naturally, as a Princeton man, I am simply delighted at the impression made; for the fault of New England is its provincialism, and there is nothing that can ever happen to it which is of such value as an awakening once in a while to the existence and importance of things outside its own territory.

Believe me when I say even more, and tell you that some of the best and most influential men who were there that night have said to me: "It was a great address and makes certain that the Preceptorial System is an important move in education; but the chief impression made was not so much the great system as the great man behind it."

Now forgive me for unloading all this upon you, but we love Princeton and you have done for her a notable service in coming to us here and giving us the address you did.

With kindest regards,

Yours cordially,   M W Jacobus

P.S.—Might I ask if any action was taken at the meeting of the Committee on Honorary Degrees in respect of the matter concerning which I spoke to you on our way to the station?[2]

M W J

TLS (WP, DLC).
[1] A brief news report of Wilson's address is printed at Dec. 12, 1905.
[2] Jacobus had probably suggested that Princeton award an honorary degree to the Rev. Dr. William Douglas Mackenzie, President of the Hartford Theological Seminary since 1903. Mackenzie received the LL.D. at the commencement on June 13, 1906.

From Henry Burling Thompson

My dear Wilson   [Greenville P.O., Del.] Dec 21, 1905

If the enclosed clipping[1] reports the situation correctly and I assume it does, permit me to congratulate you most heartily on the position you have taken on foot ball reform. The first suggestion while radical, yet if accomplished saves a very good game for it will virtually put the game back to the English Rugby, a better game for the average American boy than the present style of play. The second suggestion is in every way admirable and would do away with all the professional elements, particularly the insidious amateur professional, who has lowered the game to present standards.

The third suggestion ought to satisfy every one, whose sense of proportion is normal.

I sincerely trust the Princeton view will be acceptable to our opponents   Yours sincerely   Henry B Thompson

ALS (WP, DLC).
1 The clipping is missing, but it was a news report about the announcement printed at Dec. 18, 1905.

To John Grier Hibben and Jenny Davidson Hibben

My dearest Friends,   Christmas Day, 1905.   Princeton

Ellen and I are delighted with our presents, and thank you with hearts full of love. You know what we think,—what every one must think,—of the picture of dear Beth,—and, as for my decanter, I think it one of the most beautiful things of the kind I ever saw. It has so much *character*,—possesses a sort of *masculine* beauty and yet has grace and distinction. It is no ordinary thing, and I shall know how to value it for its own sake.

But its chief value in my eyes is, of course, as a token of your love. Its beauty expresses your unerring taste, but the fact that it is here and is mine expresses something that goes to the quick with me,—makes life a thing to take happiness from, and courage, and every good thing. May God always bless you both in all things, and may he make me worthier of your love.

Your devoted Friend,   Woodrow Wilson

ALS (photostat in WC, NjP).

To Benjamin Wistar Morris III

My dear Mr. Morris,   Princeton, N. J.   26 December, 1905.

Allow me to acknowledge your favour of the twenty-second. I take pleasure in returning the enclosed contracts,[1] signed as you request. I keep the order you sent and the t[h]ird copy of each of these contracts for our files.

I hope that you have had a very happy Christmas.

Always

Cordially and faithfully yours   Woodrow Wilson

WWTLS (WC, NjP).
1 For finishing and furnishing the tower room in Seventy-Nine Hall as Wilson's office, for which the Class of 1879 had voted to spend about $6,000. See the news item printed at June 9, 1906.

Woodrow Wilson, Grover Cleveland and William Jay Magie to John James McCook and Charles Beatty Alexander

[Princeton, N. J.]

Dear Sir: December, 1905. [c. Dec. 29, 1905]

We, the Undersigned, members of the Board of Trustees of Princeton University, earnestly request and advise you to resign your seats on the Board.[1]

In doing this we do not wish to be understood as making any charges against you; but we cannot remain blind to the fact that, whether justly or unjustly, it has come about that the successful conduct of the affairs of the University is embarrassed by your participation in its control. Our object is to protect the University against all criticism likely to hamper either its work or its growth, and we venture to suggest, in view of the present situation, a means by which you can prove in the most effectual manner your appreciation of the delicacy of the position in which the Board is placed,—an opportunity to serve the interests of Princeton in a most patriotic and unselfish way. Our sincere desire in presenting this paper is to bring about what we are sure will be to your interest and to that of the University in the way least painful and most honorable to all parties.

Woodrow Wilson   Grover Cleveland   W. J. Magie[2]

WWTLS (WP, DLC).

[1] McCook and Alexander were members of the Board of Directors of the Equitable Life Assurance Society, one of the largest of seventeen insurance companies under investigation by a committee of the New York legislature for mismanagement and gross abuse of company funds. McCook and Alexander were also partners in the law firm of Alexander and Green, which had served as legal counsel for the Equitable at various times since 1868. The committee hearings, conducted by the chief counsel, Charles Evans Hughes, lasted from early September until late December 1905, were reported in great detail in the press, and aroused widespread public concern. Although the names of C. B. Alexander and McCook never figured prominently in the daily disclosures, their association with the Equitable was apparently enough to induce the signatories of this letter to request their resignations.

Cleveland may have instigated this request since he occupied a special position in the reorganization of the Equitable and entertained strong views concerning the misappropriation of insurance funds held in virtual public trust. In June 1905, Cleveland, at the request of Thomas Fortune Ryan, who had purchased the controlling block of Equitable stock, had become one of three trustees empowered to vote the Ryan stock in the annual selection of directors. Ryan had established the trusteeship in an effort to restore stockholder and public confidence in the company, following the highly publicized struggle for power between the president, James Waddel Alexander, and the vice president, James Hazen Hyde, son of the founder of the Equitable. Alexander and Hyde resigned their positions in June 1905. For a full discussion of the Equitable's troubles in 1905 and of the insurance investigations, see Roscoe Carlyle Buley, *The Equitable Life Assurance Society of the United States, 1859-1964* (2 vols., New York, 1967), I, 539-699.

[2] As the documents will soon reveal, copies of this letter were sent to the trustees in Philadelphia for their signatures, after which Wilson planned to circulate the letter further.

A Desk Diary

[Jan. 1-Dec. 31, 1906]
The Standard Diary 1906 with WWhw entries of engagements and appointments.

Bound desk diary (WP, DLC).

From John Aikman Stewart

My dear President Wilson   New York.   January 3d 1906
    Mr John McCook sought an interview with me yesterday and the result has led me to believe that there ought to be a personal interview between him and yourself. Thus far he has been approached in the matter of his resignation only indirectly through Mr Charles B. Alexander, and he feels that he is entitled to learn directly from the President of the University regarding the feeling in the community which prompts the request for his resignation.[1]   Very truly Yours   John A Stewart

ALS (WP, DLC).
[1] Obviously, Alexander and McCook had somehow learned about the existence of the letter requesting their resignations.

From Bayard Henry, with Enclosure

My Dear President Wilson   [Philadelphia, c. Jan. 4, 1906]
    Pyne has just asked me to send this to you, by telephone.
                                                    B.H

ALI (written on B. Henry to M. T. Pyne, Jan. 2, 1906).

E N C L O S U R E

Bayard Henry to Moses Taylor Pyne

My dear Momo: Philadelphia.   Jan 2 1906
    Your special delivery letter with enclosures, which I herewith return, received yesterday just as I was leaving home. I was unable to confer with Dr. Craven and Dr. Wood until today. Without attempting to influence them in any way whatever they both advised me they are unwilling to sign the papers sent over, and think that a simple request something similar to what I sent you, covers the situation. This as I wrote you before, was Mr. Van Rensselaer's attitude. I am very sorry that there is this difference of opinion in a matter of such vital moment. Although disapprov-

ing of the form of letter, I would have been willing to sign if it had met with the approval of Dr. Craven and Dr. Wood, but when their judgment coincided with mine, and when Dr. Wood pointed out that the various requests and suggestions would open a field for discussion, I could not help feeling that I was right in my first judgment, and, that is, that a strong, plain and simple request alleging that in our judgment their continuing on the Board was an injury to the University, was better than the draft of letter presented. Knowing the sentiments of the Philadelphia members of the Board I can meet with you or President Wilson any time within the next few days when it will be convenient for you to be in Princeton, when I can point out to you just how these gentlemen and I feel on the subject of the form of letter. In looking up the charter last evening I see no reason why if the request to resign is declined we cannot act on the ground that they have become unfit to remain as Trustees, and then (as that is a question which is to be determined according to the judgment of the Board) we can decide they are unfit to remain, and proceed to elect their successors.

With best wishes and hoping there will not be any great delay in redrafting the letter to these men[1] I remain, with best wishes

Yours sincerely   Bayard Henry

TLS (WP, DLC).
[1] Subsequent documents strongly indicate that the letter was not redrafted.

From Moses Taylor Pyne

My dear Woodrow: New York   January 5, 1906.

I have been trying to get you this afternoon, but they tell me you are out of town.

I have gone over the matter very carefully with Cuyler and Cleve Dodge, and we are of the opinion that we cannot afford to let anything interfere with the progress of matters at this time.

We think that you ought, yourself, to go to Philadelphia and see Dr. Craven and Dr. Wood, and probably Dr. [J. Addison] Henry, at once, as I think you can explain matters to them in such wise as to get them to sign it. Bayard undoubtedly said nothing adverse to them at the time he presented the papers to them, but, with his view that a different kind of a paper was necessary, he probably was not in a position to answer their questions when they first saw the paper. No one can handle the matter more diplomatically than you can with these gentlemen, and I think the matter is of sufficient importance for you to take it up at once.

If they still decline to sign it, our view is that the letter be sent to Mr. Jones and to St. Louis[1] and brought back so that Jacobus and George Stewart and the New York men can sign it. When every one else has signed it we can bring it up again before the Philadelphia men. It is of great importance that no time be lost now, and if they refuse to sign it, rather than change it, we should prefer to leave these men out till the last, and, if all the others have signed their refusal will not make much difference.

Cuyler thinks he may possibly have to go to Princeton tomorrow, and, if you are there, he will call on you, but as it is uncertain, if you could possibly see these gentlemen tomorrow it would be better.

I shall be in Princeton on Monday, and shall try to look you up in the morning sometime, but if I cannot find you then I will come in at 4 o'clock, but I should like to leave on the 3.50 if possible.   Very sincerely yours,   M Taylor Pyne

TLS (WP, DLC).
[1] That is, to the Alumni Trustee, John David Davis.

A News Report of an Address in Trenton

[Jan. 8, 1906]

ADDRESSED BY PRES. WILSON

Sons of American Revolution Might be
Styled Sons of Guns.

The teaching of American history was the subject of the address given by President Woodrow Wilson of Princeton, Saturday afternoon, when the steps were taken towards the formal organization of the Trenton conference of the association of history teachers of the Middle states and Maryland.

He said in part that the history he studied when a boy is not that taught today, as many of the valuable documents giving points of value do not get into the hands of one of the later generation until the former has passed away. Referring to the American revolution he said that the change was brought about by a minority and that those who are now sons of the revolution might be styled "sons of guns."

Replying to the criticisms of Americans because they are proud of the extent of the country he said that they have reason to be, inasmuch as they have developed the territory, although they are not responsible for its size.

The value of American history to Americans he said is the effect of facts upon ourselves. New Yorkers, he continued, might be said to know nothing about Americans.

Printed in the Trenton *True American*, Jan. 8, 1906.

From William Rainey Harper

My dear President Wilson,   Chicago, January 8, 1906.

I am greatly touched by your strong and generous Christmas greeting. It was kind of you and the Princeton Faculty to think of me and it was more kind to put your thought in such beautiful and encouraging words. I cannot tell you how much I have been aided during my illness by expressions of sympathy from my friends. Among these none have been more from the heart and therefore more valued than the message from you. Let me thank you and wish well to you and Princeton a thousand times.

Very Sincerely Yours,   William R. Harper

HwL (WP, DLC).

A News Report of a Religious Talk

[Jan. 12, 1906]

PRESIDENT WILSON'S ADDRESS.

Interesting Talk Before Philadelphian Society
Last Night in Murray Hall.

President Woodrow Wilson '79, addressed the first mid-week meeting of the year in Murray Hall last evening. He spoke on the "Newness of Spirit," taking as his text Romans 7:6: "But now we are delivered from the law, that being dead wherein we were held; that we should serve in newness of spirit, and not in the oldness of the Law." President Wilson spoke partly as follows:

I sincerely hope that these words express the spirit that is coming to this University. We all know what is right, and when we do wrong we know it. If there is an internal element urging us on to wrong doing, there is but one remedy, and that is newness of spirit, which makes the law not a burden but a pleasure. The only way to become a free man is to accept this spirit with intelligence to see that it means liberation.

As soon as we accommodate ourselves to the inevitable we gain this newness of spirit, and with it joy, ease, and power, instead of the old friction and worry. Nothing is more irksome to the mind than the rest of laziness; study brings with it its own joys, and fulfillment of duty will bring about spiritual welfare.

Touching on "Character as a by-product" I would say that if we do our duty, our character will take care of itself. Those who seek to do good for their own sakes, by that very definition do no good. The patient work of a life time will unconsciously heap up the greatest character, and pleasure will accompany it. Self-consciousness is one of the greatest curses of the world. The celebrated Oxford movement, led by Cardinal Newman, made one generation at that University memorable for all time. Let us pray for a great intellectual and spiritual revivification, so that we could look back to a certain year and say, in that year great spirits were bred in Princeton.[1]

Printed in the *Daily Princetonian*, Jan. 12, 1906.
[1] For this address, Wilson used the notes printed at Nov. 8, 1896, Vol. 10.

From Hopson Owen Murfee

My dear Dr. Wilson: Marion, Alabama.   12 January 1906

I am writing to ask if you will not contribute an article to a little volume on The Influence of Education on Character and Government, which we are endeavoring to prepare.[1] This volume is designed to present the necessity and the efficacy of self-government in educational institutions in developing moral character and in training for democratic citizenship. As you may surmise the volume will give fully the history and the principles of the Honor System; the power of its principles and practices to develop men of character and to train American youth for citizenship, is a capital aim of the work to establish. It seems to me that an Honor System of Self-Government in our schools is a necessity for the preservation of our democracy. For such a volume, will you not prepare an article on the relation of the School and College to the State, and the influence of an Honor System of Self-Government in School and College on the life of the State. We expect the volume to include articles by Professor W. M. Thornton,[2] (On the Genesis of the Honor System), President Eliot, President Hadley, Dr. C. W. Kent, of the University of Virginia.

I am aware of the magnitude of my request to one in your position; and I have presumed to make the request only because I believe that your article will be a real and permanent service to the cause of education.[3]

Very truly yours   H. O. Murfee

TLS (WP, DLC).
¹ The book was never published.
² William Mynn Thornton, Professor of Applied Mathematics and Civil Engineering at the University of Virginia, at this time also serving as Dean of the Department of Engineering.
³ Wilson eventually contributed an essay, "Education and Democracy." It is printed at May 3, 1907, Vol. 17.

A News Item

[Jan. 13, 1906]

WEST CHESTER.—The annual lecture course at the State Normal School was opened by Dr. Woodrow Wilson, president of Princeton University, who spoke upon "Patriotism."

Printed in the Philadelphia *Public Ledger*, Jan. 13, 1906.

From Charles Williston McAlpin

My dear Dr. Wilson: [Princeton, N. J.]   January 13, 1906.

Mr. Duffield has just notified me of the receipt of securities and property to the value of $100,000 from Mr. Pyne for the establishment of the Robert Stockton Pyne University Fund.¹ I write to ask if I shall give out this information to the press or wait until the next meeting of the Board?²

I remain,

Very sincerely yours,   [C. W. McAlpin]   Secretary.

CCL (McAlpin File, UA, NjP).
¹ This was Moses Taylor Pyne's gift to the Endowment Account of the Committee of Fifty Fund. It consisted of $51,000 in bonds and the deed to the property known as the Upper Pyne Building on Nassau Street in Princeton, valued at $50,000. The gift was to be designated the Robert Stockton Pyne University Fund in memory of M. T. Pyne's son, Robert Stockton Pyne, who had died on February 25, 1903, at the age of nineteen.
² See WW to C. W. McAlpin, Feb. 6, 1906.

A News Report of an Address at a Memorial Service in New York for William Rainey Harper

[Jan. 15, 1906]

Several memorial services in honor of the late Dr. William Rainey Harper,¹ President of the University of Chicago, were held in this city yesterday. The most impressive was that in the chapel of the Teachers College, Columbia University, at which the principal speakers were President Butler of Columbia, President Woodrow Wilson of Princeton, and the Rev. Dr. Charles Cuthbert Hall, President of Union Theological Seminary. This service was held simultaneously with the service in Chicago. . . .

President Wilson followed [President Butler], speaking of Dr. Harper, the strong, purposeful man.

"We have come not to bury Dr. Harper," he said, "but to recognize his immortality. Our predominant thought to-day should be not one of sorrow or personal loss, but of general obligation. Dr. Harper realized that he was dealing not with men's fortunes, but with their spirits. He not only attracted the attention of academic circles, but by his work drew to the university of which he was such a great part the eyes of the whole Nation.

"As Dr. Butler was speaking, I asked myself: What is a man? He whose self-commanding spirit is always in the saddle; he who is self-spending, whose energies are centred not on himself, or his tasks, but only so far as he and they serve his fellow-man.

"Dr. Harper was one of God's noblemen. We call men great who lift their own fortunes to the heights, but the only nobility is in the man who spends his surplus of greatness on others. He is nature's patrician. He was Dr. Harper."[2]

Printed in the *New York Times*, Jan. 15, 1906; editorial headings omitted.
[1] Who had died on January 10, 1906.
[2] There is a WWhw outline of these remarks, dated Jan. 13, 1906, in WP, DLC.

From John Meigs[1]

My dear Friend: Pottstown, Pennsylvania, Jan. 16th., 1906.

I, too, am very sorry, though not surprised to find, that on so short notice it will be impossible for you to come to us on Washington's birthday. I want, therefore, here and now, to ask you to come next year on Feb. 22nd., unless in the not unnatural developments of your presidential policy it should be important for you to be elsewhere at that time; and you know that if this is so our hearts and minds will attend you with every good wish.[2]

I cannot begin to tell you how deeply impressed I have been by the splendid preceptorial scheme which you have launched. It is royally distinctive, and should supply to Princeton what is lacking in every other university of the country.

I hope that your anticipations will be helpfully confirmed, though, of course, it is early to estimate the results of the new policy. I have, however, heard only one sentiment expressed by those who have had a chance to observe the practical operation of the plan, and I need not say that this sentiment has been wholly favorable.

Mrs. Meigs joins me in every good wish for your own and Mrs. Wilson's increasing happiness.

Faithfully yours,   John Meigs

TLS (WP, DLC).
¹ Headmaster of the Hill School in Pottstown, Pa.
² Wilson did speak at the Hill School on February 22, 1907. See the news item printed at Feb. 26, 1907, Vol. 17.

From Hopson Owen Murfee

My dear Dr. Wilson: Marion, Alabama.   18 January 1906

I thank you heartily for your kind and encouraging letter of the sixteenth. It is very gratifying to me to know that you think the work which I am undertaking is worth while; and that you may be able to contribute an article to the volume. I should have confessed in my first letter that I am indebted to you for my purpose and my plan. "Such government as ours is a form of conduct, and its only stable foundation is character"; and "Nothing establishes the republican state save trained capacity for self-government, practical aptitude for public affairs, habitual soberness and temperateness of united action," are words that have filled my mind and fired my imagination as nothing else has done since I first listened to Montesquieu and to Burke.¹ And the wonderful influence of your message to our boys last April in their life here, has made me feel that no greater service could be rendered to the youth of our country, and to those who are their teachers, than to give them in an enduring and worthy form such ideals. As I am so indebted to you for the purpose and plan of my endeavor, I have turned to you for that aid and counsel which I feel you alone can give.

Briefly, my idea is to have the volume consist of two parts: the first, historical, giving the genesis and the evolution of the Honor System; the second, expository, making plain the principles and the power of the Honor System with special reference to its influence in developing character and in training youth for democratic citizenship. It is for this second part that I would ask your aid by preparing the leading article. No one, I believe, can ever speak with such authority on the influence of an honor system of self-government in our educational institutions on the individual and the state as you are fitted to do. Other articles for this second part I shall endeavor to secure from President Hadley and President Eliot.

The first part I have thought to have made up of three articles:

The Genesis of the Honor System, by Professor W. M. Thornton

The Evolution of the Honor System:
At the University of Virginia, by Dr. C. W. Kent
At Princeton University, by Dr. E. O. Lovett

Will you not aid me also with suggestions for making the book what it should be?

I am trying to make my study like your tower retreat at Princeton; is it too much to ask for a picture to hang beside my Burke?
Sincerely and gratefully yours   H. O. Murfee

P.S. I shall not attempt to get the volume out until it is convenient for you to prepare the article.

TLS (WP, DLC).
¹ At some time and place unknown to the Editors, Murfee had heard Wilson's series of lectures, "Great Leaders of Political Thought," about which see the Editorial Note, "Wilson's Lectures on Great Leaders of Political Thought," Vol. 9.

A News Report of an Address in Charleston, South Carolina

[Jan. 19, 1906]

DR. WILSON'S ADDRESS.

The Large Audience which Assembled in Hibernian
Hall Last Night was Delighted with the Instructive Words—
Banqueted at Villa Margherita.

A delighted audience listened for more than an hour last night to Dr Woodrow Wilson, the distinguished president of Princeton, who lectured on "What it Means to be an American." Dr Wilson is one of the best known of the world's educators, and, as was expected, treated his hearers to a forceful and concise exposition of the civic ideals—marking those details where the American people have drawn away from the ideals with no uncertain voice.

The name alone of the president of Princeton would have been sufficient to draw a large number of people to the Lyceum lecture at Hibernian Hall, but beyond that was the feeling that Dr Wilson would have something more than the usual to say. One who speaks these days of the American people, the American life and the great place of influence and power to which the American people have risen, is naturally drawn to dwell upon the evils that beset our path. Dr Wilson did not evade this side of our life, but he made it plain that there is that in the American character, which, having brought so much good, will bring the country safely through transient evil.

The civic duties of a man, the value of the individual thought and the necessity for the intelligent application of the great benefits and suffrages which fall to the lot of the American were touched upon by the speaker. Dr Woodrow Wilson spoke with a great deal of feeling, as one would expect from a man who has devoted so much of his life toward solving economic and educational problems.

During his stay in Charleston, which will be brief, Dr Wilson is being entertained at the home of Mr J. P. K. Bryan,[1] No 42 South Battery. Mr. Bryan is a Princeton alumnus.

Yesterday Mr. Wilson was much interested in what he saw of Charleston. He greeted many admirers during the day, and last night a dinner was given at the Villa Margherita in his honor. There he greeted many prominent Charlestonians at a reception held after the lecture was over at Hibernian Hall.

Printed in the Charleston *News and Courier*, Jan. 19, 1906.
[1] John Pendleton Kennedy Bryan, Princeton 1873, lawyer of Charleston.

From James Calvin Hemphill[1], with Enclosure

My Dear Dr Wilson:　　　　Charleston, S. C.　Jan. 22, 1906.

You will remember some general conversation at the Princeton dinner in Charleston the other night in which the conservatism of the South was much exalted as the saving grace of the nation. Probably you will be interested in the other view of the question as expressed in the editorial article which I printed in The News and Courier today and which I enclose for your consideration.

I am very sorry that I did not see more of you while you were in Charleston. The whole town is still talking about your lecture as the best delivered in this place for many years. We should like very much to take such doses often.

Very sincerely yours,　J. C. Hemphill

TLS (WP, DLC).
[1] Manager and editor of the Charleston *News and Courier* since 1888.

E N C L O S U R E

An Editorial on Southern Conservatism

[Jan. 22, 1906]

The Conservatism of the South.

Wherever two or three are gathered together in these days of political reflection, there is almost certain to be some serious discussion about the state of the country. What direction the discussion shall take will depend largely upon the character of the company. There is such a variation of types, such a difference in the point of view that it is very hard to obtain perfect agreement upon any plan that may be suggested for the improvement of our social, economic, and political conditions. Besides being very self-conscious, the American is not altogether unselfish, and his views upon public questions are not entirely free from the influences of local considerations. It is flattering to our vanity, if not to our intelligence, to be told on occasion that of all Americans we are the most conservative, and that the safety of our institutions and the progress of our country depend in large measure upon the conservatism of the South. . . .

It is true that there is a very large conservative sentiment in the South, but there has been little evidence of its influence upon the political conduct of our people in recent years. It has suffered itself to be obscured by the political proletairism which has controlled the South. In time the conservative spirit of our people would undoubtedly have prevailed in the politics of the nation, but in no part of the country have the Socialistic tendencies of the times so largely affected the political activities of the people as in the Southern States. There has not been a question in law or government or politics so widely at variance with the fundamental principles of our institutions that has not found ready acceptance in the South. It has been suggested at different times and by many persons that the South by reason of its political solidarity and its great conservatism should take the lead in American politics, but let us be frank about it.

The conservative influence of the South is not sufficient, be it exercised with never so great activity, to shape the course of political events in this country. In order to make Southern conservatism effective in our national and political affairs it must work in harmony with the conservative spirit of the rest of the country wherever it may exist. Have we so strengthened our position in the last fifteen or twenty years as to win for us the hearty cooperation of conservative men and conservative influences in other parts of the country? The South has been held together politically mainly by one consideration—the supremacy of the white race. There would have been serious political divisions among us doubtless, but for this overshadowing issue.

In one sense the so-called solid South is to be deplored, but in another, as the true event may possibly prove, Southern unity which has been compelled by the race question, has won for us the appearance at least of genuine conservatism. Some of the younger men, who have forgotten the faith of the fathers, who have not given much thought to political study, have been rather chafing at the bit from time to time, because they could not make the Government partners with them in the conduct of their business affairs. They have coveted the material prosperity of tariff-nursed New England, and argued the question with their souls that, if Government aid could have produced millions for the New England States, Government aid might likewise make many millions for the Southern States. They have admitted that the principle was altogether wrong, but they have argued that it would be no worse for the South to prosper at the expense of the taxpayer than for the North. We protest against the downright dishonesty of such a view, and we are rather grateful upon the whole that our tendencies have been resisted by a condition which we have been compelled to consider in all our political actions.

If the conservatism of the South is ever to be of any great benefit to the country, the conservatism of the South must assert itself. It must become a living, breathing force in Southern politics first before it can be a safe guide in the affairs of the nation. Let us be honest about it. Let us deserve the compliments and confidence of the country before accepting the leadership with which the enthusiastic are inclined at times to entrust to us, and for which we have not manifested in recent years any special fitness.

Printed in the Charleston, S. C., *News and Courier*, Jan. 22, 1906.

To James Calvin Hemphill

My dear Mr. Hemphill: Princeton, N. J.   26 January, 1906.

Thank you very much indeed for your kindness in sending me your editorial on Southern conservatism. It really expresses my own opinion in a very striking way. Unquestionably the conservative elements at the South have for a long time been latent and in the background. The radical element has been allowed to play fast and loose with southern politics, because the conservative men, as I take it, were disinclined to go into affairs which were complicated by the necessity of handling the negro vote. What a great many of us hope is that this latent conservatism, stronger in the souther [South] than anywhere else in the country, will in the new and happier circumstances of the time, assert itself, particularly in the reclamation of the Democratic party.

With warm regard, and with much pleasure at having met you,
                         Sincerely yours,   Woodrow Wilson

TLS (J. C. Hemphill Papers, NcD).

Henry Woodhull Green to Moses Taylor Pyne

My dear Mo: Trenton, N. J.   January 26, 1906.

I return the three papers received from you on the 20th. Owing to an attact [attack] of grip I was prevented from seeing Dr. McPherson and Dr. Dixon until yesterday, when they both asked to be excused from signing the paper. Dr. McPherson on the ground that his interpretation of the word "advise" was that it necessarily carried with it a threat, and that he could not see his way clear to sign the paper as drawn. Dr. Dixon on the ground that he had no personal knowledge of the fact that the successful conduct of the affairs of the University are embarrassed by the participation of the gentlemen in question in its control.

I have signed because I believe it is for the best interests of Princeton that these resignations be secured. I cannot, however, help feeling that Wilson should have respected the request that was so clearly made that the words "and advise" be striken out.

I have just called up President Wilson's house and am told that he is away and will be out of twon [town] for two or three days; hence I return the papers to you.

Yours very sincerely,   H. W. Green.

P.S. I think that I ought to add that both Dr. McPherson and Dr. Dixon said that they would have been willing to have signed a direct and unqualified request for the resignations, and have expressed their willingness to so vote if it comes to that.

H. W. G.

TLS (WP, DLC).

A News Item About an Affair in Brooklyn

[Jan. 28, 1906]

UNIVERSITY CLUB DINNER.

President Woodrow Wilson Guest of Honor—
Princeton Colors Theme of Decoration.

President Woodrow Wilson of Princeton University was the guest of honor last night at the third annual dinner of the University Club of Brooklyn, held at the clubhouse, No. 127 South Elliott Place. In honor of the distinguished educator the college banners which decorated the dining room were largely those of the Tigers, the souvenir menu was an album of Princeton views, and the University Glee Club, which made the dinner a lively one with college songs, devoted itself particularly to "Old Nassau."

President Wilson took for his subject a topic of special interest to his audience, speaking on "The University Man."[1]

Printed in the *New York Tribune*, Jan. 28, 1906.
[1] There is a brief WWT outline of this speech, dated Jan. 27, 1906, in WP, DLC.

From Gwynn T. Shepperd[1]

My dear Sir: Norfolk, Va.   February 1, 1906.

I have the honor to advise you that at a meeting of the Board of Directors of the Jamestown Exposition Company, held January 23rd, 1906, you were unanimously elected a member of the Advisory Board of the said company.

Our By-Laws provide that "There may be elected annually by the Board of Directors an Honorary Advisory Board, consisting of not more than one hundred (100) persons, who shall be kept in touch with the affairs of the Exposition by mailing to them from time to time the literature of the Exposition, and they shall be required to advise the Board of Directors from time to time on such matters as they may deem of interest to this Exposition. All advice received from them shall be submitted to the Board of Governors for consideration. A meeting of said Advisory Board may be called at least once a year by the President of this Company, on such date as may be hereafter fixed, but such date shall be at the same time as meeting of the Board of Directors."

This Advisory Board consists of one hundred persons in the United States, prominent in their respective professions, a list of whom is enclosed herewith,[2] so that you may know with whom you will be associated.

Trusting that we may have your early acceptance, and be hereafter furnished with your advice whenever you think it will be helpful to the cause we are endeavoring to celebrate, I am,

Most respectfully,   G. T. Shepperd.   Secretary.

P.S.—I may mention, for your information, that Honorable Grover Cleveland has accepted the position of Chairman [of] the Advisory Board and is taking a most cordial interest in the Celebration.

TLS (WP, DLC).
[1] President of the Virginia Security and Banking Co. of Norfolk, Va., and Secretary of the Jamestown Exposition Co., incorporated on March 10, 1902, to plan for the celebration in 1907 of the tercentennial of the founding of Jamestown.
[2] The enclosure is missing.

A News Report About the Progress of the Committee of Fifty

[Feb. 3, 1906]

Next week, or as soon as it is available, The Weekly will publish the annual report of the Treasurer of Princeton University,[1] showing the present financial condition of the University, the increase in funds since the last public statement by the Treasurer, a year ago, the list of donors during the year, etc. Meantime, we are enabled to report informally on the first year's work and the plans of the Committee of Fifty prominent alumni appointed by the Board of Trustees in December, 1904, "to provide for the immediate necessities and the future development of the University."

This committee was organized with Cleveland H. Dodge '79 as Chairman and George W. Burleigh '92 as Secretary. Mr. Dodge still remains Chairman, but Mr. Burleigh, having resigned on account of the stress of his private affairs, has been succeeded as Secretary by Harold G[riffith]. Murray '93, lately Assistant Secretary of the Board of Water Supply of New York City, and who, as Chairman of the committee on the dormitory of the ten classes '92-'01, now under construction, has already had much practical experience, in coöperation with the members of that committee, in planning and carrying through to a successful issue a good Princeton work. Mr. Murray is now devoting his entire time to the task undertaken by the Committee of Fifty, visiting the principal alumni centers, laying before the graduates the needs of the University and the plans of the Committee to meet them, and perfecting the organization of a systematic and continuous canvass of the whole body of the alumni. His office is at No. 52 Wall street, New York, and he will be glad to receive subscriptions to the various funds described below, suggestions concerning the work of the committee, changes of addresses of Princeton alumni, etc. Class Secretaries, in particular, can be very helpful to Mr. Murray in his work for the University.

In order that all may participate in the privilege of providing for the immediate needs and future development of the University, the Committee of Fifty has adopted the following three forms of subscription: 1. The endowment form, by which the donor agrees to give a fixed sum, and pays five per cent. yearly interest on such sum until it is paid, and upon any unpaid balance of it. 2. The term form, in which the donor agrees to give a specified amount each year for a given term of years. 3. The "flat" gift, in which the donor gives a certain sum outright. For the general body of Princeton alumni, the second is proving the most popular form, because it is within the reach of all of us. But one of the three forms will, we assume, be found to meet the requirements of any intending donor.

During the first year of its work the Committee has received subscriptions aggregating over a million dollars, of which $500,000 is in the (1) endowment form, $199,370 in the (2) term form, $23,325 in the (3) "flat" gift form, and the balance is for the building of McCosh Hall, the foundations of which have already been laid. This is a most encouraging start. For one thing it has already enabled the faculty to begin successfully the Preceptorial System, which is now receiving recognition as the most noteworthy movement of recent years, for the improvement of higher educational methods in America. But, as stated in the Committee's circular last year, to put the Preceptorial System in full operation, with the number of teachers sufficient for its needs, "would require the income of $2,500,000; and this is only one of the large plans, formulated after earnest investigation, which the University must carry out if it is to keep its place among the foremost institutions of learning."

But as yet the Committee's canvass has reached only a small minority of the alumni. And all of us are no doubt aware that if our Alma Mater were to look upon the job of educating her sons merely as an unsentimental business proposition, she would shut up shop and wind up her affairs in short order. For, as is well known, the tuition fees paid by a student fall far short of balancing the University's actual outlay for his education. The obligation we have all incurred, therefore, in participating in Princeton's benefactions, merely from the standpoint of a just and honorable debt, need not be emphasized.

Printed in the *Princeton Alumni Weekly*, VI (Feb. 3, 1906), 309-10.
    1 The Annual Report of the Treasurer of Princeton University was summarized in the *Princeton Alumni Weekly*, VI (March 3, 1906), 391-95.

An Address to the Lotos Club of New York[1]

[[Feb. 3, 1906]]

I am sincerely obliged to Mr. Lawrence for the words, the very

1 The Lotos Club of New York was founded in 1870 "to promote social intercourse among journalists, artists and members of the musical and dramatic professions and such merchants and professional gentlemen of artistic tastes and inclinations as would naturally be attracted by such a club." From the beginning, the club was well known for its banquets given in honor of distinguished men in every walk of life. Wilson was the guest of honor on February 3, 1906. The speakers who paid tribute to him were George Harvey; Frank Richard

gracious words, of introduction which he has just uttered,[2] and yet I must say that this is not the kind of occasion to put a man most at his ease. I feel very much as the old woman did who went into the side-show of a circus, and saw, or thought she saw, a man reading a newspaper through a two-inch board. "Oh, let me out of here," she cried, "this is no place for me, with these thin things on!"

I feel that the guise of greatness with which he has clothed me is perhaps a very transparent disguise, and that, after all, is all that I need this evening. I am in the plight of the Methodist divine down in Tennessee who spent a quarter of an hour praying for power. One of his deacons said to him, taking him aside, "Parson, you are praying for the wrong thing; what are you praying for power for? You don't need any power; you ought to pray for ideas."

I think it a very graceful and interesting arrangement of yours to put the man about whom you are going to speak first on the program of speakers. I have an excellent opportunity of telling you more about myself than you can possibly know, and stealing all your thunder, and giving you that kind of discouragement it may be worth my while to give you, like the youngster they tell about who found some of his chums fishing on Sunday. He told the minister. "Well," said the minister, "did you do anything to discourage them?" "Oh, yes," replied the boy; "I stole their bait." I might do the same thing to you, and so prevent any more fishing in these now, I assure you, troubled waters.

There are many things that this country needs, gentlemen. It needs knowledge; it needs skill, and a great deal of it, and of excellent sort; it needs that scientific discovery should be pushed forward to practical invention; and I take it that above all things else it needs enlightenment, in order that these needs may be put in appropriate setting in our thoughts, and we may have a definite notion what it is they are for. Are we to have skill in order that we may be merely mechanics? Is it not necessary that there should be some general line in which we should use these things

Lawrence, president of the club; Andrew Van Vranken Raymond, President of Union College; John Huston Finley, President of the College of the City of New York; Henry Mitchell MacCracken, Chancellor of New York University; Clement Carrington Gaines, President of Eastman College of Poughkeepsie, N. Y.; and John Sergeant Wise, former Virginia congressman and a prominent New York lawyer.

[2] Lawrence had introduced Wilson with the words: "There are those who attract unwittingly and irresistibly. There are men whom we admire not because they have accumulated great fortunes, but because they have thought great thoughts. It is in honor of one of these that we assemble to-night." *New York Times*, Feb. 4, 1906.

in their proper proportions and perspective? Surely it is the duty of the universities to supply the enlightenment in order that they may see the real journey they are making, and the journey the races have made in the past, and the journey we should wish them to make in the future.

There is nothing that so disturbs my imagination as the thought that we are merely one generation; that we are merely an incident in the great story, and that our success will be judged in its relation to the history of the people. Is that success consistent with the plot? What is the plot? Is there any plot, or plan, or sequence? Do we know where we came from? Do we know whither we are going?

I remember a friend of mine telling me that he stopped on a Scotch highway, and asked an old fellow who was breaking stones by the roadside, if that was the way to such and such a place; and the old fellow said, "Where do you come from?" My friend replied, "I don't know that that is any business of yours," and was told that it was as material as where he was going to. And, if you reflect, the old man was right when he said, "I cannot tell you where you are going, whether you are on the right road or not, unless you tell me whence you come from."

To use an illustration oft repeated, but which seems indispensable to me, we very often speak of a man who has lost his way in the desert as having lost himself. If you will reflect upon that for a moment, you will see that this is the one thing he hasn't lost. He is there; he has a firm grip of himself; but he has lost all the rest of the world. If he could determine any fixed point on the globe, he would have something to steer by, but he can't steer by himself.

And it seems to me that the only method of guiding ourselves in life is by determining fixed points and steering by them. You can't steer by yourselves; you must have an established direction which is not centered in your own person. When that direction is established, it gives you general control, that is, the way of the rest of the world. This is what I mean by the map of life, by those roads which the race travels.

There are certain things which the race has found out as a means of enlightenment, and one of the things which it is finding out is that the way for material mastery to be found is not to devote yourself to the processes of material mastery, but to the principles of material mastery, that is to say, not the processes of manufacture, but to the sources, the pure sciences.

The world which intends to live by science must know science, and in order to know science it must constantly refer and resort to men who bury themselves in the laboratories and seek the foundations of the forces used, the men who are not seeking anything in the making of money or the extension of manufactures, but are studying to find out the most profound secrets of nature.

You know that we are sometimes laughed at for bragging of the size of this continent, for manifestly we didn't make it; and foreigners think us very ridiculous for saying abroad that America is so big. It is not at all ridiculous, because we have conquered all of it. We are as big as the things we get. Our progress is measured by the size of America. If it had proved too big for us, we should have to be ashamed; it is because it has not proved too big for us that we are proud of its size. If you can recall the history of this race you will remember that when we came to these shores, we came helpless as infants; and when you remember the miles of continent that lie between us and the Pacific, and the character of the thick forests, and the hills upon hills, and remember that there wasn't any road made for us that we knew how to travel or find, and that we have sped our way from the Atlantic to the Pacific chiefly by knowing the processes of nature, you will see that we have conquered the country by having from first to last knowledge of the sciences, and that we never should have had this knowledge if there had not been laboratories in which men who didn't care either for commerce or civilization were constantly getting to this simple foundation of the hidden forces, and man's best relation to the great streams that drive our mills and make progress possible. So that if men want to keep the greatness of the race they must constantly see that it resorts to pure science, and that is the business of the university.

I have sat beside very successful men on occasions, and heard them explain the philosophy of their lives, and wondered how they had attained what they termed their successes. And yet it shows one thing, that a man can steer in this great uncharted ocean of our life if he steers by some sort of compass, and the compass that he should steer by is the compass of experience, the knowledge of the human mind and human nature.

I suppose that some very distinguished philosophers have a very limited practical knowledge of human nature, but all distinguished philosophers I have ever known have had a great deal of human nature themselves. It is worth your while to know what ridiculous notions people have had about themselves, as well as the notions of a nation. Preachers are right, whether you want them to be or not, in saying that we have got to have a philosophy of life and conduct. The trouble with us is that we can get along with very inconsistent philosophies of life and conduct. De Tocqueville said it was no argument that the American philosophy was consistent because it worked, for, he said, Americans can work any combination; and so it is no argument for the excellence of your philosophy that it works: you can work anything. The different parts don't have to be consistent, but it is a distinct characteristic of the two most successful races, the Romans and ourselves, that they have blazed their minds with a theory about themselves, and then practised whatever theory suited their convenience, and the very best, naturally, have been those who reduced their experience and practice to a philosophy. For example, what better generalization could you have as a description of the distinguished man who now heads the nation, than De Tocqueville's characterization of a constitutional statesman: "A man of ordinary opinions and extraordinary abilities."

I have often said that I have learned a great deal more politics from the poets than from the systematic writers of politics. I have been a systematic writer of politics myself, and I don't wonder at it. Any systematic writing is immoral writing. I say immoral writing, because no man knows enough about anything to write about it systematically. No man knows more of a certain subject than some parts. Suppose he starts to write systematically. He must have some sort of a table of contents, a systematic scheme of chapters. It may be possible he has to talk about things he doesn't know, in order to make the chapters about the same length. Some contain things he knows; some contain things he doesn't know, but has taken from somebody else; and he fixes the surface so that all will look alike, the parts not being divided, so that nobody may understand and stand on the weak parts long enough to break through.

Now, I say that that is immoral, and I am materially opposed to systematic writing. The poets are not systematic. The poets talk about only the things they have come definitely to understand, and they are interpreting to you in the phrases and language that the systematic writer has not been able to incorporate in the volume. Take this list of qualifications which might be headed "Political Workers":

Some sense of duty; something of the faith;
Some reverence for the laws the wise have made;[3]

[3] The stenographer's error. Wilson undoubtedly quoted the lines correctly: "Some sense of duty, something of a faith, Some reverence for the laws ourselves have made."

Some patient force to change them when we will;
Some civic manhood, firm against the crowd.[4]

Where can you find this better depicted than in these lines?

I will not trust a man to understand the song of a people who is not deeply read in the literature of his own people—in the imaginative literature of his people. For, gentlemen, we are lifted from achievement to achievement by imagination. No man ever demonstrated an achievement; he conceived the achievement. There was a vision dreamed in some moment of lofty feeling, and he is elevated to it by something in him that aspires to a height that the race has not yet attained, and in which, therefore, he is guided by feeling or by imagination; and that is the way of the men who lift their figures above the general crowd and are picked out as the leading men, the distinguished men, the achieving men of our generation.

Is it not worth while that somewhere young men should draw apart from active life for a little while to study these things, to contemplate these things, and be lifted out of the rut of general experience into the road of special experience? There are some things that are very material characteristics of the nation we belong to. Two things I shall mention: one, the extraordinary authority of the majority in this country; the practically overwhelming compulsion of the majority. I would speak with deference of the majority, because at the present time I belong to the minority—at least the part of it I belong to is so select and small that I suppose you must regard us as the guests of the majority, and I must speak with that respect with which the guest speaks of his host. We are at present being entertained in this country by the Republican party.

I will make my obeisance to my entertainers, but, notwithstanding, I should like to suggest that it is worth while sometimes to be very impertinent to the majority, and that university men are, if they are worthy of the name, the men especially qualified by their training to entertain independent opinions. There are moments when I actually regret being an imperialist, because the anti-imperialists are put down as though they had no right to their opinions; whereas they are entitled to their opinions, even if they are inconsistent. This reminds me of a story of Mr. [John] Hay's. He said that the anti-imperialists, in their demand that this country give up the Philippines, because it was not right that this nation should hold dependencies, and that they should

4 From Tennyson's "The Princess, Conclusion."

be turned over to Germany, reminded him of the young lady who was much given to dress and self-adornment, and who experienced religion. When she was asked by some of her friends who noticed how plainly she was garbed, what she had done with all her pretty things, she replied, "Oh, when I found that my jewelry was dragging me down to hell, I gave it to my sister."

I don't mean that I am desirous of belonging to these inconsistents, these anti-imperialists, but they have a right to their opinions even if they are inconsistent. The time may come when we need "civic manhood firm against the crowd," and have a majority that under no consideration must prevail, when the crowd is not worthy of our respect, and there should be civic manhood enough to stand firm against it until it turns out that the crowd knows what it is about; and we won't know until somebody does stand out against it worthy [of] its respect.

Then there is another thing; that is, the extraordinary influence in this country which the accomplished fact has. If you throw yourself against anything that has been done, you will be told, "What is the use? The thing has been done; we must accept it." I remember the impatience with which the law class to which I used to lecture on constitutional law, and which endured many things at my hands, used to hear my arguments to the effect that the Supreme Court of the United States was in error in the Dartmouth College case, and based its decision upon a misunderstanding of the English law and elementary rights as laid down in Blackstone.

The youngsters looked at me in amazement to see me run up against the Supreme Court of the United States, and, in the second place, they said, "Suppose they were wrong; the Dartmouth College case is law, and that settles it." The Dartmouth case is law; if it is mistaken law, must it always be law? Is there no such thing as reversing in some conservative fashion the mistakes of the Supreme Court? Is there such a thing as the justification of men, who can reason of their own will, accepting an unreasonable opinion? I am assuming now that you will confess it is unreasonable; if you were to confess it is unreasonable, would you say that because it is law it should stand, and say nothing as to its validity as reason?

Must we not have, gentlemen, some scheme of life, some particular hope, some great set of principles? Shall we forget that our eternal Judge was the judge of men who are convinced of the principles of their life? Must we not always have the spirit of learning, which is the open-minded spirit, the catholic spirit of appreciation, the spirit which desires the best, that is truth; the

spirit which is correctly convinced that there are principles at
the heart of things, and that things are worth while only in proportion to the sound principles that lie at their heart?

Printed in *Speeches at the Lotos Club*, arranged by John Elderkin *et al.* (New
York, 1911), pp. 292-301.

Colonel Harvey's Speech Proposing Wilson
for the Presidency

[[Feb. 3, 1906]]

Said your guest in his masterful response, "We need not flatter
ourselves that we are a story, or even a plot; we are a mere incident." For the purpose of this occasion I think that I may go a
step farther. That veteran editor, Mr. Henry M. Alden, has de-
duced from his long experience and intensive knowledge the conclusion that the most important feature of a story is its background. Whether or not he would make the application to an individual, I cannot say. Probably not. In any case there can be
no doubt of the interest one must feel in the influence of the
lights and shadows that encompass a character. Of your distinguished guest as an educator, as a scholar, as a historian, there
are others here far better equipped than I to speak, and the few
words that I shall venture to utter will apply only to the minor
phases. Back of the president is the university; back of the man
is his native State of Virginia. Of the former it is probably sufficient to recall that simultaneously with the installation of its
present head it planted itself firmly against the tendency to
shorten and make easy the courses of study for undergraduates.
Other colleges responded promptly, but it was Princeton that carried the flag, and it is to Princeton and its new young president
that the chief credit is due.

Of Princeton as a community, as a growing loadstone of philosophy, idealism, and sane comprehension of affairs, it suffices
to say that it meets all requirements. But recently we have had
a notable example. When, last summer, a Princeton man, a
famous Princeton man, and as honest a man as ever came out of
Princeton, was harassed into resigning his well-earned position
as the president of a great insurance company,[1] another was
found ready and fully equipped to assume the responsibility.
As the one stepped out, the other with sturdy tread walked in,
and hanging his hat upon the hook, he said, at least by inference, "They say things have been going on here that ought not
to have gone on. They won't any more. I say to my countrymen

that they need have no further apprehension. I am the original square-dealer—beware of imitations! We will now proceed to business." What business they have proceeded with since has not yet been made clearly manifest. The point is that Princeton filled the gap. May it always find for such emergencies a man of the qualities of Grover Cleveland.

Woodrow Wilson was born in an atmosphere surcharged with true statesmanship. The fates directed his steps in other paths, but the effect of that association with the traditions of his fathers remains. That he is preëminent as a lucid interpreter of history we all know. But he is more than that. One who reads understandingly the record of his country as set down by him cannot fail to be impressed with the belief that he is by instinct a statesman. The complete grasp of fundamentals, the seemingly unconscious application of primary truths to changing conditions, the breadth of thought and reason manifested on the pages of his books, constitute as clear evidence of sagacity, worthy of the best and noblest of Virginia's traditions, as was that truly eloquent appeal which last year he addressed to his brethren of the South, to rise manfully from the ashes of prejudice and lethargy and come back into their own.[2]

It is that type of man that we shall soon, if indeed we do not already, need in public life. Nobody would think of criticizing the general reformation of the human race now going on by executive decree. But progress in that direction is making so rapidly that the great work itself is sure soon to be accomplished, of course to the complete satisfaction of all concerned.

When that time shall be reached, the country will need at least a short breathing-spell for what the physicians term a period of perfect rest. That day, not now so far distant, will call for a man who combines the activities of the present with the sober influences of the past. If one could be found who should unite in his personality, in addition to these qualities, the instinct of true statesmanship, as the effect of early environment and the no less valuable capacity of practical application as the result of subsequent endeavors in another field, the ideal would be at hand. Such a man it is my firm belief, and I venture earnestly to insist, is to be found in Woodrow Wilson of Virginia and New Jersey.

As one of a considerable number of Democrats who have become tired of voting Republican tickets, it is with a sense almost of rapture that I contemplate even the remotest possibility of casting a ballot for the president of Princeton University to become President of the United States.

In any case, since opportunities in national political conventions are rare, and usually preëmpted, to the enlightened and enlightening Lotos Club I submit the nomination.

Printed in *Speeches at the Lotos Club*, arranged by John Elderkin *et al.* (New York, 1911), pp. 309-12.
    1 James Waddel Alexander, who had resigned the presidency of the Equitable Life Assurance Society in June 1905 after several months of dissension within the company. See WW *et al.* to J. J. McCook and C. B. Alexander, Dec. 29, 1905, n. 1.
    2 See the news report of Wilson's address to the Society of the Virginians in New York, printed at Nov. 30, 1904, Vol. 15.

To George Brinton McClellan Harvey

University Club [New York]
My dear Col. Harvey,   3 Feby, 1906.

Before I go to bed tonight I must express to you, simply but most warmly, my thanks for the remarks you made at the Lotos dinner. It was most delightful to have such thoughts uttered about me, whether they were deserved or not, and I thank you with all my heart.

With much regard

Sincerely Yours,   Woodrow Wilson

ALS (WP, DLC).

From the Minutes of the Session of the
First Presbyterian Church of Princeton, New Jersey

1906 Feb 3rd.

The Session met, directly after preparatory service—

Present, Sylvester W Beach,[1] Moderator and Elders, Walter B Harris, J. C. Conover[,] Robert M. Anderson, Henry E Hale. . . .

After consideration of the matter the Session decided to propose the election of additional Elders at the next annual meeting of the congregation. The Pastor to give due notice from the pulpit of such election.

The following persons were nominated by the Session. Viz:

Dr. Woodrow Wilson[2]

Prof. William F. Magie

Prof. Samuel R. Winans. . . .

The session adjourned

Henry E. Hale.   Clerk.

"Minutes of Session   1st Presbyterian Church   Princeton, N. J. [1892-1908]," bound minute book (NjPT).

1 The Rev. Sylvester Woodbridge Beach, born in Woodville, Miss., July 24, 1852. A.B., College of New Jersey, 1876; studied at Princeton Theological Seminary, 1876-80. Ordained by Baltimore Presbytery on May 26, 1880, he held pastorates in Baltimore, Bridgeton, N. J., and Paris, France, before becoming pastor of the First Presbyterian Church of Princeton in 1906. He served at the First Church until 1922 and died on Nov. 16, 1940.

2 Wilson declined the nomination, undoubtedly on the ground of lack of time for proper service. Nominated for membership on the Session again in 1908, he once more declined election and never served on the Session of the First Church.

From Colyer Meriwether[1]

Washington, D. C.   Feb. 4, 1906.

You can count on *all* of my votes in South Carolina *and* elsewhere.[2]   C. Meriwether

ALS (WP, DLC) with enc.: clipping, "Wilson for President," from the *Washington Post*, Feb. 4, 1906.

1 Head of the Geography Department of the Business High School of Washington, D. C., and Secretary-Treasurer of the Southern History Association.

2 Harvey's "nomination" of Wilson was widely reported in the press and evoked many favorable editorials. A representative sample is printed in "Woodrow Wilson as a Candidate[,] Some Press Comments," *Harper's Weekly*, L (March 10, 1906), 330.

From Harold Griffith Murray

Dear Dr. Wilson: New York   February 5, 1906.

My trip to Philadelphia was immensely successful. I only met with one flat refusal and Mr. Dodge is very much encouraged.

I met Tom Wanamaker[1] and extracted a promise from him to give $2,500 toward the establishment of a scholarship. This is the thin end of the wedge and if I can get this matter settled to his satisfaction, I feel very much confident that I can get more from him and from Rod Wanamaker,[2] whom I was not able to see. Tom is worth, they tell me, six or eight million dollars and I think that he wants to give to Princeton but does not know just how to do it. His idea in giving a scholarship is to educate men for newspaper work and he is anxious that the men educated under his scholarship should join the staff of the North American, his paper, and he has asked me to devise a way by which this can be done. I was unwilling, of course, to commit the University to anything in the matter until hearing from you, but I told him that I did not think that the University would place any such restrictions on a scholarship. If they will, if you will let me know, the matter can be very easily settled between us, but if the University will not accept under those conditions, I will endeavor to induce him to give without this restriction, and with the understanding that if he can induce the man to join the staff of the North American, the work shall be entirely on his part. It seems to me that there should be no difficulty in inducing a man to join his paper, for it is a big paper in a big city, and men who are in college are anxious to have a position secured for them as soon as they graduate. I suppose of course the man would make a specialty of English and your courses. Will you kindly let me know as soon as possible just how this gift should be made to the University and what the restrictions should be and the conditions governing it? On receipt of this information I will at once communicate with Mr. Wanamaker.[3]

Will you also write out for me fully but briefly as possible, the preceptorial scheme and also of the graduate school. I have the thing fairly well in my own mind, but Tom and Rod Wanamaker and several other men want the thing all spread on paper before them. I feel that this is a matter of very considerable importance and I should hesitate on my slight knowledge to commit myself on paper.

With regard to the list whom you are to see, will you kindly make a note that they are: [Henry Clay] Frick, J. H. Converse of Philadelphia, Norman B. Ream, and John E. [D.] Rockefeller. J. Pierpont Morgan is to be seen by Mr. Cleveland H. Dodge and Mr. Cadwalader. The Pittsburgh list I will send you shortly when I have some more information relative to it.

Yours very sincerely,   H. G. Murray   Secy

TLS (WP, DLC).
    [1] Thomas Brown Wanamaker, Princeton 1883, partner in his father's mercantile enterprises in Philadelphia and New York and owner of the Philadelphia *North American.*
    [2] Lewis Rodman Wanamaker, Princeton 1886, also a partner in his father's mercantile concerns.
    [3] Thomas Wanamaker never established the scholarship.

John James McCook to the Board of Trustees of Princeton University

[Dear Sirs:]   New York, February 5th. 1906.

I hereby tender my resignation as a Trustee of Princeton University to take effect immediately.   John J McCook

TLS (Trustees' Papers, UA, NjP).

Charles Beatty Alexander to the Board of Trustees of Princeton University

[Dear Sirs:]   New York, February 6th. 1906.

I hereby resign my position as a member of the Board of Trustees, such resignation to take effect immediately.

Charles B. Alexander[1]

TLS (Trustees' Papers, UA, NjP).
[1] The extant documents shed no light on the immediate circumstances of McCook's and Alexander's resignations. The fact that W. Wilson, G. Cleveland, and W. J. Magie to J. J. McCook and C. B. Alexander, Dec. 29, 1905, remains in the Wilson Papers indicates that it was never sent. As earlier letters have revealed, Wilson and others involved in the movement to secure McCook's and Alexander's resignations did not succeed in obtaining many, if indeed any, additional signatures to other copies of the letter.
    Wilson saw McCook and Alexander in New York, most likely on February 5, told them that the vast majority of the trustees wanted them to resign in the best interests of the university, and then said that if they did not resign he would move their removal at the next meeting of the Board of Trustees. (See Ray S. Baker, *Woodrow Wilson: Life and Letters* [8 vols., Garden City, N. Y., 1927-39], II, 177-78.) Their letters of resignation were written on the same typewriter.

To Charles Williston McAlpin

My dear Mr. McAlpin: Princeton, N. J.   6 February, 1906.

I find that I have overlooked your letter of January 13th, asking whether Mr. Pyne's gift of $100,000 for the establishment of the Robert Stockton Pyne University fund should be announced at once or withheld for announcement until the next meeting of the Board.

I think that it would be best to reserve all such announcements until the Board meets again.[1]

Pray excuse my delay in replying.

Cordially and faithfully yours,   Woodrow Wilson

TLS (McAlpin File, UA, NjP).
[1] The announcement was made only to the Board of Trustees and not to the newspapers.

From Henry Smith Pritchett

My dear President Wilson: New York   February 6, 1906.

With this I enclose a memorandum[1] containing my suggestions as to the actual method in which, first, a list of accredited institutions shall be formed; and second, the rules under which pensions shall be granted.

I ask the careful attention of the Executive Committee[2] to these tentative plans, and trust that it may be convenient for the Executive Committee to meet on Saturday, February 17th, at 2 o'clock, at the offices of The Carnegie Foundation in New York,[3] to consider these suggestions and other business which may be presented.

I expect to be able to present at that time, a tentative list of accredited institutions.[4]

Yours very sincerely,   Henry S. Pritchett

TLS (WP, DLC).

[1] It is missing.

[2] The members are listed in the news report printed at Nov. 17, 1905.

[3] Wilson undoubtedly attended this meeting. On the same day, presumably in the morning, he addressed the Friends School in New York. No news report of this address has been found.

[4] Pritchett was compiling his tentative list from information culled from the replies to a circular sent during the summer of 1905 to 627 institutions in the United States and Canada, requesting each to report on the amount of its endowment, requirements for admission and graduation, its relation to the state or province in which it was situated, and its sectarian ties and obligations, if any. See Joseph F. Wall, *Andrew Carnegie* (New York, 1970), p. 873. For additional information about the initial work of the trustees and the establishment of standards of accreditation and eligibility, see *The Carnegie Foundation for The Advancement of Teaching   First Annual Report of the President and Treasurer* (New York, 1906).

From Benjamin Wistar Morris III

My dear Dr. Wilson: [New York]   February 6, 1906.

I was sorry to have missed you on the occasion of my last trip to Princeton, but I hope to run down at the end of this week on Friday or Saturday and would like to talk matters over with you if you can spare me a few minutes, on the presumption that you will be in town at that time.

I see that the Wilson boom for 1908 has been started and trust for Princeton's sake that there is nothing in it.

Very truly yours,   B.W.M. Jr.

CCLI (WC, NjP).

To Benjamin Wistar Morris III

My dear Mr. Morris: Princeton, N. J.   7 February, 1906.

I have been unfortunate in missing you so often and am sorry to say that the end of the week is the time when I am least likely to be found at home. This week I am to go to Providence, R. I. of [on] Friday[1] and cannot get back until Saturday evening. If you could manage to come down the first of next week, you would be almost sure to find me.

You may take it for granted that the "Wilson boom" is in no way serious.

With warm regard,

Cordially yours,   Woodrow Wilson

TLS (WC, NjP).
[1] To address the Commercial Club of Providence. See the news report printed at Feb. 10, 1906.

To Henry Smith Pritchett

Princeton, N. J.

My dear President Pritchett: 8 February, 1906.

I have read your letter of February 6th with a great deal of interest. I think with you that the change in the charter of the Foundation, with regard to the principal office, was immaterial and that you did right in yielding the point.

I am sorry to find that I do not know a single member of the Senate Committee, and I fear that a letter from me would be of little more consequence than my signature to the application,[1] which they already have.

Let me congratulate you on the progress of the business. It seems to me most satisfactory.

Cordially and sincerely yours,   Woodrow Wilson

TLS (Carnegie Foundation for the Advancement of Teaching).
[1] For a federal charter for the Carnegie Foundation for the Advancement of Teaching.

From Winthrop More Daniels

My dear Wilson: Princeton, N. J.   Feb. 8, 1906

Your enclosure of F. Robertson Jones's[1] letter of inquiry was received yesterday.[2] I will try to discover something about him. Besides Marsh (F. B.)[3] recommended by Corwin, the names of several others have been presented, or suggested. Among them are Robt C. Brooks, of Swarthmore.[4]

Edgar Dawson of Newark, Delaware.[5]

Emerson D. Fite[6] (now at Harvard, but a Yale, A.B., and strongly recommended by Shipman)

John Kelso—of Allegheny Seminary.[7]

I told the Department that you wanted a "still hunt" made for possible additions to the Preceptorial staff, but that publicity was to be avoided.   Very sincerely yours,   W M Daniels

ALS (WP, DLC).
[1] Frederick Robertson Jones, Associate in Economics at Bryn Mawr College.

2 The enclosure is missing.
3 Frank Burr Marsh, Instructor in History at the University of Michigan.
4 Robert Clarkson Brooks, Joseph Wharton Professor of Economics at Swarthmore College.
5 A.B., Davidson College, 1895; M.A., University of Virginia, 1899; Ph.D., University of Leipzig, 1902, at this time Professor of English and History at Delaware College (now the University of Delaware). He was appointed Preceptor in History, Politics, and Economics at Princeton in 1906, which position he held until 1909.
6 Emerson David Fite, Austin Teaching Fellow at Harvard, where he had received the Ph.D. in 1905.
7 John Bolton Kelso, Instructor at Western Theological Seminary in Pittsburgh.

From George Brinton McClellan Harvey

My dear Mr. Wilson,   New York City.   February 8th, 1906.

If not too much trouble and you should care to do so, I sincerely hope you will get the stenographer's notes and fix up your remarks for publication. In this case, time is not the essence of publication. I am so strongly convinced of the desirability of giving your thought wider expression, that I cannot refrain from urging you to take the necessary trouble.[1]

Sincerely yours,   George Harvey

TLS (WP, DLC).
1 Wilson apparently did not heed Harvey's advice, for his speech to the Lotos Club never appeared in *Harper's Weekly*. However, Harvey did print a slightly altered portion of his own speech in *Harper's Weekly*, L (March 10, 1906), 324 (this issue, incidentally, carried a large photograph of Wilson on the cover), as part of an editorial explaining in some detail his reasons for believing that Wilson would be a good presidential candidate.

From Harold Griffith Murray

My dear Doctor Wilson: New York   February 8th, 1906.

I thank you very much for your communication of the 7th inst. I can well understand your reasons for not going into exhaustive details with regard to the Preceptorial plan, particularly on paper. I have called and talked with several hundred Princeton men since I last saw you; each and every one has shown the most intense interest in the plan, and they have unanimously said it was the best thing that ever had been done at Princeton in educational lines, and they believed that it was the best thing for Princeton. I am glad to tell you this, for it will show thoroughly the Alumni are back of you. Their interest has made them ask me for the minutest details: with my knowledge of the subject given to me by you verbally and what you have sent me in your letter, it will enable me to give Mr. Wanamaker sufficiently full and accurate details of the system.

I have spoken to Mr. Pyne about the advisability of my seeing the class secretaries in the '80's and interesting them in carrying on the Alumni dormitory extension around Brokaw Field.[1] I shall be in Princeton again in the near future and will call on you.

Yours very truly,   H. G. Murray   Secy

TLS (WP, DLC).

[1] An indication that Wilson was now ready to begin the extension of Alumni Dormitory, soon to be named Patton Hall, as originally planned to form an extended dormitory complex along the eastern side of Brokaw Field. Announcement of the plans for Alumni Dormitory and its relation to the "peripheral scheme" of extended dormitories as exemplified by Blair and Little Halls first appeared in the *Princeton Alumni Weekly*, III (Jan. 17, 1903), 244. For a description of the entire complex, see B. W. Morris to WW, Aug. 16, 1904, Vol. 15. A colored drawing of the projected series of dormitories near Brokaw Field, made late in 1904 (see B. W. Morris to WW, Dec. 12, 1904, n. 1, Vol. 15), now hangs in a small dining room on the second floor of Prospect, the faculty club of Princeton University.

From Benjamin Wistar Morris III

My dear Dr. Wilson: New York, Feb. 8, 1906.

I thank you very much for your favor of February 7th and following your suggestion will arrange to come to Princeton on Tuesday next, when I hope I may have the pleasure of seeing you.

I had a call yesterday from Mr. Murray and Dr. McAlpin, the object of whose visit I dare say you are already advised of. I should like to talk it over with you. I beg to enclose a copy of the letter which I wrote to Mr. Murray.[1]

Very truly yours,   Benj. W. Morris Jr.

TLS (WP, DLC).

[1] This enclosure, B. W. Morris to H. G. Murray, Feb. 7, 1906, CCL (WP, DLC), is not printed. In this letter, Morris provided a detailed cost analysis and estimate of the proposed extension to Alumni Dormitory, or Patton Hall.

From Edith Gittings Reid

Dear Mr Wilson   [Baltimore] Feb. 9th 1906

I want to write you a little about Dr [William Starr] Myers[1] of the Country School who tells me that he is going to see you sometime this month. He is an incomparable teacher, earnest and devoted and a hard student. An able minded, clean souled young fellow with a very scrupulous conscience. He is very young and impulsive where he alone is concerned and extremely reticent where others are involved. A cheerful companion, a poor gossip, something lacking in subtlety of thought perhaps and in the order of imagination that would make for very distinguished original work—but I imagine that he will give us some of our best text books and do work of quite a high order. Dr [Herbert Baxter] Adams said some years ago that he was "the best student he ever had and was certain to make a name for himself." However that may be, he will always be a blessing to those associated with him. I am much concerned that whatever step he now takes may be the right one and it's not at all clear to me what is best. Will you then give my young man an interested ear? He is very thin skinned, and a kind word sinks deeper with him than with almost any one I know and bears an astonishingly big harvest.

With love for you all I am

ever faithfully your friend   Edith Gittings Reid

ALS (WP, DLC).
[1] Born in Baltimore on June 17, 1877. A.B., University of North Carolina, 1897; Ph.D., the Johns Hopkins, 1900. Master of History at the Gilman School in Baltimore, 1900-1906; Preceptor in History, Politics, and Economics at Princeton, 1906-11; Assistant Professor and Preceptor, 1911-18; Professor of Politics, 1918-43. Author of numerous books on politics, government, and history and editor of and contributor to *Woodrow Wilson: Some Princeton Memories* (Princeton, N. J., 1946). Died on Jan. 28, 1956.

A News Report of an Address in Providence

[Feb. 10, 1906]

TWO COLLEGE PRESIDENTS SPOKE.

Addressed Commercial Club Last Evening.
Woodrow Wilson A Speaker.

Presidents of two universities, Woodrow Wilson of Princeton and Dr. [William Herbert Perry] Faunce of Brown, addressed the members of the Commercial Club at the dinner of the organization, held in the Narragansett Hotel last evening. "The Relation of the University to Commerce" was the subject of the evening and the polished and interesting addresses were listened to with close attention by an audience comprising the representative commercial interests of the State and city. . . .

Dr. Wilson said in part:

"Mr. President and Gentlemen of the Commercial Club—It is a real pleasure for me to stand in the presence of a company like this. Occasions like this are familiar. They are like the old darkey whose master tried to persuade him to go to the Episcopal Church. He went for a time, but finally went back to the Methodist. When his master asked him why he had gone back on the Episcopalians he said: 'Well, Marse George, I don't like that Church because it takes too long to read the records of the previous meeting." I would like to say something to-night on the relation of the university to commerce. All of us, I suppose, may be said to a certain degree to live within the commercial idea. It seems to me that Providence, this ancient seat of commerce, where merchant princes, the old and the new, have so long been honored, is one of the pleasantest in which to discuss the principles of commerce. The universities are called upon to prepare young men for a business life, but what sort of a preparation do they chiefly need to become business men? Could modern business subsist upon graduates of the Eastman College of Business, at Poughkeepsie? There they learn to draw all sorts of business papers, but you do not expect them to be great masters of commerce. They become the servants of the masters of commerce.

"The manufacturer and the merchan[t] are in the same class. They sometimes forget this when they discuss the tariff, utterly obscuring their relations, one to another. Business is an abstract and invisible thing. There isn't any man here who ever saw his business. You probably haven't seen all the persons in your employ. It is a figment of your mind as far as you are concerned, and you sit like a blindfolded chess player, imagining your moves and moving your men from memory. Except that you can conceive things that you haven't seen, and things that you never have seen you cannot become supreme in business.

"The trouble with us is that we don't often realize how ridiculous we are. Did you ever stop to think how ridiculous the clothes that we have on to-night are? We too often think that we ourselves are all right, and that the rest of the world is ridiculous, and for that reason they won't buy the goods which we think are right. So, if we are going to prepare men for commerce, we must prepare men who will know their fellow men. You must conceive commerce with a recognition of its proper dignity. We remember that business of the 16th century when the great merchants spread the wings of their fleets to the countries that they had never seen. Those were the days when the world began to be young and fresh and new again, because men believed when they could not see. And do you not see the influence that commerce has had on the history of our country? In those of old days the rivers, the arteries of commerce, were the arteries that carried the blood of nations. The nation that we rejoice in was welded together chiefly by the mercantile interests. Am I wrong in saying that it is a most statesmanlike pursuit? The work of making the Constitution of the United States was the work of a minority, a commercial minority, the minority of those who followed this statesmanlike pursuit.

"How then shall the universities prepare the young men for business? If you had 20 technical schools assembled in one place would you have a university? We can't live on mechanical skill, and if we stop with mechanical skill we stop short of commercial supremacy. We admit our supremacy, but why do we admit it? We are not equal in our technical skill with some of our rivals. Let us recognize, therefore, that the universities are for a minority, for a directing minority. The universities are beginning to understand the world, and the world will soon begin to understand the universities.

"I am beginning to predict a time when you will be the guests of the universities. The business of a university is enlightening. It is to put light into things that are not generally understood. They can study the history of commerce, for there is a great saving of time in doing [knowing] what the past has done and has not succeeded in doing. If we had any memories we would not vote on the currency question every generation. We would not vote for Mr. Bryan in every generation. Mr. Bryan is a mere historical recrudescence. He is simply something that we have forgotton [forgotten] and which we shouldn't have forgotten had we remembered the past. A man can't get any light into his business unless he knews [knows] the intellectual geography of the world. The fact of the matter is, gentlemen, that we are spirits.

"How much of your work do you plan out in advance? Do you plan to take a cocktail before each meal? If you were wise, you would not plan to do anything every day. Nothing kills a man like regular habits. Nothing will wear a tool out like doing the same things with it every day. It lasts much longer with using at different angles. Don't deceive yourselves by supposing you are building anything permanent except your characters, but don't think that if you set out to build your characters you are going to succeed. Attend to your business and your character will take care of itself. It is a favorite saying of mine that character is a by-product. Bad character is a by-product of bad conduct, and good character is a by-product of good conduct.

"There is another thing the university can do for business. The university can set an example in this way. The comradeship of the college is advantageous in that if you help young gentlemen in the atmosphere of the truth [it] is bound to result advantageously on their friendships. Men are held in their moral equilibrium not only by their own conscience but by the thought of what those among whom they have lived will think of them. Now I do not know where such an atmosphere prevails as at the university."

In speaking of the tendency to cut down the college course Prof. Wilson said: "The idea of a college course is to put a boy through a process, and the process isn't complete in three years. The sap of manhood may be rising in a Sophomore, but it hasn't got to his head. It isn't so much a matter of what they have studied as what they have been through. The object of the university is not to teach men that the university is not preliminary to life but a part of life."[1]

Printed in the *Providence Journal*, Feb. 10, 1906; one editorial heading omitted.
    [1] For this address, Wilson used the notes referred to in n. 8 to the address printed at Nov. 29, 1902, Vol. 14.

From De Witt Clinton Blair[1]

My dear Mr. Wilson: New York, February 10, 1906.

I have been considering for some time past the continuation of Blair Hall as far as the observatory, according to certain plans originally made for this work, and I have before me a letter addressed to Mr. Russell[2] by the architects, Messrs. Cope & Stewardson of Philadelphia, in which they state that according to the working drawings and specifications which were originally made for this work, but with the addition of plumbing and heating, the cost of this extension will amount to $61,000.00, and I write to say that if it meets with your approval, and the approval of the Board, I shall stand ready to advance this sum from time to time as the work proceeds: contracts to be entered into by the college and you to have entire charge of the work.[3]

There is only one condition that I would like to impose in connection with the gift, and that is that students from the Blair Academy at Blairstown should have the preference on the drawings as far as Blair Hall is concerned. I would like this done in order to stimulate the interest at Blair Hall in Princeton, and while I believe that many students at Blair Academy would not care to take the rooms in Blair Hall, owing to the rental which would necessarily be higher than certain other dormitories, I would like to feel that they have the preference, as I think this would result to the mutual advantage of both institutions.

                    Very sincerely yours,   D C Blair

TLS (WP, DLC).
    [1] Princeton 1856 and member of the Board of Trustees since 1900. Blair Hall, completed in 1897, was the Sesquicentennial gift of his father, John Insley Blair, a trustee from 1866 to 1899.
    [2] Archibald Douglas Russell, a member of the Committee on Grounds and Buildings of the Board of Trustees.
    [3] On March 8, 1906, the trustees authorized the firm of Cope and Stewardson to proceed with plans for the extension. For a description of the plans, see the news report printed at April 7, 1906.

From George Hutcheson Denny[1]

Lexington, Virginia
My dear President Wilson: Feb. 10th, 1906.

Professor Edgar Dawson of Delaware College informs me that he expects to apply for one of the preceptorships in History at Princeton University.

I desire to commend him to you, and to say that I have known him for a number of years and greatly esteem him as a man of fine capacity, character and promise. He has had the best training to be secured in this country and abroad. I am sure his claims will receive, as they deserve, careful consideration at your hands.

With kindest regards, I remain,
                Yours very truly,   George H. Denny   President.

TLS (WP, DLC).
[1] President of Washington and Lee University.

A News Item

[Feb. 10, 1906]

President Wilson was elected a Vice-President of the American Academy of Political and Social Science at its annual meeting held recently in Philadelphia.

Printed in the *Princeton Alumni Weekly*, VI (Feb. 10, 1906), 329.

From Edgar Dawson

Dear Sir: Newark, Delaware, February 14, 1906.

Pursuant to a conversation I had with you some weeks ago relative to a perceptorship [preceptorship] in English or History, I am sending to you several papers.[1] The curriculum vitae is meant to give merely an outline which I hope the letters that I shall submit from time to time will to some extent fill out.

Professor Robinson's[2] letter refers only to my dealings with students outside the class-room.
                Very respectfully yours,   Edgar Dawson.

TLS (WP, DLC).
[1] The enclosures are missing.
[2] Probably Frederic H. Robinson, Professor of Civil Engineering and Secretary of the Faculty at Delaware College.

From the Diary of William Starr Myers

Friday, February 16 [1906].

Gloriously beautiful day. At eleven o'clock called by appointment at the home of Pres. Woodrow Wilson ("Prospect"). As he was sick in bed I was taken up to his room, and had a most delightful talk with him for twenty minutes. A most attractive man. I came to inquire as to prospects for getting a position in the historical department here next year.

The Diary of William Starr Myers, Vol. 6, bound book (W. S. Myers Papers, NjP).

From Robert Digges Wimberly Connor[1]

Dear sir: [Raleigh, N. C.]   February 16, 1906.

I have the pleasure to extend to you in behalf of the Executive Committee of the North Carolina Teachers' Assembly an invitation to be present at the Assembly which will be held in this city June 12 to 15 inclusive.

We should like to have you to speak to the Assembly selecting whatever day or night session will best suit your convenience. We expect of course to meet whatever compensation you expect for you[r] services.

Indications now point to the largest gathering of North Carolina teachers in the history of the State; we expect something more than 1000. Your presence will add much to the interest and value of the session, and I feel that I voice the sentiments of the entire profession in the State when I say that no man will receive a warmer welcome among us than yourself.

I sincerely trust that you can arrange to come and that you will let me have a favorable reply from you at as early a date as possible.   Very truly yours   [R. D. W. Connor]
Sec'y N. C. Teachers' Assembly.

CCL (Nc-Ar).

[1] Historian and educator, at this time Secretary of the Educational Campaign of North Carolina, of the North Carolina Teachers' Assembly, and of the North Carolina Historical Commission. In 1934, he became the first Archivist of the United States, serving in that post until 1941.

A Memorandum on the Clubs at Princeton

17 Feby, 1906.

A general club situation involving:

Social questions with regard to both Freshmen and Sophs.[1]
What is the future of the Upper Class Clubs?

More and more expense and only social aims or
University aims?
Danger that we will develop *socially* as Harvard did and as Yale
is tending to do.
Effect on the under classes

WWhw MS (WP, DLC).
¹ These cryptic notes yield the earliest evidence that Wilson was beginning
to focus on the club situation at Princeton. For his later full analysis of the
problem and radical plan of reorganization, see his Supplementary Report to
the Board of Trustees printed at Dec. 13, 1906.

To Robert Digges Wimberly Connor

My dear Sir,   Princeton, N. J.   20 February, 1906.
    I greatly regret to say that it will not be possible for me to ac-
cept the kind invitation conveyed by your letter of the sixteenth.
The dates at which your Assembly is to come together lie so near
our Commencement that I cannot, without neglecting many duties of the first importance, leave Princeton for so long a journey
and and [sic] absence of so many hours.
    I am very sorry, and hope that you will express to your Com-
mittee my very warm appreciation and great regret.
                    Sincerely Yours,   Woodrow Wilson

WWTLS (Nc-Ar).

A News Report of an Address in Washington

[Feb. 23, 1906]
THE UNIVERSITY CLUB
More Than Four Hundred Guests at Annual Banquet.

PROMINENT MEN PRESENT

Addresses by Woodrow Wilson,
Speaker Cannon and Others.

"There never was a greater success in the way of a banquet,"
was maintained last evening by every one of the 403 guests at
Rauscher's, the occasion being the second annual banquet of the
University Club.
    Mr. L. A. Coolidge, former president of the Gridiron Club,¹
presided. Addresses were made by President Woodrow Wilson of
Princeton, Justice [David Josiah] Brewer, Secretary Wilson,²

¹ Louis Arthur Coolidge, journalist, president of the Gridiron Club in 1904.
² James Wilson, Secretary of Agriculture.

Speaker [Joseph Gurney] Cannon, Brig. Gen. Elliott,[3] William Dudley Foulke,[4] A. M. Cooley[5] and others. College songs of exceptional merit were sung by the Johns Hopkins University Glee Club, with J. H. Uhlig as soloist.

The halls were a riot of colors, the flags of more than one hundred colleges being interspersed with the national colors.

"Words of wisdom, with a spice of wit," was the motto for the toasts, and the songs, pictures, gifts to the members and the addresses thoroughly exemplified the savor of spice and wit.

President Wilson was greeted with cheers and cries which impelled him to remark:

"While I do not know many of your faces, your manners are familiar."

In speaking of George Washington as an ideal American, President Wilson said that nothing was left to be added about the man whose birthday the club was celebrating. All that could be done was to look particularly handsome and repeat the old remarks.

"Washington," the speaker said, "was so completely rounded, so symmetrical, that it is more or less impossible to make particular remarks upon him. His qualities are not separate and distinct, but so thoroughly balanced, blended into such poise that there is no one upon which to fasten. He possessed the peculiar and independent attribute of greatness. And it is rather what Washington was than what he did that has left its mark on the country. He was essentially American, and it is his Americanism that distinguishes him from his great contemporaries Hamilton and Franklin.

It was proper and natural, the speaker went on to say, that in the early days many of its master minds should have been more of the old than of the new world. Illustrating his point he told a story of an Englishman, who derided a Scotchman for claiming everything. "Why," the Britisher said, "You will be claiming Shakespeare next." "And why not?" replied the Scotchman, "he had mind enough."

Continuing, Mr. Wilson referred to another Scotchman who had a cow to sell which he offered for "twa pun." "Why," an Englishman said, "if you had that cow in London you could get ten pounds." "Yes," the seller replied, "and if I had Loch Somond [Lomond] in hell I could get six pence a glass for the water."

"The power to adjust oneself to all conditions, to have the fit-

[3] George Frank Elliott, Commandant of the United States Marine Corps.
[4] Author and public speaker, member of the Indiana Senate, 1883-85, and of the United States Civil Service Commission, 1901-1903.
[5] Alford Warriner Cooley, United States Civil Service Commissioner.

ness for the frontiers is the peculiar characteristic of Americans, and the universality and scope of Washington's genius, his influence upon his time and effect of his works, is due to the fact that his mind was at the frontier," the speaker further said. "The necessity of surmounting the Alleghanies, of connecting the head waters of the Potomac with those of the Ohio, was a constant idea with him. The fear of two empires, a coastal and an interior, was before him. His mind turned to the great plains where the real America is, and was never bounded by the provincialism of the Atlantic seaboard."

The speaker maintained that the inability to think in terms of the place where one is not is a fatal limitation in statesmanship. The American mind must be continental in scope, it must comprehend the terms of the Philippines, of Porto Rico and of all the states. Washington was able, he said, to appreciate the contemporary truths. There were those who did not see the times that were to come, and whose aim was to stick fast in an old practice. He saw visions. What had been was not enough for him. He could initiate examples. The task at hand he attacked with progressive statesmanship, with the energy of conviction and poise. There was neither a leaning backward nor a too forward attitude. The terms of order and progress without alarm or revolution were to him clear.

There was in him no contemporary weakness of cynicism. Not purity against temptation, but strength for right doing is the essential of progress. It is not enough to clean house, but to provide for the house a tenant that can't abide impurity.

No cant of the day is more tiresome than the talk of developing character. Character is not produced by speculation upon its nature and offices, but by attending to business.

It is made up of energy and decision, which are produced in activities. Character is a by product.

It is the character of Washington, which shows itself in the extraordinary ability with which he carried out his convictions, that entitles him to the claim of statesmanship. Ordinary opinions and extraordinary ability make a statesman. Unfortunately too many candidates for political preferment have extraordinary opinions and ordinary abilities.

Concluding, President Wilson said, to quote from Chalmers, nothing is more beneficial to an individual or a nation than the "expulsive power of a new affection."[6] He felt that the nation in general is returning to old affections, is beginning again to do the

6 See ns. 4 and 5 to Wilson's address to the New England Society in New York City printed at Dec. 22, 1900, Vol. 12.

things that are known to be right, is emulating the Washington courage.

"A great consolation it is," he said, "that a nation can catch the flavor of a great personality, and in arousing itself to the nature of Washington, the whole country is imbibing the spirit of independent conviction and absolute courage."

At the conclusion of the address a screen was suddenly lowered from the balcony and a view of Nassau Hall appeared.

Mr. Coolidge congratulated President Wilson and regretted that the club could not give him its support for the presidency of the United States, which has recently been suggested, but that the club has its own candidate, whereupon the entire assemblage broke out with a song to the tune of "Tammany":[7]

> "Taft for me, Taft for me;
> He is our big President.
> Far away on pleasure bent;
> Taft for me, Taft for me.
> U-ni-U-ni-U-ni-Versity."

A picture of the Princeton president and tiger on the screen was followed by one of Secretary Taft digging the canal and then called off to the White House. . . .

Printed in the Washington *Evening Star*, Feb. 23, 1906; some editorial headings omitted.

[7] A popular song published in 1900 and filled with humorous allusions to politicians and public figures. Although most of the words quickly lost their contemporaneity, the words of the chorus and the tune remained popular and were frequently heard at political conventions.

To Henry Green Duffield

My dear Mr. Duffield: Princeton, N. J.   26 February, 1906.

I inclose a check for $50 from Mess. Steinway and Sons. This is for the piano which we found in "Prospect" when we moved here. It proved entirely worthless: so much so as not to make it worth while to undertake the expense of repairing it. We learned from Mrs. Patton that it had long been of no use.

At my own expense, therefore, I have replaced it with a new piano, and with the permission of the chairman of the Committee on Grounds and Buildings have sold the old piano for what it was worth to Mess. Steinway and Sons, from whom the new piano was purchased. This check is their payment for it. It was of course the property of the University and I accordingly hand the check to you.   Very truly yours,   Woodrow Wilson

TLS (WC, NjP).

From Theodore Roosevelt

[Washington]

My dear President Wilson: February 26, 1906.

I wish I could have seen you when you were down here, but I was told you were not going to stay long enough to lunch with me on Friday, and on Thursday I was engaged all through. Are you coming down again? It would be a real pleasure to see you.

Sincerely yours,   Theodore Roosevelt

TLS (Letterpress Books, T. Roosevelt Papers, DLC).

Notes for an Address

North Carolina Society,   New York, 27 Feb. '06.

THE YOUNG MAN'S BURDEN.

To mediate between past and future.

The world lives on ordinary opinions, curiously compounded of elements old and new, infinitely diversified by all varieties of ignorance and knowledge.

It is the proper business of the young man to draw all the skeins forward, alter the pattern, renew the stuff, introduce new elements, adapt, confirm.

What does the young man find now in the field of politics and economics? A set contest between the conservative and the radical: between those in whose interest the system works and those whom it puts at a disadvantage.

Note the splendid energy called forth in this new world of ambition and effort: the statesmanlike qualities, the fine powers of organization and cooperation.

What is lacking is, the final accommodation and synthesis between private enterprise and public interest.

This synt[h]esis the young man's task. He should do his work with poise, without passion, seeing the world as a thing to be taken whole, not in *disjecta membra*. He should work constructively, not in revolutionary spirit. A task here for the university.

WWT MS (WP, DLC).

A News Report of a Talk to the North Carolina
Society of New York

[Feb. 28, 1906]

WILSON BLAMES SPEEDERS.

Auto Racing One of the Menaces of the Day,
Says Princeton's President.

President Woodrow Wilson of Princeton University talked before the North Carolina Society of New York at its eighth annual
dinner at the Waldorf-Astoria last night. President Wilson's topic
was "The Young Man's Burden," but he discussed a variety of
subjects, and among them the automobile.

"I think," he said, "that of all the menaces of to-day the worst
is the reckless driving in automobiles. In this the rights of the
people are set at naught. When a child is run over the automo-
bilist doesn't stop, but runs away. Does the father of that child
consider him heartless? I don't blame him if he gets a gun. I am
a Southerner and know how to shoot. Would you blame me if I
did so under such circumstances?

"The young man of this generation and the next will see many
interesting things in this country. What we should do now is to
get ready the old-fashioned morals and apply them to the new
forms of business. Policy holders in life insurance companies
hereafter are going to think straight and at a long distance from
headquarters. The companies are bound to respond with better
principles of business.

"The duty of the university is to see that as much as possible
of the old truths is handed down to a new generation, introducing
the youth to the highroads which lead to the legitimate goal.
Some splendid men have recently made big mistakes because in
their business excitement they have not seen the true principles
of business honor.

"I don't believe you realize the growth of Socialism in this
country," concluded President Wilson. "To stop it you must do
more and better thinking. You must sit tight and stand pat, for
perhaps you don't know the beast you are riding."

Representative Claude Kitchin of North Carolina, in responding to the toast "North Carolina," talked about the negro. He said
the black man was better protected in the South than in New
York.

Printed in the *New York Times*, Feb. 28, 1906.

From Bayard Henry

Philadelphia.

My dear President Wilson: February 28, 1906

In reply to your favor of the 27th inst., in relation to the proposed act authorizing the governing body of any municipality within whose limits is located a college or university, to authorize the Board of Trustees of said college or university, under certain circumstances, to condemn property, received.

I have had a bill drafted, which I had intended to submit to the Committee on Grounds & Buildings, and, if approved by that Committee, to have requested someone to introduce it in the New Jersey Legislature. As nearly every municipality in this country now has authority to take private property for park purposes, and as our grounds and campus are open to the public, and take the place, practically, of a public park for the residents of Princeton, I see no reason why such a measure should create any prejudice against the University. Where men from various parts of the country are spending large sums of money for the development of a village and a university and where, as above stated, the grounds and buildings belonging to the University are, in a large measure, open to the public, there are many reasons why individuals (when fully compensated) should give way to common good. I am in hopes that we may be able to buy Carpenter's property[1] without a measure of this kind, but if he and his daughter should determine not to sell their property for years to come, I see no reason why we should not avail ourselves of an act of Assembly, the same as if we were acting for a municipality in the case of a public enterprise.

I am obliged to you for your letter, but I had no idea of taking any action in this matter without fully discussing it at a meeting of the Grounds & Buildings Committee, and with you and several of the trustees.[2]

With regards, and hoping to see you on the 8th of March, if not before, I am,   Yours sincerely,   Bayard Henry

TLS (WP, DLC).

[1] He was referring to a large rooming house at 39 Nassau Street owned and run by Emory W. Carpenter and his family, including his daughter, Jennie R. Carpenter. This was the last piece of property on the south side of Nassau Street between the First Presbyterian Church and University Hall not owned by the university.

[2] Henry's proposed bill apparently never reached the stage of formal discussion. The Minutes of the Board of Trustees for March 14, 1907, record that the Carpenter property had been purchased with funds donated by friends of the university.

To Henry Green Duffield

My dear Mr. Duffield: Princeton, N. J.   1 March, 1906.

I should have given you the facts about the piano just sold more fully than I did, though I knew them only by hearsay.

I understand that the piano was given to "Prospect" by Mrs. Alexander at the time Dr. Patton became President. I am not sure whether it was Mrs. Henry M. or Mrs. Charles B. Alexander.

The piano was then already old and out of repair and Mrs. Patton made very little use of it in consequence.

Sincerely yours,   Woodrow Wilson

TLS (WC, NjP).

To Charles Williston McAlpin

My dear Mr. McAlpin: Princeton, N. J.   2 March, 1906.

Will you not be kind enough to send out notices to the members of the Committee appointed to consider the affairs of Whig and Clio Halls that there will be a meeting of that committee, by order of the chairman Mr. Dodge, on Wednesday evening next, March 7th, at half past nine at "Prospect."

Very sincerely yours,   Woodrow Wilson

TLS (McAlpin File, UA, NjP).

From Marx Warley Platzek[1]

My dear Dr Wilson   [New York]   March 2nd 1906

I have the honor to acknowledge your favor of yesterday[2] and thank you for your promptness. Let me say at the outset that we only intend to have four speakers this year[.] Experience has taught us that more than that number is unfair and unsatisfactory to all. Up to this writing Mayor McClellan is the only speaker on our list. We have invited Hon Wm Bourke Cockran[3] and are awaiting his acceptance. We are now considering several names which I am not at liberty to mention now. You may be assured however that no one will be asked who is not possessed of distinguished ability and of national renown[.] We would very much like to assign to you the toast of "Thomas Jefferson." The subject of the toast of course implies that it is to be the most important of the evening. Do please make it possible to be with us[.]

Awaiting a favorable response[4] and with much esteem I remain

Yours Truly   M. Warley Platzek

ALS (WP, DLC).

[1] New York lawyer, trustee of the College of the City of New York; and Treasurer of the National Democratic Club of New York, an organization closely associated with Tammany Hall.

[2] Platzek's earlier letter and Wilson's reply are missing.

[3] Famous orator and Democratic congressman from the Twelfth New York District.

[4] Wilson did give the address. It is printed at April 16, 1906.

To Grover Cleveland

My dear Mr. Cleveland: Princeton, N. J.   5 March, 1906.

I should think that a birth-day would bring you very many gratifying thoughts, and I hope that you realize how specially strong the admiration and affection of those of us in Princeton who know you best has grown during the years when we have been privileged to be near you. It has been one of the best circumstances of my life that I have been closely associated with you in matters both large and small. It has given me strength and knowledge of affairs.

But if I may judge by my own feeling what a man specially wants to know on his birth-day is how he stands, not in reputation or in power, but in the affection of those whose affection he cares for. The fine thing about the feeling for yourself which I find in the mind of almost everyone I talk with, is that it is mixed with genuine affection. I often find this true even of persons who do not know you personally. How much more must it be true of those who are near you.

With most affectionate regard and with a hope that you may enjoy many another anniversary in peace and honor and affection,   Faithfully yours,   Woodrow Wilson

TLS (G. Cleveland Papers, DLC).

From Moses Taylor Pyne

My dear Woodrow: New York   March 6, 1906.

Regarding the Brown property in Princeton,[1] you will remember that Mr. Huntington offered to pay $35,000 for the property. This with the 2-½% commission, would amount to $34,125.

My sister[2] authorizes me now to offer to the University the price of $35,000 flat for the property.[3] She does not wish to have any restrictions put on the property, but her idea is to tear down the present house and erect one large handsome house on the property which, I think, would be satisfactory to every one and would improve the whole street.

Very sincerely yours,   M Taylor Pyne

Please say nothing about this to anyone until I see you on Thursday   M T P

TLS (WP, DLC).
  [1] The home of the late Susan Dod (Mrs. David) Brown of 65 Stockton Street, which the university had inherited.
  [2] Albertina Pyne (Mrs. Archibald Douglas) Russell.
  [3] The trustees accepted the offer and authorized the sale at their meeting on June 11, 1906.

To Walter Hines Page

My dear Page: Princeton, N. J.   7 March, 1906.

Thank you sincerely for your letter of March 6th.[1] It is the kind of letter which it is most heartening to get. It is most pleasant to think that you look on with keen interest and approve.

It was a real pleasure to get a glimpse of you the other evening at the dinner of the North Carolina Society. Always—

Cordially and faithfully yours,   Woodrow Wilson

TLS (W. H. Page Papers, MH).
  [1] It is missing.

From Raleigh Colston Gildersleeve

My dear President Wilson: N. Y.   March 7th, 1906.

Acting on your letter, I shall proceed to make drawings of the ornamented parts of the Council Chamber, of which you complain, and shall obtain estimates on the cost of removing the plaster ornamentation and replacing it with carving. Before sending the drawings out for estimates, however, I shall submit them to you for your approval.

I have a letter from Mr. Bunn in which he tells me that none of the chairs sent to the Council Chamber met with your approval, and that you will communicate with me in regard to them. In this connection I shall be glad to be of any service to you that I can.

Faithfully yours,   Raleigh C Gildersleeve

TLS (WP, DLC).

The Special Committee on the Halls to the
Board of Trustees of Princeton University

Princeton, N. J.   7 March, 1906.

The Special Committee on the Halls recomend that

The fixed fees of the Halls be put on the college bills. All moneys thus paid in to be subject first to the order of the Curator of Grounds and Buildings, for the satisfaction of all fixed charges and for the payment of the cost of all repairs; the balances to be subject to the order of the Treasurers of the Halls upon the countersignature of the Curator.

That

Authorization be given the Faculty to make any possible arrangement whereby the University may supply the Halls with training in public speaking and debate in connection with the courses of the English Department.

Cleveland H Dodge   Chairman[1]

WWTRS (Trustees' Papers, UA, NjP).

[1] The trustees adopted the recommendations of the special committee at their meeting on March 8, 1906.

Henry Burchard Fine to the Board of Trustees'
Committee on Morals and Discipline

Gentlemen: PRINCETON UNIVERSITY, MARCH 8, 1906.

Since my last report was written the Faculty has been asked to suspend four students for intoxication and a fifth for disorderly conduct. The excesses which called for this discipline occurred in the period between the mid-year examinations and Washington's birthday.

The number of men dropped at the end of the first term because of failure in their studies was the same as last year, namely 71. They were distributed as follows among the several departments and classes:

	A.B.	B.S., Litt.B.	C.E.	Total
Seniors	2	2	1	5
Juniors	4	1	0	5
Sophomores	7	11	3	21
Freshmen	10	14	11	35
Specials	2	3	0	5
	25	31	15	71

This year, as last, a little over one-half of the dropped students were Freshmen or first year Specials. About 9% of the Freshmen failed and about 4% of the men in the three upper classes. It is to be expected that a class will lose many more men at the end of its first term in college than at any other time. Entrance examinations are the best preliminary test that we have been able to contrive of a student's preparation for college, but they are by no means a perfectly satisfactory test. By the aid of skilful coaching a student may succeed in passing them who lacks a broad and thorough knowledge of the subjects to which they relate. Last year I was inclined to attribute the failures of the Freshmen almost as largely to lack of diligence as to lack of preparation. But this year, generally speaking, the Freshmen have been industrious. That the number of failures has not materially decreased is, I think, due to the fact that the preceptorial method of instruction has led to the earlier and more complete discovery of those who were not fitted to do the work required of them here.

Five less Juniors were dropped than last year, and five less specials, but, on the other hand, two more Seniors and eight more Sophomores. A considerable number of the Sophomore failures were due in part to conditions in Physics, the one required Sophomore subject which was taught by the lecture method without preceptorial aid.

The B.S. Department makes a decidedly better showing, relatively speaking, this year than last, especially in the Freshman class, which indicates that students are already entering that Department more fully prepared to meet the requirements of our revised course of study.

Some surprise may be felt that the preceptorial method of instruction has not reduced the number of failures, but a little reflection will convince one that this result should not have been expected of the method, at least at the outset. The preceptorial system was not introduced for the purpose of keeping weak students in college, but for the purpose of promoting scholarship in the University. Its immediate effect has been greatly to increase the diligence of the body of our students and the intelligence and satisfaction with which they pursue their studies. More work, and a better quality of work has been done by most of the students in all courses to which it has been applied. As a consequence it has become more difficult, rather than less difficult for weak and idle students to pass in such courses. In particular, it is a necessary condition in a preceptorial course that a student do good and consistent work throughout the term. In such a course a student cannot make good the damage done his record through neglect of term work by cramming for the final examination. When it is remembered how largely it has been the practice of our students to neglect term work, and to rely upon cramming for the final examinations to carry them through, it will be seen that at the outset the preceptorial method was quite as likely to increase as to diminish the number of failures. That the method has been introduced without increasing the number of failures shows how generally our students have responded to its stimulus. The majority of the men whose habit it has been to do only work enough to remain in college have become really interested in their studies.

Respectfully submitted,   H. B. Fine
Dean of the Faculty.

TRS (Trustees' Papers, UA, NjP).

To Benjamin Wistar Morris III

My dear Mr. Morris: Princeton, N. J.   9 March, 1906.

The drawings for the screen work in '79 Hall[1] please me entirely and the arrangements you have made seem to me altogether suitable and convenient. I hope that you will go forward with the arrangements for the work at once.

Sincerely yours,   Woodrow Wilson

TLS (WC, NjP).
[1] That is, for the President's Room in the tower of Seventy-Nine Hall.

A News Report of a Talk in Philadelphia

[March 10, 1906]

WOODROW WILSON ON "LIBERAL TRAINING"

President Woodrow Wilson, of Princeton University, last night addressed several hundred members of the Private Secondary School Association, which began its third annual meeting yesterday afternoon in the chapel of the University of Pennsylvania. Another session will be held this morning to discuss the classics in the curriculum. The present meeting is the largest ever held, and the members expressed much gratification at its benefits. The subject of Doctor Wilson's address was "A Liberal Training."

"It has been my observation," said he, "that certain secondary schools have taken on an amount of moral enthusiasm of late which disposes them to the belief that they must make character. As this is rather apt to be at the expense of the real purpose of preparation, pursued too rigorously it cannot but result in [h]arm. Let it be assumed that the moral character is there. The main endeavor of the secondary school should be concentrated on preparation. Deviation from the fixed purpose is injurious to the school and pupil alike. The youth must be instructed to know and to know why he knows.

"A gentleman spoke to me some time ago about a young man who had failed of admission to Princeton.

" 'He is such a fine boy,' pleaded the gentleman. 'It is a mistake not to let him in.'

" 'But he failed to pass his entrance examination,' I suggested.

" 'Yes, I know that,' was the reply. 'But consider what an exceptionally fine moral character he has.'

" 'Admitting that,' I was forced to respond, 'he would have been dropped in half a year, and that would have meant half a year wasted.'

"But the gentleman, hopelessly impressed by the 'fine moral character' under discussion, went away unconvinced that justice had been done.

"So if you have young men of fine moral character, have them ready for their examinations, for character of any sort can be dealt with in only one way—performance of the tasks of the hour.

"We made a mistake at Princeton once when we admitted a revivalist. He inspired much interest, to be sure, but it was soon apparent he was interfering with the real educational work. One student, a youth of keen perception and wit, recognized the disturbing element and gently uttered a protest, for one morning the good revivalist was surprised to find tacked on the boy's door this legend:

" 'I am a Christian, but studying for examinations.'

"Education is a score of things, and I wish all minds were broad enough to see that the acceptance of one thing is not the exclusion of other things. It is like critical appreciation of Browning. The man who admires Browning fails to perceive the beauties in the works of another poet. Few can utter an appreciation of one without making a foil of another.

"There is an education of skill, not only of the eye, the hand, etc., but in the communication of information. And yet I believe that nothing so prevents the general development of the mind as a great body of information."

By this, Doctor Wilson explained, he meant information acquired to no particular purpose or indifferently understood.[1]

Printed in the Philadelphia *Public Ledger*, March 10, 1906; some editorial headings omitted.
[1] There is a WWT outline of these remarks, dated March 9, 1906, in WP, DLC.

A News Item About the Naming of Patton Hall

[March 10, 1906]

Still another announcement of much interest was that by the unanimous vote of the Alumni Dormitory Committee the dormitory presented to the University by the members of the ten classes '92 to '01 has been named Patton Hall, in honor of Dr. Francis Landey Patton, and that an appropriate inscription to this effect is to be carved in the west wall of the four-story tower of the building,—this notable addition to the campus being the gift of ten of the eleven classes whose undergraduate courses were wholly under the administration of President Patton.

Patton Hall, by the way, is now nearing completion, its gray limestone walls looming up imposingly on the east side of Brokaw Field. The stone work is practically finished, and the strong, simple, classic outlines of the building, in harmony with the long line of Gothic bordering that side of the campus, make a fine impression. The interior finishings are now being installed, plastering will be started early in April, and it is expected that Patton Hall will be entirely completed before Commencement, and ready for the students at the opening of the next college year.

Printed in the *Princeton Alumni Weekly*, vi (March 10, 1906), 410.

A News Item About McCosh Hall

[March 10, 1906]

The contract for McCosh Hall, the new recitation building to be erected on the academy lot east of Marquand Chapel, has been awarded to Mr. William R. Matthews of Princeton, builder of the Fitz-Randolph Gateway, the new Cottage Clubhouse, etc. The price stated in the contract is $364,365, this fund, together with the sum required for building the foundation of the hall, being the gift of several friends of the University whose names have not been announced.

Printed in the *Princeton Alumni Weekly*, vi (March 10, 1906), 411.

To St. Clair McKelway

My dear Dr. McKelway,   Princeton, N. J.   11 March, 1906.

I was very much surprised to learn from Mr. Tirrell,[1] whom you sent last week to see me, that you thought that Colonel Harvey's suggestion that my name be considered in connection with the next Democratic nomination for the presidency might be worth taking up seriously.

It has, of course, been very gratifying to me that Colonel Harvey should have thought of me in that way; and I quite understand that such a man as he would not put forward a suggestion of that kind in the deliberate and formal way in which he has given utterance to it without meaning it in all seriousness. But I have myself interpreted it as meaning, not that he thought that such a suggestion might lead to an actual nomination, but only that he hoped that its consideration might lead to a careful canvas of the possibility of putting in nomination some one who held views and a position like my own: views which would hold liberal and reforming programmes to conservative and strictly constitutional lines of action, to the discrediting of rash and revolutionary proposals; a position disassociated from past contests and suggestive of personal independence, the position of a man whose views had not been formed under the influence of personal ambition. To discuss such a name would be to discuss and perhaps ascertain the possibility of drawing together into common political action the men who wish a change in our present political methods and policies but not in our traditions of statesmanship. Certainly it never occurred to me to attach any other practical significance to the use of my name.

I told Mr. Tirrell that, so far as I was concerned, I should expect that you would take the name up, if you took it up at all, in the same way,—that is, not in the least with the idea that it was desirable to obtain the nomination for me, but only with the purpose of seeing what the country was willing to think of by way of a rehabilitation of some of the older ideals of the Democratic party, or, rather, by way of organizing an Opposition with which conservative men could without apprehension ally themselves.

And I have feared that if you adopted Col. Harvey's suggestion immediately a misapprehension might arise which would put another colour on the matter. On the sixteenth of April next I am to speak at the annual dinner of the Democratic Club of New York. The Club is to celebrate Jefferson's birthday on that date instead of on the thirteenth, this year. I am to respond to the toast "Jefferson"; and it will be necessary for me to speak of Jefferson's opinions as if I were reminding Democrats of the first principles of the party. Such a speech would be flat and pointless were I not to speak also of the proper application of these principles in our own day. I accepted this invitation before Colonel Harvey had made his sugggestion; but it occurs to me that if any-

Oil painting of Wilson, by Frederic Yates

Drawing of Ellen Axson Wilson, by Frederic Yates

Drawing of Wilson in 1906, by Frederic Yates

Frederic Yates

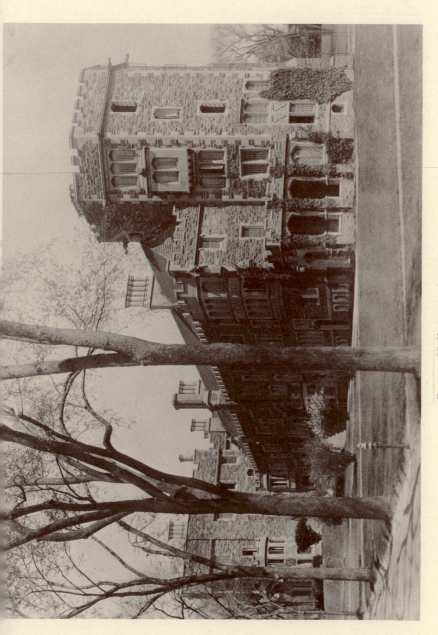

Patton Hall, erected 1906

Andrew Carnegie

Lake Carnegie

Fitz-Randolph Gateway, erected 1905

thing more were made of that suggestion before I speak at the dinner of the Democratic Club, my speech would sound like a personal platform and a self-nomination. That would mortify me profoundly.

It would, of course, make me ridiculous. But that is the least of the matter. It would entirely belie my whole character. Nothing could be further from my thoughts than the possibility or the desirability of holding high political office. That is as little in my mind now as it was before Colonel Harvey published his kind editorial characterization of me. I should like to have some part, if only a nominal one, in providing the country with an Opposition which its citizens would some day be glad to put into power, but I should not like to have that part the silly part of seeming seriously to consider myself a presidential possibility.

You know me so well, and I know and trust you so entirely that it is not necessary for me to apologize for writing this letter. You will understand and appreciate it as in all respects meaning what it says and will see how necessary it was for me to write it.

With warmest regard,

Cordially and faithfully Yours,   Woodrow Wilson

WWTLS (draft) (WP, DLC).
1 George L. Tirrell, reporter for the *Brooklyn Eagle*.

From Hopson Owen Murfee

Marion, Alabama.

My dear President Wilson: 12 March 1906

I fear that I may appear to be importunate in writing you again in regard to the volume I am endeavoring to get together on education and government. The material for the book is now all promised except the two chief articles; and tonight I am making bold to write again to you and to Dr. Lovett to ask for these two. The following plan of the volume will indicate the nature of the papers which, I fear, I have jeopardized friendship to ask:

EDUCATION AND DEMOCRACY

I

Education and Democracy: President Woodrow Wilson
Political Education: President Arthur T. Hadley
Republican Education: President Charles W. Eliot

II

Student Self-government
Historical Notes

III

The Genesis of the Honor System: Professor W. M. Thornton
The Honor System: Dr. E. O. Lovett
The Honor System and the Christian Ideal: Dr. John R.
   Sampey[1]
The Honor System and Democratic Citizenship: Mr. Erwin
   Craighead, Editor The Mobile Register.

I have set my heart on having the leading and chief article
of the little book, your words; and I hope that you will consent
to write them.[2] As I wrote you in my letter of the 18 of January,
some words of yours have been the seed from which my endeavor
has sprung; and I am desirous to have you put in the first chapter
of this little book, the insight and inspiration which I have found
in each of your books.

"Such government as ours is a form of conduct, and its only
stable foundation is character." "Nothing establishes the republican state save trained capacity for self-government, practical
aptitude for public affairs, habitual soberness and temperateness
of united action." These are the truths I should like to have you
bring home to our schools and colleges, and people, in this article.
For the work's sake I hope and pray that you will do this service.

Very sincerely yours   H. O. Murfee

TLS (WP, DLC).
   [1] The Rev. Dr. John Richard Sampey, Professor of Old Testament Interpretation at the Southern Baptist Theological Seminary since 1892.
   [2] As has been previously noted (H. O. Murfee to WW, Jan. 12, 1906, n. 3),
Wilson did contribute the essay, "Education and Democracy." It is printed at
May 3, 1907, Vol. 17.

A News Report of an Address in Youngstown, Ohio

[March 15, 1906]

PATRIOTISM

Is discussed by President Woodrow Wilson of Princeton

President Woodrow Wilson of Princeton University lectured to
the People's Institute[1] in First Presbyterian Church last evening,
a fair sized audience being present. His theme was "Patriotism,"
and was a plea for better citizenship, a wider knowledge of and
participation in matters political.

The greatest patriot, he said, is not he whose voice is loudest
in praise of his country, nor whose heart swells greatest at sight
of the flag; but rather the one who in his calmer moments seeks
conscientiously to work out the greatest good for the largest number of his countrymen. "We are justified in being proud of the

size of the United States, even though we did not make it," he said. "We have held it intact from the assaults of other nations for over a century. But there is still more to do in the future. As yet we are all but untouched by real art. We are underdeveloped, lack thoroughness, and completion. For the first time in three hundred years we are without a frontier (save in the colonies). All this time we have been beginning. Now civilization is closing in upon us. We must finish what we have begun—a much more difficult task, and one which will require the highest grade of patriotism."

Referring to the recent disclosures in the insurance investigations in New York, President Wilson did not consider it a sign of decadence in the country, but rather of its virility that condemnation should be so quick and sure. The three heads[2] are dying simply from the unswerving, honest gaze of a disapproving public. Not that the masses are any better than the principals, but that a dispassioned verdict comes nearest to being a correct one. This is ever the balance which makes public opinion the greatest power in American civilization. . . .

During the afternoon Mr. Wilson addressed the students at Rayen School.[3]

Printed in the *Youngstown Vindicator*, March 15, 1906; some editorial headings omitted.

[1] A local version of the People's Institute of New York, an educational enterprise organized in 1897 by Charles Sprague Smith, former professor at Columbia University, to provide classes, lectures, and dramatic and musical opportunities for men and women from all walks of life and of all creeds. The idea of such an institute spread to cities across the United States.

[2] He was referring to three presidents of life insurance companies subjected during the autumn of 1905 to a searching investigation by a committee of the New York legislature. One of the presidents, John A. McCall of the New York Life Insurance Company, had died on February 18, 1906, shortly after his resignation. The other two, Richard A. McCurdy of the Mutual Life Insurance Company of New York and James W. Alexander of the Equitable Life Assurance Society, had resigned in 1905 and were reported in poor health in early 1906. However, each recovered; Alexander lived until 1915, McCurdy until 1916.

[3] A news report of this address is printed at April 1, 1906.

From Benjamin Wistar Morris III

My dear Dr. Wilson: New York   March 15, 1906.

I was glad to see in your last letter that the proposed arrangements of the partitions, etc. in the '79 Hall meet with your approval.

I would now request an expression of your wishes regarding the furniture. I will make the following suggestions, and if you will be good to revise them in accordance with your wishes, I will then take up the matter with the Committee and as soon as a decision is reached will proceed at once with the work.

In order that the character of the furniture may be in keeping with the importance of the room and its future use, it seems to me that while the design should be dignified and simple, yet it should have enough richness of treatment to be in keeping with its surroundings, and to this effect I should very much like to see the furniture executed by Mr. W. F. Paris,[1] who is by all means the best available person in New York. He will give an approximate estimate on the cost and says that the work can very properly be done for from $1200. to $1500.

I would therefore suggest a large table in the ante-room opposite the fireplace about 3 by 6 feet, sturdily built with good heavy legs and braces; six or eight chairs, the type of the Windsor or library type, and in your room a flat top working table, at which you would sit with light coming over your left shoulder, and back of you, if you desire, a roll top desk for the keeping of papers in a permanent way and for temporary reception of papers and documents which you may desire for reference in the near future and yet would not like to have them lying around on top of your desk. Do you desire a chair with a swivel seat so that you may turn from the flat top desk to the roll top, which will be placed behind you? Or, have you furniture at the present time which will satisfy your requirements for your own use, and shall we confine ourselves merely to the furniture for the ante-room?

I would suggest that the seats built in with the wainscot be covered with a dark golden brown or red leather cushions and that a tan or fawn color be adopted for the hangings of the curtains, and that a similar tone be used on the plaster surfaces above the wainscoting and between the beams of the ceiling.

Hoping to hear from you regarding these matters as soon as you can conveniently write, I am with kind regards,

Yours very sincerely,   Benj. W Morris Jr

TLS (WP, DLC).
[1] William Francklyn Paris, architectural decorator, 26 W. 35th St., New York.

From Robert Hunter Fitzhugh[1]

Dr. Wilson,   Lexington, Ky.   March 15th, 1906.

Please be president, and let us have less of strenuosity and more of Washingtonism, fewer victories, and more justice and mercy.

Your urged candidacy revives my political interest which has been dead 46 years.

Enthusiastically yours,   R. H. Fitzhugh.

APS (WP, DLC).

¹ Born in Caroline County, Virginia, in 1836, he was the son of George Fitzhugh, the famous pro-slavery apologist of the Old South. Trained as a civil engineer, Robert Hunter Fitzhugh settled in Kentucky, where he engaged in pioneer work in the extension of railroads and the development of the state's mineral resources. About 1899 he retired to devote full time to writing, philanthropy, and educational work, especially among Negroes. For many years he was general superintendent and tireless promoter of the Colored Orphan Industrial Home in Lexington. As subsequent documents in this series will disclose, Wilson responded to many of his appeals for contributions to the home. Fitzhugh died in Lexington on November 17, 1919.

To John Preston Searle¹

My dear Sir: Princeton, N. J.   16 March, 1906.

Allow me to acknowledge with much appreciation your kind favor of the 10th² and to say that it will give me great pleasure to be present at the inauguration of Dr. Demorest on the 20th of June next,³ and to say a few words of greeting from Princeton.

With much appreciation,

Sincerely yours,   Woodrow Wilson

TLS (Special Collections, NjR).

¹ Member of the Board of Trustees of Rutgers College and President of the Faculty of the New Brunswick Theological Seminary.

² It is missing.

³ That is, at the inauguration of William Henry Steele Demarest as President of Rutgers College.

To Benjamin Wistar Morris III

My dear Mr. Morris: Princeton, N. J.   17 March, 1906.

Concerning your suggestion in your letter of March 15th, with regard to the furnishing of the hall in the '79 dormitory, I would make the following replies.

The table by which I sit every day measures 3' 6" by 7', and does not seem large even for my study. I should think that the table in the large room ought to be at least of that size. In my room, your suggestion of a flat top working table suits me exactly. I think that this table should have a couple of generous size drawers with locks, and that instead of a roll-top desk there ought to be a filing cabinet of the most improved pattern, which could also be locked. There should be a chair entirely wood, for myself, and of some pattern fitted to the sitter. You will know the type of chair I mean. And there should be a couple of other simple but comfortable chairs.

I like your suggestion about the type and character of the furniture very much. Bridges and I discussed the colors of the seat cushions and the hangings and also of the plaster surfaces, and I like them very much indeed.

Thanking you for your letter,

Cordially and faithfully yours,   Woodrow Wilson

TLS (WC, NjP).

From Harold Griffith Murray

Dear Dr. Wilson: New York   Mar. 17th, 1906.

Will you please accept this letter as a memorandum of our conversation of yesterday. The list of Philadelphians that Mr. Barringer and Mr. Henry thought it advisable for you to see consists of the following names;[1]

James C. Brooks,[2]	Samuel M. Vauclain,[9]
Samuel Rea,[3]	J. H. Converse,
Edwin N. Benson,[4]	John Wanamaker,
Edwin P. Borden,[5]	Tom Wanamaker,
S. Rulon Miller[6]	Rod Wanamaker,
Alba B. Johnson,[7]	Joseph Wharton,[10]
Franklin L. Potts,[8]	Thomas Potter, Jr.[11]

Mr. Barringer and Mr. Henry can give you detailed information about these men.

The Pittsburg list consists of

Jas. Laughlin, Jr. '68	Jas. H. Lockhart, '87
Jas. B. Laughlin, '86	Andrew Carnegie
B. F. Jones, '91	H. C. Frick
W. L. Jones, '87[12]	

and I suppose Mr. Peacock.[13]

I will write you a letter about the result of my interview with Bill Edwards.[14] I will tell Mr. Dodge Monday what you told me of Mr. [Norman Bruce] Ream. I hope that he will give up.

Very truly yours,   H G Murray   Secretary.

TLS (WP, DLC).

[1] Only those persons not already identified in this series will be identified here.

[2] President of the Southwork Foundry and Machine Co. of Philadelphia.

[3] Fourth Vice President of the Pennsylvania Railroad Co.

[4] Edwin North Benson, stockbroker, whose son of the same name had been graduated from Princeton in 1899.

[5] Probably Edward Payson Borden, retired businessman and philanthropist.

[6] John Rulon-Miller. His son, John Rulon-Miller, Jr., had been graduated from

Princeton in 1905, and another son, Sumner Rulon-Miller, was a member of the Class of 1907.

⁷ Alba Boardman Johnson, partner in Burnham, Williams and Co., locomotive builders.

⁸ Franklin M. Potts, President of the Philadelphia Warehouse Co.

⁹ Samuel Matthews Vauclain, an officer of Burnham, Williams and Co. His son, Jacques Leonard Vauclain, was a member of the Class of 1906.

¹⁰ Prominent manufacturer and founder of the Wharton School of Finance and Commerce of the University of Pennsylvania.

¹¹ President of Thomas Potter Sons and Co. of Philadelphia, oilcloth manufacturers.

¹² William Larimer Jones, Princeton 1887, Vice President and General Manager of the Jones & Laughlin Steel Corp.

¹³ Alexander Rolland Peacock, an executive of the United States Steel Corp.

¹⁴ William Hanford Edwards, outstanding athlete of the Class of 1900, at this time an insurance broker in New York.

From Hopson Owen Murfee

Marion, Alabama.
My dear President Wilson: 18 March 1906

I thank you with all my heart for your kindness in consenting to write the first chapter for the little volume on Education and Democracy. I am endeavoring to have all the material ready for the printer by the first of August; but if it is not perfectly convenient for you to prepare your portion by this time, any delay will not be of consequence.

The enclosures¹ will acquaint you with the nature of some material for Part Two and Part Three of the book. Part Three deals with the Honor System, and I have asked Lovett to write the chief chapter for this part: "THE HONOR SYSTEM: ITS NATURE AND ITS INFLUENCE IN THE LIFE OF THE INDIVIDUAL AND THE COMMUNITY." As he has not yet definitely consented to do this, I hesitate to ask him to prepare also an account of the Honor System at Princeton. Could you suggest some one to whom I may write for this article? Princeton and the University of Virginia are the glasses through which the world must look at the Honor System, and I wish the glasses to give as fine a view as possible of the object.

Again thanking you for your generous aid in this work, and for the vision and purpose and hope you have given to life for me, I am ever

Faithfully and gratefully yours   H. O. Murfee

TLS (WP, DLC).

¹ They were a printed questionnaire and a typed announcement, both undated, concerning his projected book, "Student-Government in School, College, and University." Both documents are in WP, DLC.

To Robert Hunter Fitzhugh

My Dear Maj. Fitzhugh: [Princeton, N. J.]   March 19, 1906.

Thank you very much for your post card. There is nothing serious about the mention of my name for the presidency; but it is truly delightful to hear such a note of cordial friendship as that sounded in your card.

Faithfully yours,   Woodrow Wilson

Printed in the Trenton *True American*, July 26, 1912.

To Azel Washburn Hazen

My dear Dr. Hazen: Princeton, N. J.   20 March, 1906.

Thank you very much for your delightful little note of yesterday.[1] It is always a real delight to hear from you.

I am not taking at all seriously the suggestion made by Colonel Harvey, and am only afraid that the discussion will be carried so far as to be a little embarrassing.

Mrs. Wilson joins me in the most affectionate messages to you all.

Always—

Faithfully and affectionately yours,   Woodrow Wilson

TLS (photostat in RSB Coll., DLC).
[1] It is missing.

From Harold Griffith Murray

Dear Dr. Wilson: New York   Mar. 20th, 1906.

I had a long talk with W. H. Edwards, '00, today about Mr. Peacock of Pittsburg. Mr. Edwards, as you probably know, is very close to him, visits him in his home and enjoys unusual confidential relations. He thinks it is most inadvisable for any one at present to approach Mr. Peacock on the subject of giving to Princeton. He says that Mr. Peacock will give and give generously to Princeton some day, but that at present he does not care to do so, as he has a son in College.[1] I have asked Mr. Edwards to keep me informed about Mr. Peacock, and whenever he has an opportunity to do so, to say a good word for the University and its needs, and I think we can rely on him to do it. I am sending this information as Mr. Peacock was on your list of Pittsburgians.

Very truly yours,   H G Murray   Secretary.

TLS (WP, DLC).
[1] Clarence Neilson Peacock '10.

From Benjamin Wistar Morris III

My dear Dr. Wilson: New York   March 21, 1906.

I wish to acknowledge your kind favor of the 17th explaining your wishes about the character and quantity of furniture for your office and the ante-room.

I have taken the matter up with Mr. Dodge and have secured his authority to have W. F. Paris, #26 West 35th St. do the work, and have subsequently called there with Mr. Bridges and gone over the matter in detail. We are all (Mr Bridges, Paris & I) of the opinion that it would be by far the best way to have you made as thoroughly familiar as possible with the work in advance in order that there may be no misunderstanding or disappointment on your part in its execution.

To this intent, I would ask if you are coming to New York in the near future, and if you can spare the time, to call at the office of Mr. Paris, letting him know in advance in order that he may arrange to be there and have all the documents and illustrations at hand for your inspection.

In compliance with your wishes it is my understanding that we are to provide as follows:

For the ante-room a table somewhat larger than your present work table in your study, to wit: about 3'8" or 4' in width by about 8' long and about 34" or 36" high, which is somewhat higher than the customary table. This idea is in order to keep the furniture in scale with the wood work in the room and with the fireplace. At each end of the table, for proper dignity of effect, the suggestion is for a large dignified arm chair with high back and four straight back chairs without arms, strongly built but light enough to be easily moved from place to place; two chairs of this same design to be provided in addition for your own office. Further in your office, your flat top work table about 3'6" x 5'6", but Mr. Paris would suggest that it be made not more than 3'1" in width if this is large enough for your purposes; two drawers to be provided to pull from the side at which you sit, and if you so desire, two shallower drawers at the opposite side. For your own chair a dignified high leather back chair of roomy dimensions and long comfortable arms with a shaped wood seat, on which if you so desire, a cushion can be used at any time.

Realizing the extreme importance of having the chair comfortable and of a proper relative height to the table, Mr. Paris has suggested that if you can conveniently do so it would be well to give him the desired height of your work table from the floor, the height of the seat of the chair from the floor and its width and depth together with the height of the back, and also whether you desire the back to be absolutely perpendicular or slightly sloping, or a little more than slightly sloping.

With this information, Mr. Paris will at once proceed with his drawings which can be submitted to you within a week.

Regretting the necessity of troubling you to this extent, which I would not do if there were any other means of assuring a result in accordance with your desires, I am,

Yours very sincerely,   Benj. W Morris Jr

TLS (WP, DLC).

A News Report of an Address on Americanism
at Oberlin College

[March 22, 1906]
Woodrow Wilson.

The last lecture in the U.L.A.[1] course was given by Woodrow Wilson on the subject, "What does it mean to be an American?"[2] This number was by far the best one of the course, and the pleasant recollections of Mr. Wilson's stirring message will go far to blot out the troubled memories which we hold of some former speakers.

"America is coming to a crisis in her national life," says Mr. Wilson. We have from the beginning risen steadily, and the rising action is drawing on to the climax. The great problem before us as a nation is to meet this climax wisely. For three centuries we have been starting things, but we have finished nothing. To the world this is the strongest evidence of weakness. We hurry and rush and live a strenuous life, and at the end of it we see many things begun, but nothing finished. Our first great weakness then is the lack of even the desire for artistic finish. Wisely did Mr. Wilson speak when he said, "The man who takes time for artistic perfection takes time to be immortal." We have not lived long enough yet as a nation to care greatly for perfection—we have lived the sordid, coarse life of commercial prosperity, without ever raising our eyes or our thoughts to higher things. In the century before us, if America is to take the place in the congress of nations that we of today fondly hope that she may take, we must study the fine arts of building, of politics, and of trade. Thus far, the world has endured our coarseness, and has even listened to the words of the unsophisticated lover of peace. But a far finer sense of diplomacy and statecraft must be attained if nations are always to hear and to heed our counsels.

Our customs, our literature, and our government, all these are but in the first stage of development. Any one with a literary nose can smell the odor of death on much of our current literature, if such it may be called. Our customs are crude, our manners shocking. Our cities are still in the muck and mire of political corruption. What have the men who govern cities learned, or what do they care, about the fine art of politics? This insensibility to artistic perfection is the great source of weakness and it must be remedied if we expect to live as a nation.

Yet with all these elements of weakness in our national character, the things that we have done we have done well. Our foundations are well builded. One of our most valuable assets is our political liberty. In older countries men have fought and died for that very liberty which here every man receives as a part of his life. Our strong and rugged Americanism is of a sort that will take well the higher polish of culture and refinement, when once we set about the acquirement of perfection. This crudeness is perhaps due to the fact that we have as yet been too busy in our battle with the wilderness to gain power and finish. Now that our frontier has vanished we may seek the higher art.

One of the most characteristic marks of an American is his power of adaptability. The most typical American of his time, Benjamin Franklin, is our great model. Whether he was in Paris, London or on the wild frontier of his native country, he was perfectly at home. He compelled respect and attention through his power of adapting himself to the occasion. There is so much strong, young vitality among us that it will insist on seeking the frontier, wherever it is. Now it is the Phillipines and Alaska. Soon it will be the shore of Asia, and then Autocratic Europe shall hear us knocking at their back door, demanding admittance for American ideas, customs, and arts. If we want to make the thoughts of America the thoughts of the world, we must study perfection.

The ideals and sentiments which move us most, and which inspire us most are expressed today in Socialism. The Socialist motive is that of Christ himself, but the method is madness. Into the future we must go with the watchword of perfection on our lips, and the spirit of the artist to guide us. The day of common work is gone: to attain, to conquer, henceforth, we must seek finished perfection in all things.

This talk—it was too informal and free to be called a lecture—was greatly enriched by the pleasing personality of Mr. Wilson. He was most unconventional in his attitudes; and spoke and moved always with a certain charming grace that added greatly to the interest of his remarks.

Printed in the *Oberlin Review*, xxxiii (March 22, 1906), 431.
¹ The Undergraduate Lecture Association.
² On March 13, 1906, as an announcement in the *Oberlin Review*, xxxiii (March 8, 1906), 399, discloses.

To Benjamin Wistar Morris III

My dear Mr. Morris: Princeton, N. J.   22 March, 1906.

Thank you for your letter of yesterday. I will take pleasure in sending Mr. Paris the details you suggest and will make an early appointment to consult him about the furniture. I have only these amendments to make to your detailed suggestions. I think that all eight of the chairs of which you speak as suitable for the large room, should be placed in that room, inasmuch as Committees will often meet there which will require quite as many chairs as that; and that the chairs for my office ought to be of a different and simpler style. They will stand in a room with a low ceiling, and I should think ought to be rather broad and low than high-backed and stiff. I should not think it at all necessary to have chairs specially made for the office. They ought easily to be picked out from stock ordinarily in existence.

I like Mr. Paris' suggestion about the table for the small office, but in the case of my own chair again I would suggest that it have no high back, but that it be rather of the type which I would describe as the mission type adapted to the human shape. I will try to be more explicit in writing to Mr. Paris, and will let him know when I can see him. I shall not overlook the matter of the University shield.

Always—
        Cordially and faithfully yours,   Woodrow Wilson

TLS (WC, NjP).

From Charles Williston McAlpin

My dear Dr. Wilson: [Princeton, N. J.]   March 22, 1906.

I enclose a copy of a letter received from Mr. Cassatt.¹ If you wish me to do so shall I say to Mr. Cassatt that the invitation holds good for June 1907?

Judge Phelps,² who has accepted the invitation to receive the degree of Doctor of Laws, asks me to send him the copy of the Latin formula used in conferring the degree. Will you be good enough to furnish me with a copy of this formula?

        Sincerely yours,   [C.W. McAlpin]   Secretary.

From Frederick A. Duneka[1]

My dear Dr. Wilson: New York   March 22, 1906.

In the absence of Mr. Alden who is in Europe (and by the way
Colonel Harvey is there also) I am replying to your very attractive
letter of March 20.

The proposed "Life of Thomas Jefferson" would, I am sure, be
a very attractive feature for the Magazine, but it would only be
fair to say that the installments in each number would probably
have to be somewhat shorter than the installments of your great
History.

The "Life" is, as you say, a thing of the future—I heartily wish
it were not—but as it is two years distant, the object of this letter
is to say that we should be very glad to make arrangements for
serialization and to make a book of it afterwards.

Please accept the sincerest thanks of the House for the opportunity you are giving, and believe that we appreciate it.

Yours very truly,   F A Duneka   General Manager.

TLS (WP, DLC).
1 General Manager of Harper and Brothers.

To Charles Williston McAlpin

My dear Mr. McAlpin: Princeton, N. J.   23 March, 1906.

I have received your letter of yesterday about Mr. Cassatt's
inability to be present at Commencement. I would be very much
obliged if you would inform him that the invitation holds good for
1907.[1]

The Latin formula for which Judge Phelps asks is as follows:

"Auctoritate mihi a curatoribus Universitatis Princetoniensis
commissa te ad summum gradum in legibus honoris causa
admitto."   Faithfully yours,   Woodrow Wilson

TLS (McAlpin File, UA, NjP).
1 He died on December 28, 1906.

A News Report of Remarks in New York to the Alumni of the Lawrenceville School

[March 25, 1906]

GEN. PORTER[1] RECALLS SCHOOL DAYS OF '54

Lawrenceville Alumni Honor Him at Waldorf Banquet.

William H. Edwards, President of the Alumni Association of the Lawrenceville School, a preparatory institution near Princeton, recently met Gen. Horace Porter, a graduate in the class of '54.

"General," he said, "we want to give a dinner in your honor."

"All right; it's up to you," responded Porter.

Last night the association put it back to Gen. Porter, when they offered the dinner at the Waldorf-Astoria. Mr. Edwards was toastmaster, and introduced Gen. Porter, who told several stories of school life at Lawrenceville. . . .

After John Reid, the Yale golf player, had sung several Scotch ballads in baritone, Mr. Edwards introduced President Woodrow Wilson of Princeton.

"It's 9:38, time for a Wilson," said Mr. Edwards by way of salutation. Dr. Wilson talked about the advantages of college athletics. He repeated that many of Great Britain's battles had been fought at Eton before they reached the actual field of carnage.

"The men who come out of the schools," he said, "should be the men to carry the ideals of the Nation and conceive the standards of fellowship. We should remember the connection of school and college sport with the future battlefields of the world and the future diplomacy of the universe. Remember that sportsmanship on the playground is the sort of diplomacy which the sort of men like John Hay have displayed. Remember that a man can't do a dirty thing on the ball-field and then speak a truth in the presence of the nations of the world. What America has stood for always has been fair play, and what she ought to keep her hands from is anything that is foul or unfair. The boys from college constitute our fountains of renewal, and in honoring Gen. Porter we are lifting the type that inspires the growth of the typical American." . . .

Printed in the *New York Times*, March 25, 1906; some editorial headings omitted.
    [1] Horace Porter, Civil War hero, Ambassador to France, 1897-1905, and prominent businessman.

From Grover Cleveland

My dear President Wilson   Stuart Fla   Mch 25, 1906

I am especially gratified and comforted by the generous words contained in your congratulatory letter.[1] You are quite right in believing that at the age of sixty nine one seeks in the past for friendship he has gained and kept, rather than for things achieved.

And so your expressions of attachment and personal trust are among the things I carefully hoard among those whose possession will be a delight and comfort to me as long as I live.

With grateful appreciation of your kind remembrance of me at this time, I am   Faithfully Yours   Grover Cleveland

ALS (WP, DLC).
[1] WW to G. Cleveland, March 5, 1906.

A News Report

[March 29, 1906]

EIGHTH ANNUAL BANQUET

Of The Daily Princetonian, Held at the Inn
Last Evening.

The eighth annual banquet of The Daily Princetonian was held last evening at the Princeton Inn. The dinner was the largest ever given by the Princetonian, one hundred and twenty-five covers being laid. . . .

The final speaker of the evening was President Woodrow Wilson. He declared that he always looked forward to a Princetonian banquet as an opportunity for giving expression to the ideas which are held by the administration of the University. There is a prevalent but nevertheless false impression among undergraduates that college years are a series of drudgeries. Not until the college course is viewed as a means to an end will its true relationship to life be appreciated. In reality, undergraduates should regard study as a business and not as a school-boy task. The one thing that should distinguish university men from others is the light in which they look at rumors. It should be a rule always to investigate before reaching conclusions. Premature judgments should be avoided. In addition, there is a moral obligation dependent upon all to investigate the sources before forming an opinion upon a report. In this line there has been a big improvement in the undergraduate body. Finally it should be born in mind that the right temper of mind is greatly to be desired in the management of national affairs.

Printed in the *Daily Princetonian*, March 29, 1906.

A Religious Address[1]

[[March 30, 1906]]

THE MINISTER AND THE COMMUNITY

There are two ideals between which the Church, first and last, has oscillated in respect to the position that a minister ought to hold in the community. The one is the ideal which expects the minister to hold himself aloof from the ordinary transactions of life, and to devote himself exclusively, and I was about to say almost ostentatiously, to the things which are spiritual. This is the ideal which has led to asceticism, to practices of the Church which have absolutely shut the priesthood off from the life of the community, which have forced upon them an unnatural way of living and an unnatural separation from the ordinary interests of the world.

Then there is the opposite idea—that the minister ought to be part of everything in a community that makes for its betterment, its improvement, its amelioration, its reformation—that he should take a deep interest in everything that affects the life of the community and be at particular pains to live as other men live, and not in any way show himself separate from the world, not in any way, that, at any rate externally, changes the current and method of his life. Certain men in our own generation have taken the position that, though they wish to preach the Gospel and influence men to come to Christ, they will have a greater influence if they do not accept the ordination of the Church, but remain laymen. It is their impression that a layman can preach straighter to the hearts of laymen than ministers can. There is something of the idea creeping in in various quarters, that the lay instrumentalities find the straightest roads to the hearts of men, and that the ministerial instrumentality is tainted a little by the professionalism which is in it; that the advice of the professional spiritual adviser is less cogent than the advice of the amateur spiritual adviser. This is the extreme form of this view.

Let us acknowledge at the outset that in our time we have been trying to unfrock the ministerial profession, literally and metaphorically. We are afraid of the frock, we are afraid of the sign,

[1] A news report of this address is printed below.

we are afraid of the touch of professionalism. It is a characteristic of our time that we wish to combine all things without differentiation in one single thing that we call life, and the consequence is that we do not know what we would be at. The consequence is that no man sees distinctly enough the particular road that he is trying to tread, the particular function which he is trying to perform in society. He says, "I must be a man," by which he means an added general force in society and not a specialized force in society; by which he means that he must disperse his powers and not concentrate them. And yet the difficulty of modern times is this very dispersion of professional energy, this obliteration of the lines that run and should run between one calling and another. The soldier is proud of his uniform and of the straps over his arms and shoulders, the marks of his rank; and every man who counts for as much of direct force as the soldier counts for ought to be proud of the things that distinguish his calling. I trust that no man will go into the ministry with the hope that he can conceal himself in the crowd, so that no man may know that he is a minister. I hope that he may plan his life so that nobody may ever associate with him without knowing that he is a minister.

How are we going to do this? By resuming the costume, by resuming the ritual, by resuming the aloofness and separateness from the world? That would be better than nothing. It is true, whether we like the fact or not, that the Roman Catholic priesthood, when its members have really remembered their consecration and lived true to it, have made a deeper impression upon the communities they lived in than the Protestant clergy, because they were men whom to look upon was to recall the fact that they were commissioned out of the unseen, that they did not live as other men lived, that they did devote themselves to something separate and apart; that it was intended that when they came into a company of men, those men should be reminded that here was a commissioner who was not a commissioner of the world; and when these men have been true to that standard they have been incomparable forces in the world.

The Protestant minister has too much forgotten the ideals of this separate priesthood. What is it that the minister should try to do? It seems to me that the minister should try to remind his fellow-men in everything that he does and in everything that he says, that eternity is not future, but present; that there is in every transaction of life a line that connects it with eternity, and that our lives are but the visible aspect of the experiences of our spirits upon the earth; that we are living here as spirits; that our whole

conduct is to be influenced by things that are invisible, of which
we must be constantly reminded lest our eyes should be glutton-
ously filled with the things that are visible; that we should be reminded that there lurks everywhere, not ungraciously and with
forbidding mien, but graciously and with salvation on its counte-
nance, the image and the memory of Christ, going a little journey
through the earth to remind men of the fatherhood of God, of
the brotherhood of men, of the journey that all spirits are taking
to the land that is unseen and to which they are all to come.

It is very interesting to note how miscellaneous the Church of
our day has become in its objects and endeavors. It is interesting
to note how central it regards its kitchen in the basement, the
bowling alley attached to the church, the billiard table where
youngsters may amuse themselves, the gymnasium—the things
that naturally associate themselves with what we call the institutional work of the Church. Did you ever ask yourself what an
institution is? An institution is merely a way of doing some particular thing. Now, I am not now making any objection to enter-
tainments, fairs, and amusements, but I do want to call your
attention to the fact that the persons whom we lead to do these
things are not often reminded of why it is that we ask them to do
them there, at the church. I have been in some churches where,
when these things were going on, the minute the minister came
into the room, you somehow got the impression that you had been
reminded of something. The walls of the room were no longer as
solid as they were; you saw bigger spaces; the mind seemed to go
back to dreams that had seemed vague before you at your mother's knee, and that gentle figure there seemed to say: "It is delightful that we should so disport ourselves, but we are spirits.
We know each other only as we know each other spiritually, and
only as these things bind us together in an eternal brotherhood is
it worth while to be here." I have been at other such gatherings
when the entrance of the minister did not suggest anything of the
kind—when only another human being had come into the room
—a human being who had no more suggestion of the eternal
about him than the youngest person present, a man who did not
carry in his mien and attitude and speech any message whatever, whose personality was not radiant with anything.

Now, it does not take a great man to radiate a pure spirit, because the most modest gifts can be associated with very deep
and real religious experiences, and the spirit may speak when the
tongue is tied. I have myself witnessed the history of a pastor
whose preaching was impossible but whose life, divine; and in
twenty years there was built up a power out of that church, out

of what I might call that speechless church, which did not radiate from the most eloquent pulpit in the other churches of the place; where eloquence seemed empty alongside of radiant godliness; where the spirit seemed to have a thousand tongues and the mind only one; where the doctrine was more expounded by the daily life of the one pastor than by all the expositions of the others. If you can combine the two, if your life can display the secret and otherwise not readily understood principles of the Gospel and your sermons expound the life exemplified, then you have something irresistible for the regeneration and revolution of a community; but as compared with each other, the reminder of the life is worth a thousand times the suggestion of the pulpit.

Is not that the supreme lesson of the life of Christ? I have sometimes thought that we would be unspeakably enriched if we had known some of the incidents of the days that Christ lived on the earth which were quite distinct and separate from His teaching—the ordinary, now unregarded incidents of His day. For I am sure that there we should have had an example infinitely fruitful for our own guidance, and should have been conscious that in everything that He said, every little thing that He did, there was a divine suggestion, a suggestion of divinity which was not a rebuke to humanity, but which heartened and revealed all that was best of itself, seemed like a sweet air out of some unattained country, like a light coming from some source that other men could not uncover; and that it must have been infinitely gracious to have Him lodge in the house. There must have seemed an atmosphere lingering there which made it impossible to forget that time was part of eternity.

Now the world is not going to be saved except the minister model himself on Christ. The world is not going to be evangelized unless the minister distinguish himself from the community. The Church is not going to recover its authority among men until its ministers display their credentials in their lives, by showing that the thought that is in them is always the thought that makes for salvation; that they will not teach the things that are impure; that they will not play with the things that are dangerous; that they are not reformers, but ministers of Christ. Did you ever notice that Christ was not a reformer? Not that He would have frowned upon a reformer, but He was not a reformer. He was not organizing men to do what is necessary to be done in order to reconstruct and better human life. He was supplying the whole motive force of that and everything else. It is just as much of a reform to go into a household where there is not the sweetness of Christian feeling and introduce it there by contagion, as it is to sit on a platform at a public meeting intended to set forward some missionary enterprise.

I remember—for I have had the unspeakable joy of having been born and bred in a minister's family—I remember one occasion which made a very profound impression upon me when I was a lad, in a company of gentlemen where my father was present, and where I happened to be, unobserved. One of the gentlemen in a moment of excitement uttered an oath, and then, his eye resting upon my father, he said with evident sincerity: "Dr. Wilson, I beg your pardon; I did not notice that you were present." "Oh," said my father, "you mistake, sir; it is not to me you owe the apology." I doubt if any other one remark ever entered quite so straight to the quick in me as that did, the consciousness that my father, taken by surprise, was at once so conscious that he was not the person offended, that he should so naturally call the attention of the man who had uttered the oath to what was the simple fact, that the offense was not to him but to his Master. It was exactly as if a disrespectful word had been spoken of the President of the United States in the presence of an ambassador of the United States, the apology would be due not to him but to his Government. And if ministers could always so contrive it that in their presence the presence of God was manifest, the whole problem of the ministry would be solved and evangelization would be irresistible.

There is only one way by which fire is spread and that is by contact. The thing to be ignited must touch the fire, and unless the fire burns in you, nobody will be lighted by contact with you. No amount of studious knowledge of the subject-matter or of the methods of your profession will do you the least degree of service unless it is on fire, and has communicated its fire to your very heart and substance.

Let every man, therefore, who goes into the ministry set himself apart; let every man who goes into the ministry go into it with a determination that nobody shall fail to know that he is a minister of the Gospel. It can be graciously done, without austerity, without rebuke, without offensiveness; it can be done by the simple method merely of being conscious yourself that you are the minister of God. For what a man is conscious of believing, he communicates to those who consort with him; what a man is known to stand for, he transmits to those who are in his presence though he speak never a word. And this consciousness of his will be the consciousness of every company he moves in, a sweet consciousness that will make his presence very gracious and everything he does acceptable to those with whom he consorts—not shutting him off from the ordinary relationships of life, but irradiating those relationships, making them the means of spreading the consciousness he has of what he is.

When I hear some of the things which young men say to me by way of putting the arguments to themselves for going into the ministry, I think that they are talking of another profession. Their motive is to do something, when it should be to be something. You do not have to *be* anything in particular to be a lawyer. I have been a lawyer and I know. You do not have to *be* anything in particular, except a kind-hearted man, perhaps, to be a physician; you do not have to *be* anything, nor to undergo any strong spiritual change in order to be a merchant. The only profession which consists in *being* something is the ministry of our Lord and Saviour—and it does not consist of anything else. It is manifested in other things, but it does not consist of anything else. And that conception of the minister which rubs all the marks of it off and mixes him in the crowd so that you cannot pick him out, is a process of eliminating the ministry itself.

Now, it is all very easy to say these things; it is impossible to do these things except by the influence and power of the Holy Spirit. If I could do the various things the right method of doing which I understand, I should be a most useful person. I know that we all should in some measure be ministers of Christ, and a man does not like to say the things that I have said and remember how little he has used his own profession to express that ministry. But, because we are imperfect, is it not the more necessary to know what the ideal is, to see it clearly, to see it steadily enough not to lose sight of it? If you lost the vision where would you go? If you did not know what you would be at, how would you ever find the way again? If you did not know what it was that you were embarking in, how could you make sure that you had found the right course of life? And the beauty of the Gospel is that it is a Gospel which leaves us, not the barren hope that in our own strength we can be useful, but the splendid, fruitful hope that there is One who if we but rely upon Him can inform us with these things and make our spirits to be the true spirits of God.[2]

Woodrow Wilson, *The Minister and the Community* (New York: Student Young Men's Christian Association, 1909).

[2] There is a WWT outline of this address, dated March 23, 1906, in WP, DLC.

A News Report of a Religious Address in Hartford

[March 31, 1906]

COLLEGE MEN URGED TO THE MINISTRY.

The third annual conference of the Christian men of Eastern colleges met at Hosmer Hall in the Hartford Theological Seminary at 8 o'clock last evening for the first session of a three days' conference. The object of the conference is to present to Christian young men in the universities and colleges the claims upon them of the Christian ministry as a profession and upwards of 150 delegates were present last evening.

The exercises last evening began with singing, "Thou, Whose Almighty Word," after which President William Douglas Mackenzie of the Seminary gave an address of welcome. . . .

After the hymn, "Ye Servants of God Your Master Proclaim," had been sung President Woodrow Wilson of Princeton University spoke on "The Relation of the Minister to the Community" saying in part:

"I hope that no man in the ministry will have the idea that he ought to conceal himself so that no man will think he is a minister. It is a fact that the Roman Catholic priest who is really devoted to his work often exerts a greater influence than the Protes[t]ant because, wherever he is seen, every man realizes that here is one who has received his commission from the Invisible. Protestants have too much forgotten the separate priesthood. The minister should try to remind men that eternity is a present thing and not something in the future and that a line connects every transaction of today with eternity; that we live here as spirits; that our conduct must be influenced by the things that are invisible and that about us there is the gracious memory and image of Jesus Christ."

Printed in the *Hartford Courant*, March 31, 1906; three editorial headings omitted.

A News Report

[March 31, 1906]

PRINCETON ALUMNI GREET PRESIDENT WILSON.

Luncheon at Hartford Club with Mayor Henney Presiding.

When it was learned that President Woodrow Wilson of Princeton University was coming to Hartford to address the Student Conference at the Hartford Theological Seminary, alumni of the university in this vicinity bestirred themselves and decided to give him a welcome. He was entertained at luncheon at the Hartford Club yesterday afternoon, twenty alumni participating. . . .

Mayor Henney[1] presided and speeches were made by President Wilson, Professor Martin of Trinity College[2] and Professor Jacobus of the Hartford Theological Seminary. Much enthusiasm was manifested at the suggestion of forming an alumni association.

Printed in the *Hartford Courant*, March 31, 1906.
  [1] William Franklin Henney, Princeton 1874, Mayor of Hartford since 1904.
  [2] Winfred Robert Martin, Princeton 1872, Professor of Oriental Languages at Trinity College.

From Hopson Owen Murfee

Marion, Alabama.
My dear President Wilson: 31 March 1906

The Trustees of the Institute have given to our boys the hall[1] in which you spoke last April for their Hall of Commons; and the boys have already begun to carry out your suggestions for it. They purpose to furnish it handsomely and to fill it with memorials of ideals, and, we hope, achievements. I am persuaded that this will do much to establish in their minds noble ideals, and to inspire indomitable endeavor. This, and much else of promise which has appeared in the school this session, I feel is the fruit of your coming to Marion. Certain it is that the boys think so. And they wish, in carrying out a policy they have adopted to put each year a stained gladd [glass] window in the Hall of Commons, to have the first memorial window in their Hall bear your name and words. In the center of the window:

WOODROW WILSON, PH.D., LITT.D., LL.D.
PRESIDENT PRINCETON UNIVERSITY
GOVERNMENT DAY ORATOR
1905

And at the bottom of the sash:

"THE TRUSTWORTHINESS OF MEN TRUSTED SEEMS OFTEN
TO GROW WITH THE TRUST."[2]—Woodrow Wilson

I am now writing to ask if you would suggest any changes. These words of yours have become the creed of us all at Marion, but I thought that you might wish to suggest others; and we should certainly like to have your approval of the wording in the upper section of the window,

The 1906 window will bear the name and words of Aristotle:

"A state can be virtuous only when the citizens who have a share in the government are virtuous."

"That which contributes most to preserve the state is the adaptation of education to the form of government."

Do you think that Aristotle would approve of that use of his words?   Faithfully yours   H. O. Murfee

TLS (WP, DLC).
1 The chapel of Marion Military Institute.
2 From "When a Man Comes to Himself," printed at Nov. 1, 1899, Vol. 11.

A News Report of an Address on Secondary Education[1]

[April 1906]

President Wilson's Address

Our opportunities! The subject is not a new one to us. At school, the faculty and at home, our parents are very mindful of their duty to us in this regard. But never has it been put before us in a more interesting way than on Wednesday, March thirteenth [fourteenth], when Dr. Woodrow Wilson honored Rayen with a visit. To see and hear the president of Princeton College was in itself a great opportunity. By being a student at Rayen School on that Wednesday afternoon each of us enjoyed a privilege which the greater part of the High School students of America never have.

A great many people read his books, but to see him and to feel the personality of the man adds weight and interest to his words. President Wilson has a strong face and a frank, direct way of speaking which gains and holds the attention of all. We wish that we might put down the words of President Wilson's speech exactly as he said them, but that is not possible. This is the substance of it:

The thing which impresses him most when he sees a large body of young people is, what a pity it is that men of years cannot give their experience to the young, to keep them from making the mistakes which they have made. Young people sometimes wonder what good all these dry studies do them and why they must waste so much time over them now and never use them again after leaving school. The system of education used today is the result of the experience of generations and it must be accepted as the best whether the student understands its advantages or not.

The so-called practical man declares that practical education is needed, that the classical is of no value, but when one considers exactly what studies are used after leaving school—if that is what "practical" means—the number is found to be extremely small.

The thing which is used is the power of analytical thinking which all of these studies give.

Everybody admits that the gymnasium is an excellent thing, everybody approves the course in it, but which of the exercises done in the gymnasium will anybody use in the real business of life? Just as the exercise in the gymnasium develops the body so do these branches taught in the High Schools and Colleges develop the mind. One must do the things in school which he will never do afterwards, just to get his mind in such a condition that he can do what he wishes to with it.

The trouble with a great many young people is that they lack imagination. They go along with their eyes on the path directly in front of them and never look up. Everything in life is imaginary. The greatest and most powerful forces in the world cannot be seen. It is necessary to lift the eyes and grasp the idea of things as a whole, to see that the accomplishment of each little duty goes toward the development of character.

There are great opportunties lying open to all. There are teachers ready to furnish explanations but they cannot furnish anything more. The great trouble with the schools today is that the teachers do all the work. One prominent professor in a preparatory school said that the young mind had the greatest imaginable power to resist the introduction of knowledge.

President Wilson says that we must *learn* and not be taught. Everything works in our favor and if we do not profit by our opportunities we have only ourselves to blame.

Orre Hazeltine, '06.

Printed in the Youngstown, Ohio, *Rayen Record*, April 1906, pp. 322-23.
[1] Delivered at the Rayen School in Youngstown, Ohio, on March 14, 1906.

From John James Moment[1]

My dear Dr. Wilson: Hartford, Conn.   April 2nd 1906

May I be allowed an added word of appreciation of your splendid services to our Conference! Your address was easily the event of the conference and continues to be the leading topic of conversation among the students. I am safe in saying that you made what happens at present to be an unpopular phase of the minister's life seem to those who heard the address the only phase of his life which was much worth while. My only regret is that several thousand more men might have heard your words.

For the success of the Conference, both in regard to the number of delegates present and with respect of their satisfaction while here, you were in a large measure responsible. We feel ourselves under no common obligations.

Your address at the dinner[2] also deserves much more than I dare say regarding it. At all events it had the effect I believe of starting our Connecticut valley alumni on a career of more lively activity than they have displayed in the past.

With heartiest thanks and kindest regards I am

Most sincerely yours John J. Moment.

ALS (WP, DLC).
[1] A.B., Princeton, 1896; studied at Princeton Theological Seminary, 1897-98; B.D., Hartford Theological Seminary, 1906.
[2] He referred to the luncheon given Wilson by the Princeton alumni in Hartford.

A News Report About the Addition to Blair Hall

[April 7, 1906]

Through the courtesy of Mr. H. C. Bunn, the Curator of Grounds and Buildings, we are enabled to present in this issue a double-page drawing of Blair Hall, showing the addition to that handsome dormitory which is to be built through the generosity of DeWitt C. Blair '56,—supplementing the Sesquicentennial gift of his father, the late John I. Blair.

The addition to Blair Hall will extend from the western end of the present building to the Halsted Observatory, about 175 feet on University Place. The architecture of the extension will, of course, be similar to that of the completed hall,—and with this addition and Patton Hall, now nearing completion, at the other end of the line, there will be almost half a mile of the imposing collegiate Gothic along the western side of the campus, the original portion of which, by the way, was Blair Hall itself. As shown in the picture, the extension on University Place is to be relieved by a tower, with an arch giving access to the campus, at the present entrance near the Observatory, and on a line with the western tower and arch of the University library. The plans provide for three entrys on the campus side of the extension, adding to the capacity of Blair Hall thirteen suites, each with a study and two bedrooms, and providing rooming accommodations for say thirty students,—for three students frequently room together in the large Blair Hall suites. With this addition and Patton Hall completed, about 150 students now compelled to find accommodations in the town will be enabled to room on the campus.

Printed in the *Princeton Alumni Weekly*, VI (April 7, 1906), 489.

An Announcement

[April 7, 1906]

UNIVERSITY BULLETIN

SUNDAY, APRIL 8. . . .

7.10 p.m. 1909 class prayer meeting in lower east room, Dodge Hall, [to be] addressed by President Wilson.

Printed in the *Daily Princetonian,* April 7, 1906.

To Arthur W. Tedcastle

My dear Mr. Tedcastle: Princeton, N. J.   10 April, 1906.

Mrs. Wilson is very much distressed that Mrs. Tedcastle should have been anxious about her, and yet there has in fact been a certain amount of justification for it. The strain of last Winter showed its effects upon Mrs. Wilson this year. She has all the year been suffering from a painful stiffness in the back and limbs, which has made constant massageing necessary and has held her off from a great many of her ordinary activities.

Still, there is no ground for real anxiety and I sincerely hope that with the warm weather she may be very much improved.

It is very kind of you to invite me to stay with you when I come up to the Boston dinner of the Princeton Alumni.[1] It seems like little more than making a convenience of you, for I cannot leave home until the day of the dinner and must return the next day. But rather than not see you at all I accept the invitation with pleasure. I will write to you before starting, by what train to expect me.

Mrs. Wilson joins me in most affectionate messages to you all.

Cordially and sincerely yours,   Woodrow Wilson

TLS (WP, DLC).

[1] On May 3, 1906. See the news report printed at May 4, 1906.

To Benjamin Wistar Morris III

My dear Mr. Morris,   Princeton, N. J.   12 April, 1906.

Will you not be kind enough to tell me the name and address of the people who are to do the wood-work, the panelling, of the large room in Seventy-nine Hall? I think you said they were Germans who did the work much more inexpensively than some of the well known contractors.

With much regard,

Sincerely Yours,   Woodrow Wilson

WWTLS (WC, NjP).

From Webster E. Browning[1]

Dear Dr. Wilson: Santiago de Chile, April 12, 1906.

Some of the recent home papers speak of you as a "Presidential Possibility" on the Democratic ticket in 1908. Our United States' Minister[2] in a recent conversation mentioned the same fact.

Although I am a long way from New Jersey and Old Nassau yet I wish to be one of the many who will assure you that such a nomination would be "muy acertado," as they say in the soft tongue of Spain. As a son of Princeton it would meet with my heartiest support; as a descendant of generations of Kentuckians I can think of no more fitting thing that the Democratic party could do. As a loyal American, though at present an exile from the home land, your election is what I would most ardently wish.

I hope to be at home about the time for the next election and will do my little best to help in taking you from the presidency of the greatest university to the presidency of the greatest nation known today.

With very kindest regards, I am,
                    Very sincerely yours,   W. E. Browning, '94

TLS (WP, DLC).
[1] Princeton 1894, Director of the American Presbyterian College in Santiago.
[2] John Hicks, Envoy Extraordinary and Minister Plenipotentiary to Chile since 1905.

A News Release of a Speech on Thomas Jefferson

[c. April 13, 1906]
(To be released Tuesday morning, 17 April.) 1906
Democratic Club Dinner:

Mr. Wilson said, in substance: Those who have never felt or sympathized with the spirit of Jefferson wonder why his memory is still celebrated, his name still appealed to by those who seek guidance or inspiration in political action. They will wonder in vain so long as they suppose that we seek to be governed by Jefferson's opinions or search among his policies for measures to suit our own times. Some of Jefferson's opinions were thought out in action and constituted a definite programme of practical policy; others were part of a philosophy of politics which had come to him from his reading and from the spirit of his time. Neither the one sort nor the other held him fast when it seemed to him that some favourite object could be served better by a departure from them than by an adherence to them.

This has given him the air, and in some quarters the reputation, of a charlatan, a man without principle, a mere politician who preferred what was expedient to what was right. A deeper view of his character displays him more justly. His opinions were meant to express two main ideals: the right of the individual to opportunity and the right of the people as a whole to a free development. His philosophical way of forming opinions belonged to a side of his nature not exercised in action. His thought was often purely academic, and showed him a proper contemporary of the French philosophers with whom he had so intimately consorted. The air of the philosophical, theorizing eighteenth century blows mildly through all that he wrote. But all this was the mere literary dress of a few simple convictions which really ruled his life and which always burned strongly within him, now in the gentle lambent flame of theory, again in the eager flame of action. Whatever turn he gave what he said, he believed always in the right of the individual to a free opportunity and in the right of the people to the unmonopolized benefits of the nation's development. If theory as he had spun it stood in the way of these, theory gave way to the best practicable means. The legislation which he urged, the policies which he adopted might not always square with his abst[r]act statements of political doctrine, but they did always square with what he conceived to be the interest of the individual and of the people.

We are too apt to think of Jefferson as a literary politician endowed with an uncanny gift of contriving popular issues, organizing parties, and directing campaigns; we do not often enough see him as what he really was, a typical American of his region and generation. He was born upon a frontier: for Albemarle county, Virginia, was as truly a frontier in the days of his youth as was the Waxhaw Settlement in North Carolina in the still primitive days of the eighteenth century when Andrew Jackson was born. He was familiar throughout his life with the simpler, plainer sides of American life, for he was constantly in contact with them, constantly immersed, even in the midst of his books, in the interests which he shared with his plainer neighbours,—as, indeed, all Virginian gentlemen were. He saw the processes of the young nation's life there in the western counties as Washington also had seen them, as processes that widened to a great and spreading growth, full of a vigour and a promise which it were folly to check or impede. Living among planters and frontiersmen who knew and controlled their own lives with an easy mastery, he believed in the capacity of the free people of the whole country to see their own interests and pursue them as his own neighbours about him did. He was an idealist and a dreamer, as popular leaders amongst us have always been, and as all Americans are who have not lost the spirit of those first days of confidence and hope. He was fond of protestations of right and broad generalizations, those utterances at once of hope and of purpose which have made the Declaration of Independence immortal and Americans the leaders of all who believe in liberty.

When it came to a profession of practical political doctrine, Jefferson declared his belief in as little government as possible, his belief, that is, that the natural processes of the people's life, which seemed to him so spontaneous and self-sufficient, should be as little rest[r]ained as possible; and he believed that such little government as there was could be better contrived and conducted under the eyes of the people themselves in the states and counties of a time which was without railways and telegraph lines, than at a national capital.

But these practical means by which he thought to realize his ideals do not now concern us. They were but means to an end. It is the end we are interested in: the realization of the rights of individuals and an impartial development of the people's life. Jefferson's objects have not fallen obsolete and out of date. They are our own objects, if we be faithful to any ideals whatever; and the question we ask ourselves is not, How would Jefferson have pursued them in his day? but How shall we pursue them in ours? It is the spirit, not the tenets of the man by which he rules us from his urn. The present maladies of our politics will not be cured by tenets; they can be cured only by a new spirit of candour, of honour, and of devotion to the general interest. It is not even news [new] laws that we need, but a new spirit in the enforcement of existing laws, an enlightened and purified intention. The wrong of our day is to be rectified, not so much by wisdom as by an effectual purpose to be pure and unselfishly serviceable. The infection of such a spirit will more surely clear our thinking and reform our affairs than the action of legislatures and the decisions of courts.

We, also, should act as those who are familiar, and lovingly familiar, with the simpler, plainer sides of American life: the sides upon which virtue shows robust and unsophisticated, ready to take the shocks of circumstance. We, too, should see the plan of the nation's life as a widening process, full of vigour and promise only if free and natural, full of danger if narrowed by the preferment of any particular set of interests. We, too, should believe in the capacity of a free people to see their own interest and follow it when told the truth and given leave to choose disinterested counsellors. We, too, should be idealists, never growing weary of earnest protestations of right and comprehensive views of human liberty.

It is in the spirit of Jefferson, for example, to prefer the interests of the many to those of the few in such matters as the tariff; to introduce into all sorts of business, private and public, the plain morals we profess among our neighbours and in all the simple, direct, and wholesome relations of our lives; to open all things that affect the general welfare to scrutiny and to the purification of the light; to apply to the railways, alike to those which thread our streets and to those which cross states and the continent itself, and to all the great undertakings which feed the industrial life of the nation, the principle that their object is service, the service, not of private interests, but of the general development.

No doubt great corporations have come to stay; no doubt a certain degree of monopoly is inseparable from their size and accumulated might; but they may, by scrutiny and regulation, be freed from the spirit of monopoly. The statesmanship we need is not the statesmanship of destruction but the statesmanship of enlightenment and of unselfish devotion.

If we were to act now in the spirit of Jefferson in dealing with the affairs of our own day, what would we do? First and foremost, we should turn away from socialism, as no remedy but only a worse danger, a danger of the very sort we seek to escape, a danger of centralized and corruptible control. Our remedy, if we seek it in the spirit of Jefferson, would be to individualize men alike in their energies and in their morals, not to lump and merge them. The whole trouble now is, not that they unite in corporate undertakings, but that they sink their consciences in the corporations of which they form a part and act as instruments rather than as men,—men with consciences and an individual responsibility to God and their fellow men. The defect of our legal system is that it allows individuals thus to lose and hide themselves,— hide themselves from the community not only but almost from their own eyes, in the business of the organizations whose affairs they conduct. Law and opinion alike should single them out, hold each to a strict accountability for his own part in the common transaction, accountable for what he did and for what he neglected, and make clear the application of old-fashioned morals to new-fashioned dealings.

It would be folly to pull down the great structures of commerce and manufacture which have been reared about us in our day and which constitute the modern economic world; but they must be dominated by a clear sense of what the individual who takes part in their administration must do and must leave undone if he would keep our respect and his own privilege.

Neither, if we acted in the spirit of Jefferson, would we permit law to take sides in the struggle between capital and labour. If it takes sides now, we must readjust the balance and hold it even. The struggle is not in itself evil; it makes in the long run for right. It is evil only in so far as one side or the other is unfair, unjust, unmanly, unscrupulous in the use of an advantage. Law must, in this as in all things, individualize the participants in the struggle and hold them severally to the responsibility of clean morals, righteousness, forbearance. We have come upon no new region of morals: the difficulty is only to recognize old principles amidst novel surroundings.

If we would act now in the spirit of Jefferson, we must be careful not to depend too much upon the federal government or turn too often from the remedy which is at hand in the power of the states. It is easier to apply morals in limited communities than in vast states, easier for neighbours to understand one another than for fellow citizens of a continent. The best searchings of morals are those which are made at home, about our own doors. We should be careful not to lose our individual sense of responsibility in the aggregate action of the nation. A revitalization of the parts is true Jeffersonian method.

With such principles we would turn again, and turn with confidence, to the common people of the country, whose eyes still perceive character and are unblinded by high finance. They do not think in corporate terms but in terms of individuals and persons. They see men singly and speak in their judgments the true and simple spirit of all just law.[1]

WWT MS (WP, DLC).
[1] There is a WWsh draft of this press release entitled "Thomas Jefferson–Toast–Dem. Club dinner, N. Y 16 Apr. '06," in WP, DLC. There are also WWhw and WWT outlines of the press release in WP, DLC.

An Address on Thomas Jefferson[1]

[[April 16, 1906]]

Mr. Chairman, ladies, and gentlemen of the Democratic Club. I often wonder why you draw modest academic persons out of their

[1] Delivered at the annual Jefferson Day Dinner of the National Democratic Club of New York in the Waldorf-Astoria Hotel on April 16, 1906. Wilson responded to the toast, "Thomas Jefferson." Other speakers, all of whom were introduced by John Fox, president of the National Democratic Club, were George B. McClellan, Mayor of New York; Judson Harmon, Attorney General

seclusion to speak to you on public occasions. I suppose it is because you feel so much immersed in affairs and know so much
about them that you occasionally want to hear someone talk who
doesn't known anything about them, for the refreshment of that
removed and impartial point of view which you are sure to get
from such persons. And yet I suppose that academic men are no
more removed from the present scene than Jefferson himself;
(applause) and therefore you give me as my toast a person as remote as I am from public affairs.

It is a singular thing to reflect upon that a body of active men
like yourselves should gather about the shrine of a ghost. It is
interesting to reflect that the man is dead and gone whom we
meet here to celebrate to-night, and that it is only by the recollection of the historian that we are reminded of his career and of his
principles; and yet it is one of the reassuring circumstances of
human affairs that men of this sort do not die, that they rule us
by their spirits from their urns; that there is something, as has
already been so eloquently said, that is immortal in their principles.

I must confess that looking back to the life of Jefferson he
seems to me a rather dim figure. He was not a man who appeared
on occasions like this, for example. He was not a man who undertook to make public addresses or often let his voice be heard
among his fellow citizens. He preferred the closet. He preferred
the written paper. He preferred that quiet utterance of the statesman which comes through the printed word. We think of him, not
as a man who mixed with the people, but rather as a man withdrawn, aristocratic, exclusive, who nevertheless gave to a nation
the law of popular action.

A great many persons look upon him as a literary man who
had an uncanny gift for making party programmes and organizing party victories, a sort of secret, Machiavelian, Italian hand
in politics; and yet if you look back to the real Thomas Jefferson
you will find him a typical American. Did you never reflect that
Albermarle County, Virginia, when he was born in it, was a frontier, and that this man whom you think of as the quintessence of
a civilized community was a frontiersman? He was born at the
front of American life. His was that wide view of American affairs which revealed itself also to Washington when he threaded
the western forests, and met the French at their outposts upon
the waters of the Ohio. He lived among the plain, the plainest

of the United States, 1895-97, who was at this time practicing law in Cincinnati
and teaching law at the University of Cincinnati; and Senator John McDermeid
Gearin of Oregon.

people of his time and drank directly at the sources of Democratic feeling. It is true that he consorted with philosophers on the other side of the water. It is true that he found himself a very suitable companion for them. But while in his abstract thinking, he was a child of his age, in his action he was a child of his country. That is the apparent contradiction in the man, that while he preached the abstract tenets of a speculative political philosophy, he nevertheless took leave to act like a wise American politician.

There seemed to be a touch of charlatanry about him, but in fact there was none. What he undertook to do was to push certain definite principles forward. When he wrote they assumed an abstract aspect. When he acted there was no abstraction about them. He did not believe that the Constitution of the U. S. warranted the purchase of the Louisiana Territory; but he advocated its purchase, saying in a letter that he was very well aware it made waste paper of the Constitution. He preferred to make waste paper of the Constitution rather than make a waste of America, devastated by wars between European powers and the power to which by plain destiny it really belonged. He had two principles and only two. He believed in the right of the individual to opportunity, and in the right of people to a free development and he knew that anything which checked either the one or the other of these checked the growth of America. He had the good sense to make theory yield to practice when theory jeoparded either one of these principles. He was a poet and a dreamer, as every man is who ever led a free people, and he never realized the practical difficulty of Democracy. The difficulty in believing in the people is that you know so many of them. (Applause.) It takes a man who can abstract the poetry from the most unpromising subject, namely, the person he knows, to construct a real, sound, water-tight theory of Democracy. I cannot make Democratic theory out of each of you, but I could make a Democratic theory out of all of you. (Appl.) And what Thomas Jefferson did was to learn the alchemy by which a great many imperfect persons are made to find impulse for the realization of visions and dreams. (Appl.) For, if you will compound with your neighbor the things which you and he believe, you will find that there is gathering in your head some little theory and vision of the destiny of the human race, if you will embark with him in a common enterprise and hope that common men, united, embody the progress of the race. (Appl.) It was thinking at once in visions and in concrete politics that made this man the great prototype of all true Democracy. Gentlemen, we do not return to Thomas

Jefferson to borrow policies. We return to Thomas Jefferson to renew ideals. (Appl.)

It were impossible to apply the policies of the time of Thomas Jefferson to the time we live in. There are no common terms in which to describe his time and ours, and unless you are going to make light of the things which now exist you cannot return to the policies of Thomas Jefferson. But you can and must return to the ideals of Thomas Jefferson[.] (Appl.) If you do return to those ideals, what will you do? for we do not take counsel with each other as fellow citizens merely to ask each other what shall we think. There is something much more important than that in hand, and that is to determine what we shall *do*. (Appl.) For this country waits upon sound action for its salvation. We shall not be saved by good thinking, but we shall be saved by honest action. (Appl.) There are maladies in the body politic. They are not incurable, if the patient should obey the instructions of the physician, and we return to Thomas Jefferson to-night to hear the instructions of the physician. Many prescriptions of health, which are prescriptions of intellectual health as well as political wisdom, remain in the spirit of Thomas Jefferson.

For one thing, we shall reject, as we would reject poison itself, the prescriptions of Socialism. (Appl.) Thos. Jefferson's creed was a creed of individualism, not of Socialism. See what it is that you would do if you accepted the nostrums of the Socialists? You would enslave the individual by making him subject to the organization. You would make the biggest, most dangerous, corruptible organization that you could possibly conceive, combining the state along such lines that each one of us would constitute not an integer, but a fraction, not a whole man, but a fraction of a great body politic. The fundamental idea of Thos. Jefferson is individualism; is a vitalization of the parts, in order to a vitalization of the whole. You cannot vitalize a whole made up of individuals without first vitalizing the parts. (Appl.) Do you say that that is an abstract doctrine? Is it abstract doctrine? What are we struggling for now? To curb the power of corporations because we do not believe in corporations? No, I think not. I don't see how our modern civilization could dispense with corporations. I don't see anything but the utmost folly in entering upon a course of destruction in respect to the present organization of our economic life. We are not afraid of the corporations except in so far as we are afraid of the men who constitute them, and we are afraid of the men who constitute them because we have not picked them out for accountability by our laws, but have submerged them in the corporation to which they belong. We have organized corporations in such a way and administered law in such a way that men hide in the corporations; not only hide from the community, but hide from their own eyes, and are not themselves aware when they are dishonest. And courts tell you that you cannot pick out Mister A., the President of the corporation and Mr. B. the Secretary of the organization, can't put him in jail. And you know you can't put the organization into jail; you know that fines won't reach the disease. Somebody has got to go to jail. (Laughter.) And the only way to get anybody into jail is to act upon Jeffersonian principles, and individualize men. Individualize men so that they will discover that if they are directors and don't direct they are going to be put in a place where they can't direct anything, not even their own selves; where men will find that the law don't deal with combinations, but with persons. It is persons who do wrong, not corporations, and when persons do wrong they should suffer the penalty of the law.

Do not answer to the Socialist, 'Yes, we will go further in the process yet, and so adjust our very politics that men will be dealt with still less as persons and become mere members of an organization.['] Will you carry this step of hiding the individual and sinking his individuality a step further so that we shall never discover the guilty person any more? The old, sane, tested processes of law are processes which have picked out the individual and said to him, 'There is nothing in which you take part for which you may not sooner or later be held responsible.' Why, gentlemen, what is it we have learned in recent investigations? That things were corrupt? No, we knew that already; but that men whom we trusted and still respect were dishonest and didn't know it. (Applause) That men whom we still respect, I repeat, so merged their own individual sense of honor in the practices of the corporations they belonged to as not to be able to distinguish personal honor from corporate interest. This republic will not be recalled to the days of heroic achievement until every man knows that his honor cannot be compounded,—that he must stand by himself, singly, alone, ready to take any shocks of circumstances and any light of exposure. (Applause.) The men whom you really honor are not men who allow their consciences to be put in harness. This, it seems to me, is one of the best teachings of Thomas Jefferson,—the individualization of men and the basing of the law upon that individualization.

But what is going to govern our consciences? Merely a fear of being found out? Are we not going to be lifted to something better than that,—"something of a faith, some reverence for the laws ourselves have made"? Are we not to have a social sense of responsibility as well as an individual sense of responsibility? While we excercise our economic energy, through corporations, are we not to subordinate corporations to the public interest? Gentlemen, there is one thing that underlies a great deal of the corporation question, as you do not need to be told. I refer to the tariff. That has too much been made upon the principle of selecting particular interests for particular privileges. Certain interests which need not be named have been allowed to stand in the way of justice,—bare, naked justice—to the inhabitants of the Philippine Islands;[2] and particular interests have been suffered both to check and to determine the economic growth of the United States. The Jeffersonian principle means this: all interests upon an equal footing and every man singled out for his personal responsibility. (Applause.)

Gentlemen, we do not, in my opinion, need more laws, but we do need laws which shall find the men. (Appl.) It seems to me to be of no little significance that we meet here to submit ourselves to the spirit of a man who is dead and gone, for what we need in affairs is not so much a programme as a new spirit. We need a rejuvenation of the principles by which we have professed to live. We need to have the scales taken away from our eyes, to see the national life as it is, and to insist that the remedies, the old and tried remedies, be once more applied in public service.

We talk about the contest between capital and labor. I do not see anything essentially evil in that contest itself. Every good thing is worked out by contest. There is a pretty story of a gentleman who was watching a chrysalis—a little creature releasing itself from the chrysalis and becoming a butterfly. One wing had loosenen [loosened] itself and the creature, apparently with torture, was trying to loosen the other wing from the retaining chrysalis. The man in pity cut the chrysalis and the creature fell, —with but a single wing. It was maimed and imperfect because he had not permitted it to struggle to its perfect life.

There is nothing evil in struggle itself. The best service you can render me if I want something from you and you want something from me, is to lay your mind squarely alongside of mine and let each one of us determine his muscle and his virtue in the contest.

Capital will not discover its responsibilities if you aid it.

2 He referred to the protectionist opponents of the Philippine Tariff bill, who had succeeded in killing it in the Senate Committee on the Philippines on March 2, 1906. This measure, providing, among other things, for a drastic reduction in the tariffs on Philippine sugar and tobacco, and for the free importation of these products after three years, had passed the House in January.

Labor will not discover its limitations and ultimate conditions if you coddle it. You must see to it that your law does not take sides,—and that is Jeffersonian principle. (Appl.) Not that the law should intervene to ease the strain, but to prevent an unmanly advantage. Law is your umpire; it must not go into the ring until one or the other opponents hits below the belt. Law does not object to blows, but it objects to fraudulent or dirty blows. It insists that the contestants be manly, sportsmanlike, righteous, courteous. Its duty is fulfilled when it has enforced the rules of the game, not when it has entered and taken part in the game. Do not conceive for yourselves a commonwealth in which the law will assist its citizens class by class, but conceive to yourselves a commonwealth in which it will preside over the life of its citizens, condescending to assist nobody, but umpiring every move of the contest. We do not have to lay down policies; we have only to remind ourselves of principles that are as old as the world. And mark my word, insofar as modern states forget these old lessons, they will get deeper and deeper into the mire of hopeless struggle and men will see a time—God forbid that it should ever come—a time of despair, when we shall look in each other's faces and say, "Are we men no longer? Are we wards? Each of us wards of all of us? Can no man take care of himself? Must I always consult you and you always consult me? Must we seek to be children or seek to be men?'['] It was a principle of Thos. Jefferson's that there must be as little government as possible,— which did not mean that there must not be any government at all, but only that men must be taught to take care of themselves. I heartily subscribe—so heartily that if I could see the way to prevent litigation I would not take it, because moral muscle depends upon your showing men that there is nobody to take care of them except God and themselves.

The handsomest pictures in the history of individuals are the pictures of those who have stood out independent of Government, —individuals who made such replies as that historic reply of two recalcitrant subjects to whom the King said, "Do you know that I can hang you?" "Aye," they replied, "and we can die cursing you." (Appl.) We should crave the spirit that will not be subdued: only under the government of unsubdueable individual spirits shall we return to the great days of Jefferson.

Gentlemen, let us not forget the events of our youth, of the youth of our nation. Let not the complexity of modern circumstances obscure for us the memory of that heroic age—let us lift our eyes above the confusion of the signs that are about us and hark back to those simple and manly principles under which we were born and under which we shall prove worthy of our heritage.[3]

(Prolonged applause.)

Printed in National Democratic Club, *Annual Dinner on Jefferson Day April the Sixteenth One Thousand Nine Hundred and Six, At the Waldorf-Astoria* (n.p., n.d.), pp. 18-27.
[3] There is a WWT outline of this address, dated April 16, 1906, in WP, DLC.

To Benjamin Wistar Morris III

My dear Mr. Morris: Princeton, N. J.   17 April, 1906.

In the matter of the wainscoting in Reunion Hall in Seventy Nine, I on the whole very much prefer the coloring of the large and darker of the two specimens of wood sent to me, and I would be very much pleased if you would have directions given to have that color and finish adopted.

Always—   Cordially yours,   Woodrow Wilson

TLS (WC, NjP).

From Palmer Eddy Pierce[1]

Dear Sir: West Point, New York   April 17, 1906.

I am taking the liberty of writing a personal letter to call your attention to a circular letter included with the Constitution and By-laws of the Intercollegiate Athletic Association formed as a result of the football conference of December 28, 1905, which were sent to you some days ago.[2]

I desire to call your attention to the following provisions of the Constitution and By-laws:

The object of the Association shall be "the regulation and supervision of college athletics throughout the United States, in order that the athletic activities in the colleges and universities of the United States may be maintained on an ethical plane in keeping with the dignity and high purpose of education."

"The colleges and universities enrolled in this Association severally agree to take control of student athletic sports, as far as may be necessary, to maintain in them a high standard of personal honor, eligibility, and fair play, and to remedy whatever abuses may exist."

"The Association at its annual convention shall choose a committee to draw up rules for the playing of the game of football during the succeeding season, and this committee shall report the same to the executive committee for promulgation."

"The football rules committee shall make a report to the annual convention on the rules of play adopted and their practical working during the preceding season."

"Each institution which is a member of this Association agrees to enact and enforce such measures as may be necessary to prevent violations of the principles of amateur sports such as:

a. Proselyting.

b. The playing of those ineligible as amateurs.

c. The playing of those who are not bona fide students in good and regular standing.

d. Improper and unsportsmanlike conduct of any sort whatsoever, either on the part of the contestants, the coaches, their assistants, or the student body.

"The acceptance of a definite statement of eligibility rules shall be not a requirement of membership in this Association. The constituted authorities of each institution shall decide on methods of preventing the violation of the principles laid down."

The quotations plainly set forth the reason for the organization of this Association and the methods by which the abuses that exist will be corrected.

The framers of the Constitutions and By-laws had in mind the necessity for wide co-ordination on the part of the colleges and universities of our country in order that athletic reform should be made effective. They also considered the necessity for control of athletics and athletic sports by the faculty of each institution. After mature consideration it was decided that the best results could be accomplished by introducing as far as possible the honor system in athletic life just as in the other conditions of student life. Hence, the very widest latitude is allowed the institutions in the methods necessary to bring about the desired results. No system of eligibility rules is required for joining the Association. What might fit the case at one institution might be entirely lacking at another; therefore, it was decided to give the greatest of independence to institutions, only asking that the desired results be accomplished.

If your university should join this Association it would not thereby lose its independence, it would simply put itself on record as being in favor of pure athletics and of desiring to control them in a rational manner. Any local agreements would not be interfered with at all by the fact that you belong to this Association.

In fact, the Association is endeavoring to encourage the formation of local association[s] in order to carry on the work of control
and reform outlined in the Constitution and By-laws above referred to.

The appointment of a football rules committee by an association composed of a great majority of the colleges and universities
of the land seem[s] necessary in order that a football rules committee may be secured, which will be representative of all the
interests and desires of such institutions throughout the land.
One of the sources of discontent during the past years with the
football rules made by the old committee[3] was the suspicion that
these rules were formed to suit conditions at great universities
without regard to the needs of the smaller. If your institution and
the six others allied with it should endeavor to control the rules
as in the past without giving the smaller institutions any representation the discontent will be greater than ever. From the remarks and conversations I heard at the conference last December,
when some seventy institutions from all parts of the land were
represented, I learned that they did not desire to do away with the
old rules committee, but that they *did insist on representation.*
This seems perfectly reasonable, and the only way it can be accomplished is by amalgamating all the institutions into one common association and electing annually a rules committee which
will control during the next year.[4] I think I am in a position to
say that your university will certainly be represented on that
committee if it should join the Association and should desire to
be so represented.

We ask then your university to join this Association and become one of its leaders. It is only by a great union such as this
that we can properly control and co-ordinate athletics in our
institutions of learning throughout the land.[5]

Yours very sincerely,   Palmer E. Pierce,
Captain, 13th Infantry, U.S.A.   President.

TLS (WP, DLC).

[1] Associate Professor of Chemistry at the United States Military Academy.
He had represented the Academy at the meeting on December 28, 1905, and was
chosen first president of the new association, a position he retained until 1913.
He was re-elected president in 1916, serving until 1929.

[2] The circular letter with its enclosures is missing.

[3] That is, the Intercollegiate Rules Committee, about which see n. 1 to the
announcement printed at Dec. 18, 1905.

[4] The two rules committees had in fact met on January 12, 1906, and agreed
to sit jointly thereafter under the name of the American Intercollegiate Football
Rules Committee.

[5] Although Wilson's letter is missing, he replied in the negative, probably
after consulting the Faculty Committee on Out-Door Sports and members of the
University Athletic Association. There was no discussion of this matter by the
University Faculty or the Board of Trustees. Princeton did not join what was
later called the National Collegiate Athletic Association until 1913.

To Winthrop More Daniels

My dear Daniels: Princeton, N. J.   18 April, 1906.

I return Taussig's and Andrews'[1] letters. My own judgment would be that Mr. Wright[2] is not far enough advanced in academic connection to be considered for a Preceptorship, and unless we are to begin someone in Economics as an Instructor with the view to possible promotion, I do not think he can be encouraged. Do you think it would be worth while in the circumstances to have him visit us?

Always—   Cordially yours,   Woodrow Wilson

TLS (Wilson-Daniels Corr., CtY).
[1] Frank William Taussig, Henry Lee Professor of Economics at Harvard, and Abram Piatt Andrew, Princeton 1893, Assistant Professor of Economics at the same institution.
[2] Probably Chester Whitney Wright, who was at this time a graduate student in economics at Harvard, where he received the Ph.D. in 1906.

From George Brinton McClellan

My dear Mr. President: New York.   Apl. 18, 1906.

I want to congratulate you on your speech, which I heard from the gallery.

It was the clearest and most forceful and eloquent oration that it has been my good fortune to hear in many a day.

Sincerely yours,   Geo B McClellan

TLS (WP, DLC).

From St. Clair McKelway

My dear President: Brooklyn, N. Y., April 18, 1906

I did not answer your welcome and enlightening letter of March 11 as I thought that time and events would best do that. They have. I have left the final form of other matter about you to Mr. Tirrell and our Managing Editor,[1] and that as news matter will take care of itself by journalistic gravitation. I let the dinner take the same course as none could tell in advance what wreck of matter and crash of booms might there be accomplished. It was converted, I see, into a McClellan-Hearst collision,[2] leaving your address as the sane national contribution to what should not have been allowed to become a local or factional sensation.

In yesterday's comment, which I enclose,[3] I took the addresses as a topic and yours, like Abou Ben Adhem's name, led all the rest in my estimate. Frankly, this was due neither to friendship nor to strategy, but to sincerity and to my estimate of Jefferson which I do not prescribe to you, but which I have long held myself. My treatment of the matter does not represent you and cannot embarrass you. It satisfies my sense of justice and I am convinced that all my readers of all parties will severally agree with bits of it.   Sincerely yours,   St Clair McKelway

TLS (WP, DLC).
[1] Arthur Millidge Howe.
[2] In his address to the National Democratic Club, Mayor McClellan made a not very subtle attack upon the publisher, William Randolph Hearst, then a prominent candidate for the New York Democratic gubernatorial nomination in 1906.
[3] The enclosure is missing, but it was an editorial, "The Jefferson Celebration," from the *Brooklyn Daily Eagle*, April 17, 1906. After comparing all the speeches at the dinner, McKelway wrote, "Woodrow Wilson, we think, was more successful in his method of construing Jefferson than any other man who took part in the dinner. . . . He advised an application of the principles of Jefferson to the conditions of the twentieth century, which even Jefferson never anticipated, but to which many things that Jefferson, now and then, advanced could be readily adjusted. On this account, we commend Woodrow Wilson's speech—and Woodrow Wilson—to the consideration of all thoughtful Democrats and of all thoughtful Republicans."

To George Brinton McClellan

My dear Mr. Mayor: Princeton, N. J.   19 April, 1906.

Thank you most cordially for your note of yesterday. It is a great pleasure to me to know that you thought my speech at the Democratic Club dinner a good one. I appreciate the opportunity given me and I can assure you that I went with you in everything that you yourself said and that it was admirably said besides.

Always—
          Cordially and sincerely yours,   Woodrow Wilson

TLS (G. B. McClellan [Jr.] Papers, DLC).

From Nicholas Murray Butler

My dear Mr. Wilson: New York   April 25, 1906

Columbia University has recently received a sum of money to establish a professorship of politics, the intent of the donor being that the income of the fund shall be used to pay the salary of a professor who will give instruction in the practical matters of government. The chair is intended to supplement and not to duplicate the work of the professors of history, law and administration in our Faculty of Political Science.[1]

It has been decided that for the year 1906-7 no appointment to the chair shall be made, but that instead two courses of lectures shall be arranged for, to be given by scholars of eminence, before the University, on topics lying in the general field of practical politics. It is hoped that before the beginning of the year 1907-8 a satisfactory incumbent for the permanent chair of politics may be found.

It is with the greatest possible pleasure that I tender you an invitation to deliver the first course of lectures upon this foundation. I hope very much that your often demonstrated interest in the subject will lead you to accept.

The suggestion that I venture to make is that the general topic of the lectures be the working of the American constitution, and that in some such fashion as was done in your "Congressional Government" years ago, you should treat in successive lectures the President, the Senate, the House of Representatives, the judiciary, the civil service, the military service, the relations between the national and state governments, and the process of constitutional amendment. The more practical and concrete the treatment, the better would the intentions of the gentleman who established the foundation be carried out.

The lectures should, I suggest, be eight or even ten in number if you prefer, and should be delivered one lecture a week in successive weeks, at the time most convenient to you during the months of November, December, January and February.

It is part of the plan that the lecturer shall, as soon as practicable after the conclusion of the lectures, furnish his manuscript for publication, at the expense of the foundation, by the Columbia University Press. The terms of the publication would be such as to secure to the author a satisfactory percentage of the net proceeds from the sale of the volume.

The honorarium that we are able to offer for the lectures themselves is $2,000.

With warm regards, I am,

Sincerely yours,   Nicholas Murray Butler

TLS (WP, DLC).

¹ George Blumenthal, a New York banker, had given the university $100,000 to establish a chair of politics. The Columbia trustees on February 5, 1906, designated the fund so established as the George Blumenthal Fund. The first incumbent of the new chair, which incidentally bore no name, was Charles Austin Beard, who was appointed Adjunct Professor of Politics in 1907.

A News Report

[April 26, 1906]

PRESS CLUB BANQUET.

Third Annual Dinner Held at the
Princeton Inn Last Evening.

The third annual Press Club banquet held at the Inn last evening was one of the most successful and interesting ever given.

During the evening the following officers of the club for the next year were elected: President, Bird LeG. Rees 1907; Vice-President, Courtland N. Smith 1908; Secretary and Treasurer, Thomas B. Reed 1908. . . .

President Woodrow Wilson '79, the last speaker, responded to the toast, "The College Man in Journalism." He said that he had been very much pleased to note that since the organization of the Press Club there has been no violation of class room courtesy in publishing things said in the lectures. A University man should always be careful to keep from distorting the facts. This is a habit into which many newspapers have fallen. No man who is really looking toward the ultimate wellfare [welfare] of the country will stand as the champion of any particular class in the community. The ferocious criticism of the United States Senate for instance, accusing it of treason and other similar crimes,[1] is manifestly unfair. It is against such distortion of the facts that University men should guard.

What is needed for the education of a man for Journalism is a broad and liberal education. A journalist must be educated to see at a glance all the phases of a subject.

Printed in the *Daily Princetonian,* April 26, 1906.
[1] He was referring to the first article, and perhaps also the second, in the sensational series by David Graham Phillips, Princeton 1887, "The Treason of the Senate," indicting the leaders of the Senate for being the tools of power, privilege, and special interests. Phillips' series ran in *Cosmopolitan* from March to November 1906.

To Nicholas Murray Butler

My dear Mr. Butler: Princeton, N. J.   26 April, 1906

You must have known how ardently a man who has been drawn off into administrative work longs for his old absorptions and activities as a student and professor. Your letter of April 25th interests me very deeply.

It is very clear to me that I would not have time to write a set of lectures. Would it be compatible with your plans for the course you suggest, that I should speak from notes and that the lectures should be taken down by a competent and experienced stenographer and that his notes should be afterwards revised by me for publication? I not only have not the time to write out a set of lectures, but they hamper me greatly in delivery when written.

Would the lectures be public or would they be delivered only to a University class?

You will see by these questions that I am tempted to do what you desire and your answers to them will greatly assist me in forming a judgment. I very much appreciate the invitation which you have conveyed to me and can assure you that it would be a delightful excursion into my old fields of study.

With much regard,

Sincerely yours,   Woodrow Wilson

TCL (RSB Coll., DLC).

To Winthrop More Daniels

My dear Daniels: Princeton, N. J.   26 April, 1906.

My judgment is that we had better drop consideration of Mr. Wright.

With your approval I will write to Mr. Mussey[1] at once and ask him if he would accept an appointment.

I have written to Edgar, offering him a Preceptorship,[2] and I have also offered one to Mr. Spencer's[3] brother.[4] Everything that I learned about him was so exceptionally favorable that, as you know, I was strongly inclined in his favor, and I found that he had to accept or decline a very attractive offer at Ohio State University to-day.[5]

My judgment would be that Mr. Marsh,[6] of the University of Mich., Mr. Corwin's friend, and, if we can get him, Mr. Mussey, should be the other appointees.[7]

Cordially and sincerely yours,   Woodrow Wilson

TLS (Wilson-Daniels Corr., CtY).
[1] Henry Raymond Mussey, Associate Professor of Economics and Politics at Bryn Mawr College. If Mussey was offered an appointment, he did not accept it.
[2] That is, Edgar Dawson, who accepted.
[3] Charles Worthen Spencer.
[4] Henry Russell Spencer.
[5] He accepted Wilson's offer.
[6] Frank Burr Marsh, Instructor in History at the University of Michigan.
[7] Marsh did not accept an appointment if it was offered.

Two Letters from Harold Griffith Murray

Dear Dr. Wilson: New York   April 26, 1906.

An accounting of my books shows that the income from the Committee of Fifty Fund from August 1, 1905 to August 1, 1906 is $94,055. This income is exclusive of any derived from the Jesup Fund. I am very anxious, indeed, to be able to report at the June meeting that the income of the fund for the year is $110,000., the sum necessary to take care of the preceptorial System.

I have been wondering since I saw you yesterday whether it would be possible for you to ask Mr. Ream to contribute his

$5,000. between now and the 1st of August. I do not know whether you would care to ask Mr. Ream to do this or not; if it would embarrass you in any way please disregard my suggestion.

Yours very truly,   H G Murray   Secretary.

Dear Dr. Wilson: New York   April 26, 1906.

Following is a list of men in Pittsburg who are kindly disposed toward Princeton, and who will, with a little cultivation I think, contribute to the university:

Nathaniel Ewing,	'69	
George C. Wilson,	'72	
John K. Bryden,	'76	(This is the man I told you about yesterday who said that next year he would give liberally to Princeton and would include her in his will).
Robert W. Patterson,	'76	
J. O. H. Denny,	'77	
George A. Howe,	'78	
Mortimer C. Miller,	'79	
J. G. Jennings,	'84	
George A. Kelly,	'87	

The list of men who are not Princeton graduates, but who are residents of Pittsburg, that are favorably disposed towards Princeton you already have.

Yours very sincerely,   H. G. Murray

TLS (WP, DLC).

Notes for a Religious Talk[1]

26 Apr. 1906.

"For to be carnally minded is death; but *to be spiritually minded* is life and peace."—Romans, viii., 6.

Specific meaning, "the minding of the Spirit," *the Holy Spirit*
   But it may be given a broader signification, which will but heighten the emphasis of its specific meaning.
      To be *mindful of the things,* in whatever sphere, *which can only be spiritually perceived in life.*
         Among these: The face of Nature: "Behold, I show you a mystery." We feel "a presence that disturbs" us

"with the joy
Of elevated thoughts; a sense sublime
Of something far more deeply interfused,
Whose dwelling is the light of setting suns,
And the round ocean and the living air,
And the blue sky, and in the mind of
man."[2]

Our relations with our fellows. Here our
standards are always in the last analysis
spiritual.

Relations of intellectual truth.

Here, we all perceive, is *the realm in which man attains
his* best dignity and most distinctive title to *overlord-
ship.*

Here is the realm of earthly immortality, whether in *literature* (the record of the spirit) or in *science* (the record
of insight).

The "spiritually minded" of the text is *the crown* of the whole
process and principle: perception of the permanent and interior relationships of character and motive, of *the invisible
things which are eternal.*

Then only come life and peace. "Peace" the text has all to itself.

WWT MS (WP, DLC).
  [1] Wilson originally dated these notes "Sunday, 7 January, 1894." He used
them for the talk in Marquand Chapel referred to in the announcement printed
at Jan. 5, 1894, Vol. 8, and for a talk to the Philadelphian Society on May 14,
1903, a news report of which is printed at May 15, 1903, Vol. 14.
  [2] From Wordsworth's "Lines Composed a Few Miles Above Tintern Abbey."

A News Report of a Religious Talk

[April 27, 1906]

PRESIDENT WILSON'S ADDRESS

Before Philadelphian Society in Murray Hall
Last Evening.

President Wilson delivered the regular mid-week address before the Philadelphian Society in Murray Hall last evening. He
took for his text Romans 8:6, "For to be carnally minded is death
but to be spiritually minded is life and peace."

He said in part: None of us feel that our bodies are ourselves.
We feel as did the man who said, "This is *mine* not *me*." No man
confesses [confuses] his body with his personality. In every age
and in every race there has been the idea that within the body,
and distinct from it, there is a spirit which is immortal. The real
life of each of us is in our spirits, and only so far as we develop

and strengthen them have we benefited ourselves. What distinguishes us one from another is our spiritual nature.

There are men who find enjoyment and pleasure among the crowds of a great city and there are others whose delight is to be outdoors, in communion with the outward forms of nature.

The pity of a man who is a slave to vice is that he has cut himself off from all that gives him kinship to the living and the eternal. There are kinds of life which cannot be satisfying; they may be truly vital but if they are not infused with the spiritual they cannot bring peace.

Peace, not idleness, is essential to true living. There is a kind of intellectual peace, it is true, but it cannot take the place of spiritual peace. The life of a university is not well-rounded and truly good unless it is infused with this essential spiritual peace.

Printed in the *Daily Princetonian*, April 27, 1906.

To Harry Augustus Garfield

My dear Mr. Garfield: Princeton, N. J.   28 April, 1906.

In view of Daniels' expected absence next year[1] I am writing to ask if you will not be kind enough to accept appointment as head of the department of History, Politics and Economics. I am sure that everyone will recognize the appointment as in every way fortunate.

Always—
          Cordially and sincerely yours,   Woodrow Wilson

TLS (H. A. Garfield Papers, DLC).
[1] He was on leave during the academic year 1906-1907.

From Ernest Cushing Richardson

My dear President Wilson: Princeton, N. J.   April 28, 1906.

I enclose carbon of letters to and from Mr. Arthur Scribner[1] which tell the tale of a $1,000 contribution of which you should be advised on general principles and to explain that this is one of the cases covered by your general permission—merely the reaping of ripe opportunity, not special solicitation. The library of a friend of Mr. Scribner was offered him by the Anderson Auction Co. for about $1100 and he was minded to give it. I examined the library and judged that $500 would buy all the books which did not duplicate material in our library or that of Dr. Bingham and Dr. Bingham has already agreed to purchase all the material in relation to Spanish South America if we would concentrate whatever attention we could on the remaining Latin American field. I than [then] saw Mr. Scribner and he considerately raised the question whether a $1,000, to be expended at our discretion, would possibly serve us better than the gift of the library. This was good business for both of us and I could only jump at this perfect opportunity to round up a complex and somewhat difficult proposition in an ideal manner.

You perhaps remember that Dr. Bingham has given us about 400 volumes. These are on Spanish and Latin American history outside of Spanish South America and he will undoubtedly some-time give us his very remarkable collection on Spanish South America if nothing breaks. In any event by supplementing his collection we have the whole Latin American problem decently attended to for practical purposes for the present. You will per-haps like to mention this matter to Mr. Scribner and, for that matter, to Dr. Bingham for his gift was quite valuable. I judge that his 400 volumes have a fair market value of $1200 to $1500.

Very faithfully yours,   E. C. Richardson
Librarian.

TLS (WWP, UA, NjP).
[1] Arthur Hawley Scribner, Princeton 1881, Vice President and Treasurer of Charles Scribner's Sons. The enclosures, not printed, are E. C. Richardson to A. H. Scribner, April 25, 1906, TCL (WWP, UA, NjP), and A. H. Scribner to E. C. Richardson, April 27, 1906, TCL (WWP, UA, NjP).

From Henry Russell Spencer

My dear President Wilson,   Columbus [Ohio], April 30, 1906.

Permit me to acknowledge the receipt through my brother of your proposition that I come to Princeton to a preceptorship in History, Politics and Economics, at a salary of eighteen hundred dollars, the appointment to run during two years. I desire to sig-nify my acceptance of the same.

Sincerely yours,   Henry Russell Spencer.

ALS (WP, DLC).

A News Report of an Address in Newark, New Jersey

[May 1, 1906]

PRESENT NEEDS OF EDUCATION

School Teachers Hear Talk by President
Wilson, of Princeton, on the Subject.

President Woodrow Wilson, of Princeton University, made an address to about 1,000 pedagogues in the First Presbyterian

Church yesterday afternoon, at a joint meeting of the Essex County Teachers' Guild and the Newark Principals' Association. Preceding the address, about 100 pupils from Elliot Street School sang a number of choruses under the leadership of Principal Charles G. Shaeffer. Corliss F. Randolph, president of the association, introduced Dr. Wilson, who spoke on the topic "A Liberal Training."

Dr. Wilson said the purpose of education was discipline, enlightenment and orientation. The elements that go to make up a liberal education, he stated, were pure science, philosophy, literature, history and politics. There was a ripple of laughter when "pure politics" was mentioned.

"This is an age of utilitarianism—an age when we want to know the reason for the existence of things, and of what use they are," said the Princeton president. "We are getting to realize that a liberal education is not something that is for the majority. In a country like this it is absolutely necessary that skill of the hand should prevail over skill of the head. Of the majority of our boys and youths we must make skilful mechanics, mechanics of the hand or mechanics of the brain: masters of some particular skill or technical education. To the minority we must give the equipment of those who are more than mechanics and are free for the larger uses of society.

"Technical education should dominate. It is only for the minority that liberal education is provided. The latter can justify itself only by working with the technical education. There ought not to be two sharply separated attitudes toward life. The minority are out of the line of the liberal education, not because they are not welcome, but because duty calls them elsewhere. Taxation can be justified just so long as the State provides a suitable education; otherwise the State should not take the money for the public schools.

"The most unwise thing ever done is to allow boys and girls to choose their own studies. I have seen this work in college. They choose those branches in which they are already strong. The discipline in school has gone from the pupil to the teacher. Almost all the hard work nowadays is done by the teacher, and all the psychologists warn us not to give any hard work to the pupils.

"The very word discipline carries with it the idea of doing what is hard. I am disciplined by having to sit still and listen to some things which I don't believe. I believe in compulsory education. I believe in making the child do what he does not want to do for the discipline of it. People admit that a gymnasium is a very beneficial thing, yet I never saw anything done in business which is practised in a gymnasium. Men don't exercise because they need that kind of action in business, but because they need red blood in their veins."

Printed in the *Newark Evening News*, May 1, 1906; one editorial heading omitted.

To Edward Graham Elliott

My dear Mr. Elliott: Princeton, N. J.   2 May, 1906.

It seems best, in order that a single set of men may not be too constantly burdened with committee work, that the very important committee on Entrance should be re-constituted, and I am taking the liberty of asking if you will not be kind enough to serve on that committee under the chairmanship of Professor S. R. Winans. You will confer a very great favor upon me and do the Faculty a real service by accepting this appointment.
                    Sincerely yours,   Woodrow Wilson

TLS (WC, NjP).

From Moses Taylor Pyne

My dear Woodrow: New York   May 2, 1906.

I saw Mr. Carton of Chicago[1] yesterday and struck him for something for the Committee of Fifty. He rather turned me aside, though, on the theory that he did not feel that the Dean had treated his younger son[2] very well, who was dropped last Spring and has just returned this February to College. He said he thought his son was entitled to a hearing. However, I do not think he had any hard feeling in the matter, but it was just enough to throw me off.

I think that if in about two weeks you will write him a letter, asking him to do something, it will have more effect than from me or from the Committee of Fifty. I do not think he would do very much but he ought to be able to give something. It would probably be in the nature of a single amount or a yearly payment.

He is, I believe, the Treasurer of the Swift people in Chicago, the great packers, and had one son, who graduated last year and another son who graduates next February.[3] I cannot remember his first name, but the Treasurer can undoubtedly give it to you.
                    Very sincerely yours,   M Taylor Pyne

TLS (WP, DLC). Enc.: H. G. Murray to C. H. Dodge, April 27, 1906, TLS
(WP, DLC), and F. A. Steuert to H. G. Murray, April 23, 1906, TLS (WP, DLC).
    [1] Laurence Arthur Carton, Treasurer of Swift & Co. of Chicago.
    [2] Laurence Roberts Carton of the Class of 1907 who was not graduated until
1908.
    [3] Alfred Thomas Carton '05 and Laurence.

From Harold Griffith Murray

Dear Dr Wilson   New York   May 2/06

    Unless I hear from you to the contrary I will call on you Tues-
day to discuss The Press Bureau[,] The Quarterly[,][1] B. F. Jones
'91[,] The Dormitory extension[2] and the Cleveland meeting of
western alumni.[3]
    Matters above enumerated are near a settlement and if I can
have fifteen or twenty minutes with you I will appreciate it
                    Yours very sincerely   H. G. Murray   Secy

ALS (WP, DLC).
    [1] About the news bureau and the alumni review, see H. G. Murray to WW,
May 10, 1906, and H. G. Murray to C. H. Dodge, June 5 and Oct. 17, 1906.
    [2] That is, the extension of Patton Hall.
    [3] A news report of this meeting of the Western Association of Princeton Clubs
is printed at May 26, 1906.

From Nicholas Murray Butler

My dear Mr. Wilson: New York   May 3, 1906

    I have been off in Canada for a week and only to-day have your
kind letter of the 26th.
    The suggestion which you make is an admirable one and I am
sure that it will add greatly to your convenience in connection
with the proposed lectures. We shall be most happy to provide
for a competent stenographer to report the lectures verbatim,
this report to serve as the basis for your revision for the Press.
    The lectures would be delivered, in our technical phrase, "be-
fore the University." This means that while they would be largely
attended by students and officers of instruction, the public generally would also be admitted and might be expected to attend in
considerable numbers. I hope very much indeed that you may be
able to accept our invitation, which is as earnest and as urgent
as I dare attempt to make it.
    With warm regards, I am,
                    Sincerely yours,   Nicholas Murray Butler

TLS (WP, DLC).

A News Report of a Talk to Princeton Alumni in Boston

[May 4, 1906]

TECHNICAL EDUCATION

AMERICAN YOUTH NOT GETTING ENOUGH OF IT.

Pres. Wilson of Princeton Says Too Much
Dependence Is Placed on Natural Ability—Annual
Dinner of N. E. Alumni.

The Princeton Alumni Assn. of New England held its annual dinner at the University Club last evening, the guest of honor being Pres. Wilson, of the college, who spoke on the operation of the newly balanced curriculum and preceptorial system which has been introduced at Princeton since his election to the presidency in 1902, and the working out of which educators all over the country are watching with interest. Other speakers included Prof. A. L. Lowell, of Harvard, Prof. W. R. Martin '72, of Trinity college; Rev. Clay McCauley '63, who recently returned from educational work in Japan; Rev. Edward H. Rudd '83, of Dedham, the newly elected president.

The retiring president, Francis L. Coolidge, '84, presided. . . .

Pres. Wilson in opening said the majority of the young men of this country must take a technical education. They are not taking it enough now.

"In Germany," he said, "there are more technical men, and it gives that country a great advantage in the industrial world. We depend altogether too much upon the natural gifts of our American young men. While he undoubtedly has some superior gifts, he must also get the superior knowledge in order that we may successfully compete with other countries."

Speaking of the new preceptorial system, he said that it is not wise to allow a youth to take whatever subjects he chooses, because he will take those subjects in which he is already developed, and ignore those in which he has no intellectual development.

"The preceptorial system is not a system," he said. "I have spent most of the year preventing the faculty from making rules. The most important thing about it is that it should have no written constitution. What we are trying to do is once and for all to get rid of the idea that a university course consists in attending a certain number of lectures and reading collateral books. The purpose is for the student to get and to take, not to receive. He is not under a master, not being taught. He is learning and he is reading. The Oxford idea of reading during the vacation period and discussing that reading with the professors during the term has great results."

In closing the speaker said the only uncertainty of the so-called system is the financial means to carry it out.

Printed in the *Boston Daily Advertiser*, May 4, 1906.

From Winthrop More Daniels, with Enclosure

My dear Wilson: Princeton, N. J., May 4, 1906.

This afternoon's mail brought the accompanying letter from Whittlesey,[1] accepting the proposition you asked me to make him. A copy of my tender I attach hereto.[2] This gives us three of our four men for next year. Will you kindly write to Whittlesey, officially confirming my overture to him. He evidently wants some such communication from you, as his letter will indicate.

Yours ever sincerely W. M. Daniels

[1] Walter Lincoln Whittlesey, Assistant in Politics at Cornell University.
[2] W. M. Daniels to W. L. Whittlesey, May 1, 1906, HwCL (WWP, UA, NjP).

ENCLOSURE

Walter Lincoln Whittlesey to Winthrop More Daniels

Dear Professor Daniels: Ithaca, N. Y. May 3, 1906.

Your kind letter of the first is just received. I am glad to accept the proposition as made and do so accept it, cheerfully and unreservedly. I understand the situation as regards permanency and am obliged to you for putting the matter so explicitly. Please let me know if this is final for the arrangements for next year will be made here before the end of the month. The chances are I will be in New York City about June first, for a couple of weeks, and will be able to come over to Princeton any time if you desire.

Thanking you for your kindness,

Very sincerely yours, W. L. Whittlesey

ALS (WWP, UA, NjP).

To Winthrop More Daniels

My dear Daniels: Princeton, N. J. 5 May, 1906.

I am taking pleasure in writing to Whittlesey to confirm your offer, and am very glad indeed to learn that he is willing to come.

I am meaning to write at once to Myers.

Always— Faithfully yours, Woodrow Wilson

TLS (Wilson-Daniels Corr., CtY).

To James Mathers[1]

My dear Mr. Mathers: Princeton, N. J.   5 May, 1906.

Allow me to acknowledge the receipt of your kind note of the third.[2] I am a little at a loss to name a subject. Would it not be best to book me simply for "Princeton University"? That would afford me an opportunity to say anything about our work here that seemed most desirable to say on that occasion.

Professor West and I are looking forward to the visit with keenest anticipation and pleasure.

Cordially yours,   Woodrow Wilson

TLS (TxU).
  [1] Princeton 1890, prominent lawyer of Cleveland, and Secretary and Treasurer of the Western Association of Princeton Clubs, who was making arrangements for that association's meeting in Cleveland on May 19.
  [2] It is missing.

Two Letters to William Starr Myers

My dear Mr. Myers: Princeton, N. J.   5 May, 1906.

I am writing to ask if you would be willing to have me nominate you to the Board of Trustees as Preceptor in History, Politics and Economics for the Academic year 1906-1907 at the salary of $1500.

I make this proposition in the confident hope that the relationship will prove mutually satisfactory and that a longer appointment would ensue, and I trust that you will think the position worth your acceptance.

Very sincerely yours,   Woodrow Wilson

My dear Mr. Myers: Princeton, N. J.   7 May 1906.

In reply to your letter of May 6th[1] I would say that our Board of Trustees meets on the 11th of June and that all elections to positions in the Faculty take place on that day.

In the meantime I would be very happy to have you visit Princeton again and consult with the members of the department as to the work you will have next year. It is almost impossible to predict my own orbit, but there will always be someone here who can give you all particulars, and I am sure you will be cordially greeted whenever you care to come.

If you will write before-hand to Professor W. M. Daniels, he will either make an appointment with you himself, or suggest whom you should look up.

Cordially and sincerely yours,   Woodrow Wilson

TLS (W. S. Myers Papers, NjP).
    1 It is missing.

From Harper and Brothers

Dear Mr. Wilson: New York City   May 7, 1906.

In order to meet the competition of the Elson History[1] which
has been issued in five volumes and is selling at what amounts to
about $5.00 net, (published rate $12.00 per set) we propose issuing your great work in a $12.00 form (four dollars for the
periodical[2] and eight for the history).

This should not interfere with the trade sales at the usual price
and we shall continue to sell by subscription the leather bound
sets at the usual price.

We are desirous of pushing this cheaper set to very large sales,
and to do this we must go to very great expense in the way of
advertising and agents' commissions. It is customary when a set
of books is put upon the market at a lower price, for the author to
accept a reduced royalty, with the result that in the end his royal-
ties are larger as to the gross amount yearly. It is impossible to
meet the expenses of selling unless there is such reduction. This
custom is practically universal.

We suggest that we pay a royalty of fifty cents a set on the
$12.00 edition only—with the guarantee that the returns to you
from this source during the year, shall be double the amount
paid to you from all subscription sales during the past year.

This arrangement has to do with this $12.00 set only of "THE
AMERICAN PEOPLE"—all the other editions remaining unchanged
in price and royalty.

Trusting that this may meet with your approval, we are,
                    Yours very truly,   Harper & Brothers.

TLS (WP, DLC).
    1 Henry William Elson, *History of the United States of America,* 2nd edn.
(5 vols., New York and London, 1905).
    2 *Harper's Magazine, Harper's Weekly, Harper's Bazar,* or the *North American
Review,* whichever the subscriber selected.

From Raleigh Colston Gildersleeve

Dear President Wilson: N. Y.   May 9th, 1906.

I have forwarded to the two contractors which you mentioned
in your letter the drawings and specifications for the carving in
the Council Chamber, and also sent them to another firm. The
figures received are as follows,—Catok & Beller $5040.00; Amer-

ican Wood Carving Co. $7000.00, $500. less for plain frieze. After having telephoned repeatedly to Samuel Lakow, as he had failed to give me an estimate as he had promised to do on different dates, I had a communication to-day from him and he promised to give me an estimate on the work some time next week if I wanted it, but he thought it would be about $7000.00. I do not know Catok & Beller, but I imagine their estimate is too low to secure the kind of work we would want, and I am inclined to think The Hiss Co's estimate was high in order to make up some of their loss on the original contract. It looks to me that the correct figure for this work would be about $7000.00

Awaiting your further instructions, believe me,

Faithfully yours,   Raleigh C Gildersleeve

TLS (WP, DLC).

To Hiram Bingham

My dear Mr. Bingham: Princeton, N. J.   10 May, 1906.

I am sincerely sorry that I have not been able to see you since you have been out of the Infirmary. Professor Daniels explained to me fully your feeling, and the plans you wish to make, and of course I hope that you will feel free to make them. I sincerely regret that your health necessitates a leave of absence and hope that the year will fully restore you.[1]

I must frankly say that I have serious doubts as to whether it would be wise to bring Mr. Roberts[2] here. With the additional Preceptors just appointed, it is possible that we may be able to manage without any further appointments, but of course I will consider Mr. Roberts's claim very carefully.

Hoping soon to see you,

Cordially and sincerely yours,   Woodrow Wilson

TLS (WC, NjP).

[1] He planned to retrace the line of march of Simon Bolivar and his army in 1819 across Venezuela and Colombia. His experiences were recorded in *The Journal of an Expedition Across Venezuela and Colombia 1906-1907* . . . (New Haven and London, 1909).

[2] Perhaps Guy Hall Roberts, a fellow graduate student of Bingham's in history and government at Harvard from 1900 to 1904. He received the Ph.D. in the latter year. In the autumn of 1906, he went to the University of California as "Acting Assistant Professor of Political Science."

To Thomas Raynesford Lounsbury[1]

My dear Professor Lounsbury: Princeton, N. J. 10 May, 1906.

I think I do know the field of choice in history pretty thoroughly, and because I do, I must say that I am at a loss to sug-

_ ch n g

gest anyone for your chair in the Sheffield School. Many men are coming on in this field, but there are not many available whose reputation is established both in the field of scholarship and in the field of teaching. If anyone should occur to me later, I will of course take pleasure in sending you an intimation.

Cordially and sincerely yours,   Woodrow Wilson

TLS (T. R. Lounsbury Papers, CtY).
[1] Professor of English Language and Literature and Librarian of the Sheffield Scientific School at Yale University.

From Harold Griffith Murray

Dear Doctor Wilson: New York   10 May 1906

Tuesday I called to see you but found you were out of town. The Press Bureau has been arranged for,[1] as well as the three-times-a-year issue of the "Alumni Weekly," which will be a review of the preceding three months, and will be sent to every one whose name appears in the Alumni catalogue; this will take the place of the publication I discussed with you when I last saw you. The Second Class Postal Laws do not permit of our issuing a quarterly periodical and having it entered as "Second Class Matter" unless over 50% of the people to whom it is sent are paid subscribers. Does it not seem best to you that the matter should be collected and put in shape by Mr. McAlpin, the Secretary? He is in a better position, under your guidance, to issue the Review, it would seem to me; he knows what it is wise to say in regard to the Trustee Meetings, and if you are willing to lend us your name as Editor and allow him to get the stuff into shape, it would be, I think, an excellent plan. Will you let me know your opinion on the matter? Is there anything new in regard to Mr. Ream?

Mr. Pyne, I presume, has talked to you about the extension of the new dormitory; it looks to me now as though another ten classes would build a section.

If you are going to the Cleveland Meeting of the Western Alumni Association would it be too much to ask you to say something about the Committee of Fifty, if it becomes convenient for you to do so? I believe it would help us.

Yours very truly,   H G Murray   Secretary

TLS (WP, DLC).
[1] See H. G. Murray to C. H. Dodge, Oct. 17, 1906.

From Harper and Brothers

Dear Mr. Wilson: New York City   May 11, 1906.

We beg to thank you for your letter of yesterday.

If our plans for the subscription sale of your history meet with your co-operation and approval, it is our intention to make a house-to-house canvass through all the most popular parts of the United States in the belief that in this way we shall be able to sell many thousand sets. We have one of the largest and most permanent organizations of this kind (subscription) in existence (perhaps the largest) with branch houses equipped with office staffs and corps of agents in nineteen cities outside of New York. In addition to these we have general agents in other places. An office like Chicago, for instance, has its agents working in nine states, so the entire country is well covered.

We have asked the opinion of the managers of our branch houses as to the outlook for the sale of this proposed edition of your history and their reports are uniformly favorable. Our own belief is that the results will be more than satisfactory to you—but, we cannot definitely promise more than our letter indicated at this stage. It has been a matter of general comment that our performances usually exceed our promises.

In the hope that we may hear from you favorably,[1] we are,

Yours very truly,   Harper & Brothers.

TLS (WP, DLC).
[1] They did. See Harper and Brothers to WW, May 24, 1906.

From Ernest Cushing Richardson, with Enclosure

My dear President Wilson: Princeton, N. J., May 12, 1906.

Enclosed is memorandum regarding proposal to have Mr. Morgan[1] take ordinary executive duties for one semester each year, releasing me for more general tasks. In answering your inquiry as to what was meant by "Ordinary executive duties" and "More general tasks," I venture, under the second head, to be rather detailed and long in order to put you fully in touch with what I am proposing to do.

(1) By ordinary executive duties is meant the entire administration of the Library as organized but without initiation of radical changes, the constructive work to be done [during] the librarian's semester and questions of policy in general to be settled when both librarian and associate are on the ground. The ordi-

[1] Junius Spencer Morgan, Associate Librarian of Princeton University.

nary duties are, as regards things internal: official signatures of orders, acknowledgment of gifts, etc., presiding at the weekly staff meeting and in general keeping the members of the force adjusted to one another and to their work. The external relations concern students as regards conduct, fines, and any other matters of appeal, faculty in sundry matters of purchase and privilege, occasional references to or from the president or the library committee, and in general the relations, personal or by correspondence with givers or alumni, and finally representative duties towards visitors from other institutions or in gatherings outside of Princeton. The ordinary duties involve a large number of authoritative small decisions but do not necessarily involve the interminable decisions on detail[ed] technical matters of cataloguing, classification, etc. which cut so seriously into the librarian's time by their constant interruption. The librarian himself allows this in order to keep fully in touch with the detail but the heads of departments are supposed to be trained to the point of responsible decision in such matters and it will be an advantage for their training to have them exercise this responsibility for one semester under competent business administration. If Mr. Morgan does not have to go deeply into these details it need not cost him more time than he can give.

(2) The "more general tasks" to which the librarian proposes to devote his time include: strictly technical tasks, the study of manuscripts and literary production.

Direct technical tasks include such things as the following: — (a) The study and making lists of best books. At present I am definitely at work on the three matters of: best reference books for the Chancellor Green Library, the most important periodicals, and the most important historical sources. I make a point of looking over collections everywhere and examining carefully the books which I am not already familiar with and, as I find it, no amount of bibliographical tools can take the place of this personal work. (b) The study of prices and sources of purchase. This too is best done by frequent visits to the dealers and such visits are of some advantage for ordinary routine purchasing as things are needed although they have not the importance with us at present that they would have if we had larger funds for general purchasing. (c) The actual purchase of books. This is perhaps the least of justifications of travel at the present moment, as the amount that can be spent for books during a bibliographical journey is insignificant. I am greatly in hope, however, that the preparation of careful lists and the evidence of such command of market value as to insure maximum results from money invested, will lead friends of the institution to supply means to make this a real factor. (d) The study of technical methods in the library business is much like keeping up with the newest machinery in manufacturing and it is by visiting libraries that one keeps fresh in this matter. (e) Another class of work outside the routine tasks includes such matters as the perfecting, indexing and printing of our classification and the very important and extensive work of revising subject headings. There will always be something to be done of this class and, although the actual work will be better done chiefly during the semester of residence, the planning for and laying out the detailed principles is much better done in part in comparison with other libraries and in part in some place where uninterrupted attention can be given. Summer vacation, of course, gives some opportunity for self-recollection but this is work which fairly belongs to the work of the year.

Tasks which may be called semi-public are work on the American Library Association Advisory Committee on rules for cataloguing, which is thrashing out an agreement with the British Library Association in this important matter on which depend many fundamental questions of economy in cataloguing. I have also retained the chairmanship of the American Library Association Committee on international co-operation because I am rather more in touch with foreign libraries than other members and can do most general good in this way especially under this proposed plan of campaign.

Work with the manuscripts includes such general gathering of data as will be most profitable for the graduate course that I have been offering in paleography. The offering of such course is probably not of first importance but if offered one must work on the manuscripts. My own knowledge of the subject is not as good, I fear, in some aspects as that of some of these new men but it is more or less comprehensive and has been gained by persistent contact with quite a wide variety of manuscripts. I have a certain start or advantage which, so far as I can judge, few of the increasing number of Americans who are going into the matter have and, as a specialty of some twenty years standing, it seems worth keeping up for the University as well as for myself and if kept up must, of course, be made first rate.

The *literary tasks* which I have in mind are pretty closely connected with the technical ones and concern the bringing to completion of various books in library science or bibliography for which I have been gathering material. I have been working and planning for twenty years past on a somewhat ambitious scheme for what might be called a bibliographical history of ancient and

mediaeval literature, beginning with the Greek and Latin literature from the Christian era to the invention of printing. This involves a very comprehensive list of manuscripts such as has been
three or four times attempted but very much needs being done
again better, as the very foundation of all good work on the history of the Middle Ages. It would involve on my part the visiting
of a great many small libraries—probably the first step as supplementing the printed catalogues of the large collections. I have
already by this means fished out quite a series of works known by
allusion but lost for literary use and I can fairly expect to recover
hundreds of such books as well as identify thousands of mss,
whose real nature is unknown to their possessors. How nearly I
shall be able to reach my ideal in this will be partly a question of
how my funds hold out, but some substantial contribution to
scholarly apparatus, it seems fairly sure, can be made. My first
product—an account of the 13th century literature, I hope surely
to attain, and probably first fruits of this in a biography of Jacobus de Varagine in a very short time.[2] With the ability to make
a somewhat frequent round of various libraries this matter would
be taken up systematically and give point to both the visiting of
libraries and the study of the manuscript for general purposes.

This work of research and publication is, of course, University
work only in the sense that the literary production of a teacher
is but it is here in large measure a by-product of more direct work
and in a broad aspect it is a University task.

There is a certain amount of productive work on which I am
engaged which lies in the field of theology and cannot be counted
a very direct contribution to the efficiency of this library but this
work I count as my diversion and do not intend to put more time
on it in the aggregate than may fairly be applied to keeping ones
mind fresh by complete change of theme.

Very faithfully yours,   E. C. Richardson
Librarian.

[2] Richardson eventually published *Materials for a Life of Jacopo da Varagine*
(New York, 1935).

Ernest Cushing Richardson to the President
and the Chairman of the Library Committee of the
Board of Trustees of Princeton University

Gentlemen: Princeton, N. J., May 12, 1906.

Your approval is respectfully asked of a proposed distribution
of labor between the Librarian and Associate Librarian by which
the latter shall take the ordinary executive duties for one semester
each year leaving the Librarian free for more general tasks which
call for travel or more uninterrupted study.

The general ground of this proposal is the belief that it will
give a greater total of effectiveness for the Library and make a
contribution to general university efficiency as well through the
librarian's work with manuscripts and his publications. In principle it does not differ from the policy approved by the library
committee some years ago by which the librarian was authorized
to extend his vacation when traveling abroad and occupied
wholly or partly with library business. The point is not unlike
that which sometimes leads to concentrating a professor's lecturing in one half of a week and his preparation in the other
half and the plan might be, as it was formerly, justified under
ordinary circumstances. Under the particular circumstances of
the co-partnership which exist between Mr. Morgan and myself
the carrying out of this principle is unusually feasible. The
amount of time and effort involved is not beyond what Mr. Morgan can and will undertake, and it is intended that as at present
the librarian shall be responsible for the consistent working out
and application of technical methods during the year.

Under this arrangement the intention will be to apply the released time to the study of best books, prices, sources, etc., the
study and working out of technical methods, the study of manuscripts, and the preparation of matter for publication. Some of
the proposed publications do not bear directly on library work
but it is not intended to devote more time to these recreative
specialties than would be justified under present circumstances.

Some detail as to "Ordinary executive duties" and also as to
the librarian's "more general tasks" is given in separate memorandum in response to the President's inquiry.

While under this arrangement the librarian does not intend
to render anything less than a full years service to the University
he is not unmindful of the agreeable and, in some degree, unusual
aspects of his work as here defined. It is perhaps not improper to

suggest in this connection: (1) that the librarian's salary reflects the agreeableness of the position, relatively, both to the standards of other libraries and to the compensations of the heads of departments in this library; and (2) that under it certain expenses of travel cordially assumed by the Committee under previous understanding are spared for the library; (3) Certain positive advantages are secured to the University which could not be had in the case of one less free to travel at his own expense or traveling less.[1]

Respectfully submitted,   E. C. Richardson
Librarian.

TLS (WWP, UA, NjP).
[1] The trustees approved the proposed arrangement on June 11, 1906.

To Nicholas Murray Butler

My dear President Butler: Princeton, N. J.   14 May, 1906

With not a few misgivings as to the feasibility of doing well what you desire, because of the multitude and the exacting nature of my administrative duties, but yielding to my very ardent desire to return to my old fields of discourse, I accept the kind invitation you have extended to me to deliver a course of lectures during the first half of the next academic year on the Government of the United States.

I would suggest the following as the topics of the lectures:

I. Constitutional Government
II. The Place of the Government of the United States
    in Constitutional Development
III. The President of the United States
IV. The House of Representatives
V. The Senate
VI. The Judiciary
VII. The States and the Federal Government
VIII. The Civil Service

Thanking you for your kind readiness to make the arrangements with regard to the lectures which I suggested,

With much regard,

Sincerely yours,   Woodrow Wilson

TCL (RSB Coll., DLC).

To Jerome Davis Greene[1]

My dear Sir: Princeton, N. J.   14 May, 1906.

I take pleasure in accepting the kind invitation of the Governing Boards of Harvard University[2] to attend the Commencement Exercises in Sandars [Sanders] Theatre on Wednesday, June 27th, next.[3]   Very truly yours,   Woodrow Wilson

TLS (MH-Ar).
[1] Secretary to the Corporation of Harvard University.
[2] It is missing.
[3] As WW to J. D. Greene, May 30, 1906, discloses, Wilson had been asked to deliver the annual Phi Beta Kappa Oration at Harvard. The same letter explains why Wilson was unable to do so.

From Nicholas Murray Butler

My dear President Wilson: [New York]   May 15, 1906

I thank you most heartily for your letter of the 14th, and am truly delighted that your other duties will permit you to give the course of lectures in the next academic year on the working of the American Constitution. Just as soon as you can conveniently suggest appropriate dates for the lectures, we shall be glad to have them, in order that in due time accurate public announcement may be made.

The title which I suggested for the course, namely, "The Working of the American Constitution," may not approve itself to you. If so, will you be so good as to suggest some better title?

All necessary arrangements for the stenographic recording of your lectures, in order that they may be speedily revised for publication, will be made without further trouble to you.

With best regards, I am,
                    Faithfully yours,   Nicholas Murray Butler

TCL (RSB Coll., DLC).

A News Report of an Address in Cleveland

[May 19, 1906]

HEAD OF PRINCETON DEFINES EDUCATION

A reception was given last night at the University Club in honor of Dr. Woodrow Wilson, president of Princeton University, who is in the city to attend the seventh annual convention of the Western Association of Princeton Clubs.[1]

Following a dinner given in his honor, Dr. Wilson spoke to the members upon a general subject touching the needs of the universities in the United States.

In the course of his remarks he laid down the following definition: "Education—a university education—is the process of causing the sap of manhood to rise in a freshman until it reaches his head and he becomes a senior. I haven't consulted any of my biological friends, but I believe the process will be found to be a biological one—that this sap rises through cellular tissues."

This caused considerable merriment until Dr. Wilson explained that he was perfectly serious in making the assertion. He said that a university education is not intended to give universal knowledge. On the contrary, it gives but little knowledge. It is intended to create in a man a condition of receptiveness to knowledge—to teach him the process of arriving at the truth.

"There is another thing," Dr. Wilson continued. "What we need most here is discrimination in what is taught. I deplore the degree of imitation of each other that has grown up in our schools. We are all trying to teach all there is to know, instead of showing merely the process by which knowledge may be struggled for. No one man ever summed up all the knowledge in the world."

Another idol of the public was shattered when Dr. Wilson said that the college "fellow" was the most conservative of men instead of the most recklessly radical. He touched the subject in a general way and cited no instances of what the public might think was radicalism on the part of the college man.

"I contend that the college man is the most conservative in the community, because he never wishes to see things change. That is because he has the ideals and tenets of his father, but lacks his experience. He is so filled with the ardor of following these ideals that he comes to be termed radical instead of conservative, as he really is.

"This, by the way, is the glorious legacy which came with the Declaration of Independence. The nation's most popular men to-day are those who are known to believe in things for the truth there is in them rather than for personal reasons. The surest way to reach a public downfall is to let it be known that your public beliefs are influenced by your private interests."

The annual convention of the club will begin this morning at the Hollenden Hotel.[2]

Printed in the *Cleveland Leader*, May 19, 1906; some editorial headings omitted.
[1] Wilson had spoken earlier in the day—May 18—at the University School, East High School, and Central High School in Cleveland.

[2] The full text of Wilson's address to the Western Association of Princeton Clubs is printed at May 26.

From Henry Burchard Fine

Am Bord des Postdampfers
My dear Tommy,   den 19. Mai 1906

A line as I am drawing out into the bay to thank you again for so generously arranging things that I am to have the great joy of soon being with my dear ones again. But it seems selfish to be so happy as I am today when I reflect upon how much work I am sailing away from this summer afternoon.

Jack Hibben gave me full instructions regarding the Norman Smith affair[1] and I shall expect a cablegram of the sort arranged between us on my arrival at Dover.

I saw Mr. [Stephen S.] Palmer this morning regarding the Physical Laboratory. He put me off with advice about seeing Mr. Frick—but when I said that if we failed in other directions we should expect him to do the thing for us a couple of years hence at any rate, he didn't seem much shocked. He only said that he had been thinking that perhaps his son Edgar would in time be interesting himself in doing that kind of thing for Princeton. I am by no means convinced of the impossibility of getting our laboratory through Mr. Palmer after a little while—if he becomes convinced that we cannot get it from some outsider.[2]

I do hope that you are going to have the best sort of summer possible—and that my running away will not cause you any serious inconvenience.

With kind regards to Mrs. Wilson, I am as ever
Affectionately Yours   H. B. Fine

ALS (WP, DLC).

[1] That is, arrangements to offer the Stuart Professorship of Psychology, made vacant by the recent resignation of Frank Thilly, to Norman Kemp Smith, Assistant Professor of Philosophy at the University of Glasgow. For a biographical sketch of Smith, who accepted Princeton's invitation, see Wilson's Annual Report to the Board of Trustees printed at Dec. 13, 1906. Thilly had resigned to accept a professorship of philosophy at Cornell. His letter of resignation is missing, but see F. Thilly to WW, June 19, 1906.

[2] In fact, Stephen S. Palmer did give the Physical Laboratory, which was named for him. It was completed in 1908.

From Lucius Hopkins Miller

My dear President Wilson,   Princeton, May 19, 1906.

I desire to submit the following report concerning the Senior Course in Biblical Literature:

I. *Facts.*

   1st Term.

      35 regular students

      6 optional   "   (who took practically all the term's work)

      ―――

      41 Total.

   2 Grads.   5 B.S. and 34 Academic.

These 41 men were handled in a 4 preceptorial divisions of 10 men+ each. 3 Failures occurred―all three conditions being removed at the conditional examination.

Of these 41 men, not more than 8 intend to enter the ministry. (This is partly from actual knowledge & partly guess-work as I did not ascertain the facts)

Of these 41 men, 16 did not re-elect the course. Of these 16, however, 5 graduated in February, leaving a net total of 11 men who, for one reason or another, did not continue. Of the 3 men who failed, two re-elected.

   2nd Term.

      43 regular students

      2 optional   "   (one continuing throughout & the other 1½ months)

      ―――

      45 Total

These 45 men were handled in 8 Preceptorial Divisions of 6 men each. There will probably be not fewer than two and not more than 5 failures. Of these 45 men, not more than 5 intend to enter the ministry, 3 of the 1st term's candidates having dropped out of the course.

20 men[,] new men[,] elected the course, making a total for the year of 61 different men, out of a possible 240-250, who came under the influence of the course.

3 of the 1st Term optional students became regular in the 2nd Term.

The complexion of the class this term was Grads. 2, Specials 1, Scientific 2, Academic 40.

II. *The Ground Covered.*

It was the original intention (cf. Catalogue) to take up Old Testament Literature 1st Term and New Testament Literature 2nd Term, but it was found unwise to attempt to cover so much ground & therefore the whole year has been spent upon the Old Testament.

Having spent several weeks, at the outset, on propaedeutic material, in order to discuss some of the general questions concerning the Bible & Religion & in order to get the teacher & students en rapport, we took up the literature in chronological order and traced the Religious Development from the very beginnings of the Hebrew Religion in Moses down to the Exile & its climax in the Great Prophets of the Pre-Exilic Period.

In a word, the men have been given a chance to understand thoroughly the Religion of the Hebrews, or, more properly speaking, Prophetism which is the essential thing, for time did not allow any treatment of the Exilic & Post Exilic Periods which are, of course, less important than the Pre-Exilic Period, belonging as they do to the more or less decadent Priestly Development.

In addition to this, the nature of Essential Christianity has been thoroughly discussed in order to bring out its superiority and the essential connection between it & its Hebrew ancestor.

III. *Methods*

Lectures have been given twice a week and the third hour given over to the Preceptorial Divisions in which the material of the Lectures, as well as that of some of the required books, was reviewed.

The Required Reading of the 1st Term comprised (1) Ottley "Short History Hebrews,"[1] (2) Dods "Bible—Its Nature & Origin"[2] (3) Art. in Hastings Bible Dict. "Hexateuch"[3] (4) Books of Genesis & Judges. *The Required Work of the 2nd Term* included (1) an essay of not less than 2000 words, upon assigned books or parts of books of the Old Testament, or subjects pertaining thereto. (For this essay 6-12 books or articles apiece had to be consulted) (2) Cornill "Prophets of Israel"[4] (3) Knox, Brown, McGiffert "The Christian Point of View"[5] (4) Amos, Hosea, Isaiah (authentic parts of chaps. 1-39) Micah, Deuteronomy & Jeremiah to be read.

IV. *Efficiency.*

I cannot say much for the efficiency of the work of the 1st term. Besides those things, incident to all beginnings, that tend to lower efficiency, the size of the preceptorial divisions and the failure to conduct them so as to induce the proper amount of

[1] Robert Lawrence Ottley, *A Short History of the Hebrews to the Roman Period* (New York, 1901).
[2] Marcus Dods, *The Bible: Its Origin and Nature* (New York, 1905).
[3] "Hexateuch," in James Hastings (ed.), *A Dictionary of the Bible . . .* (5 vols., New York, 1898-1904), II, 363-76.
[4] Carl Heinrich Cornill, *The Prophets of Israel*, trans. by Sutton F. Corkran (Chicago, 1895).
[5] George William Knox, Arthur Cushman McGiffert, and Francis Brown, *The Christian Point of View: Three Addresses* (New York, 1902).

definite weekly work and so as to be able to tell just how much was being done, militated against securing good results. The 2nd Term has been far more efficient. Definite work & rigid requirement in the smaller-sized divisions have necessitated far more consistent work and have enabled me to know just where each man has stood and to get at him more directly.

The Essays are quite above the average & represent a considerable amount of 1st Hand Reading. The Subjects cover practically the whole Old Testament and most of the men have been obliged to make a study of periods quite beyond the scope of the year's work in the class. Each man was met alone in the Stacks & given ½ hour explanation as to literature & method of preparation for the Essay. Coming at the beginning of the Term, this enabled me to meet each man in a peculiarly personal way and the effect upon the attitude of many men toward the whole course was apparent at once. In working up the essays each man was obliged to read & study primarily the text of the Book upon which he wrote.

The Results have been gratifying. Most, if not all, have thus seen that pieces of literature in the Bible, of whose existence, oftentimes, they were not even aware, were interesting and eternally valuable.

We may safely leave it to them to make the fair inference from that which they discovered to that which is to be discovered in all the others.

V. *Purpose of the Course*

The Purpose of this course, broadly speaking, is, I take it, twofold—

1st, to bring out the essentially Religious & Ethical nature of the Literature in such a way that all who take the Course may ever after have a deeper & more intense, because more intelligently held, faith in the eternal & supreme value of the whole Bible.

2nd So to awaken in men the feeling of the need among us for a better realization of what the Bible has to give, as to lead them to enter the Ministry.

VI. *Concluding Remarks*

I think that the first of the two purposes above indicated has been measurably accomplished. As to the second, I do not think anyone has been led, through the influence of this year's course, to take up religious work as his life-work—at least, so far as I know, and so far as one can tell at this time, when many are still uncertain as to their ultimate desire in this matter.

For the most successful carrying out of both of the above purposes, I am convinced that, if curriculum arrangements at all permit, this course ought to extend over both Junior and Senior Years.

I should like to see Princeton become, more than it is today, a place whence may come many of the most gifted & useful men in the Ministry of our land.

Among many other reasons, certainly this is one great reason why more of our best men now are not entering the Ministry—they are either ignorant of, or have a doubt concerning, the message of the Bible. If they do not have this ignorance or doubt dispelled before Senior Year, the chances are greatly against their making, in one year, the adjustments necessary to permit them to decide for the Ministry.

Furthermore, the experience of the year has shown conclusively that it is impossible to cover, in a proper way in one year, the whole Bible.

It is necessary to a proper orientation to spend the whole year upon only one of the Two Testaments. If but one year is possible for this course then two more or less defective alternatives are open—1st, to offer a Course in the New Testament each year—2nd To offer an alternating two-year Course covering the Old Testament one year and the New Testament the other.

From my point of view there is only one sane solution and that is to authorize a Course for Junior Year as well as Senior Year, so that I may take those who wish it over the whole ground, and, by beginning earlier, influence more good men in the direction of the Ministry.

Under this arrangement the Old Testament Course would fall in Junior Year & the New Testament Course in Senior Year. Besides tracing thus the development both logically and chronologically, by treating the Old Testament first I shall be able better to accustom the men to the modern point of view, which I apply in a thoroughgoing way, before the most vital parts of the Bible are taken up, thus leading the men more gradually, and therefore more safely, up to those intellectual explanations of the Old Faith that are necessitated by the changes in our modern Life & thought.

Even if this suggestion is looked upon with favour—and I leave the question of practicability with those who know more about it than I—it is not my desire to have the change made next year. The course in the New Testament, to be given next year, will be new and will give me all that I can effectively handle, but I trust the suggestion may be considered as seriously as it has been made, and that it may be adopted for the year 1907-1908.[6]

Yours very truly,   Lucius Hopkins Miller

ALS (WP, DLC).
[6] The course was offered, as before, only to seniors during 1907-1908. However, beginning the following year, the second of Miller's "defective alternatives" was adopted, the Old Testament being offered to seniors one year and the New Testament the next.

From Benjamin Wistar Morris III

My dear Dr. Wilson: New York   May 21, 1906.

I enclose herewith a rough sketch as requested by you showing the proposed arrangement of connecting the next group of dormitories with Patton Hall by a stone wall and gate. This, as you will notice, retains the scheme originally suggested and which you told me you do not desire to depart from. As I am being pressed by Mr. Murray for a perspective of the new groupe [group] for money raising purposes, may I ask you to let me know as soon as possible if a development of this arrangement will meet your approval. The design is not submitted as a finished study but merely to illustrate the scheme, which is of course lacking in study of detail. It however illustrates the composition of this particular portion in general mass.

Trusting that this answers the spirit of your request, I am,

Yours very sincerely,   Benjamin W Morris

P.S.—I am still inclined to the opinion that at the south end of the buildings on the east side of Brokaw Field that the effect will be better if the Avenue of Elms were allowed to remain unobstructed and that the building have its own termination but designed of course in relationship to the remaining dormitories on the south side of the Field extending east and west and terminating in the quadrangle. The arrangement, of course, must be made so that continuity and co-relation of the parts will be preserved. I do not, however, consider it absolutely essential and feel that another solution is possible though I do not think it would look as well.

Will you be good enough to give me your opinion on this point also?   B W M

TLS (WP, DLC). Enc.: rough pencil sketch of Patton Hall.

To Catherine Gansevoort Lansing[1]

My dear Madam: Princeton, N. J.   23 May, 1906.

Allow me to acknowledge with the utmost appreciation your very generous kindness in sending to the University your check for $2500 for the endowment of a scholarship in memory of your brother Henry S. Gansevoort of the class of 1855.

I am sure that I express the feeling of all my colleagues on the Board of Trustees in assuring you of our warm appreciation and of the real service that this gift will do. It is peculiarly gratifying to have friends who think of us in this way.

Cordially and sincerely yours,   Woodrow Wilson

TLS (NN).
[1] Widow of Abraham Lansing, prominent lawyer of Albany, N. Y.

From Lawrence Crane Woods[1]

Pittsburg, Penna.   May the Twenty-third,
My dear Dr. Wilson: Nineteen Hundred and Six.

Of all the times that I have had the pleasure of listening to you, I cannot recall a single one of the many splendid addresses you have made which interested me and seemed so timely, forceful and helpful as that one given in Cleveland Saturday night. I have been attempting in a very feeble way to repeat a number of your ideas to my brother,[2] Rev. Dr. Campbell[3] and a number of the Princeton fellows.

I fear that you have no notes of your remarks. If you had, I should appreciate them very much. In fact, I doubt whether anything could help Princeton more throughout the great West than the distribution among thoughtful men of just such a paper. I have always loved Princeton, but never did I feel more intelligent faith and pride in her than I do today.

Very truly yours,   Lawrence C. Woods

TLS (WP, DLC).
[1] Princeton 1891, Assistant Manager of the Equitable Life Assurance Society agency for western Pennsylvania.
[2] Edward Augustus Woods, manager of the agency of the Equitable Life Assurance Society in Pittsburgh.
[3] The Rev. Dr. William Oliver Campbell, pastor of the Sewickley, Pa., Presbyterian Church.

From Harper and Brothers

Dear President Wilson: New York   May 24, 1906.

We thank you for your letter of yesterday accepting our proposition of the 7th inst.

As you point out, the outlay for advertising, circulars, and other expenses in working out our proposed scheme will be very great, and if the venture should prove unsuccessful the loss would be entirely borne by us. If, however, our expectations are realized, we look for a large sale, and a sale outside of the usual channels of the book business.

We hope that in carrying out our plan, we may dispose of a sufficient number of copies to satisfy your most sanguine anticipation.   Very truly yours,   Harper & Brothers

TLS (WP, DLC).

To Robert Bridges

My dear Bobby: Princeton, N. J.   24 May, 1906.

Thank you for your letter of yesterday. I will take pleasure in keeping an eye on the furniture sent for our Hall. The work on the wainscoting is going forward very steadily; not as fast as I had expected, but no doubt as fast as it can be well done.

I am in a dreadful rush of work, but shall hope to have part of an evening for the smoker.[1]

Always—   Affectionately yours,   Woodrow Wilson

TLS (WC, NjP).
[1] The '79 smoker at commencement.

A News Report

[May 26 and June 2, 1906]

THE ANNUAL CONVENTION OF THE WESTERN ASSOCIATION
OF PRINCETON CLUBS

By James Mathers '90

The seventh annual convention of the Western Association of Princeton Clubs was held at Cleveland, Ohio, May 19th. A large number of delegates responded to the invitation of the Princeton Club of Cleveland, and by nine o'clock in the morning the lobby of the Hollenden Hotel was filled with enthusiastic Princeton men. They came from all over the West and brought the Princeton spirit with them. As soon as classmates had settled identities, the association met in business session, with John H. Thacher '95 of Kansas City, Mo., President of the association, presiding. The invitation of the Princeton Club of Chicago was accepted for the 1907 meeting of the association. . . .

In the evening the seventh annual banquet was held at the Hollenden Hotel, tendered to the delegates by the Princeton Club of Cleveland. The toastmaster was H. S. Johnson '78, President of the Cleveland Club, and the following toasts were responded to: "Princeton University," President Woodrow Wilson '79; "Maintaining the Standards," Professor Andrew F. West '74; "The Princeton of Former Days," John H. Voorhees '41 of Cincinnati; "Princeton in the South," William L. Granberry '85 of Nashville; "Princeton, Pittsburgh and the West," George R. Wallace '91, Pittsburgh. Unannounced subjects were responded to by John D. Davis '72 of St. Louis, David B. Jones '76 of Chicago, and Judge Harry White '54 of Indiana, Pa.

◊

. . . Responding to the toast "Princeton University," President Wilson said:

Mr. Toastmaster and gentlemen: I am always at a loss to determine whether I would rather come at the beginning of a list of speakers, or at the end. At the beginning I have no speech to make but my own; at the end I may have gathered a number of suggestions from the speakers who have already spoken. You are at my mercy if I come first, because I can do nothing but deliver you my well-known speech.

I always feel, upon an occasion like this, that I am a responsible minister reporting to his constituents. And I think that Professor West will bear me out in saying that the report of the present year, now about concluded, is in every way satisfactory. I do not know that it is particularly satisfactory to the eighty men who were dropped at the mid-year examinations; but I think that all of them are coming back next year, and will probably regard themselves as able to report progress at that time. I do know that the new spirit of study which has come upon Princeton would surprise some of you. (Laughter and applause.) About this table I recognize the faces of some who were ingenious in resisting the processes of learning—and if they have applied as much ingenuity to their business as they did then to their pleasure, I congratulate them upon their success. One of the undergraduates the other day said, in a tone of great condemnation, that Princeton was not the place it used to be—that men were actually talking about their studies at the clubs. He evidently regretted that as an invasion of the privileges of undergraduate life. But the beauty of the situation is that the studies of the University are becoming, I will not be so bold as to say they have already become, a part of the life of the University, and for my part I don't care a peppercorn for studies which do not constitute a part of the life of the men who are pursuing them. (Applause.) I believe that there has been in all our universities in years past too much of the spirit of schoolboys; not because the men there were not often really interested in their studies, but because the processes of the university kept them schoolboys in their attitude toward their studies; now at Princeton they are beginning to feel that they are coming into the privileges of manhood.

You have heard a great deal, I dare say, first and last, about the Preceptorial System, and most of it has been from the old point of view, namely, that it brought the teacher into personal and intimate contact with the pupil. But the point I would dwell upon is that the relationship is not so exclusively that of pupil and teacher as it used to be; that the new thing we are introducing is the independent pursuit of certain studies by men old enough to study for themselves and accorded the privilege in their studies of having the counsel of scholars older than themselves. It is not merely that they are being led, but that they are becoming what every university student ought to be, namely, reading men.

I have sometimes said to the men I knew best in the University that it did not make so very much difference with me what a man read, but it did not seem to me that any man had the title to call himself a university man who was not a reading man, who merely gathered the transitory impressions of the day in which he lived and did not put himself into the main currents of thought that flow out of the old centuries into the new, that constitute the pulse and life of the race. Men are in universities in order to come into contact with the vital forces that have always beat through the centuries in making civilization and in making thought (applause), and if they do not voluntarily put themselves into contact with those forces, those forces are of no avail to them. For what a man reluctantly receives he does not retain, and it does not constitute any part of his life.

The thing which has pleased me most in regard to the Preceptorial System is not only the splendid fact that the alumni have given us the money to conduct the system, but the significant fact that the undergraduates have welcomed the change and have felt that it enriched their own life. It would be a very petty life to live if we were merely schoolmasters; it would not interest me for twenty-four hours to be a taskmaster in respect to the studies of a lot of youngsters. Unless I can lead them to see the beauty of the things that have seemed beautiful to me, I have mistaken my profession. (Applause.) It is not the whip that makes men, but the lure of things that are worthy to be loved. (Applause.) And so we feel that we are entitled to be full of hope in regard to the increasing intellectual life of Princeton. For, gentlemen, I am covetous for Princeton of all the glory that there is (applause), and the chief glory of a university is always intellectual glory. The chief glory of a university is the leadership of the nation in the things that attach to the highest ambitions that nations can set themselves, those ideals which lift nations into the atmosphere of things that are permanent and do not fade from generation to generation. (Applause.) I do not see how any man can fail to perceive that scholarship, that education, in a country like ours, is a branch of statesmanship. It is a branch of that general work of enabling a great country to use its energies to the best advantage and to lift itself from generation to generation through the stages of unbroken progress.

When I look about upon the generation in which we live, I, like every man who looks with thoughtful eyes upon it, am very much sobered by what I see; not disconcerted, not robbed of hope, not cooled even in my optimism, but nevertheless very much sobered by the seriousness of the task which confronts us. Every age is compounded of things old and new, and the men of middle age are more involved in the things that are old than are the men in the generation that is coming on. And I always think of the change that must constantly be expected in a complex age as residing more with the younger generation than with the generation that is actually in charge of affairs. I see these young men drawing on all the complicated skeins that make up the pattern of our modern life, modifying that pattern, renewing the stuff where it is old, changing, confirming, doing all those things that draw on the forces of one age to be the forces of another. Because only they, when they are competent, can see the pattern as a whole. I believe that in spite of all the things which we deplore, and which bring the blood to our faces, there is a great deal that is splendid about the civilization of our day. The things that have been done in this country by way of its material advancement could not have been done without great gifts, without great powers, individual and corporate. There is a sense in which the individual in the modern industrial world is necessarily greater, if he be noticeable at all, than the individual of any other generation. For no man can do anything in this generation by and of himself. He must rule his fellow men and draw them into coöperation with himself, if he would accomplish anything. There is a touch of statesmanship about every piece of modern business, about every piece of modern engineering. It is as if all the powers of the world were organized and the captains of industry were making their way forward in the ranks to be generals in command of the forces of mankind. There is a great deal of planning and energy by which men have won their material supremacy—as well as the other side of the picture, which for the present I do not care to draw.

Now, young men coming with new forces into this complicated plot, have freer hands than other men in the generation, cleaner hands and freer hands than anybody else. And when one asks one's self what sort of education these men should have in order to carry what will be the young man's burden for many a day to come, it seems to me evident that the education they receive should not be such as to catch them at once in the web of the complicated interests which they must touch without prejudice and without favor. To put it in plainer, less abstract terms, if you merely train men for business, directly for business, they are immersed in the business, so far as their thoughts are concerned, throughout their education, and are committed to the prejudices of their occupations before even they enter upon them. (Applause.) You cannot train men for a particular business without filling their heads with the atmosphere of that business; and we want a great body of young men going into the active affairs of this world untouched by the atmosphere of any particular interest. We must in our processes of education, somewhere, put ourselves in a position to give young men a view of life which shall not be touched by the interests which will engross them when they seek to make their living. (Applause.)

For, gentlemen, there are many complications of human motive. When we speak of a man's making his living, we forget that he is also making somebody else's living in nine cases out of ten. Many a man would draw out of the business he is in, when he saw it was touching him with corruption, if it did not mean privation to a woman he loves, to children he loves; if it did not mean he was bringing upon others a kind of suffering and a sort of anxiety which he might be willing to bring upon himself singly, but is not willing to bring upon them. If men acted singly and each for himself, the aspect of affairs would be very different; and many a man is debased by some of the noblest impulses of his nature, his love for those who are not concerned in the things which have involved him. Many a man would be morally independent if he were in fact independent, but he is carrying the fortunes of others.

Look, therefore, how impossible it is for him to assess any problem in a disinterested fashion, if from the first he has been taught, in college as well as elsewhere, that the chief end of man is to make a living! If the chief end of man is to make a living, why, make a living any way you can. But if it ever has been shown to him in some quiet place where he has been withdrawn from the interests of the world, that the chief end of man is to keep his soul untouched from corrupt influences, and to see to it that his fellow men hear the truth from his lips, he will never get that out of his consciousness again. There will always come up within him with a great resurgence, some way or other, those lessons of his youth, and there will come a voice from the conscience which will arrest the very progress of a generation. But if you never teach him any ideal except the ideal of making a living, there will be no voice within him, he will know no other ideal.

I believe, therefore, that there must be some universities in this country which undertake to teach men the life that is in them, by teaching them the disinterested truths of pure science, by teaching them the truths of pure philosophy, and that literature which is the permanent voice and song of the human spirit, letting them know that they are not going a lonesome journey, but that generations of men behind them are crying them on to do better things than they could otherwise even attempt, and that generations beyond them are beckoning them on to a day of happier things. (Applause.) There must sound in the halls of the true university this eternal voice of the human race that can never be drowned as long as men remember what the race has hoped and purposed.

And so, gentlemen, the ideals that we talk about, the ideals that we try to translate into definite programmes of study, are not things which we can take or leave as we please, unless you believe that we can take or leave life itself as we please. There is no choice in the matter. I am not daunted by the prediction that we are going to be submerged in waves of materialism, because any man who has read ever so superficially the history of the race knows that there are certain things that cannot be absolutely submerged or crushed. If there remain any little band of men keeping the true university spirit alive, that band will, after a while, seem to be all that there is of a great nation, so far as the historian is concerned.

It affords me very great satisfaction sometimes to see how certain public men are misjudged, and to know that quiet gentlemen, sitting in university chairs, will, when the noise of that

generation is over, readjust the balance and tell future generations who were really the great men of that generation. (Applause.) We are the jury that sits last, and future generations
will know from us alone who were the great men that were our
contemporaries. The noisy talk of the day will pass with the day
itself, and then that eternal voice of literature will continue to
sound, that voice which is purged of passion, which at any rate
seeks to speak the thing which is just and true and of good repute.

And so, our ambitions for a university which retains this spirit
are not hopes so much as definite confidence that certain things
must come to pass. The best thing, to my thought, about what we
call the Princeton spirit is the manliness and the unselfishness
and the truthfulness that there is in it. Why should any of you
love Princeton? Because it is a beautiful place? Because the
trees are beautiful to look upon in the spring? Because the sward
is green and the buildings are handsome? Are you in love with a
physical image? Are you in love with a thing the life of which is
all over for you, simply because you remember the good times you
had in those pleasant places? Your love would die in you tomorrow, if you did not know that you got while in Princeton the
thing which made you better citizens and better comrades and
more honest and just men than if you hadn't gone there. That is
what gives you the Princeton spirit, that is the reason that the
Class of '41 is modern; that is the reason that there is no difference whatever in the conception which Mr. Voorhees has and
the conception which members of the present senior class of
Princeton University have. The life is different, but the personality of the place is the same; it is the same place you have all
loved, and praise God it shall always remain the same place.
(Applause.)

And so, gentlemen, I feel the spirit of all the ideals which we
entertain for Princeton made greater, the effort made more confident to partake of such things as can never be conquered or
lessened, when I come into contact with companies like this. I
don't know that I do you any good in going from gathering to
gathering, but I certainly know that in coming I drink of the wine
of the spirit which is the life of the place which I am entrusted to
govern. (Applause.) We all intend the same thing, we all share
the same thoughts, we all feel the same impulse, and that is the
ground of our confidence as to the future. (Prolonged applause
and cheers.)

Printed in the *Princeton Alumni Weekly*, vi (May 26 and June 2, 1906), 632,
651-55.

To Jerome Davis Greene

My dear Sir: Princeton, N. J. 30 May, 1906.

I have just been told to-day, after an examination by my physician, that I am on the verge of a very serious break-down, which might have very lasting results,[1] and that it is absolutely necessary, therefore, for me to withdraw from all public engagements and to reduce my work to the smallest possible amount.

I appreciate the very great embarrassment I may be putting Harvard University to in asking if it is possible at this late day to find someone else than myself to deliver the Phi Beta Kappa address at your approaching Commencement. I need not assure you that nothing but evident necessity would lead me to make so extraordinary a request at this time. I cannot help hoping that, if you will be generous enough to seek a substitute, one may even yet be found, and I feel certain that I may count upon the generosity of Harvard authorities in this unusual exigency.

Pray express to President Eliot my very keen feeling of chagrin that such a request should be necessary.

Very sincerely yours, Woodrow Wilson

TLS (MH-Ar).
[1] On Monday, May 28, Wilson had awakened blind in his left eye. John Grier Hibben accompanied him to Philadelphia, where he was examined by the famous ophthalmologist, Dr. George Edmund de Schweinitz, who found that a blood vessel had burst in the eye. Dr. de Schweinitz told Wilson that this was a manifestation of a general disease of the arteries and advised him to give up active work. However, Wilson also visited Dr. Alfred Stengel, an internist in Philadelphia, who, although he discovered a moderate degree of arterial tension, believed that a rest of three months would restore him fully. As subsequent documents reveal, Wilson followed this advice immediately. For a description of the attack and its immediate impact upon the Wilson family, see EAW to Mary E. Hoyt, June 12, 1906, and EAW to Florence S. Hoyt, June 27, 1906. For a diagnosis of what seems to have been in fact a very severe stroke and its impact upon Wilson's personality, see Edwin A. Weinstein, M.D., "Woodrow Wilson's Neurological Illness," *Journal of American History*, LVII (Sept. 1970), 334-37.

From Charles Williston McAlpin

My dear Dr. Wilson: [Princeton, N. J.] May 31, 1906.

I was distressed to hear of your indisposition from the Hibbens today and I hope and pray that it may not prove to be serious.

I have just received word from Dr. van Dyke that owing to absence from Princeton on Commencement Day he will be unable to present Dr. McClure[1] for the degree of Doctor of Divinity.

Very sincerely yours, [C.W. McAlpin] Secretary.

CCL (McAlpin File, UA, NjP).
[1] The Rev. Dr. James Gore King McClure, President of McCormick Theological Seminary.

To Nicholas Murray Butler

My dear President Butler: Princeton, N. J.   1 June, 1906

Various circumstances have made me dilatory in replying to your recent letters about the lectures I have promised to give at Columbia next year.

I have just had the misfortune to suffer a hemorrhage of one of the blood vessels of my left eye and the doctor tells me that it is absolutely necessary that I should give the eye rest for the entire summer. This inevitably makes me fear that it is possible I may have to disappoint you altogether, and I must ask you if you are willing to take the risk.

It is clear that I cannot carry out the plan I had formed of making preparation for the lectures this summer. I hope you will tell me very frankly whether you are willing to have the lectures come in January and February next, and whether you are willing to take the risk, which seems to be slight, that I shall not be able to prepare them at all, even in the autumn. I cannot tell you with what chagrin I find myself obliged to ask these questions, and I shall count upon you to give me the frankest possible answers.

In respect to the topics, I am quite willing to substitute for one of those I suggested, the one you suggested as a substitute, viz., "Party government in the United States."[1]

Cordially and sincerely yours,   Woodrow Wilson

TCL (RSB Coll., DLC).
[1] The letter in which Butler made this suggestion is missing.

A Draft of a Letter to John Grier Hibben[1]

My dear Jack,   Princeton, N. J.   4 June, 1906.

There is a matter to come before the Board[2]

Our life has broadened to new aspects since the Grad. Col. was conceived. It is all some day to be of a kind in the methods of its life. Groups, groups, groups

Admirable statement,—and quite conclusive enough for action if the School were considered apart from the general interests of the Univ.

Except *administratively*,—not a legal or theoretical question.

But seclusion and separation not synonomous, E.g. Oxford.

We are studying an organic problem—which only the trustees see as a whole and handle with full responsibility—and the Grad. College must be treated as part of it.

Geographical separation out of the question. I stand for the original and only complete conception (See Inaugural and Grad.
Book[3])

Separate teaching: "The several professors are each to have definite responsibility for the counsel and direction of a small
group of students, whom they are to meet outside the regular
courses in a very intimate way, both in the Grad. Col. and in
their own houses.["][4]

WWT, WWhw, and WWsh MS (WWP, UA, NjP).
[1] Since Dean Fine was in Europe, Wilson had asked Hibben to represent
him at the meeting of the Board of Trustees on June 11, 1906.
[2] The location of the proposed Graduate College. At a meeting of the trustees'
Committee on the Graduate School on May 12, 1906, Wilson had proposed as a
site the Bayles Farm, a tract adjacent to the campus off Washington Road.
(Andrew F. West, "A Narrative of the Graduate College of Princeton University
. . . ," mimeographed MS [UA, NjP], pp. 22-23.) As Wilson's draft of this letter
makes clear, West argued for a location away from the campus, most probably
the Merwick estate. This encounter marked the beginning of the great controversy between Wilson and West over the Graduate College.
[3] That is, that the Graduate College should be located in or near the heart
of the campus. In his inaugural address, "Princeton for the Nation's Service,"
printed at Oct. 25, 1902, Vol. 14, Wilson, talking about the Graduate College
had said: "We shall build it, not apart, but as nearly as may be at the very
heart, the geographical heart, of the university; and its comradeship shall be for
young men and old, for the novice as well as for the graduate."
The "Grad. Book" was West's *The Proposed Graduate College of Princeton
University* (Princeton, N. J., 1903), in the preface of which Wilson had described West's conception of the Graduate College as "this little community of
scholars set at the heart of Princeton." West himself had clearly implied that
the Graduate College ought to be in the center of the campus because of "the
direct and invaluable help" it would "supply in harmonizing, invigorating, and
elevating the life and thought of the undergraduate students." He had also
said that every undergraduate would pass the Graduate College in his daily
walks. Insofar as the Editors know, the meeting of May 12, 1906, was the first
occasion on which West proposed an off-campus location.
[4] Wilson was here quoting from *The Proposed Graduate College of Princeton
University*, p. 17.
It seems likely that Wilson never sent a letter along the lines of this draft to
Hibben but rather talked with Hibben about the matter and asked him to
present his views in the event that the location of the Graduate College should
come before the Board of Trustees. As it turned out, the trustees did not discuss
the site of the Graduate College at their meeting on June 11 because the
Committee on the Graduate School reported to the Board as follows: "We have
at this time no suggestion to offer regarding a site for the building or the details
of its [the Graduate College's] construction, and inasmuch as the [Swann]
bequest will not be available until the expiration of a number of months,
abundant time is allowed for the consideration of these very important questions." About the Swann bequest, see W. M. Sloane to WW, Oct. 15, 1906, n. 1.

From Nicholas Murray Butler

My dear President Wilson: [New York]   June 4, 1906

I am very sorry indeed to hear by your letter of the 1st that
one of your eyes is giving you trouble. We shall be only too happy
to adapt ourselves to your wishes and necessities in regard to the
lectures, but we could not contemplate the possibility of their not

being given. They may be given at any time next year that you prefer, and, if necessary, Dr. Albert Shaw, who is to be the second lecturer on the same foundation and who is to deal with present day problems of practical politics, will certainly be only too happy to adapt his convenience to yours.[1]

I do not know that I ought to suggest another topic to you, for I do not see how we can get along without all of the topics that you had proposed to treat. Therefore, if "Party Government in the United States" involved dropping a topic, perhaps the suggestion better be treated as not having been made. It had occurred to me, however, that the party system as it has grown up has so changed the theory of the Constitution in many ways that perhaps it ought to be treated specifically.

With high regard and hoping for your prompt recovery from your misfortune, I am,

Sincerely yours,   Nicholas Murray Butler

TCL (RSB Coll., DLC).
[1] Shaw did agree to give his lectures first in January and February 1907, as WW to N. M. Butler, Dec. 6, 1906, discloses. Wilson delivered his series in March and April 1907.

From F. Tompkins[1]

Dear Sir: New York, June 4th, 1906.

Herewith please find enclosed ten shares of stock of THE TAMMANY PUBLISHING COMPANY. We more than appreciate your kindness, and sincerely trust that we may be able to pay you a dividend of at least five per cent this year.

If we can serve you at any time do not hesitate to command us.

Very truly yours,   F. Tompkins   Managing Editor.

TLS (WP, DLC). Enc.: stock certificate for five shares in the Tammany Publishing Co., dated June 4, 1906.
[1] Managing Editor of the *Tammany Times*, a weekly published between 1893 and 1914.

Harold Griffith Murray to Cleveland Hoadley Dodge

Sir: New York   June 5th, 1906.

The following is a report of the Committee of Fifty to date. In studying it, will you please bear in mind that the fiscal year of the University ends on July 31st, and that, for the symplifying of accounts, the Committee of Fifty's fiscal year is synchronous.

The Committee was organized in December, 1904, the first subscription on record being received February 15th, 1905.

At a meeting of the Trustees, held in June, 1905, the following pledges were reported:

For Permanent Endowment, $420,000, (not including Mr Jesup's gift of 60,000.00) at 5 percent and yielding an annual income of $21,000

Promises of annual gifts   51,610

Specific gifts   22,950

Total $95,560

Since the report of a year ago, the Committee has received a pledge for a permanent endowment of $20,000, bearing interest at 5 percent and yielding an annual income of $1,000

Promises of annual pledges and specific gifts,   26,400.

Total $27,400.

The total income for the fiscal year ending August 1st, 1905, including interest from the endowment pledges, was $31,500

The total income to date for the fiscal year ending August 1st, 1906, approximates,   102,000

We have secured in pledges, to date, for the fiscal year ending August 1st, 1907,   79,688.

Of this amount $14,685.00 was subscribed this Spring.

The shrinkage between the income for the present fiscal year and that ending in 1907, of $22,312, is due to the Annual or Third Form Pledge, in which the donor makes no pledge for succeeding years. The fact, however, that the men who have given in this form are all generous and loyal friends of the University, makes it certain that the same amount will be contributed by them next year.

In the first, or Endowment Form, we have secured $500,000, of which $135,000 has been paid in to the University.

In pledges under the Term Form for five years, the Committee has secured $42,000. The bulk of the subscriptions, however, are subject to cancellation at pleasure. The fact, however, that to date we have had but one cancellation, equivalent to a one-hundredth part of one percent of the amount raised so far by this Committee, is a fair indication that we may count upon the continuation of pledges running "until further notice" for an indefinite period.

The amount of money that the Committee has raised during the past year does not, however, in any way represent the work that has been done, for nearly 1,000 graduates have been interviewed, either by Mr. Burleigh, the former Secretary, or myself, and fully one-half of those seen who have not contributed have signified their intention of doing so within the next year. A sys-

tematic record is kept of all visits made, and an efficient "follow
up" system which is being pursued will undoubtedly result in a
material increase in the number of subscribers in the near future.
The lamentable ignorance of a majority of the alumni body with
regard to the financial condition of the institution, has made
necessary a large amount of educational work, but the last six
months has undoubtedly made practically every graduate cognizant with the needs of Princeton, the advantages of the Preceptorial System and the work of this Committee.

Chicago, Philadelphia, St. Louis, Baltimore, Cincinnati and
Newark have been visited this Spring, so that the large centres
have been fairly well canvassed.

In addition to the regular work of collecting funds, by this
Committee, a plan has been formulated by which the various
classes desiring to make memorial gifts to the University will be
enabled to contribute individually an entry to the proposed dormitory on the east side of Brokaw Field, in the manner in which
Patton Hall was built by the ten classes from '92 to '01 inclusive.
Not a little of the Secretary's time has been devoted to the evolution of this plan, and it appears at present entirely probable that
within a year ground can be broken for a dormitory with at least
ten entries, at a cost of, approximately, $170,000.

While it is too soon to announce definitely what classes will
contribute these entries, it is safe to say that the class of '81 will
make its memorial gift an entry, the money being already practically raised. Other classes, ranging from '73 to '05, have the
matter under advisement, and several of them have started to
raise the amount necessary for an entry. Some $35,000 or $40,-
000 has been raised already in this way. Many men are willing to
contribute generously to a Class Fund, who are not willing to
contribute to a general maintenance fund of the University, and
this dormitory scheme has met with universal approval.

While it is true that money contributed by the classes for a
memorial gift is not money actually raised by this Committee, it
seems only fair—in view of the time that the Secretary has been
obliged to devote to the carrying through of this plan, the enthus-
ing of various class secretaries and interviewing of numerous
prominent alumni—that the Committee should receive a certain
amount of credit for the funds raised for the erection of the new
dormitory.

So large a percentage of the alumni reside in small towns,
where they can be reached only by letter, it appears advisable to
the Committee to appeal to them through local pride, and a plan
formulated to put in operation this Fall is for the alumni in small

centres to club together, guaranteeing a certain amount each year to the University, the gift to be known by the name of the town or locality from which it comes. An example of this is the town of Albany, N. Y., the alumni of which place, numbering about a dozen, have agreed to pay in to the University Treasury, each year, a sum not less than $250. Plainfield, N. J. has signified her intentien [intention] of underwriting a sum yet to be determined, and on the publication of the new alumni catalogue —which it is understood has grouped the graduates by localities[1]—it will be a very easy matter to start these clubs all over the country.

The Committee has made arrangements with the "Alumni Weekly," through which there will be published in October, January and May of each scholastic year, a review of all matters pertaining to Princeton since the previous issue, and sent to every living graduate free of cost. By this means the entire alumni body will be kept thoroughly in touch with what is being done at Princeton, and there will be no excuse in future for an alumnus being ignorant of Princeton affairs.

In addition to this, a press bureau has been organized through which, starting in the Fall, will be sent out from Princeton to 1,200 daily newspapers, from time to time, general articles of interest relative to the University. These articles, while of a timely nature, will be scholarly in tone, and will in no way tend to advertise the University in an undignified manner, but rather to disseminate academic or scientific information in a manner which will reflect credit on the University.

The work done by this Committee during the past year will undoubtedly be cumulative in result, and the full effect will not be felt for several years. It has been the policy of the Secretary to coerce no one. Every subscription that has been received has been given spontaneously, which is the best assurance that the subscriptions will continue.

The policy pursued, while not productive of the most satisfactory immediate results, will undoubtedly place the Committee on a firmer basis, and if this policy can be pursued it is my belief that we will ultimately have every man giving—who can afford to —to the support of the University, voluntarily—a consummation devoutly to be desired.

Respectfully,   H G Murray   SECRETARY.

TLS (Trustees' Papers, UA, NjP).
[1] *Directory of the Living Graduates and Former Students of Princeton University* (Princeton, N. J., 1905 [1906]).

From Henry Smith Pritchett

Dear President Wilson: New York   June 9, 1906.

I have the honor to inform you that, in accordance with your recommendation, at the meeting of the executive committee on June 7th, the following retiring allowances were voted to professors of Princeton University:

Professor Charles A. Young	$2430.
Professor Wm. A. Packard	2020.
Professor George Macloskie	1700.
Total	$6150.

This sum will be paid in monthly installments of $512.49 by check to the treasurer of Princeton University or such other official as you may designate, the first check being mailed about July 25th.

I beg that you will, in conveying this announcement to the distinguished men to whom these retiring allowances are granted, assure them of the high regard and esteem in which they are held by the trustees of the Carnegie Foundation for the Advancement of Teaching.

I am   Very sincerely yours,   Henry S. Pritchett

TLS (WP, DLC).

A News Item

[June 9, 1906]

President Wilson's Class, which marked its quarter-century year by the gift of Seventy-Nine Hall, is celebrating its annual reunion this year by finishing and furnishing the Tower Room of that dormitory, at an expense of about $6,000. The room will be turned over to President Wilson to be used as his office. The enthusiastic Class Secretary, William R. Wilder, announces that the class will sit together at the Yale game, adjourning to "a large and very enjoyable reunion in the Tower Room Saturday night, which will be conducted in our usual informal and unostentatious manner."

Printed in the *Princeton Alumni Weekly*, VI (June 9, 1906), 673-74.

To the Class of 1906[1]

[Princeton, N. J.]

Gentlemen of the Graduating Class: June 10, 1906.

I cannot tell you with how deep and sincere regret I find myself unable to address to you in person the words of affectionate farewell I have had it in my heart to speak to you to-day. I have felt a peculiarly intimate interest in your class, a special solicitude for its welfare. You will always be associated in my mind with the four years during which some of the most significant things I had planned and hoped for in the life of the University took shape and came to a happy realization. You have been patient under change, intelligent and loyal in all that it fell to you to do as the face of our life was altered,—in all things true sons of a great university springing forward to new days of achievement. If the things done in Princeton during these years have not touched your thought quite as deeply as they have touched ours, I am sure that they have touched your feeling for the place as deeply and have made you as vividly conscious as we are of its manifest destiny among American universities. I feel that in letting you go we are saying good-bye to trusted junior partners in a deep and far-reaching business whose issues are to make Princeton greater and greater with every year of her life.

In parting with you we do not think chiefly of ourselves, but of you. Your circle is now to be broken; but not in spirit. Our thoughts should not be wholly sad in the parting. Wherever we go we shall be bound together. The imperishable spirit of what we have done and enjoyed here goes with us. And this solemn hour, this sacred place remind us of what is deepest and most imperishable in what we have been as comrades and as lovers of good books and good men since we came to this place. The love of God and of his truth has always been our chief fountain of life in Princeton. May you always drink of it, deeper and deeper draughts as the years go by, for all other fountains shall dry up; and may God in all things guide and bless and keep you. Our good-bye is not ⟨yet⟩ a final word of parting. It is an affectionate greeting at a turning of the way. We shall ever be comrades in all true things and all worthy aspirations, lifted by the same spirit through all toils and all achievements.[2]

WWT MS (WP, DLC).

[1] Dr. Henry van Dyke read Wilson's message to the graduating class at the end of his baccalaureate sermon on June 10, 1906.

[2] This message was printed in the *Princeton Alumni Weekly*, VI (June 16, 1906), 694.

The Curriculum Committee to the Board of Trustees
of Princeton University

Gentlemen of the Board: [Princeton, N. J., c. June 11, 1906]

Your Committee does not desire to review the curriculum work of the year further than to say that all the expectations regarding the success of the reorganization of the courses of study on the Departmental basis, including the Preceptorial System, have been more than fulfilled. Faculty and students are not merely satisfied with the practicability of the new order of things, but have given it the hearty co-operation of work which it has demanded of their hands. No better proof of enthusiasm could be desired. . . .

Your Committee desired to present for your action the following recommendations from the President:

I. Re-appointments:

As Preceptor in History and Politics, Royal Meeker,	4 years, at $2000. per annum
" " " " " E. S. Corwin,	4 years " $2000 " "
" " " English, Nathaniel E. Griffin	1 year " $2000 " "
" " " Modern Languages, George T. Northup	1 year " $1400 " "
As Preceptor in Modern Languages, Henry [Harvey] W. Thayer,	3 years at $1800 per annum

II. New Appointments:

As Preceptor in Art & Archaeology, Chas. R. Morey,[1]	2 years, at 1500 per annum
" " " English Morris W. Croll,[2]	3 years at $1800 " "
" " " " Louis W. Miles,[3]	3 years at $1800 per annum
" " " History & Politics, Wm. S. Myers,	1 year at $1500 per annum
" " " " " Edgar Dawson	1 year at 1800 per annum
" " " " " Henry R. Spencer	2 years at 1800 per annum
" " " " " W. M. Adriance	1 year at 2000 per annum
" " Modern Languages, Varnum L. Collins[4]	4 years at 2000 per annum
" " " " Jacob N. Beam[5]	3 years at 1500 per annum
As Professor of Latin for one year in place of Professor J. B. Carter— Hamilton Ford Allen.	
As Assistant Professor in Physics,—Edwin Plimpton Adams[6]—	$1500

III. That Prof. George Macloskie of the Department of Biology in the School of Science, be at his own request, retired from active service with the title of Professor of Biology Emeritus, at a salary of $2000 per annum.

IV. That leave of absence during the first term of the coming academic year be granted Professor Thomas Marc Parrott, of the Department of English—the period designated being intended to fill out the year's leave he was to receive on understanding with the President, six months of this year having been already taken.[7]

Respectfully submitted,   M W Jacobus

From the Minutes of the Board of Trustees of Princeton University

[June 11, 1906]

The Trustees of Princeton University met in stated session in the Trustees' Room in the Chancellor Green Library, Princeton, New Jersey, at eleven o'clock on Monday morning, June 11, 1906.

In the absence of the President of the University the Senior Trustee occupied the chair. . . .

PRESIDENT WILSON REQUESTED TO PROLONG HIS VACATION

On motion of Mr. Cleveland and seconded by Mr. Pyne the following resolution was adopted:

RESOLVED that we desire to express our solicitude on account of the condition of President Wilson's health which deprives him of active participation in our Commencement activities. And in recognition of the fact that this condition is the direct result of close application and unremitting devotion to his labours in behalf of the University, we request, and especially enjoin it upon him, that he prolong his vacation to such an extent, as to time and manner of enjoyment, as may promise the complete restoration of his health and vigor. . . .

EXECUTION OF PAPERS IN THE ABSENCE OF THE PRESIDENT OF THE UNIVERSITY

On motion of Mr. Pyne, duly seconded, it was

RESOLVED that in the absence of the President, the Dean of the Faculty and in his absence, the Acting Dean be authorized to sign, execute and affix the Seal of the University to all such papers as the President would be entitled to execute.

PROFESSOR HIBBEN APPOINTED ACTING DEAN

RESOLVED that Professor John Grier Hibben be appointed Acting Dean during the absence of the Dean.

Ellen Axson Wilson to Mary Eloise Hoyt

My dear Mary,   Princeton   June 12 [1906]

Thank you very much for seeing about the Bryn Mawr matter;[1] Jessie is not willing (and neither am I!) to consider a three year course, so we must consider the incident as closed. The Woman's College requires even *more* hours weekly than Bryn Mawr, so it seems a pity that things are not more adjustable,—when the course is elective too. However Jessie is in such *very* good physical condition at the end of this year that I am less concerned about the Balt. climate for her, so perhaps it is all for the best.

This is the reception day & of course I am writing in extreme haste—please excuse everything,—but I cannot delay longer explaining the situation here. Two weeks ago yesterday Woodrow waked up perfectly blind in one eye!—it turned out from the bursting of a blood-vessel in it. Of course we had a dreadful week; all sorts of tests were made to determine the cause,—it is something wrong with the circulation due entirely to a general condition of overstrain. The doctors said he must stop *all* work at once, that it was impossible to exaggerate the critical nature of the situation. But now there is every cause for encouragement. The clot in the eye is being absorbed with extraordinary rapidity; and the doctor say[s] he has practically no doubt now that all will be well, —that the eye will be saved, and that if he takes a long summer of *perfect* rest & quiet he himself will be perfectly restored to health in the fall. Of course, he says that the eye will never be quite so strong as the other. In the meantime we are all making every effort to keep him free from anxiety and worry and above all to keep things quiet for him. He is of course *very* nervous—annoyed by the things he usually enjoys,—as for instance the lively chatter of the young people. He is making rather uncomplimentary remarks about the confusion caused by "seven women in a house" and asking when I "supposed Sister A[nnie]. & little A. were going"! So if he feels thus about his own sister, I know you understand, dear, that I ought not to add to the number of the household;—even *you* and our dear Florence, whose sweet, quiet, gentle ways are so exactly to his taste. Of course he would probably object if he knew I was writing this, but you will doubtless agree that my duty is clear. I am *so sorry* to miss your visit!

Woodrow is sleeping at Mr. Westcott's to be out of the commencement confusion[.] He did not even attend the Trustee meeting yesterday, but I had the luncheon as usual. Dean West receives with me today,—Dean Fine having been in Europe several weeks,—leaving his work on Woodrow; which doubtless contributed to this result. Now Mr. Hibben has to do nearly all! But it is time to dress. Don't be too much worried; all will be well in the end. We may all go to Europe,—to the Eng. lakes,—if he continues to improve at his present rate. We may sail June 30.

Devotedly,   Ellen.

I am as well as usual.

ALS (in possession of William D. Hoyt, Jr.).

[1] That is, whether Jessie Wilson should transfer from the Woman's College of Baltimore (now Goucher College) to Bryn Mawr College.

From the Alumni of Princeton University at Their Annual Luncheon

President Wilson: [Princeton, N. J.]   June 12, 1906.

We, the Alumni of Princeton University assembled at the 159th Commencement beg to express our great joy that our prayer for your speedy and complete recovery is being answered, and to assure you of our unceasing desires for your good health and the long continuance of your valued services to our Alma Mater.

TL (WP, DLC).

From Henry Burling Thompson

My dear Wilson   Princeton   June 12 1906

Yesterday was a memorable day for me, but it was clouded by the knowledge of the cause of your absence. First may I extend my sincere sympathy for your present illness and pray it may only be temporary. My election as a Trustee[1] was such a complete surprise to me I have not yet adjusted myself, to think of it normally. I do however appreciate the honor and responsibility but can not think of it lightly, but service rendered with love makes all burdens easy, and it is in this spirit I must approach its duties. It is a delight to think of working with so many men, who are to me, the best men I have ever known and the best men I shall ever know

Yours sincerely,   Henry B Thompson

ALS (WP, DLC).

[1] He and Joseph Bernard Shea of Pittsburgh had been elected Life Trustees at the meeting of the Board of Trustees on June 11, 1906, to replace John J. McCook and Charles B. Alexander, whose resignations had been accepted by the trustees on March 8, 1906.

From Cleveland Hoadley Dodge

Dear "Tommie"   New York.   June 14th 1906

I left yesterday directly after Commencement without getting
a chance to say à Dios to you[.] You were an awfully good boy to
take such care of the President & although we missed you terribly
we were happy that you were literally obeying the Doctor's orders,
& it was almost worth while to have you away, to see how your
understudy rose to the occasion. It was beautiful. Hibben represented you with great dignity & tact—absolutely effacing himself
& without a suspicion of slop over.

God bless you old man & put you all right again

Don't forget that you are enjoined by the Board to recover your
health, & stay away until that is un fait accomplis

Let me know if I can do anything for you while you are away

With warmest good wishes

Ever yours faithfully   Cleveland H. Dodge

Don't think of answering this

ALS (WP, DLC).

John De Witt to John Grier Hibben

My dear Dr. Hibben,   Princeton, N. J.   14th June 1906

Several months since I had a conversation with Prof. Hoskins[1]
on the influence of German learning and literature on the theological thought & religious life of America. It led to several conversations and finally to my inviting him to take up the subject
seriously and prepare two or three articles for the *Princeton
Theological Review*. Not knowing him before, I was not prepared
for the breadth and exactness of his knowledge and his grasp of
a large, complex, new (in the sense that it had never before been
adequately treated) and historically important subject. Of course
after our first talk I sought his company and took several walks
with him—the fine impression he made on me being always deepened; until, finally, I asked him for the articles. The first article
is in my hands. It deals with the colonial period. It has the admirable qualities I have already mentioned and is a valuable contribution to the subject. We shall publish the first half of it
in the January number of the Review.[2]

Of course, one cannot talk with a man as much as I talked
with Prof. Hoskins during these walks without learning more
about him than his relation to the subject that brought us together. I found him a mature man of wide intellectual interests,

broadly cultivated, strongly attached to the University[,]
thoroughly and intelligently believing in it and in the new departure in teaching, affectionate and loyal in his allusions to his
colleagues, and, *me judice*, sane in his judgments on matters
connected with his profession. I have come to have for him a
high respect and warm regard.

It has lately come to my knowledge through my Assistant Dr.
Loetscher,[3] his near neighbor, that Prof. Hoskins is a good deal
depressed. Loetscher tells me that Prof. Hoskins salary is only
$1500 a year and that his household has to be maintained with-
out a servant. The language of Loetscher's father's household is
German, and Loetscher is himself a lover of German literature.
In this way Loetscher and Hoskins have been brought together
often. On inquiry, I found that Loetscher—whose opinion on such
a subject I think of great value—thinks very highly of him both
as a scholar and as a man. He gave me what seemed to me to be
the very best reasons for his belief that Hoskins can scarcely
fail to become a man of distinction in his department and increasingly valuable as a member of the University Faculty.

This morning I met Mrs. [Willard] Humphreys on the street
and had quite a long talk with her about the relations between
Dr. Humphreys and Prof Hoskins, and Dr Humphreys opinion
of Hoskins. I found that Dr. Humphreys opinion was just that
of Loetscher. Mrs Humphreys spoke with deep feeling of the
warm friendship between Prof. Hoskins and her husband. I am
sure that Dr. Humphreys would join me, as Mrs. Humphreys
would also, in the petition I am about to make.

That is that Prof. Hoskin's salary be increased $500.00, and
that Dr. Wilson will as soon as possible encourage him to believe
that it will be done in the Autumn when the Trustees will meet.
This would, I am sure, be a great help to him during his vacation.

I write this with less hesitation than I should feel, but for
Hoskin's own reserve on the subject. He has not asked me to do
it, though once or twice allusions to the difficulty one has in "making ends meet in Princeton" have been made by him. I write it
because of the circumstances in which I have learned to believe
in his value to the university, & because through his friends
Mrs. Humphreys and Dr. Loetscher I have learned of the hard-
ships of a scholar.

I write to you rather than to Dr. Wilson, because I do not know
just when Dr. Wilson's physician will permit him to take up
questions like this one.[4]

                    Very sincerely yours,   John De Witt

ALS (WP, DLC).

1 John Preston Hoskins, Princeton 1891, Assistant Professor of German since 1898.

2 John Preston Hoskins, "German Influence on Religious Life and Thought in America During the Colonial Period," *Princeton Theological Review*, v (Jan. and April 1907), 49-79, 210-241.

3 Frederick William Loetscher, Princeton 1896, Instructor in Church History at Princeton Theological Seminary.

4 Hoskins' salary was not increased until 1911, when he received $2,000. He was promoted to professor in 1912 at a salary of $2,500.

Two News Items

[June 16, 1906]

President Woodrow Wilson expects to spend the summer abroad, and will sail on the Caledonia two weeks hence.

◊

Owing to ill health, Dr. Woodrow Wilson, president of Princeton University, has been compelled to cancel his engagement to speak at the inauguration of President Demarest, of Rutgers College on June 20.

Printed in the *Princeton Press*, June 16, 1906.

From Howard McClenahan

Princeton, N. J.

My dear Dr. Wilson—   June seventeenth [1906].

On Monday last, Mr. Pyne told me, entirely to my surprise, that my salary had been increased seven hundred dollars.

I want to express to you my great appreciation of this most welcome addition to my income, as well as my gratification at the at the [sic] manner in which it was brought about. While I should prefer to be in Princeton on a small salary rather than elsewhere on a larger one, yet life in Princeton has many financial problems. This larger salary comes to me as a most welcome relief from some of these problems, for which I am very grateful.

Most gratifying is the manner in which this increase has come. I can think of nothing more pleasing than what has happened to me, to have such a thing happen without solicitation or suggestion on my part. Such things, which we must regard as evidence of your interest and watchfulness, can only increase the great loyalty which we all have for you, and only make us put even more energy and enthusiasm into our work.

I can not at all sufficiently thank you for my good fortune for which I believe you to be wholly responsible. I am indeed very grateful to you.

I sincerely hope that the summer's rest is going to enable you to come back to us in the fall with restored health, and to take the direction again of the magnificent work which has been done by, and with, you during the last four years.

Mrs. McClenahan[1] joins with me in my expressions of gratitude and in the hope for your speedy and complete recovery.

I am   Very sincerely   Howard McClenahan.

ALS (WP, DLC).
[1] Bessie Lee McClenahan.

From Moses Taylor Pyne

My dear Woodrow: New York   June 19, 1906.

Shipley[1] writes me as follows: "Will you ask Mr. Pyne to let it be known in the right quarters that Mr. O. W. Richardson,[2] who, I hear by last mail, is likely to accept a post at Princeton,[3] is 'without being in the least a weak man,' easy to get on with, considerate of others' views and capable of seeing more than one side to a question.["]

                    Very sincerely yours,   M Taylor Pyne

TLS (WP, DLC).
[1] Arthur Everett Shipley, Fellow and Lecturer on Natural Science at Christ's College, Cambridge.
[2] Owen Willans Richardson, Fellow of Trinity College and Director of Natural Science Studies at Corpus Christi College, Cambridge.
[3] He did accept appointment as Professor of Physics and joined the faculty in the autumn of 1906.

From Frank Thilly

Dear President Wilson: Princeton, June 19th, 1906.

Before leaving Princeton I wish to express to you my sincere appreciation of all the kindness you have shown me and to thank you most heartily for the courteous and generous treatment I have always received at your hands. It has been a pleasure and an honor to be associated with you, and I shall never cease to be glad to have known you. I have always admired your scholarship, which is a credit to the nation, but since coming to Princeton I have also learned to respect you as a man. It grieves me to hear that you are not in good health, but I earnestly hope, as I believe, that you will soon regain your strength and resume the duties which you perform with such great fidelity and efficiency.

                    Cordially yours,   Frank Thilly.

ALS (WP, DLC).

From William Alfred Packard

Rangeley Lake House,
My dear Prest Wilson: Rangeley, Maine   June 20th 1906

I have just received here, and replied to, a letter of Profr Hibben informing me of my being placed upon the Carnegie Foundation, with a salary of $2020. I accept the benefaction with a very grateful sense of its value as a mark of regard and esteem from the Prest and Trustees of the Fund, as well as a pecuniary benefit. I have replied accordingly to Prof. Hibben's letter, but I wish also to thank you especially for your own kind part in the award, and to add my best wishes for your speedy and complete recovery from your temporary disablement, and for your happy and healthful trip abroad to make it sure and permanent.

Believe me, ever,
Very Truly and Faithfully yours.   Wm. A. Packard.

ALS (WP, DLC).

To Cleveland Hoadley Dodge

My dear Cleve,   Princeton, N. J.   21 June, 1906.

I cannot refrain from writing just a line to tell you how your kind note about myself and about Hibben delighted and comforted me. Nothing could exceed the kindness and generosity with which you have all treated me. It has touched and heartened me immensely. Your affectionate friendship, in particular, has made and will always make me very happy. As for your devotion to Princeton, it is her great asset!

May God bless you, my dear fellow. I mean to come back well and try to justify your confidence in me.

Always,
Gratefully and affectionately Yours,   Woodrow Wilson

WWTLS (WC, NjP).

Ellen Axson Wilson to Florence Stevens Hoyt

My dear Florence,   Princeton   June 27 [1906]

Just a little word of good-bye,—for I am simply overwhelmed with work. What would I not give to see you and dear Mary [Hoyt] before I leave!

I told Mary to send you my letter,[1] as I would not have time to write to both in detail. But I know now more exactly than I did then what is really threatening Woodrow. It is hardening of the arteries, due to prolonged high pressure on brain and nerves. He has lived too tensely. It is, of course, the thing that killed his father; as a rule it is the result of old age. Mr. [Herbert Baxter] Adams, there in Balt., died of it,—"premature old age" they called it in his case.

Of course, it is an awful thing—a dying by inches, and incurable. But Woodrow's condition has been discovered in the very early stages and they think it has already been "arrested." But I will quote for your satisfaction a letter of Dr. Stenger's:[2] "I find a very moderate grade of arterial trouble and of a character that does not suggest any progressive course as likely in the near future. You were fortunate in having the local (ocular) trouble because it called attention to the general condition which would otherwise have passed unnoticed. I feel entirely confident that a rest of three months will restore you fully. Of course 50 year old arteries do not go back to an earlier condition, but I expect that you will be as well as you need be for any work you can reasonably wish to undertake next Fall. The warning simply indicates that excess of work is dangerous. You have doubtless done too much in the last few years."

I do not quite understand all this, as some of the sentences seem to contradict each other; but I am told that I *ought* to consider it "very reassuring." He sent it today expressly *to* reassure.

I am afraid, dear, that I ought not to write you tonight when I confess I am rather overwhelmed. Of course I shall get myself more in hand soon. But this was my only time to write—& now I *must* stop! We sail Sat.[3] Our address will be the "British Linen Co Bank, London."

With devoted love believe me, my dear, *dear* Florence, as always—   Yours most fondly,   Ellen.

ALS (in possession of William D. Hoyt, Jr.).
  [1] EAW to Mary E. Hoyt, June 12, 1906.
  [2] That is, Dr. Alfred Stengel.
  [3] June 30, 1906, on *Caledonia* of the Anchor Line.

To Charles Williston McAlpin

Loughrigg Cottage,[1] Rydal,
My dear McAlpin,   Ambleside, Westmoreland. 19 July, 1906.

I know that the doctor would let me write this letter, if he knew how much it lay on my heart to send you a greeting.

The voyage was most easy and prosperous, the landing prompt and propitious; and we thanked you and Mrs. McAlpin every day of the journey for the abundant supply of delightful fruit you so thoughtfully sent us. It was most kind and generous of you, and we appreciated it deeply. I appreciated even more the chance to see you at the steamer. How I wish I could have brought you along!

We have been established now eight days in our tiny cottage. It is most picturesquely and delightfully situated, close by Rothay stream and under the shadow of Loughrigg, and, though we are a tight fit, I am sure we shall be most comfortable and happy in it. It is at the very heart of the region we most love.

I am feeling very well indeed,—even better than when I left. I feel confident that rest in this remote place will set me up in short order. I find that the spirit of doing nothing has already come most graciously upon me. I look at the poor, strenuous tourists with pity, and think comfortably how much better it is to stay in one place. The sight of my eye does not perceptibly improve; but I shall be very patient about that, and be more than content if my general health is re-established.

My full and accurate address is as typewritten above. Will you not be kind enough to ask [John] Rogers Williams to send it to Momo,[2] to Mr. Duffield, to Cleve Dodge, and to any others entitled to have it who may ask for it?

Mrs. Wilson joins me in warmest messages of regard to you both; and I am, as always,

Faithfully and affectionately Yours,   Woodrow Wilson

WWTLS (photostat in RSB Coll., DLC).
[1] The Wilsons were subletting the cottage (owned by John Tolson, a draper of Rydal) from Adelaide Troutbeck (Mrs. Henry Curwen) Wordsworth. Henry Curwen Wordsworth (1834-68) was a grandson of the poet.
[2] Moses Taylor Pyne.

To Charles Freeman Williams McClure

My dear McClure,   Rydal, Ambleside, 2 August, 1906.

Thank you for your letter of July fourteenth. I am gratified to learn that your negociations with Professor Calkins have prospered and that you are so confident that he will decide to come to us.[1] My mind is set at ease.

Fine is to sail on the sixteenth of this month and when he reaches Princeton will be both Dean and President until my return, as Hibben is until Fine returns. If anything further is necessary in regard to Mr. Calkins before I get back, you need not take the trouble to send a letter over sea. Fine or Hibben will act for me in all the steps now remaining to be taken. I am sincerely obliged to you for your prompt and successful conduct of this important piece of business.

I hope that you will have a most refreshing vacation and that your new associate will be everything we expect.

With warm regard,

Faithfully Yours,   Woodrow Wilson

WWTLS (McClure Zoological Autograph Coll., NjP).
[1] Gary Nathan Calkins, Professor of Invertebrate Zoölogy at Columbia University. For the denouement, see WW to C. F. W. McClure, Oct. 21, 1906, n. 1.

To Annie Wilson Howe

My precious Sister,   Rydal, Ambleside, 2 August, 1906.

Nellie has told you of our safe arrival and settlement here; but I must indulge myself in a line or two to send my love and tell you how constantly we think of you.

Dear Nellie would have fulfilled the promise of her letter and written again at once had she not gone down with an attack of the German measles. Apparently she picked it up in Glasgow as we passed through: it developed just ten days after we got here. It was a deep disappointment and distress to us all, but she is all right again now, though still partially quarantined. We shall not know for a few days yet certainly whether the others are to develop the disease or not. They were of course with her before the nature of the trouble disclosed itself. There was nothing serious about the thing itself, but it has sadly disordered our comfortable plans,—for which the dear child considers herself quite responsible!

We are at rather close quarters in the tiny cottage we have taken, but comfortable withal and very content. The spot is delicious, and we explore this delightful country up and down, good weather or bad. It rains a great deal, but very gently and sweetly, and the whole countryside is kept fresh for the bright days.

We are all well (even Nellie, now). I am puzzled what to report about myself. I have never *felt* as if there were anything the matter with me, you know, except for the eye; and I can only guess that I am improving from the unmistakable increase of energy that comes to me from week to week: my enjoyment of long walks (I have tramped as much as fourteen miles in a day), and all that sort of thing. This place contents me entirely, and more as the time goes on. You need not be in the least anxious about me.

Thank you, dearest sister, for the letters that came to us on the steamer as we left New York.[1] They were as sweet letters as ever were written, and made us very happy. Who should turn up here the other day but Miss Carrie Stribling.[2] We had two delightful glimpses of her; and she told me that you had not been obliged to go up the hill after all. I am so glad.

Take good care of yourself. All join me in the deepest love; and I am always

Your devoted brother,   Woodrow Wilson

WWTLS (WP, DLC).
[1] They are missing.
[2] Undoubtedly the daughter of Col. Robert M. Stribling, proprietor of Mountain View in Markham, Fauquier County, Va., where Mrs. Howe was vacationing.

To Leslie Mortier Shaw[1]

Rydal, Ambleside, England,
My dear Mr. Shaw,   11 August, 1906.

I take the liberty of writing to ask if an exception to the ordinary tariff regulations might not be made in regard to certain possessions of my friend, Professor O. W. Richardson, of Cambridge University.

Professor Richardson has won a very enviable reputation as a physicist, and is about to throw in his lot with us at Princeton, to my very great satisfaction. He was married about two months ago[2] (before his plan of moving to the United States was formed) and a number of the household goods which he wishes to take with him were received at that time by Mrs. Richardson as Wedding presents. They have, therefore not been in his possession, or in hers, for the required period of one year. It seems to me very clear that it would be no violation of the spirit of the law if these goods were admitted as immigrants' household possessions, free of duty; and I am writing in the hope that you will think it equitable in the circumstances to rule to that effect. The goods are not of great value, but Professor Richardson does not feel able to pay the duty.

Hoping most sincerely that you may be able to authorize this arrangement for my colleague; and with many apologies for troubling you in so small a matter,

With much regard,

Sincerely Yours,   Woodrow Wilson

WWTLS (Bureau of Customs Files, DNA).
[1] Secretary of the Treasury, 1902-07.
[2] To Lilian Maud Wilson on June 12, 1906.

To Robert John Wynne[1]

My dear Sir,   Rydal, Ambleside, 12 August, 1906

I take the liberty of writing to you in the interest of my friend, Professor O. W. Richardson, of Cambridge University, who is about to transfer his residence to the United States.

Although a young man, he has attained real eminence as a physicist, and will be a most valuable addition to our roll of learned men. He is of the temper to throw himself very heartily into our life and undertakings.

I write to ask if you will not be kind enough to recommend to the Treasury Department that an exception be made in his case to one of the tariff regulations. Some of his household effects Professor Richardson has only recently acquired. He was married only some two months ago and they came to him as wedding presents. This was before his plan for removing to the United States had been formed. It seems to me that in the circumstances they clearly do not fall within the meaning of our law, if interpreted in its spirit rather than in its letter.

I am myself writing to the Secretary of the Treasury to-day, and would very much value your support in this matter.

With much regard, and many apologies for troubling you with this matter,   Sincerely Yours,   Woodrow Wilson
                         President, Princeton Univer[sity]

WWTLS (WC, NjP).
[1] United States Consul General in London.

To Owen Willans Richardson

                                        Rydal, Ambleside,
My dear Professor Richardson,   15 August, 1906.

I quite understood that Mr. Fine's letter was written before you got into direct communication with me.[1]

I wrote to the Consul-general in London, and he replied[2] that you had just called at his office, and had decided to leave the goods in question in this country for a twelvemonth. No doubt you had merely discussed this and he was hurrying to the conclusion that would give him the least trouble. I wrote also to the Secretary of the Treasury, but of course he has not yet replied.

Mr. Fine tells me that the transportation of your furniture, etc., will cost you about three hundred and fifty dollars in charges. I think it fair in the circumstances that the University should relieve you of that expense, and I will write to-day to Mr. Pyne, the chairman of the Finance Committee of our Board of Trustees requesting him to authorize that arrangement.

Sincerely hoping that all difficulties will dwindle as you face them, and that we shall have a happy meeting on the other side, and again assuring you of the pleasure we had in seeing you both,

Cordially Yours,   Woodrow Wilson

WWTLS (in possession of Henry Bartholomew Cox).
[1] As this letter will subsequently reveal, the Richardsons had visited the Wilsons at Rydal.
[2] His letter is missing.

To Andrew Fleming West

My dear West,   Rydal, Ambleside, 20 August, 1906.

Let me express my warmest sympathy with you in the loss of your father.[1] I know what the loss means, and I am sure that the difference after the departure of a man of such force and genius will be very great for you. For him it was a release from ill health and failing strength, but for you is it not a veritable revolution in all that has shaped your life hitherto? I trust that you know how deep and genuine our feeling is for you in the circumstances.

I have just received a letter which rather upsets me.[2] It seems that, amidst the wholesale upheaval of my plans in June I neglected to notify the University of North Carolina that I would not be able to fulfil my promise to speak on their next founder's day, the twelfth of October. I have just written to President Francis P. Venable to beg his forgiveness

I also expressed the strong hope that he would invite you in my stead, assuring him that we should all be proud to have you speak for Princeton. Whether he will do so or not, I can only conjecture; I hope he will, and I trust that nothing will prevent you from going down and giving them the orthodox educational tradition if he does.[3]

I am faring very well indeed. I feel more vigourous and bumptious every day, and am feeling quite confident that by the sixth of October the doctors will be without all excuse for keeping me from sailing.

I hope that you are well in spite of the fierce summer.

With warm regard,

Always Faithfully Yours,   Woodrow Wilson

WWTLS (UA, NjP).
[1] The Rev. Dr. Nathaniel West, who had died in Washington, D. C., on July 7, 1906.
[2] It is missing.
[3] President Venable did invite West to deliver the address, but he was unable to accept on account of a previous engagement.

Eight Letters to Ellen Axson Wilson[1]

My precious darling,   Rydal, 21 August, 1906.

We have missed you all dreadfully. You would have been sorry for us if you had seen us[2] playing two-handed euchre last night in an empty house. But one can be lonely and happy both, and we are deeply happy to think of the good time our dear ones are having.

And we are both well. I still think that I can see more with my left eye, and for the rest I am absolutely all right. I am spending this morning writing letters. The day is what the weather bureau people call "fair."

Ah, darling, how fully and poignantly I know how I love you when you are away from me! Our lives have been so knitted together that we cannot really *live* apart. God bless you and keep you. Unbounded love from us both.

                              Your own   Woodrow

The opera glasses and the eye-drops went to York yesterday.

[1] Mrs. Wilson, Jessie, and Eleanor had just left for a two weeks' tour of England.
[2] That is, Wilson and Margaret Wilson.

My sweet darling,   Rydal, Wednesday, 22 August, 1906.

It was such a delight to get your letter from Durham,[1] saying that everything had gone well with you and that even "The County" was delightful. I hope with all my heart that the pleasure of it all will grow upon you with every step of the little trip, and that you will all of you come back with shining eyes. Ah, how I love you, and what a delight it is to think of your pleasure!

It still rains here. It relented a little yesterday and we got out for short walks, but it could not keep up its pleasant humour all day and by the middle of the afternoon the clouds were down on the hills again and the rain had returned. This morning is of the same kind. But it does not affect our spirits in the least. We write letters and are content. And we are perfectly well.

I will despatch the London Beadeker [Baedeker] to meet you at the Thackeray[2] to-day; also a line asking them to reserve rooms for you.

Nothing has happened to us. As I walked through Ambleside yesterday a lady, the sister of a very fine Princeton graduate of whom I have always been fond, stopped me and spoke to me very cordially. They think at police headquarters that Margaret's vest has been found, the picking up of such a garment being reported, but we cannot be sure until it is brought in to-day.

I hope that your lodgings are proving satisfactory and that my dear ones are all well and happy.

With love, love, love,—as much as you want,

Your own,   Woodrow

[1] All of Mrs. Wilson's letters to her husband during this trip are missing.
[2] The Thackeray Hotel in London.

My sweet love,   Rydal, 23 August, 1906.

I am to go this morning to sit to Mr. Yates.[1] Margaret is to go with Mary[2] and Honor[3] over Wansfell to Troutbeck, while all the world hereabout is going in the other direction, to the Grasmere Sports. The wind has swung into the North and is blowing cold.

It was nasty as could be all day yesterday until about four in the afternoon, when everything smiled again and was beautiful. I woke out of a delightful nap to see blue sky and sunshine everywhere, and got up and took a walk.

Margaret brought Mrs. Yates[4] and the girls in to tea (I was walking), and I came back to find them playing games in high glee. They stayed until dinner time, and we took Elsie's[5] breath away by having them stay. Mr. Yates had gone to Keswick to see how his pictures were hung at the exhibition and was not to be back until nine. Fortunately there was enough to eat, though not clean napkins enough. Then we walked up to the quar[r]ies while the sun set, and Margaret and I came back to our usual game of euchre. I have won only two games since we began Monday night!

We are perfectly well, and, if I may judge by myself, we think of you all the time.

I dare say this will be in time to catch you still at Lincoln.

Margaret sends dearest love to you all; and I love you more than I dare try to tell at this time, when I miss you so. But, remember, it is a happy, happy loneliness. I want everything to be just as it is, and would not be made happy, but miserable, if it were changed.   Your own,   Woodrow

[1] Frederic Yates, born September 15, 1854, of Rydal, Ambleside, an English painter of portraits and landscapes of the English lake district who had studied in the studio of Léon Bonnat in Paris. He was a frequent exhibitor at the New Gallery, the New English Art Club, and the Royal Academy. Wilson, soon after his arrival in Rydal, had met Yates on Pelter Bridge over the Rothay River, and the two men at once struck up a warm friendship that lasted until Yates's death on February 11, 1919.

Wilson's letter to Moses Taylor Pyne of December 31, 1906, discloses that Pyne, perhaps in correspondence that is missing, had commissioned the portrait on behalf of Princeton University. The portrait, actually a gift to the university of Pyne's wife, Margaretta Stockton Pyne, now hangs in the foyer of Prospect. It is reproduced in the photographic section of this volume.

  2 Yates's daughter.
  3 Honor Browne of London, a close friend of Mary Yates.
  4 Emily Chapman Martin Yates.
  5 Presumably a servant.

My own darling,   Rydal, 24 August, 1906.

I am so sorry to hear of your discomfort in York. It is too bad, for I know that your nights are everything to you

By the way sweetheart, I wrote to the Thackeray Hotel in London telling them of your coming and promising them that as soon as possible you would telegraph them the exact time (I do not mean exact as to hour) at which to expect you. You telegraph from the post office, you know, and their telegraphic address is simply "Thackeray, London." I find that on their very courteous letter of reply. The sooner you send them word after reaching Cambridge the better, but do not hurry yourself in Cambridge. You can tell the cabby in London that you wish to be driven to the Thackeray Hotel on Great Russell Street, opposite the Museum.

Your letters are so sweet and satisfactory, My darling, and make me so happy with their record of enjoyment. Bless you all three! Have as much fun as you can pack into the time, make the time any length you want, and do everything with a light heart.

We are "perfectly all right" in every respect. All yesterday morning and all this I have sat to Mr. Yates. I do not quite know yet what to make of what he has done, but he is himself enthusiastic and is evidently working *con amore*, with the ardent desire to present you with something stunning, as he puts it, when you return. No doubt he will.

Yesterday afternoon I performed quite a feat (for me) in walking. I climbed straight to the top of Wansfell Pike (the path would permit nothing else, being quite uncompromising[)]; went down the other side into Troutbeck village (we *must* buy Mr. Brown's house[1]); and came home by the high-road we drove upon and I walked before returning from the Kirkstone. Margaret and Mary and Honor took the same walk. They started at at [sic] half-past ten in the forenoon, I started four hours later, at half-past two; and I got home just ten minutes later than they did! They were an hour and a half on the top, eating their lunch;

picked mushrooms and frolicked as they went (among other things burying a dead field mouse with due form and feeling), and lingering again in Troutbeck for tea and sandwiches, while I paused nowhere so much as ten minutes, though, as you may imagine, I went up that long steep at a snail's pace, and made the round in a little less than four hours and a half. It was fine! I had not stretched my legs in a long time.

By this token you may see how well I am. I wish I knew the token by which to let you really know how much I love you, and how entirely and happily I am

Your own   Woodrow W (habit)

1 Townend, owned by one Browne, a yeoman farmer. This house, built in 1696, was occupied by the Browne family until 1944. It is now a National Trust property.

My precious darling,   Rydal, 25 August, 1906.

Two letters from you yesterday, one from York, one from Lincoln, both redolent with your own sweetness, God bless you. It is beyond measure delightful to think of the beautiful things you are seeing with your two bairns, and how their capacity for enjoying must be growing under your guidance. Please do everything you *feel* like doing for them, even if it takes longer,—will you not, my darling?

I forwarded to you this morning two letters from home, both from Madge,1—one addressed to Jessie, one to you. No letters have come across the sea this week for either Margaret or me.

Nothing happens to us and we are very happy. It rains too constantly for long walks, but the afternoons are beautiful and we get out for short ones between showers. I still sit for my picture, and it is beginning to come into shape in a very interesting way. I think it will be strongly individual and unusual and that you will like it very much. I sit three hours at a time, and usually Mrs. Yates is with us.

Margaret and I are to make up your bundle of four gauze vests, two shirt waists, two embroidered collars, and two pairs of cotton stockings this afternoon, and I am to take them into Ambleside and send them off to your London address by parcels post. They ought to be waiting there for you.

Margaret is a great comfort to me, as thoughtful and sweet as she can be. Dearest love from us both to all three of our dear ones; and for yoorself [yourself], my darling more love than tongue can tell from   Your own   Woodrow

1 Mrs. Wilson's sister, Margaret Randolph Axson.

Rydal, Sunday morning,

Eileen mavourneen,   26 August, 1906.

Two letters having come on Friday, we had none from our dear ones yesterday, and to-day we are cut off; but I trust and believe that they are all right. Perhaps to-morrow we shall have a feast of two more letters.

It is raining, as usual this morning, and Margaret and I are not going to church. The afternoons lately have been bright and beautiful: we are trusting that this afternoon, too, will be. If it is we shall go to afternoon service at Grasmere. Mr. Peterson[1] does not preach to-day; and to-morrow he is off for three or four weeks in the Tyrol.

I called on him last night. It came about in a most characteristic Yatesian way! Mr. Yates having postponed asking him to call so late that it was impossible for him to find the time, yesterday, without so much as saying by your leave to me, despatched a note to him to ask when I could find him at home! Mrs. Peterson rode out to the Yates's on her wheel to answer the note: to say that her husband had a bad knee, else he would have come out to see me at once, and that they would be at home that evening. I was horribly embarras[s]ed. It was so like a situation that an ordinary American would have been expected by these conventional people to have created. But there was nothing for it but to call, and call I did, at eight, the hour named. At nine the three Yateses and Margaret called for me. They announced their coming by singing outside the window, most beautifully, and of course stayed an hour when they came in. After the first embarrassment was over I enjoyed the call very much indeed. Of course Mr. Peterson was worth meeting and in every way most interesting and attractive, and Mrs. Peterson is quite lovely. They are going to try to see you just as soon as they get back. I sincerely wish the acquaintance had begun earlier; you would enjoy them so.

We are perfectly well, darling, and very peaceful in our minds and doings. God bless you all and keep you from all harm. We love you all three with all our hearts.

My heart is full of you, my sweet pet. I am sure you know how deeply and tenderly and passionately I love you.

Your own   Woodrow

[1] The Rev. Magnus Fraser Peterson, curate of the Church of St. Mary Virgin at Ambleside.

Rydal, Monday afternoon,

My precious sweetheart,   27 August, 1906.

Today the weather suddenly changed its mood altogether and is giving us a perfect feast of sunshine. We have been very patient and cheerful under the dispensation of rain, rain, rain; but we are none the less delighted to see the sun again, especially since he comes with such a reassuring smile, as if inclined to stay. Margaret and Mary and Honor have gone up Fairfield, intending to go *down* (!) to the Kirkstone and thence back home by the short way. They are saving the finest walk there (Fairfield Round) for Jessie and Nellie when they return. This big walk is a parting treat for Honor, who goes home on Thursday. I did not feel equal to quite so heroic a climb, and sat to Mr. Yates instead.

The portrait lacks something of being fine, but every touch now brings it nearer to what it ought to be, and I feel sure that, especially after he has acted on your suggestions concerning it, you will like it thoroughly,—since you have an inexplicable weakness for the original. His trouble is that he sits too near me and gets the lower part of my face at a different angle from that at which he sees the upper part.

What a pure delight your sweet letters are, my Eileen. The air of enjoyment, of excitement among beautiful and noble things, which they breathe fills me with a peace and delight it would be hard for me to find words for. You are making me very happy by this expedition. Mrs. Yates brought over yesterday a letter from Mrs. Brown,[1] which Margaret forwarded to you at once; but *please* do not take its suggestion: you know how eager I am to have you do the whole thing yourself; and you *Must* know how much more delightful and *profitable* it is to the children. How perfectly delightful the opening of our dear Nellie's eyes and heart to these things must be. I envy you the sight of it!

It did not exactly clear up yesterday afternoon, but it at least *held* up, and dear Margaret and I walked over to service at Grasmere. They had the evening service in all it[s] simplicity, and it was very sweet and soothing. The somewhat simple-minded younm [young] man who conducted the service preached on Elijah! The contrast with what we had heard last Sunday afternoon was of course very marked; but I rather enjoyed the little discourse on the whole for its simplicity and obviousness. Our walk home in the waning twilight, with the mountains *very* solemn about us gave the proper final touch to our spirits. We had supper, counted the clothes for the laundry, and went to bed with peaceful, quiet minds.

Margaret sends a heartful of love: my heart fairly aches with its messages of love. Above all things else I love, love my darling.

Your own,   Woodrow

1 The Editors have been unable to identify her.

My precious one,   Rydal, 28 August, 1906.

Another glorious day of sunshine leads us to hope that August has relented and that the good weather of September is at hand.

This is our precious Jessie's birthday. Give her love without measure, and most loving congratulation, and tell her how deeply proud we are of her sweetness and character. May God bless and keep her, and bring her happiness!

We are sending to-day the nightgowns, the phenacetine, and some handkerchiefs from the wash. Do not think that you are giving us trouble: we delight to do these things.

There is no news. I have sat another morning for the portrait. There is something the matter with the lower part of the mouth, none of us exactly knows what. We are to drop it now, therefore, until the end of the week when Mr. Yates can go back to it with fresh eyes. You know what that means, and how wise such a resolution is. He wants to make it perfect, and was yesterday a bit discouraged. I begin to feel confident that it will come out all right. I think he has been trying to catch some fleeting expression.

A letter from Dr. Jacobus to-day[1] also bids me stay through the winter! Alas, I do not see how I could. He admits Pyne put him up to it.

We are well and vigourous. We love and think of you always. Bless you for your sweet letters. They make me very happy. Everything about you makes me more and more

Your own   Woodrow

WWTLS (WC, NjP).
1 It is missing.

From James Burton Reynolds[1]

Sir: [Washington] August 28, 1906.

In reply to your letter of the 11th instant, relative to the free entry of the wedding presents of Prof. O. W. Richardson and wife who are about to take up their residence in this country, I transmit herewith a copy of Department circular of February 1, 1904,[2]

from which you will observe that "nonresidents of the United States are entitled to bring with them as baggage, free of duty, all wearing apparel, articles of personal adornment, toilet articles, and similar personal effects in actual use and necessary and appropriate for the wear and use of such persons and their present comfort and convenience, not intended for other persons or for sale."

Only "professional books, implements, instruments, and tools of trade, occupation, or employment, in the actual possession at the time, of persons emigrating to the United States," are free of duty as immigrants effects, nor could the wedding presents you mention be admitted free of duty as household effects, since, as you state, they have not been in the use of the present owners for the required period of one year.

Respectfully,   J. B. Reynolds. Acting Secretary.
A.J.

CCL (Bureau of Customs Files, DNA).
[1] Assistant Secretary of the Treasury.
[2] It is missing.

Five Letters to Ellen Axson Wilson

My own darling,   Rydal, 29 August, 1906.

Another bright day! The weather seems indeed to have changed its mood. Margaret is to go to the Taylor's[1] this afternoon, but I am going on a tramp to Easedale Tarn, making a day of it. I was not nearly so tired after my climb over Wansfell as I have been after other long walks. I think I am quite fit, and it makes me very happy to be so.

But not as happy as to read your letters, you dear thing, and learn what sweet weather and what delightful times you and the dear ones with you are having. That is tonic for my mind and heart.

There is no news of us, for, happily, it is no news that we are well. Margaret takes care of me most sweetly and our days go most smoothly.

You left for London half an hour ago. How delightful! I cannot sufficiently thank you, my pet, for your letters, with all their love and sweetness.

Love unmeasured from us both to all three. I love you more than I can ever make you know.

Your own   Woodrow

[1] The Editors have been unable to identify them.

My own darling,   Rydal, 30 August, 1906.

I am off for Edinburgh this afternoon, by the same train you took to Durham. I wrote to the doctors I am to see there,[1] asking when I could see them, and they have both fixed to-morrow. Their letters came this morning at breakfast time. I am grieving to leave Margaret alone; but she says she does not mind a bit.

I enjoyed my long walk yesterday immensely, and it refreshed me greatly. It was nine miles, and some of it hard climbing, but I got back quite fresh. Margaret went out to the Taylors' in their motor car and had a very pleasant and amusing time. They are evidently only about half baked, and Margaret suspects Mrs. T. of dropping her aitches. It was Margaret's first ride in a motor car, and she enjoyed it very much. They took her for a spin around Thirlmere.

We are both well, and both happy so long as the letters from you and the dear girls tell of health and pleasure.

Ah! my sweet one, my love for you is past words. I will write from Edinburgh.   Your own, Woodrow

WWTLS (WC, NjP).
[1] See WW to EAW, Aug. 31, 1906, ns. 1 and 2.

                                        The Royal Hotel, Edinburgh,
My precious one,   31 August, 1906

My worthless pen hand will not hold out to write much, but all that it does write will please you. The eye doctor[1] is evidently very well pleased—agreeably surprised—at the condition of the eye, and my blood-pressure, general-condition doctor[2] is inclined to think that it would be rather better for me to go back to (moderate) work than not to go. He wants to see me again, however, after a week's trial of certain medicine, before giving his final decision. He was *very* encouraging. Jessie may come with me *next* Thursday, therefore.

By all means see Ellen Terry.[3] Take a cab for the evening, and see her at night—but stay to the matinee rather than not see her at all! I think, by the way, that there are some London and North Western trains wh. have a through section to Windermere. Make the Thackeray porter find out for you.

I leave to-morrow and shall be due at Windermere at 5.15 P.M.

Bless you, dears. Love immeasurable to all three of you! I am well and happy. I love you beyond all words!

                                        Your own   Woodrow

[1] George Andreas Berry, M.B., F.R.S., Senior Ophthalmic Surgeon, Royal Infirmary, Edinburgh, and Lecturer in Ophthalmology at the University of Edinburgh.

2 Francis Darby Boyd, M.D., Assistant Physician, Royal Infirmary, Edinburgh.
3 Ellen Terry was playing in Herbert Beerbohm Tree's production of Shakespeare's *The Winter's Tale* at His Majesty's Theatre in London.

My sweet one,   Edinburgh, 1 Sept. 1906
I went to the Royal Infirmary to have my blood pressure tested (it is very little off) and at noon am off for Rydal. I am all right. Nothing more to report. I just drop this line as a token of love. I am altogether   Your own   Woodrow

ALS (WC, NjP).

Eileen mavourneen,   Rydal, 2 September, 1906.
I reached home safe and sound, although after an exceedingly hot and disagreeable journey, yesterday afternoon, finding Margaret on the bridge waiting for me, very well and bright. I have been uneasy at the reports of the extreme heat in London. I hope my precious ones are not suffering from it, and that they are prudent about exposure. I found that Margaret had forwarded the letter from you which I expected to find awaiting me here to Edinburgh yesterday morning, not having her thinking cap on at the time! It was a sore trial to me, being very dependent on my darling's letters.
Now that I am back at my type-writer, I can give you a more particular account of what the doctors said. I went first to Dr. Berry, the eye specialist, a very quiet but very satisfactory person. He said that he found the eye in excellent condition, perfectly healed, and that it would be quite safe for me to read, indeed he seemed to think that it would be best for me to use it in that way, with moderation. Altogether he was very encouraging, and did not hesitate to say that I could go back to work without risk.
The other doctor was less confident, but only, I think, because he was younger and had a bigger question to decide. Dr. Gibson,[1] to whom Dr. Stengel[2] referred me, is away, attend[ing] a medical convention in Canada, as Dr. Stengel feared he would be, and the Dr. Boyd to whom I went has charge of his practice in his absence. Dr. Stengel said that he thought it would be perfectly safe to go to any one whom Dr. Gibson might depute; and I found that Dr. Boyd had the full letter which Dr. Stengel had written to Dr. Gibson about my case. After looking me over very carefully and thoughtfully, Dr. Boyd said that he thought that it would probably be better for a man of my temperament to go back to work than to lead an aimless and perhaps anxious year on this side the water; and he said that, with proper moderation

in work, I could return with perfect safety. "If," he said, "we should lay off from work every man whose blood tension is slightly off the normal, a great many very useful and important men would be idle." He evidently felt the responsibility of making the decision on so brief an acquaintance with me and with the case; and said that while he really had no doubt about the matter that was worth dwelling on, he would rather wait a week to see the effect of some medicine he gave me and to consult Dr. Berry, the oculist, on whose judgment he greatly relies, before finally forming a judgment. Yesterday morning I went, by his direction, to the Royal Infirmary and had the tension of my blood tested by an attractive young intern. It was not much off the normal. The only thing that disquieted me at the Infirmary was a charming young nurse whom I met in the corridor and of whom I asked my way. Her smile and her bewitching Scots speech nearly stole my heart away. I had to hurry on out of danger. And so you see, my darling, that I have practically no doubt about our sailing, a very happy family, on the sixth of October. My spirits have gone up delightfully since the consultations. Both doctors seemed so simple and so sincere that I knew just how to read what they said, and was very much reassured. It is delightful to send you such news, to brighten the close of your little pleasure excursion.

Of course if you stay for the Wednesday matinee I will not go to Edinburgh on Thursday, but will wait until Monday. That will suit the doctor just as well, I am sure. He named an early day because he knew how important it was for me and the University that a decision should now be made practically at once.

Margaret joins me in dearest love to all three of our loved ones. As for my own love for you, my pet, absence always makes it a bit intolerable, my precious darling, but I at least know to the depths of my heart how I am linked to thee. I love you with all my heart.   Your own   Woodrow

Both perfectly well.

WWTLS (WC, NjP).
  [1] George Alexander Gibson, M.D., Physician to the Royal Infirmary, Edinburgh.
  [2] That is, Dr. Alfred Stengel of Philadelphia, whom Wilson had consulted soon after his stroke.

From Charles Williston McAlpin

My dear Dr Wilson   Seal Harbor Maine   Sept 2d, 1906.

Pray do not attribute my neglect to reply to your letter of July 19 to any lack of appreciation on my part. Your letter has been my constant companion this summer and the expressions of

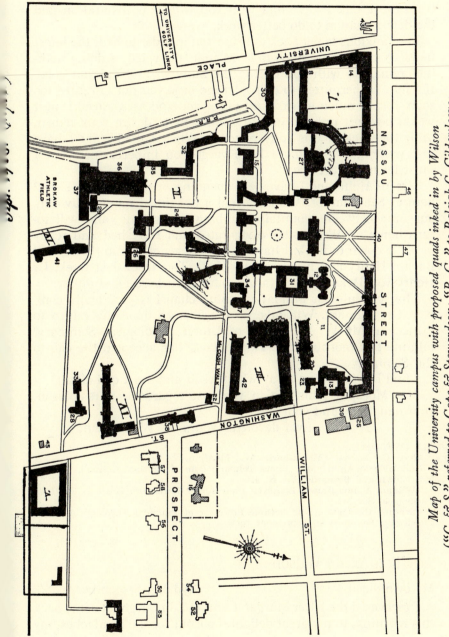

Map of the University campus with proposed quads inked in by Wilson
("C. & S." referred to Cope & Stewardson; "R. G.," to Raleigh C. Gildersleeve;
"M.," to Benjamin W. Morris III. All were architects.)

friendship contained in it have made me a proud and happy man. I am not given to gushing, but when I read your words and feel that I can call you my friend I feel that I must let you know of my admiration and affection for you. Association with you has made my work at Princeton a labor of love and I have come away from every talk I have had with you with new inspiration and the determination to do better work.

I am anxious to get back to Princeton in order to hear the latest news from you, and hope to learn that "the spirit of doing nothing" remained with you during the Summer and did you good. If I may be permitted to do so, let me urge you not to return too soon, for, as much as we want to see you and as we need you, it would be most unkind and unwise for us to desire your return, until your health was fully restored. When I read what I have just written, I feel that I have verged on impertinence, but I must let my heart speak.

Mrs McAlpin[1] and I have been spending August with my sister[2] here at Seal Harbor. We have had a delightful month, dividing our time between mountain climbing and sailing, and will return home on Wednesday invigorated and refreshed and ready to settle down to work. I have had glimpses of Momo [Pyne] and Bayard Henry and lunched with H. D. Thompson last week. Dr Henry van Dyke and his family have been here all summer.

The schedule for Sunday morning chapel is practically completed to January. Will take up the balance upon my return to Princeton. Mr W. A. Brown of Union Theological Seminary[3] told me this morning that Hugh Black[4] has accepted the call to the Seminary.

I find I am running away with myself and must call a halt.

Mrs McAlpin joins me in warmest regards to Mrs Wilson, your daughters and yourself

Ever devotedly yours   C W McAlpin.

ALS (WP, DLC).

[1] Sara Carter Pyle (Mrs. Charles W.) McAlpin.

[2] Adelaide McAlpin (Mrs. James Tolman) Pyle of McAlpin Corners, between Morristown and Bernardsville, N. J.

[3] William Adams Brown, Roosevelt Professor of Systematic Theology at Union Theological Seminary.

[4] Scottish theologian, who became Professor of Practical Theology at Union Theological Seminary in September 1906.

To Ellen Axson Wilson

My own darling,   Rydal, 3 September, 1906.

I recovered the letter Margaret sent to Edinburgh: it came back this morning, to my great delight. Lookout for the headaches, my sweet pet. "Don't overdo" is a duty as obligatory upon you as upon me. Think how my mind and body are bound up with yours, and spare yourself for my sake. Dear love! I mean all this very deeply.

It is delightful to see from your letters that London is not proving so formidable, after all, and that your days are pass[ing] easily as well as delightfully. Bless you all!

We went to Rydal church yesterday morning and heard *two* inarticulate curates conduct the service. In the afternoon we walked over to Grasmere and enjoyed the simple service there, with a discourse from an interesting young curate from a London East End mission: a fellow of some charm and force.

I am afraid that Mr. Yates is a bit discouraged over the portrait; but there is no sufficient reason why he should be, and we go at it again this morning. He says that if he does not get it right in one more sitting, he hopes I will do him the service of kicking him. There must be something hard to do about the lower part of my face. Mr. Yates encourages me to talk all the time I am sitting,—says he does not want me to sit quiet,—and the result is that he is trying to draw something that is altered, even in line, I dare say, every moment.

Nothing happens to us. We are perfectly well and shall be perfectly happy when we get you all back again. Margaret is a brick. She joins me in warmest love to you all and is as happy as I am that you are having such a delightful time.

I love you, Eileen, oh how tenderly and how passionately! God bless and keep you, mavourneen.

Your own,   Woodrow

WWTLS (WC, NjP).

To Harry Augustus Garfield

Rydal, Ambleside, 3 September, 1906.

My dear Garfield
(if I may take the liberty of dropping the Mister),

I have come to the conclusion that it would not be prudent for me to plunge right into lecturing on my return home. Fortunately my course of the first term, in Jurisprudence, in no way depends on the lectures for its definiteness and coordination now that the men really read. I write to ask, therefore, if you will not arrange in the Department for the experiment of making that course an entirely preceptorial course, without lectures. That arrangement need not involve more work for the preceptors, and it will free the lecture hours (Mondays and Tuesdays from nine to ten) for their conferences with the men in the class. It is, I think, an interesting and valuable precedent to set, even if there were no other reason for doing it.

I am feeling greatly improved, and have no doubt that I could take up the lectures again without real risk; but I want to vindicate my prudence by beginning very leisurely and sedately to pull the load again. The doctors shall have no indictment against me this time.

We are booked to sail on the sixth of October, from Glasgow, in the *Caledonia*, of the Anchor Line, one of the few boats of that line which actually "make" their schedule time. We ought, therefore, to be in on the eighth day, the fourteenth; but I am saying, for good measure, the fifteenth.

I need hardly say how eager I am to get back. One never knows until they threaten to lay him off how he loves the work he is doing or the men with whom he is doing it. It will be such a pleasure to see you again. The last time I was on this side I got your letter saying that you would come to Princeton.[1] That was one of the happiest satisfactions that has come to me.

I hope that you are all well and that you have had a refreshing summer. Mrs. Wilson and my daughters join me in warmest regards to you all.

Cordially and faithfully Yours,   Woodrow Wilson

WWTLS (Wilson-Daniels Corr., CtY).
[1] H. A. Garfield to WW, July 14, 1903, Vol. 14.

To Ellen Axson Wilson

My precious darling,   Rydal, 4 September, 1906.

How delightful it is to think that this is the last letter that can reach you before you start for home! Ah, my sweet one, how I want you,—how I long to have you in my arms again, and always close at hand to turn to upon any impulse! You are all the world to me.

We are all right in every way. I will meet you at Windermere. There is a coach which meets your train and comes strait through Ambleside for Grasmere, so that we can be set down at Pelter Bridge without change. What a happy day it will be!

Mr. Yates is doing a new picture, with Pelter Bridge in it and it promises to be a beauty,—not so poetical as the other (which, by the way, he has in part restored to its first dark beauty), but very sweet and desirable. And the portrait is all right. After much

travail and discouragement, he has hit it at last. I am to sit a
little while this morning, and then it will be ready for your inspection. I feel confident that you will be delighted. It is quite
unlike any other attempt to show my looks. I do not see how he
has had the patience to finish it.

There is no news. We did nothing yesterday but watch Mr.
Yates draw and write letters, except that after tea we walked
over to Grasmere and bought you a copy of the new edition of
Canon Rawysley's "Literary Associations of the English Lakes"[1]
and the volume of Mrs. Ewing you ordered,[2] which, by the way,
does *not* contain "Our Field"!

You must all know how much love we would send. How much
I love you, my darling, I shall try to tell you and make you feel
when I am once more released from loneliness and longing by
your sweet presence.

With a full heart,   Your own,   Woodrow

WWTLS (WC, NjP).
[1] Hardwicke Drummond Rawnsley, *Literary Associations of the English Lakes*,
3rd edn. (2 vols., Glasgow, 1906).
[2] One of the numerous collections of children's stories by Juliana Horatia
Gatty (Mrs. Alexander) Ewing.

To Robert Bridges

My dear Bobby,   Rydal, Ambleside, 9 September, 1906.

It was a great pleasure to get your letter,[1] and a great surprise
to get it from Antwerp. How delightful it would be if you could
go back with us. We are to sail on the sixth of October from Glasgow, on the Anchor Line's fine "Caledonia," the same boat we
came over on. She is most satisfactory, though the food on the
Anchor Line boats is to be praised with reserve. Would she be
impossible to you? Come if you possibly can. It would be a genuine delight to me.

Except for two trips to Edinburgh, one for a Professor of Psychology[2] and one to see my doctors there, I have stayed here:
and with perfect delight. No doubt God *could* have made a love-
lier country than this Lake District, but I cannot believe he ever
did. We have been here something over two months now, and the
month that remains to us will be all too short for the completion
of our enjoyment. I have come to love the region like a second
home. We have had a little cottage all to ourselves, placed in
perhaps the most beautiful spot of all, and our love of the hills
and walks has come to be very intimate indeed. I have come to
prefer rainy weather!

And it has been very good for me. I feel entirely rested and refreshed, and my eye has made the full progress that was expected. When I saw the Edinburgh doctors about ten days ago, they thought me quite fit to go back to any reasonable amount of work. Indeed they were of the opinion that for a man of my temperament it would probably be a mistake to spend too many idle weeks away while the University was in session and all my thoughts and desires inseparably bound up in what was going forward there. I go to see them again to-morrow, for their final examination and judgment. But I have little doubt what the decision will be. I mean to put in a thoroughly sensible year. I am not going to lecture; I am not going to make any outside engagements that can be avoided; I shall superintend, and push all important plans forward; and I shall take several short rests, in Florida or elsewhere. It will beat Europe in its tonic and quieting effect all to pieces.

I am sorry you were so tired out, and hope with all my heart that you will get the fullest rest and refreshment. Do not stand the heat in Italy any longer than is prudent. Come this way and see   Your affectionate friend,   Woodrow Wilson

WWTLS (WP, DLC).
   [1] It is missing.
   [2] He had gone earlier to Edinburgh to interview Norman Kemp Smith.

To Charles Howard McIlwain

                                        The Royal Hotel, Edinburgh,
My dear Mr. McIlwain,   10 September, 1906

The sad, sad news of Mrs. McIlwain's death[1] has just reached me, and I venture to write you this line of deepest sympathy, not because any word of mine can really be a word of comfort as against such a loss, so sudden, so irreparable, but because my heart bade me tell you at least how profoundly Mrs. Wilson and I feel for you in your distress and how we wish that there were some direct way in which we could make you feel our friendship and sympathy. May God bless and sustain you and give the comfort and strength which only he can give in such a tragedy.

                          Your sincere friend,   Woodrow Wilson

ALS (WC, NjP).
   [1] McIlwain's wife, Mary Irwin McIlwain, had died on August 24, 1906.

To Cleveland Hoadley Dodge

My dear Cleve.,   Rydal, Ambleside, 16 September, 1906.

We sail on the sixth of October, from Glasgow, on the Anchor Line steamer "Caledonia," on which we came over and were very comfortable; and we ought to reach New York by the fourteenth. The doctors not only consent: they think it best, provided I take decent care of myself. You may imagine how happy their decision makes me. I have not only appreciated your advice and the advice of all the friends who have begged me to take time to get well: I have known that it was the only wise advice, and I left the doctors absolutely free to say whether I should return now or not. They were keen enough to see that for a man of my disposition several months of idleness over here would be so irksome as to be positively hurtful unless I knew them to be necessary; and they did not think them necessary. They thought, on the contrary, that equable and reasonable work would be good for me. I have promised them, moreover, to take special care of myself next winter: to break the year with a little vacation in Florida, to make as few outside engagements as possible, and to keep myself within bounds while at home. I have every disposition to obey them! I love my work too much to be willing to run the risk of rendering myself unfit for it!

Momo has written me[1] of your contribution of nine thousand dollars toward wiping out last years deficit. I do not know how to express my admiration of this kind of thing on your part and on his. I know you too well to be surprised, and yet every act of this kind on your part seems to strike me afresh, with a new delight, and a new access of affection. How delightful it is that we should be a group of friends who are working heart and soul for the University which has in it the making of the best and most distinguished institution of its kind in the world: that we should believe in each other, and should feel the same enthusiasm for the same ideals. I have indeed fallen upon a happy fortune to be the leader in such an enterprise, so backed and so conducted!

The summer has brought to maturity the plans for the University which have for years been in the back of my head but which never before got room enough to take their full growth.[2] I feel richer for the summer, not only in health but also in thought and in ability to be of service. A year such as I have planned next year to be ought to set all sorts of processes in order, and that without undue strain on me.

I have learned to love Rydal like another home. I have not stirred from this enchanting region once since the tenth of July, except to go to Edinburgh to see the doctors and get our new Professor of Psychology, Norman Smith, a fellow I feel sure everybody will like. The new man in Physics, Richardson, came here to see me. Our Faculty will be more interesting than ever before this winter.

My daughters are off on a visit to Sir William Mather's[3] in Scotland, where he has taken a place for the summer. I have been so careful of myself that I would not go. I should like to come to this place of healing every summer if I could afford the ocean passage so often!

I have written Momo about an item or two of business about which he will no doubt speak to you, so that I need not repeat here what I said to him.

Mrs. Wilson joins me in warmest regards to you all, and I am, as always,   Your devoted friend,   Woodrow Wilson

WWTLS (WC, NjP).
   [1] Pyne's letter is missing.
   [2] He was referring to his plan, soon to be presented to the Princeton trustees, to divide the university into residential colleges. See his Supplementary Report to the Board of Trustees printed at Dec. 13, 1906.
   [3] For a re-identification of Sir William Mather, see H. I. Triggs to WW, Oct. 26, 1906, n. 2.

A News Report

[Oct. 2, 1906]

WOODROW WILSON'S STAND

Refuses to be a Candidate for Senate from New Jersey.

For a week past the name of Dr. Woodrow Wilson, president of Princeton University, has been mentioned as the one on which the Cleveland Democrats of New Jersey would unite as their candidate for the United States Senate.[1] Dr. Wilson, who is now abroad, was asked yesterday by the *Evening Post* to cable his position. The telegram sent to him was:

"Your name is being used as a candidate for United States Senator from New Jersey. Did you authorize this?"

President Wilson's reply, sent from Ambleside, England, was received to-day. It reads:

"Did not authorize use of my name. Very much complimented that I should be thought of for Senate, but could not leave my work at Princeton."[2]

While Dr. Wilson is thus eliminated as a candidate, the Democrats will continue their quest for a man whose candidacy will appeal to all the citizens of the State. Now that the danger of political manipulation is fully appreciated by those in charge, it is believed that the right man will be found—one whose candidacy will be authorized, and whose record and personality will be such as to commend him to the independent voters.

Opposition within the Republican party, to the reelection of United States Senator Dryden[3] is being taken advantage of by New Jersey Democrats of the better class. They are casting about for a candidate on whom the anti-Dryden men can unite. In effect, a popular vote for Senator is planned, for the intention is to announce to the voters of the State, irrespective of party, that the election of the assemblymen and senators named on the Democratic ticket means the election of a first-class Democrat to succeed the Prudential president. There have been many consultations by those concerned in the movement, and there are strong hopes expressed that it will take shape and become formidable.

This plan is to leave no doubt to the issue by naming the candidate for Senator, and drawing attention to his fitness to represent the State in place of the present corporation Senator, against whom a large part of his own party is now in revolt.

Printed in the New York *Evening Post*, Oct. 2, 1906; one editorial heading omitted.

[1] The introduction of Wilson's name into Democratic discussions about the senatorship came at the instigation of George Harvey through his friend, James Smith, Jr., of Newark, former United States Senator, Democratic leader of Essex County, and owner of the *Newark Advertiser*. In fact, the *Newark Advertiser* had promoted Wilson's candidacy as early as September 6, 1906, when it printed a long dispatch from its Trenton correspondent saying that Cleveland Democrats in the state might unite behind Wilson's candidacy. If, as seemed likely, the Republicans controlled the legislature when it convened in January 1907, the senatorial nomination of Wilson by the Democratic minority would of course have been only honorific. However, Harvey saw it as an opportunity to give Wilson national political exposure and as a first step in grooming Wilson for the Democratic presidential nomination in 1912. See Willis Fletcher Johnson, *George Harvey, 'A Passionate Patriot'* (Boston and New York, 1929), pp. 123-25, and William O. Inglis, "Helping to Make a President," *Collier's Weekly*, LVIII (Oct. 7, 1916), 15. Subsequent documents and notes will disclose the outcome of this matter.

[2] There is an undated WWhw draft of this cablegram in WP, DLC.

[3] John Fairfield Dryden of Newark, United States Senator since 1902. He was also the founder and President of the Prudential Insurance Company of America, one of the companies investigated by the special committee of the New York legislature headed by Charles Evans Hughes in 1905.

To Frederic Yates

My dear Yates,   S.S. *Caledonia* [Glasgow]   6 Oct. 1906.

We are on board well and happy—except that we are leaving dear friends; the ship is steaming out of harbour, and we are actually homeward bound. All join me in the most affectionate messages to you all. God bless you.

Faithfully   Woodrow Wilson

ALS (F. Yates Coll., NjP).

From George Ballantine and Son

Dear Sir,   Glasgow, 13 October 1906

We have now the pleasure to hand you B/L[1] and copy invoice (for Customs purposes) of one case Glen Grant, Finest Old Scotch Whisky, shipped in accordance with your instructions per SS "Astoria["] from Glasgow to New York, under through bond to Newark, N. J.

We trust this will arrive safely and give you satisfaction as regards quality.

We enclose address of our agent in New York for our G.G. Brand, Finest Old Scotch Whisky.

We think this would give you every satisfaction and you could draw your supplies from stock there and save heavy freight on small shipments.

We are, Dear Sir,

Yours faithfully,   Geo. Ballantine & Son

TLS (WP, DLC). Enc.: invoice dated Oct. 13, 1906 (WP, DLC).
[1] That is, bill of lading.

A Report of a Statement

[Oct. 15, 1906]

WOODROW WILSON'S POSITION.

Again Repudiates Senate Candidacy—
Essex Democrats, However, Stick to Him

Woodrow Wilson, president of Princeton University, returned yesterday on the Caledonia, from his summer trip abroad. He had this to say of the persistence of a certain element of the New Jersey Democrats in holding to him as a candidate for the United States Senate, notwithstanding his cabled denial that he was in any sense in the field:

"The mention of my name was without any authority from me, and was a great surprise. Although I am an old-line Democrat, and would do any service to restore the party to power, I cannot see that it would be any help for me to accept such an offer. I do not know anything more about it than was cabled. My duty is to Princeton, and I should be reluctant to give up my work there."

The eleven Essex County, New Jersey, Democratic candidates for the Assembly met Saturday night in Newark, and adopted the following resolution:

We, the Democratic candidates for General Assembly of Essex County, unanimously pledge ourselves that, in the event of our election, our choice for United States senator from the State of New Jersey will be Dr. Woodrow Wilson, president of Princeton University.

We take this action without any reservation, believing that in Dr. Wilson the State of New Jersey will have a senator who will bring to the Senate the purity of purpose and the high intellectual powers which will add honor and prestige not only to New Jersey but to the entire nation.

We believe that Dr. Wilson will obey the voice of his party and, as a loyal Democrat, truthfully serve his country and his party in the highest legislative body in our nation.

This resolution is in line with the report that the Democrats would pledge themselves to some well-known man, who was certain to refuse, then, after getting Republican votes on the strength of the pledge, vote for ex-Senator James Smith, jr.

Printed in the New York *Evening Post*, Oct. 15, 1906.

From Cleveland Hoadley Dodge

Dear Mr President   New York. Oct. 15th 1906

Welcome home! Your delightful letter rejoiced my heart & the good news of your improved health made all our hearts very happy.

We are awfully glad to have you back & are going to save you all we can & see that you take care of Princeton's most valuable asset.

Looking forward to seeing you very soon

Yrs faithfully   C H Dodge

ALS (WP, DLC).

From William Milligan Sloane, with Enclosure

My dear Wilson   [Princeton, N.J.]   Oct. 15, 1906

You are welcome home, all the more so as I hear you bring great store of health and vigour. Inasmuch as the trustees meet this week I send you this communication written for Mrs. Swann's[1] executors by Bayard Stockton notifying the university of the bequest and its probable amount. Since the inventory was made for the surrogate some of the securities have risen in value and my personal, unofficial opinion given to you for your own use, only, is that after the legacies of about $100000 are paid the residuary estate will be nearer $275000.

Yours ever   Sloane.

1 Josephine Ward Thomson Swann, about whom see EAW to WW, Aug. 28, 1902, n. 1, Vol. 14. She had died in Washington, D. C., on March 2, 1906. Her will provided that Princeton University should be the residuary legatee of her estate, the proceeds to be used to construct "upon the grounds of the said University" a residence for graduate students to be named "The John R. Thomson Graduate College of Princeton University" in memory of her first husband, John Renshaw Thomson, United States Senator from New Jersey from 1853 until his death in 1862. Thomson had attended Princeton briefly as a member of the Class of 1817.

ENCLOSURE

William Milligan Sloane, Bayard Stockton, and Francis Larkin, Jr., to the Board of Trustees of Princeton University

Princeton, N. J.   Oct. 15, 1906.

The late Mrs Josephine A. Thomson Swann, being much interested in the plan of a Graduate College as outlined by Professor A. F. West, in her will left her residuary estate to you for the promotion of this purpose. We send herewith a copy of her Will.

This bequest will, so far as we can now see, amount to $250,-000—and her executors expect to be ready to turn it over to your body shortly after January first next.

Respectfully yours   William M. Sloane
Bayard Stockton
Francis Larkin Jr.   Exrs

ALS (WWP, UA, NjP).

Harold Griffith Murray to Cleveland Hoadley Dodge

Sir: [New York] Oct. 17th, 1906.

The following is a report of the Committee of Fifty to date:

At the meeting of the Committee held in Princeton, June 11th, 1906, I reported that at that time for the fiscal year ending July 31st, 1906, pledges aggregating in the total of $102,000. had been secured. I have now to report that at the end of the fiscal year the total amount of the pledges secured and *paid in*, with interest from the moneys collected or paid in under the endowment form, amounted to $126,917.25 and an even $500,000. secured in the endowment form. Of this latter sum $185,000. has been paid in. For the present fiscal year ending July 31st, 1907, pledges aggregating $104,708. have been secured. This is inclusive of interest on the sums pledged to endowment. At the June meeting the amount pledged for this year amounted to $79,688.

ALUMNI DORMITORY.

The plan for erecting a dormitory to the South of Patton Hall and east of Brokaw Field by various classes under the same plan as that pursued in the erection of Patton Hall, has made some progress since the June meeting. It was them [then] hoped that at this meeting the exact number of classes willing to go into this scheme would be known. The summer months, however, delayed the various classes who had the matter under advisement in reaching a conclusion, and at the present, the following classes are the only ones who have definitely agreed to erect entries. [blank]

The following classes have the matter before them for consideration, and it is hoped they will reach a satisfactory and definite conclusion in the near future.—76, 77, 80, 81, 84, 87, 02, 03, 04, 05, 06[1]

Neither time nor trouble has been spared by me in endeavoring to bring these latter classes to a determination, but more time has been asked for consideration, and it does not seem probable at present that we shall know definitely just what classes will enter into the agreement before the middle of winter.

The Trustees of the Alumni Fund have agreed to devote their principal sum, some $35,000., to this dormitory. The money received through this channel will be sufficient to erect two entries, so that at present, we can count on four entries as definitely contracted for.

THE PRESS BUREAU.

Arrangements have been concluded with the managers of The Alumni Weekly, through which there will be published hereafter three times in each academic year a short but complete review of all important matters pertaining to the University since the previous issue. The numbers of The Weekly containing these reviews will be sent to every alumnus of Princeton. The dates of publication will be the second issue in the fall, the first issue after the Christmas holidays, and the first Saturday in May. Through the general distribution of these numbers of The Weekly, the Alumni will be kept thoroughly informed of all matters of special interest relating to the University. Professor John G. Hibben, '82, has kindly consented to act as editor. The first issue of this review has already made its appearance in The Weekly under date of October 6th.

I would suggest that each one of these special issues of The Weekly contain a condensed but comprehensive review of some

---

[1] The figures are in Wilson's handwriting.

department of the University written by its head, so that gradually the Alumni may be put in touch with and thoroughly understand each department, its aims, and methods. During the past
year eight articles written by graduates of Princeton University
appeared in the Newark Evening News. By the courtesy of that
paper, they have been republished in booklet form[2] by the Committee of Fifty, and are being distributed free to the Alumni and
friends of the University. Some 700 of these booklets have already been sent to libraries of the principal preparatory schools
throughout the United States, and to the libraries of the leading
universities in this country and abroad. The contents of the booklet consist of "Historic Princeton," "Royal Charters of Princeton,"
"The Plans, Corriculum [Curriculum]," "The Preceptorial System," "The Honor System," "The Graduates School," "Undergraduate Life, Freshman and Sophomore," "Undergraduate Life,
Junior and Senior Years."

The Press Bureau has been thoroughly organized and is already in operation. Special thanks are due to Mr. Ivy Lee of the
Class of '98 for his material help and advice in carrying this
plan through to a successful termination. We are now sending
weekly to some 1200 newspapers throughout the United States
short articles descriptive of the University, its life and aims.
These articles are dignified in tone and can only reflect credit
on the University. I am endeavoring to make these articles of a
suggestive nature with the hopes that various editors might make
editorial comment. Through the effort of Mr. Luther Price, '88,
(correspondent for the London Tribune, London, England) our
press notices and other literature are sent to the English papers.
Descriptions of the Preceptorial System have already made their
appearance in papers published in Constantinople, Syria, Tan-
giers, and Africa. Illustrated articles of some length are being
prepared for Sunday Supplements of the daily papers, and it is
hoped the first of the series will appear in the Spring.

In addition to this work, the Secretary has endeavored to answer any strictures on Princeton which have appeared in print,
and which have been brought to his attention.

THE ALUMNI FUND

At the last meeting, I reported to the Committee that Mr.
[John Conover] Ten Eyck, '75, Secretary of the Alumni Fund,
and Mr. T. F. Humphrey, '94, Manager, had expressed a desire
to meet our wishes and were willing to have their fund absorbed

---

[2] *Princeton University: Some Characteristic Features* (n. p. 1906).

by the Committee of Fifty Fund. After the meeting held in Princeton, Mr. Ten Eyck agreed to supply me with a list of the subscribers of the Alumni Fund and to use his efforts to induce them to transfer their subscriptions to our Committee. In July Mr. Ten Eyck rescinded his decision, and I have therefore been unable to make any great progress toward the absorption of this fund.

PLAN FOR REORGANIZATION.

At the June meeting it was unanimously voted that at the next meeting the Chairman present a plan of reorganization and suggest a policy to be pursued in the future. As a result of my experience during the last six months as Secretary, I should like to submit to you for your consideration the following:

The Committee has been in existence for nearly two years. This period has been of sufficient length for us to ascertain what members of the Committee can be of material assistance to us in our work and those who through stress of personal affairs, or lack of interest are not. There are members of the Committee who have not attended a meeting during the past year nor contributed to the fund, nor answered the letters of the secretary. It would seem advisable, therefore, to elect men to the committee, in place of the latter[,] who can give active assistance to us in our work. An over ruling majority of the present members of the Committee were graduated prior to 1890. When it is taken into consideration that over one-half of the Alumni of the University were graduated since 1895, it does not appear as if the younger half of the Alumni were fairly represented on the Committee, and if we hope to have the classes more recently graduated as loyal and intelligent supporters of the University as the older ones soon after graduation, I think it would be advisable to educate them in the needs of the University at the earliest possible date. With rare exceptions, I have found that the more closely in touch with Princeton a graduate is, the more readily he gives.

The Alumni of Princeton respond most readily I find to the call of the Class Secretary. It is but natural that this should be so as classmate can write to classmate more intimately than it is possible for one not a member of the Class. Knowing the men individually, their financial condition, their personality, it is much easier for a popular member of a Class to raise money than anyone else, and I would suggest that in the reorganization of this Committee, representatives of each class from 1870 to 1906, inclusive, be appointed, and that as each succeeding Class is graduated a representative be appointed from it.

If this plan meets with the approval of the Committee, the term of appointment should be limited to one year, so that if the appointed did not prove worthy, he could soon be dropped. If the Trustees or President of the University would make the appointments they would undoubtedly be considered a great honor, and would prove an extra incentive to good work.

The man selected should be, where he has proved his value, the Class Secretary. Where the man appointed is not the Class Secretary it is quite possible he might be selected for this office by his Class when he proves his fitness to fill the position. By this method it would be easy for this Committee to amalgamate with the Class Officers Association, which is to-day a confessed failure. By this method of organization we should have on the Committee a man from each Class thoroughly in touch with the work of the Committee, with the conditions of his class, its ability to give money, and with the wishes of the Trustees.

Geographical representative [representation] is undoubtedly desirable, but it is not so important to the work, as Class representation and as several of the efficient Class Secretaries are in other centers than New York and Philadelphia, we would, if this scheme is adopted, have, to a certain extent, geographical representation.

In addition to the advantages already given I believe one of even greater importance is having in close touch with the Trustees a representative man from each class who can answer for the ability of the individual members of his class. Princeton has for many years depended upon a very few men to manage the affairs of the University, with the result that to-day we have men serving on various Committees, many of which are organized to carry on work with which they are unfamiliar. In the future, for example should the University desire to form a Committee to look after matters pertaining to the Library, it would be an easy matter to ask each member of the Committee of Fifty to send to the President of the University the name or names of those in his Class whom he deems best fitted to serve on the Committee.

In suggesting this plan, it is not my idea to have the Class representative do the work of soliciting now being done by me, but to give assistance in cases of men living in small centers who cannot be reached through personal solicitation, or who are abroad, or who have not responded to my efforts. They would, moreover, be of very material assistance to the Secretary of the Alumni in keeping a correct list of the names and addresses of the classes.

The Alumni of Princeton has [have] in the past few years subscribed several million dollars toward the support of the University, and many of us have straightened ourselves financially to meet demands. In a circular put forth by the Committee in the Spring the statement was made that an Alumnus subscribing to the Committee of Fifty would be immune from farther solicitation so far as the University per se was concerned. Several classes at this time are, at the request of the Committee of Fifty, raising funds to erect entries in the new Dormitory. It would seem unwise to ask a class to contribute an entry and then solicit individual members of that class for funds for the Committee. Moreover I believe it is a bad financial policy, for it delays the raising of the Entry Fund. Men who are subscribing to both funds, split the amount they give. I would recommend that this Committee agree not to solicit the members of the Classes contributing entries, or other memorial gifts until the amount of their memorial fund is raised. After the Fund has been collected the Committee can then take up the work of soliciting the Class. The majority of men who give to Princeton are willing to give a certain amount each year, but do not like to be making several payments to several funds, nor to be continually solicited. If this idea is adopted, it will be only a few years before the Classes building entries will have finished their work. It might be wise to use our efforts to have each Class as it is graduated agree to erect an entry in the new dormitory by its decennial, and after that period to contribute individually to the Committee of Fifty, and thus systematize the method of giving.

Respectfully submitted, H G Murray Secretary.

TLS (Trustees' Papers, UA, NjP).

A News Report on Wilson's Return to Princeton

[Oct. 20, 1906]

President Wilson '79 returned to Princeton the first of the week, very much improved in health as a result of his summer in the English lake district, where he had a cottage at Rydal and spent three months in out-door life, tramping and rusticating in the Wordsworth country. Sailing from Glasgow on the "Caledonia" on Oct. 6th, after a rough voyage Dr. Wilson and his family reached New York on Oct. 14th.

The President's office is now in the tower of Seventy-Nine Hall, where he transacts the administrative business of the University, and receives callers between the hours of two and four on Monday, Tuesday, and Wednesday. A very handsome suite of rooms has been finished and furnished for this purpose by the President's classmates of '79, which is hereafter to be the official headquarters of the President of Princeton University.

Dr. Wilson's first out-of-town engagement of the academic year will be with the Princeton Alumni Association of Tennessee, at their annual reunion at Chattanooga on Oct. 27th.[1] During the year he will make his speaking engagements as few as possible, in order to enable him to devote his time to the administrative work of the University. He is not delivering his usual classroom lectures during the first term, this course being conducted entirely under the Preceptorial System. Next term, however, he will continue his class-room work as usual.

Printed in the *Princeton Alumni Weekly*, vii (Oct. 20, 1906), 63.
[1] A news report of Wilson's address to the Tennessee alumni is printed at Oct. 28, 1906.

A News Item

[Oct. 20, 1906]

Dr. Andrew Fleming West, Dean of the Graduate School, has been formally invited to accept the presidency of the Massachusetts Institute of Technology, as the successor of Dr. [Henry Smith] Pritchett. Dean West issued the following signed statement on Wednesday evening:

"The announcement made to-day from Boston that the Executive Committee of the Massachusetts Institute of Technology has invited me to accept the presidency of that institution is correct. I am not prepared to make any further statement at present.

(Signed)   Andrew F. West."

Printed in the *Princeton Press*, Oct. 20, 1906.

The Curriculum Committee to the Board of Trustees of Princeton University[1]

Gentlemen of the Board: Princeton, October 20, 1906.

Your Committee on Curriculum recommend to you for action the following new appointments, the salary in each case having already received approval from the Finance Committee:

Howard McClenahan of Princeton, to be Professor of Physics at a salary already determined

Augustus Trowbridge of Wisconsin (Ph.D. Berlin) to be Professor of Physics at a salary of $2,000.

Owen Williams [Willans] Richardson of Cambridge (D.Sc. Univ. of London) to be Professor of Physics at a salary of $3,500.

Norman Smith, of Glasgow, to be Stuart Professor of Psychology at a salary of $4,000.

H. Lester Cooke, of McGill (M.A. Cambridge) to be Assistant Professor of Phsyics [Physics] at a salary of $1,500.

Philip Ely Robinson, of Princeton (Ph.D. Giessen) to be Assistant Professor of Physics, at a salary of $1,500.

Edmund H. Hollands, of Cornell (Ph.D.) to be Instructor in Philosophy at a salary already determined.

Walter Lincoln Whittlesey, of Univ. Oregon, to be Instructor in History, Politics, and Economics at a salary already determined.

Walter Woodburn Hyde, of Cornell, to be Instructor in Classics at a salary already determined.

George D. Brown, of Johns Hopkins, to be Instructor in English at a salary already determined.

Maxwell Struthers Burt, of Princeton, to be Instructor in English at a salary already determined.

Charles William Kennedy, of Columbia, to be Instructor in English at a salary already determined.

Herbert Spencer Murch, of Univ. Oregon, to be Instructor in English at a salary already determined.

Sigmund Gottfried Spaeth, of Haverford (A.M.) to be Instructor in Modern Languages at a salary already determined.

Donald Clive Stuart, of Univ. Michigan, to be Instructor in Modern Languages at salary already determined.

Robert Lee Moore, of Univ. Texas, (Ph.D. Univ. Chicago) to be Instructor in Mathematics at a salary already determined.

Walter Daniel Bonner, of Nebraska Wesleyan Univ. to be Instructor in Chemistry at a salary already determined.

John Davison Rue, Jr., of Princeton, to be Instructor in Chemistry at a salary already determined.

Ralph Andrew Barry, of Princeton, to be Instructor in Civil Engineering at a salary already determined.

Elliott Chipman Brown, of Princeton, to be Instructor in Civil Engineering at a salary already determined.

Lynden Brown Shoemaker, of Princeton, to be Instructor in Civil Engineering at a salary already determined.

Respectfully submitted,   Melancthon W Jacobus
Chairman.[2]

TRS (Trustees' Papers, UA, NjP).
1 There is a WWhw outline of this report, dated Oct. 19, 1906, in WWP, UA, NjP.
2 The trustees approved these recommendations at their meeting on Oct. 20, 1906.

Henry Burchard Fine to the Board of Trustees' Committee on Morals and Discipline

Gentlemen: PRINCETON UNIVERSITY, OCTOBER 20, 1906.

I beg to submit the following report:

The number of students dropped last June for deficiencies in scholarship was 46 as against 57 in June, 1905. Of these dropped students 6 were Juniors, 15 were Sophomores, 20 were Freshmen and 5 were Special Students. Of the 41 who were regular students, 13 were A.B. men, 12 were C.E. men and 15 either B.S. or Litt.B. men.

Four students were suspended this fall because of intoxication at Commencement time when one of them was a Junior, and the remaining three Freshmen. Three Seniors were suspended for intoxication in connection with the "Senior Parade," which occurred on October 13th. I have no other cases of discipline to report.

The total number of new students is 358 as against 427 last year. The following table indicates the number of Freshmen candidates for each of the degrees—A.B., B.S. & Litt.B., and C.E. For purposes of comparison the corresponding figures for last year are also given:

	1906	1905
Freshmen A.B.	138	188
B.S. & Litt.B.	92	109
C.E.	95	92
Total	325	389
Specials & Upperclassmen	33	38
Grand Total	358	427

It should be added that practically all of the 33 students entering this year who are classified above as Specials and Upperclassmen are men who have been admitted from other colleges. Most of them have been given provisional enrolment as Specials in accordance with our new regulations, but are in reality candidates for one of our degrees.

There is a noticeable falling off in the Freshman class as compared with last year, but the mere fact that 422 men took preliminary examinations this year as against 360 last year is enough to indicate that this falling off in the number of candidates for admission is likely to be only temporary. The high quality of preparation shown by the present Freshmen in their entrance examinations would also seem to indicate that the loss this year is merely in the number of students of inferior preparation who just contrive to do enough to meet our entrance requirements but are not really equal to doing the work required of them here. Of the present Freshmen 42% were admitted without any conditions whatsoever and 65% with either no condition or but one condition.

Of the entering students 39% are Presbyterians and 28% Episcopalians. There are 22 Congregationalists, 20 Methodists, 15 Baptists, 14 Catholics, 10 Dutch Reformed, 8 Jews, 5 Lutherans, 5 Unitarians, 2 Quakers, 1 Christian, 1 Evangelical, 1 Universalist, and 14 enroll themselves as belonging to no denomination. About one-half of the entering Presbyterian and Episcopalian students are communicants, and about one-third of those belonging to other evangelical denominations.

The average age of the Freshman class at entrance is eighteen years and two months.

Respectfully submitted,   H. B. Fine

TRS (Trustees' Papers, UA, NjP).

A Resolution

[c. Oct. 20, 1906]

Resolved: That the Board learns with the utmost concern of the possibility that Professor Andrew F. West may accept a call which would take him away from Princeton. The Board would consider his loss quite irreparable. By his scholarship, by his ideals, by his fertility in constructive ideas, he has made himself one of the chief ornaments and one of the most indispensable counsellors of the place. The Board has particularly counted upon him to put into operation the Graduate College which he conceived and for which it has planned. It begs to assure him that he cannot be spared and that the Board trusts that, should he remain, its hopes and his may be the sooner realized because of this additional proof of his devotion.[1]

WWhw and WWT MS (Trustees' Papers, UA, NjP).

[1] This resolution was adopted and spread on the minutes of the Board of Trustees of Oct. 20, 1906.

Resolved: That the Board learns with the utmost Concern of the possibility that Professor Andrew F. West may accept a call which would take him away from Princeton.

The Board would consider his loss quite irreparable. By his scholarship, by his ideals, by his fertility in con-structive ideas, he has made himself one of the chief orna-ments and one of the most indispensable counsellors of the place. The Board has particularly counted upon him to put into operation the Graduate *College* ~~School~~ which he conceived and for which it has planned. It begs to assure him that he cannot be spared and that the Board trusts that, should he remain, its hopes and his may be the sooner realized be-cause of this *additional* ~~addition~~ proof of his devotion.

Wilson's draft of his resolution concerning West

From the Minutes of the Board of Trustees of Princeton University

[Oct. 20, 1906]

The Trustees of Princeton University met in stated session in the Trustees' Room in the Chancellor Green Library, Princeton, New Jersey, at eleven o'clock on Saturday morning, October 20, 1906.

The President of the University in the chair. . . .

PRINCETON UNIVERSITY
DECLARED A NON-SECTARIAN INSTITUTION

On motion of Mr. Cuyler duly seconded the following preamble and resolutions were adopted:

> WHEREAS by the terms of the Act of Incorporation of The Carnegie Foundation For The Advancement of Teaching, sectarian institutions are excluded from the benefits of the Foundation and

WHEREAS Princeton University is a non-sectarian institution therefore be it

RESOLVED, that we the Trustees of Princeton University hereby formally declare that no denominational test is imposed in the choice of trustees, officers or teachers, or in the admission of students, nor are distinctly denominational tenets or doctrines taught to the students, and be it further

RESOLVED, that the Secretary of the Board be directed to send a copy of these resolutions, properly attested, to the President of the Carnegie Foundation For The Advancement of Teaching.

To Charles Freeman Williams McClure

My dear Mr. McClure: Princeton, N. J.   October 21st, 1906.

I shall be at home this week until Wednesday noon, when I shall be obliged to go away for about a week. If it is not postponing the interview too long, perhaps you could arrange with Professor Calkins to see me on Thursday, Friday or Saturday of next week. I sincerely hope he is thinking favorably of our calling.[1]
Always faithfully yours,   Woodrow Wilson

TLS (McClure Zoological Autograph Coll., NjP).
[1] Calkins decided to remain at Columbia.

To Frederic Yates and Emily Chapman Martin Yates

Our dear, dear Friends,   Princeton, N. J.   22 October, 1906.

Forgive us for having let a whole week go by before telling you of our arrival home,—but if you could know what has been happening to us! Such another breathless week I never had in my life! The Board of Trustees of the University met on Saturday, less than a week after we set foot upon land, and a whole year's body of business and of complications large and small crowded in to those six days. I have hardly got my breath yet. I shall have to loaf for the better part of a week to get back my Rydal calm.

We did not have a comfortable voyage. Gale succeeded gale; the decks were wet; mist and rain penetrated our marrows; there were but two days of generous sunshine; all of us but Jessie were sick at the outset, and that destroys one's self-respect for the whole voyage; so that New York seemed to us very beautiful on the quiet Sunday morning as we steamed to our wharf. We left Stockton Axson to deal with the customs officials and hurried to dear Princeton, where loving friends greeted us and we were happy. How like a truant I felt, and how delightfully glad every-one seemed to see us again!

This morning came two delightful letters from you,[1] that made our hearts glow, and our thoughts rush back to Rydal. You may be sure they had never lost consciousness of you. What a happy, happy thing our meeting and our summer-long companionship was! I am sure that it has made us all richer in love and in happiness. Strange longings stir in us now as we turn over our photographs of the dear Lake country. It seems like another home, where hearts wait for us.

How pleased we are over the success of the little exhibition. I could not but feel a little immodest as I read the list of pictures,—so many Wilsons standing up to be looked at! But we did not stand up to be looked at ourselves, but only to exhibit the genius of the dear artist. By the way, please send the landscapes[2] in their frames and a receipted bill (if you can trust me!) for the frames. With the duty added they will cost less than like frames would cost here. And would you send also a statement that the drawings[3] are presents! Such generosity I never heard of before, or such a delightful way of exercising it.

There is nothing to tell of ourselves. Jessie is in Baltimore,[4] Nellie is in Raleigh:[5] only dear Margaret is left us. We are well and happy; and mean, now that that hectic week is over, to rest.

All join me in dearest love to you all.

Your affectionate friend,   Woodrow Wilson

WWTLS (F. Yates Coll., NjP).
  [1] They are missing.
  [2] These were two landscapes, "Morning" and "Evening," purchased by Wilson for £30 apparently for Junius Spencer Morgan. There is a handwritten receipted bill, dated October 1, 1906, and signed by Yates, in WP, DLC.
  [3] Pastels of Wilson and Mrs. Wilson. They are reproduced in the photographic section of this volume.
  [4] At the Woman's College of Baltimore (now Goucher College), where she was a junior.
  [5] At St. Mary's School, an Episcopal boarding school and junior college for girls in Raleigh, N. C., where she was a freshman in the college department.

To Henry Edward Rood[1]

My dear Mr. Rood: Princeton, N. J.   October 24th, 1906.

It gives me sincere pleasure to comply with the request contained in your letter of yesterday.[2] I have the warmest feeling for Mr. Alden, and I should be pleased to add anything that might increase his pleasure at the celebration you are planning.

Sincerely yours,   Woodrow Wilson

TLS (Alfred W. Anthony Coll., NN).

1 Assistant Editor of *Harper's Magazine.*
2 Rood's letter is missing. He had asked Wilson to write a letter to Henry Mills Alden congratulating Alden on his seventieth birthday, and to attend a dinner in his honor on that occasion in New York on November 10, 1906. Wilson's letter is printed as the following document. He also attended the dinner and sat at the head table with, among others, the guest of honor and the host, Colonel Harvey. An account of the affair, with photographs, is printed in *Harper's Weekly,* L (Dec. 15, 1906), 1810-40.

To Henry Mills Alden

My dear Mr. Alden,   Princeton, N. J., October 24, 1906.

I hope that on your seventieth birthday you will think of your life with as much pleasure as your friends feel in looking back upon it. I hope that you will realize, as they do, its efficiency, its completeness, its gracious influence upon those who have come into direct contact with it, its elevating influence upon those whom it has touched silently and indirectly the world over throughout an entire generation. My own association with you has brought me only pleasure, profit, and stimulation, and with all my heart I wish you many, many more years in which to enjoy the satisfaction of a well-spent life.

Always cordially and faithfully yours,

Woodrow Wilson.

Printed in *Harper's Weekly,* L (Dec. 15, 1906), 1814.

From John Cawley[1]

My Dear Doctor Wilson   Newark, N. J.   Oct 25th/06

Since I landed I learned that your name has been prominently before the public in connection with the *United States Senatorship for N. J.*

Feeling as I do that your present field of usefulness is almost unlimited it seems almost a pity you should be called upon to consider the relatively small honor of U. S. Senatorship and yet—but it is an awfully *big* yet—it seems a much greater pity that a man of your proportions should not push out of the way men such as our present senatorial representatives. It means sacrifice, of course, but some sacrifices are worth while. As one of your fortunate shipmates I think I may say "as one speaking with authority" that if your election depended on the votes of your shipmates you would win "hands down."

Faithfully yours   John Cawley

ALS (WP, DLC).
1 Vice President of Cawley, Clark and Co., paint manufacturers of Newark.

From Henry Inigo Triggs[1]

Dear Sir,   London W.   October 26th 1906.
Proposed Sundial   Princeton Univ:[2]

I am sending herewith the foundation plan of the Sundial[.] You will see that I have made the foundations in 3 circular rings varying in depth according to the weight they will have to sustain. The reason that they are circular is that it is impossible just at present to fix the position of the sundial in relation to the points of the compass and as the plan is octagonal it can fit anywhere on the circle.

We have not yet received permission from Corpus Christi Coll: but I hope to be able to cable you almost as soon as you receive this drawing which is sent forward in order that there may be no delay. I presume you will not start before we have this permission[3]
                    Yours very faithfully   H. Inigo Triggs

ALS (WWP, UA, NjP).
[1] British architect and designer of gardens, author of several books on these subjects.
[2] The sundial was to be a gift to Princeton University from Sir William Mather, British industrialist and M.P., 1885-86, 1889-95, and 1900-1904, who had received an honorary LL.D. from Princeton in June 1905.
Mather himself explained the origin of the project in his letter of presentation to Wilson of July 4, 1907 (printed as an Enclosure with W. Mather to WW, Aug. 22, 1907, Vol. 17): "In wandering around the lovely grounds of Princeton, and reading in its buildings its history, commencing with the foundation of the College in British Colonial days, from simple 'Old Nassau' to the most recent splendid architectural erections; and further in reading the terms of the Royal Charter which conferred on Princeton the rank of Oxford as to its degree and purpose as a classical University, I conceived the idea of sending over from England on my return some object that should symbolise the connection not only between Oxford and Princeton, but between Great Britain and America. Under the guidance of the eminent architect Mr. Inigo Triggs, I found the famous Turnbull Sun-dial in the quadrangle of Corpus Christi College, Oxford."
The sundial at Corpus Christi was constructed in 1581 by Charles Turnbull, a mathematician at the college.
It seems highly likely that Wilson discussed this project with Mather during his stay in England. Mather's letter to Wilson of December 3, 1906, intimates that this was true, although it does not say so explicitly.
[3] The President and Fellows of Corpus Christi College gave permission for the replica to be made soon after Triggs's letter was written, as Mather's telegram to Wilson of November 19, 1906, indicates. Subsequent documents in this and the following volume will detail the construction of the sundial and its erection and dedication at Princeton.

From Ernest Cushing Richardson, with Enclosure

My dear President Wilson: Princeton, N. J.   Oct. 27, 1906.

I had a talk with Mr. Pyne about the question of utilizing Mr. [George Allison] Armour's services; enclosed is copy of my report to him attempting to meet your wish that it should be something real. The proposed solution only occurred to me after Mr. Pyne had left the problem with me to think over but it embodies the result of a lot of thinking and observation which I had hoped at sometime to go over with you, when the time should be ripe, and the more I think of it the more it seems to me that this particular opportunity might serve to focus the involved matters most admirably if it, or any variations of it, proved sympathetic to your plans.   Yours very sincerely,   E. C. Richardson, Libr.

TLS (WWP, UA, NjP).

Ernest Cushing Richardson to Moses Taylor Pyne

Dear Mr. Pyne: Princeton, N. J., Oct. 27, 1906.

The problem suggested by President Wilson and yourself is, I understand, to utilize Mr. Armour's services in such a way as to give dignity enough to satisfy him and sufficient real service to justify the dignity. I greatly covet unutilized service but very strongly believe in President Wilson's well known view against the titles of honor without service. I have been frank to express to you the difficulty of using men who are in a position to be so independent as Mr. [Junius Spencer] Morgan and Mr. Armour but this trouble ceases when service is clearly understood to be real.

Within the limit of present organization I only see two possible suggestions, (1) keeper of classical books and (2) keeper of seminary and department libraries.

I have some doubt whether either of these would appeal sufficiently to Mr. Armour. There is a way, however, by which through a little expansion of organization the situation could be well met and two or three excellent points gained for university organization with no necessary increase in expense, present or prospective, save as resources for development might be developed by Mr. Armour in his office.

The organization of all the libraries and museums of a university in one is a matter that has been a good deal talked of and written about and approached in practice in recent years. We have here, as you know, gradually and quietly, one after another, gathered all department and seminary libraries into a federate organization. The idea of the unification of all the libraries and museums of an institution (the apparatus of research) is now riper than the unification of the libraries of a university was fifteen years ago. I suggest, therefore, the creation of a Department of research and publication which shall be, at present, if you like, simply the library, the seminary libraries, the department libraries and our small publication plant, but which may conceivably, with the good will of the respective departments, gradually absorb the general administration of the common interests of museums and of which I shall be director (excuse the lack of modesty), Mr. Armour vice-director, and Mr. Morgan librarian, re-emphasizing the fact that within this domain I have the same character of authority as regards all that the President has towards professors and librarians however wealthy or poor. While the plan does not necessitate any extension beyond the three classes of libraries and the amount of publication now carried on by the library and need not even be extended to museums, I could, if the President thought well of it, gradually develop an organization, stimulation, and guidance of research work which should be of a good deal of assistance to the dean of the graduate school and might, with the right instrumentalities, develop a movement of some distinction for us, now that research has come to be recognized as one of our defined functions. I think that Mr. Armour . . . might likely be made as valuable in this work as Mr. Morgan and Mr. McAlpin have proved themselves to be in their line. And if university sentiment should ripen rapidly towards the united organization of libraries and museums I think his services might be made invaluable in the developing of the proper housing and disposition of our collections.[1] I am sending a copy of this to President Wilson and hope that your joint request will be enough apology for any lack of modesty that may seem to lie in a proposition which might involve creating me director of research and publication. I assure you that I would cordially accept an order which put some one else into that position if he better suited President Wilson's judgment and plans.

Very sincerely yours,   [E. C. Richardson]

CCL (WWP, UA, NjP).

[1] For reasons unknown to the Editors, nothing was done about this proposal, and Armour never held a position in the library or elsewhere in the university administration.

Two News Reports of Addresses in Chattanooga, Tennessee

[Oct. 27, 1906]

MANY MEET DR. WILSON

Mountain City Club Entertains Princeton's President.

The Mountain City club royally entertained those members of the Tennessee Princeton Alumni association and their guest,

President Woodrow Wilson, last night with a reception in their elegant club house and with a generous luncheon. Fully one hundred representative gentlemen, including citizens of the city, visiting Princeton men, members of the club and officers from Fort Oglethorpe, were present to do honor to Princeton's chief executive, and in doing which they were delightfully entertained.

After an hour spent in pleasant conversation, introductions and greetings, President Wilson was asked by Mr. Herbert Bushnell, president of the club, for a talk on some live question of the day, and to which Dr. Wilson responded very happily and to the delight and pleasure of his listeners. He chose for the subject, "Americanism and What It Means," and treated it in most unique and characteristically vigorous manner. President Wilson is one of the really wonderful public talkers of his day and possesses the gift to a remarkable degree of first understanding what he is to talk about; how he is to talk and exactly how to say what he is going to say in logical and clear fashion so that when he finishes his hearers have absorbed the ideas he conveys and are thoroughly impressed by the force of his conclusions. It would be impossible in a few paragraphs to give even a satisfactory synopsis of his address, but the central idea was that what Americanism should mean is the abandonment of theoretical reforms and the adoption of practical, common sense, business methods in dealing with all those public questions now so heroically decried by a certain class of public persons [as] being evils and which the dreamers and theorists foolishly conceive may be cured by certain classes of legislation. We cannot be said to legislate morals or right principles into men, and the thing to do is to apply to each abuse the test of common sense and make as near impossible in the future the creation of such abuses. For instance: the trouble with the trusts, and the socalled criminal corporations, was not so much the combination of capital to engage in a certain business, but the over-capitalization, the watering of securities, the losses of which as well as the profits on which must be borne by the people. The simple remedy he said was to pass laws prohibiting over-capitalization—"a proposition so effectual and simple," he observed, "that it is strange our friends the politicians have never thought of it,"—a bit of artistic sarcasm everybody present thoroughly enjoyed.

The inelasticity and inaccessibility of the currency was one of the national evils of which he complained and against which he charged much of the dissatisfaction and unrest among the people. These points he explained strongly and from a standpoint that caught the attention of his auditors. He believed in the branch banks with the powerful backing of the government scattered throughout the country as one of the solvents of this problem.

The speaker closed what he had to say by a reference to the pleasure he had already had from this his first visit to Chattanooga and expressed his great pleasure at the cordiality of his reception and greeting among Chattanooga people. . . .

It was a pleasant affair, and it may be safely said that the president of Princeton university established himself at once in esteem and high regard of every Chattanooga[n] who met him.

It is the purpose of the local association to accompany President Wilson and the visitors from other states to Lookout mountain this morning leaving the Read House at 9:30 o'clock and returning at about 12:30 in a special car thoughtfully and kindly tendered by the Chattanooga Railways company.

In the afternoon leaving the Read House at 2 o'clock the party will be driven to the park in automobiles courtesly [courteously] offered by the owners of private machines in the city as a mark of respect for President Wilson and the Tennessee association of Princeton men.

Tonight, beginning at 8 o'clock, will be held the regular association banquet at which President Wilson will be the chief speaker.

Printed in the *Chattanooga Times*, Oct. 27, 1906; some editorial headings omitted.

[Oct. 28, 1906]

DR. WILSON ON IDEALS

Princeton Alumni Have a Second Annual Banquet.

"Hip, hip, hoo-rah" and many cheers for Princeton rang through the Read house last night. It was the occasion of the second annual banquet of the Princeton Alumni association of Tennessee and President Woodrow Wilson was the guest of honor. . . .

He was greeted by cheers for himself and for the university. "It is with sincere pleasure that I find myself in this company, enhanced by the presence of so many Princeton guests as well as Princeton's sons. Mr. Granberry[1] has certainly pitched the tune most delightfully for what I am about to say. I have but one speech and that one I must vary to suit different occasions. It is time for us to sing with all the powerful orchestration we can get for it the needed idealism in practical life. We have not sufficient discussion of education in this country. There is not any kind of education that the country does not need. We must not only make the material portion greater, but the spiritual portion greater. There must be education not only for particular callings, but for that spiritual training that makes real greatness.

"The use that is made of hands dies with the hands themselves, but the voice that education gives with its spirit is itself immortality. We ought not to hide our faces in books, but we should know more of the world that we live in." Dr. Wilson referred to the ideals for which our forefathers fought and declared that they should be taught and impressed into the minds of every generation. He declared that he loved the ideals for which the men of the army fought, saying that he would feel a greater pride in a brother who died at twenty in the service of his country and whose picture is left on the mantlepiece than one who had lived his life in selfishness. Mr. Wilson advised every man to get married so that he would have at least one other person to live for besides himself. He referred to the selfishness in human beings and urged that people should forget this and come to think more of the ideals, to think more of humanity and less of self. He said that when a man was married he was given new responsibilities, he was put in a harness from which he could not break at liberty and declared that without harness a man was not pulling anything but himself.

"Ought we not to become idealists because it is only the ideals that will survive? The only typical thing about this nation is its ideals. Power and wealth will not disturb America. What we need is only proof that it has not forgotten the past, the simplicity of its original faith, the responsibility of the individual." Dr. Wilson inveighed against socialism, declaring that the socialist turned his face opposite to America's first principles. He said that individualism was the hope of the nation and that organization was something that could have been devised by the devil himself. He said that learning, pure learning, is the salvation of the race, and that what the people need to do is to keep in mind the things that are pure and beautiful. "You can kill truth by forgetting it, you can serve it only by remembering it." At the end of his address Dr. Wilson was greeted with continued applause and renewed Princeton cheers.

Printed in the *Chattanooga Sunday Times*, Oct. 28, 1906; some editorial headings omitted.

1 William L. Granbery '85, who had introduced him. He is identified more fully in n. 1 to the news report printed at Nov. 29, 1905.

From Andrew Fleming West

Dear Wilson—   Princeton, N. J., October 30 1906

It has been a stiff and wearing strain—but it is over—and I need hardly tell you the relief of finding I am to stay in Princeton. A few days more of this sleepless worry and there would be nothing left of me either to send to Boston or to stay in Princeton.

I am sending you in this a copy of my declination mailed this afternoon to Boston and of a note to the Trustees of Princeton.[1]

Now for team work—DEO GRATIAS   ORA PRO NOBIS

                    Ever yours   Andrew F. West

ALS (WP, DLC).
[1] A. F. West to the Executive Committee, Massachusetts Institute of Technology, Oct. 30, 1906, TCLS (WP, DLC), and A. F. West to the President and Board of Trustees of Princeton University, Oct. 30, 1906, TCLS (WP, DLC).

Andrew Fleming West to the President and Board of Trustees of Princeton University

Gentlemen: Princeton, N. J.   October 30 1906

After full deliberation and in compliance with the desire so generously and finely expressed in the minute adopted by your honorable body on October twentieth, I deem it proper to state that I have this day declined the office of President of the Massachusetts Institute of Technology. It is my desire to spend the rest of my life in Princeton and to do all I can to advance both the general interests of the University and the cause of the proposed Graduate College to which I regard myself bound by a relationship of peculiar interest and obligation.

And I beg to remain

                    Very Respectfully Yours,   Andrew F. West

ALS (Trustees' Papers, UA, NjP).

To Fred Lewis Pattee[1]

My dear Professor Pattee: September [Nov.] 1st, 1906.

Thank you for your letter of October 26th.[2] The death of John Rogers Williams was a great shock and a very great grief to us all.[3] He was a fellow of the most sterling and serviceable qualities, and we shall find it very hard to replace him. His illness came very suddenly, and death ensued with startling promptness.

With much regard, I am,

                    Sincerely yours,   Woodrow Wilson

TLS (F. L. Pattee Papers, PSt).
¹ Professor of English Literature at Pennsylvania State College (now Pennsylvania State University). Pattee was editing *The Poems of Philip Freneau* (3 vols., Princeton, N. J., 1902-1907), which appeared under the auspices of the Princeton Historical Association, of which John Rogers Williams had been "General Editor."
² It is missing.
³ Williams died of tuberculosis in McCosh Infirmary on the Princeton campus on October 21, 1906. He had been in the infirmary only about three weeks before his death.

Notes for a Talk at the Opening of the Faculty Room in Nassau Hall¹

2nd Nov., 1906.
Opening of Fitz Randolph Hall

The gift originated in a sentiment,—one of the strongest, most honourable,—the cement of nations. *Piety.*

It has been used to satisfy the same sentiment,—the most wholesome and most stimulating a university, or a nation, can feel.

This ground, the historical centre of Princeton's life[,] this Hall the heart of that life,—though for a time thrown out of function.

We shall expect to live here always in the presence of the past. But all the past of America is progressive,—all consciousness of the past stimulates to attempt a better future

Her universities—if not reduced to bread and butter standards—the nurseries of the nation's ideals.

WWhw MS (WP, DLC).
¹ A news report of this affair is printed at Nov. 10, 1906.

From Frederic Yates

My dear Doctor,   Rydal, Ambleside.   Novr. 3rd, 06

Of course we were glad to get your delightful letter but you mustn't do it again. No, this is just why I have written Margaret because I thought the dear girl would have time to write. We are quite sure you ought not to do anything that is not absolutely imperative. Now then!

Well, it was good to hear nevertheless, and when the postman handed me your two letters I advertized it with a loud shout to my two dear ones. They made me promise I wouldn't read a word until they were by my side, so there was great settling down and then—the feast began. I tell you you may count on it—we love you dearly and if ever you get so that you arn't quite sure just come over again.

We all felt sad about the sea trip—that is something that I love so much that I wanted to come along too apart from all idea of going with the Woodrow Wilsons, of course—but that you had only two fine days; for the Atlantic, that is disgraceful. Well comfort your dear selves and know that you have escaped a series of delicacies of Rydal weather. Not only has it rained and rained and the river out of all bounds, and misbehaving itself by almost coming over the road in front of your cottage,—all that meadow your side of Pelter Bridge was under water, and on the 29th Oct. down came snow 1½ inches—and I got a lovely picture of Silver How all covered, and all the lake looking oh so cold. It was then, the following day, quite warm,—and thunder and lightning and now pouring again while my dear ones are at Burneside, singing part songs in delightful company. I go to meet them at Ambleside at 7.40—the last motor does not come through Rydal.

Julius Caesar has found his Brutus. Mary will tell of the tragedy. I am busy preparing the show at Grafton St. Invitations out next week, for the 26 Novr—until 1st Decr. at the Dutch Gallery, 14 Grafton St London W

I will send cards that you can send to friends you may have in London.   Yours with all my heart,   Fred Yates

ALS (WP, DLC).

From Melancthon Williams Jacobus

Private
My dear President Wilson: Hartford   4th Novr 1906

The New York papers give me the information of Dean West's decision to remain at Princeton, which I take for granted is correct.

Of course for the sake of the Graduate School I am glad that he has so decided, but the meeting of the Graduate School Committee, which I was privileged to attend after the Trustees lunch,[1] impels me to write you for assurance that his remaining is on the basis of a thorough understanding of the position which he occupies in relation to your Presidency of the University.

I would be greatly relieved to know that you are perfectly satisfied with the decision and are without misgivings as to the future   Ever loyally   M W Jacobus

ALS (WP, DLC).
[1] This meeting took place on October 19, 1906, at the home of Grover Cleveland, the committee's chairman. After routine business was disposed of, there ensued a discussion of the situation created by West's call to the presidency of the Massachusetts Institute of Technology, which apparently soon focused

on the relationship of West to Princeton University and, more specifically, on relations between West and Wilson. West, the only participant who has left an account of what transpired at the meeting, alleges that a rather heated exchange took place between Wilson and himself, during which West cited many instances of Wilson's failure to support West's plans as Dean of the Graduate School. According to West, Wilson replied only that the Dean had a "remarkable memory." See Andrew F. West, "A Narrative of the Graduate College of Princeton University . . . ," mimeographed MS (UA, NjP), pp. 25-28. Brief summaries based on West's "Narrative" appear in Arthur S. Link, *Wilson: The Road to the White House* (Princeton, N. J., 1947), pp. 62-63, and in Henry W. Bragdon, *Woodrow Wilson: The Academic Years* (Cambridge, Mass., 1967), p. 315.

To Frederic Yates and Emily Chapman Martin Yates

My dear Friends,   Princeton, N. J.   6 November, 1906.

It is exactly a month to-day since we sailed from Glasgow. You have been in our thoughts constantly, and with every thought want deep abiding affection. It would be hard to say now what a mere summer in the dear Lake District would have done for me if I had got mere rest and recreation. It is always affection that heals me, and the dear friendships I made were my real tonic and restorative. It would be hard to overstate what "the dear Yates" did for me; and I shall forever bless them and seek them as I turn hither and thither in my journey.

The evidence your last letter[1] contained of the Petersons' generous affection and appreciation touched us very deeply. I wish I knew how to tell them of the value and deep pleasure and encouragement I take from their friendship and could let them know how warmly we reciprocate all their feelings about us! How heartening it is to feel that such people have freely turned their hearts towards you! Please give them our love.

We have settled to our winter's life. The first week was a tremendous one. The Board of Trustees of the University met in quarterly meeting, and there was one continuous rush of business, expected and unexpected, from the time I set foot in Princeton until the Board had adjourned. And even then the tide merely ran in another direction. There were four months' of business to catch up with, and all sorts of questions faced me which had all the vacation through been lying in wait for me. I did not take a long breath for two weeks. And then I had to start on a long journey. I went down into Tennessee to meet a body of our alumni, visited my brother at Nashville on my way home, and did not get back again for another week. At last I seem to have settled to something like a level pace. I got back last Wednesday.

Meanwhile, we have been duly distributed. The third day after we got home Jessie started for Baltimore and Nellie for Raleigh, north Carolina. I cannot tell you what it cost us to give up our

482 NOVEMBER 7, 1906

baby and let her go so far away from us. I cannot bear to speak much of it yet. The dear thing seems already, to judge by her letters, to have fallen very happily into the life of the school,—but what a gap there is in our lives every day!

Margaret has plunged into all sorts of innocent gaieties, and it is delightful to see what a good time she is having. She has a sweet, enjoying nature, and everything goes with a zest with her: she extracts pleasures from very simple things. She looks and seems better than we have seen her look in several years and our hearts are light about her. She is deep in her music, practicing with a peculiar pleasure at her Steinway because of the deprivation of the summer, in not having a decent instrument to sing to.

Madge is still in the South, and we have not seen her. She is so much sought after by friends in every direction that we are beginning to wonder whether she will be home by Christmas.

Mrs. Wilson is delightfully well. The summer did her as much good as it did me. We both rejoice in being ourselves again. The plunge into work does not seem to have harmed me at all.

I have so far escaped actual entanglement in politics, though the meshes were spread for me by wireless telegraphy before I landed. An effort more serious than I had anticipated was made to induce me to become a candidate for the Senate; but grace was given me and I declined. I hope that that will quiet other dangers.

We grow impatient for the pictures,—not because you are not doing just what we wanted you to do, but only because we love and desire them. How content I shall be when I get the drawing of Ellen hung here in my library!

As much love as you want from all of us.

Your affectionate friend,   Woodrow Wilson

To Mrs Yates[2]

Dear, dear love to all & thanks for the letters! Will write very soon. I have been as busy as Woodrow—indeed *busier* (!) for *I* have no secretary and "runners" to help *me*!

WWTLS (F. Yates Coll., NjP).
[1] This letter is missing.
[2] EAWhw.

From Moses Taylor Pyne

My dear Woodrow: New York   November 7th, 1906.

You have undoubtedly heard of the renewal by the Boston Tech. of their attack on our Faculty, this time reaching out for probably the most important and valuable man we have.[1] The problem is entirely different here as I believe he would be entirely competent to handle the proposition they make, but I do not see how we can possibly spare him at the present moment. He looks at it simply as a question of where his duty lies and, while I believe that he will decide to remain in Princeton, nevertheless, I think that everything should be done to show him that it is his duty to remain here, and that if he remains here he will not be hampered in any arbitrary manner. I know that he feels very strongly on the subject of the School of Science, and I would suggest that he be made Dean of that Faculty. I think that he will be in a position to do an immense amount of good there, and some head for the School is absolutely needed at the present day if we are to preserve and conserve that side of the University. If this were done it seems to me that he might feel the possibilities and the responsibility placed upon him there so strongly as to make it the turning point in his decision. This is simply a suggestion on my part but I wish you would give it very thorough and careful consideration. I shall see you in a day or two about it.[2]

Regarding the utilization of George Armour's energies, it seems to me that the best suggestion that comes to me yet is that of Director of Seminary and Department Libraries. This, I think, would give him as much occupation or as little as he desired. It would put a certain amount of responsibility on him, subject, however, to that of the Librarian, who has plenty of tact for cases of this kind and can work very well with him. I think the result would be of advantage to the University in getting Armour's direct interest concentrated on a part of the University in which he is most interested. If he will take it it will be an honorable and dignified position for him and in every way would be valuable. If you approve of this would it be possible for me to see him shortly, and, if he care to take such a position to ask the Chairman of the Library Committee to authorize it at once, so that it can go in the Catalogue, knowing that the Board will approve it at the next meeting. I should like to see it in this year's catalogue, if possible, as he may be going abroad next year and it would be pleasant to have it in this year.

Very sincerely yours,   M Taylor Pyne

TLS (WP, DLC).
   [1] The Massachusetts Institute of Technology search committee had just offered the presidency of that institution to Henry Burchard Fine.
   [2] Actually, Fine did not become Dean of the Departments of Science until 1909.

To John Grier Hibben and Jenny Davidson Hibben

My dear, dear Friends,   Princeton, N. J.   8 November, 1906.

I dare say I have told you all that is in my heart concerning you, and I know of no new or better way of telling it; but I *must* pour out some of what is in my heart to-day.[1]

Possibly even I, whom I know you love, may be intruding by speaking at all to-day,—the day sacred to all that is deepest and dearest in your lives and also most separate and exclusive; but your love for each other seems to me a clear evidence of what you *are*, and therefore a crowning indication of what has made you so dear to all who have had the privilege of knowing you intimately,—your truth, your loyalty, your unfailing insight and quick sympathy, your love of purity and sweetness and of the charm that goes with grace and tempered character; and these things have tied you to innumerable friends and given me a sort of excuse to intrude. You never showed better taste than in choosing each other, and perhaps your friends may hope that in preferring them you found in them something at least a little like yourselves. May God bless you and give you many, many more happy anniversaries,—is the prayer of two friends who have known the same happiness.

Your devoted friend   Woodrow Wilson

ALS (photostat in WC, NjP).
[1] Their nineteenth wedding anniversary.

From Melancthon Williams Jacobus

Personal

My dear President Wilson: Hartford   9 November 1906

I wish to thank you for the confidence of your letter, which will not be betrayed.

I regret that it confirms my suspicions and my fears; but for this reason I am all the more anxious to reassure you not only of my own loyalty, but also of the conviction of the Graduate School Committee that the President is the head of the University and that whatever may be our ideals for the Graduate Department, it is to be recognized as but a part of the University organization and its interests as subordinate to those of the institution in general

May the future encourage the good heart you are keeping.

Yours very sincerely   M W Jacobus

ALS (WP, DLC).

A News Report

[Nov. 10, 1906]
The Opening of the New Faculty Room

The occasions are very rare when Ex-President Cleveland makes a public address. Such an occasion was the formal opening of the new Faculty Room in Nassau Hall, which was celebrated with appropriate ceremonies on Nov. 2nd. Several members of the family of Augustus Van Wickle, who bequeathed to Princeton the fund for erecting the Fitz Randolph Gateway and restoring the large room in Nassau Hall for the use of the faculty, were Princeton guests on this notable occasion.

The academic procession, marshalled by Prof. William Libbey '77 and led by President Wilson '79 and Mr. Cleveland, marched from the University Library to Nassau street, thence through the Fitz Randolph Gateway to Nassau Hall. When the procession arrived at the new entrance to the campus in front of Old North [Nassau Hall], Miss Marjorie Van Wickle, a daughter of the donor, opened the big iron gates under the granite eagles.

The exercises in the Faculty Room began with prayer by Prof. Henry van Dyke '73, which was followed by the singing of "America." On behalf of the family Prof. John Grier Hibben '82 formally presented the bequest of Augustus Van Wickle. . . .

In accepting the Van Wickle bequest on behalf of the Trustees, President Wilson expressed the appreciation of the University, saying that there could be no more appropriate gift from a descendant of Nathaniel Fitz Randolph than one which touched with added beauty his original gift. Ex-President Cleveland then delivered the following address: . . .

The exercises were closed with the singing of Old Nassau.

Printed in the *Princeton Alumni Weekly*, VII (Nov. 10, 1906), 120-21.

From Frederic Yates

[Rydal, Ambleside] Nov. 15 [1906]
Bless you for your second letter just received.

We are filled with thankfulness that you speak so happily of each one of your (*our*) dear ones, and that all goes well. " 'Pears like" you are to have "fame *with* peace"—a combination impossible, one would say, except by declining proffered honours.

You are constantly in our thoughts too, with oh what love & peace. "The thirst that from the soul doth rise demands a drink divine" and after knowing you dear people we are hard to please again—and feed on memories rather than seek new ties.

Nothing can rob of us what we have had, I continually & gloatingly reflect.

For over an hour I've been cleaning the glass on your drawing and also that of our dear little "da Vinci"—hers having been cracked while at Bell's[1] during the "Show." I've replaced it. Tell her I fain would be her "secretary" and Mary her glad "runner." God watch between us—& keep us all.

ALS enclosed with Emily C. M. Yates to WW, Nov. 14, 1906, ALS (WP, DLC).
    [1] The studio of Herbert Bell, Ambleside photographer.

Alfred Ernest Stearns[1] to Charles Grosvenor Osgood[2]

My dear Osgood: Andover, Massachusetts
                                     November 15, 1906.

Your good letter of the 11th inst. has been acknowledged I believe in my absence by our mutual friend, and at times fellow laborer, Bancroft.[3]

I appreciate deeply the spirit of your note. I am interested too in your reference to the situation at Princeton, for I have attemped with great interest to watch that experiment, if such it may be called. I do not believe that there is any one today who more thoroughly appreciates the improvements which have taken place at Princeton the last three years than do I. Two days after my appointment to my present position I was called upon to pass through an experience which I am not likely soon to forget, and which in all its disagreeableness could be attributed in a large measure to the lax conditions and standards against which both Dr. Bancroft[4] and I had offered formal protests to the Princeton authorities.[5] At that period in Princeton's history she was gathering in from Andover, and so far as I could learn, from other schools as well, the weaker brothers. With President Wilson's advent the whole situation changed, and for over a year I have felt strongly that Princeton bade fair not only to equal the other institutions of her class, but possibly to wrest from them the leadership in scholarship and the best kind of college spirit. This is the view of an individual merely, and one whom I confess has had no opportunity to examine thoroughly into the conditions existing in the various institutions involved, but who is obliged to be governed by impressions largely. If Princeton by her tutorial system is able to save the universities and large colleges from ignoring the individual and the deeds of the individual, she will have done a splendid thing for the higher American education.

Please accept my thanks for your kind words to me personally. I hope I may be able to hold the good old school true to her early and cherished traditions. If I cannot, my failure will not be due to lack of inspiration or desire.

With kind regards and best wishes to you personally, believe me,   Very sincerely yours,   Alfred E. Stearns

TLS (WC, NjP).
[1] Principal of Phillips Academy, Andover, Mass.
[2] Osgood was a member of the Class of 1890 at Andover.
[3] Cecil Kittredge Bancroft, Instructor in Latin, Registrar, and Assistant to the Principal at Phillips Academy, Andover.
[4] Cecil Franklin Patch Bancroft, Ph.D., Principal of Phillips Academy, 1873-1901.
[5] He referred to an episode of cheating by Andover students on Princeton entrance examinations, about which see EAW to WW, July 18, 1902, n. 2, Vol. 14.

From Sir William Mather

                                    London   Nov. 19th [1906]
Proceed with sundial foundations

                                                      Mather
Hw telegram (WWP, UA, NjP).

To Whom It May Concern

                                              Princeton, N. J.
To Whom It May Concern: November 20th, 1906.

I take pleasure in introducing my friend Mr. Malcolm S. Taylor, who was graduated from Princeton University with the class of 1903, and in recommending the cause which he represents[1] to all public-spirited Christian people.

I happen to have a considerable acquaintance with the conditions of life in the North Carolina mountains. I know, therefore, how admirably suited to their needs such a school as Mr. Taylor expects to establish would be. It would touch their lives where their need is greatest, on the religious side and on the industrial side, and would be much better than any school on the ordinary lines could possibly be. I sincerely hope that Mr. Taylor will meet with generous support.

                    Very sincerely,   Woodrow Wilson

PCL (WP, DLC).
[1] Malcolm Slicer Taylor was at this time a student at the General Theological Seminary in New York, from which he was graduated in 1907. He spent his summer vacations while in seminary as a lay missionary among southern mountaineers. "In 1908," he later wrote, "I . . . went into the North Carolina mountains to start an agricultural and industrial school for southern mountaineer boys. . . . It took five years to establish the Patterson School." *Decennial Record of the Class of 1903, Princeton University* (n.p., 1914), pp. 283-84. The Patterson School, located at Legerwood, N. C., was named for Samuel Legerwood Patterson (1850-1908), former North Carolina Commissioner of Agriculture, who gave his estate for the school.

From Robert Bridges

My dear Tommy: New York, November 20 190[6]

I find that we have a balance of $156.64 in the Class Room Fund, and you are hereby authorized to spend that amount on the furniture as you see fit. Will you kindly O. K. the bills as they come in and send them on to Cuyler, who will immediately pay them?

I went in the room on Saturday and thought it looked very attractive. We had hoped to have enough money for some more chairs, but the balance is better expended as you suggest.

Very truly yours   Robert Bridges

TLS (WP, DLC).

From Edgar Odell Lovett

Princeton, New Jersey

Dear President Wilson: 21st November, 1906.

I have made two unsuccessful attempts to see you this week. I am writing now to ask you to keep in mind the matter of equipping a Princeton Astronomical Expedition to South Africa, which I barely suggested to you in a letter last year.[1] The more I think about the idea, the larger the reasons for the undertaking grow. I have been trying hard not to talk about the matter before finding out your wishes. I have done too much talking about it already. I have asked no one to give. Mr. McAlpin has kindly offered to take the question up as seriously as he has that of the Syrian Expedition[2] as soon as the latter is completely provided for.

Professor Young writes:

> "It would certainly be a splendid thing for the University to send such an Expedition as you have in mind. There is now a magnificent opportunity for a big telescope properly mounted and manned to do important work in the Southern hemisphere: and I certainly do most heartily wish you success in carrying out the idea."

There is enormous and increasing pressure from without. Swarthmore College is ordering a refracting telescope of twenty-four inches aperture; the Harvard College Observatory is installing a reflecting telescope of five feet aperture; the proposed New York Observatory and Nautical Museum (a future adjunct of Columbia University) has placed an order for a refractor of thirty inches aperture; Yale University has appropriated fifty thousand dollars for the publication of Professor Brown's lunar tables;[3] the Western University of Pennsylvania[4] has a thirty inch refractor making; the University of Michigan has ordered a three foot reflector; Harvard and the University of California have permanent stations in South America; the Carnegie Institution is about to go to the Southern hemisphere with a definite problem (the site will be determined in a few days); there is a gigantic scheme preparing at Harvard parading under the guise of a proposal for an International Southern Observatory.

I believe that it is quite possible for us to fold our dome quietly and as silently steal in ahead of this procession. In five or ten years we should have results with which every future student of the structure of the sky would have to reckon, real contributions to knowledge which would occupy a permanent place in the history of astronomy.

For thirty years astronomy at Princeton has consisted of a great man and his reputation, neither of which was made in Princeton.[5] That great man has gone.

Is it too much to hope that you will be able to give this project (the details of which are being worked out) an early place among your many plans for Princeton?

Awaiting your commands, I beg to remain

Faithfully yours,   Edgar Odell Lovett

TLS (WP, DLC).

¹ It is missing.

² About this expedition, see n. 1 to the report to the Board of Trustees printed at June 13, 1904, Vol. 15.

³ Ernest William Brown, at this time Professor of Mathematics at Haverford College and soon—in 1907—to occupy the same post at Yale University. His "lunar tables" were not published until 1919 under the title, *Tables of the Motion of the Moon* (3 vols., New Haven, Conn., 1919).

⁴ Founded in 1787 as the Pittsburgh Academy, it was reorganized as the Western University of Pennsylvania in 1819 and became the University of Pittsburgh in 1908.

⁵ That is, Charles Augustus Young, Emeritus Professor of Astronomy, renowned for his pioneering studies in solar physics, particularly his spectroscopic researches. His most notable discoveries occurred while he was Professor of Natural Philosophy and Astronomy at Dartmouth. He joined the Princeton faculty in 1877.

To Charles Grosvenor Osgood

Princeton, N. J.

My dear Professor Osgood: November 22nd, 1906.

I am sincerely obliged to you for your thoughtful kindness in sending me Mr. Stearns' letter. Such letters give me no little comfort and encouragement. I hope it will not be many years before we have converted all the leading schoolmasters of the country to the view this letter expresses, and certainly it ought to make us the more careful to deserve the opinion.

Always cordially and sincerely yours,

Woodrow Wilson

TLS (WC, NjP).

From Cleveland Hoadley Dodge

Dear Mr. President: New York   November 22, 1906.

Apropos of the conversation we had last Sunday evening in regard to the new building for the geological and biological departments, would it not be well, before I settle anything definite with my mother, to wait until you have had your talk with Mr. [Henry Clay] Frick, which I hope will come off very soon?

It is quite possible that he may not be prepared to give on the scale necessary to thoroughly launch the graduate college, and he may not care to give a large sum for endowment purposes, and might prefer decidedly to provide for some definite, concrete purpose like the proposed geological building, which could be identified with his name.

I should think it would be just as well for you to have this to present to him in case he is not attracted by other propositions. I feel quite sure my mother would give about as much to other purposes, if Mr. Frick should decide to assume the responsibility for this.[1]   Very sincerely yours,   C. H. Dodge

TLS (WP, DLC).
[1] As it turned out, Frick did not give any money for the purposes that Dodge mentioned. Dodge's mother, Sarah Hoadley (Mrs. William Earl) Dodge, gave the money for what became Guyot Hall, used to house the Departments of Geology and Biology.

A News Report

[Nov. 23, 1906]

MURRAY HALL ADDRESS.

President Wilson Delivers the Third Address
of Series, on College Men's Problems.

President Wilson delivered a very forceful address before the Philadelphian Society last evening, taking as his text "We are unprofitable servants: we have done that which is our duty to do."

This is the spirit, President Wilson said, which is characteristic of the present generation—to do those things which are indispensable to its welfare. Fundamentally, the unprofitable servant is the man who has merely accomplished his duty.

Every university is the place where knowledge should be diffused, for knowledge was never intended for private consumption or satisfaction, but to enlighten the world and be increased by constant usury. In some cases, however, it is only an instrument of a subtle kind of egotism. Men absorb it, but are ever afterwards like dim glow-worms, hiding their light from the rest of mankind, when, in fact, the only way by which they are able to be of consequence is to join all their forces into one mighty effort. Such men are unprofitable in the literal sense of the word, and are only satisfied with the execution of necessary duties. They neither do justice to themselves nor to their university, for the object of this institution is to provide the world with men who will help it in every stage of its progress. They must be willing to perform hard tasks and speak out the truth which was instilled into them, though it be directly opposed to popular opinion.

Printed in the *Daily Princetonian*, Nov. 23, 1906.

To Cleveland Hoadley Dodge

My dear Cleve.   Princeton, N. J.   November 23rd, 1906.

I think that the suggestion of your letter of November 22nd is a very wise one, and that I had better keep that card to play in my interview with Mr. Frick.

My only fear is that this will mean serious delay in our plans. If we could get an early promise of the physical laboratory and the geological-biological building, it would enable us to effect an immediate reorganization on the scientific side, that would be of immense benefit. I mean by putting Fine in charge, as I know he has always wished to be put. But I am afraid that Mr. Frick is going to avoid an interview for some time to come.[1]

I think I could not exaggerate what these two gifts would mean to the University. We are trying hard to get, for example, an excellent biologist, and our utter lack of equipment defeats us at almost every turn. The moment a man now working in a well equipped laboratory comes to Princeton and looks around, he knows that he would sacrifice everything by coming. Until this condition of things is remedied, we are really hopelessly embarrassed in our effort to make the University strong where it is weak.

Thank you sincerely for your letter.

Always affectionately yours,   Woodrow Wilson

TLS (WC, NjP).
[1] He seems to have succeeded entirely.

From William Kelly Prentice

Dear Dr. Wilson   Princeton, N. J.   Nov. 23rd, 1906
 I thank you very much for your letter, and for the friendly spirit in which it is written. I am glad also that you understood the spirit of my communication of some weeks ago.[1]
 I am sure that you know that my heart is in the work here and that I wish to cooperate with you in every way for the success of this University of ours. And, because I ask for a full salary[2] and you are obliged to refuse it, there really is no reason why there should be any unfriendliness between us, is there?
 So I hope you will not be personally offended when I tell you that I am not satisfied with my present salary.[3]
      Yours very sincerely   William Prentice

ALS (WP, DLC).
[1] It is missing.
[2] That is, $3,000 a year.
[3] His salary at this time was $2,500 per annum. It was increased to $3,000 in 1907.

From Robert Hunter Fitzhugh

My dear Doctor Wilson   New York.   November 23d, 1906
 The promptness and tenderness with which you responded to my begging letter of day before yesterday[1] really humbles me with a sense of gratitude. For a man of your eminence, and many duties to treat with such kind consideration an appeal by an obscure man for so small, and remote a matter is certainly enough to invoke the gratitude and loyalty of any reflecting man.
 I salute you for yourself and as a Virginian reverting to the dear old state's ancient glory,
 With great and affectionate consideration,
      Very truly yours   R. H. Fitzhugh

ALS (WP, DLC).
[1] It is missing.

From Charles Williston McAlpin

My dear Dr. Wilson: [Princeton, N. J.] November 27, 1906.
 In accordance with your instructions I have sent out a call for a meeting of the Committee on Honorary Degrees on Wednes-

day evening, December 12th., at eight o'clock in the President's Room in Seventy-Nine Hall. I am sending this note to you as a reminder of the meeting.

     Sincerely yours,   [C. W. McAlpin]   Secretary.

CCL (McAlpin File, UA, NjP).

A Fragment of a Letter from Ellen Axson Wilson to Anna Harris

                     [Princeton, N. J., c. Dec. 1, 1906]

. . . There is simply no end to the "functions" I am called upon to have. This one is to the graduate students. There are three or four large receptions in the year,—five or six hundred at each, some smaller ones, four or five formal luncheons to trustees & others, from 24 to 80 each, and a formal dinner every week or two, to from 10 to 24. Then of course there are guests constantly coming to a meal or overnight and people invited more informally to meet them at dinner,—also the University preacher from Saturday to Monday of every week. Do you wonder I am glad when summer comes and we leave for a while this great (though charming) house with its 35 rooms?

     We had a most delightful time last summer. We spent the summer (all of us,) in England,—took a picturesque rose-bowered cottage on the banks of the Rothay, "under Loughrigg," and kept house for three months. It was at Rydal,—close to Wordsworth's "Rydal Mount," and still closer to "Fox Howe" the home of Dr Arnold and Matthew Arnold. Indeed our cottage was the home of a Mrs. Wordsworth whose husband was the poets grandson, and it is her daughter who now lives at Rydal Mount.[1] They were all very agreeable and attentive to us. Miss Arnold,[2] Matthew's sister[,] is one of the most interesting and attractive women I ever met and added greatly to the pleasure of our summer. But of course the country itself is the main joy. It is indescribably beautiful; Woodrow is so infatuated with it that he could hardly be withheld from buying a sumer home there,—a reckless thing to do when one considers the expense of taking a whole family over. The fact that we were all together was of course what made it so ideal. All except Nellie had travelled abroad before, but had gone in detachments!

     But now I really *must* close! Remember that I am simply setting you an example and must have a letter in return telling me all about *your*selves. I hear next to nothing of Rome friends now that all the Hoyts have left, and I am hungry for news of everyone. That *beautiful* large lace centre-piece that you sent me is still the joy of my heart,—one of my two *best* table decorations,—so that although I do not *need* a reminder of my dear old friend, I have very constant occasion to think gratefully and lovingly of you. With warm regards to all friends, I am, dear, as ever,

Yours most affectionately,   Ellen A. Wilson.

ALS (WC, NjP).
[1] Violet (Mrs. John Fisher Jones) Wordsworth. On his marriage to Violet Wordsworth in 1885, Jones was authorized by Royal Licence to take the surname Wordsworth.
[2] Frances Bunsen Trevenen Arnold (1833-1923), the youngest of Matthew Arnold's four sisters and the only one who never married. She became mistress of Fox How, the Arnold family home near Ambleside, after the death of her mother in 1873.

From Sir William Mather

My dear President Wilson,   London.   Decbr. 3d/06

I hope my cable saying that the foundations might now be laid for the Sun-dial monument duly reached you.

The sculptors are now engaged on the work & I am assured that all will be finished in good time to enable the erection to be completed before the 12th June next.

Have you considered the question of the Custom house? It would be almost an act of international discourtesy if you were to meet opposition in your desire to have this bit of Old England treated as an article not coming within the tariff laws. Yet strange things do occur through officialdom all the world over, & you would be wise to get consent well in advance. For your information I may say the value will be about £500 on this side. I have engaged a high class firm to carry out the work.

I sincerely trust you are restored and that you are going easy all the time in your great work at Princeton.

I sent a letter to your Hotel St Enoch at Glasgow, but I am afraid rather late to reach you. As a matter of curiosity I should like to know whether I succeeded in getting our "send off" to you in time.[1] Of course it required no acknowledgment.

We are all settled again in London & my wife & daughters send heartiest greetings to you all.

Very Sincerely yours   W. Mather

ALS (WWP, UA, NjP).
[1] In any event, it is missing in the several collections of Wilson's papers.

From Arthur Hobson Quinn[1]

My dear Dr. Wilson: Philadelphia.   December 3, 1906.

I have the honor to inform you that at a meeting of the Association of Colleges and Preparatory Schools of the Middle States and Maryland, held on December 1st, you were unanimously elected President of the Association for the year 1906-07. I trust that you may feel willing to accept the election.

The duties of the office will consist mainly in presiding at the next Convention, and in attending two or three meetings of the Executive Committee during the year. These meetings can, of course, be arranged at a time and place to suit your convenience.

Very truly yours,   Arthur H. Quinn   Secretary.

TLS (WP, DLC).
[1] Assistant Professor of English at the University of Pennsylvania and Secretary of the Association of Colleges and Preparatory Schools of the Middle States and Maryland.

From Charles Williston McAlpin

My dear Dr. Wilson: [Princeton, N. J.]   December 5, 1906.

Mr. Cadwalader has written that he expects to attend the meeting of the Committee on Honorary Degrees on next Wednesday evening.

The accident on the Southern Railway in which President Spencer and General Schuyler were killed[1] has been a great shock to Mr. Cadwalader. It seems that this Thanksgiving hunting trip was an annual affair and heretofore Mr. Cadwalader has always been a member of the party, but for some reason he was unable to go with them this year.

Very sincerely yours, [C. W. McAlpin]   Secretary.

CCL (McAlpin File, UA, NjP).
[1] Samuel Spencer, President of the Southern Railway Co., Philip Schuyler of New York, and two other friends were killed on November 29, 1906, when Spencer's private car, attached to a stalled train, was struck from behind by another train near Lynchburg, Va. The party was on its way to Spencer's game preserve near Friendship, N. C., to hunt quail. For an extensive account of the accident and biographical sketches of the victims, see the *New York Times*, Nov. 30, 1906.

To Nicholas Murray Butler

Princeton, N. J.
My dear President Butler: December 6th, 1906

Dr. [Albert] Shaw and I had a brief conversation yesterday about our lectures at Columbia, and he very generously offered to give his course in January and February, if you would consent to the arrangement, in order that I might have the longer time to make ready. I sincerely hope that this arrangement will be agreeable to you. Dr. Shaw said that he would communicate with you at once about it.

Always cordially yours,   Woodrow Wilson

TCL (RSB Coll., DLC).

From Nicholas Murray Butler

Dear President Wilson: [New York]   December 7, 1906

I thank you very much for your kind note of the 6th, and am today writing to Dr. Shaw asking him to choose his dates in January and February.

Perhaps you will, at your convenience, select the dates most convenient for you in March and April. We could advise you here which afternoon in the week will prove freest from conflict with ordinary stated courses in law and political science. Of course we are anxious to have as many of those students as possible come to your lecture, and, therefore, we shall want to fix upon a day and hour when their attendance will not be expected elsewhere. Four o'clock in the afternoon is probably the best time from our point of view.

I have only one regret in your taking March and April, and that is that since I have promised to be in California in March it would not be possible for me to be present and present you at the opening lecture, as I had hoped to do, not only for reasons of academic courtesy, but because of our personal friendship.

With warm regard, I am,

Faithfully yours,   Nicholas Murray Butler

TCL (RSB Coll., DLC).

From William Henry Rideing[1]

Boston, Massachusetts.

Dear President Wilson: Dec. 7th, 1906.

I find that very often if a contributor bears in mind the character of the *Companion's* constituency, which though it includes adults as well as younger readers is in the majority an audience of people in the formative period of life, he generally discovers some more or less imperative message for them in his own mind. However, two subjects occur to me at the moment which may appeal to you:

1. Vocational Training and the University. Is the coordination all that it might be?
2. The Evolution of Human Kindness (Humane education). I think this by illustration and allusion could be made very inspiring.

If neither of these seems workable to you, please let me know, but the latter has such rich material connected with it that I am encouraged to believe you will accept it.[2]

I am, dear President Wilson,

Yours Faithfully,   William H. Rideing.

ALS (WP, DLC).
[1] Associate Editor of *Youth's Companion*.
[2] See W. H. Rideing to WW, Dec. 18, 1906, n. 1.

A News Report

[Dec. 8, 1906]

THE FORMAL OPENING OF LAKE CARNEGIE[1]

Enthusiastic Reception to the Donor, His Presentation Address and President Wilson's Acceptance

Lake Carnegie, finally finished and forming a beautiful sheet of water below the college campus and northward to Kingston, was opened on Wednesday, December 5th, with appropriate ceremonies, formal and informal. Marking the culmination of a great engineering enterprise, which has changed the map of Mercer County and given to Princeton, an inland town, the advantages of location on the water, it was a gala day on the campus and in the village, and an occasion of joyful celebration. The colors of the college and the nation were flying from the campus towers and along Nassau street, and town and gown joined in giving the donor of the lake a most hearty and enthusiastic reception.

Mr. and Mrs. Carnegie, with a large party of guests, arrived at 11 o'clock in a special train from New York. From that hour the college exercises were suspended for the day, and the entire undergraduate body was at the station to give the visitors a Princeton welcome. President Wilson '79, Dean Fine '80, and M. Taylor Pyne '77, of the Board of Trustees and the lake association, formed the official reception committee at the station, and when Mr. Carnegie emerged from his car the students cut loose with rousing cheers. As Mr. Carnegie, walking with President Wilson, ascended the steps to the campus, he pointed to a banner sus-

[1] For information about the planning and construction of Lake Carnegie, see ns. 1 and 2 to the news item printed at Nov. 29, 1903, Vol. 15.

pended from a student's room in the Blair Hall tower, and laughed heartily with the crowd at the legend—

WELKUM TO

THE

LAIRD OF SKIBO

That was the beginning of the mutual understanding between the simple students and their guest and benefactor, and thereafter they needed no formal introduction. A few minutes later the academic procession, marshalled by Prof. William Libbey '77 and headed by President Wilson and Mr. Carnegie (who wore the purple hood of Doctor of Laws), emerged from the Faculty Room in Nassau Hall and marched to Alexander Hall, which was crowded to the roof. Surrounded by the trustees and faculty, the President occupied the baldachino, with the guest of honor sitting at his right. No sooner was the dignified academic procession seated than the gallery, packed with undergraduates, broke in on the formal programme and sang with great gusto—

> Carnegie, Carnegie,—
> He is giving us a lake,
> You can hear the breakers break,—
> Carnegie, Carnegie,
> Andy, Andy,
> You're a dandy,—
> Carnegie!

The verse was repeated with enthusiasm, and there was no doubt that Mr. Carnegie enjoyed it.

In beginning the formal exercises, President Wilson said: "I am sure I need not tell you for what purpose we have assembled. It is our distinguished honor to have with us to-day Mr. Andrew Carnegie, whom I have great pleasure in introducing to the audience." Which was followed by prolonged cheering as Mr. Carnegie arose to speak, holding in his right hand a large envelope, the contents of which were readily guessed by the audience. His address of presentation of the lake was in part as follows:

> Mr. President, Gentlemen of the Faculty, Ladies and Gentlemen:
> We are assembled upon this occasion that I may hand over the deed for the lake and the property which the committee of your graduates has so zealously labored to construct. I feel, as a Scotchman, that if my foot is not on my native heather it is on the campus of the Scotch university of this country. [Cheers.] You have a wonderful history, Mr.

President. Princeton emerges from obscurity under the rule of one of the most conspicuous characters that has yet appeared in American history. Dear old Dr. Witherspoon, when he was a young man in Scotland, and an established church minister, no less, rebelled against the practice of the landed proprietors having a right to impose the minister upon the congregation, and so zealous was he that he was actually arrested for creating a riot, which I think the injustice largely excused. He came to Princeton and Walpole said in the House of Commons that the American colonies had been run away with by a Presbyterian minister. From that day to this there has never been a call made upon the patriotism of this country in which students of Princeton have not lead the van.

I have read more than once that this is the only educational institution that stood firmly for the cause of American independence. There certainly was no other university in that contest which excelled Princeton in patriotism. I am very sure that if my parents had been able to give their son a university education—and I wonder whether that would have benefited the son; I think it would; at all events I would have pursued a different career—but if they had had to choose a university it is dead sure that it would have been Princeton, and that their son would have approved the choice. [Cheers.]

Well do I remember the day that I first visited Princeton with my friend Howard Russell Butler. I had been building lochs at Skibo—we don't have lakes over there, that is so English—and my practiced eye saw this valley and this stream. And I said, "O, what a place for a lake"—I mean loch —and Mr. Butler said "Yes, for thirty years the students of Princeton have longed for a lake upon which to row and for aquatic sports." And I said, "Indeed." [Cheers and laughter.] Now just think how duty calls. Even more than that, see how the hand of Providence works. There stood the situation presented to me, all the features ready. There stood my Princeton friend telling me that it was a want that Princeton felt. And then I was in the loch-building business. And the spirit moved me and I said, "Well, Butler, see what you can do. I would like to give Princeton, that Scotch university, a loch."

Mr. Carnegie then referred to the "serious and delicate subject of sport," saying that aquatics have a spotless reputation, and that he hoped that the influence of aquatics upon Princeton would be to lift every other sport to that level. He deplored the commercial spirit of football introduced by professional coaching, but rejoiced that the game is becoming cleaner, and congratulated Princeton upon its share in the reform. Also he said that it would give Mrs. Carnegie and himself the greatest pleasure to present a trophy for the first competition in aquatics held on the lake.

In conclusion Mr. Carnegie said: It remains now only my duty to hand over the deeds to your President, and I tell you, ladies and gentlemen, this is the occasion when a man realizes the great truth that it is much more blessed to give than to receive.

As Mr. Carnegie finished speaking, amid tremendous cheering, he handed to President Wilson the envelope containing the documents conveying his gift to the Lake Carnegie Association, which has been incorporated under the laws of New Jersey, and is composed of John W. Aitkin '69, William Allen Butler '76, M. Taylor Pyne '77, Dr. Jasper J. Garmany '79, C. C. Cuyler '79, Alexander R. Gulick '89, Henry W. Green '90, Mr. A. D. Russell and Mr. R. A. Franks.

On behalf of the association, President Wilson formally accepted the lake, Mr. Carnegie standing and facing the speaker, who said:

Mr. Carnegie:

It is with the greatest pleasure that we welcome you to Princeton. We recognize in you, as all the world does, a man devoted with a singular directness of aim to promoting the peace of the world, and the true intellectual interests of the two nations your life has most intimately touched. We have loved Princeton so much, perhaps I should say have so idealized it in our affections, that we deem it a place especially fitted to welcome a great Scotsman and a great citizen who devotes his thought and his wealth to the public welfare, and especially to the highest interests of education. At least two great Scotsmen, John Witherspoon and James McCosh, have made an imperishable record for themselves here. Indeed these two men may be said to have formed the place and given it its character and distinction, Witherspoon when the nation was forming, McCosh when it had seen its second birth by civil war. I like to believe that from Witherspoon, who held it steady to a young nation's cause when other institutions of its kind faltered and lost their vision of the days to come, Princeton derived that sense of public obligation and that tradition of public service which have been so characteristic of it ever since, and I know that it derived from McCosh the impulse to scholarship which has made it a great University, ready for the tasks of the modern world. James Madison was Witherspoon's pupil, and the Constitution of the United States, which he was so largely instrumental in framing, may be said to have been the fruit of Princeton's teaching in days which waited for and expected revolution. You have adopted America as truly as those great men did, and we may welcome you as an American of their principles.

The errand upon which you come to-day is a very gracious one, to present to a company of gentlemen in the interest of this place and its vicinity a beautiful lake, destined to grow more and more beautiful as verdure creeps to its banks, and stately trees grow more and more upon its shores and islands. It was characteristic of you, if you will permit me to say so, that you saw so instantly what Princeton needed to complete its charm and still further promote the healthful pleasures of those who frequent it. Of course, those of us who had known and loved the place for many years had often commented upon the fact that an unsightly marsh marred its outer skirts, a marsh which could never be redeemed except by replacing it with broad and wholesome stretches of water. A single visit showed you the need not only, but the opportunity also, and you have availed yourself of the opportunity with a generosity and frank simplicity which the world has learned to expect of you, but which are none the less delightful and admirable in each new instance of their display.

I deeply regret the fact that Mr. Croes,[2] the distinguished engineer who devoted himself with so much interest to the execution of this noble project, did not live to see its happy completion.

I do not think that it is merely our doting love of the place that has led us to think of it as a place which those who love this country and like to dwell upon its honorable history would naturally be inclined to adorn with their gifts. Nassau Hall, the ancient building from which we derive our familiar designation of ourselves as sons of Old Nassau, carries us back by association to the revolution which established constitutional government in England, for it was named in honor of the Prince of Orange, and its history

2 John James Robertson Croes, civil engineer of New York, who had died recently.

has been worthy of the tradition of which its name is significant. It is interesting to remember that in 1770 the letter of the New York merchants, announcing that they had broken their non-importation agreement and inviting the merchants of Philadelphia to join them in their breach of faith and of patriotism, was seized on its way through Princeton and burned by the undergraduates in front of Nassau Hall. In the same place, four years later, the students burned the college steward's store of tea. The Declaration of Independence was at the earliest possible moment proclaimed from the steps of Nassau Hall, the reading being greeted by a triple volley of musketry. In August, 1776, the first legislature of the State of New Jersey sat in the library room of the building. In the memorable days which saw the despairful closing months of 1776 brighten into the hope of January, 1777, the actual storm of war beat about its walls, and for several months Washington was obliged to use it as a hospital for his own men and his British prisoners. For five months of 1783 the Continental Congress used its great hall as its meeting place. There Congress gave Washington its formal thanks for his great service rendered the country. There they received the first diplomatic representative accredited to the United States, Peter Van Berckel, Minister Plenipotentiary from the Netherlands, and there they received the news of peace. We could not but be patriotic here, and I know that you yourself, sir, feel the compulsion of this noble tradition.

I suppose that most of us here present today think chiefly of the pleasures this gift will bring. I wish I knew how to tell you the appreciation of this remarkable gift which is felt by these young gentlemen, as eloquently and as convincingly as they could do if they stood in my place [cheers]. We older men will get a great deal of pleasure out of Lake Carnegie by reason of our appreciation of its beauty. These young gentlemen will use it and will bless you for the fun they get out of it. By its use your name and memories of your generosity will be closely associated with some of the happiest days of their lives, and perhaps with some of the most momentous, if they go boating with young ladies [applause and laughter]. It is interesting to reflect, too, that no traveler will approach Princeton without receiving as his first impression of the place the pleasure of seeing those placid and beautiful stretches of water, which, we are happy to say, will bear your name.

In receiving this unique and noble gift, I am, I know, speaking, by their gracious permission, as a representative of the gentlemen who are to be the legal owners of this lake, rather than as the official head of the University, and yet I feel as if I were in some sense receiving you into our university body. I should like to feel that you will hereafter regard yourself as an adopted son of Old Nassau [prolonged cheering], and it is delightful to feel that we are adding your name to the list of those who have been put upon our roll of honour as having known how to be nobly generous and wisely public-spirited.[3]

The exercises in Alexander Hall were concluded with the singing of Old Nassau, during the last verse of which Mr. Carnegie, catching the spirit of the song, stepped to the front of the platform and led the singing, waving his arm in unison with the waving hats in the audience. Finally there were rousing cheers with "Carnegie" and "Princeton" on the end of them.

At one o'clock President and Mrs. Wilson entertained Mr. and Mrs. Carnegie and their guests at luncheon, at Prospect. After luncheon Mr. Carnegie and his party were conducted by automobiles around the lake, returning in time for the special train, which left for New York at four o'clock. Before his departure Mr. Carnegie called upon Mr. Cleveland.

Printed in the *Princeton Alumni Weekly*, vii (Dec. 8, 1906), 182-86; some editorial headings omitted.
[3] There is a WWsh draft of this speech, dated Dec. 5, 1906, in WP, DLC.

To Moses Taylor Pyne

My dear Momo: [Princeton, N. J.] December 8th, 1906.

Mrs. Wilson and I should both feel our self-respect a good deal damaged if anyone but ourselves should pay for an entertainment at Prospect, particularly an entertainment which we offered and were delighted to give. I shall take the liberty of paying for Wednesday's lunch myself, and know that you will understand and sympathize. I want you, however, to know that we are none the less deeply appreciative of the liberal intention in this matter of those of you who were generous enough to pay for the successful affair of Mr. Carnegie's reception.

Always affectionately yours,   [Woodrow Wilson]

CCL (WWP, UA, NjP).

To Edward Field Goltra[1]

My dear Mr. Goltra: Princeton, N. J.   December 8th, 1906.

I learn through a letter of Mr. Murray's to Mr. McAlpin, the Secretary of the University, that you are hopeful of obtaining the funds necessary to build a physical laboratory, from Mr. W. K. Bixby,[2] about whom I remember you spoke to me once. I need not tell you how deeply I appreciate your efforts in behalf of the University, or how useful they are likely to be. I take the matter up with you at this moment, only because it now seems extremely likely that a group of gentlemen will give us, not merely enough for a physical laboratory, but enough to equip and endow it. I thought that I owed it to you to tell you this, in strict confidence, in order that you might not find yourself in the unpleasant position of having obtained a gift for something already provided for.

The money is equally needed for a biological laboratory, which we most earnestly desire and which would be of untold value to all of the Princeton men who are likely to study medicine or go into the teaching profession in this most important branch of study.

I know that you will appreciate the motives which lead me to write thus, and I hope that if I can assist you in any way, you will not hesitate to call upon me for all the information you desire.

With warm appreciation and sincere regards,

Sincerely yours,   Woodrow Wilson

TLS (E. F. Goltra Papers, MoSHi).
1 Princeton, 1887, iron and steel manufacturer of St. Louis.
2 William Keeney Bixby of St. Louis, prominent manufacturer, banker, businessman, philanthropist, and generous patron of scholarship.

From Arthur Hobson Quinn

Philadelphia.

My dear Dr. Wilson: December 8, 1907 [1906].

I am very glad to receive from you your acceptance of the Presidency of the Association for 1906-07. I am enclosing to you a list of the officers of the Association for your information.

There is usually a meeting of the Executive Committee in January, and, if you will indicate to me a convenient time and place for that meeting, I will notify the other members of the Committee, which consists, as you see, of four members, and the President, Secretary and Treasurer, ex officio.

Our usual habit has been to meet at 1 o'clock, take luncheon together, and then discuss the business afterwards; but I feel that this year we might institute a reform by having the meeting earlier, say 11 o'clock A.M., thus getting the routine business out of the way before luncheon and having more time to discuss the program and the speakers in the afternoon. I shall be glad to have your opinion as to the change when you set the date of the meeting.

Very sincerely yours,   Arthur Hobson Quinn
Secretary.

TLS (WP, DLC). Enc.: "Officers of the Association 1906-1907," T MS

From Mark Antony De Wolfe Howe

Dear Sir,   Boston, Massachusetts   12 December 1906

For one of our April numbers in which *The Companion*'s eightieth anniversary is to be celebrated we wish to secure a special article of unusual importance. As the time so nearly coincides with the opening of the Jamestown Exposition, it has occurred to us that an article related to this theme would be most appropriate. Accordingly I am writing to ask whether this article may not come from you. The title of the paper I have in mind might be "The Southern Type of Colonist"—or something of the sort. The debt of the nation to the settlers of the southern states has certainly received far less general recognition than the corresponding debt to the northern colonists. With the Jamestown Exposition as the point of departure, it seems to me that a significant and valuable article might well spring from the topic I have suggested. *The Companion* would rather have this paper from you than from any one else. Its length should be approximately 3500 words, and the manuscript should be in our hands early in March. In method of treatment the philosophic aspect of the matter should be suggested rather than elaborated—the emphasis being laid rather upon what is strikingly human and picturesque. May I not hear that you can see your way to undertaking such a paper for us? I need not say how much it would be appreciated, both [by] my colleagues here and by our wide circle of impressionable readers.[1]

Believe me, Sir, Respectfully yours,

M. A. De Wolfe Howe
(Corresponding Editor)

ALS (WP, DLC).
    [1] See W. H. Rideing to WW, Dec. 21, 1906, n. 1.

From Frederic Yates

My dear Doctor,   [London]   12th Decr. o6

The enclosed note[1] will arrive ahead of the Portrait. I hope it reads as it ought to read[.] I felt rather like beginning "My Lords & Gentlemen!" but Uncle Sam wouldnt tolerate that. I put in another "Times" cutting[2] if by chance you'd like it for the Trustees to see.

Remember that the underwriters risk ceases at New York. I would like to feel sure of your covering the picture against all risks until it reaches Princeton.

I did not varnish it before it went off, but it could have a thin coat of *copal,* before you hang it up. Let this be done by proper picture people.

Van Wisselinghs agent in New York is Macbeth—Picture Dealers. Do not let the picture be varnished until it reaches Princeton. When they do varnish it they lay it flat on the ground which insures the varnish lying flat.

The Bills of Lading will follow this.

One case contains the big portrait[,] the smaller case contains the two landscapes, and four drawings.

                                        Truly Yours   Fred Yates.

ALS (WP, DLC).
    [1] The enclosed "note" is missing because Wilson forwarded it in his letter to Moses Taylor Pyne of December 31, 1906. It was, as Wilson put it, a "formal letter of Mr. Yates . . . stating the price for the [Wilson] portrait itself. . . ."
    [2] A clipping of a news item in the London *Times,* Nov. 6, 1906, saying that Yates had exhibited Wilson's portrait and a number of oil paintings at Mr. Van Wisselingh's, 14 Grafton St., London.

To the Board of Trustees of Princeton University

                    [Princeton, N. J.]   December 13th, 1906.
GENTLEMEN OF THE BOARD OF TRUSTEES:

I have the honor to submit my annual report for the year 1905-1906.

Since my last report, our colleague Dr. George Macloskie has retired from active duty on the teaching force of the University, after a service of thirty-two years. Dr. Macloskie came to Princeton as Professor of Biology in 1874 from Trinity College, Dublin, and throughout the years which have ensued has constantly grown in our esteem and confidence. His services became of increasing value to the University as the years went by, and he now retires to a well-earned rest,—and yet not to an entire rest. He sought the

leisure of retirement from the exacting duties of teacher at this
time in order to make sure of an immediate opportunity to complete his portion of our important Pategonian Reports.[1]

The additions to our teaching force this year, though not so
numerous as those which I had the pleasure of reporting a year
ago, are noteworthy, both in number and in quality.

Dr. Norman Smith, who comes to us from Glasgow University,
to succeed Professor Thilly as Stewart [Stuart] Professor of Psychology, was graduated Master of Arts at St. Andrews University
in 1893, and after graduation spent two years in study at the
Universities of Zürich, Berlin and Paris. In 1896 he was appointed Assistant Professor of Philosophy at the University of
Glasgow. The following year he received the additional appointment of Lecturer in Philosophy at Queen Margaret College. In
1903 he received the degree of Doctor of Philosophy from St.
Andrews University. For ten years before coming to us, Mr. Smith
had steadily grown in the confidence and admiration, not only of
his colleagues at the University of Glasgow, but also of all those
who observe the progress of philosophical thought in Great Britain. In him we once more bring from Scotland some of the most
vigorous influences of our thought.

Dr. Owen Williams [Willans] Richardson, Professor of Physics, was graduated Bachelor of Arts from Cambridge University
in 1900, having taken First Class Honors in Part I of the Natural
History Tripos in 1899, and First Class Honors in both physics
and chemistry in Part II of the Natural History Tripos in 1900.
The year following his graduation he was elected to the Coutts
Trotter Studentship for Research in Physics at Trinity College; in
1902 he was appointed Fellow of the same college; and in 1903
obtained the Clerk Maxwell Studentship for Research in Physics
in Cambridge University. In 1904 he received the degree of Master of Arts. At the same time that he matriculated at Cambridge
University, he matriculated also at London University, where he
earned similar honors in his chosen branches of study, and from
which he received in 1903 the degree of Doctor of Science, for
research in physics. At the time of his appointment here he was a
Fellow and Sub-Lector of Trinity College, Cambridge, Director

1 William B. Scott (ed.), *Reports of the Princeton University Expeditions to
Patagonia, 1896-1899* (8 vols. in 19, Princeton, N. J., 1901-32). The chief object
of the expeditions was the collection of vertebrate and invertebrate fossils.
By 1906, Macloskie had contributed two parts to the eighth volume on botany:
"Ferns and Fern-like Plants of Patagonia" and "Flora Patagonica." He planned
to revise these sections in retirement and completed this task in 1914 with the
publication of a supplement to the eighth volume entitled *Botany—Section III
Revision of Flora Patagonica.*

of natural science studies at Corpus Christi College, Cambridge, Clerk Maxwell Student in the University, and a demonstrator in the Cavendish Laboratory.

Dr. Augustus Trowbridge, Professor of Physics, studied at the Columbia School of Mines from 1890 to 1893, leaving without a degree to accept an engineering position at the World's Columbian Exposition in Chicago. In 1894 he entered the University of Berlin as a student of mathematics and physics, and in 1898 received from that University the degree of Doctor of Philosophy. The same year he was appointed Instructor in Physics at the University of Michigan. From 1900 to 1903 he was Assistant Professor of Physics at the University of Wisconsin, a position which he left for a single semester to study at the University of Bologna, returning to fill a full professorship at Wisconsin, the chair which he held until he came to us.

Dr. Edward Plimpton Adams, Assistant Professor of Physics, was graduated Bachelor of Arts, from Beloit College in 1899. From 1899 to 1901 he was a student in the graduate school of Harvard University, receiving from that University in the latter year the degree of Master of Science. From 1901 to 1903 he held the appointment from Harvard as John Tyndall Scholar, and pursued studies at the universities of Berlin, Göttingen, and Cambridge. In 1904 he received from Harvard the degree of Doctor of Philosophy. Since 1903 he has been Instructor in Physics at Princeton, where he has completely established himself in our confidence.

Dr. Philip Ely Robinson, who is also this year promoted from an Instructorship in Physics to an Assistant Professorship, was graduated Bachelor of Arts from Princeton University in 1898. He pursued special studies in science at Princeton from the time of his graduation until 1900, holding during the first of his two years of graduate study here the Class of 1861 Fellowship in Experimental Science, and receiving at the end of his fellowship year the degree of Master of Arts. From 1900 to 1903 he studied at Berlin and Giessen, receiving the degree of Doctor of Philosophy from the latter University in 1903. Since 1903 he has been Instructor in Physics at Princeton.

Mr. Hereward Lester Cooke, Assistant Professor of Physics, was graduated from McGill University in 1900, taking first rank honors in philosophy. From 1901 to 1903 he was Demonstrator in Physics at McGill, and in 1903 he received from that University the degree of Master of Arts. In the same year he was awarded the 1851 Exhibition Scholarship, placed at the disposal of McGill University, an appointment which he held by special extension for three years, during which period he was engaged in research work at the Cavendish Laboratory at Cambridge University. In 1903 he was also awarded the Advance Student Exhibition, offered by Emanuel College, Cambridge. He thus comes to us directly from the Cavendish Laboratory.

Mr. Walter Maxwell Adriance, Preceptor in History, Politics and Economics, was graduated Bachelor of Arts from Yale University in 1900. During the two years following his graduation he taught French and German in Westminster School at Simsbury, Connecticut. The next three years he spent in graduate study in the Department of Economics at Yale, from which University he received in 1903 the degree of Master of Arts. During the academic year 1905-1906 he served as Instructor in Debating at Yale, and as coach of the debating teams.

Dr. Edgar Dawson, Preceptor in History, Politics and Economics, was graduated Bachelor of Arts from Davidson College, North Carolina, in 1895, and Master of Arts from the University of Virginia in 1897, holding at the University of Virginia the John Y. Mason Fellowship in History. From 1897 to 1899 he was Principal of New Providence Academy in Virginia; from 1899 to 1900 he was a student of history, English philology, and modern philosophy at Heidelberg University, and at Leipzig University from 1900 to 1902, receiving from that University in 1902 the degree of Doctor of Philosophy. Since 1902 he has been Professor of History and English at Delaware College, Newark, Delaware.[2]

Dr. William Starr Myers, Preceptor in History, Politics and Economics, was graduated Bachelor of Arts from the University of North Carolina in 1897. During the three following years he was a graduate student in History, Politics and Economics at the John Hopkins University, receiving from that University in 1900 the degree of Doctor of Philosophy. From 1900 until the present year he was Master of History in the Baltimore Country School for Boys.[3]

Dr. Henry Russell Spencer, Preceptor in History, Politics and Economics, was graduated Bachelor of Arts from Colby College in 1899, Master of Arts from Columbia University in 1901, Doctor of Philosophy from Columbia University in 1905, holding the University Fellowship in American History at Columbia during the year 1902-1903. After 1903 he was not in residence at Co-

[2] Now the University of Delaware.
[3] Now the Gilman School.

lumbia, but served as Instructor in American History and Political Science (1903-1905) in the Ohio State University. In 1905 he was advanced to the rank of Assistant Professor.

Mr. Charles Rufus Morey, Preceptor in Art and Archaeology, was graduated Bachelor of Arts from Michigan University in 1899, Master of Arts in 1900. From 1900 to 1903 he was Fellow in the American School of Classical Studies at Rome, being also during two of those years Buhl Fellow of the University of Michigan. From 1903 to 1904 he held the Fellowship in Archaeology at Princeton; from 1904 to 1905 he was Instructor in Classics at the Princeton Preparatory School; from 1905 to the present year Instructor in Classics in Princeton University, a position from which he is now promoted to be Preceptor in Art and Archaeology.

Dr. Morris William Croll, Preceptor in English, was graduated Bachelor of Arts from Pennsylvania College, Gettysburg, Pennsylvania,[4] in 1889. After teaching several years he entered the senior class of Harvard University, from which in 1894 he received the degree of Bachelor of Arts, and in 1895 the degree of Master of Arts. For four years he was Instructor in English in the University School at Cleveland, Ohio, and for two years studied as Harrison Fellow at the University of Pennsylvania, from which University, in 1891 [1901], he received the degree of Doctor of Philosophy. From 1901 to 1905 he occupied the position of Associate Editor of the revised edition of Worcester's Dictionary, planned by Mr. Lippincott.[5] In 1895 [1905] he came to Princeton as Instructor in English, a position from which he is now advanced to be Preceptor.

Dr. Lewis Wardlaw Miles, Preceptor in English, was graduated Bachelor of Arts from the Johns Hopkins University in 1894. After graduation he studied medicine for three years, at the University of Maryland, receiving in 1897 the degree of Doctor of Medicine. After graduating in Medicine he turned again to study at the Johns Hopkins University, devoting his attention to French, German and English, and receiving in 1902 the degree of Doctor of Philosophy. From 1903 to 1905 he served as Instructor in German in the Baltimore Country School for boys, from whence in 1905 he was invited to a instructorship in English at Princeton. He is this year promoted to membership in the faculty as Preceptor.

Dr. John [Jacob] Newton Beam, Preceptor in Modern Languages, was graduated Bachelor of Arts from Princeton Univer-

[4] Now Gettysburg College.
[5] *Worcester's Academic Dictionary*, the revised edition of which was published by J. B. Lippincott Co. of Philadelphia in 1908.

sity in 1896, and immediately after graduation became Instructor in German and French at the Princeton Preparatory School, where he remained three years. In 1899 he received the degree of Master of Arts from Princeton, and became an Instructor in the University, teaching German during the year 1899-1900, and French during the year 1900-1901. He then went abroad for study, and after two years at the University of Jena, received from that University the degree of Doctor of Philosophy. In 1903 he returned to Princeton as Instructor, and has served the University continuously since that time.

Mr. Varnum Lansing Collins was graduated Bachelor of Arts from Princeton University in 1892, Master of Arts in 1895. During the year following his graduation he was Professor of Classics at Moore's Hill College, Indiana; the year 1893-1894 he devoted to the study of modern languages at Princeton; in 1894 he accepted the position of Secretary to the University Librarian, and he has continuously served the University in connection with the administration of the Library from that time until his present appointment as Preceptor in Modern Languages, first as Secretary to the Librarian (1894-1895), then as Assistant in charge of circulation (1895-1896), and finally for ten years (1896-1906) as Reference Librarian.

The following new appointments have been made in the staff of Instructors:

In History, Politics and Economics, Walter Lincoln Whittlesey, A. B., University of Oregon, who has had five years experience in teaching at the University of Oregon and at Cornell University. *In English*, George Dobbin Brown, A.B., Johns Hopkins University, 1895, Ph.D. 1901, recently English Master in the Country School for Boys, Baltimore; Maxwell Struthers Burt, A.B., Princeton University, 1904, graduate student at Munich, 1904-1905, at Oxford University, 1905-1906; Charles William Kennedy, A.B., Columbia University, 1902, Ph.D. Princeton University, 1906, having been Scribner Fellow in English 1905-1906; and Herbert Spencer Murch, A.B., University of Oregon, 1898; Doctor of Philosophy, Yale University, 1906; Assistant in English in the academic faculty, Yale University, 1901-1906. *In Modern Languages*, Sigmund Gottfried Spaeth, A.B., Haverford College, 1905; A.M. 1906, and Teaching Fellow in English, 1905-1906; and Donald Clive Stuart, A.B., University of Michigan, 1903, A.M. 1904, graduate student at Columbia University, 1904-1905, and at the Sorbonne, 1905-1906. *In Mathematics*, Robert Lee Moore, B.S. and M.A., University of Texas, 1901; Ph.D. University of Chicago, 1905; Assistant Professor of Mathematics, at the

University of Tennessee, 1905-1906. *In Physics*, Philip Thomas, B.Sc., Ohio State University, 1904, and from 1904 to 1906 in the employ of the Western Electric Company, Chicago. *In Chemistry*, Walter Daniel Bonner, B.S., Nebraska Wesleyan University, 1906; and John Davison Rue, B.S., Princeton, 1906; *In Civil Engineering*, Ralph Andrew Barry, C.E., Princeton, 1906; and Elliott Chipman Brown, C.E., Princeton, 1904.

Our new method of instruction has now had a full year's test, and has stood the test most satisfactorily. It has produced more and better work; it has systematized and vitalized study; it has begun to make reading men; and it has brought teachers and pupils into intimate relations of mutual interest and confidence. I speak of it as a "system" of instruction, but we have not given it the symmetry or the uniform rules of a system. We have sought to preserve the utmost elasticity in its use, in order that the individual gifts and personal characteristics of the Preceptors might have free play. Not only must instruction in each subject have its own methods and points of view, but each instructor must be as free as possible to adapt himself to his pupils as well as to his subject. What is true of all teaching is particularly true of this intimate way of associating teacher and pupil: the method is no more effective than the man who uses it. His whole makeup conditions his success and determines its character. The almost uniform success of last year's work means that the teachers were singularly fitted for the new and delicate task for which they had been selected.

There were marked varieties of success, of course. The new way of teaching demands for its ideal success a very intimate and cordial sympathy between the preceptor and his pupils, and of course not all of the preceptors have been of the temperament to make close friends of the men they taught. Some are a little too much inclined to be mere faithful taskmaskers [taskmasters], the supervisors of their men's work, and the intimacy between them and their pupils is hardly more than the intimacy that must in any case come from such relations of mutual responsibility. Some have succeeded because they stimulated their men; some because they understood and helped them; some because they knew how to hold them to strict and frequent reckonings; some because they interested; others because they had the gift for congenial conference. But amidst all the variety there has been no failure, and the beginning of the second year of the system already shows interesting results in the new attitude of the undergraduates and the manifest fruits of the year of training. Each class shows a distinct stage of advance. It is not merely a year further along in the subject of study, but also a year further along in the ability to study, and in intelligence of approach and facility in work.

I am sure that you will read with interest and pleasure what the Lib[r]arian of the University says, in the report hereto appended, of the effects of the new system as shown in the use of the library. There has been a general intellectual quickening. It followed, of course, from the new requirements of study involved in the new method of instruction that more books would be used and the library more habitually resorted to, but something much more interesting than that has taken place. The voluntary use of the library has very greatly increased. Required work has produced a general inclination and desire to read, which has been gratified by reading of all kinds. Moreover, the too great engrossment of the teacher in his work with the men assigned him, to the exclusion of original work of his own, which we so much feared, has not as a matter of fact followed the introduction of the system. The Lib[r]arian informs us that the library was never before so much used for research and original study. I think that these facts should give all who are interested in the advancement and distinction of the University peculiar gratification.

The most noteworthy change affecting the subject matter of the undergraduate course of study which was made during the year, was the introduction of a special honors course in mathematics and physics. When the present course of undergraduate study was under discussion in the faculty, it was generally agreed that the more serious students who wished to be candidates for honors in some special field of study ought to be offered an opportunity for more intensive and definite study in their departments, after passing through the drill of freshman and sophomore years, but it was thought best to postpone the formulation of such special courses until the new scheme of study had been tried in its entirety for a little while, and until there should be special opportunities of instruction because of increases in our staff or equipment, or because of the disclosure, as we gained experience, of special opportunities for a suitable rearrangement or adaptation of courses. Towards the close of the last academic year such a special opportunity seemed to have disclosed itself in the mathematical and physical studies. Our staff of instruction in those subjects has been notably strengthened. The study of the preparatory mathematics runs far back into the school years, and our undergraduates may be presumed to have ascertained their tastes and aptitudes in studies of that kind quite definitely: and the combination of mathematics and physics affords a sufficiently broad and various body of the subject-matter of exact science to render it feasible to arrange for intensive study which shall not be specialization. Moreover, those subjects lie within a field of study which students are not likely to enter from mere whim or taste and without serious purpose,—the purpose of really stretching their minds to consistent endeavour. The faculty therefore consented to the formulation, somewhat earlier than would otherwise have been deemed wise, of an honors course in mathematics and physics.

The course begins in sophomore year. All sophomores are required to take a three-hour course in general physics. Those who seek honors always take the elective course in mathematics. Under the new arrangement those who seek honors are required to take, not the ordinary three-hour elective in mathematics, but a four-hour course designed for the purpose; and in order that they may have more time for these special studies, they are released from one of the additional elective courses which they would otherwise have been obliged to select. Thus they take, as all sophomores do, the required course in logic and psychology and, if they are candidates for the degree of Bachelor of Arts, the required Greek of the first term and the required Latin of the second term; and they are obliged to add to their elective mathematics only one other elective study, if they are candidates for the B.S. or Litt.B. degrees, and if candidates for the Bachelor of Arts degree, take no elective but mathematics. Their whole number of hours is thirteen instead of fifteen. In junior year the concentration becomes more complete. Out of a list including a course in pure mathematics, a course in analysis, a course in applied mathematics (mechanics in junior year, electricity and magnetism in senior year), a course in theoretical physics and a course in experimental physics, each candidate for honors is permitted to choose three consecutive courses, his senior courses being also consecutive with his junior courses, and he is obliged to add to these nine hours of work in mathematics and physics only one additional elective. This additional elective must, however, lie entirely outside the field of mathematics and physics. His total number of hours is twelve instead of fifteen.

It is hoped that this new arrangement of studies for men seeking honors in this particular field will encourage at least a small body of specially qualified men to attempt serious achievement in exact science, and the members of the faculty directly concerned by the change have entered upon the new undertaking with a great deal of enthusiasm.

The year which has passed since my last report has confirmed us in our confidence that our plans for a graduate college are not only wise but also sure to be singularly fruitful along the very lines which are most characteristic of them. Instead of being scattered here and there through the town, wherever they could find lodgings, a large number of our graduate students have been living together at Merwick, and their close and constant contact with one another, their free life, their refined and agreeable environment have not only added greatly to their pleasure, but have brought, as we expected, a contagion of high ideals and of scholarly ambitions whose influence it has been very delightful to witness. The life at Merwick under Mr. Butler and Dean West has proved another of those innovations which recent years have witnessed at Princeton, which were not experiments but parts of a development along well thought out lines.

It is the more gratifying, therefore, that Mrs. Josephine E. Thompson Swann should have enabled us, by her generous bequest, to take immediately the next step, and enlarge this community life of our graduate students to something like an adequate scale. Mrs. Swann's bequest will amount to fully $250,-000, and will be paid into the University treasury about the first of January next. Mrs. Swann directs by her will that this sum be devoted "as soon as practicable, to the erection and construction upon the grounds of the said University of a building to be known as the John R. Thompson Graduate College of Princeton University; the said building to contain sitting and sleeping rooms for professors and students, with a dining hall, kitchen and the necessary appurtenances in a portion of the building entirely separate and apart from such sitting and sleeping rooms. The living rooms shall be rented at the best prices they will command . . . and the income derived from such rentals, after deducting the cost of maintaining said building, shall be devoted to the maintenance of as many fellowships of $400 each as the funds will provide. These fellowships . . . shall be given to Bachelors of Arts of the male sex, of high character and ability, who would not otherwise be able to continue their studies at the University. The fellows, to a number not exceeding thirty, shall have unfurnished rooms in the building free of rent. The tuition fees of the fellows shall be remitted by the Trustees as a condition of this gift. . . . The said fellowships shall be bestowed upon Bachelors of Arts who are engaged in scientific and literary research other than that directly connected with professional studies, so-called;" shall be known as The John R. Thompson Fellowships; and in awarding them "Bachelors of Arts of Princeton University shall have preference in the order named: First, from the Borough of Princeton: Second, from the County of Mercer, and Third, from other parts of the State of New Jersey, provided always that the attainments of such persons are fully equal to those of other applicants. In default of such candidates, the appointments are to be open to male Americans holding the degree of A.B. from any approved college or university. No one of said fellowships shall be given to or held by a married man." It is further directed that resident fellows of the college shall eat at the common table and pay the charges fixed therefor.

These provisions agree in every substantial particular with the plans already made for the development of graduate life at Merwick, and the beginnings made there will very easily lend themselves to this expansion. We may congratulate ourselves that we have thus immediately at hand the opportunity to build a graduate college which may be so readily and so consistently combined, as first a model and then an auxiliary, with the great graduate college for whose erection and endowment we are so eagerly seeking funds. Wisely planned and placed, Thompson College will always stand as one of the ornaments of our campus, and as a most interesting evidence of Mrs. Swann's generosity and foresight. It is a significant link in our chain of consistent development.

The number of graduate students, which was last year 106, is this year 115. Of this number 38 are devoting themselves exclusively to graduate study as against 33 last year, and 77 are combining graduate study in the University with graduate work in Princeton Theological Seminary. Of the 38 regular graduate students 11 are in residence at Merwick and sixteen take their meals there. When Thompson College is completed, we shall have accommodations for a very much larger proportion.

The following table shows the number admitted to the University as undergraduates this year, as compared with last:

	1905	1906
Freshmen without conditions	134	146
Freshmen with conditions	277	202
Specials	48	13
Seniors	5	2
Juniors	3	4
Sophomores	8	11
	475	378

Of the freshmen admitted upon examination in 1905, twenty for one reason or another did not come. Of those admitted this year twenty-six did not come. So that the corrected figures for the two years are: 1905, 455; 1906, 352. The actual number of freshmen who entered the University in 1905 was 391, in 1906, 322, a loss of 69 in the entrance figures of this year as compared with those of last year. To these statistics the following should, for the full information of the Board, be added:

	1905	1906
Examined but not admitted	69	72
Preliminary and partial examination	437	455

There was thus a gain of eighteen in the number of preliminary and partial examinations this year as compared with a loss of forty-eight last year, as compared with the year preceding. The comparative stability of these latter figures and the falling off in entrance indicate, so far as we can ascertain, the same thing. Formerly, because our examinations were often less difficult or our standards less rigidly maintained than those of other universities of the same rank and reputation, a large number of ill-prepared and unstudious boys came to Princeton from the secondary schools, particularly the private schools. Now, it being generally understood that our requirements are rigidly insisted on and that poor preparation means almost certain failure at the term examinations after entrance, none but boys who can hope to meet our requirements are inclined to attempt our tests. Slowly the number of well-prepared applicants is increasing. You will notice that the proportion of the present freshmen admitted without conditions is much larger than last year, and the figures given do not indicate the full extent of the improvement, because the proportion of very lightly conditioned men is not indicated. The best secondary private schools are sending a larger number of their men to us, but such changes are always slow. The tide will take several years to turn, but with the improving quality of our students, we are quite willing to wait.

The total undergraduate enrollment of the University is 1236 and was last year 1280, a decrease of forty-four. The number of instructors of all grades has increased since last year from 153 to 164, an average of about one teacher to seven and one-half pupils.

Patton Hall was completed during the summer and is now occupied. It seems to be in every way excellently adapted to its uses, and, with the addition to Blair Hall and the other dormitories now in prospect through the generosity of other classes, bids fair somewhat to lighten our burden with regard to the housing of the undergraduates.

The construction of the addition to Blair Hall has been delayed by the slowness of one of the contractors in supplying the stone for the interesting skewed arch which is to span the roadway, but the other portions of the building are progressing more satisfactorily and are already under roof. They constitute as satisfactory an addition to the beautiful line of Blair Hall as we had expected, and will add greatly both to the charm and to the convenience of that part of the campus.

The central portion of McCosh Hall is now under roof, and it is hoped that the class rooms which it contains will be ready for use by the beginning of the second term. The other portions of the building go forward more slowly. As the walls of the building near completion they show an unusual beauty of form and proportion, and promise to make this noble memorial to our beloved one-time leader one of the finest ornaments, as it will be one of the most useful buildings, of the campus.

The Treasurer's Report will be found this year to be in a more convenient form for reference than hitherto. As now formulated, it forms a very plain and satisfactory exhibit of the resources and the expenses of the University. The item which will no doubt chiefly attract your attention is the $120,538 received through the Committee of Fifty. The splendid work being done by this committee is a truly extraordinary evidence of the loyalty and generosity of the alumni of the University. And yet the Committee feels that their work is but just begun and that their efforts "to capitalize the good will of the alumni" will from year to year show yet much larger results. It is immensely encouraging to feel that the strength of the alumni is behind us in the execution of our plans for the development of Princeton. The total gifts for immediate expenditure, including those received through the Committee of Fifty, amounted to $158,071.27, and besides this there was received for endowment and permanent investment $365,451.31, making the total gifts for the year $523,522.58. The total income for the year, including the gifts for immediate expenditure, was $568,131.06.

During the year three of our professors emeriti have been put upon the roll of the Carnegie Foundation for the Advancement of Teaching, to receive retiring allowances.[6] This admirable foundation bids fair to be of the highest usefulness in relieving college teachers of the anxieties of old age, and will

6 Charles Augustus Young, William Alfred Packard, and George Macloskie. See H. S. Pritchett to WW, June 9, 1906.

certainly render the administration of a system of retirements henceforth comparatively simple.

Respectfully submitted, WOODROW WILSON.[7]

Printed document (WP, DLC).
[7] There is a WWsh draft of this report, dated Dec. 13, 1906, in WP, DLC.

A Supplementary Report to the Board of Trustees of Princeton University

[Princeton, N. J.,
GENTLEMEN OF THE BOARD OF TRUSTEES: c. Dec. 13, 1906]

I take the liberty this year of submitting a supplementary report, because I wish to bring to your attention certain matters concerning our University life, a discussion of which it would, I think, at this time be unwise to make public.

The questions I am about to approach and their proper solution have been taking form in my mind for many years, and the suggestions I shall make, though radical in character, are the fruit of very mature consideration.

As the University has grown in numbers and in popularity elements have been introduced into its life which threaten a kind of disintegration, which would unquestionably mean, also, a deep demoralization. These elements center in the Upperclass Clubs. They are, I believe, susceptible of being dealt with and removed now without serious friction and with the best feeling on all hands, but I am not sure that they would be a year or two hence. We have dealt with the studies of the University and have put them upon an admirable footing. The life of the University is the atmosphere of its studies. We must now turn to that and make it such an atmosphere as will best sustain study and every other wholesome thing.

The undergraduate is much more affected by his relations outside the classroom and outside the conferences with his preceptor than by his relations to his teachers, as our life is at present organized. In regard to his studies, he is either steadied or distracted by the social influences about him. His morals in all matters of conduct, his standards of success, his ambitions and his aversions are determined for him very largely by what he sees the older men of the college, or the most influential and attractive men of his own class, seeking and avoiding. His ideals are formed by what takes place around him. In our close-knit little University world the winds of habit and opinion hold as steady as trade winds, from season to season, and every undergraduate, except here and there a man of unusual force and initiative, trims his sails to them with cautious precision.

No one who has watched this influence in recent years can doubt that the spirit of the place is less democratic than it used to be. There is a sharp social competition going on, upon which a majority of the men stake their happiness. It seems to grow more and more intense and eager from year to year, and the men who fail in it seem more and more thrust out of the best and most enjoyable things which university life naturally offers—the best comradeships, the freest play of personal influence, the best chance of such social consideration as ought always to be won by natural gifts and force of character.

A certain amount of disintegration has inevitably come by mere growth. The growth of such universities as Harvard has shown that, as our American universities are now organized, unity disappears with increase of numbers. The Harvard authorities are casting about with deep anxiety for some means of drawing the scattered fragments of their undergraduate body together again under some one set of influences, and they have so far sought in vain, after costly experiments such as that of the Harvard Union,[1] by means of which they sought to bring the University together into a common club life. But in our case,

[1] The idea of a Harvard Union, resembling somewhat those at Oxford and Cambridge, had been discussed since the mid-1890's, and in 1899 Henry Lee Higginson gave $150,000 to build a university club on land owned by Harvard University. The building, which was dedicated as the "Harvard Union" on October 15, 1901, contained a restaurant, library, common and meeting rooms, and ten bedrooms for overnight guests, as well as certain service facilities. The Union was intended to be a common meeting ground for all students of the university along with faculty members and alumni, and it was hoped that it would promote democracy and fellowship among all members of the university community.

Whether or not the experiment of the Union was a success by 1906 is difficult to determine. Between 1899 and 1906, the total resident undergraduate and graduate enrollment of Harvard University, including the medical and dental schools in Boston, averaged around 4,000 students a year. By February 1, 1902, three and a half months after the opening of the Union, there were 1,773 "active members" and 1,942 "graduate members." As of October 29, 1906, there were 2,007 active and 2,009 graduate members, and the Union was reported to be in sound financial condition. It was only after 1908 that the total membership declined drastically to less than 2,000. In the 1930's, the Harvard Union became the dining hall and student center for all freshmen at Harvard.

In view of Wilson's comment about the "deep anxiety" of the "Harvard authorities," it should perhaps be stressed that the movement for the Union was initiated and carried through by alumni. Though the President and Dean of Harvard College indicated approval of the experiment in their annual reports, there is no indication that they were deeply concerned about the Union. Indeed, President Charles W. Eliot was well known for his lack of interest in the real or alleged social problems created by the expansion of Harvard University.

For further details, see the *Harvard Graduates' Magazine*, VIII (Dec. 1899), 239-43; *ibid.*, X (Dec. 1901 and March 1902), 214-35, 390; and *ibid.*, XV (Dec. 1906), 272. See also Samuel Eliot Morison, *Three Centuries of Harvard, 1636-1936* (Cambridge, Mass., 1936), pp. 418-19, 478.

growth in numbers is being accompanied by disintegration, not into individual units, but into social groups, a disintegration which means demoralizing struggle and competition. Such influences are peculiarly hostile to that quietness of mind and that calm assurance that merit and achievement will tell, which constitute the best atmosphere of study, and we cannot as university authorities turn our eyes away from them or decline to deal with them.

Let me describe what is taking place.

As the years have gone by, the Upperclass Clubs have assumed a more and more prominent place in our university life, and membership in them has become more and more desirable; and men in the lower classes, instead of waiting to be individually elected into them, have of late years actually organized to obtain admission. The elections to these clubs take place in the spring of sophomore year. Formerly, the clubs, of course, made choice of individual sophomores who seemed to the upperclassmen of the clubs desirable companions, just as any other similar organizations would recruit their membership. But by degrees all that has been changed. For some time covertly, and now quite openly, groups of sophomores get together in certain eating clubs for the purpose of gathering to themselves by their own choice the men who are to go into the several upperclass clubs. The chief of these sophomore eating clubs are distinguished by well known badges, and their membership is each year perpetuated by the introduction at the end of the year of a group of freshmen who are to inherit their opportunities. Their badges are hats of a particular color or a particular combination of colors in the hat and hat-band, and they are known as 'hat lines.' One has a soft felt hat of red, another of green, another of light blue, another of dark blue, another of white with a gray band as its distinctive emblem. Of course, admission into these hat lines (some of which are supposed to be preferable to others) becomes the immediate ambition of freshmen, and plans are quickly laid by members of the entering class to commend themselves to these groups of sophomores; because admission into a hat line almost certainly means ultimate election into one of the upperclass clubs. A sharp rivalry sets in between groups of freshmen having this ambition in view, and the freshman eating clubs come to have a distinct social object, as the sophomore eating clubs have; so that the year closes for them either in success or in bitter disappointment,—a disappointment so keen as to embitter many a young fellow's whole subsequent life at the university. A good many, in their disappointment, withdraw from the university.

This ferment of anxious hope and fear, this busy planning for the coveted social advantage is said to be even more noticeable this year than usual. Hitherto the freshmen clubs have been scattered through the town. Now that they are collected into a single building[2] and drawn into close contact with each other, the contagion is more immediate and more violent, and a much larger proportion of men than usual are absorbed by the passionate desire to get into one of the desired hat lines.

The hat lines are by no means always conducive to good comradeship even, because, being made up by force of ambition rather than because the members are congenial to one another, they are often disturbed by interior divisions and hopeless incompatibilities of temperament. Instances have been known of a hat line whose members were divided into two or more groups who had nothing to do with each other, either in their club rooms or elsewhere.

Moreover, the whole system works to the serious detriment of the upperclass clubs. Their choice is between groups, not among individuals; because they want one or two particular men, they must take a whole "following" (for such is the undergraduate name for a hat line group), the men they do not care for along with those they would like, and there are very serious embarrassments about picking out members from more than one following. The sophomores organized into followings are virtually in a position to dictate who of their classmates shall be selected.

I need hardly comment upon the influence of this system of life. You see how all university "politics" must spring out of it. You see how certain it is that many a modest fellow, who did not happen to be aggressive enough or lucky enough in freshman year to get into a favorite following may easily miss the pleasures and the influence in university life to which he may be entitled by gifts and character. I do not mean to say that a majority of the men who do not "make" a following and an upperclass club are crushed by that circumstance, but it does make a serious difference in their lives at the University. Many men deliberately stay out of these organizations by choice or because they cannot afford the extra expense which membership entails, and it has often happened that some of the most highly esteemed and some of the most popular men of a class are outside, not inside, the clubs and followings. The democracy of the place is not destroyed. But it is impaired, and social preferences in themselves undesirable are put by the system of hat lines upon a clearly artificial and unnatural footing.

2 All freshmen were now required to eat in the commons in University Hall.

The upperclass clubs have, the while, been growing less and less simple in their appointments and in their standards of living, and graduates who were themselves members of the clubs when they were in Princeton, express their deep concern at the growth of what they, with perhaps some exaggeration, call the luxury of life at the clubs, as they erect more and more costly buildings and add this, that, and the other elaboration to their lives. More serious than these things is the slow, almost imperceptible and yet increasingly certain decline of the old democratic spirit of the place and the growth and multiplication of social divisions. There is something singularly fine and unselfish in the Princeton spirit—a spirit of solidarity and of love for the University, and it does constantly overcome and obscure these tendencies; but they are there and do become more and more noticeable and disturbing.

These influences not only prevent the simplicity and naturalness of life which should belong to a university, not only introduce a spirit of social competition which interferes with the natural intercourse and comradeship of the undergraduates, but are also distinctly and very seriously hostile to the spirit of study, incompatible with the principles of a true republic of letters and of learning. We shall not have done our duty by the University until we have succeeded in discovering and applying a remedy.

The remedy I suggest is to oblige the undergraduates to live together, not in clubs but in colleges. I propose that we divide the University into colleges and that we induce the stronger upperclass clubs themselves to become colleges under the guidance of the University.

By college I mean not merely a group of dormitories, but an eating hall as well, with all its necessary appointments, where all the residents of the college shall take their meals together. I would have over each college a master and in it two or three resident preceptors, and I would have these resident members of the faculty take their meals in hall with the undergraduates; but I would suggest that the undergraduates of each college be given a large measure of self-government, in the spirit of our later development, so that the rules of the college life should be administered, if not framed, by committees upon which undergraduates should have full representation. Each college would thus form a unit in itself, a largely self-governing unit.

No member of a college, of course, could arrange to take his meals outside his college at a club, and undergraduates could not be members at once of a college and of such clubs as we now have, founded on the habit and convenience of eating together. Because I greatly respect and admire the history and traditions of our present upperclass clubs, I would make great sacrifices in the carrying out of such a plan as I have suggested, rather than destroy them or even break the continuity of their life and development. They have been the center of many wholesome and honorable influences, and only their recent developments have made their continuance upon their present plan a menace to the right guidance of our university growth. I would propose therefore that they be induced, by every proper suggestion and influence, themselves to develop into colleges.

The changes necessary to effect the transition would be, in form at any rate, very slight. The devotion of their graduates supplies them and seems likely to supply them more and more abundantly with money for expansion, and as things stand at present they are tempted to spend it upon the enlargement and beautification of their homes. In order to convert themselves into colleges of the sort I suggest, it would be necessary for them only, (1st) to undertake as soon as and as rapidly as their resources permitted, the building of dormitories attached to their present clubhouses, until they had enough apartments to house their members; (2nd) to admit to residence one or more unmarried members of the faculty, nominated by them to the President of the University and approved by the Board of Trustees or by the President, upon their delegation; and (3rd) to put the guidance of their affairs from day to day partly in the hands of these resident teachers, a concession which need sacrifice no essential point of their self-government.

It would not be necessary for them to give up their privilege of choosing their undergraduate members. Constitutions could be agreed upon for them, which would leave them practically as free in that matter as they were before the creation of the hat lines. They could select from the Junior members of the other colleges and make their membership up upon any principle of congeniality that commended itself to them. So far from losing anything by the change, they would certainly gain a unique distinction in the history of American education and American university life, and add to their own vitality and interest, while serving their university in an extraordinary degree.

Relieved by the club-colleges of a portion of the campus population, the University could the sooner provide dormitory room for all its students and the exceedingly desirable end would be immediately attained of having the freshmen in the dormitories and under the direct influence of University life. In the colleges those influences would be stronger than ever and more wholesome, for classes would be merged, not separated, in their common life, and the older men would exercise a healthy influence, by way both of restraint and example, upon the freshmen and sophomores. Our senior class would be more than ever our governors, to their great benefit and ours.

In brief, then, I would substitute the college for the club. Our present social life is based on the eating club. Intercourse in the eating clubs furnishes us with the whole social atmosphere, alike of our athletics and of our studies, and it is in principle an organization by clique, by severed groups, with no common uniting object. In the new comradeship of the college a common object and association would be supplied, and the spirit of letters could, under the proper fosterage, creep into the general consciousness. The ugly rivalries and jealousies of the present system would be reduced to a minimum; college life would be once more unified and once more given a collegiate object. The negative argument for the change is that it would pluck present abuses up by the roots. The positive argument is that it would foster a new spirit and a new principle of union and of comradeship. Other universities are likely to try this method of reintegration, but none has such materials for it or such bases of cooperative enthusiasm as we have. We have put teacher and pupil into a new relation of comradeship almost forgotten elsewhere. We must now provide a new comradeship for pupil and pupil.

I know that it will be objected that this is, so far as college is to be divided from college in the reorganization of the University, a method of dividing, not a method of reuniting the University, but it has already grown beyond the point where it would be possible to make of it a single unit again. The disintegration is taking place, a disintegration into atoms too small to hold the fine spirit of college life. We must substitute for disintegration a new organic process. The new body will have divisions, but all the parts will be organs of a common life. It is reintegration by more varied and more abundant organic life. This is the time to act, when the fluid mass trembles upon the verge of some sort of final crystallization.[3]

TR (Trustees' Papers, UA, NjP).

[3] There is a WWhw outline, dated Dec. 1906, and a WWsh draft of this report, dated Dec. 13, 1906, in WP, DLC.

From the Minutes of the Board of Trustees
of Princeton University

[Dec. 13, 1906]

The Trustees of Princeton University met in stated session in the Trustees' Room in the Chancellor Green Library, Princeton, New Jersey, at eleven o'clock on Thursday morning December 13, 1906.

The President of the University in the Chair. . . .

COMMITTEE TO CONSIDER SUPPLEMENTARY REPORT
OF THE PRESIDENT

After a discussion of the supplementary report of the President on motion of Mr. Jones, seconded by Mr. Henry, the following resolution was adopted:

> RESOLVED, That a committee of seven, of which the President of the University shall be the Chairman, be appointed by the chair to consider the proposition of the President as outlined in his supplementary report and to report thereon at the March meeting of the Board.

In accordance with this resolution the President of the University appointed the following Committee:

> Woodrow Wilson, Chairman
> M. Taylor Pyne
> Melancthon W. Jacobus
> Bayard Henry
> David B. Jones
> Cleveland H. Dodge
> Robert Garrett[1]

[1] The committee's report (drafted, actually, entirely by Wilson) is printed at June 10, 1907, Vol. 17.

From Annie Wilson Howe

My darling brother,   Chapel Hill, N. C. Dec. 13th, 1906

I suppose I should take the telegram you sent me as an answer to my letter of welcome home. I was certainly glad to receive it and enjoyed seeing dear Nell so much. I am so glad she is happy at St. Marys. The first week or two after her arrival was so dismal and she was so disgusted with *every*thing that although I was just as sorry for her as I could be, and full of sympathy, I could not help being amused. You know whatever Nell does is done energetically, and her expressions of disgust were not exceptions to her usual style. Of course it was to me alone that she gave vent to her feelings, and she was sweet about it too—saying that she thought things would look brighter soon. She was very much disappointed that she could not come to us on Thanksgiving. She had enjoyed her first little visit so much. I hope she can come oftener after Christmas.

Woodrow, I have felt very sorely tempted to borrow thirty five hundred or four thousand dollars and buy a little house here. I can buy a pretty lot and build a house to suit myself for that sum, the only trouble being that I may not be able to borrow at five per cent. I wish I had spent what father left me for this purpose. The advantage of building here is that I could most probably sell or rent at *any* time—houses being in great demand. Dr. Pratt,[1] who is probably the most practical business man here, says they will be more and more so, as the college is growing. What do you think about it? The great trouble is that I would *never* be able to pay off the mortgage as there will never be any money coming to me from outside.

I was so distressed to hear of Ellie's trouble about finding a cook—and the price you have to pay for her now that she is found.

Please kiss Ellie and Margaret for me, and *beg* them both to write to me some time when they can find leisure.

Madge has just left for Richmond. She has been with us for a week this time. She has made many friends here, and was *very* much admired of course. She looks so pretty in bright colors.

In speaking of my pet scheme, I forgot to say that there is a charming little house, just next door to George's house, for sale. The price is thirty five hundred, and five hundred would put it in perfect shape.

All in the house unite with me in warmest love to every one of you. A heart full from

Your devoted sister,   Annie W. Howe.

ALS (WP, DLC).
[1] Joseph Hyde Pratt, Professor of Economic Geology at the University of North Carolina and State Geologist since 1906.

From Melancthon Williams Jacobus

En Route Thursday Evg
My dear President Wilson: 13th Decr 1906

If the enclosed prophesy[1] is realized, would it be wise to nominate Mr Bryce for a Princeton degree?

He may have been honored already by us—I confess ignorance —or he might possibly be unwilling to accept our offer: but there can be no question of his coming within our "Canons."[2]

I wish to thank you for forwarding to me the request for a pastor from the Aberdeen Church. I am placing it in the hands of our Faculty Committee on Supplies at whose hands it will receive careful consideration

Finally—You placed before us today one of the most significant measures ever taken under the thought of the Board. Have no question as to its ultimately successful working out; it only needs a wise and patient handling

Hurriedly   M W Jacobus

ALS (WP, DLC).
[1] It was an unidentified newspaper editorial speculating on the likelihood of the appointment of James Bryce as British Ambassador to the United States.
[2] Wilson was not able to make arrangements for the award of an honorary degree to Bryce until 1907.

From John Howell Westcott

Dear Woodrow: [Princeton, N. J.] Dec. 13, 1906

The work of the preceptors is distributed this term, as follows:

	Total		class		Precept.	
Anderson	Total	17	class	6	Precept.	11
Basore	"	15	"	6	"	9
Cameron	"	15	"	3	"	12
Hastings	"	16	"	6	"	10
Hutson	"	17	"	6	"	11
Kellogg	"	15	"	6	"	9
MacRae	"	18	"	6	"	12
Magie	"	15	"	6	"	9
Rankin	"	16	"	6	"	10
Stuart	"	16	"	4	"	12
Van Hook	"	13	"	2	"	11

173

2 Instructors   26
5 Professors   30

Total fresh. & soph.
hours. . .   229 hours.

The effort is to equalize the number of hours as far as physical considerations of the schedule allow, & the inequalities of one term are compensated, as far as possible, in the other term of each year.   Yours always faithfully   J.H.W.

ALI (WWP, UA, NjP).

A News Report of an Address to the Southern Society of New York

[Dec. 15, 1906]

WOODROW WILSON ATTACKS PATERNALISM

Government Can't Do Everything, He Tells Southern Society.

Woodrow Wilson, President of Princeton University, came out against the income tax and in favor of proper application of present laws, rather than the passage of new laws, at the twenty-first annual banquet of the Southern Society, held in the grand ballroom of the Waldorf-Astoria last night. . . .

It was the occasion of the coming of age of the Southern Society, and was a brilliant affair. The room was decorated with fir trees and smilax, and the boxes were filled with women, who sat through the dinner in order to hear the speeches. . . .

Mr. Verdery[1] introduced Dr. Wilson, who got a Princeton College yell from one corner of the room. Dr. Wilson said that America was growing anxiously thoughtful about herself, and took as the topic of his remarks "Patriotism," quoting Tennyson's lines:

> A nation still, the rulers and the ruled;
> Some sense of duty,
> Something of a faith;
> Some reverence of the laws ourselves have made,
> Some patient force to change them when we will,
> Some civic manhood, form [firm] against the crowd.[2]

"Patriotism, properly considered," said Dr. Wilson, "is not a mere sentiment; it is a principle of action, or, rather, is a fine energy of character and of conscience operating beyond the narrow circle of self-interest. Every man should be careful to have an available surplus of energy over and above what he spends upon himself and his own interests, to spend for the advancement of his neighbors, of his people, of his nation.

"Each line affords a text for the matter I speak of. It requires constant effort of the imagination and constant studious attention to the variety of conditions which diversify the life of the country from [ocean] over to ocean, and an ever persistent catholicity of sympathy and of judgment to think of this country as every citizen should, as a single whole, a thing to be served not merely in its parts and in its separate interests, as the States are intended to serve it, but also in its entirety as the Federal Government is intended to serve it, keeping all interests harmonious, all powers co-operative—as a nation compact of rulers and of ruled, moving together under those who make the laws and by reason of the virtue of those who obey them.

"And yet only upon such a conception can an intelligent sense of duty be based. Genuine patriotism cannot be based upon a sense of private advantage or upon any calculation of interest. It can be based only upon a sense of duty. And duty must conceive its object, the country, the Nation we would serve. It was in America that patriotism first conceived this large way of thought and action for the ordinary citizen and put him in the way of statesmanlike thinking.

"I like to recall that passage of de Tocqueville's in which he marvels with eloquent praise at the variety of information and excellence of discretion which our polity did not hesitate to demand of its people, its common people. It is in this rather than in anything we have invented by way of governmental form that we have become distinguished among the nations, by what we expect of ourselves and of each other. I believe that there is enough red blood in the body politic to overcome any disease. Every loyal citizen should look upon this country singly and as a whole.

"America has fallen to the commonplace level of all the other nations which have preceded her, if she has not something of that faith that makes of her public idealists and of her citizens men to whom principles seem a sustaining motive of action. When she ceases to believe that all men shall have equal opportunity she goes back upon the principle on which the Nation was founded.

" 'Some reverence for the laws ourselves have made.' We have reverence enough for the laws if it be an evidence of reverence that we think that making law consists of legislation. I don't know that this country needs any more laws. I think we have laws enough. What this country needs is a more searching process in the application of the laws and less regard for persons in that application."

"How'll we get it?" some one in the hall cried out.

"Oh, we'll get it all right. It is proposed now that taxes shall be punitive; that men shall be punished for getting rich by a Government which has given them extraordinary facilities for getting rich.[3] A Government which has a discriminating tariff cannot in conscience punish a man for getting rich. [Applause.] In my opinion there is only one sort of taxation that is just, and that is taxation that does not discriminate. I know of only one legitimate object of taxation, and that is to pay the expenses of the Government.

"Revenue ought always to be obtained from such sources that taxation will assist rather than check or discourage industry and enterprise. It is, in part, by the examples of Governments in such matters that individuals have used the revenue-getting powers of corporations to penalize rivals. The Government sets the example both of fosterage and of destruction.

"The right objects of law are to facilitate the life of society and to keep the conditions of profitable action upon a footing of equity, fair dealing, and equal advantage. Governments should supply an equilibrium, not a disturbing force.

"To keep such conceptions at the front in public policy is not easy in a striving and restless age. It requires not a little civic manhood, 'firm against the crowd,' to resist the admission that the Government should do everything, acting as general providence for its people, but the time has come for such sober counsel as will relieve Government of the business or [of] providence and restore it to its normal duties of justice and of impartial regulation, a mastery over what is evil, a fosterage of what is good, but not a management of affairs of society.

"Patriotism is a mere sentiment and is blind alike to its opportunity and to its duty if it does not seek to perceive and to act upon large principles."[4]

Printed in the *New York Times*, Dec. 15, 1906; some editorial headings omitted.

[1] Marion Jackson Verdery, President of the Southern Society of New York.

[2] From Tennyson's "The Princess: Conclusion."

[3] President Theodore Roosevelt, in his Annual Message to Congress on December 3, 1906, had urged Congress to consider the enactment "in the near future" of a law providing for a graduated inheritance tax and to explore the "possibility of devising a constitutional income-tax law," or, if that failed, to pass an income tax amendment to the Constitution.

[4] There is a WWT outline of this address, dated Dec. 14, 1906, and a WWsh draft of a press release, dated Dec. 14, 1906, in WP, DLC. A typed copy of the press release is in WC, NjP.

To George Brinton McClellan Harvey

Princeton, N. J.

My dear Colonel Harvey,   16 December, 1906.

I have had a great many troubled thoughts about the subject of our recent interview at the Century Association. I know that what we discussed was a mere possibility: I am not exaggerating it: on the contrary, I believe that I think it slighter and more remote than you do; but one ought to be as careful about possibilities as about probabilities, and I wish to think my course of action out as clearly and upon as definite data as possible.

I do not deem myself a suitable person to be a presidential candidate on the ticket of a party so divided and so bewildered as the Democratic party is at present; still less do I deem myself a suitable person to be President. The party should be led at this time by a man of political experience and of extraordinary personal force and charm, particularly if he is to lead as a representative of the more conservative and, by the same mark, less popular section of the party.

I think, therefore, that I am justified in begging you to tell me what men of large political experience and of recognized political authority regard me as an available and desirable man for the purpose. You spoke the other day of a large number of men, whose names I would be surprised to hear, having spoken to you in support of the idea of my nomination. Do you not think that it would be wise and right to let me know who they are, and what information it is that has led you to go forward with the idea you were generous enough to originate at the Lotos Club dinner? I feel that I cannot afford (my own judgment in the matter being what it is) to go even so far as to accept a complimentary vote for Senator without this information. I could not, without it, deliberately put myself into a position that would make it necessary for the politicians to consider me.

I write this in fulfilment of my promise to let you know with perfect candour my thoughts about this important matter.

With warm regard,

Sincerely Yours,   Woodrow Wilson

WWTLS (WP, DLC).

From George Brinton McClellan Harvey

My Dear Mr. Wilson,   [New York]   Dec. 17, 1906.

I quite appreciate your feeling and, while I cannot hope to recall all of the conversations I have had with various persons, a few stand out rather prominently in my recollection. I have never sought an interview on the subject with anyone. Such talks as I have had have been not casual quite, but naturally general in character. For example, walking up the street the other day, August Belmont[1] remarked "Mr. Wilson is the type of man to win with, if we hope to win at all." Henry Watterson[2] said "My dear boy, you have the ideal in mind, and ideals don't often go in politics." Mr. Laffan,[3] proprietor of the "Sun," just returned from Washington told me there was a surprising amount of talk there and no little apprehension in official circles; hence his editorial[4] supplemented by another on your speech in Saturday's Evening Sun.[5] Mr. Ochs,[6] proprietor of the Times, told me on the steamer last summer that he had remarked to Miller,[7] his editor, that it was a splendid suggestion and Miller had agreed but advised waiting a bit. I ran across Thomas F. Ryan[8] the other day and he immediately began to ply me with questions, saying that he was hearing little else from his political acquaintances. Major [James Calvin] Hemphill of the Charleston News & Courier took to the idea at once and still holds; every week or so I get from him some sort of reference to it. Then among the steady-going bankers, Democrats who have been voting the Republican ticket, such as Dumont Clarke, President of the American Exchange bank, favorable comment has been universal. Invariably the phrase would be something like "I only wish we *could* nominate such a man as that because we could elect him. The country is sick of too much government." Naturally a good many letters came to me while I was printing opinions on the suggestion, but I refrained from publishing any for fear it might seem that I was trying to create a "boom." In a word, I have never heard an *unfavorable* comment, the reference almost always being to you as a type rather than as an individual—which also has been the crux of my own expression, even in the little speech at the Lotos Club.

If I should cudgel my memory, other names would occur but these are fair samples.

That was a fine speech the other night. [Adrian Hoffman] Joline says it got the reception it deserved, too.

If you want to have a really good time, read my piece on Root's speech in the next North American Review.[9]

Faithfully Yours   George Harvey

Am sending you a copy of what I said at Charleston two years ago.[10]

ALS (WP, DLC).

  [1] The prominent New York banker and conservative Democrat.

  [2] Editor of the Louisville *Courier-Journal*.

  [3] William Mackay Laffan, publisher and editor of the New York *Sun* and New York *Evening Sun*.

  [4] An editorial on the inheritance tax, in the New York *Evening Sun*, Dec. 15, 1906.

  [5] An editorial in *ibid.* on Wilson's speech to the Southern Society of New York on December 14. Entitled "Plainly Disqualified," this editorial said that any dreamy, impractical man who said that the country could not be saved by new laws was obviously disqualified for the presidential nomination on the Democratic ticket. "No further proof," the editorial concluded, "should be needed to convince those who have spoken of President Wilson as a possible candidate for the Democratic nomination to be Chief Executive of the nation that he is an impossibility. The Democrats are given more wild-eyed and breathless advocates for new laws to make everybody good and rich and happy than the Republicans, and President Wilson is plainly disqualified, on last night's showing, to be the Democratic standard bearer."

  [6] Adolph Simon Ochs, publisher and principal owner of the *New York Times*.

7 Charles Ransom Miller.

8 Thomas Fortune Ryan, the noted financier and conservative Democrat.

9 In "The Editor's Diary," CLXXXIV (Jan. 18, 1907), 213-19.

10 The enclosure is missing, but he was referring to his address at the 175th anniversary dinner of the Saint Andrew's Society in Charleston, S. C., in November 1904. In this speech, Harvey had exhorted the South to take a prominent role in the rehabilitation of the Democratic party and through new leadership to "reassert the broad statesmanship of the past." For an excerpt from the address and a discussion of its impact, see Willis Fletcher Johnson, *George Harvey, 'A Passionate Patriot'* (Boston and New York, 1929), pp. 105-109.

A Memorandum

[c. Dec. 18, 1906]

Interested.	Favourable (to type)
Mr. Laffan	August Belmont
Thos. F. Ryan	Henry Watterson
	Ochs-Miller
	Dumont Clark

Favourable to Man
Major Hemphill
J. H. Eckels[1]
John G. Carlisle[2]

WWhw memorandum written on verso of G. B. M. Harvey to WW, Dec. 17, 1906.

1 James Herron Eckels, United States Comptroller of the Currency, 1893-97, at this time President of the Commercial National Bank of Chicago.

2 John Griffin Carlisle of Kentucky, United States Secretary of the Treasury, 1893-97, at this time practicing law in New York.

From William Henry Rideing

Boston, Massachusetts.

Dear President Wilson: Dec. 18th, 1906.

Did you like either of the subjects I proposed to you? If they do not draw you I will attempt some others. I should like to know which of them you accept, though it may be necessary for me to wait for the MS.[1]

I am,   Yours, Sincerely,   William H. Rideing.

ALS (WP, DLC).

1 Wilson eventually submitted "The Personal Factor in Education," printed at Aug. 1, 1907, Vol. 17.

From Cleveland Hoadley Dodge

Dear Mr. President: New York December 19, 1906.

Your good letter of yesterday came this morning and I at once ascertained that Miss Wickham[1] and her partner could go down tomorrow morning in the train reaching Princeton about 11 o'clock, and I have telegraphed you to that effect. I think you will find that these young ladies have excellent taste, and I hope that Mrs. Wilson will be pleased with what they have to suggest.

Mr. Cleveland sent for me this morning and asked me to come up and see him at the Equitable Building, where he is superintending the elections,[2] and I found that he was a good deal worried about your plans for the development of the University into colleges, fearing that it might postpone indefinitely the interest in the Graduates' School. I assured him that all of us, and especially yourself, were deeply interested in the Graduates' School, and I knew that you had no intention of doing anything to injure that plan. I think, if you have a chance, when he gets back to Princeton, it would be very desirable for you to go in and talk it over with him a little.

Of course the plans for the college development will take a great deal of money, and whilst I think it very desirable for us to have the thing in mind, I do not see how we can carry out your ideas immediately.

My mother has arranged for the fund to provide for the geological and biological department, and I should think it would be just as well for you and the men in charge of the departments to be now considering pretty definitely what you want so that, before long, we can put the matter in the hands of the architect.

If you are going to be in New York before leaving for Bermuda[3] I hope very much I may have a chance of seeing you and talking over some of these matters.

Wishing, most heartily, you and yours the "Compliments of the Season,"   Very sincerely yours,   C. H. Dodge

As to the architects I feel that Parish & Schroeder[4] whose plans for McCosh Hall we all considered the best & who were put No 1 by Hamlin,[5] ought to have a chance at the new building

TLS (WP, DLC).

[1] Dodge had engaged Julia P. Wickham of New York and her partner to design a new window for Prospect.

[2] As one of the three trustees of the majority bloc of Equitable stock, Cleveland was overseeing the election of the new directors of the life insurance company.

[3] This is the first indication in the documents that Wilson intended to take a mid-winter vacation in Bermuda.

[4] Wainwright Parish and James Langdon Schroeder, architects of New York. They were in fact later chosen to design the building.

[5] Alfred Dwight Foster Hamlin, Professor of Architecture at Columbia University since 1904.

To Cleveland Hoadley Dodge

My dear Cleve: Princeton, N. J.   December 20th, 1906.

Thank you for your letter of yesterday. I am writing early in the morning, so that Miss Wickham and her partner have not yet come, but we are looking forward with much interest to their visit, and with great pleasure to what they are to do.

I will take pleasure in seeing Mr. Cleveland as you suggest. There need be no antagonism at all between the plans I suggested to the Board and the plans we had already set our heart upon.

I cannot tell you with what delight I learn that your mother has arranged for the funds to provide for the geological and biological departments. It makes my heart very light to think that that side of the University is to be so splendidly taken care of, and I shall enter into the plans with all my heart.

My purpose is to consult Wick Scott and the biological men and set them to work to make out a very careful statement of the sort of building and the sort of equipment they will need. I should say that this would take some time, and that it would not be prudent to put the matter in the hands of architects before these suggestions were worked out with the utmost detail. I should imagine that everything would be ready and brought up to that stage by the time I return from Bermuda, but if you think that my absence at this time will delay or embarrass the matter, I will gladly forego the trip or postpone it. I should not think a month, however, too much for the maturing of these plans.

I think your suggestion about Parish and Schroeder a very proper one indeed, and one that ought if possible to be acted upon.

I dare say I shall be in New York some time next week, and I will make a point of seeing you if I do come.

Always affectionately yours,   Woodrow Wilson

TLS (WC, NjP).

To Sir William Mather

My dear Sir William: [Princeton, N. J.] December 20th, 1906.

My delay in writing in reply to Mr. Triggs's letter and to your cable has been due, I am sorry to say, to our inability to handle the matter of beginning work on the foundations of the sun dial at our end. Winter has pounced upon us very early, the frost has got into the ground, and we are really afraid to put in the foundations at present. We hope and think, however, that by beginning promptly in the spring, as soon as the frost permits, we can easily accomplish the task of completing the structure by June, because of your kind intention of sending us the material for the super-structure in marked and fitted parts.

Everyone to whom I speak about the matter is delighted with the whole plan.

I am taking up the matter of the possible[1]

CCL (WWP, UA, NjP).
[1] The balance of the copy of this letter is missing.

From Joseph R. Wilson, Jr.

Dear Brother: Nashville, Tenn.   Dec. 20, 1906.

We have heard nothing from you since your delightful visit here, but presume that you and yours are all well.

I wish it were possible for me to send some evidence of my love for you and all the members of your household that would appropriately express all I feel, but it is the spirit that prompts a remembrance at this happy season, not the intrinsic value of any gift that may be given, so I will have to content myself with a note of love and best wishes for a happy, happy Christmas and a most successful New Year. In this sentiment, Kate and Alice join with sincerity.

Kate, Alice and I will spend Christmas in Clarksville, going there Saturday night. I will remain until the following Tuesday night and Kate and Alice will be absent for several days longer. We anticipate a pleasant visit to our former home and the many kind friends there.

Dr. Bull,[1] our pastor has left us, having accepted a call to the pastorate of the First Presbyterian Church at Scranton, Pa. We learned to love him and his family and greatly regret their departure. Among the members of Dr. Bull's Scranton congregation, are two gentlemen who own the most prominent daily newspapers of the town, and Dr. Bull declares his purpose to secure a call for me to that place. I do not especially desire a move so far North, but would, of course, consider a proposition that would mean something better along financial lines.

Great interest is being manifested here in the Wilson presidential boom and nearly every day my opinion on the subject is asked by men of prominence in this section. I am hardly in a position to reply satisfactorily for I know so little of your desire and views on the subject. Please enlighten me at once, for if you do desire such a thing as the nomination, it would not hurt to "push it along" you know, although I am free to confess to those who speak of it that there is no great desire on my part to have you enter the National political arena because of the tactics required to secure desired results along political lines. The more I am in public life and the more I see of politicians, the more am I disgusted with them and their methods.

I wish I could chat longer, but pressing work calls me to return to the routine of the daily newspaper slave.

Again wishing you a very happy Christmas and glad New Year, and with unbounded love to you and yours from us three,

Your aff. brother,   Joseph.

TLS (WP, DLC).
¹ The Rev. Dr. Griffin William Bull, pastor of the Moore Memorial Presbyterian Church in Nashville, 1904-1906, and of the First Presbyterian Church of Scranton, Pa., 1906-16.

From William Henry Rideing

Boston, Massachusetts.
Dear President Wilson: Dec. 21st, 1906.

If you can let us have the article on the Southern Type of Colonist by March 1st we shall be able to use it in the No. which will be devoted to the Jamestown celebration. Can we count on having it by that date or earlier? Hoping you will say "Yes"¹ I am

Yours Faithfully,   William H. Rideing.

ALS (WP, DLC).
¹ Wilson agreed. His essay, "The Southern Colonist," is printed at March 1, 1907, Vol. 17.

To William Henry Steele Demarest

Princeton, N. J.
My dear Dr. Demarest: December 22nd, 1906.

I am notified by the agent of the Rhodes Trust, that the qualifying examinations preliminary to the next appointment from this State will take place on January 17th and 18th next.

I have been assuming that you would be kind enough to take Dr. [Austin] Scott's place on the New Jersey Committee, a committee the appointment of which was put in my hands, and I am writing to ask if you have any suggestions or wishes with regard to advertising the coming examinations.

I think that the same arrangement can be made this year that was made last, namely, that the examinations be held at the Public Library in Trenton, and I would suggest that as before some representative of your faculty and some representative of ours be present to superintend the examinations.

As for advertising, the only thing that has occurred to us hitherto has been to give the information about the examinations out to newspaper men as news, as soon and as often as possible.

With warm regard,

Sincerely yours,   Woodrow Wilson

TLS (Archives, NjR).

To William Sulzer[1]

Princeton, N. J.

My dear Mr. Sulzer: December 22nd, 1906.

Allow me to thank you very much for your kindness in sending me copies of your speeches on the American Merchant Marine. It is a subject in which I am very much interested.

Always sincerely yours,   Woodrow Wilson

TLS (WC, NjP).
[1] At this time a congressman from New York.

To Charles Richard Van Hise

Princeton, N. J.

My dear President Van Hise,   26 December, 1906.

I am sincerely obliged to you for your letter of the twentieth of December,[1] and for the kind invitation which it conveys. It would give me the sincerest pleasure to come to the University of Wisconsin on Founders Day, and I should deem it a privilege to speak to the audience I should have there; but I am sorry to say that I am promised for the twenty-second of February.[2]

Please accept my warmest thanks and my sincerest regrets.

Cordially and faithfully Yours,   Woodrow Wilson

WWTLS (Presidents' File, WU).
[1] It is missing.
[2] He had promised to speak at the Hill School on Washington's birthday, 1907.

From Edwin Augustus Stevens[1]

My dear "Tommy":   Hoboken, N. J.   December 29th, 1906.

Some of my friends have told me of their interview[2] with you some time since. I am still confined to the house or I should try to see you.

It seems to me best that we should each know exactly how the other feels and his reasons.

I am very loath to accept the report of the interview with you as expressing your views[3] and I think you are entitled to know my reasons for this feeling.

You will recall that when I saw you last fall I urged you to allow the party the use of your name and promised as far as I could control them to get my friends to support you and to make the same kind of a canvass for you as I then intended making for myself.

You will also remember that I told you that I did not want the office, that I did not expect to be elected, that my object in making the run was to inaugurate better party conditions, that your candidacy would accomplish this end better than mine, but that the use then being made of your name was so far as I could see not in good faith. I cannot remember whether I told you that it had been intimated to me that the support of the Essex delegation could be secured at a figure, but I believe this did not reach me until after I had seen you.

You will probably recall that after stating that you could not be a candidate you gave me as a reason for not complying with my request that you ask those who had endorsed you to support me (as I had offered to do for you) that you had nothing that you could give me, that your name was being used against me in bad faith and in spite of your statement that you could not take the office and that you could not place yourself in the position of asking these parties to do you a favor.

I will confess that I felt after that interview that your name would not be used against me and I still feel that I had good reason to so believe.

You may wonder why I should take so much trouble for the empty compliment of a minority nomination. In itself, it is only a compliment, one that I have already enjoyed and one to which I would gladly surrender any claim I may have if good would come of my doing so.

My reasons for troubling you about this are twofold.

First. I made my run for the avowed purpose of bringing about better party conditions. The very men who opposed me in this, the ones who in the past have controlled the state machine, the ones from whom came the intimation I have mentioned, are the ones who have been and are backing you. It is not because I want the compliment but because I feel that the welfare of the party demands that their methods should not succeed.

Second. Your name has been mentioned for the Presidency. Your running against me will be taken by my friends under the conditions as an act of bad faith, as a sign of your willingness to allow the use of your name as a club by the very men who every good Democrat feels to have been the bane of the party and whose leadership has made the state hopelessly Republican.

Do you want to enter active politics in such a way? Your doing so, in my judgment, would be a fatal mistake. You will array against you the very men who must control if the party is to succeed.

A gentleman, wihtout [without] whose support you cannot win, wrote some time ago to a friend of mine that if I would put up the money necessary there was no reason why I should not receive the general support of the party. In other words, if I should become a liar, I would be acceptable.

Remember this is not a personal fight. Those behind me are supporting me only because I stand for something, for rescuing the party from its past leadership, for better political conditions. Your candidacy to them is an attempt to retain control by those hitherto at the helm and they will fight it as such. They know all the facts as I have given them to you.

Whatever your decision I shall do my utmost to prevent anything that would injure you politically, but remember I do not pretend to be able to control.

I have written you, my dear Tommy, with the utmost frankness, such as should obtain between old friends. I feel that your present position, as stated to me, is not fair to me, nor to your own interest, and I have given you my reasons for this feeling. I trust that you will treat me as I have treated you. If I am wrong, I hope you will set me right.

Very truly yours,   E. A. Stevens

TLS (WP, DLC).

1 Wilson's old friend and classmate, a prominent engineer, and son of the founder of the Stevens Institute of Technology in Hoboken. Active in Democratic politics in New Jersey for many years, he was at this time a leader of the anti-Smith, progressive wing of the party and had earlier announced his candidacy for the Democratic senatorial nomination.

2 As later letters will reveal, Wilson had been visited by a delegation of reform Democrats headed by Charles Clarke Black, Princeton 1878, a prominent lawyer of Jersey City and member of the State Board of Taxation and Equalization since 1891.

3 That is, Wilson had told his visitors, somewhat to their dismay, that he would be willing to accept a complimentary senatorial nomination by the Democratic members of the legislature.

To Moses Taylor Pyne

My dear Momo: Princeton, N. J.   December 31st, 1906.

The portrait has arrived, and I enclose the shipping bill showing a charge for freight of $19.05. I also enclose the formal letter of Mr. Yates, the artist, stating the price for the portrait itself, namely 200 guineas. In addition to that there is a charge of 25 pounds for the frame of the picture, which Mr. Yates thought it best to have put on the canvas in London, and which should be remitted to him at the address given on his letterhead.

I feel a good deal abashed at sending these bills to you, for a photograph of myself, but I hope that you will not feel that I have in any way exceeded the instructions you were kind enough to give me about having the painting made.

Will you not be kind enough to send the proper shipping instructions to Downing's Foreign Express?

Always affectionately yours,   Woodrow Wilson

TLS (V. L. Collins File on Princeton Portraits, UA, NjP).

A Desk Diary

[Jan. 1-Dec. 31, 1907]

The Excelsior Diary 1907 with WWhw and WWsh lists of names and addresses, important engagements, various memoranda, bibliographical references, and some entries for 1908.

Bound desk diary (WP, DLC).

A Desk Calendar

[Jan. 1-Dec. 31, 1907]

Bound desk calendar with no cover or title page, with WWhw and other entries of Wilson's engagements.

Bound calendar (WP, DLC).

From Henry St. George Tucker,[1] with Enclosure

My dear Mr. Wilson: Norfolk, Va.   January 1, 1907.

I enclose copy of the resolution of the Board of Governors of the Jamestown Exposition Company passed at their meeting on December 28, 1906. A perusal of these resolutions leaves me but little to say in inviting your acceptance of the position which is tendered you. Our Exposition, primarily historical and educational, of course, to meet the demands of a considerable constituency must embody a commercial feature, and I count it a most fortunate incident that the Board has been able to find in you, distinguished as an educator and historian in our country, a man in whom they are glad to entrust the delicate and important position suggested in these resolutions. To allay any fear which you may have as to your inability to discharge this duty I am informed by the Governor of this department that your work will be but slight and need not begin seriously until about the time your University closes, that it would then last only about three or four weeks. The experience we have acquired from other Expositions makes us the more solicitous for your acceptance of this position, that the country may be aware long in advance, of perfect fairness and justice in the department of awards. The detail of this work can be fully given you and we will wait your acceptance of this position with keen interest and expectant hope.

With my best wishes for you in the coming year and always, I am,

Yours sincerely, H. S. G. Tucker President.

[1] Lawyer of Staunton, Va., and President of the Jamestown Exposition Co.

ENCLOSURE

Gwynn T. Shepperd to Henry St. George Tucker

Dear Sir: Norfolk, Va. January 1, 1907.

The following resolution was unanimously adopted by the Board of Governors at a meeting held December 28th, 1906:

"WHEREAS, the commemoration of the first permanent English Settlement in this Country next year makes the occasion of such importance as to lead the Board of Governors to desire that in the matter of the allotment of premiums and awards at the close of the Exposition, that the work shall be done in such a manner as to give entire satisfaction to all who may in any way be interested in such result, we, therefore, feel that we should have at the head of this department one of the very highest character and whose distinguished reputation will guarantee that every action taken in this department will have the cordial and hearty approval of those whose interests are affected; and

"WHEREAS, we believe that no one possesses these qualifications or requirements more completely than Dr. Woodrow Wilson, of New Jersey, and believeing [believing] that his just exercise of Judicial functions would make him invaluable to us, be it therefore

"RESOLVED: by the Board of Governors of the Jamestown Exposition Company that the position of Director of Juries and Awards be tendered Dr. Wilson on the part of this Company; and in doing so, the wish of the Company is thus expressed that he will be willing to perform this service for the benefit of the Exposition Company, the State of Virginia, the commercial interest of New Jersey and the Country at large.

"RESOLVED FURTHER: That in the event of the acceptance of the tender thus made, the Company will promptly co-operate with him in the organization of the Department, and furnish such assistance necessary to put same on the highest plans [plane], which cannot but result in successful and satisfactory service to all exhibitors."[1]

Very truly yours,   G. T. Shepperd   Secretary.

TLS, (WP, DLC).
[1] Wilson did not accept the position of Director of Juries and Awards.

To Ellen Axson Wilson

My own darling   Princeton, N. J.   2 January, 1907.

It was a real delight to see your handwriting by my plate this morning and to read the sweet reassuring letter. How thankful I am, and how intensely and with how unbroken a consciousness I love you and our blessed baby, whose sweetness nearly broke my heart throughout all the terrible trial.[1] May God bless and keep you both!

We are all well. Jessie's eye is better, and so far the other one is not affected. I have written to Dean Van Meter[2] that she cannot return until she is cured of the trouble. She is very cheerful and sweet, of course.

I am *so* sorry about the germicide, dearest. It was used up, in another spray, for Jessie. Do you remember what Dr. Hough[3] called it, or where you put the memorandum? If you do, telephone me and I will forward it at once.

I hope you will go to the theatre! How I wish I were there to go with you! To-night I take dinner, just family dinner, with the Ricketts.[4] They are exceedingly sweet and sympathetic.

Mr. [Stephen S.] Palmer came in yesterday to say that I could rest assured that the physical laboratory would be built and provided with a maintaining endowment. It is still to remain a secret because we hope to use these prospects in other quarters as an argument for endowment for the scientific side, but the strain of anxiety and doubt is off, and I am light-hearted again about it. What a delightful boom it will give us. I believe it is the making of the tide!

The Hibbens came back this morning. Jack has just called me up on the telephone. I have not seen them yet.

All join in love without measure, my sweet one. My heart yearns for you with positive pain. It is a sweet pain only because I know that you love and want me.

Your own Woodrow

WWTLS (WC, NjP).
¹ Eleanor had been operated upon in Philadelphia for removal of tubercular glands in the neck. See EAW to Anna Harris, Feb. 12, 1907, Vol. 17.
² John Blackford Van Meter, Dean of the Woman's College of Baltimore.
³ Probably Dr. Perry B. Hough, 123 E. 76th St., New York.
⁴ Mrs. Palmer Chamberlaine (Eliza Getty) Ricketts and her daughter, Henrietta.

To Edwin Augustus Stevens

My dear Ned., [Princeton, N. J.] 2 January, 1907.

You may be sure that there will be no misunderstanding between us if frank friendship can prevent it.

Possibly it [is] because I am such an outsider and so inexperienced in such matters, but the whole difficulty is that I cannot bring myself to see the situation as you seem to see it. It seems to me that if I were to do what you suggest I would be quite gratuitously taking part in the factional politics of the State, with which I will not in any circumstances connect myself.

When it was a question of actual election to the Senate I felt bound to say that I could not accept the office; but a complimentary vote, tendered by a minority, involves no responsibility on the part of the recipient, and therefore it seems to me that it would be quite gratuitous of me to say that, if it were tendered me, I would not accept it. That would be intervening *for the sake of settling factional differences*, and that my position forbids my doing upon any occasion. I have already said with sufficient emphasis that I am not a candidate for anything; and no one, I take it, will venture to doubt my sincerity.

I shall be sincerely grieved if this decision seems to you unreasonable or ungenerous; it seems to me only common sense and common dignity on my part, and I beg that you will accept it in the spirit in which it has been made.

I was very much distressed to hear of your illness, and trust that you are entirely recovered. I hope it was not imprudent of you to come north again so soon.

Always

Cordially and faithfully Yours, Woodrow Wilson¹

WWTCL (WP, DLC).
¹ There is a WWsh draft of this letter in WP, DLC.

To Harry Laity Bowlby[1]

My dear Mr. Bowlby: Princeton, N. J.   January 3rd, 1907.

Thank you very much indeed for your kind New Year's letter. It has given me the greatest gratification, and I beg to assure you that your regard and thoughtfulness have given me a great deal of pleasure in all our relationships. May [e]very good fortune and blessing be with you during the year.

Cordially and sincerely yours,   Woodrow Wilson

TCL (RSB Coll., DLC).

[1] Princeton 1901; Princeton Theological Seminary, 1904; at this time pastor of the First Presbyterian Church of Altoona, Pa.

To Ellen Axson Wilson

My precious darling,   Princeton, N. J.   4 January, 1907

There is no news to tell of ourselves to-day. Everything goes as happily with us as it can with our two loved ones away,—especially since I have seen our darling baby sitting up and looking so well and so sure of health and strength again.

Jessie's eye makes provokingly slow progress, but the other eye is not infected and the malady is behaving as well as could be expected. She was out in the garden, with the doctor's consent, for a little while To-day.

Florence[1] will probably see you to-morrow, almost as soon as this letter can reach you. It has been a great pleasure to have her here.

We love you both more than I know how to put into words, and my love for my own darling seems to grow deeper and more passionate with every stroke of fortune.

Your own,   Woodrow

WWTLS (WC, NjP).

[1] Florence Stevens Hoyt, Mrs. Wilson's first cousin, who was an English teacher at the Bryn Mawr School in Baltimore.

To Henry Smith Pritchett

[Princeton, N. J.]

My dear President Pritchett: January 4th, 1907.

I am sincerely sorry to hear of your illness, and trust that you are making real progress towards complete recovery. I hope the new year will contain for you no more trials of this kind.

I have no hesitation in ratifying, so far as I am concerned, the bestowal of a retiring allowance upon Judge Cole.[1]

Always cordially and sincerely yours,
[Woodrow Wilson]

CCL (WWP, UA, NjP).
[1] Chester Cicero Cole, former Chief Justice of the Supreme Court of Iowa and Dean of the Drake University College of Law since 1892, who had recently retired.

From Edward Henry Wright, Jr.[1]

My dear Pres. Wilson: Newark N. J.   Jany 4/07

I have been asked to make the speech at the coming session of the Legislature placing your name in nomination for the United States Senatorship. My father Col. Wright[2] of the class of '44 you have met, & I am a '94 man, but was compelled to abandon my college course through illness. I note these facts that you may take what I say as from one Princeton man to another. Col. Stevens as you know was a candidate. I took particular interest in the stand he took against the corrupt use of money. He made a gallant fight, & as a type of good citizen is respected from one end of the state to the other for his own true worth, & the principles he represents. I think that the complimentary vote should be his, & I feel sure you would not stand in his way. I dont think you thoroughly understand the situation here. We have urgent need of good men & for his honest efforts the Col. deserves the recognition & support of his party. I trust that you will consider this communication confidential. Nothing would give me greater pleasure than to see such a democrat as yourself in the White House. I remain, my dear Sir,

Sincerely & respectfully yrs.   Edwd H. Wright Jr

ALS (WP, DLC).
[1] A lawyer of Newark.
[2] Also a Newark lawyer.

To Moses Taylor Pyne

My dear Momo: [Princeton, N. J.]   January 5th, 1907.

I have just written to Mr. Ream, begging that he would send his $5000. to Mr. Murray, and I have no doubt he will do so.

I am delighted to say that Nellie is improving very rapidly, and that there is every prospect that she will be able to sail with me for Bermuda on the 12th.[1]

Always affectionately yours,   [Woodrow Wilson]

CCL (WWP, UA, NjP).
¹ As it turned out, she was unable to accompany him.

From Edwin Augustus Stevens

My dear "Tommy,"　　　　　Hoboken, N. J.　Jan. 5th '07

I want to thank you for your kind & frank letter of the second.

You seem to have missed my meaning. You can not prevent someone's nominating you &, as there are no duties connected with a minority nomination, if you tried to, you could not make your refusal effective.

It seems to me that as things now are you are, passively it is true, "taking part in the factional politics"

It also seems to me that it is very important that there should not be even an apparent contest with your name on one side & mine on the other. Usually there would be no special reason against such a contest.

To meet this & to prevent such a misunderstanding as leads you to think that I want you to refuse to accept a minority nomination, if tendered, I make the following definite suggestion.

Will you write to Mr Lethbridge,¹ the nominee for speaker & one of your supporters, saying that you had at no time authorized the use of your name in connection with the Senatorship, in fact had stated that you could not undertake the duties of the office; that in reliance on this statement I have made a fight for the position; that we stood for the same things & that while under the circumstances you had nothing to ask & there was nothing you could refuse, you wanted it understood that the use of your name against me was without authority & (if you will add it) distasteful to you?

I take it from the tone of your letter that you will not write such a letter, which is all I have ever wanted of you. Before going further, however, I want to be sure of my ground, as we do not seem to have fully understood each other. In case of my being right I shall at once do all I can to get my name out of the unfortunate muddle. As I have been an avowed candidate, my position is a little different from yours. I shall, however, write as nearly a similar a letter as circumstances will allow & I shall add the request that my friends vote for you.

You will understand that having gone into the fight there is an implied promise to stay in as long as I can do any good & that I can not set myself up as the final judge of that question. You will also realise that the fight is not on the question of an empty compliment, but on one of party control, & that the Senatorial fight has its importance mainly on account of its prominence. Its effect is moral, but none the less of importance. If it is felt that I can not withdraw without injury to the cause of party reform I shall have to stay where I am, but it will only be after my friends are informed of my views & wishes. I trust you will think this over very carefully, especially as it bears on your own political prospects. I don't suppose that these worry you much, but the party is sadly in need of good men & specially of those who have not been embroiled in past party strife.

I have already written you how I thought this would affect you in this respect. I see to-day no reason for changing this opinion, but rather the contrary.

If you are in any doubt as to what to do, ask some of your friends who have been in touch with state politics.

I may be utterly wrong as to their advice, but I feel sure that it will be to do as I suggest.

I want to ask you one question. Do you mind telling me whether you have a friend or even know any one among those who are presenting your name?

Remember that whatever your decision I shall accept the same as taken in a spirit of friendship & that, while I cannot but feel that after our last interview I had a right to feel that your name would not be used against me, without some protest on your part, I shall recognise & respect your right to a contrary opinion &, the incident being closed, shall regard & treat this matter as one of those differences of opinion that will arise among friends.

Very Truly Yours   E. A. Stevens

ALS (WP, DLC).
1 Edgar E. Lethbridge, Democratic representative from Orange, Essex County. He was in the marine insurance business.

To George Brinton McClellan Harvey

My dear Colonel Harvey,   Princeton, N. J.   7 January, 1907

Intimations come to me from so many quarters that, were I to consent to receive the complimentary vote of the members of the legislature for the United States senatorship, I would be thought to have acted in bad faith towards Colonel Stevens, to whom I left a free field, and all the work of the campaign, when it was a question of winning an election, that I feel that I must withdraw my name from consideration. I have, as you know, been entirely passive in this matter from the first. I declined to be considered a candidate for the senatorship; and I would have accepted the honour of a complimentary vote only if it could have come to me without casting the least reflection upon my old friend Colonel Stevens. Now that I know that his friends would consider my acceptance of the vote as depriving him of the honour earned by his campaign, I cannot think of accepting it. It would do me nothing but harm and would involve me in a way wholly foreign to my character. I can remain passive no longer. I must beg that you will point out to me the most courteous and convenient way in which to convey to the gentlemen who were intending to pay me this honour my inability to accept their kindness.

You have played so generous, so thoughtful, so admirable a part in this whole matter that my chief regret is that you will be disappointed. I hope that I may have many opportunities of showing my appreciation and admiration, and that you will not think me too exacting a friend in asking you now to show me the way of extrication.

With warmest regard,
Cordially and faithfully Yours,   Woodrow Wilson[1]

WWTLS (WP, DLC).
[1] There is a WWsh draft of this letter in WP, DLC.

To Cleveland Hoadley Dodge

My dear Dodge: [Princeton, N. J.]   January 7th, 1907.

The following is a full memorandum of what must be done to put the scientific work of the University upon a proper footing of efficiency.

We have splendid geological, paleontological and biological collections, some of these unique, others unusual in their completeness or in the perfection of their several specimens (notably the collection got together by our expedition to Patagonia), which we are unable either to exhibit or to use in instruction because of the lack of a museum, and which we are unable to make the subject of a complete classification and study because of the lack of proper laboratories and apparatus of investigation. Undoubtedly the greatest single need of the University at the present moment is the need of a natural history museum and laboratories of instruction for the Departments of Biology, Paleontology and Geology. Indeed, the need is so great that these departments must stand still until it is supplied, and the University yearly lose credit.

This means that we should have a museum, not such as New York is attempting,[1] but a museum of instruction where our unique collections can be displayed entire and our other collections by properly selected specimens, and that this museum should be so built as to be central to the laboratories of the several departments served by it. Our idea is a central museum, with long wings upon either hand, containing the laboratories, lecture rooms, rooms of preparation, work shops, etc.: on the one hand those for the Department of Geology and Paleontology, on the other those for biology and its allied branches. It is difficult to estimate the cost of such a building without plans drawn in detail by architects and reckoned upon by practical builders, but according to the best advice I can obtain, it would cost, with the proper margin for its maintenance (a thing very essential, if the University is not to be impoverished by its possession) quite $600,000.

I am the more anxious that such a building should be obtained, and obtained at once, because we have definite assurances that if the means for its erection can be secured, an equal amount will be forthcoming for the endowment of our scientific courses. No promise could be better fitted to put us upon our metal. It is not the usual tiresome condition involved in the familiar promise of so much if as much more is given, but a much more satisfactory promise of a specific sum for a definite purpose, and adequate for that purpose, if an equal sum can be obtained for an equipment which would make the money worth while and productive of the greatest service to the University and its pupils. It is with the greatest eagerness and anxiety that I await the outcome of the effort to make sure of the one gift by securing the other. The growth and excellence of the University seem to depend upon it.

Very sincerely yours,   [Woodrow Wilson][2]

CCL (WWP, UA, NjP).
[1] That is, the American Museum of Natural History.
[2] There is a WWsh draft of this letter in WP, DLC.

To Edward Henry Wright, Jr.

My dear Mr. Wright: Princeton, N. J.   January 8th, 1907.

I have read your letter of January 4th, which reached me only yesterday afternoon, with the greatest interest and concern. As you know, I have been in no way concerned personally in the movements which have led to my name being made prominent in connection with the United States Senatorship. I have thought that I owed it to the University as well as to myself to take no part in politics that would push my own interest. Being a complete outsider, I am necessarily wholly ignorant of the forces at work. I would esteem it a real favor if you would tell me very frankly what lies behind the suggestion of your letter. You may be sure that I will treat it as an inviolable confidence. I should wish, as soon as informed of the real circumstances, to act very promptly.[1]

Thanking you for your letter,

Sincerely yours,   [Woodrow Wilson]

CCL (WP, DLC).
    [1] Wright's reply, if he wrote one, is missing. Perhaps he conferred personally with Wilson.

To Moses Taylor Pyne

My dear Momo: [Princeton, N. J.]   January 8th, 1907.

Did you not, before I came back from my trip to Tennessee, make some special arrangements for rates at the Princeton Inn for University Preachers sent there instead of invited to Prospect? I have no doubt that the enclosed bill for my guest of last Sunday[1] is at the usual rates, though they seem to me very great. I am not complaining, I am only asking for information.

I mailed, by the first post this morning, the memorandum you suggested that I should send to Dodge, and I hope it will be satisfactory. Do you not think that you could induce Mr. Ledyard Blair[2] or someone else who would be personally influential with him, to ask Mr. Norman Ream for the other $600,000 we wish?

I asked him some time ago for the physical laboratory, and in writing to him the other day, asking that his subscription of $5000 be sent to Murray, I told him that we had obtained the building. The best plan, therefore, would be to ask him for the endowment, and I should think that if the proper persons urged it, he would be very likely to give something. He certainly seems most friendly to us.

Always affectionately yours,   [Woodrow Wilson]

CCL (WWP, UA, NjP).
    [1] He was the Rev. Dr. William Hamilton Spence, pastor of the First Presbyterian Church of Uniontown, Pa.
    [2] Clinton Ledyard Blair, Princeton 1890, son of De Witt Clinton Blair. Both father and son were partners in the New York banking firm of Blair and Co., with offices at 24 Broad St., New York. Norman Bruce Ream also occupied office space at the same address.

From Harold Griffith Murray

Dear Dr. Wilson,   New York   January 9, 1907.

I saw Mr. Struthers Burt[1] after I saw you, and had a very satisfactory interview with him. He strikes me as being a very wideawake and intelligent gentleman. He has, by this time, I presume, seen you and had a talk with you.

I would like to make a suggestion to you with the hope that it will meet with your approval, and that is, when you are going to make a speech anywhere, to let Burt have an advance copy with a release date. This date will be religiously kept by all the papers, and if we can get your speech three or four days in advance, it will permit of 1200 newspapers publishing what you have to say on any subject the morning after the speech is made. We cannot depend upon the Associated Press for this kind of service. Moreover, by this method there will be no danger of anything you say being garbled or twisted to give a meaning which you did not intend.

Yours very truly,   H. G. Murray   Secretary

TLS (WP, DLC).
[1] Maxwell Struthers Burt '04, Instructor in English, who had agreed to serve as the campus representative of Murray's Press Bureau.

To Moses Taylor Pyne

My dear Momo: [Princeton, N. J.]   January 10th, 1907.

I cannot think of allowing you to pay Dr. Spence's bill at the Inn. All that I meant was that I thought special rates had been arranged for my ministerial guests. I am more than willing to pay the bills, but I didn't want to pay them without knowing what the rates were. Do be kind enough to send the bill back to me.

It was a pity that I should have told Mr. Ream that the physical laboratory was secured, but you know I asked him, indeed urged him, to give us such a laboratory some months ago, and I felt that on the whole it would make the most impression on him to tell him that we had secured the laboratory without his assistance. I think, at any rate, that the matter is not prejudiced, and that it is possible that if someone to whom he would very much dislike to say no were to approach him, he might give at least a considerable amount to our much wished-for scientific endowment.

Nellie, unfortunately, will have to stay at home and have her neck dressed for some weeks to come, and I am condemned to go

off to Bermuda by myself on Saturday. You know there is a cable
by which you can always get hold of me, if I am needed for any
sort of counsel or service.

Always affectionately yours,   [Woodrow Wilson]

CCL (WWP, UA, NjP).

To William Kelly Prentice

Princeton, N. J.
My dear Professor Prentice: January 10th, 1907.

It goes hard to be obliged to say no to any request so interesting
as that made in your letter of January 7th.[1] It is just the kind of
thing that I should like to assent to in every instance.

But I am bound to have a hard official conscience in such matters, and it does not seem to me that it would be wise, in view of
the fact that I am to recommend to the Board that you have a full
year's leave of absence on salary for 1908-1909, that you should
take a month from the teaching duties of the year preceding.

Pray regard this decision as most reluctantly made.

Faithfully yours,   Woodrow Wilson

TLS (UA, NjP).
[1] His letter is missing.

From George Brinton McClellan Harvey

Dear Mr. Wilson,   New York City.   January 10th, 1907.

I spent all of yesterday in a meeting of an Association of pub-
lishers who were scared out of their boots by the "big stick" and
Anti-trust Act, and have been in Jersey City all day on a legal
matter, so I have only this minute reached your letter.

I quite appreciate your predicament in view of the importu-
nities of the friends of Colonel Stevens, and recognize the necessity on your own account of defining your position. It seems to
me that the most straightforward and effective way of complying with their request would be to write to Mr. Black, or one of
the other gentlemen who waited upon you, substantially to this
effect:

"In view of the probability of my departure for Bermuda
at an early date I think, to avoid the possibility of any misunderstanding, I should place in your hands a concise statement of my attitude respecting the nomination of the candidate for United States Senator by the Democratic Members
of the Legislature, such as I endeavored to make clear to

you on the occasion of your recent call upon me. It is simply
this: I have never been and am not now a candidate for the
nomination. I took no part in the campaign and do not feel
that I am in any sense entitled to the honor. I have no information from any Democratic members of the Legislature
of their intention to vote for me; consequently if there be
any having such a purpose in mind, I cannot address them
directly. But I am quite willing and desire to authorize you
to request, on my behalf, that my name be withheld from
consideration in the Democratic caucus. It is perfectly clear
to my mind that the compliment should be paid to some one
of those who were active in the canvass whose result so
closely approached a complete Democratic victory. If, then,
as you informed me, some members of the Legislature are
still disposed to vote for me, I earnestly urge them to reconsider their determination and to give their votes to some
one who by his efforts fairly won the tribute of that recognition. To make certain that no further doubt may exist respecting my attitude or wishes, I think it would be well for
you to publish this letter.

With kind regards, I am etc."

I have put this suggestion into words simply because it is the
easiest way for me to convey my idea of the best method. Your
own phraseology would be naturally much better. I do not think
that the friends of Colonel Stevens ought to expect you to declare
in favor of his candidacy, as that would involve you immediately
in a faction. If something of this sort should not satisfy them,
they must be hard to please indeed. Incidentally, I am still convinced that the nomination will not go to Colonel Stevens under
any circumstances, as those to whom I have talked feel that it
would be folly from a party standpoint to name one simply rich
man against another. However, time will have to settle that.[1]
Personally I feel that the Stevens people are unwarrantably
greedy of an empty honor, in view of a greater purpose from a
party standpoint, but since they take that position I fully appreciate the fact that it is virtually impossible for you to refuse to
accede to their demands. Of course I only make this suggestion of
method in response to your request and shall feel no chagrin
whatever, if you should see fit to ignore it entirely.

Thanking you for your expressions of confidence and friendliness, believe me   Faithfully yours,   George Harvey

TLS (WP, DLC).
  [1] Harvey was right. Stevens did not get the Democratic nomination, which
went instead to James Edgar Martine of Plainfield. For further details on the

senatorial balloting by the joint session of the New Jersey legislature, see n. 1 to WW to C. C. Black, Jan. 11, 1907, printed as an Enclosure with WW to C. C. Black of the same date.

From Charles Williston McAlpin

My dear Dr. Wilson: [Princeton, N. J.]   January 10, 1907.

I had intended to call upon you today in order to wish you bon voyage, but the meeting of the Trustees of the Book Store[1] consumed most of my afternoon. The only matter that I wish to ask you about is what I shall do when I receive Judge Ewing's[2] letter in reply to mine. I presume that his request must be complied with if he still persists in asking me to notify the alumni of his decision not to accept a renomination or reelection. If you think, however, that I should try to bring pressure to bear on him by some of the Trustees I will do so. Will you advise me on this matter, before you leave?

Trusting that you may have a very pleasant and beneficial trip, I remain with kindest regards,

Ever faithfully yours,

[C. W. McAlpin]   Secretary.

CCL (McAlpin File, UA, NjP).
   [1] He was referring to the Princeton University Store, Inc., in the organization of which in 1905 he and Dean Fine had been prime movers. Before 1905, the Book Store was a small operation managed by students. In 1907, the University Store occupied three rooms in West College and sold athletic supplies as well as books.
   [2] Nathaniel Ewing, an Alumni Trustee, who did not wish to stand for reelection.

From Emanuel Raphael and James Everett McAshan[1]

Dear Sir: Houston, Texas.   January 10th, 1907.

The Wm. M. Rice Institute for the advancement of Literature, Science and Art is now being organized. It has an endowment of Five Million Dollars, or more. It will be non-sectarian and non-political, free tuition to whites. It will be located here.[2]

It is our desire to do the greatest possible good with the money at our command, and to cover the whole field as indicated in our title, as rapidly as we can. We think it was the intention of the founder to give manual training, applied science and liberal arts preference in the organization. It is our desire to realize his wishes if possible and at the same time be affiliated with the school system of the country. In order to hasten our work, we need for the head of the institution the very best man to be had.

We need a young man, a broad man, and we need him at once; and we are able to pay him such a salary as such distinguished services should command, and will gladly do so if we can get the right man.

Our object in writing to you is to ascertain if you know of such a man, and if so advise us and place us in correspondence with him,— such a man as you yourself would select.

Feeling that the importance of our work is its own excuse for this intrusion upon your time and attention, and requesting an early reply, we beg to remain,[3]

Yours truly,   E. Raphael

J. E. McAshan

Committee of the Board of Trustees.

TLS (WP, DLC).

[1] Raphael, in the real estate business in Houston, was Secretary of the Board of Trustees of Rice Institute; McAshan, a Houston lawyer, was Vice-Chairman of the board. Together, they constituted the search committee for the first president of the new institution.

[2] William Marsh Rice (1816-1900), after making a large fortune in Texas real estate and cotton exporting during the Civil War, moved to New Jersey and later lived in New York. He had chartered the William M. Rice Institute for the Advancement of Literature, Science and Art (to be located in Houston) in 1891 and in his will left the bulk of his estate to the institution. In 1900, Rice was murdered by his valet, Charles F. Jones, who did the deed at the instructions of Rice's lawyer, Albert T. Patrick.

[3] As E. Raphael to WW, March 21, 1907, Vol. 17, will reveal, Wilson nominated Edgar Odell Lovett, who became the first President of Rice Institute.

From Motokichi Takahashi[1]

Dear Sir: Rock Springs Wyo   Jan. 10th 1907.

It was four month ago, when I have gone up to Princeton, to bid my farewill to you; but unfortunately I have found you in absence there.

Since October I have been staying in this place, working as superintendent for Japanese coal miners in Central Coal and Coke Co. On the contraly [contrary] with my earnest desire to write to you, was so busy not able to do so.

Meantime I have been pleasing myself, by report of my friends in Princeton that your health is very well this year and the University is growing steadily. So I herewith want to express my hearty congratulation to you.

In last month I have read a text of your valuable speech for Southern club, with great interest.[2] I assume that all of your students are everywhere looking upward you, and your publications are giving them very powerful enlightment and encouragement.

By the way may I venture to ask your opinion about the school separation question in San Francisco?[3] I having myself most pleasant life in Princeton, am appreciating an[d] thanking for the friendship of this country; but can not find any reason to wellcome such a treatment like San Francisco.

In this part I have found new fact that our labourers are most reliable for their employers; of becours [because] they are very energitic and clever and faithful. They can work fourteen hours in a day throughout the year, and easily masters their work, so other labourers can not competate [compete] with them, unless they, foreign labourers, will use the power of union which exclude Japanese labourers. On other hand our labourers' daily life is higher than other ones, they spend most part of earnings for their lifing, so that merchants in the town like my boys. Therefore I can not justify the attacks on our labourers, as cheap laborours, like Senate Gearin.[4] The attacking is noncence, just like to attack on labour saving michine by weak laboure[r]s.

So I want to be optimist on this problem, so far while we can believe the "free competition" is the golden doctrine of economic movement. Is my view mistake? Please kindly enlight me in this matter.

Now I have a pleasure to tell you that I am going to leave this place, by the 19th inst., for San Francisco where I will take the steamer for my mother land. Though my stay in this place is very short I have quite satisfied myself with the result of my work, so am very much thankful for Princeton, who educated and upheld me.

On this occation I am going to send you a "Satsuma Vase" by express. If you will accept the same as a token of my love and respect to you, it will be great pleasure of me.

Finally I hope you can arrange your valuable time to come arround to our country in near future. I am sure that your visit will be a great benevorent work, to enlighten our people.

With sincere wish of season to you and your famiry, faculty, I remain   Yours most respectfully   Moto Takahashi

ALS (WP, DLC).
[1] He had been a graduate student at Princeton, 1903-1905, and had received the A.M. degree in 1906.
[2] See the news report printed at Dec. 15, 1906.
[3] A controversy over the rapidly increasing immigration of Japanese laborers into the states on the Pacific coast, especially California, had been developing since 1900. It came to a sudden head on October 11, 1906, when the San Francisco School Board adopted a resolution requiring all Chinese, Japanese, and Korean children to attend an "Oriental Public School," thus segregating them from the white children in the school system. The Japanese government, reflecting the keen sensitivity of Japanese public opinion to the obvious racist overtones of this action, protested strongly to the United States Government.

President Roosevelt, although aware of the problem of the competition of Japanese labor with American workers in the Pacific coast area, well knew that the Japanese government and people had been humiliated, and did all he could both to mollify the Japanese and to secure revocation of the exclusion order. He sent Victor H. Metcalf, Secretary of Commerce and Labor, to California to investigate the situation and attempt to negotiate the revocation of the School Board's order. Roosevelt himself gave wide publicity to the affair by excoriating the action of the School Board in his Annual Message to Congress of December 4, 1906. This action pleased the Japanese but exasperated the Californians. The release of Metcalf's report on December 18, 1906, only increased the recalcitrance of the San Francisco authorities and their constituents.

The controversy continued into the early months of 1907. Meanwhile, negotiations by the Roosevelt administration with the Japanese government and the San Francisco School Board were gradually bringing about an acceptable solution. By late February, the Japanese and American governments had agreed upon the informal arrangement later known as the "Gentlemen's Agreement," by which Japan would not issue passports to Japanese laborers going to the mainland of the United States in return for the rescinding of the School Board's segregation order. The entire School Board, together with the School Superintendent and Mayor of San Francisco, went to Washington in early February to negotiate directly with the President and other administration officials. An agreement was reached on February 15, 1907, and the School Board rescinded its order on March 13.

The most thorough study of this affair and its related issues is Thomas A. Bailey, *Theodore Roosevelt and the Japanese-American Crises* (Stanford, Calif., 1934). A more recent study centering on the international aspects of the crisis is Raymond A. Esthus, *Theodore Roosevelt and Japan* (Seattle, Wash., 1966), pp. 128-66.

[4] John McDermeid Gearin, who filled an unexpired term as United States Senator from Oregon, serving from December 13, 1905, to January 23, 1907. On January 7, 1907, Gearin made a lengthy speech in the Senate in which, after first defending the legal right of the San Francisco School Board to adopt its exclusion order, he devoted most of his efforts to a discussion of the immigration of Japanese laborers to the West Coast, predicting that they would inevitably drive out white labor altogether. His arguments reflected much evidence of racial prejudice against Orientals in general and Japanese laborers in particular. See the *Congressional Record*, 59th Cong., 2nd sess., pp. 674-84.

An Announcement

[Jan. 11, 1907]

PRESIDENT WILSON SAILS FOR BERMUDA TOMORROW.

President Wilson will sail from New York City to-morrow for Bermuda, where he will remain until February 9, when he will again return to Princeton. The trip is made for the purpose of securing rest and an opportunity of doing some work for which concentrated effort is needed,[1] the conditions here being unfavorable for his purposes. After his return to Princeton he will be a guest at the annual banquet of the Princeton Club of Western Pennsylvania, at Pittsburg, where he will deliver an address on April 2.[2]

Printed in the *Daily Princetonian*, Jan. 11, 1907.
[1] That is, work on his Blumenthal lectures at Columbia University on constitutional government in the United States.
[2] A news report of this address is printed at April 3, 1907, Vol. 17.

To George Brinton McClellan Harvey

My dear Col. Harvey: Princeton, N. J.   January 11th, 1907.

Thank you most heartily for your kind letter of yesterday, received this morning. It is really a great relief to me to have my judgment of the obligations of the situation confirmed by yours. I particularly thank you for your suggestions as to the form of my action, and I shall take real pleasure in adopting them.

I am starting for Bermuda tomorrow, and shall take away with me a much lighter heart by reason of the solution of this singular difficulty, together with the most delightful recollections of your kindness.

With much regard,

Faithfully yours,   Woodrow Wilson

TLS (WP, DLC).

To Charles Clarke Black, with Enclosure

My dear Mr. Black: Princeton, N. J.   January 11th, 1907.

I have made many inquiries and done a great deal of thinking since you were kind enough to visit me the other day, and I am now convinced that I was deceiving myself in supposing that by maintaining the position I then indicated to you, I would really be keeping myself aloof from the differences which separate the several groups of Democratic members of the legislature. I therefore take pleasure in sending you the enclosed letter, in the hope that you will make any use of it that you deem judicious.

Faithfully yours,   [Woodrow Wilson]

E N C L O S U R E

To Charles Clarke Black

My dear Mr. Black: Princeton, N. J.   January 11th, 1907.

It is probable that I shall be leaving for Bermuda at an early date. I think it best, therefore, in view of our recent conversation and in order to avoid the possibility of any misunderstanding, to place in your hands the following statement of my position with regard to a possible nomination by the Democratic members of the legislature, for the United States senatorship.

As you know, I have never been and am not now a candidate for the nomination. I took no part in the campaign, and do not feel that I am in any sense entitled to the honor. I have no information from any Democratic members of the legislature of their intention to vote for me. Consequently, if there be any having such a purpose in mind, I cannot address them directly. But I desire to authorize you to request on my behalf that my name be withheld from consideration in the Democratic caucus.[1]

It is perfectly clear to my mind that the compliment should be paid to someone of those who were active in the canvass whose result so closely approached a complete Democratic victory. If then, as you informed me, some members of the legislature are still disposed to vote for me, I earnestly urge them to reconsider their determination and to give their vote to someone who by his efforts fairly won the tribute of that recognition.

To make certain that no further doubt may exist respecting my attitude and wishes, I think it would be well for you to publish this letter.[2]

With kind regards,

Faithfully yours,   [Woodrow Wilson]

CCL (WP, DLC).

[1] In spite of his request, Wilson was nominated in the Democratic legislative caucus when it met on January 22, 1907. He and Stevens both received fifteen votes. On the first ballot in the joint legislative session on the following day, Wilson received ten votes and Stevens sixteen. The Republican incumbent, Senator Dryden, received thirty-six votes, five short of a majority. On the second ballot on the same day, Wilson picked up five votes, Stevens held firm at sixteen, as did Dryden at thirty-six. No further balloting occurred until January 29, when in the course of three ballots Wilson slipped from fifteen to twelve, Stevens held firm at sixteen, and Dryden leveled off at thirty-five. Before the next balloting six days later, February 5, Republican leaders prevailed upon Dryden to withdraw, and replaced him with Frank Obadiah Briggs, State Treasurer and Chairman of the State Republican Committee. Meanwhile, the Democrats, foreseeing further deadlock between the supporters of Wilson and Stevens, selected as a compromise candidate James Edgar Martine of Plainfield, who had received no more than nine votes in any of the earlier ballots. In the final ballot on February 5, Briggs was elected Senator with forty-one votes, while Martine received thirty-five.

It might be added that the core of Wilson's support came from members of the Essex County Democratic organization controlled by former Senator James Smith, Jr., and that the balance of Wilson's votes came from men outside Essex County friendly to the Smith machine.

[2] Wilson's letter was published on January 21, 1907. See, e.g., the *Newark Evening News*, Jan. 21, 1907.

To Edwin Augustus Stevens

My dear Ned: Princeton, N. J.   January 11th, 1907.

My delay in replying to your last letter has been due to the fact that I have been very busy making such inquiries as would enable me to act upon the fullest possible information in the matter which has disturbed me and you.

I want to thank you for the delightful friendliness and generous spirit of your letter, and to assure you that these puzzles of judgment as to what line I should take, have only bound me closer to you.

I am at last convinced that you are right in saying that to remain passive now is to defeat my own end, which has all along been to maintain a perfect disconnection from the differences which have arisen between Democratic groups in this State. I think that it would be a mistake for me to write to the Speaker of the House, as you suggest, because I have had absolutely no communication with any official spokesman of any of the groups in the legislature. Indeed, so far as I know, I have no acquaintance with any Democratic member of the legislature. I am therefore taking the liberty of writing to Mr. Black, with the suggestion that if he pleases he may print the letter I send him. I know that you will understand my wish to take this action outside politics, so to speak, and I think that you will be convinced that the form of my letter to Mr. Black takes me entirely out of the choice for even a complimentary nomination. I am convinced that I could not accept such a nomination.

Allow me, in closing, to thank you for having done so much and done it so frankly, to set me right in this delicate matter.

Always cordially and sincerely yours,

[Woodrow Wilson]

CCL (WP, DLC).

To Charles Williston McAlpin

My dear McAlpin: Princeton, N. J.   January 11th, 1907.

I don't think that it would be wise to urge a reconsideration upon Judge Ewing any further than we have already urged it, and I think that the wise thing, if he insists upon withdrawing, would be to accept his decision and act upon it, as he requests.

I take the liberty of enclosing a letter,[1] to which I have already replied, so that you may if you choose send some definite information in the matter to the Dr. Bickford mentioned.

I am off tomorrow morning, I am sorry to say, and hope that while I am gone there will be nothing to distress and everything to hearten you and all of us. Au revoir.

Always cordially and faithfully yours,

Woodrow Wilson

TLS (McAlpin File, UA, NjP).
1 It is missing.

From Charles Clarke Black

My dear President: Jersey City, January 12, 1907

I beg to acknowledge the receipt of your letter of January 11th, addressed to me, in behalf of the candidacy of Colonel Stevens for the United States Senatorship. In reply thereto I can assure you that I thoroughly appreciate the apparently delicate position in which you have been placed in this matter.

My interest arose out of the fact that Colonel Stevens was a worthy candidate, representing the higher things in politics. It has been a great pleasure for me to contribute some effort in his behalf. I think ultimately his candidacy will be productive of some good. What our politics is suffering from is the lack of participation therein by men of high character, who stand for the public good, as opposed to private interests.

I will endeavor to make judicious use of your letter, and have handed it to Mr. Alexander,[1] a member of the Assembly, and a loyal Princeton man.

By way of a passing interest, you might be interested in knowing that in an address which I made a week ago to-night in Jersey City, I brought forward your name as a nominee for the Presidency, whom Jerseymen should and ought to delight to advance. It met with many evidences of favor.

Believe me, your friend,   Sincerely,   Chas C Black.

TLS (WP, DLC).
[1] Archibald Stevens Alexander, Princeton 1902, a member of the General Assembly from Hudson County.

To Ellen Axson Wilson

                         On board Twin Screw S.S. Bermudian
My own darling,   12 Jany 1907

I send this line by the pilot to say that I am well and my spirits as light as it would be reasonable to expect in the circumstances. The boat seems very comfortable and my room is most pleasantly situated on the deck corresponding with the one we were on coming home.

And I love my darling with a love which makes me tremble with tenderness and yearning and solemn joy. Ah, if you but *knew how* and how much!

Love to all. God bless you!   Your own   Woodrow

How I do wish for Nen!

ALS (WP, DLC).

ADDENDA

To James Hampton Kirkland[1]

Princeton, New Jersey,

My dear Sir, 9 December, 1897

It has taken me several days to make up my mind what I could do about your kind invitation[2] to speak at Vanderbilt next Commencement; for my engagements away from home, running into next winter, are already so numerous as to daunt me. But I have at last determined to stretch a point and come to you. I cannot now announce my subject, but you may book me for June fourteenth, and I will announce my subject later.

I very keenly appreciate the cordial terms of your invitation; and shall look forward to the occasion with the liveliest anticipations of pleasure.[3]

With warm regards,

Very sincerely Yours, Woodrow Wilson

WWTLS (J. H. Kirkland Papers, TNJ).
[1] Chancellor of Vanderbilt University.
[2] It is missing.
[3] A news report of Wilson's address is printed at June 15, 1898, Vol. 10.

To Henry Eldridge Bourne[1]

My dear Sir, Princeton, New Jersey, 27 September, 1900.

I am sincerely obliged to you for the suggestion of your kind letter of the twenty-second,[2] that I undertake this winter a course of lectures on American history before the Cleveland branch of the Daughters of the American Revolution. I should be delighted to do so were it possible, or, rather, prudent. But my winter is to be more engrossed than ever with literary work, and I have already made as many speaking engagements away from home as I feel I have the right to add to that work and my college duties.

Pray convey to the Committee of the Society my warm thanks for their kind desire to hear me, and believe me,

With sincere regard and appreciation,

Very truly Yours, Woodrow Wilson

WWTLS (H. E. Bourne Papers, OClWHI).
[1] Professor of History, College for Women, Western Reserve University.
[2] It is missing.

To Bayard Henry

Princeton, New Jersey,

My dear Mr. Henry,   25 November, 1900.

I am sometimes a very indiscreet man, and my promise of last year is undoubtedly a case in point.[1] I must have known then what a desperately busy man I was to be this winter getting up an al[l]-the-year serial for Harper's Magazine for 1901, and that, under the circumstances, I ought to stick like wax, the winter through, to my desk. But I made the promise out of genuine affection for the stock of my "own kith and kin," which was a most proper motive, and I stand ready to redeem it.

In brief, I accept with appreciation and pleasure the invitation you so kindly extend to me[2] to be present at the dinner of the Scotch-Irish Society on the evening of the twenty-first of February next; and shall only ask such indulgence for the speech I shall make as a hard-headed people may be willing to vouchsafe in the case of a voluntarily overworked brother labourer.[3]

With much regard, and many thanks for your letter,

Sincerely Yours,   Woodrow Wilson

WWTLS (in possession of Bruce Gimelson).

[1] Wilson had promised Henry to speak to the Scotch-Irish Society in Philadelphia on February 8, 1900. The illness of Stockton Axson had prevented him from fulfilling this engagement. See WW to EAW, Feb. 6, 1900, n. 1, Vol. 11; WW to EAW, Feb. 9, 1900, *ibid.*; and WW to EAW, Feb 11, 1900, *ibid.*

[2] It is missing.

[3] See n. 2 to the announcement printed at Jan. 5, 1901, Vol. 12.

To William Alexander MacCorkle[1]

Princeton, New Jersey,

My dear Mr. MacCorkle,   31 January, 1901.

Like hundreds of others of your fellow countrymen, I was especially pleased with the whole of your very able address delivered at the recent conference on the negro race.[2] I am the better prepared, therefore, to enjoy and appreciate the address on Universal Suffrage which you have been kind enough to send.[3] I shall read it with attention, and, I expect, with agreement; and thank you most sincerely for your thoughtfulness in letting me see it.

With much regard,

Very sincerely Yours,   Woodrow Wilson

WWTLS (photographic copy in William A. MacCorkle, *The Recollections of Fifty Years of West Virginia* [New York and London, 1928], facing p. 586).

[1] Governor of West Virginia, 1892-97, lawyer, and publicist of Charleston, West Va.

[2] William Alexander MacCorkle, *The Negro and the Intelligence and Property Franchise. Address of Wm. A. MacCorkle, late Governor of West Virginia, before*

the Southern Conference on Race Problems, Montgomery, Alabama, May 9, 1900 (Cincinnati, 1900).

In this address, MacCorkle argued that the constitutional exercise of the right of the franchise was the vital and underlying principle of the life of the free American people, and that "the infraction of this principle is surely attended with ultimate ruin to our system of republican government." The Fifteenth Amendment, he said, was as much a part and parcel of the organic law governing the country as any section of the Constitution. The Negro's right to the suffrage was as sacred as the white man's, and should be as sacredly guarded. Yet the white South had never intended that the Negro should rule or largely participate in political affairs. The crucial question was how to give the Negro his franchise without imperiling southern civilization. The answer was to give the vote to the Negro when he qualified for it by education and acquisition of property. No danger of Negro domination lay in such a policy, for whites would continue to control southern state governments. However, as the South industrialized, it would divide politically, and the Negro vote would play a significant role. The political and civil advancement of the Negro was not only desirable but also inevitable. He was improving rapidly, economically and culturally. Once the intelligent Negro was enfranchised, he would ally with the intelligent white Southerner, and the time would come when the South would need the Negro vote. The present franchise policy of many southern states was repression, which bred discontent, drove away intelligence, and exacerbated sectional feeling. The South desperately needed the help of the North in solving the race question.

3 "The Experience of this Republic as to the Elective Franchise," which MacCorkle delivered before the Nineteenth Century Club of New York on January 15, 1901, and later included in his *Some Southern Questions* (New York, 1908), pp. 149-214. No copy of the reprint which MacCorkle sent to Wilson seems to have survived.

"The Experience of this Republic as to the Elective Franchise" was an eloquent and vigorous defense of universal suffrage as the cornerstone of free government. Universal suffrage strengthened local government, provided a stimulus to the political education of immigrants in the great cities, offered no danger to an independent judiciary, protected civil liberties, and strengthened the organic powers of the state governments. Turning to the South, MacCorkle said that circumstances during Reconstruction had forced white Southerners to drive Negroes from political power. He had advocated an educational or property qualification that would apply impartially to both races. The South was now in process of giving Negroes their rights in consonance with the spirit of the Constitution. In the balance of this address, MacCorkle discussed the effect of universal suffrage upon federal-state relations, the mutual relations of classes, party politics, and the rights of minorities; the present dangers to democracy in the United States; the general good effects of a literacy test; and the need for political regeneration and reform.

To Cleveland Hoadley Dodge

My dear Cleve,   Princeton, 27 Sept., 1903

Not till night before last, when I opened the last pile of mail which I found awaiting my return, did I learn of your father's death.¹ I was deeply shocked and grieved,—not grieved for him but for those who are left without him. Four several times have I sat down to write to you, but not till this (Sunday) evening have I been permitted to say in pease [peace] what it was in my heart to say.

You know,—at least, I hope you do,—how much I admired him. It seems to me a singularly noble thing to be what he was, a great man of business who used his influence like a statesman and his wealth like one who loves his fellowmen. Every one seems to have thought so of him.

My thoughts, when the news came upon me, sprang at once to you and the grief I knew it would bring to you seemed in some way personal to myself. I am sure you must know my affection; but I could not let it go at that. I felt that I must put it into words even if I did not find the best words.

Hoping for a chance to see you soon,

Affectionately Yours,   Woodrow Wilson

ALS (in possession of Phyllis Boushall Dodge).
[1] William Earl Dodge, who died suddenly at Bar Harbor, Maine, on August 10, 1903.

Two Letters from Stockton Axson to John Van Antwerp MacMurray[1]

My dear Mr. Macmurray: Princeton, N. J.   Dec. 14, 1905

You probably think that I have forgotten my promise to ask President Wilson for the letter you spoke of. But this is not the case. He has been out of town a great deal since I saw you, and only this week have I had an opportunity to talk to him on the subject.

He remembers you vividly and has for you much respect and the kindest regard, so that I did not at all have to expatiate to him on your qualities. But as I predicted, he was interested to get a clear account of your purpose, motives and plans for going into the diplomatic service. He is very conscientious about writing letters of recommendation, and especially letters recommending men to the public service. It seems that he has many requests of this sort and makes it an invariable rule to decline such requests unless he is completely satisfied that the applicant has not only admirable qualities of character and intelligence but also special fitness for the thing which he seeks. Mr. Wilson tells me that he has complied with only three out of a great many requests for letters of this kind.

Could you, unobserved, have heard our conversation about you, you could not but have been gratified by the opinions which he expressed of you, but he felt that your traits, as he knows them, better adapt you to a life of letters or teaching than to aggressive public life. How high an opinion he holds of you was shown in a very remarkable manner when last spring he gave his consent to have you called to Princeton as a preceptor,[2] waiving your lack of special graduate training and experience. So far as I know you were the only man who received such a consideration from him, and I can not exaggerate the significance of this. It was such a complete departure from his general policy that I was amazed when I heard of it. As you know, when you and I talked together I was unaware of this—and you were too modest to tell me. Much as I myself should like to have you here, I simply assumed that it was impossible that you could be invited to a preceptorship without training and without experience. But it seems you *had* been invited. This thing, done with the consent and approval of a man like Mr. Wilson, ought to inspire you with a fresh confidence in yourself.

So he is very willing to write a letter testifying to your innate qualities and your acquisitions. But he is unwilling to give you a specific recommendation to the diplomatic service until he knows more. So—and this is the point of it all—he wants you to write him a letter, clearly stating your purpose and plans for applying for a diplomatic position. If you wish to make this your life's career and can show him that you have ideas on the subject which will satisfy him that you have a reasonable chance to succeed in this career, he will, I am sure, be glad to recommend you. If on the other hand you wish merely to have a few years of foreign residence as an attaché,—as a sort of general culture course,—I am afraid he will not consent.

I think it will help to make the situation clear to you if I give you a bit of our conversation. I said to him, "Macmurray certainly has all the qualities and equipment to make him a valuable attaché, breeding, education, a fair command of foreign tongues, charm of manner." "Yes," said Mr. Wilson, "he has, but it would be doing him no service to assist him in spending his life as an attaché." "But," said I, "we should hope that he would advance from that position." *Dr. Wilson*: "To do that, it would be necessary not only that he have inherent qualities, but that he devote himself with singleness of heart to the service, that he have it as his sole object to fit himself for the service. Do you know that this is his sole object?" *Axson*: "I can not say that I do." *Dr. Wilson*: "Does he not perhaps feel that the position of attaché will afford him an opportunity to acquire the knowledge of the world which will help him later to succeed in creative literature?" *Axson*: "I do not know. But even if this is the case, will this interfere with his doing good work as an attaché?" *Dr. Wilson*: "But I cannot recommend him to the service if he merely wishes to use it for this purpose."

This, I think, will help you, more than any exposition of mine, to see his point of view.

Now, with this in mind, write him a clear letter, as full as needs be, setting forth your objects, both immediate and ultimate, and he will then be able to act with a satisfaction of knowledge which I could not give him.

I have written at this great length so that you might fully understand Mr. Wilson's attitude. I hope sincerely that you will be able to satisfy him, and that you will get from him a letter which will assist you.

I have here in my study a folding lounge which is just as good as a bed. Won't you come down and occupy it some night? I should love to have you.

Wishing you all success,

Yours sincerely always   Stockton Axson

P.S. Please remember me to Mr. Camp[3] when you see him.

[1] Princeton, 1902; LL.B., Columbia University, 1906; afterward a distinguished Foreign Service officer who, among other things, was Minister to China, 1925-29, and Ambassador to Turkey, 1936-42.
[2] In the Department of English.
[3] MacMurray's classmate, Charles Wadsworth Camp.

[Princeton, N. J.]
My dear Mr. Macmurray: Saturday afternoon [Dec. 16, 1905]

Though I have but a moment at my disposal I want to spend it in acknowledging your letter which came a little while ago. I shall not have a chance to see Dr. Wilson today and so shall not know until tomorrow whether he has heard from you. But I want to say just this to you, that it seems to me that your letter to me meets and answers any doubts which may have been in his mind, and I think he will be willing to write the letter which you desire, and if he is willing he will be glad. By which I mean that his warm regard for you is such that it will be a pleasure to him to assist you in attaining your object when he can do that conscientiously as I feel sure he can in the light of your statement —for of course you will make to him practically the same statement which you have made to me.

I hope his letter may serve your turn, and that you will be able to acquire whatever "influence" is necessary from your congressman, and that President Roosevelt and Mr. Root[1] will give you just the very best berth at their disposal, and that you will find all the direct and indirect results from that all which you can desire.

With all best wishes for health, happiness and success (and about the latter I feel a great deal more confidence than you, judging from the tone of your letter), I am

Very sincerely yours   Stockton Axson

P.S. Indeed it never occurred to me that there was anything "discourteous" in your not mentioning overtures from the English department when we were discussing possibilities at Princeton. I ascribed it (when I learned that such overtures had been made) to just what I said, your modesty. Harper told me that a definite offer had not been made to you, but said that had you been inclined to teach you could have had the position, because the Department wanted you and the president cordially approved. My only reason for referring to it was to show you the really extraordinary esteem in which Mr. Wilson holds you.

P.S. 2. I am under the impression that one of the most useful men in the U. S. diplomatic service is Mr. [Henry] White. And he entered the service just as you plan to. After many years as secretary in England, he has found his reward in an ambassadorship.[2] Of course all political chances are more precarious than those of business or professional life, but I shall hope that your own history will be like that. There is no *reason* why it shouldnt be.

ALS (J. V. A. MacMurray Papers, NjP).
[1] Secretary of State Elihu Root.
[2] White was Ambassador to Italy at this time.

Two Letters to John Van Antwerp MacMurray

Princeton, N. J.

My dear Mr. McMurray,   21 December, 1904 [1905].

Allow me to thank you for your very satisfactory letter of the eighteenth.[1]

My feeling of uneasiness in all such cases rests chiefly on my knowledge of the great temptations connected with foreign secretaryships. There is little of serious importance to do; the activities are those of society rather than those of business; the unimportant things are always at the front; there is no provocation to study; impulses are cooled and principles are exposed to rust. In brief, it does not seem as yet a vital thing with us; and a man must have aims unusually definite, interests unusually well defined and serious to avoid demoralization. I feared you were going into the service for literary ends: to see the world. Pardon me if I ask whether you have considered all this. You are too good a man not to choose something that will really be worth stretching your gifts to.

Faithfully Yours,   Woodrow Wilson

[1] It is missing.

Princeton, N. J.

My dear Mr. MacMurray,   26 December, 1905.

I have read your letter of the twenty-fourth with a great deal of pleasure.[1] I want to assure you that my questions were not founded on any doubts as to your essential seriousness, but only on the desire to be of real service to you. It will give me pleasure to write to Mr. Root to express the hope that, should such an appointment as you desire become available he will take your name under serious consideration.[2] I sincerely hope that it will have some favourable effect upon your chances. It would be very pleasant to me to think that I had been in some part instrumental in starting you upon the career you have chosen.

With much regard and all good wishes,

Sincerely Yours,   Woodrow Wilson

WWTLS (J. V. A. MacMurray Papers, NjP).

[1] It is missing.

[2] Wilson's letter to Secretary Root is missing in the Root Papers in DLC and in the State Department files in DNA.

INDEX

NOTE ON THE INDEX

THE alphabetically arranged analytical table of contents at the front of the volume eliminates duplication, in both contents and index, of references to certain documents, such as letters. Letters are listed in the contents alphabetically by name, and chronologically within each name by page. The subject matter of all letters is, of course, indexed. The Editorial Notes and Wilson's writings are listed in the contents chronologically by page. In addition, the subject matter of both categories is indexed. The index covers all references to books and articles mentioned in text or notes. Footnotes are indexed. Page references to footnotes which place a comma between the page number and "n" cite both text and footnote, thus: "624,n3." On the other hand, absence of the comma indicates reference to the footnote only, thus: "55n2"–the page number denoting where the footnote appears. The letter "n" without a following digit signifies an unnumbered descriptive-location note.

An asterisk before an index reference designates identification or other particular information. Re-identification and repetitive annotation have been minimized to encourage use of these starred references. Where the identification appears in an earlier volume, it is indicated thus: "*1:212,n3." Therefore a page reference standing without a preceding volume number is invariably a reference to the present volume. The index supplies the fullest known forms of names, and, for the Wilson and Axson families, relationships as far down as cousins. Persons referred to in the text by nicknames or shortened forms of names can be identified by reference to entries for these forms of the names.

A sampling of the opinions and comments of Wilson and Ellen Axson Wilson covers their more personal views, while broad, general headings in the main body of the index cover impersonal subjects. Occasionally opinions expressed by a correspondent are indexed where these appear to supplement or to reflect views expressed by Wilson or by Ellen Axson Wilson in documents which are missing.

INDEX

Aberdeen, 528

Abridgement of the Indian Affairs . . . Transacted in the Colony of New York, from the Year 1678 to the Year 1751 (Wraxall; ed. McIlwain), 42n1

Adams, Edwin Plimpton, 421,n6, 508

Adams, Herbert Baxter, *2:391,n1; 309, 430

Adams, John, 53

Adams, John Quincy, 144

Ade, George, 115

Adelbert College, 131

Adler, Felix, 211,n2

Adriance, Walter Maxwell, 421, 509

Aitken, John William, 5, 500

Alabama Educational Association, 113

Alaska, 341

Albany, N.Y.: Princeton alumni, 418

Alden, Henry Mills, *9:311,n1; 299, 343, 470-471

Alderman, Edwin Anderson, 35-36,n1, 195

Alexander, Archibald Stevens (Princeton 1902), 563,n1

Alexander, Charles Beatty, 276,n1, 277f, 304,n1, 424n1; Mrs. (Harriet Crocker), 322

Alexander, Henry Martyn, Mrs. (Susan Mary Brown), 322

Alexander, James Waddel, 5, 276n1, 299n1, 333n2

Alexander & Green, New York law firm, 276n1

Alger, Frederick Moulton, 43,n4

Allen, Hamilton Ford, 106-7, 130, 248, 421

Allen Academy, Chicago, 248

Ambleside, Westmorland, 436, 439, 450, 480

American Academy of Political and Social Science, 313

American Exchange National Bank, New York City, 533

American Intercollegiate Football Rules Committee, 371,n4

American Journal of Archaeology, 187n1

American Library Association, 392

American Line, 179

American Merchant Marine, 539

American Museum of Natural History, 550,n1

American Philosophical Society, 36, 56-57

American Revolution, 143

American School of Classical Studies at Athens, 247, 253, 254

American School of Classical Studies at Rome, 166, 167, 247, 253, 510

American Wood Carving Company, 387-88

Americanism defined, 53

Amherst College, 240

Anchor Line, 430n3, 450, 451, 453

And Gladly Teach: Reminiscences (Perry), 180n

Anderson, Andrew Runni, 55, 132, 252, 528

Anderson, Anna E., 234

Anderson, Carrie, 234

Anderson, Robert M., 301

Anderson Auction Company, New York City, 379

Andrew, Abram Piatt, 30,n1, 41, 372,n1

Andrew Carnegie (Wall), 55n3, 305n4

Ann Arbor, Michigan, 60; WW address, 44-45

Ann Arbor Daily Argus, 45n

Annapolis, *see* U.S. Naval Academy

Annin, Robert Edwards, 215

Antaeus, 216

Anthony, Alfred W., 470n

Archaeological Institute of America, 253

Archer, 92,n2

Aristotle, 354

Armour, George Allison, *9:516,n3; 472-74, 483

Army-Navy football game, Princeton, 1905, 172-73, 175, 242-43

Arnold, Frances Bunsen Trevenen, 493,n2

Arnold, Matthew, 493, 493n2

Arnold, Thomas, 493

Ashe, Samuel A'Court, 187n1

Associated Press, 553

Association of Colleges and Preparatory Schools of the Middle States and Maryland, 495, 504-5

Association of History Teachers of the Middle States and Maryland, 279

Astoria, S.S., 456

Athens: Archaeological Congress, 93

Atherton, Thomas Henry, 5

Atkins, V. B., 73

Atlantic Monthly, 170, 180n2

Autocrat of the Breakfast Table (Holmes), 226,n5

automobile: menace of reckless driving of, 320

Axson, Edward Stockton, nephew of EAW, 86,n1, 88

Axson, Edward William, brother of EAW, *2:372,n2; 86,n1, 88-89, 154n1; Mrs. (Florence Choate Leach), 86,n1, 88-89

Axson, Margaret Randolph (Madge), sister of EAW, *2:417n1; 28, 158, 187, 439,n1, 482, 527

Axson, Stockton (*full name:* Isaac Stockton Keith Axson II), brother of EAW, *2:386n1; 28-29,n3, 154n1, 155,n1, 158, 180, 187, 469, 565n1, 567-70

Brown University, 213n1
Browne, Honor, 437,n3, 438, 441
Browne (yeoman of Troutbeck, West-
morland), 438,n1
Browning, Robert, 328
Browning, Webster E., 358
Bryan, John Pendleton Kennedy,
286,n1
Bryan, Pendleton Taylor, 5
Bryan, William Jennings, 43, 49, 50-
51, 69, 311
Bryce, James, Viscount Bryce, 97, 527-
28
Bryden, John Kerfoot, 377
Bryn Mawr College, 58-59, 79, 132, 255,
423,n1
Buffum, Douglas Labaree, 60, 132, 256
Buley, Roscoe Carlyle, 276n1
Bulkeley, Frances Hazen, 13n
Bull, Griffin William, 537,n1
Bunn, Henry Conrad, 176, 324, 356
Burke, Annie R., 234
Burke, Edmund, 284, 285
Burleigh, George William, 5,n3, 134,
291, 416
Burt, Maxwell Struthers, 465, 511, 553
Bushnell, Herbert, 475
Butcher, Samuel Henry, 28
Butler, Ed, 216n3
Butler, Howard Crosby, 140n3, 186,n1,
198, 247, 263, 515
Butler, Howard Russell, 499
Butler, Nicholas Murray, 224, 282,
283, 373-74, 375-76, 383, 395, 396,
413, 414-15, 495-96
Butler, William Allen, 500

Cadwalader, John Lambert, 5, 39, 266,
303, 495
Caesar, Julius, 119, 221, 480
Caledonia, S.S., 427, 430,n3, 450, 451,
453, 455, 456, 463
Calhoun, John Caldwell, 53
California, University of, 110, 250,
252, 489
Calkins, Gary Nathan, 431,n1, 469
Cambridge, England, EAW in, 436
Cambridge, University of, 46, 81,n2,
83, 156-57, 157, 163, 164, 165, 198,
246-47, 434, 465, 507, 508, 509;
Cavendish Laboratory, 508, 509; Ob-
servatory, 83, 83n2
Cameron, Donald, 67, 104, 132, 252,
528
Cammack (of Kansas City), 98
Camp, Charles Wadsworth, 569,n3
Campbell, Henry Monroe, 43,n4
Campbell, John Alexander, 64,n2
Campbell, William Oliver, 404,n3
Cannon, Joseph Gurney, 315, 316
Carlisle, John Griffin, 534,n2
Carnegie, Andrew, 4, 54, 67, 78, 139,
224, 336, 497-503; Mrs. (Louise
Whitfield), 497, 500, 503
Carnegie Corporation of New York,
55n3

Carnegie Foundation for the Advance-
ment of Teaching, 55n3, 67, 78n2,
224, 304-5,n2,3,4, 306, 306n1, 419,
429, 468, 469, 518
Carnegie Institution of Washington,
54, 82n2, 83, 489; Bureau of His-
torical Research, 106
Carnegie Teachers Pension Fund, see
Carnegie Foundation for the Ad-
vancement of Teaching
Carnegie Trust for the Universities of
Scotland, 54,n2
Carow, Emily, 233,n1
Carpenter, Emory W., 321n1
Carpenter, Jennie R., 321n1
Carter, Jesse Benedict, 130, 166-67,
176, 180, 248, 421; Mrs. (Kate
Benedict Freeman), 166, 167, 176
Carton, Alfred Thomas, 382,n3
Carton, Laurence Arthur, 382,n1
Carton, Laurence Roberts, 382,n2,3
Carver, Thomas Nixon, 41,n6
Cassatt, Alexander Johnston, 342,n1,
343
Catok & Beller, 387, 388
Cawley, John, 471,n1
Centre College, Kentucky, 247, 254
Century Association, New York City,
531
Chalmers, Thomas, 317
Chambers, James Julius, 110
Chapel Hill, N.C., 526, 527
Chapin, Charles Sumner, 219,n2
character: a by-product, 228, 230, 311,
317; moral character, 327-28
Charleston, S.C., 285-86; Hibernian
Hall, 285, 286; Saint Andrew's So-
ciety, 533,n10; Villa Margherita,
286; WW address, 285-86
Charleston News and Courier, 286,
286n, 286n1, 288n1, 533
Charlottesville, 192
Chattanooga: Chattanooga Railways
Company, 476; Read House, 476;
WW address, 474-77
Chattanooga Times, 476, 477
Chautauqua, 253
Chicago: Princeton alumni, 405
Chicago, University of, 33, 159, 179,
198, 248, 251, 253, 254, 257, 258,
259, 272n1, 282, 465, 511
Chinese culture and society, 121
Christian Point of View: Three Ad-
dresses (Knox, McGiffert, Brown),
400,n5
Churchman, Philip Hudson, 27,n1
Clark, George Rogers, 144n3
Clark, Kenneth Sherman, 24n2
Clark, William (1770-1838), 143-44,-
n1,3,4
Clark University, 59n1, 61n1
Clarke, Dumont, 533, 534
Clay, Henry, 53
Clemons, William Harry, 38
Cleveland, Grover, 102, 136, 197,

flag, worship of, 30-31
Flanagan, Edith L., 234
Fleming, Matthew Corry, 5
Flinn, John William, 87,n2
Folk, Joseph Wingate, 216,n3
football, intercollegiate, 238-40n2,3, 242, 271, 274-75, 369-71, 500
Ford, Henry Jones, *11:262,n2; 43-n2, 97
Ford, Jeremiah Denis Matthias, 172n1
Fordham University, 240
Forsyth, Andrew Russell, 157,n3, 163
Forsyth, William Holmes, 5
Fosdick, Raymond Blaine, *138,n1
Foster, William, Jr., 11,n1, 198, 247
Foulke, William Dudley, 316,n4
Fountain, F. S., 113
Fox, John, 362n1
Fox How, Ambleside, Westmorland, 493, 494n2
Franklin, Benjamin, 53, 56-57, 226, 316, 341
Franks, Robert A., 78, 224, 500
Frazer, David Ruddach, 131, 199
Freiburg i.B., University of, 257
Freneau, Philip, 479n1
Freund, Katie, 234
Freund, Louis W., 104,n1, 105, 206, 234, 235
Freund, Wilhelmina, 234
Frick, Henry Clay, 303, 336, 398, 490, 491
Frothingham, Arthur Lincoln, Jr., 93-94, 103, 130, 245, 246

Gaines, Clement Carrington, 292n1
Gansevoort, Henry Sanford, 404
Garfield, Harry Augustus, *14:486-87,-n1; 206n2, 379, 449-50
Garfield, James Rudolph, 15n1
Garmany, Jasper Jewett, M.D., 500
Garrett, John Work, *11:113,n2; 18,-n1, 20, 204, 205
Garrett, Robert, *11:113,n2; 5, 19,n1,-2, 20, 204, 205, 233, 266, 526
Garrett, Thomas Harrison, Mrs. (Alice Dickinson), *8:461,n2, 18,n2
Gauss, Christian Frederick, 61, 132, 256-57
Gearin, John McDermeid, 362n1, 558,-n4
Genesee, Society of the, 231
Geneva, University of, 257
George Harvey, 'A Passionate Patriot' (Johnson), 455n1, 534n10
German Influence on Religious Life and Thought in America During the Colonial Period (Hoskins), 425,n2
Gerould, Gordon Hall, 52, 58, 79, 132, 255
Gerrans, Henry Tresawna, 165,n3
Gettysburg College (formerly Pennsylvania College), 258, 510
Gibson, George Alexander, M.D., 445,-n1
Giessen, University of, 465, 508

Gildersleeve, Basil Lanneau, 104
Gildersleeve, Raleigh Colston, 104, 144-45, 150-151, 152-53, 154, 161-62, 176, 181-83, 184, 185, 191, 212, 324, 387-88, 447
Gillespie, William, 132, 159, 160, 162, 258
Gilman School, Baltimore, 308, 509,n3, 510, 511
Gimelson, Bruce, 102n, 565n
Girton College, Cambridge, 163
Gladden, Washington, 227n2
Glasgow: 432; St. Enoch Hotel, 494
Glasgow, University of, 398n1, 465, 507
Glass, Frank Potts, 75, 78, 168
Glass, Franklin Purnell, 168,n5
Goltra, Edward Field, 5, 504,n1
Göttingen, University of, 258, 508
Goucher College, 28n2, 423, 424n1, 470, 544
Granbery, William Langley, 236,n1, 406, 476,n1
Grand Army of the Republic, 30-31, 35
Grant, Frederick Dent, 11,n4
Grant, Ulysses Simpson, 12n4, 221
Granville, Ohio, 253
Grasmere, Westmorland, 437, 440, 441, 449, 450
Graustock, University of, 257
Green, Andrew White, 223,n2
Green, Henry Woodhull, 266, 289, 500
Greene, Clayton Wellington, 203,n2
Greene, Jerome Davis, 396,n1, 412
Greenwood, Joseph Rudd, 199
Greer, David Hummell, 228,n1, 230
Grenoble, University of, 256
Griffin, Nathaniel Edward, 132, 255, 421
Grindelwald, Switzerland, 178
Grinnell College, 16, 16n2,3,4
Groningen, University of, 82
Groton School, 192n1
Gulick, Alexander Reading, 500
Gustavus Adolphus College, St. Peter, Minn., 256

Hadley, Arthur Twining, 281, 284, 331
Hale, Henry Ewing, 301
Hall, Charles Cuthbert, 282
Halle, University of, 249, 250, 253
Hamill, Hugh Henderson, 5
Hamilton, Alexander, 53, 206, 316
Hamilton College, 45-47, 47n1, 239, 247, 257
Hamlin, Alfred Dwight Foster, 535,n5
Hampden-Sydney College, 132, 252
Hanover, N.H., 194, 245
Hardaway, Prof., 73
Harlan, James Shanklin, 5
Harmon, Judson, 362n1
Harper, George McLean, *3:571,n1; 570; Mrs. (Belle Dunton Westcott), 159
Harper, William Rainey, 224, 273, 280, 282-83

WOODROW WILSON

AND ELLEN AXSON WILSON

Our lives have been so knitted together that we cannot really *live* apart, 436

APPEARANCE

Described by interviewer, 115-16
Frederic Yates portrait, 437, 438, 441, 442, 449, 506, 541-42
striking resemblance to George Ade, 115

FAMILY LIFE AND DOMESTIC AFFAIRS

Lyme, Conn., vacation 1905, 153,n1, 154,n1, 155, 156, 158, 160,n1, 161, 163, 167, 168, 169, 171, 172, 174, 175, 178, 181
English lake holiday, June 30-Oct. 14, 1906, 424, 427, 429-93 passim
WW sends home case of Ballantine whisky from Scotland, 456

HEALTH

Recuperation from hernia operation and phlebitis at Palm Beach, 3, 12-13, 28-29
Stroke of May 28, 1906, blindness in